How to Find What You Need in

THE CANADIAN WRITER'S HANDBOOK

1. **Consult the table of contents.** The table of contents (pages v–xv) offers a comprehensive list of the *Handbook*'s chapters, sections, and subsections. Chapters are designated with Roman numerals, from I to VIII. Sections, numbered consecutively without regard to chapters, are designated with Arabic numerals, from 1 to 81. Subsections are designated with letters within each section (for example, 1a, 1b, 1c). Appendices are numbered from A1 to A3.

2. **Use the thumb index.** The thumb index, used together with the key on the next page, will help you find the chapter you're looking for. In addition, a quick glance at any thumb tab will tell you what section and subsection are being discussed on that page.

3. **Refer to the list of marking symbols.** The list of marking symbols, located on the inside back cover, will direct you to the sections that discuss specific writing problems, such as *faulty parallelism* or *dangling modifiers.*

4. **Check the index.** The detailed index (pages 635–54) will direct you to the pages where you will find information on specific topics (such as dangling modifiers) and words and phrases (for example, *altogether, all together*).

5. **Look over the list of exercises.** Exercises, with page references, are listed by title on pages 655–56.

Chapter Index

THE CANADIAN WRITER'S HANDBOOK

FIFTH EDITION

William E. Messenger

Jan de Bruyn

Judy Brown

Ramona Montagnes

OXFORD
UNIVERSITY PRESS

70 Wynford Drive, Don Mills, Ontario M3C 1J9
www.oup.com/ca

Oxford University Press is a department of the University of Oxford. It furthers the University's objective of excellence in research, scholarship, and education by publishing worldwide in

Oxford New York

Auckland Cape Town Dar es Salaam Hong Kong Karachi Kuala Lumpur Madrid Melbourne Mexico City Nairobi New Delhi Shanghai Taipei Toronto

With offices in

Argentina Austria Brazil Chile Czech Republic France Greece Guatemala Hungary Italy Japan Poland Singapore South Korea Switzerland Thailand Turkey Ukraine Vietnam

Published in Canada
by Oxford University Press

First published 2008

Library and Archives Canada Cataloguing in Publication

The Canadian writer's handbook / William E. Messenger . . . [et al.]. — 5th ed.

Includes bibliographical references and index.
ISBN 978-0-19-542755-4

1. English language—Composition and exercises. 2. English language—Grammar. I. Messenger, William E., 1931–2003.

PE1408.C35 2007 808'.042 C2007-901972-2

Cover Design: Sherill Chapman

1 2 3 4 – 11 10 09 08

This book is printed on permanent (acid-free) paper ♾.

Printed in Canada

Contents

dedicated to William Edmund Messenger

1931–2003

Preface

The fifth edition of *The Canadian Writer's Handbook* is a blending of the old and the new. Like the previous editions, this one is written to help you in what we see as the ongoing (even lifelong) project of improving written communication. We know that the improvement of our own writing is a work in progress, and we believe that the same may be true for our readers. Whether you are a longtime writer of English seeking to refresh and refine your abilities or one who is writing in English as an additional language, we hope that the suggestions, examples, exercises, and guidelines in this new edition will provide a trustworthy resource that will enable you to write with greater confidence and skill.

This fifth edition represents something new primarily in its organization and focus. While previous editions were organized in binary fashion, this edition has a tripartite organization that opens and closes with an emphasis on the larger units of discourse. We begin with a chapter on principles of composition ranging from the design of paragraphs to the design of the whole essay and the principles of effective planning and argument; we close with an updated chapter on research-based writing. In the middle section of the book, we explore principles of grammar, syntax, and usage at the word and sentence level. As in previous editions, we devote considerable space to examination of sentence patterns, parts of speech, and sentence structure and variety; we also include chapters on punctuation, mechanics and spelling, and diction—all accompanied by the kinds of exercises our readers have found useful in previous editions. The three appendices of this edition provide sample essays (a number of them marked and graded), detailed explanation of marking symbols, and omnibus checklists designed for use at the revising and editing stages of your writing projects.

Overview

The Canadian Writer's Handbook is intended for you to use as a reference work, to consult on particular issues arising from the everyday writing activities, challenges, and questions you encounter. It may also be used as a class text for discussion and study in writing courses, programs, and workshops. We suggest that you begin by considering the ways in which you will be using this book. Then, start to familiarize yourself with it by seeing what it has to offer you. Browse through the table of contents and the index. Look up some sections that arouse your interest. Flip through the pages, pausing now and then for a closer look. Note the running heads at the tops of pages and the thumb index; note also the chapter index at the beginning of the book, the list of marking symbols inside the back cover, and the list of exercises at the end of the book: these, together with the guide at the end of this preface, can help you find things in a hurry.

Organization

Notice how the material is arranged. Begin to think about how you can best approach it. You may want to begin at the beginning and proceed carefully through the book; some points in later sections won't be clear to you unless you understand the material in the early chapters. But if you already understand basic grammar—the functions of the parts of speech and the principles governing English sentences—you may need only a quick review of chapters II, III, and IV. Test yourself by trying some of the exercises in each chapter and check your answers with your instructor or consult this book's website (www.oup.com/ca/he/companion/brownmontagnes5).

For Readers and Writers of English as an Additional Language

Our experience as university instructors has given us the opportunity to work with a number of writers engaged in the challenging project of reading and writing in English as an additional language (EAL). Because English is a third, fourth, or fifth language to many such students, we have long felt that the term "ESL" (English as a second language), used to describe or even to label these writers, is something of a misnomer. Still, at several points in this new edition, we offer information and direction of particular importance to those of you who are approaching English as a relatively new language and have designated those relevant sections with the symbol ▲.

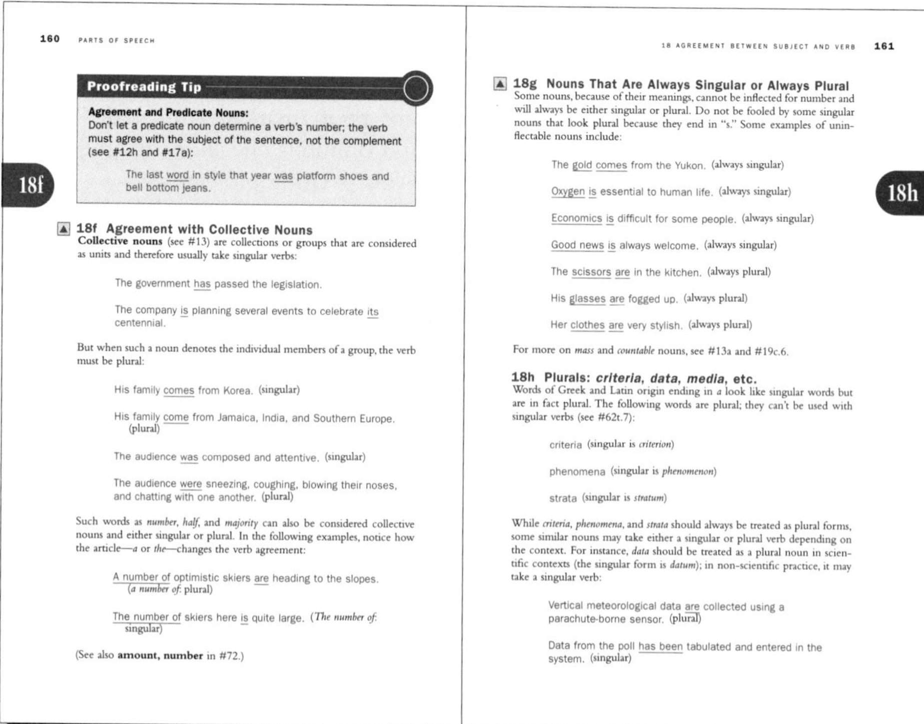

160 PARTS OF SPEECH

18f

Proofreading Tip

Agreement and Predicate Nouns:
Don't let a predicate noun determine a verb's number; the verb must agree with the subject of the sentence, not the complement (see #12h and #17a):

The last word in style that year was platform shoes and bell bottom jeans.

▲ **18f Agreement with Collective Nouns**
Collective nouns (see #13) are collections or groups that are considered as units and therefore usually take singular verbs:

The government has passed the legislation.

The company is planning several events to celebrate its centennial.

But when such a noun denotes the individual members of a group, the verb must be plural:

His family comes from Korea. (singular)

His family come from Jamaica, India, and Southern Europe. (plural)

The audience was composed and attentive. (singular)

The audience were sneezing, coughing, blowing their noses, and chatting with one another. (plural)

Such words as *number*, *half*, and *majority* can also be considered collective nouns and either singular or plural. In the following examples, notice how the article—*a* or *the*—changes the verb agreement:

A number of optimistic skiers are heading to the slopes. (*a number of*: plural)

The number of skiers here is quite large. (*The number of*: singular)

(See also **amount, number** in #72.)

18 AGREEMENT BETWEEN SUBJECT AND VERB 161

18h

▲ **18g Nouns That Are Always Singular or Always Plural**
Some nouns, because of their meanings, cannot be inflected for number and will always be either singular or plural. Do not be fooled by some singular nouns that look plural because they end in "s." Some examples of uninflectable nouns include:

The gold comes from the Yukon. (always singular)

Oxygen is essential to human life. (always singular)

Economics is difficult for some people. (always singular)

Good news is always welcome. (always singular)

The scissors are in the kitchen. (always plural)

His glasses are fogged up. (always plural)

Her clothes are very stylish. (always plural)

For more on *mass* and *countable* nouns, see #13a and #19c.6.

18h Plurals: *criteria, data, media*, etc.
Words of Greek and Latin origin ending in *a* look like singular words but are in fact plural. The following words are plural; they can't be used with singular verbs (see #62t.7):

criteria (singular is *criterion*)

phenomena (singular is *phenomenon*)

strata (singular is *stratum*)

While *criteria*, *phenomena*, and *strata* should always be treated as plural forms, some similar nouns may take either a singular or plural verb depending on the context. For instance, *data* should be treated as a plural noun in scientific contexts (the singular form is *datum*); in non-scientific practice, it may take a singular verb:

Vertical meteorological data are collected using a parachute-borne sensor. (plural)

Data from the poll has been tabulated and entered in the system. (singular)

Checking Your Work Before Submitting It

When you finish a piece of writing, go through the omnibus checklists in Appendix 3. If you find you're not sure about something, follow the cross-references to the sections that will give you the help you need.

Correcting and Revising Returned Work

When you get a piece of writing back with marks and comments, first look it over alongside Appendix 2, "Marking Symbols Explained." The information there may be enough to help you make the appropriate changes. But if you need more than a reminder about a specific issue or pattern—if you don't understand the fundamental principles—follow the cross-references and study the sections that discuss and illustrate those principles in greater detail. You should then be able to edit and revise your work with understanding and confidence.

An important feature of this book is that it discusses and illustrates various issues in several places: in the main discussions and in the exercises that accompany them, in the review exercises at the ends of sections and subsections, in writing and proofreading tips, in the sample essays in Appendix 1, and in Appendix 2. If the information you find in one or another of these places isn't enough to clarify a point, remember that you may not yet have exhausted the available resources: try the index to see if it will lead you to still other relevant places.

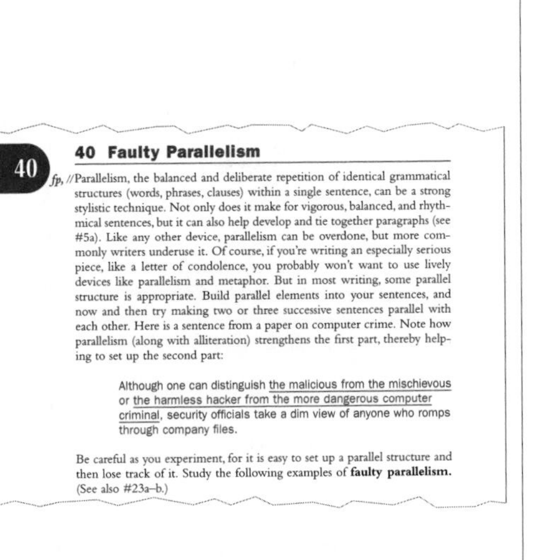

40

40 Faulty Parallelism

fp, //Parallelism, the balanced and deliberate repetition of identical grammatical structures (words, phrases, clauses) within a single sentence, can be a strong stylistic technique. Not only does it make for vigorous, balanced, and rhythmical sentences, but it can also help develop and tie together paragraphs (see #5a). Like any other device, parallelism can be overdone, but more commonly writers underuse it. Of course, if you're writing an especially serious piece, like a letter of condolence, you probably won't want to use lively devices like parallelism and metaphor. But in most writing, some parallel structure is appropriate. Build parallel elements into your sentences, and now and then try making two or three successive sentences parallel with each other. Here is a sentence from a paper on computer crime. Note how parallelism (along with alliteration) strengthens the first part, thereby helping to set up the second part:

> Although one can distinguish the malicious from the mischievous or the harmless hacker from the more dangerous computer criminal, security officials take a dim view of anyone who romps through company files.

Be careful as you experiment, for it is easy to set up a parallel structure and then lose track of it. Study the following examples of **faulty parallelism.** (See also #23a–b.)

MARKING SYMBOLS EXPLAINED 611

fp // **Faulty Parallelism**

Revise by making coordinated elements grammatically parallel.

> ***fp:*** For me England brings back memories of pleasant walks in Cornwall on some windblown lea, looking out to sea dressed in warm woollen jerseys, and feeling a warmth brought about by being with my family in that place.

The three objects of the preposition *of* here are all nouns, but *looking* and *feeling*, unlike *walks*, are gerunds. Repeating *of* before each gerund would help, but it is better to make the three grammatically parallel (and the phrase "dressed in warm woollen jerseys" seems more appropriate to the windblown lea than to looking out to sea):

> ***revised:*** For me England brings back pleasant memories of walking on some windblown lea in Cornwall dressed in warm woollen jerseys, looking out to sea, and feeling a warmth brought about by being with my family in that place.

There is also the kind of awkwardness that occurs when a parallel structure breaks down—or isn't sufficiently built up:

> ***fp:*** During my trip I had the chance to learn some of the language and to help with the shopping and cooking—all of which helped make the experience enjoyable.

The sentence structure implies that we're going to be given more than two things—and the phrase "all of which" makes it sound as though we have been. Perhaps the writer subconsciously thought of "shopping" and "cooking" as separate items; but the parallelism is in the verbs *learn* and *help*. That is, the implied parallel series after *to* is not fulfilled.

> ***revised:*** During my visit I had the chance to learn some of the language and to help with the shopping and the cooking; these activities helped make the experience enjoyable.

Alternatively, a third element could be supplied, or *cooking* could be governed by a third verb, such as "participate in."

See #40.

A2

Numbering and Cross-Referencing

The book's sections are numbered consecutively throughout, without regard to chapters. Cross-references are to section and subsection numbers, or, occasionally, to chapters. In the index, references are to page numbers. Exercises are numbered according to their sections; note that some sections do not include exercises.

Important Terms

The first one or two times an important term occurs, it is in boldface. Pay attention to these terms, for they make up the basic vocabulary necessary for the intelligent discussion of grammar, syntax, and style.

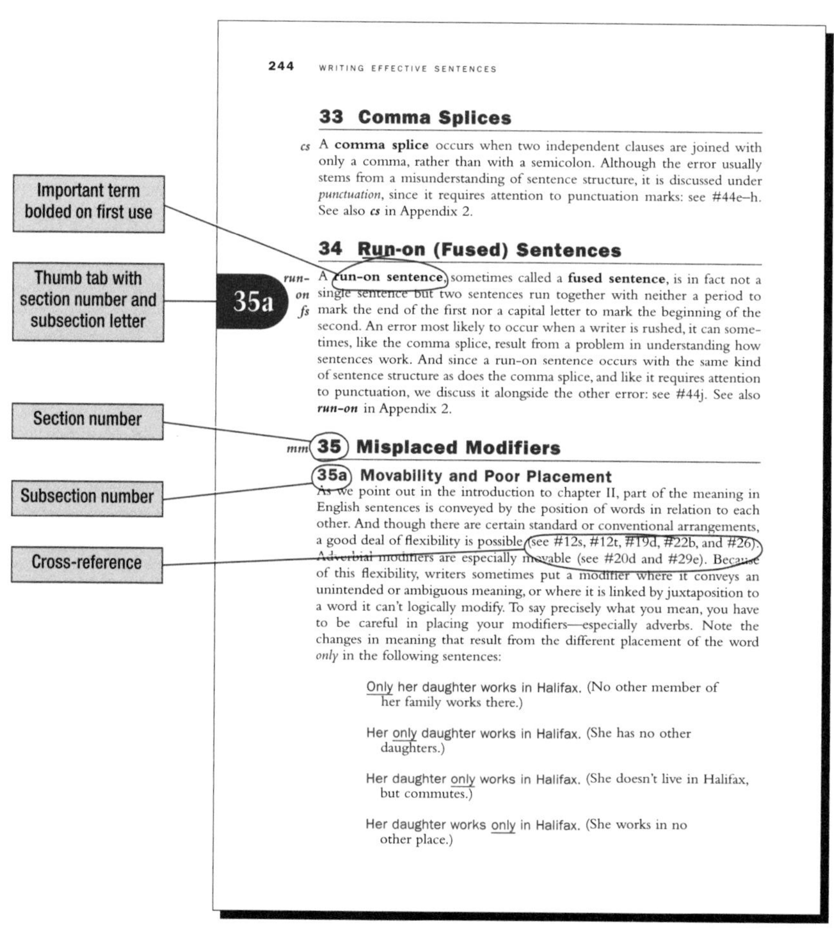

244 WRITING EFFECTIVE SENTENCES

33 Comma Splices

cs A **comma splice** occurs when two independent clauses are joined with only a comma, rather than with a semicolon. Although the error usually stems from a misunderstanding of sentence structure, it is discussed under *punctuation*, since it requires attention to punctuation marks: see #44e–h. See also ***cs*** in Appendix 2.

34 Run-on (Fused) Sentences

run-on fs A **run-on sentence**, sometimes called a **fused sentence**, is in fact not a single sentence but two sentences run together with neither a period to mark the end of the first nor a capital letter to mark the beginning of the second. An error most likely to occur when a writer is rushed, it can sometimes, like the comma splice, result from a problem in understanding how sentences work. And since a run-on sentence occurs with the same kind of sentence structure as does the comma splice, and like it requires attention to punctuation, we discuss it alongside the other error: see #44j. See also ***run-on*** in Appendix 2.

mm 35 Misplaced Modifiers

35a Movability and Poor Placement

As we point out in the introduction to chapter II, part of the meaning in English sentences is conveyed by the position of words in relation to each other. And though there are certain standard or conventional arrangements, a good deal of flexibility is possible (see #12s, #12t, #19d, #22b, and #26). Adverbial modifiers are especially movable (see #20d and #29e). Because of this flexibility, writers sometimes put a modifier where it conveys an unintended or ambiguous meaning, or where it is linked by juxtaposition to a word it can't logically modify. To say precisely what you mean, you have to be careful in placing your modifiers—especially adverbs. Note the changes in meaning that result from the different placement of the word *only* in the following sentences:

Only her daughter works in Halifax. (No other member of her family works there.)

Her only daughter works in Halifax. (She has no other daughters.)

Her daughter only works in Halifax. (She doesn't live in Halifax, but commutes.)

Her daughter works only in Halifax. (She works in no other place.)

Other Key Features

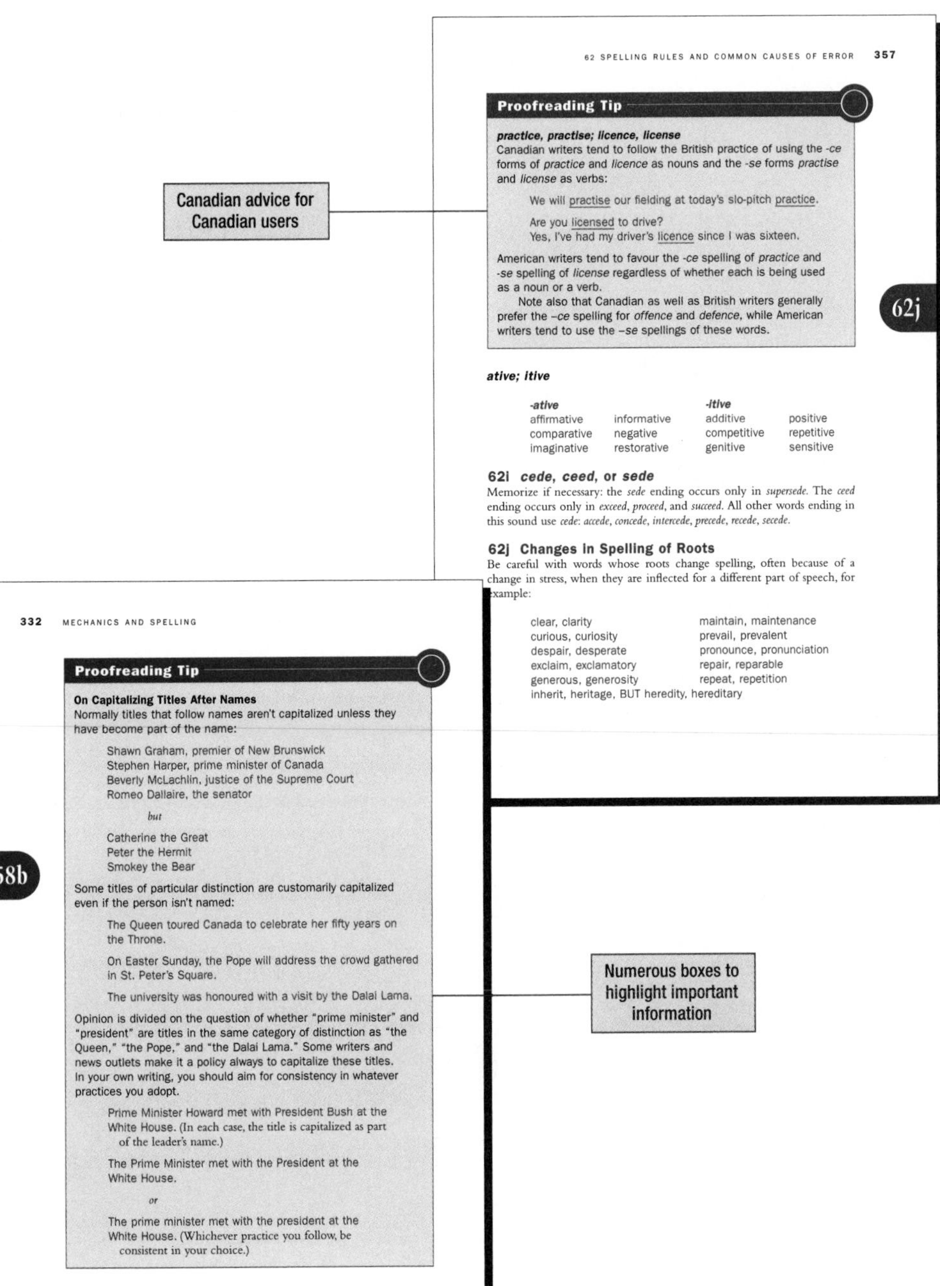

62 SPELLING RULES AND COMMON CAUSES OF ERROR 357

Proofreading Tip

practice, practise; licence, license
Canadian writers tend to follow the British practice of using the *-ce* forms of *practice* and *licence* as nouns and the *-se* forms *practise* and *license* as verbs:

We will practise our fielding at today's slo-pitch practice.

Are you licensed to drive?
Yes, I've had my driver's licence since I was sixteen.

American writers tend to favour the *-ce* spelling of *practice* and *-se* spelling of *license* regardless of whether each is being used as a noun or a verb.

Note also that Canadian as well as British writers generally prefer the *–ce* spelling for *offence* and *defence*, while American writers tend to use the *–se* spellings of these words.

62j

ative; itive

-ative		***-itive***	
affirmative	informative	additive	positive
comparative	negative	competitive	repetitive
imaginative	restorative	genitive	sensitive

62i *cede, ceed,* or *sede*
Memorize if necessary: the *sede* ending occurs only in *supersede*. The *ceed* ending occurs only in *exceed*, *proceed*, and *succeed*. All other words ending in this sound use *cede*: *accede, concede, intercede, precede, recede, secede*.

62j Changes in Spelling of Roots
Be careful with words whose roots change spelling, often because of a change in stress, when they are inflected for a different part of speech, for example:

clear, clarity	maintain, maintenance
curious, curiosity	prevail, prevalent
despair, desperate	pronounce, pronunciation
exclaim, exclamatory	repair, reparable
generous, generosity	repeat, repetition

inherit, heritage, BUT heredity, hereditary

332 MECHANICS AND SPELLING

Proofreading Tip

On Capitalizing Titles After Names
Normally titles that follow names aren't capitalized unless they have become part of the name:

Shawn Graham, premier of New Brunswick
Stephen Harper, prime minister of Canada
Beverly McLachlin, justice of the Supreme Court
Romeo Dallaire, the senator

but

Catherine the Great
Peter the Hermit
Smokey the Bear

58b

Some titles of particular distinction are customarily capitalized even if the person isn't named:

The Queen toured Canada to celebrate her fifty years on the Throne.

On Easter Sunday, the Pope will address the crowd gathered in St. Peter's Square.

The university was honoured with a visit by the Dalai Lama.

Opinion is divided on the question of whether "prime minister" and "president" are titles in the same category of distinction as "the Queen," "the Pope," and "the Dalai Lama." Some writers and news outlets make it a policy always to capitalize these titles. In your own writing, you should aim for consistency in whatever practices you adopt.

Prime Minister Howard met with President Bush at the White House. (In each case, the title is capitalized as part of the leader's name.)

The Prime Minister met with the President at the White House.

or

The prime minister met with the president at the White House. (Whichever practice you follow, be consistent in your choice.)

Other Key Features

Abundant exercises and examples throughout

17 VERBS 149
Exercise 17h (2) Using auxiliary verbs
Select ten or so of the sentences you wrote for the preceding exercise and try using do and some of the modal auxiliaries (see #17e) with them to produce different meanings.
Example: I do paint pictures. I should be painting the garage.
I did paint pictures. I should have been painting pictures.
Didn't you paint pictures? I shouldn't have tried painting the ceiling.
I may have painted pictures. Could I have been painting in my sleep?
Can you paint? They must have been painting all night.
17i
17i Sequence of Tenses
When two or more verbs occur in the same sentence, they will sometimes be of the same tense, but often they will be of different tenses.
1. Compound sentences
In a compound sentence, made up of two or more independent clauses (see #12z), the verbs can be equally independent; use whatever tenses the sense requires:
I am leaving [present progressive] now, but she will leave [future] in the morning.
The polls have closed [present perfect]; the clerks will soon be counting [future progressive] the ballots.
He had made [past perfect] his promise, and the committee decided [past] to hold him to it; therefore they will expect [future] his cooperation in drafting a new business plan in the weeks ahead.
2. Past tense in independent clauses
In complex or compound-complex sentences, if the verb in an independent clause is in any of the past tenses, the verbs in any clauses subordinate to it will usually also be in one of the past tenses. For example:
I told her that I was sorry.

SAMPLE STUDENT ESSAYS WITH COMMENTS AND GRADES 569
A Cathy,
This essay was a pleasure to read. You made a valid argument, using authority to back your statements, and you acknowledged and refuted the opposition's views while keeping a friendly tone. In addition, the essay combines a variety of sentence types and styles that keeps the readers engaged with the topic.
For the next essay, however, you may want to proofread carefully for spelling mistakes.
Sample Essay No. 6
Contrasting Vancouver and Abbotsford
v.t. use present perfect
Unbelievably, I lived in almost 10 different places in Canada. When I first came to Canada, I lived in Lethbridge and then I moved to Calgary. After that my family moved to BC where I subsequently lived in Nanaimo, Langley, Aldergrove, Abbotsford, Walnut Grove, Surrey and Vancouver.
correct verb tense
Truthfully, I have attended about 15 different schools. Different places evoke a different atmosphere, due to the surrounding and the people.
sp: "surroundings"
I moved from Abbotsford to Vancouver just a year ago; they are the two most recent places that I've lived in. Abbotsford and Vancouver have many similarities and differences.
can you list them? or explain why?
Abbotsford is a rural place where agriculture is the main economy. Driving through the country, we can breathe in the fresh air and look at the farm animals grazing on the grass. I love the fresh open land of green grass everywhere and large spaces between the houses. Fortunately, houses here are much cheaper than the houses in Vancouver, hence, there is a lower demand for land in the country. The road is less crowded here because there are fewer occupants, less likely to get into car accidents.
unnecessary
art. (use "the" with a limiting phrase)
one? or many? plural
you need to add a conjunction & subject & verb
A1
Vancouver is an urban place where the land is more valuable. Everywhere on the sidewalk there would be people walking. I made many friends here because there are more opportunities for me to encounter them. Sometimes I feel that there is no fresh are here because of the busy traffic at every hour of the day, polluting the air. The houses here
idiom: "On the sidewalks everywhere"
people?
use present tense – not conditional form
sp
transition

Marked student essays that serve as models for how to edit and format written work

Other Key Features

Detailed guidelines for documenting sources in MLA, APA, Chicago, and CSE styles

An article in an edited book

Kaplan, A. (2003). Women, film, resistance: Changing paradigms. In J. Levitin, J. Plessis & V. Raoul (Eds.), *Women filmmakers: Refocusing* (pp. 15–28). Vancouver: UBC Press.

An article in a reference book

Fernandez, D. (2002). Rice cake of the Philippines. In A. Davidson (Ed.) *The Penguin companion to food* (pp. 792–797). London: Penguin.

A multivolume work

Smelser, N.J. & Baltes, P.B. (Eds.). (2001). *International encyclopedia of the social and behavioural sciences* (vols. 1–26) Amsterdam: Elsevier.

An anonymous article

Riopel takes world junior silver. (2007, 24 February). *The Globe and Mail*, p. S5.

A republished book

81a

McLuhan, M. (2002). *The mechanical bride: Folklore of industrial man.* Corte Madera, CA: Gingko Press. (original work published 1951).

A translated work

Benjamin, W. (2006). *Berlin childhood around 1900* (H. Eiland, Trans.). London: Belknap Press.

A review

Cohen, L. (2003). Metaphor and alienation. [Review of the book *The age of immunology: Conceiving the future in an alienating world*]. *Anthropological Quarterly, 76*, 343–350.

Woolley, P.J. (2002). Review of the book *Terrorism in the mind of God: The global rise of religious violence. The Journal of Conflict Studies, 22*, 152–153.

The first review by L. Cohen is entitled "Metaphor and alienation." The second review by P.J. Woolley is untitled, as are many reviews appearing in scholarly journals in the behavioural and social sciences.

A dissertation abstract

Ing, N.L. (2002). Dealing with shame and unresolved trauma: Residential school and its impact on 2nd and 3rd generation adults (Doctoral dissertation, University of British Columbia, 2001). *Dissertation Abstracts International 62/08*, 2664.

A letter

Wright, A. (2007, February 24). War cover-up? [Letter to the editor]. *The Globe and Mail*, p. A18.

An audio recording

Ma, Y. (2007). *Appassionato* [CD]. Toronto: Sony BMG Music Canada.

A musical recording (by musicians other than the original artist)

Foster, S. (1851). Sweetly she sleeps, my Alice fair [Recorded by C. LaRue, C. Norman, & K. Robertson]. On *Lullaby journey* [CD]. Troy, New York: Dorian. (1996) 81a

A television program

Weissman, A. (Director). (2006, July 16). Blue Buddha: Lost secrets of Tibetan medicine [Television series episode]. In *The Nature of Things with David Suzuki*. Toronto: Canadian Broadcasting Corporation.

A videotape

Lapointe, P., Wong, G.Y.G., & Menard, J. (Producers) and Isacsson, M., & Lapointe, P. (Directors). (2002). *View from the summit: Quebec City—April 20–22, 2001* [Motion picture]. Canada. (Available from the National Film Board of Canada, P.O. Box 6100, Station Centre-Ville, Montreal, PQ H3C 3H5)

Acknowledgements

As with the previous editions of *The Canadian Writer's Handbook*, the fifth edition owes much to the contributions of reviewers, colleagues, friends, fellow writers, and talented and committed editors.

For their determination to strengthen and polish their work and their commitment to grow and change as thinkers and writers, we thank our students. We are especially grateful for their generosity in allowing us to use their questions and insights about writing in this book.

We deeply appreciate the encouragement, advice, and support we receive from the talented and enthusiastic staff of Oxford University Press—especially from David Stover, Phyllis Wilson, Kathleen McGill, Molly Armstrong, and Peter MacDonald. Special appreciation goes to our meticulous, ever-patient, and gifted manuscript editors, Eric Sinkins and Janna Green.

To all of you, many thanks.

Jan de Bruyn, Ramona Montagnes, and Judy Brown
University of British Columbia

Principles of Composition

I

Introduction: Paragraphs, the Writing Process, Argument, and In-class Writing

Writing is paradoxical, when you think about it. It is, on the one hand, the most commonplace of activities—something many of us do in one way or another every day of the week, every week of the year. On the other hand, writing is one of the most astonishing and complex acts of communication any of us is asked to undertake in the course of getting an education, doing a job, or living a life.

Writing calls upon us to exercise creativity in generating ideas out of our own experience; it asks us to practise synthesis in entering the world of ideas and in discovering and integrating the ideas of others with insights of our own; it expects us to develop our powers of communication in shaping and presenting our arguments to different audiences of readers; it challenges us to demonstrate our talents for organization, reflection, and revision in working through the writing process from that first idea to the printing of our final draft.

Chapter I investigates the principles of unity, coherence, and emphasis that apply to the larger units of communication, the paragraph and the essay. It provides a guide to the process of composing and writing an essay, and along the way, will offer advice on writing argument and on composing in-class essays and essay examinations.

1 Kinds of Paragraphs

A paragraph can be classified in two ways:

1. according to its function in its larger context;
2. according to the kind of material it contains and the way that material is developed.

1a Functions of Paragraphs

Introductory, **concluding**, and **transitional paragraphs** are especially designed to begin or end an essay or to provide links between major sections of a longer essay. Other paragraphs in an essay, the **body paragraphs**, contribute to the development of a topic.

1b Kinds of Paragraphs: Methods of Development

Body paragraphs can be classified according to the way their material is developed. There are several **methods of development** to choose from. The method(s) you use for any given paragraph or essay will depend on the nature of your topic and on your audience and purpose. Principal methods include: *description*, *narration*, *definition*, *classification*, *analysis into parts*, *process analysis*, *comparison and contrast*, *cause and effect*, and *example and illustration*. The following questions can help you approach essay topics with these methods in mind. In each question, "X" represents the topic being developed.

- *description*: What are the physical features of X?
- *narration*: What is the story/history of X?
- *definition*: What is X?
- *classification*: Into what categories or types can X be divided?
- *analysis*: What are the parts of X and how do they contribute to the whole of X?
- *process analysis*: What are the steps of X, or what are the steps leading to X?
- *comparison and contrast*: How is X similar to Y? How is X different from Y?
- *cause and effect*: What are the causes of or reasons for X? What are the effects or consequences of X?
- *example and illustration*: What are some concrete/specific examples or instances of X?

These methods of development are seldom mutually exclusive. Two or more are often combined in a single paragraph, and a whole essay may use several. Even narration can be used in an expository (explanatory) essay: for example, a case study may provide narrative evidence to support an observation.

Some methods are combined in other ways. For example, when you are comparing or contrasting you are also necessarily classifying and defining. And almost any method can be thought of as supplying examples to support or clarify an assertion made early in a paragraph or essay. As long as you maintain the fundamental requirements of unity and coherence, you can mix and combine these methods in any way that serves your purpose.

To demonstrate the ways in which the questions we have listed would operate in the development of a topic, consider the following scenario. (For further examples and exercises, see #1–7 Review later in this chapter.)

Suppose that you were asked to write a short paper of 500 words or so on the broad subject area of contemporary air travel. At first, you might draw a blank in thinking about ways in which to focus the topic to allow you to write something distinctive—something to engage your own interest and to earn the respect and interest of your potential readers. Applying the questions we have listed would very likely help you to open up the possibilities for development.

The process would look something like this:

SUBJECT: air travel today

narration: What is the story? Tell the story of recent air travel to the United States.

analysis: What were the steps in the process of the journey?

effect: What are the consequences of air travel?

- the stress of travelling during times of heightened security/terrorism alerts
- the boredom of sitting for hours in the boarding lounge, the airline cabins, the line-ups for luggage
- cramped quarters and claustrophobia for those travelling economy class

comparison: What are the essential differences between travel to the US by air and travel by car, train, or bus?

description: What might I describe to enhance my paper?

- the terminal building
- the security gate or customs desk
- the cramped quarters in the airline cabin
- the noise of the aircraft, of fellow passengers

In this stage of the process, you might see the methods of definition, classification, process analysis, and example/illustration as being less promising. Keep in mind that you may return to them at a later point, for the process of thinking your way through a topic is *recursive*—back and forth—rather than linear.

Following is an example of one of the paragraphs that might result from this process:

My most recent trip to New York City brought home to me the ways in which airline travel has changed for the worse since the events of September 11, 2001. Concerns	**narrative opening**
about security were evident from the moment we made our way to the security gates at Vancouver Airport. Passengers were asked to remove overcoats and shoes; they were required to dispose of gels and liquids in carry-on luggage; their photo identification was studied carefully; every adult passenger was questioned about travel plans by members of the security staff. After a four-hour	**analysis: the steps in the security process**
delay in our departure time, armed air marshals apparently boarded the aircraft with us, and the cockpit was	**time transition: "after a four-hour delay"**
locked. These measures put many	**effects of the process**

of us passengers on edge and added a large dose of nervousness to the boredom and claustrophobia long associated with cross-border flights in less dangerous times.

2–6 Unity, Coherence, and Emphasis in Paragraphs

To be effective, all paragraphs, but especially body paragraphs, require **unity**, **coherence**, and well-controlled **emphasis**. Writing a paragraph involves designing the best possible package to contain and convey your ideas. You have a sense of what point you wish to convey (your topic), and, usually early in the process, you have an array of items to include as well (your supporting ideas and evidence). You arrange your ideas and evidence in the package by ordering them logically, linking them to one another using strategies for coherence. You may well spend some time rearranging to make the package look the way you want it to—to give each item the appropriate emphasis.

2 Paragraph Unity

An effective body paragraph ordinarily deals with one main idea; its singleness of purpose engages its readers by focusing their attention on that main idea. If a paragraph is disrupted by irrelevant digressions or unnecessary shifts in point of view or focus, readers will lose the thread of the discourse and become confused. In other words, a paragraph has unity when every sentence in it contributes to its purpose and nothing in it is irrelevant to that purpose.

3 Paragraph Coherence

Though a paragraph is unified because every sentence contributes to the development of its single theme or idea, it could still come apart if it doesn't have another essential quality: coherence. Coherence can be defined as the connection of ideas. Some inexperienced writers assume that simply placing one sentence after another guarantees coherence. In fact, coherence is achieved only by carefully packing the contents of a paragraph and linking the ideas to one another. You can ensure coherence in your writing in two ways:

1. by carefully organizing your material, and
2. by using a variety of transitional devices that create structural coherence.

4 Coherence Through Organization: Beginning, Middle, and Ending

A body paragraph has a *beginning*, a *middle*, and an *ending*. Good organization means rational order. Typically, the beginning introduces the main idea; the middle clearly and logically follows from and develops the statement of that idea, and the ending is a natural conclusion that unobtrusively closes the discussion or provides a hook for the next paragraph. (But see the **Writing Tip: On Positioning Transitional Material** in #4a.)

4a The Beginning: Topic Sentences

Body paragraphs typically open with a statement of the main idea, called a **topic sentence**.

1. Functions of topic sentences

A good topic sentence indicates what the paragraph will be about. It is, in effect, a promise that the rest of the paragraph fulfills. If the paragraph is part of a larger context, such as an essay, the topic sentence will usually perform two other functions:

1. It will refer to the subject of the essay and at least suggest the relation of the paragraph to that subject.

2. It will provide a transition so that the new paragraph flows smoothly from the preceding paragraph.

On Positioning Transitional Material

It is sometimes possible, but often difficult, to provide forward-looking material at the end of a paragraph. Don't struggle to get something transitional into the last sentence of a paragraph. The work of transition should be done by the first sentence of the next paragraph. In other words, tampering with a paragraph's final sentence merely for transitional purposes may diminish that paragraph's integrity and effectiveness. See #4c.

2. Efficiency of topic sentences

Since it has so much to do, a good topic sentence, even more than other sentences, should be efficient. Here is one that is not:

> The poet uses a great deal of imagery throughout the poem.

4a

The sentence indicates the topic—the poem's imagery—but promises nothing more than to show that the poem contains a lot of it. But offering a long list of images wouldn't develop an idea; it would merely illustrate what is self-evident. Trying to revise this weak topic sentence, the writer inserted the adjective *good* before *imagery*; now the paragraph must at least try to show that the abundant images are good ones (not as easy a task as the writer may have thought). But the focus is still largely on the quantity of imagery, which is not where the focus should be. What is most important is the function of the imagery: What does the poet do with the imagery? Further thought might lead to a revision like this—a topic sentence that not only has more substance in itself but also suggests the approach the paragraph will take:

> The poem's imagery, most of it drawn from nature, helps to create not only the poem's mood but its themes as well.

The same essay also contained the following inefficient topic sentence:

> In the second stanza, the poet continues to use images.

The revision didn't help much:

> In the second stanza, the poet continues to use excellent images to express his ideas.

Again, what is needed is something sharper, more specific, such as an assertion that provides a significant idea that can be usefully developed. For example,

> The imagery in the second stanza contrasts vividly with that of the first.

or

> In the second stanza, images of death begin the process that leads to the poem's ironic conclusion.

A good opening topic sentence should be more than just a table of contents; it should be a significant part of the contents of the paragraph. Pay close attention to the formulation of your topic sentences, for they can help you achieve both unity and coherence not only in individual paragraphs but also in an essay as a whole (see #8a–b).

3. Notes on the placement of topic sentences

In many paragraphs, the development fulfills the promise made in an opening topic sentence. Or, by conscious design, a topic sentence may be placed at the end or elsewhere in a paragraph. Sometimes delaying a topic sentence can increase readers' interest by creating a little mystery to get them to read on. And stating a topic at the end of a paragraph takes advantage of that most emphatic position (see #6). Note for example the paragraph in #4b.1 labelled *Coherence through orderly development*. The topic sentence identifies the topic, which has two elements. But the paragraph itself refers to "development" only at the end, where the short final sentence explicitly ties it all to the idea of coherence. That part of the topic, in other words, we delayed until the end, or climax.

A paragraph's topic, then, though single, may consist of more than one part. Similarly, it may not be stated all in one sentence. In this paragraph and the one preceding, for example, note that not until the end of the second sentence is the topic fully clear. It is not uncommon for a paragraph to have a second topic sentence, one that partly restates the topic and partly leads into the body of the paragraph.

And, rarely, a paragraph's topic may not be stated at all because the focal idea of a paragraph is clearly and strongly implied. This kind of paragraph occurs most often in narratives, where paragraphs begin in such a way that their relation to the preceding paragraph is sufficiently clear—perhaps indicated by no more than an opening *Then* or *When*.

See also the Notes on Beginnings, #9-l.

4b The Middle

1. Coherence through orderly development

A well-developed body paragraph fulfills the promise of its beginning. If, for example, you were writing a paragraph that began with the last example of a topic sentence above ("In the second stanza images of death begin the process that leads to the poem's ironic conclusion"), you would have to explain the process and the irony of the poem's conclusion, and you would have to show how images of death from the second stanza set that process in motion. To fulfill your promise effectively, then, you would have to decide how to organize your material. For example, you might first describe the irony of the conclusion and then analyze the images to show how they lead to that conclusion. Or you might start by analyzing the death imagery and then proceed to answer some questions that you could ask yourself: What effect do the images create? How does that effect contribute to the way the poem proceeds? How does that process lead to the conclusion? In other words, after considering the different possibilities, you would choose a way of presenting your material, and the order you choose to follow should be one that makes sense; one idea should lead logically to another until you reach your goal. Then your paragraph will be coherent.

2. Patterns of development

Orderly development sometimes occurs automatically as one works through one's ideas in composing paragraphs and essays. But most writers must give some conscious thought to how a particular paragraph (or essay) can best be shaped. The most common *patterns of development* writers use to make their paragraphs orderly and coherent are the following:

- *spatial* (moving through space, such as top to bottom or left to right; used in describing physical space)
- *chronological* (moving through time; used in narration and process analysis)
- *climactic* (moving from the least important to most important point; often used in academic writing)
- *inverse pyramid* (moving from the most important to least important point; used in reportage/print journalism)
- *inductive* (moving from data to assertions; often used in writing for sciences and social sciences)
- *deductive* (moving from assertions to supporting data or premises; often used in writing for the humanities)
- *block* (in a comparison of two items, a full discussion of the first item followed by a full discussion of the second item)
- *alternating* (in a comparison of two items, a back-and-forth discussion of the first and second items)

Further, some of the *methods of development* discussed above (see #1b) themselves impose patterns on the arrangement of ideas in a paragraph. In addition to using narration and process analysis, which focus on chronological order, or description, with its focus on spatial order, one can move from cause to effect or from effect to cause, or from a statement about a whole to a division of it into parts (analysis), or from a statement about one thing to a comparison of it with another. As with the methods of development, these patterns are not mutually exclusive within a paragraph or an essay.

4c The Ending

As you compose and revise your drafts, the endings of your paragraphs will sometimes come naturally. But they are likely to do so only if, when you begin a paragraph, you know just where it is going. The final sentence of a paragraph, like all the others, should be a part of the whole (and see the **Writing Tip: On Positioning Transitional Material** on page 7). In other words, the final sentence of a paragraph will most often be a statement growing out of the substance of the paragraph, a sentence that rounds off its paragraph in a satisfying way.

Some advice for ending paragraphs

If a paragraph doesn't seem to be ending naturally, you may have to stop and think consciously about it. Here are a few pointers to help you do that:

1. A good ending may point back to the beginning, but it will not merely repeat it; if it repeats something, it will do so in order to put it in the new light made possible by the development of the paragraph.

2. A good ending sentence doesn't usually begin with a stiff "In conclusion" or "To conclude." In fact, sometimes the best way to end a paragraph is simply to let it stop, once its point is made. A too-explicit conclusion might damage the effectiveness of an otherwise good paragraph that has a natural quality of closure at its end.

3. A good ending might have a slight stylistic shift that marks a paragraph's closing, perhaps no more than an unusually short or long sentence. Or an ending might be marked by an allusion or brief quotation, as long as it is relevant and to the point and not there simply for its own sake.

4. A good paragraph usually doesn't end with an indented ("block") quotation, or even a shorter full-sentence quotation that isn't set off. Even though you carefully introduce such a quotation, it will almost inevitably leave a feeling that you have abandoned your paragraph to someone else. Complete such a paragraph with at least a brief comment that explains the quotation, justifies it, or re-emphasizes its main thrust.

5 Structural Coherence

Careful organization and development go a long way toward achieving coherence. But you will sometimes need to use other techniques as well, providing links that ensure a smooth flow of thought from one sentence to another.

The main devices for structural coherence are parallelism, repetition, pronouns and demonstrative adjectives, and transitional words and phrases. Like the methods and patterns of development, these devices are not mutually exclusive: two or more may work together in the same paragraph, sometimes even in the same words and phrases.

5a Parallelism (See #28c and #40.)

Parallel sentence structure is a simple and effective way to bind successive sentences. Similar structural patterns in clauses and phrases work like a call and its echo. But don't try to maintain a series of parallel elements for too long. If the echoes remain obvious, they will be too noticeable and will diminish in power as they get farther from the original. Parallelism, like any other device, should not be overdone.

5b Repetition

Like parallelism, repetition of words and phrases effectively links successive sentences. But the caution against overdoing it is most applicable here. Repetition properly controlled for rhetorical effect can be powerful (as in Martin Luther King's famous "I have a dream" speech), but repetition, especially on paper, can also become evidence of a writer's limited vocabulary or ingenuity. Structure your repetitions carefully; don't put too many too close together. And generally use the device sparingly.

5c

5c Pronouns and Demonstrative Adjectives

By referring to something mentioned earlier, a pronoun (see #14) or a demonstrative adjective (see #19a) constructs a bridge within the paragraph between itself and its antecedent or referent.

Writing Tip 

Using Pronouns and Demonstrative Adjectives to Create Unity and Coherence

It is also possible, of course, to use pronouns and demonstrative adjectives to create links between paragraphs, but avoid

a. an ambiguous antecedent or referent, and
b. a distant antecedent.

If you are far beyond the antecedent, or if more than one is possible, you risk confusing your readers rather than building coherence for them. Either way, straight repetition is preferable.

And make it a point to use demonstrative adjectives rather than demonstrative pronouns. Demonstrative adjectives are clear and can add emphasis. Pronouns are not emphatic; rather they can be weak and ambiguous (see #14f, #16c, #19a, #41, and ***ref*** in Appendix 2).

5d Transitional Terms

Used strategically, transitional words and phrases can create a logical flow from one part or idea to another by indicating their relation. The best transitional signal for a particular spot in a discourse creates successful coherence. Here are some of the more common and useful transitional terms:

- terms showing addition of one point to another

and	also	another	in addition
further	besides	moreover	

- terms showing similarity between ideas

again	equally	in other words	in the same way
likewise	similarly		

- terms showing difference between ideas

but	although	conversely	despite
even though	however	yet	though
in contrast	whereas	nevertheless	in spite of
still	otherwise	on the contrary	on the other hand

- terms showing cause and effect or other logical relations

as a result	because	consequently	for
hence	of course	since	then
therefore	thus		

- terms introducing examples or details

for example	in particular	namely	specifically
for instance	to illustrate	that is	

- terms expressing emphasis

chiefly	especially	more important
indeed	mainly	primarily

- terms showing relations in time and space

after	afterward	at the same time	before
earlier	in the meantime	later	meanwhile
simultaneously	then	while	subsequently
behind	beyond	farther away	here
nearby	in the distance	next	there
to the left			

These and other such words and phrases, occurring usually at or near the beginnings of sentences, are the glue that helps hold paragraphs together. But if the paragraph isn't unified in its content, and if its parts haven't been arranged to fit with one another, then even these explicit transitional terms won't give much structural coherence to your writing.

Writing Tip

On Avoiding Overuse of Transitions

Don't overuse transitional terms. If your paragraph already contains structural elements that make it coherent, it won't need any of these. Adding a transitional word or phrase to nearly every sentence will make writing stiff and mechanical sounding.

5d

Exercise 3–5 Recognizing coherence

Point out the various means by which coherence is established in the following paragraph, and comment on their effectiveness.

> The Mercers, as David French presents them in his play *Leaving Home*, are much like real families are: essentially good people struggling for understanding and trying not to kill each other. French shows the audience a family much more authentic than the people with pasted-on smiles in those 1950s billboards and magazine advertisements. They have tremendous difficulties at times and tremendous happiness at other times. The cozy walls of their home cannot shut out past history, unhappy memories, miscommunication, and feelings of alienation. Despite, or perhaps because of their difficulties, they are heartbreakingly recognizable. The Mercer clan is the mid-twentieth-century Canadian family in all its contradictory glory—a force for both good and ill in the lives of its members.

6 Emphasis in Paragraphs

Just as in a sentence, so in a paragraph the most emphatic position is its ending, and the second most emphatic position is its beginning (see #29a). That is another reason the opening or topic sentence is so important a part of a paragraph. And an ending, because of its emphatic position, can make or break a paragraph.

But structure and diction are also important. Parallelism and repetition create emphasis. Independent clauses are more emphatic than subordinate clauses and phrases. Precise, concrete, and specific words are more emphatic than vague, abstract, and general ones. A long sentence will stand out among several shorter ones; a short sentence will stand out among longer ones. Keep these points in mind as you compose and revise your paragraphs; let emphasis contribute to the effectiveness of your writing.

7 Length of Paragraphs

There is no optimum length for a paragraph. The length of a paragraph will be determined by the requirements of the particular job it is doing. In narration or dialogue, a single sentence or a single word may constitute a paragraph. In a complex exposition or argument essay, a paragraph may go on for a page or more—though such long paragraphs are rare in modern writing. Most body paragraphs consist of at least three or four sentences, and seldom more than nine or ten. Transitional paragraphs are usually short, sometimes only one sentence. Introductory and concluding paragraphs will be of various lengths, depending on the complexity of the material and on the techniques of beginning and ending that the writer is using.

7a Too Many Long Paragraphs

If you find that you are writing many long paragraphs, you may be overdeveloping, piling more into a paragraph than its topic requires. Or you may not be weeding out irrelevant material. Or you may be dealing in one paragraph with two or more topics that should be dealt with in separate paragraphs. Any of these tendencies can damage the coherence of your writing. Keep in mind that paragraphs are at least as much for readers as they are for writers. Generally, you should give your reader regular breaks to pause and consider your main claims and evidence, which means providing one or two paragraphs per page of your writing.

7b Too Many Short Paragraphs

A common weakness among inexperienced writers is to settle for paragraphs that are too short to develop their topics sufficiently. The body of a paragraph should be long enough to develop a topic satisfactorily. Merely restating or summarizing the topic is not enough. If you find yourself writing many short paragraphs, you may not be adequately developing your main ideas. Or you may be endangering coherence by splintering your discussion into small parts: when you revise, check to see if two or more related short paragraphs can be integrated to form one substantial paragraph. Generally, a body paragraph in a piece of academic writing should set out a claim and provide evidence well-integrated into your sentence structure. It should also comment on and explain the significance of the evidence. This structure, as you might expect, calls for several sentences—more than two or three short statements, in other words.

7c Variety

Try to ensure that any extended piece of writing you produce contains a variety of paragraph lengths: long, short, medium. The reader may become unengaged if the essay has a constant similarity of paragraph lengths. (The same is true of sentences of similar length: see #28a). You should also try to provide a variety of patterns (#4b.2) and methods of development (#1b) in your paragraphs. For example, parallelism, however admirable a device, would likely lose its effect if it were the basic pattern in several successive paragraphs.

Normally, then, the paragraphs that make up an extended piece of writing will vary in length. Ensure that each of your paragraphs is as long or as short as it needs to be to achieve its intended purpose. See also #8c.

1–7 Review: A Sample Paragraph with an Analysis

The paragraph that follows illustrates principles discussed in the preceding sections of this chapter. The writer has gone on to analyze her handling of the paragraph. Consider analyzing several paragraphs of your own writing in the same way to assess your strengths and weaknesses in this important aspect of writing.

> [1] Can child characters be heroic? [2] Some adult readers might argue that heroism is something beyond the reach of a child. [3] Such readers might add that children lack the experience, the knowledge, and the power required to separate themselves from the adult-dominated communities they know and to embark on the quest into the unsafe, unpredictable world identified with the hero's quest. [4] But consider characters as different as Lewis Carroll's Alice and, more recently, Philip Pullman's Will Parry. [5] Alice quite happily chooses to enter the bizarre world of Lewis Carroll's *Through the Looking Glass*, and she holds her own in encounters with lions, twin boys, bad-tempered eggs, and transmogrifying monarchs. [6] Will Parry, for his part, leaves Oxford to seek his missing father and with Lyra Silvertongue as his companion, leads other children as well as adults through adventure, suffering, and turmoil to establish a Republic of Heaven on Earth.

Analysis of the Paragraph

Function

- The paragraph is from the body of the essay as far as a reader can determine without the context of the whole essay.
- It deals with substantial ideas about child heroism in literature.

Methods of development

- The principal method is argument.
- There is also an element of comparison in sentence 4.
- The writer gives examples to support the argument. See sentences 5 and 6.

Unity

- The paragraph focuses in each of its sentences on how child protagonists can be heroic.

Coherence and emphasis

- The topic sentence of this paragraph is sentence 1.
- Sentence 1 starts with a question to engage the reader's attention.
- Sentence 2 picks up the key words "child" and "heroism."
- Sentence 3 picks up the words "readers" and "children."
- Sentence 4 starts with a strong coordinating conjunction "but" that indicates a reversal in thought.
- Sentences 5 and 6 follow parallel structure in content and form.

Length and development

– With six sentences, the paragraph can be said to be of average length.
– Its development is sufficient for its purpose.

Review Exercises 1–7 Working with paragraphs

A. Compose topic sentences that will effectively begin paragraphs for *five* of the following:

1. to explain to a ten-year-old how to make a bacon, lettuce, and tomato sandwich
2. to describe an encounter with a panhandler
3. to tell a friend about your experience of seeing an accident happen
4. to introduce an essay on the history of clocks
5. to recount an anecdote about one of your relatives in order to illustrate his or her character
6. to describe your dream house
7. to analyze a particular article you recently read in a newspaper
8. to introduce an essay on the role of fast food in our culture
9. to introduce a short essay about something important you learned when you failed at something
10. to explain what *Canadian* means to you

B. Write separate paragraphs developing two of the topic sentences you composed for Exercise A.

C. Analyze the paragraphs you have written in Exercise B by doing the following exercises:

1. Identify and illustrate the methods of development you used in writing each of the paragraphs for Exercise 2.
2. How did you ensure that your paragraphs are unified?
3. Identify and illustrate the techniques you used to make your paragraphs coherent.
4. What did you intend to achieve with your final sentence for each paragraph?

D. Here are some body paragraphs. Analyze and evaluate each one (you may also wish to assign rankings to them). Consider specifically each of the principles discussed in the preceding pages:

- methods of development
- unity
- coherence
- emphasis
- length and adequacy of development

Review Exercises 1–7 Working with paragraphs – *continued*

(1) Physical activity is good for people. It contributes greatly to a person's physical and mental well-being. The schedules of varsity teams are very demanding. The swim team has eleven practices a week, of which eight are mandatory—two a day, each an hour and a half in length. The workouts consist of approximately four thousand metres each. The program also consists of running, weight training, and flexibility exercises. Not only does this sort of exercise keep a person in good physical shape, but it also increases mental awareness. Because you are up and active before classes begin, you are more mentally and physically awake than if you had just gotten out of bed.

(2) Although some people, like the members of my family, find it a mystery, doing laundry involves only three simple steps. First, different-coloured clothes take different temperatures of water: so put the darks in cold water, the whites in hot water, and the others in warm water. Secondly, you need to tell the machine whether your load is supposed to be cold or hot, so adjust the dial accordingly and put in your detergent. Last but not least, when the cycle is finished, throw your clothes in the dryer, but be careful not to dry them at such a high heat that your favourite cotton sweater becomes your spaniel's favourite jacket.

(3) "A home should be a sail not an anchor," so the saying goes. A home should provide inspiration for creativity whether this source for creativity lies in an astounding view or in beautiful and meaningful objects. A home should encourage you to look outwards as well as inwards.

(4) The storyteller makes use of animal metaphors to describe an individual's character by naming him after the animal whose stereotyped personality he possesses. The importance of living creatures in folk tales is twofold. First, the folk tale is used to teach the tribe's children the significance of individual species; and second, the use of animal names suggests a great deal about a character's personality.

(5) I am attending university so that I can learn more about myself and the world. So far I have learned that I, like Hamlet, am a procrastinator. And that the world encompasses grades, caffeine, and a few dear kindred spirits.

(6) The intertidal fauna in general and specifically tide-pool fauna can act as model systems for population studies (Raffaelli &

Review Exercises 1–7 Working with paragraphs – *continued*

Hawkins 1996, Johnson 2000). For intertidal organisms, the tidal cycle constitutes a major environmental disturbance, and tidal effects will be especially pronounced for protozoa, which are often abundant in tide-pools (Scherren 1900, Fauré-Fremiet 1953). Furthermore, as protozoan generation times are on the order of hours to days, they are useful model-organisms to investigate population dynamics, the effects of disturbance, and cyclic behaviours (e.g. Gause 1934, Holyoak 2000). By recognizing the behaviour and distribution of these organisms, we can provide key information about survival strategies of tide-pool fauna and offer insight into general phenomena concerning the dynamics of populations and metapopulations. This study, thus, focuses on how one protozoan survives in tide-pools; in doing so we indicate the occurrence of both general and unique adaptations to a high-disturbance environment.

(7) Although the words *ignorance* and *stupidity* are often used interchangeably, there is a difference between them. *Ignorance* is defined as lack of knowledge and *stupidity* is defined as lack of intelligence. To call a person *ignorant* implies that the person does not know all that is known or can be learned. To call a person *stupid* implies that the person lacks the ability to learn and know. The words are similar in that they both indicate a deficiency in knowledge or learning, but they differ in that one signifies a permanent condition and the other a condition that may be only temporary. Ignorant people can educate and inform themselves. Stupid people have a dullness of mind that it is difficult or impossible to change.

(8) I believe that Jean Piaget's research has clearly shown that games and rule-making contribute to child development. Children learn much about autonomy and democracy while testing the rules of games. In his early research, Piaget chose 1,100 children along with the game of marbles to reach his conclusion. The choice of the game of marbles was a good one since it requires no referee and no adult supervision. It is played from early childhood to the pre-teen years. One six-year-old, when asked who he thought had made the rules, replied, "God, my father, and the town council." At about eleven years old, children agree that they can change the rules themselves. Piaget has shown that the game of marbles provides a way for children to test the quality of rules and the necessity of rules.

7c

Review Exercises 1–7 Working with paragraphs – *continued*

(9) If beauty is in the eye of the beholder, can the blind experience beauty? Of course. Although, in our ignorance, we sighted people often assume that beauty is purely a visual concept, in truth, beauty can be defined as anything that restores our souls or at least reminds us that we have souls.

(10) Everything looks beautiful from the saddle of my horse, especially on a crisp fall day. The autumn sun glints through the fretwork of golden poplar trees that border the road. The track ahead is muddy and well-trampled by many horses' feet. I can hear the clatter of hooves on the concrete, then the soft sucking sound of the mud as we gain momentum and move out to begin our ride. After we gain considerable speed, it happens. That wondrous sensation when horse and rider become one glorious moving body. I feel it now as my horse takes full rein while the blood surges and pounds in my ears and the wind frees my hair as it stings my face. Time ceases to exist here in a world of exhilarating revelation as I become giddy with excitement. Tired, my horse slows down. The spell is broken. The sun has disappeared completely, and the wind is beginning to rise in bone-chilling forecast of the dreary winter days to come. I will be back again, soon.

8–11 The Whole Essay

8 Essays: Unity, Coherence, and Emphasis

The principles of composition apply with equal validity to the essay as a whole and to each of its parts: what holds true for the sentence and the paragraph also holds true for the essay as a whole.

8a Unity

Like a sentence or a paragraph, an essay should be unified. That is, everything in it should be about one topic. If your paragraphs are themselves unified and if you make sure that the opening sentences of each paragraph refer explicitly (or implicitly but unmistakably) to your overall subject as indicated by your title (see #4a.1), your essay itself will be unified.

8b Coherence

Coherence should pertain not only between words in a sentence and between sentences in a paragraph, but also between paragraphs in an essay. If the beginning of each paragraph provides some kind of transition from the preceding paragraph, the essay will almost surely be coherent. The transitional words and phrases listed above (#5d) and others like them are often useful for establishing the necessary connections between paragraphs, but don't overdo it by using them to begin every paragraph. Often you can create the link by repeating a significant word or two from the preceding paragraph, usually from somewhere near its end, and sometimes you can make or strengthen the link with a demonstrative adjective, or even a pronoun (but see the **Writing Tip** in #5c). Remember, though, that transitional words and phrases are meant to draw attention to links that exist in the content of consecutive paragraphs. Without an inherent connection between one paragraph and the next, not even explicit transitions will be effective. (See also #4a, on topic sentences.)

8c Emphasis

Just as in a sentence or a paragraph (see #29a and #6), the most emphatic position in an essay is its ending, and the second most emphatic position is its beginning. That is why it is important to be clear and to the point at the beginning of an essay, usually stating the thesis explicitly (see #9-1.3), and why the ending of an essay should be forceful. Don't, for example, conclude by repeating your introduction or, in a short essay, by summarizing your points. And since the last thing readers see is usually what sticks most vividly in their minds, essays often use climactic order, beginning with simple or less elaborate points and ending with more important or complex ones (see #4b.2).

Further, the length of a paragraph automatically suggests something about the importance of its contents. Although a short, sharp paragraph can be emphatic in its own way, generally a long paragraph will deal with a relatively important part of the subject. As you look over your work, check to make sure you haven't skimped on an important point, and also that you haven't gone on for too long about a relatively minor point (see #7).

9 The Process of Planning, Writing, and Revising an Essay

No effective essay can be a mere random assemblage of sentences and paragraphs. It needs a shape, a design, even if only a simple one. How does one get from the blank page to the desired finished product? By taking certain steps, because a piece of writing, like any other product, is the result of a process. The usual steps that a writer takes, whether consciously or not, fall into three major stages:

- STAGE I: PLANNING
  - finding a subject and formulating questions about it
  - limiting the subject
  - determining audience and purpose
  - gathering reliable data
  - classifying and organizing the data
  - outlining

- STAGE II: WRITING
  - writing the first draft
  - integrating evidence
  - commenting on significance of evidence
- STAGE III: REVISING
  - revising
  - preparing the final draft
  - editing and proofreading

Sometimes one or more steps may be taken care of for you; for example, if you are assigned a specific topic, finding and limiting a subject, and perhaps even determining audience and purpose, will already be taken care of. And often several parts of the process will be going on at the same time; for example, there is often a good deal of interaction among the activities in the planning stage. Sometimes the order will be different; for example, you may not be clear about your purpose until you have finished gathering and then classifying and organizing data. And sometimes in the revising stage, you may want to go back and rethink your purpose, or dig up more material, or even further limit or expand your topic. But all the activities have to happen somehow, somewhere, sometime, for a polished piece of writing to be produced.

And even though you may take some of these steps as a matter of course, relatively inexperienced writers should consider following them deliberately, particularly if the projected essay is long or complicated, like a term paper or a research paper.

9a Finding a Subject and Pre-writing

1. For writing situations that are discipline-specific

When you are enrolled in a course of study for a particular discipline (for example, Asian studies, anthropology, environmental studies, comparative literature), writing topics will not necessarily be assigned to you. Instead, an essential part of the process will involve you designing topics and projects relevant to your studies. Develop topics around researchable questions of current interest in the field and narrow them to fit the time allotted to the assignment and the length expected by your reader.

You might consider some of the following when developing the proposal or statement of purpose that is often called for in such circumstances:

- a question of definition, a key term with a history of changing denotations over time [for a cultural geography course, "What is gendered space?"]
- a central debate evidenced in the scholarly writing produced in the discipline [for a Canadian studies course, "How do scholars of the 1970s and those of today differ on the evaluation of Pauline Johnson's poetry?"]

- a review of the scholarly literature surrounding a particular question in the field [for a children's literature course, "How can theories of ecocriticism be applied to the reading of Canadian children's literature set on the Prairies?"]
- a question or issue that crosses disciplinary boundaries (for example, a question preoccupying linguists and sociologists, or economists and geographers) [for a human geography course, "How will global climate change affect birth rates in Central and South America?"]
- an idea raised incidentally in lectures or seminars that deserves further investigation [for a film studies seminar course, "Do images of children in recent Canadian films provide clues to the way Canadian culture has constructed ideas of childhood?"]

Such possibilities should make it possible for you to produce a paper distinctive in its approach—something more and better than a cutting and pasting of the views of two or three major sources that may tend to exclude the perspective of the student writer.

In working out your research and preparing a plan for the paper, devise a reasonable timeline for research, planning, writing, revising, and editing. Consider the needs and expectations of your reading audience and the availability of a variety of electronic and non-electronic sources that are both scholarly and current. Keep in mind that the use of Canadian sources may be important to your objectives and to your readers.

2. For writing situations that are not discipline-specific

If you are enrolled in a writing course that involves writing papers in a variety of forms and for a range of audiences, you may be working outside a particular discipline or area of study. In such circumstances, a specific subject area or discipline will not likely be attached to your writing assignments, and you will be seeking one for yourself. Some writers think this is among the most challenging parts of composing an essay, but it needn't be, for subjects are all around us and within us. A few minutes of free-associating with a pencil and a sheet of paper, jotting down and playing around with questions and any ideas that pop into your head, will usually lead you at least to a subject area if not to a specific subject. Scanning the pages of a magazine or a newspaper, a scholarly website or journal is another way to stimulate a train of thought; editorial and letters pages are usually full of interesting subjects to write about, perhaps to argue about. Or think about the questions or problems you may have about the course for which you are writing the essay. Often the very thing that puzzles you provides you with a good topic. The possibilities are almost endless.

Try to find a subject that interests you, one that you will enjoy working with and living with for an extended period of time. Formulate a question or series of questions worth investigating and researching. Don't, in desperation, pick a subject that bores you, for you may handle it poorly, and

9a

probably bore your readers as well. If you are assigned a topic that doesn't particularly interest you, try to make it a learning experience: immerse yourself in it; you may be surprised at how interesting it can become.

Whether your assignment is discipline-specific or more general, consider producing in the initial stages a proposal or statement of purpose that you can discuss with your instructor or prospective readers. Following is a preliminary statement of purpose for a 1,000-word paper on nineteenth-century Canadian writers.

Kevin Cheung English 222/010
10 January 2007

Paper is due:	12 March 2007 (approximately two months)
Target length:	1,000 words
Audience:	fellow students and my instructor, all with an interest in the subject
Subject:	nineteenth-century Canadian writers
Topic:	contrasting the responses of Catharine Parr Traill and Susanna Moodie to their first years in Canada
Questions:	Why did these two individuals—sisters close in age and living close to one another in their first days in Upper Canada—react so differently to their new homeland? How is it that Traill celebrates the land, the people, even the winter weather? How is it that Moodie is so critical of the land, the people (especially her neighbours), and the conditions of life?

Major sources so far:

Charlotte Gray's *Sisters in the Wilderness*
Traill's *The Backwoods of Canada*
Moodie's *Roughing It in the Bush* and Atwood's *Journals of Susanna Moodie*

9b Limiting the Subject

Once you have a subject, limit it: narrow it to a topic you can develop adequately within the length of the essay you are writing. More often than not, writers start with subjects that are too big to handle. Seldom do they come up, right away, with a topic like what people's shoes reveal about their characters, or the dominant image cluster in a particular short story, or the inefficiency of the cafeteria; they're more likely to start with some vague notion about footwear, or about how enjoyable the story was, or about campus architecture. To save both time and energy, to avoid frustration, and to guarantee a better essay, be disciplined at this stage. If anything, overdo the narrowing, for at a later stage it's easier to broaden than it is to cut.

For example, let's say you wanted to write about "travelling"; that's obviously far too broad. "National travel" or "international travel" is narrower, but still too broad. "Travelling in Asia?" Better, but still too large, for where would you begin? How thorough could you be in a mere 500 or even 1,000 words? When you find yourself narrowing your subject to something like "How to survive on $20.00 a day in Tokyo" or "What to do if you have only 24 hours in Hong Kong" or "Why I don't travel with my mother" or "The day my passport got stolen," then you can confidently look forward to developing your topic with sufficient thoroughness and specificity. (See also #66.)

Exercise 9a–b Finding and limiting subjects

List ten broad subject areas that you have some interest in. Then, for each, specify two narrowed topics: (a) one that would be suitable for an essay of about 1,500 words (six double-spaced typed pages), and (b) one for an essay of about 500 words. (Feel free to list more than two topics if you wish.)

EXAMPLES

1. Broad topic: Clothing
   a) Narrower topics: Contemporary clothing, Renaissance clothing
   b) Even narrower topics: Gender differences reflected in contemporary clothing
2. Broad topic: Nature
   a) Narrower topics: Favourite trail walks, roses
   b) Even narrower topics: The therapeutic effects of walking on trails, how not to kill your houseplants, water imagery in a sonnet

9c Considering Audience and Purpose

1. Audience

When you write a personal letter, you naturally direct it to a specific reader. If you write a "Letter to the Editor" of a newspaper, you have only a vague notion of your potential readership, namely anyone who reads that newspaper, but you will know where the majority of them live, and knowing only that much could give you something to aim at in your letter. The sharper the focus you can get on your audience, the better you can control your writing to make it effective for that audience. Try to define or characterize your audience for a given piece of writing as precisely as possible.

Some of the writing you do for school may have only one reader: the instructor. But some assignments may ask you to address some specific audience; sometimes an instructor will ask you to write "for an audience of your peers." In the absence of any other guideline, writing for your peers is not a bad idea. Your choice of the right tone and language to use and of what definitions and explanations to provide will often be appropriate if you keep an interested and serious but not fully informed audience in mind.

2. Purpose

All writing has the broad purpose of communicating ideas. In a course, you write for the special purpose of demonstrating your ability to communicate your knowledge to your audience. But you will write more effectively if you think of each essay as having one or more of the following purposes:

1. to inform
2. to convince or persuade
3. to enter into discussion or debate

Few essays, however, have only one of these purposes. For example, a set of instructions will have the primary purpose of informing readers how to do something, but it may also be trying to convince them that this is the best way to do it. And to interest readers more, the instructions may also be written in a stimulating style. An analysis of a poem may seem to be pure exposition, explaining how the poem works and what it means, but in a sense it will also be trying to persuade readers that this interpretation is a viable one. An argument will then necessarily include exposition. An entertaining or even whimsical piece may well have a satiric tone or some kind of implicit "lesson" calculated to spark debate. And so on. Usually one of the three purposes will dominate, but one or both of the others will often be present as well. (And see #10 below, on writing arguments.)

The clearer your idea of what you want to do in an essay, and why, and for whom, the better you will be able to make effective rhetorical choices. You may even want to begin by writing down, as a memo to yourself, a detailed description or "profile" of your audience and as clear a statement of your purpose as you can formulate. Tape this memo to the wall over your desk. If your ideas become clearer as the work proceeds, you can refine these statements. In any event, as you go through the process of writing, keep sight of your audience and your purpose.

Exercise 9c Thinking about audience and purpose

Choose a fairly simple subject (for example, your typical day at school or work, the state of your finances, your best or worst course, why you need to buy an expensive item, your health and fitness goals). Write two letters on the topic (300–500 words for each) to two distinctly different kinds of readers, for example different in age, background, education, philosophy of life, or closeness of acquaintance with you. In an accompanying paragraph, briefly account for the differences between your two letters. Did your purpose and/or style change when you changed audiences?

9d Gathering Evidence

An essay can't survive on just vague generalizations and unsupported statements and opinions; it must contain specifics: facts, details, data, examples. Whatever your subject, you must gather material by reading and researching, conducting formal interviews, talking to others, or by thinking about your personal experience. And don't stop when you think you have just enough; collect as much information as you can within the time you have allotted for evidence gathering, even two or three times what you can use; you can select the best and bank the rest for future use.

1. Brainstorming

If you are expected to generate material from your own knowledge and experience (instead of through formal research), you may, at first, have difficulty coming up with ideas. Don't be discouraged. Sit down for a few minutes with a pencil and a sheet of paper, write your topic in the centre or at the top, and begin jotting down ideas. Put down everything that comes into your head about it. Let your mind run fast and free. Don't bother with sentences; don't worry about spelling; don't even pause to wonder whether the words and phrases are going to be of any use. Just keep scribbling. It shouldn't be long before you've filled the sheet with possible ideas, questions, facts, details, names, examples. You may even need to use a second sheet. It may help if you also brainstorm your larger subject area, not just the narrowed topic, since some of the broader ideas could prove useful.

2. Using questions

Another way to generate material is to ask yourself questions about your subject or topic and write down the answers. Start with the reporter's standard questions: *Who? What? Where? When? Why? How?* and go on from there with more of your own: What is it? Who is associated with it? In what way? Where and when is it, or was it, or will it be? How does it work? Why is it?

What causes it? What does it cause? What are its parts? What is it a part of? Is it part of a process? What does it look like? What is it like or unlike? What is its opposite? What if it didn't exist? Such questions and the answers you develop will make you think of more questions, and so on; soon you'll have more than enough material that is potentially useful. You may even find yourself writing consecutive sentences, since some questions prompt certain kinds of responses. For example, asking *What is it?* may lead you to begin defining your subject; *What is it like or unlike?* may lead you to begin comparing and contrasting it, classifying it, thinking of analogies and metaphors; *What causes it?* and *What does it cause?* may lead you to begin exploring cause-and-effect relations; *What are its parts?* or *What is it made of?* could lead you to analyze your subject; *How does it work?* or *Is it part of a process?* may prompt you to analyze and explain a process.

Exercise 9d Generating material

Using two of your narrowed topics from Exercise 9a–b, brainstorm by peppering them with questions to see how much material you can generate. Then try the same techniques with the larger subjects to see if that will yield any additional useful material. You might also want to try getting together with one or two friends or classmates and bouncing ideas and questions off one another. This is a helpful technique for preparing for collaborative writing projects.

9e Classifying and Organizing the Evidence

1. Classifying

As you brainstorm a subject and jot down notes and answers, you'll begin to see connections between one idea and another and start putting them in groups or drawing circles around them and lines and arrows between them. It is important to do this kind of classification when you have finished gathering material. You should end up with several groups of related items, which means that you will have classified your material according to some principle that arose naturally from it. During this part of the process you will probably also have discarded the weaker or less relevant details, keeping only those that best suit the topic as it is now beginning to take shape; that is, you will have selected the best.

For a tightly limited topic and a short essay, you may have only one group of details, but for an essay of even moderate length, say 750 words or more, you will probably have several groups.

The map below was created by a student to classify and organize her ideas for an 800-word paper on the effects of war on the child characters in Joy Kogawa's novel *Obasan*.

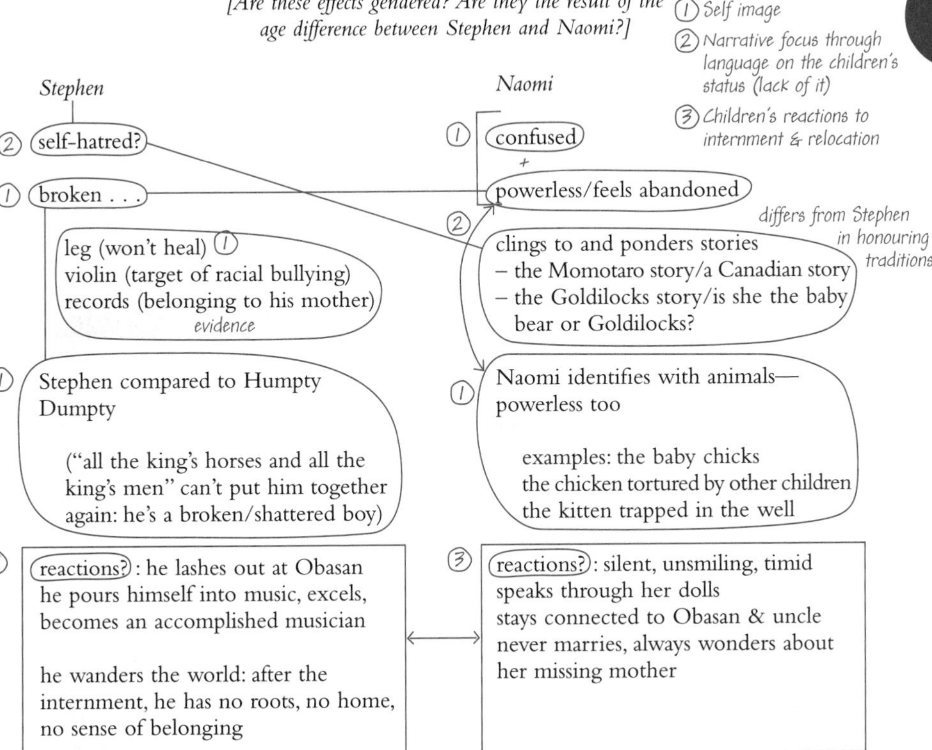

Effects of War on Stephen and Naomi Nakane
[Are these effects gendered? Are they the result of the age difference between Stephen and Naomi?]
Compare & contrast the two characters according to . . .
① Self image
② Narrative focus through language on the children's status (lack of it)
③ Children's reactions to internment & relocation
Stephen
Naomi
② self-hatred?
① broken . . .
leg (won't heal) ①
violin (target of racial bullying)
records (belonging to his mother)
evidence
① Stephen compared to Humpty Dumpty
("all the king's horses and all the king's men" can't put him together again: he's a broken/shattered boy)
③ reactions?: he lashes out at Obasan
he pours himself into music, excels, becomes an accomplished musician
he wanders the world: after the internment, he has no roots, no home, no sense of belonging
① confused
+
powerless/feels abandoned
②
clings to and ponders stories
– the Momotaro story/a Canadian story
– the Goldilocks story/is she the baby bear or Goldilocks?
differs from Stephen in honouring traditions
① Naomi identifies with animals—powerless too
examples: the baby chicks
the chicken tortured by other children
the kitten trapped in the well
③ reactions?: silent, unsmiling, timid
speaks through her dolls
stays connected to Obasan & uncle
never marries, always wonders about her missing mother

Writing Tip

On Managing Groups of Details in Classifications

Try to classify your material in such a way that you end up with several groups, each of which will correspond to a separate major section of your essay. Remember, though, that an essay with more than seven major sections may be unwieldy for both writer and reader. Similarly, an organization of only two major sections risks turning into an essay of two large lumps, sometimes referred to as two mini essays; if your material calls for organizing into only two sections, take extra care to ensure that the whole is unified and coherent.

9e

2. Organizing

Once you have classified your material into groups, put the groups into some kind of order. Don't necessarily accept the first arrangement that comes to mind; consider as many different arrangements as the material will allow, and then select the best one for your purpose and audience. (For the most common arrangements, see the *Patterns of development* in #4b.2.) The order should be logical rather than accidental or arbitrary. Ideally, the groups and their details should fall into order naturally, resulting in an arrangement that is the most effective way of presenting the material.

Exercise 9e Classifying and organizing data

Use the material you generated for the two topics in Exercise 9d. Classify each mass into groups of related items and arrange each set of groups into the best kind of order you can think of for them. In a few sentences, explain why you chose each particular order. Justify in terms of your audience and purpose.

9f The Thesis Statement and the Outline

The following section examines the process of preparing an outline for an essay. The most crucial parts of the planning or "pre-writing" stage are the formulation of a **thesis statement** and the construction of an **outline.**

During the early stages, you gradually increase your control over your proposed essay: you find and narrow a subject, you think about audience and purpose, you gather evidence and generate ideas, and you classify and arrange your material. At some point while you are doing all this you will probably have formulated at least a tentative thesis, a statement that identifies your topic and points the way to what you want to say about it.

This *thesis statement* or *thesis sentence* performs the same function for an essay that a *topic sentence* does for a paragraph. It leads off the outline; the ordered groups become *main headings*, and the details that make up each group, if they aren't simply absorbed by the main heading, become subdivisions of it in various levels of *subheadings*. And though tentative sketches of a possible beginning and ending aren't essential to an outline, it's usually worth trying to think of something of the sort at this stage; you can easily change later if you think of something better. Here is an example, a student's outline for a short essay:

THESIS STATEMENT: Students who have a social life are happier, smarter, and better prepared for the workforce than students who concentrate only on their studies.

BEGINNING: All work and no play makes a dull student. Although many people, including my parents, believe that students should spend all their time studying, I believe students are better off socializing in moderation at university. Why?

I. They are happier.
   A. develop friendships
   B. develop maturity and a more balanced perspective towards life

II. They are smarter.
   A. receive academic support in study groups
   B. receive academic support from friends who are strong in certain disciplines

III. They are better prepared for the workforce.
   A. develop an effective network of contacts
   B. develop interpersonal skills
   C. develop communication skills

ENDING: So the next time my parents tell me to get off the phone because I should be studying, I will be ready with my answer. I will tell them I am leading a balanced life, improving academically, and getting ready for my future.

Note the layout of an outline: numerals and letters are followed by periods and a space or two; subheadings are indented at least two spaces past the beginning of the first word of a main heading. Few outlines will need to go beyond one or two levels of subheading (see #9j.5), but if further subdivision is necessary, here is the way to indicate successive levels:

```
I.
II.
      A.
      B.
            1.
            2.
                  a.
                  b.
```

(1.)
(2.)
(a.)
(b.)

9g The Importance of Outlining

An outline drawn up before you write a major essay will usually save you both time and effort at later stages. Writing the draft will be easier and smoother because it follows a plan: you know where you're going. You can avoid such pitfalls as unnecessary repetition, digression, and illogical or otherwise incoherent organization. In other words, a good outline can be like a map that keeps the writer from taking wrong turns, wandering in circles, or getting lost altogether.

Keep in mind, too, that an outline should not be binding. If as you write and revise you think of a better way to organize a part of your essay, or if some part of the outline proves clumsy when you try to set it down in paragraphs, or if you suddenly think of some new material that should be included, by all means go with your instincts and revise accordingly. And as you proceed, you may want to refine your thesis to reflect changes in your ideas. The virtue of using an outline is that rather than drifting about rudderless, you are in control of any changes you make because you make them consciously and carefully, and you will have a record of your changes if you want to rethink them later.

9h Kinds of Outlines

Outlining of some kind is usually necessary for a good essay. The more complicated the essay, the more important the outline. A short, relatively simple essay can sometimes be outlined in your head or with a few informal jottings, but even a shorter essay can be easier to write if you've made a blueprint for your essay first.

The method of outlining you use may be your own choice or it may be set by your instructor or by the nature of a project. Some people like the *topic outline* with its brief headings and subheadings, as in the example above (#9f). Sometimes a *paragraph outline* will work well, one that simply lists the proposed topic or opening sentences of the successive paragraphs that will eventually form the essay. Probably the most useful outline is the *sentence outline,* for it helps to establish the foundation of your essay.

9i Sentence Outlines

A sentence outline resembles a topic outline except that brief headings and subheadings are replaced by complete sentences. The advantage of having to phrase each item as a complete sentence is that you are unlikely to fool yourself into thinking you have something to say when in fact you don't. For example, imagine you are planning an essay on various cuisines and, in a topic outline, you put down the heading "the new trends." But if you haven't been eating out recently, you might find when you sit down to write your draft that you have little or nothing to say. In a sentence outline, you are compelled to make a statement about the topic, in this case perhaps something like "Although people have their favourite meals at home, when it comes to eating out, they are willing to try different foods." With even such a vague sentence before you, you can more easily begin supplying details to develop your idea; the act of formulating the sentence guarantees that you have at least some ideas about whatever you put down.

Another benefit of a sentence outline is that, when properly handled, it is self-constructing. In a topic or other relatively informal outline, the thesis statement should set up or contain the main headings, either implicitly, as in the example in #9f, or explicitly, as in the example below. In a sentence outline the headings and subheadings work the same way. Our earlier example—"Although people have their favourite meals, when it comes to eating out, they are willing to try different foods"—automatically leads into two subheadings: "A. people have their favourite meals," and "B. when it comes to eating out, they are willing to try different foods." Such partial repetition is natural to a good sentence outline; it may seem stiff and clumsy, but it is a strength, since it fosters coherence and unity within each part of an essay and in an essay as a whole.

As an illustration, here is a student's sentence outline on the topic of the environment:

THESIS STATEMENT: Certain corporations get away with crimes against the environment because profits are all important, our society cannot easily measure the crimes committed, and when the company is prosecuted, the penalties are weak.

BEGINNING: Although corporate crimes against the environment are profound in their impact, corporations are not held accountable or are mildly prosecuted. Three important reasons seem to stand out.

I. There is a conflict between making a profit and protecting the environment.
   A. The strength of economics outweighs ideological or political views.
   B. There is the perception that corporate crime against the environment is not real crime as the people involved are often professional and respectable.

II. It is difficult to determine or measure the extent of crimes against the environment.
   A. Government and regulatory bodies resist releasing facts.
   B. Records and comments from officials that are released are not always consistent.
   C. As corporate crime against the environment is often outside the scope and the know-how of traditional investigative journalism, the media does not always uncover the extent of the activity.

III. Weak penalties and lax enforcement do not deter corporations.
   A. The wording of environmental laws is ambiguous.
   B. Sanctions and penalties are weak.
   C. Prosecution involves expense and political repercussions private citizens' groups may wish to avoid.

ENDING: (Sum up the main points and point to implications for the future or suggest possible solutions?)

9j Constructing Sentence Outlines

The following are some guidelines for putting together a good sentence outline:

1. Make every item from the thesis statement down to the last subheading a single complete major sentence.
2. Use only simple or complex sentences; do not use compound sentences. Since the independent clauses of a compound sentence could themselves be written as separate sentences, having a compound sentence in your outline may mean that two or more headings are masquerading as one; consider making each clause a separate heading.
3. In any kind of outline you need to supply at least two subheadings if you supply any at all. A subheading, by definition, implies division. For this reason, a heading cannot be subdivided into only one part as a subheading. If under "I" you have an "A," then you must also have at least a "B"; if you have a "1" you must also have at least a "2," and so on. If you find yourself unable to go beyond one subheading, it probably isn't a subdivision at all but an integral part of the main heading that should be incorporated into it.
4. The headings or subheadings at each level should be reasonably parallel with each other; that is, I, II, III, etc. should have about the

same level of importance, as should subheadings A, B, C, etc. under a given main heading, and 1, 2, 3, etc. under each of these. One way to help achieve this balance is to make the sentences at any given level as much as possible grammatically parallel.

Writing Tip

On Managing the Number of Subheadings in an Outline
As with the major sections of an essay, having more than six or seven subheadings under any one heading risks being unwieldy.

5. Few outlines need to go beyond one level of subheading for the average essay. If an essay is unusually long or complicated, you may find it helpful or necessary to break things down to a second or even third level of subheading. But remember that headings and subheadings should mostly state ideas, propositions, generalizations; the supporting facts can be supplied at the writing stage and don't need to go into the outline. If you find yourself including several levels of subheading, you may already be itemizing your facts and details.

Exercise 9f–j (1) Writing thesis statements and outlines

Return to the two topics you've been working with from Exercise 9a–b through 9e. If you haven't already done so, formulate a thesis statement for each topic. Make each a single simple or complex sentence. Try to compose the sentences in such a way that each foreshadows the major divisions of the outline to come. Then construct the two outlines. Make at least one of them a sentence outline. Include a statement of audience and purpose with each outline.

Exercise 9f–j (2) Revising weak outlines

One of the most important functions of an outline is to give you a graphic representation of a projected essay so that before you begin drafting the essay you can catch and correct structural and other flaws (repetition, overlap, illogical organization, introductory material masquerading as part of the body, inadequate thesis statements, subheadings that aren't really subdivisions, and so on). Here are some outlines drafted by students for possible essays. Analyze them critically; pretend that they are your own and that you'll have to try to write essays based on them. Detect their flaws, both major and minor, and then try to revise each so that it

9j

Exercise 9f–j (2) Revising weak outlines – *continued*

could guide you through the first draft of an essay. Do any of them seem simply unworkable, unsalvageable? If so, why?

(1) THESIS STATEMENT: Every Canadian should be fluent in both official languages.

I. It would be good for the individual.
  A. Improved job opportunities
  B. Increased communication skills

II. It would be good for the community.
  A. Increased communication and understanding between cultures
  B. Decrease in prejudice and racism

III. It would be good for the country.
  A. Increased nationalism and patriotism
  B. Establishes a Canadian identity

(2) THESIS STATEMENT: Reading is a creative exercise for the imagination.

I. Reading encourages people to visualize settings of stories.

II. Reading encourages people to visualize the appearance of characters.

III. Some plots encourage people to imagine the endings of stories or to fill in missing parts of stories.

IV. Science-fiction stories provide people with inspiration that allows their imaginations to wander.

(3) THESIS STATEMENT: The journal can play an important role in your life.

I. Motives for keeping a journal
  A. Keeping a record of life
  B. Evaluating and surveying your life

II. Topics other than the weather to write about in your journal
  A. Personal Development
    1. Health, Diet, Sports
    2. Spirituality, Dreams
    3. Books and Films, Quotes from Reviews
  B. Work Related Issues
  C. Current Events
    1. Celebrities
    2. World Events: War
  D. Travel

Exercise 9f–j (2) Revising weak outlines – *continued*

(4). THESIS STATEMENT: The negative effects of television on our lives

I. It leads to physical decay.
   A. People are less likely to exercise.
   B. Television encourages overeating.

II. It leads to mental decay.
   A. It requires no mental participation.
   B. People are less likely to engage in activities or hobbies that engage the mind or define their personalities.

III. It leads to social decay.
   A. People do not engage in communal activities together.
   B. People do not eat meals together.
   C. It encourages consumerism over connection with people.

(5) THESIS STATEMENT: The effects of television on our lives

I. There are too many shows pertaining to sex and violence on television.
   A. Many shows on TV lead people to accept violence as a way of life.
   B. Children are left to formulate their own opinions on sex.

II. Many people centre their entire lives on TV.

III. Advertising on TV disillusions people.
   A. Most ads deceive people into buying things they don't need.

IV. There are some good educational shows on TV.

(6) THESIS STATEMENT: Stress is a problem in university that must be dealt with.

I. Different types of stress and what causes them
   A. Unhealthy: stress overload, too much work, not enough rest, bad nutrition
   B. Healthy stress levels: small amounts of pressure, beneficial to some extent, help one learn and grow
   C. Emotional: family problems, love problems, depression, loneliness, unable to concentrate
   D. Physical: work too hard, overdoing it, too much pressure, health problems

II. Problems that arise with stress
   A. Sustained stress: heart attacks, health problems
   B. Common symptoms: ulcers, insomnia, irritability, sweaty or clammy hands, fidgetiness, higher pulse rate

9j

Exercise 9f–j (2) Revising weak outlines – *continued*

III. Treatments: How to cope
   A. Physical: relax, read, take up a hobby, watch TV, do something relaxing
   B. Emotional: relax mind, meditation, exercise
   C. Serious stress: psychotherapy, counselling, get mind away from problems

(7) THESIS STATEMENT: Safety and efficiency can be improved at Smithson's Store and Pharmacy.

I. Layout of Shelves
   A. Shelves in Pharmacy: the passages in between shelves are too narrow.
   B. Shelves in Front Part of Store: there are blind spots that encourage theft.

II. Placement of Equipment
   A. Tablet Counting Machine: there isn't enough counter space.
   B. Compounding Area: not enough cupboard space, temperature might affect stability of chemicals
   C. Electric Heater: it is placed in a dangerous location.

III. Organization of Medication
   A. Placement of medication: medication is organized by brand names as opposed to generic names
      1. Possible recording errors: some medications have similar names.
      2. Stock supplies: unnecessary and space consuming extra supplies
   B. Wasting of Medication
      1. Expiration of medication: some medications are hidden by the inefficient shelving technique.
      2. Ordering of medication: too many extra supplies are ordered.

When you have finished working on these outlines, go back and examine your own two outlines from the preceding exercise. Do you see any possible weak spots in them? If necessary, revise them.

Can you think of some possible titles for these potential essays—for the ones outlined in this exercise and for your own?

Exercise 9f–j (3) Constructing and using outlines

Construct outlines for proposed essays on three of the following:

1. Technology has (or has not) made our lives more complicated
2. The methods you use to overcome procrastination
3. Sixteen is (or is not) too young an age at which to learn to drive
4. The steps to take to ensure a good night's sleep
5. Tattooing and piercing are (or are not) ways of making the body beautiful
6. The importance of empathy
7. The reasons why dragon myths or legends are universal
8. Why being the only, youngest, middle, or eldest child in the family is the most challenging
9. If success is nothing more than one long patience (Flaubert), define failure
10. How to spend a Sunday afternoon

Check your outlines carefully for any weaknesses, and revise them as necessary.

9k Writing the First Draft

Once you have a good outline to follow, the work of drafting becomes smoother and more purposeful. With the shape of the whole essay laid out, you can concentrate on the main tasks of drafting: finding the right words, generating the right kinds of sentences, and constructing good transitions and strong paragraphs.

Writing Tip

On Going from an Outline to a Draft

(1) Sometimes a main heading and its subheading from the outline will become a single paragraph in the essay; sometimes each subheading will become a paragraph; and so on. The nature and density of your material will determine its treatment.

(2) It may be possible to transfer the thesis statement from your outline to the essay unchanged, but more likely you will want to change it (perhaps several times) to fit the style of the essay. The thesis is the statement of your purpose or of the position you intend to defend in the essay, so it should be as polished as possible. The kind of basic or mechanical statement that is suitable in an outline may be inappropriate in the essay itself.

9-l Notes on Beginnings

1. Postponing the beginning

Starting the actual writing can be a challenge: most writers have had the experience of staring at a computer screen or a blank sheet of paper for an uncomfortable length of time while trying to think of a good way to begin. If you have no beginning in mind at this point, don't waste time trying to think of one. Plunge right into the body of the essay and write it as rapidly as you can. Once you have finished writing the first draft, you'll have a better idea of what it is that needs to be introduced; you can then go back and do the beginning with relative ease. In fact, writers who write a beginning first often discard the original version and write a new one, either because the essay that finally took shape demands a different kind of beginning or because in the midst of composing they thought of a better one.

2. Beginning directly

Just as it isn't always a good idea to begin a final paragraph with "In conclusion," so it's generally not good practice to open routinely with something mechanical like "In this essay I will discuss" or "This essay is concerned with." On occasion, such as when your essay is unusually long or complicated or when you are presenting it as part of a seminar, conference, or panel, it may be helpful to explain in advance what your essay is about, to provide readers with what amounts to a brief outline (just as it is then often necessary to provide some summary by way of conclusion). But most essays don't require this kind of beginning and won't engage an audience with such a stiff introduction. As a rule, then, don't talk about yourself and your essay; talk about your topic. Rather than begin by informing readers of what you are going to say (and then at the end reminding them of what you have said), start with something substantial and, if possible, attention-getting. Try to end with something similarly sharp and definitive.

3. Determining subject and thesis

However you begin, it is necessary to identify your subject and to state your thesis somewhere near the beginning—usually not later than the first or second paragraph. For example, even if your title is something like "Imagery in Shakespeare's Sonnet 65," you should still, preferably in your first sentence, mention both the author and the title of the poem. The title of your essay is not a part of its content; the essay must be able to stand on its own.

Special circumstances may, on occasion, call for you to delay the full statement of a thesis to near the end, for example as part of a strategy of building to a climax. Even then, you will probably provide at least some indication of your thesis near the beginning, perhaps in general terms. Or sometimes a thesis can be broken into several parts to be stated at intervals in the course of an essay. On rare occasions, you may want to be mysterious, but readers generally don't like being kept in the dark. (See also #10d.2.)

4. Being direct, smooth, economical: some examples

Begin as directly, smoothly, and economically as you can. Here, for example, are three ways an essay with the title "Imagery in Shakespeare's Sonnet 65" might begin; note how differences in order, punctuation, and wording make each succeeding one better and shorter than the one before:

> (1) In Sonnet 65 by William Shakespeare, there is a great deal of imagery.
>
> (2) William Shakespeare in his Sonnet 65 uses imagery to . . . .
>
> (3) The imagery in Shakespeare's Sonnet 65 . . . .

Here is the beginning of an essay on one of Shakespeare's sonnets. The writer can't seem to get the engine warmed up:

> William Shakespeare, famous English poet and writer of plays, has always been known for the way he uses imagery to convey the point he is making in a particular piece of work. Shakespeare's Sonnet 65 is no exception to this, and this is one of the better examples of his work that I have studied, for illustrating his use of imagery.
>
> The best example in the sonnet comes in lines four and six, where Shakespeare compares a "summer's honey breath" and a "wrackful siege of battering days."

Compare this with another student's beginning on the same topic:

> In Sonnet 65, Shakespeare appeals to a person's knowledge of visible properties in nature in an attempt to explain invisible properties of love and time.

The second writer has taken control of the material immediately. Even though no particular image has yet been mentioned, the second writer, in one crisp sentence, is far beyond where the first writer, well into a second paragraph, is.

Here is another example of an ineffective beginning. That the writer was in difficulty is shown by the redundancy in the first sentence, the illogicality in the second sentence, and the vague reference and wordy emptiness of the third:

> Nowadays, in these modern times, different cultures celebrate different holidays in many different ways. Thanksgiving is filled with a seemingly endless variety of memories and emotions. I would imagine this is experienced by almost every family and mine is most certainly not an exception.

9-1

The writer's own revision proves that the difficulties were merely the result of floundering, trying too hard to make a beginning; had the beginning been written after the body of the essay was complete, it might have taken this form:

> Holidays help define a family. In my family, where expectations are great, Thanksgiving brings out the best and worst of our individual characteristics.

Exercise 9-I Evaluating beginnings

Here are some beginnings from student essays. Which ones are effective and which ones need revision? Point out the contrasting characteristics that enable you to evaluate them relative to each other.

(1) Leonardo da Vinci was not concerned so much with explanations of why things worked as he was with how they worked. His scientific interests were as diverse as his other interests; they covered anatomy, geography, geology, mathematics, mechanics, and physics. He dissected several cadavers and developed what are called "transparency drawings"—pictures which show both external and internal features simultaneously. He mapped several cities from an aerial perspective, and there are several entries in his notes concerning the origins of fossils and geological strata. Quite simply, he was a deeply curious man whose life shows what it means to be a true Renaissance man.

(2) Problems relating to a society affect all its inhabitants; hence, all its inhabitants must take part in curing society's ills. I find that society is plagued by problems such as degenerating neighbourhoods, growing unemployment, and increasing racism. Cultural conflicts have been the root of most of our problems; thus, if the situation is to improve, some changes must occur.

(3) For many people, their first thought after the ring of the alarm clock is of a steaming cup of coffee. Their stumble to the kitchen for this pick-me-up blends with their dreams. The sleepy eyes that measure out the fragrant brown granules flick open after their owners have savoured that first morning cup of coffee. After a strong cup of coffee, most people perform physical and mental tasks at the peak of their ability. The reason is caffeine.

Exercise 9-I Evaluating beginnings – *continued*

(4) The poem "To an Athlete Dying Young," written by A.E. Housman, structurally contains different periods of time in its stanzas. The different stanzas refer to different times. The rhythm of the poem is not uniform in beat. However, it has a consistent rhyme scheme. This poem is also an example of a dramatic monologue.

(5) "Quit while you're ahead" may be an old and worn-out saying, but it aptly applies to A.E. Housman's poem "To an Athlete Dying Young." In this dramatic monologue the speaker seizes upon this idea as a means of consoling the athlete, or those who mourn him. Beauty and victory are fleeting. Not only does the eternal passing of time always bring change, but once our "peak" has been reached, there is no place to go but down. Rather than growing old and watching new athletes break his records, the young athlete in the poem dies at an early age. His victory garland is preserved, "unwithered," by death.

9m–o The Final Steps

The product of rapid composition is a first draft. Although some first drafts may come close to being acceptable finished products, don't gamble that your draft can pass for a polished essay. There are three tasks to undertake before you should consider an essay finished: *revising*, *preparing the final draft*, and *proofreading*.

9m Revising

Revision (re-vision, literally "scrutinizing again") is an extremely important stage of writing, far too often neglected by less experienced writers. Experienced writers revise a piece of writing at least two or three times. Many writers revise five or even ten or more times before they consider a piece to be finished.

Revise carefully and slowly, looking for any way to improve what you've written. Don't aim just to correct errors made in haste, but also to remove clutter and improve diction, sentence structure, punctuation, coherence, paragraphing, organization, and so on. Some writers find that going through a draft for one thing at a time is effective—for example, going through it looking only at paragraphing, then going through it again looking only at the structure and variety of sentences, then at punctuation, then at diction, and so on. And you will want to proofread carefully for those errors you know you tend to make.

Adopt the role of an observant and alert reader looking for strengths and pinpointing weaknesses and errors. To do this effectively, try to allow yourself a cooling-off period; wait as long as possible between the drafting and the revising—at least two or three days—so that you can look at your own work with more objectivity, as a dispassionate third-party reader would. If you're having trouble, you may find the Omnibus Checklist (see Appendix 3) helpful during your revisions.

9n Preparing the Final Draft

When you are through revising a piece of writing, carefully prepare the final draft, the one that will be presented to your reader or readers. Once the work is out of your hands, it's too late to change anything; make sure it's in good shape when it leaves your hands. It should be neat, and it should be in the appropriate format for the kind of writing it is. For most of your academic writing, heed the requirements of your particular audience, and follow carefully the Manuscript Conventions listed and discussed in #56.

9-o Editing and Proofreading

Proofreading will have been taking place during revision, of course, and also during drafting, but go over what you consider to be the final copy of your essay when you believe it is ready. This final proofreading will prove worthwhile; despite earlier careful scrutiny, you will probably discover not only typographical errors but also hitherto unnoticed slips in spelling, punctuation, and grammar.

Do your proofreading with exaggerated care. Read each sentence, as a sentence, slowly (and aloud whenever possible); but also read each word as a word; check each punctuation mark, and consider the possibility of adding some or removing some or changing some. Particularly when you proofread for spelling errors, do so as a separate process. You might consider doing this by starting at the end of your work and reading backward, one word at a time, so that you won't get caught up in the flow of a sentence and overlook an error.

Do not put full trust in any of the spelling, grammar, and style checks that are part of, or designed to be used with, word-processing programs. They can't possibly cover all the matters that require attention. And remember that spell checkers can't spot a misspelled word that happens to be the same as some other correctly spelled word—for example, *form* instead of *from*, or *through* instead of *though*; nor can they tell you that you've mistaken, say, *your* for *you're*, or *principal* for *principle*.

10 Argument: Writing to Convince or Persuade

Most of the principles of composition are even more important in argument than in other kinds of writing, though as we have suggested earlier (#9c.2), other kinds of writing, especially exposition, often include an element of argumentation. But when your principal purpose is to convince or persuade, there are several additional points and principles to keep in mind. Here are some brief suggestions and some practical advice to help you write effective arguments. (See also **convince, persuade** in #72.)

10a Subject

When you are focusing on your subject for an argumentative essay, keep in mind that there is no point in arguing about easily verifiable facts or generally accepted assumptions (2 + 2 = 4; the sky looks blue; good nutrition promotes good health; oil is a nonrenewable energy source). One cannot argue about facts, only about what the facts mean. Since an argument depends on logical reasoning, when you argue about opinions based on facts you will necessarily use factual data to support your contentions. A collection of unsupported opinions is not an argument but merely a series of assertions.

Similarly, one cannot logically argue about matters of taste. You can't argue that blue is a prettier colour than green; you can only assert that *you* find it prettier, for whatever reason. The subject of an argument should be something that is capable of verification, though the fact that it is being argued about at all indicates that its verification is not automatic or to be taken for granted.

10b Audience

When your *purpose* is to convince or persuade, your knowledge of your *audience* and your constant awareness of that audience are crucial. Consider, for example, how differently you would have to handle your material and your tone depending on whether you were writing to an audience of (a) people basically sympathetic to your position, (b) people likely to be hostile to your position. Since the effectiveness of an argument depends partly on your gaining or holding the confidence of your readers, or at least getting them to listen to you willingly and with a reasonably open mind, it is important that you avoid presenting anything that might keep them from listening.

Know your audience. Are your readers largely men? women? elderly? young? well-educated? middle-class? business people? students? politically conservative? "green"? wealthy? poor? artistic? sports lovers? car owners? family oriented? animal lovers? And so on. The more you know about your potential readers and their attitude toward your topic, the better you will know what choices to make so that you can clearly communicate your position and its value as an argument worth thinking about.

10c Evidence

When you are gathering material for an argument, look especially for concrete, specific, precise, factual data that you can use to support your generalizations (see #66b). The effectiveness of your argument will, in part, depend on the quality and the quantity of the evidence you provide both to support your position and to counter your opposition. For example, try to find some statistics you can cite, or some expert you can quote (the appeal to authority), or some common experience or assumption about life that you can remind your readers of (the appeal to common sense). You may be able to make good use of your own experience or that of someone you know well.

But be sure that the evidence you gather and use is both reliable and relevant. Don't cite a rap artist as an authority on a medical question—unless she's studying for her M.D.; don't cite as support the results of an experiment that has been superseded by later experiments; don't discuss the style and upholstery of a car if you're arguing about which car provides the most efficient transportation.

10d Organization

Consider audience and purpose when laying out your material. You will find that an outline will often help you. Here are some specific points to keep in mind:

1. Emphasis

Usually, you will want to save your strongest point or points for the end, the most emphatic position of your argument. But since the beginning of your essay is also emphatic, don't open with a weak or minor point. It is usually best to begin with strength and then deal with minor points and proceed to the end in the order of climax. (See also #29, #6, #8c.)

2. Thesis

In an argument, your thesis statement is in effect a proposition that you intend to support; you want to prove it, at least to the satisfaction of your readers. For that reason, it usually appears at the beginning, just as a formal debate begins with a reading of the proposition to be debated. Occasionally, however, you can delay your statement of the thesis until near the end, letting a logical progression of reasoning lead up to it. But don't try for this dramatic effect unless it will work better than stating your proposition up front; for example, consider whether your readers might be put off, rather than drawn in, by being kept in the dark about just what your proposition is. (See also #9-1.3.)

3. Methods of development

Arguments can make use of any of the methods of development: narration (an illustrative anecdote), description (a detailed physical description of something it is important for readers to visualize clearly and perhaps feel emotion towards), comparison and contrast, analysis, and so on (see #1b). But be careful with analogy: using an analogy as the central pillar of an argumentative structure is risky, for opponents can too easily challenge it and pull it apart (see #10h.9); use analogy as an extra illustration or as one of several minor props. Definitions help establish a common ground between you and the reader. And give strong consideration to cause-and-effect analysis (*What caused it? What does it cause? What will it cause?*), often a mainstay of argument: you argue for or against something because of what has happened or is happening or will happen as a result of it.

4. Patterns of development

Similarly, an argument can use any one or more of the common patterns of development (see #4b.2). An argument is likely, for example, to follow a logical progression, to move from general to specific or from specific to general, and to rise to a climax. But there is one further pattern that often occurs in argument: like a formal debate, many arguments move back and forth between *pro* and *con*, between statements supporting your proposition and statements refuting your opponent's position (see #10f).

10e–h How to Argue: Reasoning Logically

10e Being Reasonable

Appeal to common sense; appeal to authority; above all, appeal to reason. Demonstrate your respect for your reader's intelligence by appealing to it; a reader is then more likely to respect you and your arguments. If you appeal to prejudices and baser instincts you may get through to a few, but thoughtful readers won't respond favourably to such tactics. Appeals to people's emotions (sympathy for the poor or sick, love of children, feelings of patriotism, fear of injury) can be effective additions to an appeal to reason, but they are not a valid substitute for it. Similarly, if you're conducting a reasoned argument you will usually want to adopt a moderate tone. Stridency and sarcasm will only win you points with readers who are already thoroughly in agreement with your position.

10f Including the Opposition

Be fair: bring in and address any major opposing points of view. Your readers are likely to be aware of these and will expect you to address them. If you try to sway your readers by mentioning only what favours your side, you will lose their confidence because they will conclude correctly that you are unfairly suppressing unfavourable evidence. By raising opposing points and doing your best to refute them convincingly, you will not only strengthen the logic of your argument but you will present yourself as a reasonable person, willing to concede that there is another side to the issue. Moreover, by taking on the discussion of both sides in a debate, you can often impart a useful back-and-forth movement to your argument, and you can see to it that after refuting the final opposition point, you end on your own strongest points.

10g Using Induction and Deduction

The two principal methods of reasoning, *induction* and *deduction*, occur both separately and in combination in argument. You should know how each works, and it sometimes helps to be aware of which one you are using at any given point so that you can use it effectively.

10g

1. Induction

Inductive reasoning argues from the particular to the general. That is, it uses specific examples to support a general proposition. A team of chemists will argue that their new theory is correct by describing the results of several experiments that point to it. If you want people to vote for mayoral candidate A rather than B, you could point to several instances of A's actions on behalf of the city while on city council and also perhaps point to several instances of B's harmful decisions. If you wanted to argue against a proposal to cut back on funding for the athletic program at your school, you could cite the major ways in which the program benefits the school and its students; you could also interview other students to show that the majority agrees with you.

Inductive reasoning cannot prove anything; it can only establish degrees of probability. Obviously the number of examples affects the force of such arguments. If the chemists could point to only two successful experiments, the claim for their theory would remain weak; if they could cite a hundred consecutive successes, their argument would be convincing; there would be a strong likelihood that the experiment would work again if tried for the hundred-and-first time.

Be rigorous in presenting your data, but also consider how much detail your audience really needs. If, in a speech or a written argument, you detailed fifty noble acts of candidate A and fifty ignoble acts of candidate B, you would probably lose your audience and turn them against you and your proposition. You would do better to describe a few actions on each side and try to establish that those actions were representative of the two candidates' behaviour.

Similarly, if you interviewed students about the athletic program at your university or college, you would need to talk to enough of them for your sampling to be considered representative; if you polled only elite athletes, you could hardly claim that their opinions were typical. And though the sampling would have to be large for the results to be convincing, it would be the total number that would carry weight, not the detailed opinions of each individual student.

In addition, you must be able to explain any notable exceptions among your examples, for these form the bases of possible opposition arguments. For example, if one of their experiments failed, the chemists would need to show that at that time their equipment was faulty, or that one of their ingredients had accidentally become adulterated. If candidate A had once voted to close a useful facility, you could try to show that financial exigency at that time left no choice, or that the facility, though generally perceived as beneficial, was in fact little used and therefore an unnecessary drain on the city's resources. If you explicitly acknowledge such exceptions and show that they are unimportant or atypical, they can't easily be used against you by a reader who disagrees with you.

2. Deduction

Deductive reasoning argues from the general to the particular. It begins with facts or generally accepted assumptions or principles and applies them to specific instances. For example, we know that oil and other fossil fuels are nonrenewable energy sources that will presumably someday be depleted, and we also know that the world's energy needs are increasing exponentially. Basing their argument on those two facts, energy experts have concluded that it is increasingly important for us to discover or develop alternative sources of energy.

The standard way of representing the process of deductive thinking is the *syllogism*:

MAJOR PREMISE: All mammals are warm-blooded animals.
MINOR PREMISE: Whales are mammals.
CONCLUSION: Therefore, whales are warm-blooded animals.

Syllogistic reasoning is a basic mode of thought, though commonly in everyday thinking and writing one of the premises is omitted as "understood"; for example if a student says "This term paper is due tomorrow, so I'll have to finish it tonight," the assumed second premise ("I don't want to hand the paper in late") goes without saying.

Deductive reasoning, unlike inductive reasoning, can establish proof, but only if the premises are correct and you follow the rules of logic. For example, if one of the premises is negative, the conclusion must be negative—and two negative premises cannot lead to a conclusion at all. The term common to both premises—called the "middle" term (in the foregoing example, *mammals*)—cannot appear in the conclusion. Most important, if the conclusion is to be an absolute certainty, this "middle" term must, in at least one of the premises, be all-inclusive, universal, or what is called "distributed"; that is, it must refer to all members of its class, usually with an absolute word like *all, every, no, none, always, never*. If instead it is qualified by a word like *some, most*, or *seldom*, the conclusion can only be a probability, not a certainty (and if both premises include such a qualifier, they cannot lead to a conclusion):

Most mammals are viviparous.
Whales are mammals.
Therefore, whales are probably viviparous.

Here one could reason further that since whales are not among the oviparous exceptions (platypus, echidna), they are indeed viviparous.

For a conclusion to amount to certainty both premises must be true, or accepted as true:

No mammals can fly.
Whales are mammals.
Therefore, whales cannot fly.

Here the conclusion is *valid* (the reasoning process follows the rules), but it is not *sound*, since the first premise with its categorical *no* excludes the bat, a flying mammal. Such a conclusion, even if true (as this one is), will be suspect because it is based on a false premise.

If one argues that

> All mammals are four-legged animals.
> Whales are mammals.
> Therefore, whales are four-legged animals.

The conclusion, however valid, is not only unsound but untrue as well. To be accurate, the first premise would have to refer to *some* or *many*; the conclusion would then have to be something like "whales may be four-legged animals." Here the absurdity is obvious. But it is not uncommon to hear something like "X must be anti-business; after all, he is in favour of preserving the rain forests." In such a case the absurdity may not appear so obvious, but in the syllogism underlying this reasoning the first premise would read something like "Anyone who argues for preserving the environment is against business"; again, changing "Anyone who argues" to the correctly qualified "Some people who argue" renders the conclusion unsound.

Be skeptical whenever you find yourself using—or thinking—absolute terms like *all* and *everyone* and *no one* and *must* ("Everyone benefits from exercise"; "All exams are unfair"; "[All] Scots are stingy"; "Lawyers are overpaid"; "No one cares about the elderly"; "Vitamin E must be good for you"): you may be constructing an implicit syllogism that won't stand up, one that an opponent can turn against you. Use such qualifiers as *most* and *some* and *sometimes* when necessary; you won't be able to establish absolute proof or certainty, but you may still have a persuasive argument.

3. Combining induction and deduction

Induction and deduction often work together. For example, when you cite instances from candidate A's record, you use induction to establish the general proposition of your candidate's worthiness. But then you implicitly turn to deduction, using that generalization as the basis for a further conclusion: "Candidate A has done all these good things for our city in the past; therefore when elected mayor he or she will do similar good things." (But would the unstated second premise—"A person who behaved in a certain way in the past will continue to behave that way in the future"—require some qualification?)

10h Detecting and Avoiding Fallacies

If you are mounting a counter-argument, it often pays to look for flaws in your opponent's reasoning, such as hidden assumptions and invalid syllogisms. There are several other kinds of recognized, and recognizable, logical fallacies to look for—and, of course, to guard against in your own writing.

Most of them amount to either avoiding evidence or distorting evidence, or both, and some are related to or overlap with others. Here are the main ones to watch for:

1. *Argumentum ad hominem*

Argumentum ad hominem means "argument directed at the person." It refers to an attempt to evade the issue by diverting attention to the person at the centre of the argument: "Mozart lived an amoral life; therefore his music is bound to be bad." Mozart's morality is irrelevant to a discussion of the aesthetic quality of his music. "My opponent is obviously not fit to be mayor; she never goes to church, and her daughter was arrested last year for shoplifting." Neither the candidate's non-attendance at church nor her daughter's arrest—whether or not she was guilty—necessarily has any bearing on the candidate's fitness for office. Such tactics, according to their degree of directness or nastiness, are referred to as innuendo or name-calling or mud-slinging.

A similar tactic, known as guilt (or virtue) by association, is an attempt to tarnish (or enhance) someone's or something's reputation through an association with another person or thing. This kind of argument often takes the form of an endorsement: "I always take my car to Caesar's Garage because my friend Manuel says they're great, and he knows a lot about cars." Many instances of this kind of argument turn out to be fallacious because the stated connection between the two things is either not real or irrelevant. A brand of soft drink is not necessarily better because a famous actor is paid to say it is, nor is a politician necessarily evil because he once had his picture taken with someone later convicted of a crime.

2. *Argumentum ad populum*

Argumentum ad populum is an "argument directed at the people"—an attempt to evade the issue by appealing to mass emotion. Like *argumentum ad hominem*, this technique uses appeals to prejudices, fears, and other feelings not—or not clearly—relevant to the issue. Often by using what are called "glittering generalities," it calls upon large and usually vague, unexamined popular feelings about religion, patriotism, home and family, tradition, and the like. One version of it, called the "bandwagon" approach, associates mass appeal with virtue: if so many people are doing this or thinking that or drinking this or wearing that, it must be right or good.

3. Red herring

A red herring is a false or misleading issue dragged across the trail to throw the dogs off the scent. The new matter may be interesting, but if it is fundamentally irrelevant to the question being argued, it is a red herring. For example, *ad hominem* arguments are red herrings, since they divert a reader's or listener's attention from the main question by injecting the issue of personality.

4. Hasty generalization

A hasty generalization is a generalization for which there is insufficient evidence. It occurs when an arguer jumps to a conclusion that is based on relatively little proof, for example when a team of chemists formulates a theory with only two successful experiments to point to (see #10g.1). Consider another example: just because you and a friend didn't like the food you were served once at a particular restaurant, you aren't justified in asserting that the food is always bad at that restaurant; maybe the regular chef was away that day. But if you've had several such experiences and can find other people who've had similar ones, you'll be closer to establishing that those experiences were typical and therefore sufficient to generalize upon.

5. Begging the question

Begging the question is assuming as true something that needs to be proved: "The government should be voted out of office because the new tax they've just imposed is unfair to consumers." The arguer here is guilty of begging the question of the tax's unfairness, which needs to be established before it can be used as a premise.

Similar to question-begging is circular reasoning, in which a reason given to support a proposition is little or no more than a disguised restatement of the proposition: "Her consistently good cooking is easy to explain: she's an expert at all things culinary." This is the same as saying she is a good cook because she is a good cook.

6. *Post hoc ergo propter hoc*

Post hoc ergo propter hoc means "after this, therefore because of this." It refers to oversimplifying the evidence by assuming that merely because B follows A in time, B must be caused by A. It's true that thunder is caused by lightning, but the subsequent power failure may have been caused not by the lightning but by a tree blown down across the power line. Think about common superstitions: if you always wear your green socks during an exam because once when you wore them you wrote a good exam and so you think they bring you good luck, you are succumbing to the *post hoc* fallacy. Consider another example: "As soon as the new government took office, the price of gasoline went up"; the price hike might have nothing to do with the new government, the timing being coincidental.

7. Either-or

The either-or fallacy, also called "false dilemma," refers to an oversimplification of an issue by presenting it as consisting of only two choices when in reality it is more complex than that. Some questions do present two clear choices: one either gets up or stays in bed; either one is pregnant or one is not; either one votes in an election or one doesn't. But most arguable issues are not matters simply of black and white; there is often a large area of grey between the extremes. One doesn't have to vote for either A or B; one can perhaps find a third candidate, or one can stay home and not vote for anyone. "If you aren't for us, then you must be against us!" This common cry is false; one could be neutral, impartial, uninterested, or committed to a third option. "If I don't pass this course, my life will be ruined." This can be seen as an exaggeration. "The administration at work is either indifferent to employees' needs or against employees in general." Neither unpleasant alternative is likely to be true. This insidious pattern of thinking underlies a good deal of what we think of as prejudice, bigotry, and narrow-mindedness: "If you don't attend a recognized religious institution, then you're not really religious," or "If you don't support the war, you're unpatriotic." Although it is sometimes tempting, don't oversimplify; acknowledge the rich complexity of most issues.

8. Exaggerating the trivial

When you exaggerate the trivial, you distort the evidence by treating a minor point as if it were a major one. If the point is your own, discerning readers will infer that you lack substantial evidence and have had to fall back on weak arguments. If the point is an opposing one, the audience will infer that you can't refute major points and are trying to make yourself look good by demolishing an easy target. "We should all give more to charity because being generous can give us a warm feeling inside" may be worth mentioning, but not worth dwelling on. On the other hand, don't distort the evidence by trivializing opposition points that are important.

9. False or weak analogy

A false or weak analogy occurs when one oversimplifies the evidence by arguing that because two things are alike in some features, they are necessarily alike in one or more others as well. You can say that learning to ride a bicycle is like learning to play the piano: once you learn, you seldom forget; but you would not go on to argue that one should have a bicycle tuned periodically or that one should mount a tail light on the piano for safety while playing at night. Analogies can provide interesting and concrete illustrations; by suggesting similarities they can help define, clarify, explain, or emphasize something; see, for example, the analogy comparing an outline to a road map in #9g. We would not expect our analogy to convince you of the importance of an outline, but we hope that, by adding its concrete touch, we help you to understand and perhaps to accept our assertions.

One fairly common argument claims that because city or provincial or other governments are in some ways similar to large business organizations, they need experienced business people to run them. The more similarities you can point to, the stronger the argument. The trouble with this and other arguments from analogy is that no matter how many specific similarities you can come up with, your opponents can usually keep ahead of you by citing an even greater number of specific and significant differences. After all, leading a government may be *like* running a business, but it is not the same thing.

10h

10. Equivocation

Equivocation involves using a term in more than one sense; being ambiguous, whether accidentally or intentionally: "It is only natural for intelligent people to reject this idea. And as science tells us, natural law is the law of the universe; it is the law of truth, and must be obeyed." Aside from the appeal to snobbery and self-esteem (we all like to think we are "intelligent," but just what is "intelligence"?) and the appeal to the prestige of "science" in the modern world (but just how infallible is science?) and the imposing but vague term *universe* and the glittering abstraction *truth,* do the two occurrences of the word *natural* correspond with each other? And is a natural *law* comparable to legislation passed by a government and enforced by police and the courts? Don't let the meanings of words shift as you move from one phrase or sentence to the next. Choose and use your words ethically and carefully.

11. Non sequitur

Non sequitur means "it does not follow." When for whatever reason a general proposition does not follow logically from the particular examples cited to support it, or a conclusion does not logically follow from its premises, it is a *non sequitur.* The term would apply to any of the fallacies discussed above and also to such leaps of logic as "She can French braid hair; she'd make a good mother," and "I've had singing lessons for two years; I should get the lead role in the opera."

Exercise 10 (1) Detecting faulty reasoning

Point out the weak reasoning in each of the following. Identify any particular fallacies you detect.

1. She's a liberal, so she's sure to use the taxpayer's money for all sorts of give-away programs, for that's what "liberal" means: generous.
2. Your advertisement says that you want someone with experience as a computer programmer. I've had a year's experience as a computer programmer, so I'm clearly the person you want for the job.
3. Since peanuts can cause allergic reactions, they should be taken off the market.
4. He's bound to have an inferiority complex. Look at how thin he is!
5. Novels written by women often have women as protagonists. Since this novel has a woman as protagonist, it was probably written by a woman.

Exercise 10 (1) Detecting faulty reasoning – *continued*

6. In the past, my dishwasher has always been quiet, but now that new people have moved in to the apartment next door, the dishwasher is noisy. They must have done something funny to the plumbing.
7. Dogs make better pets than cats because when they wag their tails they're happy; cats flick their tails when they're angry.
8. This critic says Mel Gibson's movies are second-rate, but since she's known to be a feminist her judgment won't stand up.
9. If I am not promoted, the company will immediately collapse.
10. Student opinion is overwhelmingly in favour of dropping the first-year science requirement. I took a poll among my fellow English majors, and over 80 per cent of them agreed.
11. The police are supposed to protect society from real criminals. When they give me parking tickets they're not doing their job, for I'm not harming society and I'm certainly not a criminal.
12. We've had an unusually warm winter, no doubt as a result of the meteorite shower last year.
13. Fashion models have slim bodies. They must be much healthier than most other people.
14. This party is for lower taxes, and so am I. That's why I am loyal to the party and always vote for its candidates.
15. People who live and work together constitute a social community, and in a democracy social communities should have a measure of self-government. Since the university is such a community, and since the vast majority of those participating in its life are students, it follows that students should have a major say in the running of the university.
16. Advertising is like fishing. Advertisers use something attractive for bait and reel out their lines to dangle the bait in front of us. They think of consumers as poor dumb fish, suckers who will swallow their stuff hook, line, and sinker. And there's a lesson for us in that: if you bite you'll get hurt, for there's always a nasty hook under the bait. The only way to protect yourself is to make sure you don't fall for any advertiser's pitch.

10h

Exercise 10 (2) Analyzing arguments and recognizing persuasive techniques

1. In an essay, analyze three or four current magazine advertisements for different kinds of products. Point out all the techniques of persuasion you can find in them. Do they appeal more to emotion than to reason? Are they guilty of any particular fallacies?
2. Look over a week's worth of the editorial and letters pages of a local city or campus newspaper. Select and analyze three or four editorials or letters in order to discover their argumentative techniques.
3. Find a more extended piece of argumentative writing in a magazine with national circulation. Try to find one arguing about some issue of national importance. Analyze it as an argument. Consider its subject, its audience, its structure, its methods of reasoning, its possible weaknesses, and so on. Assign it a grade.

Exercise 10 (3) Including the opposition

In the following sentence outline for an argumentative essay, the student took little account of points the opposition might raise. Read through it carefully, listing as many opposition arguments as you can think of; then recast the outline so as to include those arguments. You can improve the outline in other ways as well. If you find the counter-arguments compelling, you may want to recast the thesis so that you are arguing for the other side. Include in the revised outline one or more sentences each for both a possible beginning and a possible ending of the essay. Think up a good title.

THESIS STATEMENT: In my opinion, it is better to listen to music at home rather than in a concert hall.

I. By staying home instead of going to a concert, people save money on tickets, transportation, and babysitters.
   A. The cost of listening to a CD at home is a third of the cost of a ticket to get into a concert.
   B. Any kind of transportation is an additional cost to a music lover who goes to a concert.
      1. Cars require fuel and parking.
      2. Taxis are expensive and hard to get.
      3. Public transit is too slow and full of people who are coughing.

Exercise 10 (3) Including the opposition – *continued*

C. Parents who wish to go to a live concert must hire a babysitter.

II. Music lovers have the comfort and convenience of staying at home.
A. They have easy access to relatively inexpensive refreshments and to washroom facilities.
B. They can sit in an open and relaxed manner.
1. Theatre seats are too compact and uncomfortable.
2. The cost of refreshments is very expensive.
C. When one is in a large crowd it is often difficult to concentrate on the music.

III. A CD provides perfect sound every time.
A. You can listen to one piece many times using the repeat function.
B. You don't have to listen to other people coughing, applauding or scrunching candy wrappers.

Exercise 10 (4) Writing an argument

Carefully plan and write an argument of between 1,000 and 1,250 words (4–5 double-spaced typed pages) on some local issue, perhaps something you found while working on part 2 of Exercise 10 (2). Take a position you sincerely believe in. Don't pick a topic that you can't deal with fairly thoroughly. Be sure to take into account any major opposition arguments.

11 Writing In-class Essays and Essay Examinations

Writing an essay in class or during an examination is much like writing an essay in your own room, in the library, or anywhere else—except that you may have to do it faster: you don't have time to think and plan at leisure and at length. Therefore, you need to make the best use of the time you have. All the principles discussed earlier in this chapter still hold, but here is some additional advice to help you work quickly and efficiently:

1. **At the beginning of an examination, read through the whole test right away.** If it has more than one part, budget your time: before you start thinking and writing, decide just how much time you will

need or can afford to spend on each part. Make decisions about time allotment based on the mark value of each section of the examination.

2. **Read the topics or questions carefully.** Don't, in haste, misread or misinterpret. Don't read wishfully, finding in a question what you want to find instead of what is actually there.

3. **Follow instructions.** If you're asked for an argument, *argue.* If a question asks you to *analyze* a text, don't simply give a summary of it. If it asks you to *justify* or *defend* your opinions or conclusions, don't simply assert them. If it asks for *comparison and contrast,* don't spend too much time on one side of the matter. If it asks you to *define* a term or concept, don't simply describe it or give an example of it, and don't ramble on about your feelings about it or your impressions of it.

4. **Take time to plan.** Don't panic and begin writing immediately. Think for a few minutes. The time you spend planning will ensure that the job of writing is easier and the result clearer. Do a little quick brainstorming. Take the time to make at least a sketch outline, with a thesis or proposition and a list of main points and supporting details; you will then be less likely to wander off the topic or change your thesis as you proceed. It's often a good idea to limit yourself to three or four main points, or parts (in addition, that is, to a beginning and an ending).

5. **Get started.** Once you've drawn up your plan, start writing. If necessary, leave several lines or a page blank at the beginning and plunge right into your first point. Don't waste time trying to think of a beginning if one doesn't occur to you quickly; you can come back and fill it in later. Quite possibly you won't need to supply a separate "beginning" at all. Get to the point quickly and stay with it. Make your thesis clear early on; that may be all you need by way of a beginning. Often you can pick up some key words or phrases from the question or topic and use them to help frame a thesis and get yourself going.

6. **Write carefully.** Whereas in an essay written at home or in a research essay you may write your draft hurriedly and spend most of your time revising and editing, in an exam you have to make most of your changes as you go. (This is another reason it's important to have a plan: without one, you could, as you pause to tinker with a sentence, forget your thread of continuity, your line of argument.) You won't have time to do much revising; your first efforts at sentences will often have to do. And in an exam, don't waste time recopying an initial draft, because you are not being tested on your handwriting.

7. **Aim for quality, not quantity.** More is not necessarily better. Your essay should be of reasonable length, and sometimes a required minimum length will be specified. What is most important is that you adequately develop your subject by developing each of your main points. But don't try to impress by going on and on, for then you will likely ramble, lose control of your thesis and your organization, and not give yourself time to edit and proofread.

8. **Be specific.** Provide examples, illustrations, and evidence. By all means generalize, but support your generalizations with specific and concrete details.

9. **Conclude effectively.** Refer to, or restate, your thesis, and if necessary refer again to your three or four main points, but do so in a way that adds something new. Sometimes a single concluding sentence can make a good clincher, especially if it suggests or underscores some result or effect growing out of what your discussion has said. If possible, echo an idea you had in your introduction.

10. **Proofread carefully.** Leave yourself enough time to look for the kinds of mistakes and slips we all make when writing fast. Don't just run your eyes over your sentences, assuming that any errors will leap out at you, even though that may give you the illusion that you've checked your work. Read carefully. If you know that you're prone to certain kinds of errors, look specifically for them.

Understanding Sentences

II

Introduction: The Conventions of Language

II

Words are the building blocks we use to put together language structures that enable us to communicate. Combinations of words produce sentences; combinations of sentences produce paragraphs; combinations of paragraphs can form stories, detailed expositions, descriptions, summaries, arguments.

When we write, we represent speech sounds with symbols called letters, which combine to form the units called words. Those who share a familiarity with a particular language are able to communicate because each person knows the meaning of the sounds. If you said "Look" when you meant "Listen," you would fail to communicate. The success of the process depends upon the **conventions**, the shared acceptance of what particular words mean.

Putting words together to make sentences is also subject to conventions. We use particular word orders and other standard ways of showing how words are related to each other; and since writing represents speech, we use certain visual devices to help clarify meaning and make communication easier. The conventions governing the arrangement of words and the relations between them constitute the **grammar** of a language. The techniques that help us "hear" writing as something like speaking constitute the conventions of **punctuation**.

The next four chapters of this book describe and illustrate these conventions of language and ways of avoiding errors in their use. Although on occasion we use terms like "rules" and "right" and "wrong," try to think of yourself as studying not the "rules" of grammar and punctuation but their conventions; and think not in terms of what is "right" or "correct" but in terms of what is conventional—that is, mutually agreed upon, and therefore understandable, and therefore effective.

Grammar

The term *grammar* is virtually equivalent to the term *syntax*, which refers to the relations among words and the order of words in individual sentences. Chapters II through V are about sentences, the primary units of communication: how they work, what goes into them, what their varieties are, how their parts are arranged, and how they are punctuated. You may be able to write fairly well without knowing much about these grammatical principles. But if you have any difficulties writing correct and effective sentences, you'll find it much easier to overcome them if you know how sentences work. And you'll find an understanding of sentence grammar especially helpful in improving the effectiveness of your punctuation.

Don't be intimidated by the thought that you're studying "grammar." After all, if you can read and understand these sentences, you already know a great deal of grammar; chances are you absorbed it, unconsciously, as part of everyday life. Now you need only raise some of that understanding into consciousness so that you can use it to help you stick to the conventions and make your writing more effective. You may often be able to trust your intuitive grasp of the way English words and sentences work; but if you find yourself having trouble, especially if you are multilingual and English isn't your first language, you may want to consult the principles more often and apply them more consciously.

We use the vocabulary of traditional grammar both because it has, for many, the virtue of simplicity and familiarity and because it is usually the vocabulary used to study another language. It is also the vocabulary used by dictionaries and other reference books in their definitions and discussions of usage. Learning these terms shouldn't be difficult. If you find the going rough, you may be making it unnecessarily hard for yourself; if you fight the material, it may well fight back. But if you approach it with interest and a desire to learn, you'll find that it will cooperate and that the quality of your writing will improve as you increase your mastery of the conventions. Further, you will not only be learning to follow "rules" in order to produce "correct" sentences but also be learning how to choose one form or usage or order rather than another. Good writing is often a result of being able to make intelligent choices from the alternatives available to you.

This chapter introduces the basic elements and patterns of English sentences and defines and classifies different kinds of sentences. Awareness of these patterns and an ability to recognize phrases and clauses will increase your understanding of sentence grammar.

12 Sentence Patterns and Conventions

All sentences have a purpose, namely to communicate ideas and/or feelings. And there are **conventional** ways to convey these ideas and feelings. For example, if someone tells you,

> I am writing a report on student-centred learning.

you know that the sentence is stating a fact, or a supposed fact. If the same person then says,

> Are you familiar with the term "student-centred learning"?

you know that you are being asked a question and that you are expected to give an answer. If your friend then says,

> Give me your opinion of my report proposal.

you know you are being asked to do something, being given a mild command. And when your fellow student says,

> What an ambitious project!

you know you are hearing an emphatic expression of strong feeling.

We know how to interpret these different kinds of utterances because we understand and accept the *conventions* of the way sentences communicate. Sentences are classified according to the kind of purpose each has. Sentences that *make statements of fact or supposed fact* are called **declarative:**

> The United States is Canada's largest trading partner.
>
> *Anne of Green Gables* is tremendously popular in Japan.
>
> This seminar deals with the effects of globalization on education.

Sentences that *ask questions* are **interrogative**; in speech, they often (but not always) end with a rise in the pitch of one's voice; in writing, they end with a **question mark**:

> Is this computer virus affecting your e-mail?
>
> Are you going to the library?
>
> Why? What's the reason?

Sentences that *give commands* or *make requests*, that expect action or compliance, are **imperative:**

> Please print the document.
>
> Don't forget to file your income tax return.
>
> Edit your work carefully before submitting it.

Sentences that *exclaim*, that express strong feeling with vigour or emphasis, are called **exclamatory**; they customarily end with an **exclamation point**:

> That was an unforgettable race!
>
> Not if I can help it!
>
> Amazing!

Like many other traditional categories, however, the ones we've described aren't always so simple or obvious. For example, a sentence may include both *interrogative* and *declarative* elements:

> "Should the voting age be raised?" the candidate asked.

or both *imperative* and *declarative* elements:

> Please contact me about your project: I have information that's relevant.

or be both *imperative* and *exclamatory*:

Slow down!

12

And many *imperative* sentences, especially those that make requests, are at least implicitly *interrogative* even though they don't end with a question mark:

Please forward this message. (Will you please forward this message?)

Sometimes the same basic sense can be expressed in all four ways:

I need your help.
Will you help me?
Help me with this.
Help!

Nevertheless, you're seldom in doubt about the purpose of sentences you hear or read, and you're seldom, if ever, in doubt about the purpose or purposes of any sentence you speak or write. Your awareness of the *conventions* guides you: you know almost instinctively how to frame a sentence to make it do what you want.

But a more conscious grasp of the way sentences work will help you frame them even more effectively. It will help you when you're in doubt. And it will help you not only to avoid weaknesses and errors but also to revise and correct them when they do occur.

Since most sentences in written and academic discourse are *declarative*, their patterns are the ones you need to understand first. Most of the rest of this chapter, then, deals with the basic elements and patterns of declarative sentences.

12a Subject and Predicate, Noun and Verb

A standard declarative sentence consists of two parts: a **subject** and a **predicate.** The subject is what acts or is talked about; the predicate is what the subject does or what is said about it. For example:

subject	*predicate*
Grass	grows.
Birds	fly.
I	disagree.

The essential element of the subject part of a sentence is a **noun** (*Grass*, *Birds*) or a **pronoun** (*I*) (see #13 and #14); the essential element of the predicate part of a sentence is a **verb** (*grows*, *fly*, *disagree*) (see #17).

Exercise 12a

Compose five two-word sentences similar to those in the example above. Each will need a single-word noun or a pronoun as its subject and a single-word verb as its predicate.

12b Articles and Other Modifiers

Few sentences, however, consist of only a one-word subject and a one-word predicate. Frequently, for example, nouns are preceded by articles (*a*, *an*, *the*) (see #19c):

subject	*predicate*
The child	toddled.

And both subject and predicate often include **modifiers**, words that change or limit the meaning of nouns and verbs. Nouns are modified by **adjectives** (see #19):

subject	*predicate*
The young child	toddled.
A caged bird	will sing.

Verbs are modified by **adverbs** (see #20):

subject	*predicate*
The young child	toddled triumphantly.
They	flew south.

Exercise 12b

Rewrite the sentences you wrote for Exercise 12a, adding articles and single-word adjectives and adverbs to them as you think appropriate.

12c–k Basic Sentence Patterns

Such single-word modifiers as those in the example above account for only part of the richness of many sentences, which may feature impressive arrays of modifying phrases and clauses (see, for example, the sentences discussed in #26). Yet complicated as they may seem, almost all English sentences use only a few basic patterns, or combinations of them. If you can recognize and understand the sentence patterns indicated in the chart below and elaborated on in the following pages, you will be well on your way to being able to analyze any sentences you write or read.

Sentence Pattern #	*Description*
1	Subject + Verb
2A	Subject + Verb + Direct Object
2B	Subject + Passive Voice Verb
3	Subject + Verb + Indirect Object + Direct Object
4A	Subject + Linking Verb + Subjective Complement (predicate adjective)
4B	Subject + Linking Verb + Subjective Complement (predicate noun)
5A	Subject + Verb + Direct Object + Objective Complement (adjective)
5B	Subject + Verb + Direct Object + Objective Complement (noun)
6	*There* or *It* + Linking Verb (+ complement) + Subject

12c Sentence Pattern 1

SUBJECT + VERB

This is the pattern you've already looked at and imitated. The subject, consisting of a noun (with its modifiers) or a pronoun, is followed by the predicate, consisting of a verb (with its modifiers):

subject	*predicate*
The Cheshire cat	smiled mysteriously.
Birds	fly.
These large, ungainly birds	can fly quite gracefully.
They	soar majestically.

Exercise 12c

Return to the sentences you wrote for Exercises 12a and 12b, or compose new ones, this time adding a few more modifiers to some of the nouns and verbs.

12d Sentence Pattern 2A

SUBJECT + VERB + DIRECT OBJECT

In this pattern we expand the basic sentence core by adding a direct object to the predicate. A direct object, like a subject, must be either a noun or a pronoun, and the verb must be transitive—that is, it must be able to take a direct object (see #17a):

subject	predicate	
noun or pronoun	***transitive verb***	***direct object***
I	paint	urban landscapes.
Sandra	enjoys	opera.
It	intrigues	him.
Pierre	is reading	scripts.
Impatient journalists	pursue	tight-lipped celebrities.

In this pattern the subject acts, the verb indicates the action, and the direct object is the product (*landscapes*) or the receiver (*opera, celebrities*) of the action. Note that direct objects can, like subject-nouns, be modified by adjectives (*urban*, *tight-lipped*).

Exercise 12d

Compose five sentences following Pattern 2A, some with modifiers and some without.

12e Sentence Pattern 2B (passive voice)

SUBJECT (receiver of the action) + PASSIVE VOICE VERB (+ 'by' phrase: agent/performer of the action)

In this pattern the order of the main elements of Pattern 2A is reversed. That is, the former direct object becomes the subject, and the former subject moves to the end of the sentence, after the **preposition** *by* (see #22). The verb stays in the middle but changes to the passive voice—a form of the verb *be* followed by a **past participle** (see # 21d). Use the passive voice strategically—that is, when you want to emphasize the receiver rather than the performer of an action. Make your choice knowing that overuse of the passive can sometimes make writing wordy and unclear. Consider a crime scenario in which a detective might say, using Pattern 2A,

Poison killed him. (active voice)

But in the circumstances it would be more natural to say

He was killed by poison. (passive voice)

Similarly, you can write some of the sentences under Pattern 2A according to Pattern 2B:

subject	*predicate*	
noun or pronoun	***verb***	***prepositional phrase***
Urban landscapes	are painted	by me.
Scripts	are read	by Pierre.
Tight-lipped celebrities	are pursued	by impatient journalists.

But you can see that such alternatives would be preferable only in unusual circumstances, for example if you wanted special emphasis on *urban landscapes* or *scripts* or *tight-lipped celebrities*. Note that in this pattern the '*by*' phrase is often omitted as unnecessary or unknown:

He has been poisoned (by someone).

See also #17o–p and #29f.

Exercise 12e

Convert each sentence you wrote for Exercise 12d into Pattern 2B. How many now seem to be sentences you could use in effective discourse? Try to include them in contexts where they would be preferable to the versions you wrote for Pattern 2A. Then compose a few new sentences using Pattern 2B, ones that make clear sense in the passive voice.

12f Sentence Pattern 3

SUBJECT + VERB + INDIRECT OBJECT + DIRECT OBJECT

A sentence with a direct object sometimes also includes an **indirect object**. An indirect object is a noun or pronoun referring to an animate being and identifying the recipient of an action—that is, the person or other living creature to whom or for whom an action occurs.

subject	*predicate*		
noun or pronoun	***transitive verb***	***indirect object***	***direct object***
He	sent	his adviser	an e-mail message.
Grace	lent	Ari	her lecture notes.
Jason	offered	his guests	sushi.

Note that you can usually vary this pattern, and still say essentially the same thing, by changing the indirect object to a prepositional phrase that comes after the direct object:

subject	*predicate*		
noun or verb	***transitive verb***	***direct object***	***prepositional phrase***
He	sent	an e-mail message	to his adviser.
Grace	lent	her lecture notes	to Ari.
Jason	offered	sushi	to his guests.

Exercise 12f

Compose five sentences in Pattern 3. Then rewrite two of them using a prepositional phrase, with *to* or *for,* instead of an indirect object.

12g Sentence Pattern 4A

SUBJECT + LINKING VERB + SUBJECTIVE COMPLEMENT
(predicate adjective)

Some verbs—called **linking verbs** (see #17a)—require something other than an object to complete the idea, something called a **complement.** And since the complement is linked to the subject, it is sometimes called a **subjective complement.** The principal linking verb is *be* in its various forms (see #17f). In Pattern 4A, the verb links the subject with an adjectival modifier in the predicate part of the sentence; the modifier is therefore called a **predicate adjective:**

subject	*predicate*	
noun or pronoun	***linking verb***	***subjective complement (predicate adjective)***
She	is	curious.
Cell phones	have become	indispensable.
Samosas	taste	spicy.

Exercise 12g

Compose three sentences following Pattern 4A.

12h Sentence Pattern 4B

SUBJECT + LINKING VERB + SUBJECTIVE COMPLEMENT
(predicate noun)

In this pattern, a verb links the subject with a noun or pronoun acting as a subjective complement and called a **predicate noun**:

subject	*predicate*	
noun or pronoun	*linking verb*	*subjective complement (predicate noun)*
This	is	it.
Lynn Coady	is	a talented writer.
Raw vegetables	make	good snacks.

Exercise 12h

Compose three sentences following Pattern 4B.

12i Sentence Pattern 5A

SUBJECT + VERB + DIRECT OBJECT + OBJECTIVE COMPLEMENT **(adjective)**

Such verbs as *appoint, believe, call, consider, declare, designate, elect, find, judge, make, name, nominate, select,* and *think* are sometimes followed by a direct object and an **objective complement**—a complement describing the object rather than the subject. In Pattern 5A, as in Pattern 4A, the complement is an *adjective:*

subject	*predicate*		
noun or pronoun	*transitive verb*	*direct object*	*objective complement (adjective)*
The committee	considered	the proposal	unworkable.
The jury	found	them	guilty as charged.
They	made	themselves	comfortable.

Exercise 12i

Compose three sentences following Pattern 5A.

12j Sentence Pattern 5B

SUBJECT + VERB + DIRECT OBJECT + OBJECTIVE COMPLEMENT (noun)

In this variation, the objective complement that completes the meaning of the direct object is a *noun:*

subject	*predicate*		
noun or pronoun	***transitive verb***	***direct object***	***objective complement (noun)***
The party	named	her	interim leader.
The critic	declared	the artist	a failure.
We	judged	the party	a success.

Exercise 12j

Compose three sentences following Pattern 5B.

12k Sentence Pattern 6 (expletive)

***THERE* or *IT* + LINKING VERB (+ complement) + SUBJECT**

This final pattern is, like the passive voice in Pattern 2B, something that you should use judiciously: the **expletive** pattern. In such sentences the word *There* or *It* appears at the beginning, in the place usually occupied by the subject; then comes a linking verb, usually a form of the verb *be;* and then comes the subject. When used strategically, *There* and *It* enable you to make certain kinds of statements in a more natural way or with a different emphasis than you could otherwise. For example, instead of having to say

subject	*predicate*
That life begins at forty	may be true.
No solutions	existed.
No plumbing	was in the cabin.

you can, using Pattern 6, say

expletive	*linking verb*	*complement*	*subject*
It	may be	true	that life begins at forty.
There	were		no solutions.
There	was		no plumbing in the cabin.

Here are some further examples of Pattern 6:

> There were several protesters waiting to heckle the premier.
>
> It is easy to follow this recipe.
>
> It is challenging to study Sanskrit.
>
> There wasn't a cloud in the sky.

See also #18e, #29f, and #71a.

Exercise 12k (1)

Try converting the four examples above into a different pattern (for example, *Several protesters were waiting to heckle the premier*). In what kinds of contexts might the alternative—and more direct—versions be preferable?

Exercise 12k (2)

Convert the following sentences into Pattern 6:

1. Ten mugs of hot tea are on the table.
2. No way around the obstacle exists.
3. To look directly at a solar eclipse is dangerous.
4. A magnificent celebration occurred.
5. People were everywhere!
6. Waiter, a fly is in my soup.

Do some seem better in the expletive form? Why? How might context determine one's choice?

Exercise 12c–k Identifying sentence elements and patterns

Identify the pattern of each of the following sentences. Label each subject-noun or subject-pronoun *S* and each predicate-verb *V*. Then label each direct object *DO*, each indirect object *IO*, each subjective complement *SC*, and each objective complement *OC*. If you wish, also label any articles and other modifiers.

1. Food nourishes. Pattern____
2. Bruce finds gardening relaxing. Pattern____

Exercise 12c–k Identifying sentence elements – *continued*

3. The Schmidts are excellent cooks. Pattern____
4. I love lasagna. Pattern____
5. There are nine modules in our oceanography course. Pattern____
6. Poor Stephen was hit by a bus. Pattern____
7. Jacques brought me luck. Pattern____
8. Certain music can affect one's emotions. Pattern____
9. The group elected Jo spokesperson. Pattern____
10. Some people are superstitious. Pattern____

12-l Other Elements: Structure Words

Most declarative sentences use one or more of the above patterns. And the elements in those patterns—subjects, verbs, modifiers, objects, and complements—make up the substance of all sentences.

Many sentences also include words like *and, but, for, of, under, with.* Such words are important because they connect other elements in various ways that establish meaningful relations between them. Such words are sometimes called **structure words** or **function words**; most of them belong to two other classes of words, or "parts of speech," **conjunctions** (see #23) and **prepositions** (see #22). All of these elements are discussed and illustrated at greater length in chapters III and IV.

12m–r Clauses and Phrases

Before you go on to chapter III, you need to understand the differences between **clauses** and **phrases** and how they work in sentences. Clauses and phrases are groups of words that function as grammatical units or elements *within* sentences but that—except for **independent clauses**—cannot stand alone *as* sentences.

12m Independent (Main) Clauses

A clause is a group of words containing both a *subject* and a *predicate.* If it is an **independent clause**, it can, as the term indicates, stand by itself as a sentence. Each of the sample sentences in the preceding sections is an independent clause, since each contains the minimum requirement: a noun or pronoun as subject and a verb functioning in the predicate; each is a **simple sentence** (see #12z.1).

But an independent clause can also function as only part of a sentence. For example, if you start with two separate independent clauses—that is, two simple sentences:

> The exam ended.
>
> The students submitted their papers.

you can combine them to form a **compound sentence** (see #12z.2):

> The exam ended; the students submitted their papers.
>
> The exam ended, and the students submitted their papers.
>
> The exam ended; therefore the students submitted their papers.

Each of the two halves of these sentences is an independent clause; each could stand alone as a sentence.

12n Subordinate (Dependent) Clauses

A **subordinate clause,** unlike an independent clause, usually cannot stand by itself. Even though, as a clause, it contains a subject and a predicate, it is by definition *subordinate, dependent* on another clause—an *independent* one—for its meaning. It therefore must be treated as only part of a sentence, as in the following examples (the subordinate clauses are in italics); these are called **complex sentences** (see #12z.3):

> *When the exam ended*, the students submitted their papers.
>
> The students submitted their papers *as the exam ended*.
>
> The students submitted the papers *that they had written during the exam*.
>
> The exam ended, *which meant that the students had to submit their papers*.

Note that subordinate clauses often begin with such words as *when*, *as*, *that*, and *which*, called **subordinators,** which often clearly signal the presence of a subordinate clause as opposed to an independent clause (see #23c).

(Subordinate clauses can be used separately, for example in dialogue or as answers to questions, where the context is clear: Why did the students submit their papers? *Because the exam had ended.* Except in such circumstances, a subordinate clause should not stand by itself as if it were a sentence. See #12w and #12x.)

12-o Functions of Subordinate Clauses

Like a phrase (see below), a subordinate clause functions as a grammatical unit in its sentence. That is, a subordinate clause can occupy several of the slots in the sentence patterns illustrated just above. For example, a **noun clause** can serve as the subject of a sentence:

> That free speech matters is evident. [Pattern 4A]

as a direct object:

> Azin knows what she is doing. [Pattern 2A]

or as a predicate noun:

> The question is what we should do next. [Pattern 4B]

Adjectival clauses (also called **relative clauses**; see #14d) modify nouns or pronouns, such as a direct object:

> The reporter questioned the police officer who had found the missing child. [Pattern 2A]

or a subject:

> The project that I am working on is proceeding smoothly. [Pattern 1]

Adverbial clauses usually modify main verbs:

> We left because we were utterly bored. [Pattern 1]

12p Phrases

A **phrase** is a group of words lacking a subject and/or predicate but functioning as a grammatical unit within a sentence. For example, a **verb phrase** (see #17e) acts as the verb in this Pattern 1 sentence:

> Most of the wedding guests will be arriving in the morning.

A **prepositional phrase** (see #22) can be an adjectival modifier:

> Most of the wedding guests will be arriving in the morning.

or an adverbial modifier:

Most of the wedding guests will be arriving in the morning.

12p

The words *Most of the wedding guests* constitute a **noun phrase** functioning as the subject of the sentence. Any noun or pronoun along with its modifiers—so long as the group doesn't contain a subject–predicate combination—can be thought of as a noun phrase. Similarly, a **gerund phrase** (see #21f) can function as a subject:

Bungee jumping can be risky. Pattern 4A

or as a direct object:

She tried bungee jumping. Pattern 2A

A **participial phrase**—always adjectival (see #21d)—can modify a subject:

Trusting her instincts, Jane gave the candidate her support. Pattern 3

or a direct object:

I am reading an article discussing human cloning. Pattern 2A

An **infinitive phrase** (see #21a) can function as a direct object (noun):

This organization wants to eradicate poverty. Pattern 2A

or as a subject (noun):

It may be impossible to eradicate poverty. Pattern 6

It can also function as an adjective, for example one modifying the subject:

Their desire to eradicate poverty is idealistic. Pattern 4A

or it can function as an adverb, for example one modifying the verb:

They arranged the agenda to highlight the anti-poverty campaign. Pattern 2A

Adverbial infinitive phrases can also act as **sentence modifiers** (see #20a and #20d.4), modifying not the verb or any other single word but rather all the rest of the sentence:

To be honest,
To tell the truth, } the meeting ended shortly after you left.

Exercise 12m–p Recognizing phrases and clauses

Indicate whether each of the following groups of words is an independent clause, a subordinate clause, or a phrase. Label the subject (*s*) and verb (*v*) of each clause. In the case of a subordinate clause, circle the subordinator.

1. not only BC but PEI as well ____________
2. rarely have we witnessed such a performance ____________
3. for the first time in her life she was speechless ____________
4. since no one was paying attention ____________
5. down the hall from my office ____________
6. but interest rates are rising ____________
7. while looking for his cell phone ____________
8. his bubble burst ____________
9. after the conference was over ____________
10. according to the overly complicated directions in the guidebook ____________

12q Appositives

Two other kinds of phrases you should be familiar with are the **appositive** and the **absolute**.

An **appositive** is a word or group of words that renames or restates, in other terms, the meaning of a neighbouring word. For example, if you start with two simple sentences,

> Marc is our lawyer. He looks after our business dealings.

you can turn the first into an appositive by reducing it and combining it with the second:

> Marc, our lawyer, looks after our business dealings.

The noun phrase *our lawyer* is here said to be **in apposition to** *Marc.*

Most appositives are nouns or noun phrases that redefine, usually in more specific terms, the nouns they follow. But occasionally an appositive precedes the other noun:

> A skilful lawyer, Marc looks after our business dealings.

And occasionally another part of speech can function as an appositive, for example a participial (adjectival) phrase:

> Searching frantically, tossing books and papers everywhere, they failed to find the missing passport.

or a verb phrase:

> Document (provide details of your sources for) this argument.

An appositive can also be a single word, often a name:

> Our lawyer, Marc, looks after our business dealings.

And, rarely, even a subordinate clause can function as an appositive:

> How she travelled—whether she journeyed alone or not—remains a mystery.

Note that an appositive is grammatically equivalent to the term it defines and could replace it in the sentence:

> Our lawyer looks after our business dealings.
>
> A skilful lawyer looks after our business dealings.
>
> Marc looks after our business dealings.
>
> Tossing books and papers everywhere, they failed to find the missing passport.
>
> Provide details of your sources for this argument.
>
> Whether she journeyed alone or not remains a mystery.

(For the punctuation of appositives, see #48b and #55g.)

Exercise 12q (1) Writing appositives

Combine each of the following pairs of sentences into a single sentence by reducing one of each pair to an appositive. Construct one or two so that the appositive comes first.

1. Joe is an amateur astronomer. He uses his telescope to scan the skies every night.
2. Diana Krall is a talented jazz singer. She turns old standards into memorable contemporary pieces.
3. I must thank my teachers for encouraging me in my education. They inspired me with their confidence about the future.
4. My grandfather believes in hard work. He tends to his vegetable garden for hours every day.
5. You can save time by preparing carefully. That is, you can take careful notes and draft a clear plan for your argument.

Exercise 12q (2) Using appositives

Combine each of the following pairs of sentences into a single sentence by reducing all or part of one of them to an appositive. You may drop some words and rearrange others, but don't change the basic meaning. For practice, try to write some sentences in more than one way. In each case, identify the appositive phrase you have created by underlining it.

Example: Hong Kong is one of Asia's busiest ports. It is a major Pacific commercial centre.

(a) Hong Kong, <u>one of Asia's busiest ports</u>, is a major Pacific commercial centre.

(b) One of Asia's busiest ports, <u>Hong Kong</u>, is a major Pacific commercial centre.

(c) <u>One of Asia's busiest ports</u>, Hong Kong is a major Pacific commercial centre.

1. The book I read last weekend was *The Golden Compass*. It is the first volume of Philip Pullman's *His Dark Materials* trilogy.
2. To become a fine architect is not easy. It takes many years of study and apprenticeship.
3. I always look forward to April. It is the month when the cherry blossoms appear.

12q

Exercise 12q (2) Using appositives – *continued*

4. Team sports more than occupy her spare time. She plays volleyball, field hockey, and soccer.
5. Tabloid newspapers seem to go in for sensationalism. They are the smaller, easier-to-hold newspapers.
6. Canada has a larger land mass than any other country except Russia. It is a country with a small population.
7. She was relaxed and confident when she began the competition. She was sure she could win.
8. The word *hamburger* is one of the common words we take for granted. It comes from the name of a German city.
9. Dr. Snyder is our family physician. She is a dedicated person who works long hours.
10. Running marathons is not something everyone should try. It is a potentially dangerous sport.

12r Absolute Phrases

An **absolute phrase** has no direct grammatical link with what it modifies; it depends simply on juxtaposition, in effect modifying the rest of the sentence by hovering over it like an umbrella. Most absolute phrases amount to a sentence with the verb changed to a participle (see #21d). Instead of using two sentences,

> The intermission had ended. The last act finally began.

you can reduce the first to an absolute phrase modifying the second:

> The intermission having ended, the last act finally began.

If the original verb is a form of *be*, the participle can sometimes be omitted:

> The thunderstorm (being) over, the tennis match resumed.

Sometimes, especially with certain common expressions, the participle isn't preceded by a noun:

> There were a few rough spots, but generally speaking the rehearsal was a success.

> Judging by the population statistics, we have become a multicultural nation.

And sometimes infinitive phrases (see #12p and #21a) function as absolutes:

To say the least, the campaign was not a success.

You can also think of many absolutes as *with*-phrases from which the preposition has been dropped:

(With) the thunderstorm over, the tennis match resumed.

Careful measurement is a must, (with) the results dependent on this kind of due attention.

And you can think of most absolute phrases as functioning much like an adverb modifying the rest of the sentence (see #20a and #20d.4):

absolute: All things considered, it was a fair exam.
adverb: Unfortunately, I hadn't studied hard enough.

See also #21i and Exercise 21(5).

Exercise 12r Writing absolute phrases

Compose five sentences using absolute phrases. In each of your sentences, underline the absolute phrase. You may want to start with pairs of sentences or with sentences containing a *with*-phrase.

12s Order of Elements in Declarative Sentences

Even if you didn't know the names of some of the bits and pieces, chances are that the samples presented earlier in this section to illustrate the basic sentence patterns felt natural to you; they're the familiar kinds of sentences you use every day without even thinking about their structure. Note that the natural order of the elements in almost all the patterns is the same:

subject—verb
subject—transitive verb—object(s)—(objective complement)
subject—linking verb—subjective complement

The only exception is Pattern 6, the expletive, in which the subject follows the verb (see #12k).

12s

This conventional order of *subject—verb—object or complement* has proven itself the most direct and forceful pattern of expression:

War is hell.
Humpty Dumpty had a great fall.
We are such stuff as dreams are made on.
We shall defend every village, every town, and every city.

But this order can be altered to create special stylistic effects or special emphasis, and to introduce pleasing variations:

direct object	*subject*	*transitive verb*
Their generosity	I	have never doubted for a moment.

subjective complement	*linking verb*	*subject*
Long	was	the introduction to this otherwise short speech.

Such inversions aren't wrong, for conventions (or rules) are made to be broken as well as followed; but their very unconventionality demands that they be used judiciously. They are most at home in poetry or highly oratorical prose:

Thirty days hath September . . .

And now abideth faith, hope, and charity, these three;
but the greatest of these is charity.

Never in the field of human conflict was so much owed by so many to so few.

Elsewhere such variations are rare, since any unusual pattern almost automatically calls attention to itself, something seldom appropriate in expository prose. But used occasionally, and appropriately, they can be highly effective.

Exercise 12s Using alternative word orders

Try composing four or five declarative sentences that vary the standard order of elements in one way or another. Then choose one of your sentences and use it in a paragraph that you think justifies the unorthodox order.

▲ 12t Order of Elements in Interrogative Sentences

The conventional order used in interrogative sentences usually differs from that used in declarative sentences. It is, of course, possible to use the declarative order for a question—for example in speaking, when one can use stress and end with the rising or falling intonation that usually indicates a question:

They're getting married tomorrow?

thereby conveying a meaning something like

Do you mean to tell me that they are actually getting married so soon rather than waiting and planning a more formal ceremony? How surprising!

Unless you're recording or imitating dialogue, you won't use this technique too often in your writing.

Usually, an interrogative sentence, besides ending with the conventional question mark, will take one of the following patterns. If the verb is a single-word form of *be,* it precedes the subject:

verb	*subject*	*subjective complement*
Is	Nunavut	a province?

With all other single-word verbs, it is necessary to supply a form of the auxiliary verb *do* before the subject; the main part of the verb then follows the subject in the normal way:

auxiliary verb	*subject*	*main verb*	
Does	Nunavut	have	provincial status?

If the verb is already a verb phrase, the first auxiliary comes before the subject:

auxiliary verb	*subject*	*second auxiliary*	*main verb*
Are	you		daydreaming?
Will	Max		speak first?
Have	you	been	meditating?

If the question includes a negative, the *not* goes before or after the subject, depending on whether one uses the less formal, contracted form:

Aren't you going? Are you not going?

With questions using expletives (Pattern 6 see #12k), the expletive and the verb are reversed:

Were there many people at the orientation?

Was it easy to follow her argument?

With so-called "tag" questions, a statement is followed by a verb–pronoun question; note also that a *not* appears in one or the other of the two parts:

> Maria has been hiking, hasn't she?
>
> Maria hasn't been hiking, has she?

All the above questions invite a *yes* or *no* answer, perhaps extended by a short clause made up of the appropriate pronoun (or expletive) and auxiliary, such as

> Yes, she was. Yes I am. No, I haven't.
> Yes, there were. No, it wasn't. No, he hasn't. No, he has not.

Note that the negative answers include a *not* in the clause.

The only other common form of question begins with a **question word**, one of the interrogative adverbs or pronouns; these invite answers beyond a mere *yes* or *no*. When a question begins with an interrogative adverb (see #20a), a form of *do* or another already present auxiliary comes before the subject:

> Why did he say that?
>
> Where (When) are you going?

If an interrogative pronoun (see #14c) functions as subject, the sentence retains standard declarative word order:

> Who will speak first?

If the opening pronoun is the *object* of the verb or a preposition, it is followed by the added auxiliary *do* or the first part of a verb phrase, the subject, and the rest of the verb, just as in the *yes* or *no* pattern:

> Whom did you invite?
>
> To whom did you address the invitation?

A similar reversal occurs when an interrogative pronoun functions as a possessive or other adjective (see #19a):

> Whose (Which, What) political platform do you favour?
>
> To what (which, whose) problems will the speaker address herself?

See also #22b, on the placement of prepositions in questions.

Exercise 12t Constructing interrogative sentences

Select a representative variety of ten sentences from those you've written for earlier exercises in this chapter and rewrite them as questions. Try using two or more different forms of question for some of the sentences.

12u The Structure of Imperative Sentences

It is possible, especially with emphatic commands, to use the full structure of a declarative sentence:

subject	*predicate*
You	take that back!
You two in the corner	please join the rest of the group.

Still, the conventional form of an **imperative sentence** uses only the *predicate*, omitting the *subject* (an understood *you*):

Come into the garden, Maud. (*Maud* is not the subject, but a noun of address; see #13b.)

Stretch before you run.

Close the door.

Edit carefully.

Enjoy.

Sometimes, especially in dialogue or informal contexts, even the verb can be omitted; a complement alone does the job:

Careful. Easy, now. Steady.

You may think you'll have little use for imperative sentences in your writing. But if you ever want to write a set of instructions, you'll need to use a great many of them. And they can provide useful variety in other contexts as well, just as questions can. *Declarative* sentences are unquestionably the mainstay of written expression, but *interrogative* and *imperative* sentences are also useful. So consider using them.

12v What Is a Sentence?

Now for a different kind of look at these groups of words called sentences. First, just what is a **sentence**? Most standard definitions are unsatisfactory and unrealistic because they leave out the kinds of sentences we use more often in speech than in formal writing. One of them, for example, says that a sentence is a group of words with a subject and a verb. But the first sentence of this section, just above, lacks a subject–verb combination. And here are some more sentences that lack one or the other or both:

> Yes. No. When? Now or never. Oh my goodness! Wow!
>
> Who, me? Well, I never! John. Coffee.
>
> Come here. Never mind. Call me Ishmael. Sink or swim.

Out of context, such sentences don't tell us much, but they are clearly acceptable units. Moreover, some groups of words do contain a subject–verb combination but are still not sentences: an opening capital letter and a closing period don't make a subordinate clause a sentence:

> I decided to make a list. <u>Before I went shopping</u>.
>
> They bought me the bike. <u>Which I had stared at in the store the week before</u>.

The second clause in each of these is a **fragment** (see #12x).

Another common definition claims that a sentence is a complete thought. But *Yes* and *No* aren't satisfyingly complete without the questions that prompted them, nor are some of the other examples without their respective contexts. Nor is there anything necessarily "incomplete" about such words as *dog, hand, chair, freedom, love*—yet these words are not normally thought of as sentences.

Remember that language is primarily spoken. It is more realistic to define a sentence as *a satisfyingly complete pattern of intonation or expression*: that is, a complete utterance. Your voice and natural tone should tell you whether a certain group of words is or is not a sentence. Make it a practice to read your written work aloud, or at least to sound it out in your mind. Doing so will help you avoid ambiguity.

12w–y Minor Sentences, Fragments, and Major Sentences

Sentences—that is, acceptable patterns of expression—are of two kinds, which we call **minor** and **major**. Though this and similar books deal almost exclusively with *major* sentences, and though you won't have much use for *minor* sentences in academic writing, you should understand what minor sentences are so that you can use them occasionally for emphasis or other rhetorical effects, or when you are writing a piece of dialogue. And you need to be able to distinguish between the minor sentence, which is acceptable in some academic writing, and the fragmentary expression, which is not.

12w Minor Sentences

A **minor sentence** is an acceptable pattern of expression that nevertheless lacks either a subject or a finite verb, or both. But it is easy to supply the missing element or elements from context; for whereas major sentences can usually stand by themselves, most minor sentences need a context of one or more nearby sentences in order to make sense—most obviously, for example, as answers to questions. The minor sentence, however, like the major, is grammatically independent.

Minor sentences are usually one of the following four kinds:

1. Exclamations

   Oh! Well, I never! Heavens!
   Wow! Incredible!

2. Questions or responses to questions

   When? Tomorrow. How many? Seven.
   Why? What for? How come? Really?
   Yes. No. Perhaps. Certainly.

3. Common proverbial or idiomatic expressions

   Easy come, easy go. Now or never.
   Better late than never. Down the hatch.

4. Minor sentences used for rhetorical or stylistic effect: These are more common in narrative and descriptive writing, but they can be effective in other contexts as well. Here is how Charles Dickens begins *Bleak House*:

   > London. Michaelmas Term lately over, and the Lord Chancellor sitting in Lincoln's Inn Hall. Implacable November weather. As much mud in the streets, as if the waters had but newly retired from the face of the earth, and it would not be wonderful to meet a Megalosaurus, forty feet long or so, waddling like an elephantine lizard up Holborn Hill.

And so on, for three long paragraphs: not a major sentence in sight.

Clearly the beginning of a piece of writing is a good place to try the effects of a minor sentence or two. A writer might begin an essay this way:

> Time, time, time. It is our constant companion and our greatest nemesis.

And here is a paragraph from another essay:

> One of the best times of the year in Vancouver is the spring. You know, those weeks in early April brimming with sunshine and new growth. Gardens and parks filled with crocuses, cherry trees in bloom, newborn birds in their nests.

12x Fragments

frag Don't mistake an unacceptable **fragment** for an acceptable minor sentence:

> ***frag:*** I didn't see the film. Because I felt that it would be too violent for my taste.

The *Because*-clause is a fragment. The period after *film* should be deleted so that the subordinate clause can take its rightful place in the sentence. (But note that this *Because*-clause, like many other fragments, would be acceptable as an answer to a question just before it.)

> ***frag:*** It was a hilarious moment. One that I'll never forget.

The clause beginning with *One* should be linked to the preceding independent clause with a comma, not separated from it by a period. It can then take its rightful place as a noun clause in apposition to *moment.*

> ***frag:*** He gave me half his sandwich. Being of a generous nature.

The participial phrase beginning with *Being* is not a separate sentence but an adjective modifying *He*; it should be introduced by a comma, or even moved to the beginning of the sentence:

> ***revised:*** Being of a generous nature, he gave me half his sandwich.

Note that fragments tend to occur after the independent clauses that they should be attached to.

12y Major Sentences

A **major sentence** is a grammatically independent group of words containing at least two essential structural elements: a subject and a finite verb (see #12a and #17b, Note). Major sentences constitute 99 per cent or more of most college and university writing. They are the sentences whose basic patterns are illustrated in sections #12c to #12k.

Exercise 12w–x Recognizing minor sentences and fragments

Indicate whether the italicized group of words in each of the following is a minor sentence or a fragment. In examples where the italicized words constitute a fragment, suggest a revision to correct the problem.

1. We stayed at the picnic. *Until the sun went down.*
2. Just look at the way they play together. *How rare!*
3. You say you've never seen this man? *Never?*
4. We chose to eat at this restaurant. *It having a vegetarian menu, after all.*
5. How much wood can a woodchuck chuck? *Plenty.*

12z Kinds of Major Sentences

Sentences can be classified grammatically as **simple**, **compound**, **complex**, and **compound-complex.**

1. Simple sentences

A **simple** sentence has one subject and finite verb unit, and therefore contains only one clause, an independent clause:

S V
Denis works.

S V
The boat leaks.

S V
The new museum opened on the weekend.

The subject or the verb, or both, can be compound—that is, consist of more than one part—but the sentence containing them will still be **simple**:

Claude and Kim left early. (compound subject)

She watched and waited. (compound verb)

The sergeant and his men moved down the hill and crossed the river. (compound subject, compound verb)

12z

2. Compound sentences

A **compound** sentence consists of two or more simple sentences—that is, independent clauses—linked by coordinating conjunctions (see #23a), by punctuation, or by both:

S V S V
The conductor's baton fell, and the concert ended.

S V S V
The clouds massed thickly against the hills; soon the rain fell in torrents.

S V S V
We wanted to hear jazz, but they played bluegrass instead.

S V V
Gabriel's patience and persistence paid off; he not only won
V
the prize but also earned his competitors' respect.

S V S V S V
The day was mild, the breeze was warm, and everyone went for a swim.

3. Complex sentences

A **complex** sentence consists of one independent clause and one or more subordinate clauses; in the following examples, the subordinate clauses are underlined:

We believe that we have some original plans for the campaign. (noun clause as direct object)

The strike was averted before we reported for picket duty. (adverbial clause modifying *was averted*)

This course is the one that calls for the most field research. (adjectival clause modifying *one*)

Marco Polo, who left his native Venice as a teenager, returned home after twenty-five years of adventure. (adjectival clause modifying *Marco Polo*)

When the film ended, the audience burst into applause which lasted several minutes. (adverbial clause modifying *burst*, adjectival clause modifying *applause*)

Although it seems premature, the government is proceeding with third reading of the legislation. (adverbial clause of concession, in effect modifying the rest of the sentence)

Note that when the meaning is clear, the conjunction *that* introducing a noun clause, or the relative pronouns *that* and *which* can be omitted:

He claimed he was innocent.

. . . the suitcase he had brought with him.

But see the proofreading tip near the end of #48a.

4. Compound-complex sentences

A **compound-complex** sentence consists of two or more independent clauses and one or more subordinate clauses:

Because the architect knows that the preservation of heritage buildings is vital, she is consulting widely, but as delays have developed, she has grown impatient, and therefore she is thinking of pulling out of a project that represents everything important to her.

We can analyze this example as follows:

Because the architect knows (adverbial clause)
that the preservation of heritage buildings is vital (noun clause)
she is consulting widely (independent clause)
but (coordinating conjunction)
as delays have developed (adverbial clause)
she has grown impatient (independent clause)
and (coordinating conjunction)
therefore (conjunctive adverb)
she is thinking of pulling out of a project (independent clause)
that represents everything important to her (adjective clause)

12z

Exercise 12z (1) Recognizing kinds of sentences

Label each of the following sentences as simple, compound, complex, or compound-complex.

1. If you read this novel, you will find yourself questioning the narrator's credibility. ______________
2. Everybody is going to laugh on cue. ______________
3. The trombonist who performed so well at this concert is the same one we saw last summer at the Montreal Jazz Festival. ______________
4. The groom mumbled a bit; the bride spoke her vows in a clear, strong voice. ______________
5. Few things are more pleasant than a lovingly prepared and carefully presented elegant meal consisting of several courses, consumed in good company, with soft background music, and accompanied by noble wines. ______________
6. They chose the stocks they judged to be safest, but they lost money in the recession nevertheless. ______________
7. Our classmates concluded a heated debate of the issue, and then we all voted in favour of lowering the voting age to sixteen. ______________
8. A philosophy major will learn to think clearly and will acquire a sense of cultural history, and so when she graduates she should probably have the critical thinking skills and knowledge base to make herself employable. ______________

Exercise 12z (2) Constructing different kinds of sentences

Recycle one or more of the original simple sentences you composed for question #1 as you go on to the more complicated sentences. Use as many other modifiers—words and phrases—as you want.

1. Compose three simple sentences.
2. Compose two compound sentences, each with two independent clauses.
3. Compose a compound sentence with three independent clauses.
4. Compose two complex sentences, each with one independent and one subordinate clause.
5. Compose a complex sentence with one independent and two subordinate clauses.
6. Compose three compound-complex sentences.

Parts of Speech III

Introduction: The Parts of Speech and How They Work in Sentences

As you saw in chapter II, *word order* helps determine whether a sentence is asking a question or making a statement. But word order is important in another and even more basic way. The order of elements in Pattern 2A (see #12d), for example—subject, verb, direct object—determines meaning:

Students need teachers.

Clear enough. We know, from standard English word order, that *Students* is the subject, *need* the verb, and *teachers* the direct object. Reversing the order reverses the meaning:

Teachers need students.

Now we know that *Teachers* are doing the *needing* and that *students* are the objects of the need. If you know a language like German or Latin, you know how different—and in some ways more difficult—they can be; for in such languages it is the *form* of the words, rather than their position, that determines meaning. For example the following sentence would, in English, not only sound awkward but also be ambiguous.

Teachers students need.

But the same three words in Latin would be clear because the *forms* of the two nouns would show which was subject and which was object.

The change in a word's form is called **inflection**. Some words in modern English must be inflected in order for sentences to communicate clearly. If, for example, you want the noun *boy* to denote more than one young male, you change it—*inflect* it—by adding an *s* to make it plural: *boys*. If you want to use the verb *see* to denote the act of seeing in some past time, you change its form so that you can say, for example, *I saw* or *I have seen* or *I was seeing*.

English words fall traditionally into eight categories called **parts of speech**. Five of these can be inflected in one or more ways:

- noun
- pronoun
- verb
- adjective
- adverb

The other three are not inflected:

- preposition
- conjunction
- interjection

For example the preposition *in* is always *in*; the conjunction *but* is always *but*. (The only exceptions occur when words are referred to *as words*, as in "There are too many *and*s in that sentence" and "I don't want to hear any *if*s, *and*s, or *but*s," or in informal or idiomatic usages such as "She knows all the *ins* and *outs* of the process," where such words function as nouns rather than as structure words, prepositions, and conjunctions.)

Note that the term *inflection* applies only to the change of a word's form within its part of speech. That is, when the noun *boy* is inflected to make it plural, the new form, *boys*, is still a noun; when the pronoun *they* is inflected to *them* or *theirs*, the new forms are still pronouns. (Again there is an exception: when you inflect a noun or pronoun for the possessive case before a noun—the *boy's* coat, *their* idea—you turn it into an adjective; some people, however, thinking of *form* rather than *function*, prefer to call these inflected forms "possessive nouns" and "possessive pronouns.")

Many words can be changed so that they function as different parts of speech. For example the noun *centre* can be made into the adjective *central*, or the noun *meaning* into the adjective *meaningful*, or the verb *vacate* into the noun *vacation*. Such changes, however, are not inflections but **derivations**; a word can be *derived* from a word of a different part of speech, often by the addition of one or more suffixes: *trust*, *trustful*, *trustfully*, *trustfulness*. And many words, even without being changed, can serve as more than one part of speech; for example:

> She is cool under pressure. (adjective)
>
> Relations between the two may cool now that they're apart. (verb)
>
> He knows how to keep his cool in a crisis. (noun)

The word *word* itself can be a noun ("Use this *word* correctly"), a verb ("How will you *word* your reply?"), or an adjective ("*Word* games are fun"). The word *right* can be a noun (his legal *right*), an adjective (the *right* stuff), an adverb (turn *right*, do it *right*), or a verb (*right* an overturned canoe). Or consider the versatility of the common word *over*:

> At least we have a roof over our heads. (preposition)
>
> The game is over. (adjective)
>
> Write that page over. (adverb)
>
> "Roger. Message received. Over." (interjection)

The *form* of a word, then, doesn't always determine its function. What part of speech a word is depends on its *function* in a particular sentence.

The rest of this section discusses the eight parts of speech—their inflections (if any) and other grammatical properties; their subcategories; how they work with other words in sentences; and some of their important derivatives (verbals)—and calls attention to some of their potential trouble spots, such as **agreement** and a verb's **tenses**.

13 Nouns

A **noun** (from the Latin *nomen*, "name") is a word that names or stands for a person, place, thing, class, concept, quality, or action: *woman*, *character*, *city*, *country*, *citizen*, *ship*, *garden*, *machine*, *silence*, *vegetable*, *road*, *freedom*, *beauty*, *river*, *spring*, *investigation*. **Proper nouns** are names of specific persons, places, or things and begin with a capital letter: *Dorothy*, *Rumpelstiltskin*, *Winnipeg*, *England*, the *Titanic*. All the others, called **common nouns**, are capitalized only if they begin a sentence:

> Freedom is a precious commodity.
>
> Spring is my favourite season.

or form part of a proper noun:

> Spring Garden Road
>
> the Peace Arch
>
> the Ottawa River

or are personified or otherwise emphasized, for example in poetry:

> Our noisy years seem moments in the being
> Of the eternal Silence. . . .
>
> (Wordsworth)

(See #58, on capitalization.)

One can also classify nouns as either **concrete**, for names of tangible objects (*doctor*, *elephant*, *utensil*, *book*, *barn*), or **abstract**, for names of intangible things or ideas (*freedom*, *honour*, *happiness*, *history*). (See #66.)

Collective nouns are names of collections or groups often considered as units: *army*, *committee*, *family*, *herd*, *flock*. (See #15e and #18f.)

▲ 13a Inflection of Nouns

Nouns can be inflected in only two ways: for **number** and for **possessive case**.

13a

1. For number

Most common concrete nouns that stand for *countable* things are either **singular** (naming a single thing) or **plural** (naming more than one thing). And though proper nouns supposedly name specific persons, places, or things, they too can sometimes logically be inflected for the plural; for example, there are many *John Smiths* in the telephone book, there are several *Londons* (e.g. the one in England and the one in Ontario), and since 1948 there have been two *Koreas.* Most singular nouns are inflected to indicate the plural by the addition of *s* or *es*: *girl*, *girls*; *box*, *boxes*. But some are made plural in other ways: *child*, *children*; *stimulus*, *stimuli*. (For more on the formation of plurals, see #62t.)

Some concrete nouns, however, called **mass** nouns, name materials that are measured, weighed, or divided, rather than items that are counted—for example *gold*, *oxygen*, *rice*, *sand*, and *pasta*. As **uncountable** or **noncountable** nouns, these are not inflected for the plural. Also **uncountable** are abstract nouns and nouns that stand for ideas, activities, and states of mind or being; for example, *honour, journalism, skiing, happiness.*

Some nouns, however, can be either countable or uncountable, depending on the context in which they are used. For example:

> The butcher sells meat. (uncountable)
>
> The delicatessen offers several delicious smoked meats. (countable, equivalent to *kinds of smoked meat)*
>
> They insisted on telling the truth as a matter of honour. (uncountable)
>
> Many honours were heaped upon the returning hero. (countable, since an *honour* here is not an abstract quality but designates a specific thing like a medal, a citation, or at least one or another sort of verbal recognition)

(See also #15c, #18g and #19c.5.)

2. For possessive case

As we saw earlier, in English, whether a noun is a *subject* (**subjective** case) or an *object* (**objective** case) is shown by word order rather than by inflection. But nouns are inflected for **possessive** case. By adding an apostrophe and an *s*, or sometimes only an apostrophe, you inflect a noun so that it shows possession or ownership: *my mother's job, the children's toys, the students' grades.* (For more on inflecting nouns for possessive case, see #62w.)

13b Grammatical Function of Nouns

Nouns function in sentences in the following ways:

- as the subject of a verb (see #12a):

  Students work hard.

- as the direct object of a verb (see #12d):

  Our team won the championship.

- as the indirect object of a verb (see #12f):

  We awarded Yoko the prize.

- as the object of a preposition (see #12f and #22):

  We gave the prize to Yoko. It was a book about mountain-climbing.

- as a predicate noun after a linking verb (see #12h):

  Genevieve is an accountant.

- as an objective complement (see #12j):

  The judges declared Yoko the winner.

- as an appositive to any other noun (see #12q):

  Andre, the chef, stopped Roger, the dishwasher.

  We gave Yoko the prize, a book about mountain-climbing.

  My brother, Masoud, graduated last year.

Nouns in the *possessive case* function as adjectives (see #19a):

Maria's coat is expensive. (Which coat? Maria's.)

I did a day's work. (How much work? A day's.)

or as predicate nouns, after a linking verb:

The expensive-looking coat is Maria's.

Even without being inflected for possessive case, many nouns can also function as adjectives within noun phrases: the *school* paper, an *evening* gown, the *automobile* industry, the *dessert* course, and so on (see #71g).

A noun (or pronoun) referring to someone being directly addressed, as in dialogue or in a letter, is called a *noun of address.* Such nouns, usually proper names, are not directly related to the syntax of the rest of the sentence and are set off with punctuation:

Yuki, are you feeling well?

Soon, Steve, you'll see what I mean.

Exercise 13b Recognizing nouns

Underline each noun or noun phrase in the following sentences and determine whether it is functioning as a subject, a direct object, an indirect object, an object of a preposition, a subjective complement (predicate noun), an objective complement, an appositive, or a possessive adjective.

1. Canada's tenth province, Newfoundland, joined Confederation in 1949.
2. The Queen was given a Canadian encyclopedia edited by a distinguished professor.
3. Halifax's mayor presented the speed skater the gold medal.
4. We often think back with pleasure on our childhood.
5. Shakespeare wrote many plays, but *Hamlet*, a tragedy, is his best known work.

14 Pronouns

A pronoun, as its name indicates, is a word that stands for (*pro*) or *in place of* a noun, or functions like a noun in a sentence. Most pronouns refer to nouns that come earlier, their **antecedents** (from Latin for *coming before*):

Joshua offered an opinion, but he didn't feel confident about it.

Here, *Joshua* is the antecedent of the pronoun *he,* and *opinion* is the antecedent of the pronoun *it.* Occasionally an antecedent can come after the pronoun that refers to it, especially if the pronoun is in a subordinate clause and if the context is clear—that is, if the pronoun couldn't refer to some other noun (see also #16d):

> Although he offered an opinion, Joshua didn't feel confident about it.

There are eight different pronoun types:

- personal
- impersonal
- interrogative
- relative
- demonstrative
- indefinite
- reflexive (or intensive)
- reciprocal

Generally, pronouns perform the same functions as nouns: they are most often subjects of verbs, direct and indirect objects, and objects of prepositions; some can also function as appositives and predicate nouns. Some pronouns are inflected much more than nouns, and some require closer proofreading for case, reference, and agreement than you might think.

The following sections discuss the different kinds of pronoun; their inflections; their grammatical functions in phrases, clauses, and sentences; and the special problems of **case** (#14e), **agreement** (#15), and **reference** (#16).

14a Personal Pronouns

Personal pronouns refer to specific persons or things. They are inflected in four ways:

1. For person

- **First-person** pronouns (*I*, *we*, etc.) refer to the person or persons doing the speaking or writing.
- **Second-person** pronouns (*you*, *yours*) refer to the person or persons being spoken or written to.
- **Third-person** pronouns (*he*, *she*, *it*, *they*, etc.) refer to the person(s) or thing(s) being spoken or written about.

2. For number

- **Singular** pronouns (*I*, *she*, etc.) refer to individuals.

> I am writing. She is writing.

- **Plural** pronouns (*we*, *they*, etc.) refer to groups.

> We are writing. They are writing.

(Note that the second-person pronoun *you* can be either singular or plural.)

14a

3. For gender (2nd- and 3rd-person pronouns)

- **Masculine** pronouns (*he, him, his*) refer to males.
- **Feminine** pronouns (*she, her, hers*) refer to females.
- The **neuter** pronoun (*it*) refers to ideas or things, and sometimes to animals.

(Note that in the plural forms—*we, you, they*, etc.—there is no indication of gender.)

4. For case (see also #14e)

- Pronouns that function as **subjects** must be in the **subjective** case:

  I paint. She paints. They are painting.

- Pronouns that function as **objects**—whether direct or indirect—must be in the **objective** case:

  The idea hit them. Give her the book. Give it to me.

- Pronouns that indicate possession or ownership must be in the **possessive** case:

  That turtle is his. This turtle is mine. Where is yours?

(Note that pronouns in the possessive case—*yours, theirs, its, hers*, etc.—do not take an apostrophe before the *s* to indicate possession.)

The following chart shows all the inflections of personal pronouns:

		subject	*object*	*possessive pronoun*	*possessive adjective*
singular	*1st person*	I	me	mine	my
	2nd person	you	you	yours	your
	3rd person	he	him	his	his
		she	her	hers	her
		it	it		its
plural	*1st person*	we	us	ours	our
	2nd person	you	you	yours	your
	3rd person	they	them	theirs	their

Possessive (or **pronominal**) **adjectives** always precede nouns (*My* car is in the shop); **possessive pronouns** may function as subjects, objects, and predicate nouns (Let's take *yours*).

Note that *you* and *it* are inflected only for possessive case, that *his* serves as both possessive pronoun and possessive adjective, and that *her* serves as both objective case and possessive adjective.

14b Impersonal Pronouns

Especially in relatively formal contexts, the **impersonal pronoun** *one,* meaning essentially "a person," serves in place of a first-, second-, or third-person pronoun:

> One must be careful when choosing course electives.
>
> One must keep one's priorities straight.

The pronoun *it* is also used as an impersonal pronoun in such sentences as the following; note that the impersonal *it* is usually the subject of some form of *be* (see #17f) and that it usually refers to time, weather, distance, and the like:

> It is getting late. It's almost four o'clock.
>
> It's warm. It feels warmer than it did yesterday.
>
> It was just one of those things.
>
> It is a mile and a half from here to the station.

Proofreading Tip

On Using the Impersonal Pronoun "It"

You may want to edit your work to avoid overuse of the impersonal pronoun "it." The sentences that are formed using this pattern are known as weak expletives and sometimes delay unnecessarily the true subject of the sentence. The last example could easily be revised to read *The last station is a mile and half from here.*

14c Interrogative Pronouns

Interrogative pronouns are *question words* used usually at or near the beginning of *interrogative sentences* (see #12t). *Who* is inflected for objective and possessive case, *which* for possessive case only:

subjective	*objective*	*possessive*
who	whom	whose
which	which	whose
what	what	

Who refers to persons, *which* and *what* to things; *which* sometimes also refers to persons, as in *Which of you is going?* The compound forms *whoever* and *whatever*, and sometimes even *whichever* and *whomever*, can also function as interrogative pronouns. Here are some examples showing interrogative pronouns functioning in different ways:

- as a subject:

  Who said that?

  Which of these books is best?

  What is the baby's name?

- as the direct object of verb:

  Whom do you recommend for the job?

  What did you give Aunt Jane for her birthday?

- as the object of a preposition (see also #22):

  To whom did you give the book?

  To what do I owe this honour?

- as an objective complement:

  What did you call me?

  You've named the baby what?

In front of a noun, an interrogative word functions as an **interrogative adjective**:

Whose book is this?

Which car shall we take?

For more on *who* and *whom,* see #14e.

14d Relative Pronouns

A **relative pronoun** usually introduces an *adjective clause*—called a **relative clause**—in which it functions as subject, object, or object of a preposition. The pronoun links, or *relates*, the clause to an antecedent in the same sentence, a noun or pronoun that the whole clause modifies.

The principal relative pronouns are *who*, *which*, and *that*. *Who* and *which* are inflected for case:

subjective	*objective*	*possessive*
who	whom	whose
which	which	whose
that	that	

Who refers to persons (and sometimes to animals thought of as persons), *which* to things, and *that* to either persons or things. Consider some examples of how relative pronouns function:

14d

Margaret, who is leaving in the morning, will call us later tonight. (*who* as subject of verb *is*; clause modifies *Margaret*)

Joel described the woman whom he had met at the party. (*whom* as direct object; clause modifies *woman*)

At midnight Sula began to revise her descriptive essay, which was due in the morning. (*which* as subject of verb *was*; clause modifies *essay*)

She avoided working on the annual report that she was having trouble with. (*that* as object of preposition *with*; clause modifies *report*)

A relative clause is either **restrictive** and unpunctuated, or **nonrestrictive** and set off with punctuation. It is **restrictive** if it gives us information that is essential to identifying the antecedent (e.g. *whom he had met at the party*); it is **nonrestrictive** if the information it gives us is not essential to identifying the antecedent and could be left out of the sentence (e.g. *which was due in the morning*). (See also #48.) If the relative pronoun in a restrictive clause is the object of a verb or a preposition, it can usually be omitted:

Joel described the woman [whom or that] he had met.

She avoided working on the annual report [that or which] she was having trouble with.

But if the preposition is placed before the pronoun (e.g. *with which*), the pronoun cannot be omitted:

She was working on the annual report with which she was having trouble.

When *whose* precedes and modifies a noun in a relative clause, it functions as what is called a **relative adjective**:

Jana was the one whose advice he most valued.

And sometimes a **relative adverb**, often *when* or *where*, introduces a relative clause (see also #20a):

> Here's an aerial photo of the town where I live. (The clause *where I live* modifies the noun *town*.)

> My parents told me about the time when I learned to walk. (The *when* clause modifies the noun *time*.)

Sometimes *what* and the *ever*-compounds (*whatever, whoever, whomever, whichever*) are also considered relative pronouns, even though they introduce noun clauses (e.g. "Remember *what I said*." "Take *whichever one you want*."). *Who, whom*, and *which* may also introduce such noun clauses.

For more on *who* and *whom*, see #14e. For more on adjective clauses, see #19 and #26a.

14e Case (See also #14a.4.)

ca Determining the correct case of personal, interrogative, and relative pronouns is sometimes challenging. In writing particular sentences and in formal writing generally, the challenge may be to determine whether a pronoun should be in the subjective or objective case. In everyday speech and informal writing, things like "*Who* did you lend the book to?" and "It's *me*" and "That's *her*" upset few people. But in formal writing and strictly formal speech, you should use the correct forms: To *whom* did you lend the book? It is *she*. If you know how a pronoun is functioning grammatically, you will know which form to use. Here are some guidelines to help you with the kinds of sentences that sometimes cause problems:

1. A pronoun functioning as the *subject* should be in the *subjective* case.

   Whenever you use a pronoun as part of a *compound subject* (see #12z.1), make sure it is in the *subjective* case. Someone who wouldn't say "*Me* am going to the store" could slip and say something like "Susan and *me* studied hard for the examination" instead of the correct

   > Susan and I studied hard for the examination.

   If you're not sure, remove the other part of the subject; then you'll know which pronoun sounds right:

   > [~~Susan and~~] I studied hard for the examination.

   But even a one-part subject can lead someone astray:

   > ***ca:*** Us students should stand up for our rights.
   > ***revised:*** We students should stand up for our rights.

The pronoun *We* is the subject; the word *students* is an appositive (see #12q) further identifying it, as if saying "We, the students, should . . ."

2. A pronoun functioning as a direct or indirect *object* should be in the *objective* case.

   Again, errors most often result from the use of a two-part structure—here, a *compound object*. Someone who would not say "The club asked *I* for my opinion" could slip and say "They asked Ingrid and *I* to take part in the play." When you use a pronoun as part of a compound object, make sure it's in the *objective* case. Again, test by removing the other part:

   They asked [~~Ingrid and~~] me to take part in the play.

Proofreading Tip

On Hypercorrection of Pronouns
Don't slip into what is called "hypercorrection." Since many people say things like "Jake and me went camping," others—not understanding the grammar but wishing to seem correct—use the "and I" form even for an object, when it should be "and me." For example, you would say *The new tent was for Jake and me,* not *The new tent was for Jake and I.*

3. A pronoun functioning as the *object* of a preposition should be in the *objective* case:

   ca: This information is between you and I.
   revised: This information is between you and me.

   Speakers and writers who have learned not to use *me* as part of a compound subject sometimes overcorrect in cases such as this and use *I*; but the objective *me* is correct in this instance, for it is the object of the preposition *between*.

4. A pronoun functioning as a *predicate noun* (see #12h and #25d) after a linking verb should be in the *subjective* case. In other words, if the pronoun follows the verb *be*, it takes the subjective form:

   It is they who must decide, not we.

   The swimmer who won the prize is she, over there by the pool.

   It is I who will carry the greater burden.

If such usages sound stuffy and artificial to you—as they do to many people—find another way to phrase your sentences; for example:

> They, not we, must decide.
>
> The swimmer over by the pool is the one who won the prize.
>
> First prize went to that girl, over there by the pool.
>
> I will be the one carrying the greater burden.

Again, watch out for compound structures:

ca: The nominees are Yashmin and me.
revised: The nominees are Yashmin and I.

5. Pronouns following the conjunctions *as* and *than* in comparisons should be in the *subjective* case if they are functioning as subjects, even if their verbs are not expressed but left "understood":

   > Roberta is brighter than they [are].
   >
   > Aaron has learned less than I [have].
   >
   > Hiroshi is as tall as I [am].

   If, however, the pronouns are functioning as objects, they should be in the *objective case*:

   > I trust her more than [I trust] him.

   See also **so . . . as** in the Usage Checklist, #72.

6. Use the appropriate case of the interrogative and relative pronouns *who* and *whom*, *whoever* and *whomever.* Although *who* is often used instead of *whom* in speech and informal writing, you should know how to use the two correctly when you want to write or speak more formally.

   a. Use the *subjective* case for the *subject* of a verb in a question or a relative clause:

   > Who is going?
   >
   > Dickens was a novelist who was extremely popular in his own time.

b. Use the *objective* case for the *object* of a verb or preposition:

Whom do you prefer in that role?

He is the candidate whom I most admire.

She is the manager for whom the employees have the most respect.

If such usages with *whom* seem to you unnatural and stuffy, avoid them by rephrasing your sentence:

She is the manager that the employees respect most.

c. In noun clauses, the case of the pronoun is determined by its function in its clause, not by other words:

How can you tell who won? [subjective case]

I'll give the prize to whomever the judges declare the winner. [objective case, object of preposition]

For the possessive case of pronouns with *gerunds,* see #21h.

Exercise 14e (1) Using correct pronouns

Underline the correct pronoun in each of the pairs in parentheses.

1. (She, her) and (I, me) will work on the project tonight.
2. There stood Eva, (who, whom) we had just said goodbye to.
3. Is Tomi the person (who, whom) you think will do the best job?
4. This gift will please (whoever, whomever) receives it.
5. The coach advised Anwar and (I, me) not to miss any more practices.
6. (Who, Whom) do you wish to see?

Exercise 14e (2) Problem pronouns

Make up five sentences that use a personal pronoun in the subjective case (*I*, *he*, *she*, *they*) after a form of the verb *be*, and five sentences using the pronoun *whom* or *whomever* in a correct formal way. Then rewrite each sentence, keeping each one formal but avoiding the possible stuffiness of these usages.

14f Demonstrative Pronouns

Demonstrative pronouns, which can be thought of as pointing to the nouns they refer to, are inflected for *number*:

singular	*plural*
this	these
that	those

This and *these* usually refer to something nearby or something just said or about to be said; *that* and *those* usually refer to something farther away or more remote in time or longer in duration; but there are no precise rules:

> Try some of this.
>
> The clerk was helpful; this was what pleased her the most.
>
> These are the main points I will cover in today's lecture.
>
> That looks appetizing.
>
> That was the story he told us the next morning.
>
> Those were his exact words.
>
> Those are the cities you should visit on your holiday.

These pronouns also often occur in prepositional phrases with *like* and *such as*:

> Someone who wears an orange shirt like that has an unusual fashion sense.
>
> I need more close friends like those.
>
> A cute house such as this will sell immediately.

Proofreading Tip

Avoiding Vagueness in Using Demonstrative Pronouns
Useful as demonstrative pronouns can be, employ them sparingly in writing, for they are often vague in their reference. Instead, consider this alternative: When followed by nouns, these words function as *demonstrative adjectives*, and then there's no risk of vagueness: *this* belief, *that* statement, *these* buildings, *those* arguments. See #16c, #41, and ***ref*** in Appendix 2.

▲ 14g Indefinite Pronouns

Indefinite pronouns refer to *indefinite* or unknown persons or things, or to indefinite or unknown quantities of persons or things. The only major issue with these words is whether they are *singular* or *plural*. Think of indefinite pronouns as falling into four groups:

- GROUP 1: compounds ending with *body*, *one*, and *thing*. These words function like nouns—that is, they need no antecedents—and they are almost always considered *singular*:

anybody	everybody	nobody	somebody
anyone	everyone	no one	someone
anything	everything	nothing	something

- GROUP 2: a few other indefinite pronouns that are almost always *singular*:

another	each	either	much
neither	one	other	

- GROUP 3: a few that are always *plural*:

both	few	many	several

- GROUP 4: a few that can be either *singular* or *plural*, depending on context and intended meaning:

all	any	more	most
none	some		

For discussions of the important matter of grammatical **agreement** with indefinite pronouns, and examples of their use in sentences, see #15c and #18d.

Only *one* and *other* can be inflected for number, by adding *s* to make them plural: *ones*, *others*. Several indefinite pronouns can be inflected for possessive case; unlike personal pronouns, they take *'s*, just as nouns do (or, with *others'*, just an apostrophe):

anybody's	anyone's	everybody's	everyone's
nobody's	no one's	somebody's	someone's
one's	other's	another's	others'

The remaining indefinite pronouns must use *of* to show possession; for example:

That was the belief of many who were present.

When in the possessive case, indefinite pronouns function as adjectives. In addition, all the words in Groups 2, 3, and 4, except *none,* can also function as adjectives (see #19a):

any boat	some people	few people
more money	each day	either direction

The adjective expressing the meaning of *none* is *no*:

Send no attachments.

Sometimes the cardinal numbers (*one*, *two*, *three*, etc.) and the ordinal numbers (*first*, *second*, *third*, etc.) are also classed as indefinite pronouns, for they often function similarly, both as pronouns and as adjectives:

How many ducks are on the pond? I see several. I see seven. I see ten.

Do you like these stories? I like some, but not others. I like the first and the third.

He owns two boats.

Stay tuned for the second thrilling episode.

14h Reflexive and Intensive Pronouns

Reflexive and intensive pronouns are formed by adding *self* or *selves* to the possessive form of the first- and second-person personal pronouns, to the objective form of third-person personal pronouns, and to the impersonal pronoun *one* (see #14a, #14b).

singular	*plural*
myself	ourselves
yourself	yourselves
himself	
herself	themselves
itself	
oneself	

A **reflexive pronoun** is used as an object when that object is the same person or thing as the subject:

He treated himself to bubble tea. (direct object)

One should pamper oneself a little. (direct object)

She gave herself a treat. (indirect object)

We kept the idea to ourselves. (object of preposition)

These pronouns are also used as **intensive pronouns** to emphasize a subject or object. An intensive pronoun comes either right after the noun it emphasizes or at the end of the sentence:

Although he let the others choose their positions, Angelo himself is going to pitch.

The professor told us to count up our scores ourselves.

They are also used in prepositional phrases with *by* to mean *alone* or *without help*:

I can do this job by myself.

Proofreading Tip

On the Use of Intensive and Reflexive Pronouns
Do not use this form of pronoun as a substitute for a personal pronoun:

The team and I [not *myself*] played a great game tonight.

Especially don't use *myself* simply to avoid having to decide whether *I* or *me* is correct in a compound subject or object (see #14e).

▲ 14i Reciprocal Pronouns

Like a reflexive pronoun, a **reciprocal pronoun** refers to the subject of a sentence, but this time the subject is always plural. The two reciprocal pronouns themselves are singular and consist of two words each:

each other (referring to a subject involving two)

one another (referring to a subject involving three or more)

They can be inflected for possessive case by adding *'s*:

each other's one another's

These pronouns express some kind of mutual interaction between or among the parts of a plural subject:

> The president and the prime minister praised each other's policies.
>
> The computers in this office in effect speak to one another, even though the employees never do.

See **each other, one another** in the Usage Checklist, #72.

15 Agreement of Pronouns with Their Antecedents

agr Any pronoun that refers to or stands for an *antecedent* (see #14) must **agree** with—i.e. be the same as—that antecedent in **person** (1st, 2nd, or 3rd), **number** (singular or plural), and **gender** (masculine, feminine, or neuter). For example:

> Joanne wants to go to university so that she will be prepared to take her place in the world.

Since the proper noun *Joanne*, the antecedent, is in the third person, singular, and feminine, any pronouns that refer to it must also be third-person, singular, and feminine: *she* and *her* thus "agree" grammatically with their antecedent.

The following sections (#15a–f) point out the most common sources of trouble with pronoun agreement. Note that these circumstances are similar to those affecting subject–verb agreement (see #18). Note also that these errors all have to do with *number*—whether a pronoun should be *singular* or *plural.* Mistakes in gender and person also occur, but not as frequently (but see #39d, on shifts).

15a Antecedents Joined by *and*

When two or more singular antecedents are joined by *and*, use a *plural* pronoun:

> The manager and the accountant compared their figures.
>
> Both Jennifer and Chinmoy contributed their know-how.

If such a compound is preceded by *each* or *every*, however, the pronoun should be *singular*:

> Each book and periodical in the library has its own catalogue number.

15b Antecedents Joined by *or* or *nor*

When two or more antecedents are joined by *or* or *nor*, use a *singular* pronoun if the antecedents are singular:

> The dog or the cat is sure to make itself heard.
>
> Either David or Jonathan will bring his car.
>
> Neither Maylin nor her mother gave her consent.

If one antecedent is masculine and the other feminine, rephrase the sentence (see #15d).

Use a *plural* pronoun if the antecedents are plural:

> Neither the players nor the coaches did their jobs properly.

If the antecedents are mixed singular and plural, a pronoun should agree with the nearest one. But if you move from a plural to a singular antecedent, the sentence will almost inevitably sound awkward; try to construct such sentences so that the last antecedent is plural:

> ***awkward:*** Neither the actors nor the director could control his temper.
>
> ***revised:*** Neither the director nor the actors could control their tempers.

Note that the awkwardness of the first example extends to gender: if the actors included both men and women, neither *his* nor *her* would be appropriate; see #15d. For more information on agreement of verbs with compound subjects joined by *or* or *nor*, see #18c.

15c Indefinite Pronoun as Antecedent

If the antecedent is an *indefinite pronoun* (see #14g), you'll usually use a *singular* pronoun to refer to it. The indefinite pronouns in Group 1 (the compounds with *body*, *one*, and *thing*) are singular, as are those in Group 2 (*another*, *each*, *either*, *much*, *neither*, *one*, *other*):

> Each of the boys worked on his own project.
>
> Either of these women is likely to buy that sports car for herself.
>
> Everything has its proper place.

Indefinite pronouns from Group 3 (*both, few, many, several*) are always plural:

> Only a few returned their ballots.

The indefinite pronouns in Group 4 (*all, any, more, most, none, some*—see #14g) can be either singular or plural; the intended meaning is usually clearly either singular or plural:

15c

> Some of the food on the menu could be criticized for its lack of nutrients.

> Some of the ships in the fleet had been restored to their original beauty.

Here the mass noun *food* demands the singular sense for *some*, and the countable noun *ships*, in the plural, demands the plural sense (see #14g). But confusion sometimes arises with the indefinite pronoun *none*. (See also #18d.) Although *none* began by meaning *no one* or *not one*, it now commonly has the plural sense:

> None of the boy scouts knew how to fix their bicycles.

With a mass noun, or if your intended meaning is *not a single one*, treat *none* as singular:

> None of the food could be praised for its quality.

> None of the boy scouts knew how to fix his bicycle. (Here, you could perhaps even change *None* to *Not one*.)

When any of these words function as *adjectives*, the same principles apply:

> Each grandfather worked on his own project.

> Either woman may buy the car for herself.

> Only a few people returned their ballots.

> Some food can be praised for its nutritional value.

> Some ships had been restored to their original beauty.

Note: The word *every* used as an adjective requires a *singular* pronoun:

> Every grandfather has his own project.

15d Pronouns and Inclusive Language: Avoiding Gender Bias

Several indefinite pronouns and indefinite nouns like *person*, as well as many other nouns used in a generalizing way, present an additional challenge: avoiding gender bias.

In centuries past, if a *singular antecedent* had no grammatical gender but could refer to either male or female, it was conventional to use the masculine pronoun *he* (*him*, *his*, *himself*) in a generic sense, meaning any person, male or female:

15d

> ***biased:*** Everyone present at the lecture raised his hand.
>
> ***biased:*** A writer should be careful about his diction.

Today this practice is regarded as inappropriate and inaccurate, since it implies, for example, that no women were present at the lecture and that there are no women writers. Such usages reveal the unconsidered assumption that males are the norm. And merely substituting *she* or *her* in all such instances is no solution, since it represents gender bias as well.

You can and should avoid biased language. Colloquially and informally, many writers simply use a plural pronoun:

> ***agr:*** Anyone who doesn't pay their taxes is asking for trouble.

But this practice may be seen by some readers as fostering errors in agreement; and it is unacceptable to some who care about the traditions of language, for it is grammatically incorrect. (Note in the example above the clash between the plural pronoun *their* and the singular verb *is*.)

There are better solutions:

1. If you are referring to a group or class consisting entirely of either men or women, it is only logical to use the appropriate pronoun, whether masculine or feminine:

   Everyone in the room raised his hand.

   Everyone in the room raised her hand.

   If the group is mixed, try to avoid the problem, for example by using the indefinite article:

   Everyone in the room raised a hand.

2. Often the simplest technique is to make the antecedent itself plural: then the plural pronoun referring to it is grammatically appropriate, and no problem of gender arises:

   All those in the room raised their hands.

   Writers should be careful about their diction.

3. If your purpose and the formality of the context permit, you can use the impersonal pronoun *one*:

   If one is considerate of others' feelings, one will get along better.

   If this sounds too formal, consider using the less formal second-person pronoun *you* (but see #16e; you need to be careful when you address the audience directly):

   If you are considerate of others' feelings, you will get along better.

4. Another option is to revise a sentence so that no gendered pronoun is necessary:

   Everyone's hand went up.

   Sometimes the pronoun can simply be omitted:

   A writer should be careful about diction.

5. But if a sentence doesn't lend itself to such changes, or if you want to keep its original structure for some other reason, you can still manage. Don't resort to strings of unsightly devices such as *he/she*, *him/her*, *her/his*, *him/herself*, or *s/he*. But an occasional *he or she* or *she or he* and the like is acceptable:

   If anyone falls asleep, he or she will be asked to leave.

   A writer should be careful about her or his diction.

   But do this only occasionally; used often, such repetitions become tedious and cluttering.

See also **man, woman, lady, etc.** and **person, persons, people** in the Usage Checklist, #72.

15e Collective Noun as Antecedent

If the antecedent is a *collective noun* (see #13), use either a singular or a plural pronoun to refer to it, depending on context and desired meaning. If the collective noun stands for the group seen as a unit, use a *singular* pronoun:

> The team worked on its power play during the practice.
>
> The committee announced its decision.

15e

If the collective noun stands for the members of the group seen as individuals, use a *plural* pronoun:

> The team took up their starting positions.
>
> The committee had no sooner taken their seats than they began chatting among themselves.

15f Agreement with Demonstrative Adjectives

Demonstrative adjectives must agree in number with the nouns they modify (usually *kind* or *kinds* or similar words):

> ***agr:*** These kind of doctors work especially hard.
> ***revised:*** This kind of doctor works especially hard.
> ***revised:*** These kinds of doctors work especially hard.

Exercise 15 Correcting agreement errors

In each of the following, correct any lack of agreement between pronouns and their antecedents. Revise sentences as necessary to avoid gender bias.

1. Everybody is free to express their own opinion.
2. Una or Gwendolyn will lend you their textbook.
3. Anyone who thinks for themselves will not be deceived by advertising.
4. After studying his statements for over an hour, I still couldn't understand it.
5. It is usually a good sign when a person starts caring about his appearance.
6. Everyone who wants to play the game will be provided with a pencil to write their answers with.
7. In order to make sure each sentence is correct, check them carefully during revision and proofreading.

16 Reference of Pronouns

ref A pronoun's **reference** to an antecedent must be clear. The pronoun or the sentence will not be clear if the antecedent is remote, ambiguous, vague, or missing.

16a Remote Antecedent

16a

An antecedent should be close enough to the pronoun to be unmistakable; your reader shouldn't have to pause and search for it. An antecedent should seldom appear more than one sentence before its pronoun within a paragraph. For example:

> ***ref:*** People who expect to find happiness in material things alone may well discover that the life of the mind is more important than the life filled with possessions. Material prosperity may seem fine at a given moment, but in the long run its delights have a way of fading into inconsequential boredom and emptiness. They then realize, too late, where true happiness lies.

The word *People* is too far back to be a clear antecedent for the pronoun *They*. If the second sentence had also begun with *They*, the connection would be clearer. Or the third sentence might begin with a more particularizing phrase, like "Such people . . ."

16b Ambiguous Reference

A pronoun should refer clearly to only one antecedent:

> ***ref:*** When Donna's mother told her that she had won a grand piano, she was obviously delighted.

Each *she* could refer either to Donna (*her*) or to Donna's mother. When revising such a sentence, don't just insert explanatory parentheses; rephrase the sentence:

> ***weak:*** When Donna's mother told her that she (her mother) had won a grand piano, she (Donna) was obviously delighted.

> ***clear:*** Donna was obviously delighted when her mother told her about winning a grand piano.

> ***clear:*** Donna's mother had won a grand piano, and she was obviously delighted when she told Donna about it.

> ***clear:*** Donna was obviously delighted when her mother said, "I won a grand piano!"

Another example:

> ***ref:*** His second film was far different from his first. It was an adventure story set in Australia.

A pronoun like *it* often refers to the subject of the preceding independent clause, here *second film*, but *it* is also pulled toward the closest noun or pronoun, here *first*. The problem is easily solved by *combining* the two sentences, reducing the second to a subordinate element:

> ***clear:*** His second film, an adventure story set in Australia, was far different from his first.

> ***clear:*** His second film was far different from his first, which was an adventure story set in Australia.

16c Vague Reference

Vague reference is usually caused by the demonstrative pronouns *this* and *that* and the relative pronoun *which*:

> ***ref:*** The doctors are overworked, and there are no beds available. This is an intolerable situation for the hospital.

Another way of writing this would be to change *This*, after a comma, to *which*:

> ***ref:*** The doctors are overworked, and there are no beds available, which is an intolerable situation for the hospital.

In both sentences there is a problem with vague reference. *This* in the first example and *which* in the second seem to refer to the entire content of the preceding sentence, but they also seem to refer specifically to the fact that there are no beds available in the hospital. Revision is necessary:

> ***clear:*** The overworked doctors and the lack of available beds make for an intolerable situation for the hospital.

> ***clear:*** The doctors are overworked, and there are no beds available. These two circumstances make for an intolerable situation for the hospital.

A *this* or *which* can be adequate if the phrasing and meaning are appropriate:

> ***clear:*** It is not only the overworked doctors, but it is also the lack of beds which makes the situation intolerable for the hospital.

Another example:

> ***ref:*** Othello states many times that he loves Iago and that he thinks he is a very honest man; Iago uses this to his advantage.

The third *he* is possibly ambiguous, but more problematic is the vague reference of *this*. Changing *this* to *this opinion*, *these feelings*, *this attitude*, *these mistakes*, *this blindness of Othello's*, or even *Othello's blindness*, makes the reference clearer. Even the *his* is slightly ambiguous: *Iago takes advantage of* would be better—or just omit *his*.

And don't catch the "this" virus; sufferers from it are driven to begin a large proportion of their sentences and other independent clauses with a *this*. Whenever you catch yourself beginning with a *this*, look carefully to see

- if the reference to the preceding clause or sentence or paragraph is as clear on paper as it may be in your mind;
- if the *this* could be replaced by a specific noun or noun phrase, or otherwise avoided (for example by rephrasing or subordinating);
- whether, if you decide to keep *this*, it is an ambiguous demonstrative pronoun; if so, try to make it a **demonstrative adjective**, giving it a noun to modify—even if no more specific than "This *idea*," "This *fact*," or "This *argument*" (see #14f and #41).

And always check if an opening *This* looks back to a noun that is in fact singular; it may be that "*These* ideas, facts, or arguments" would be more appropriate.

16d Missing Antecedent

Sometimes a writer may have an antecedent in mind but fail to write it down:

> ***ref:*** In the early seventeenth century, the Renaissance attitude was concentrated mainly on the arts rather than on developing the scientific part of their minds.

The writer was probably thinking of "the people of the Renaissance." Simply changing *their* to *people's* would clear up the difficulty.

ref: After the mayor's speech he agreed to answer questions from the audience.

The implied antecedent of *he* is *mayor*, but it isn't there, for the possessive *mayor's* functions as an adjective rather than a noun. Several revisions are possible:

clear: When the mayor finished his speech, he agreed to answer questions from the audience.

clear: After speaking, the mayor agreed to answer questions from the audience.

clear: At the end of his speech, the mayor agreed to answer questions from the audience.

Note that in this last version, *his* comes before its supposed "antecedent," *mayor*—an unusual pattern, but one that is acceptable if the context is clear (for example, if no other possible antecedent for *his* occurred in the preceding sentence) and if the two are close together.

ref: Whenever a student assembly is called, they are required to attend.

Since *student* here functions as an adjective, it cannot serve as an antecedent for *they*. It is necessary to replace *they* with *students*—and then one would probably want to omit the original *student*. Or one could change "student assembly" to "an assembly of students" and retain *they*.

ref: Over half the guests left the party, but it did not stop the band from playing.

Again, no antecedent. Change *it* to *their departure*.

16e Indefinite *you*, *they*, and *it*

In formal writing, avoid the pronouns *you*, *they*, and *it* when they are indefinite:

informal: In order to graduate, you must have at least 120 course credits.

formal: In order to graduate, a student must have at least 120 course credits.

(The impersonal *one* would be all right, but perhaps not as effective because it is less specific and more formal.)

informal: In some cities they do not have enough recycling facilities.

formal: Some cities do not have enough recycling facilities.

formal: Some cities' recycling facilities are inadequate.

16e

Although it is correct to use the expletive or impersonal *it* (see #12k and #29f) and say "*It* is raining," "*It* is hard to get up in the morning," "*It* is seven o'clock," and so on, avoid such indefinite uses of *it* as the following:

informal: It states in our textbook that we should be careful how we use the pronoun *it*.

formal: Our textbook states that we should be careful how we use the pronoun *it*.

Exercise 16 Correcting faulty pronoun reference

Correct any faulty pronoun reference in the following:

1. Summer homes make good retreats—for those who can afford it.
2. You cannot suppress truth, for it is morally wrong.
3. The deadline was a month away, but I failed to meet it, for something happened that prevented it.
4. The tone of the poem is such that it creates an atmosphere of romance.
5. Television usually shows regular commercials, but this is more and more supplanted by product placement in movies.

17 Verbs

Verbs are core parts of speech. A verb is the focal point of a clause or a sentence. As you saw in chapter II, standard sentences consist of subjects and predicates: every subject has a predicate, and the heart of every predicate is its **verb**.

Verbs are often called "action" words; yet some verbs express little or no action. Think of verbs as expressing not only *action* but also *occurrence*, *process*, and *condition* or *state of being*. All verbs *assert* or *ask* something about their subjects, sometimes by *linking* a subject with a complement. Some verbs are single words; others are phrases consisting of two or more words. Here are some sentences with the verbs underlined:

He throws curves.

I thought for a while.

Karen is a lawyer.

Something happened last night.

I am cooking pasta.

By midnight, I will have driven two hundred kilometres.

Are you listening?

The two columns of figures came out even.

Will you be needing this DVD later?

The fresh bread smells delicious.

They will set out for Egypt in June.

The monument was built in 1976.

(For a discussion of such two-part verbs as *come out* and *set out,* see #22d–e.)

17a Kinds of Verbs: Transitive, Intransitive, and Linking

Verbs are classified according to the way they function in sentences.

A verb normally taking a *direct object* is considered a **transitive verb.** A transitive verb makes a transition, conveys a movement, from its subject to its object:

She has good taste.

He introduced me to his uncle.

Greg never neglects his lab work.

She expresses her ideas eloquently.

He stuffed himself with pizza.

Where did you put that book?

A direct object answers the question consisting of the verb and *what* or *whom*: Introduced *whom*? Me. Never neglects *what*? Lab work. Expresses *what*? Ideas. Stuffed *whom*? Himself. Did put *what* where? Book. (See also #12d, #12f, #12i, and #12j.)

A verb that normally occurs without a direct object is considered **intransitive** (see also #12c):

17a

When will you arrive?

What has happened to the aquarium's whale?

The earthquake occurred during the night.

You should rest for a while.

He gossiped with his roommate.

Please stay.

Many verbs, however, can be either transitive or intransitive, depending on how they function in particular sentences:

I ran the business effectively. (transitive)
I ran to the store. (intransitive)

I can see the parade better from the balcony. (transitive)
I can see well enough from here. (intransitive)

He wished that he were home in bed. (transitive)
She wished upon a star. (intransitive)

In fact, few verbs are exclusively either transitive or intransitive, as a good dictionary will show you. Verbs felt to be clearly intransitive can often also be used transitively, and vice versa:

She slept the sleep of the just. (In this sentence, *slept* takes the object *sleep* and therefore is transitive.)

He leaned back in the chair and remembered. (In this sentence, *remembered* takes no object and therefore is intransitive.)

A third kind of verb is called a **linking** or copulative verb. The main one is *be* in its various forms. Some other common linking verbs are *become*, *seem*, *remain*, *act*, *get*, *feel*, *look*, *appear*, *smell*, *sound*, and *taste*.

Linking verbs don't have objects, but are yet incomplete; they need a **subjective complement**. A linking verb is like an equal sign in an equation: something at the right-hand (predicate) end is needed to balance what is at the left-hand (subject) end. The complement will be either a *predicate noun* or a *predicate adjective* (see also #12g and #12h). Here are some examples:

Angela is a lawyer. (predicate noun: *lawyer*)
Angela is not well. (predicate adjective: *well*)

Mikhail became a pilot. (predicate noun: *pilot*)
Mikhail became uneasy. (predicate adjective: *uneasy*)

The winner is Nathan. (predicate noun: *Nathan*)

The band sounds good. (predicate adjective: *good*)

The surface felt sticky. (predicate adjective: *sticky*)

Occasionally a complement precedes the verb, for example in a question or in a sentence or clause inverted for emphasis:

How sick are you?

However happy he may have been, he did not let his feelings show to the other contestants.

Like an object, a subjective complement answers the question consisting of the verb and *what* or *whom*, or perhaps *how*: Is what? A lawyer. Became what? Uneasy. Is who? Nathan. Sounds how? Good. It differs from an object in that it is the equivalent of the subject or says something about it.

Such verbs as *act*, *sound*, *taste*, *smell*, and *feel* can of course also function as transitive verbs: She *acted* the part. He *sounded* his horn. He *smelled* the hydrogen sulphide. I *tasted* the soup. He *felt* the bump on his head.

Similarly, many of these verbs can also function as regular intransitive verbs, sometimes accompanied by *adverbial* modifiers (see #20): We *looked* at the painting. Santa *is* on the roof. Teresa *is* at home. We *are* here. But whenever one of these verbs is accompanied by a predicate noun or a predicate adjective, it is functioning as a **linking** verb.

17a

Exercise 17a (1) Using transitive and intransitive verbs

After each transitive verb in the following, supply an object; after each intransitive verb, supply an adverb (or adverbial phrase) or a period. If a particular verb can be either transitive or intransitive, do both.

Examples: **Moira *wants*** money. (tr.)
Moira *waited* patiently. (intr.)
Moira *speaks* loudly. (intr.)
her mind. (tr.)

1. Adriana expects ____________
2. Tony breathed ____________
3. Murray talks ____________
4. Kamala knelt ____________
5. Yvonne believed ____________
6. Ricardo bought ____________
7. They ordered ____________
8. Yukio learned ____________
9. Olivier performed ____________
10. Brian responded ____________
11. Sonya teaches ____________
12. Xian sings ____________
13. Pierre repairs ____________
14. Council vetoed ____________
15. Ann compromised ____________
16. Soolin flew ____________

Exercise 17a (2) Recognizing subjective complements

In the following, first identify the complement of each italicized linking verb, and second, indicate whether it is a predicate noun or a predicate adjective.

1. She *was* sorry that he *felt* so ill. ____________ (first), ____________ (second)
2. Because he *was* a computer expert, he *was* confident that he could write a software program for the system. ____________ (first), ____________ (second)
3. The book *became* a best seller even though it *was* scholarly in its examination of black holes. ____________ (first), ____________ (second)
4. Since the house *was* well insulated, it *stayed* warm throughout the severe winter. ____________ (first), ____________ (second)
5. Incredible as it *seems*, the casserole *tasted* as good as it *looked* odd. ____________ (first), ____________ (second), ____________ (third)

Exercise 17a (3) Using subjective complements

After each linking verb, supply (a) a predicate noun and (b) a predicate adjective.

Example: Kevin *was* (a) an engineer.
(b) energized.

1. Erika *is* (a) ________________.
   (b) ________________.
2. Priscilla *became* (a) ________________.
   (b) ________________.
3. Luigi *remained* (a) ________________.
   (b) ________________.
4. The government *had been* (a) ________________.
   (b) ________________.

Exercise 17a (4) Using verbs

Compose sentences using some common linking verbs other than *be, become, seem,* and *remain.* Then compose other sentences using the same verbs as either transitive or intransitive verbs, without complements. Can any of them function as all three kinds? Try *smell*, for example, or *act*.

▲ 17b Inflection of Verbs: Principal Parts

As well as being important in spoken and written communication, verbs are also the most complex, the most highly inflected, of the eight parts of speech. Verbs are inflected

- for **person** and **number**, in order to agree with a subject (#17d);
- for **tense**, in order to show an action's time—present, past, or future—and aspect—simple, perfect, or progressive (#17g);
- for **mood**, in order to show the kind of sentence a verb is in—indicative, imperative, or subjunctive (#17-l and #17m);
- for **voice**, in order to show whether a subject is active (performing an action) or passive (being acted upon) (#17-o and 17p).

Every verb (except some auxiliaries; see #17e) has what are called its **principal parts**:

1. its **basic** form (the form a dictionary uses in headwords, see #63c)
2. its **past-tense** form
3. its **past participle**
4. its **present participle**

17b

Verbs regularly form both the *past tense* and the *past participle* simply by adding *ed* to the basic form:

basic form	*past-tense form*	*past participle*
push	pushed	pushed
cook	cooked	cooked

If the basic form already ends in *e*, however, only *d* is added:

move	moved	moved
agree	agreed	agreed

Present participles are regularly formed by adding *ing* to the basic form:

basic form	*present participle*
push	pushing
cook	cooking
agree	agreeing

But verbs ending in an unpronounced *e* usually drop it before adding *ing*:

move	moving
skate	skating

And some verbs double a final consonant before adding *ed* or *ing*:

grin	grinned	grinning
stop	stopped	stopping

For more on these and other irregularities, see #62d–f. Further, good dictionaries list any irregular principal parts, ones not formed by simply adding *ed* or *ing* (and see #17c).

It is from these four parts—the basic form and the three principal inflections of it—that all other inflected forms of a verb are made.

Note: The basic form of a verb is sometimes called the **infinitive** form, meaning that it can be preceded by *to* to form an infinitive: *to be*, *to push*, *to agree*. Infinitives, participles, and gerunds are called **non-finite verbs**, or **verbals**; they function not as verbs but as other parts of speech (see #21a–f). **Finite verbs**, unlike non-finite forms, are restricted or limited by person, number, tense, mood, and voice; they function as the main verbs in sentences.

▲ 17c Irregular Verbs

Some of the most common English verbs are **irregular** in the way they make their past-tense forms and their past participles. Whenever you aren't certain about the principal parts of a verb, check your dictionary, or use the following list, which contains most of the common irregular verbs with their past-tense forms and their past participles (where two or more are given, the first is the more common). If you need to, memorize these forms; practise by composing sentences using each form (for example: *Choose* the one you want. I *chose* mine yesterday. Have you *chosen* your topic yet?). If you're looking for a verb that is a compound or that has a suffix, look for the main verb: for *misread*, *proofread*, or *reread*, look under *read*:

basic or present form	***past-tense form***	***past participle***
arise	arose	arisen
awake	awoke	awoken
bear	bore	borne (born for "*given birth to*")
beat	beat	beaten
become	became	become
begin	began	begun
bend	bent	bent
bet	bet	bet
bid	bid	bid
bind	bound	bound
bite	bit	bitten
bleed	bled	bled
blow	blew	blown
break	broke	broken
breed	bred	bred
bring	brought	brought
broadcast	broadcast, broadcasted	broadcast, broadcasted
build	built	built
burst	burst	burst
buy	bought	bought
cast	cast	cast
catch	caught	caught
choose	chose	chosen

basic or present form	*past-tense form*	*past participle*
cling	clung	clung
come	came	come
cost	cost	cost
creep	crept	crept
cut	cut	cut
deal	dealt	dealt
dig	dug	dug
dive	dived, dove	dived
draw	drew	drawn
dream	dreamed, dreamt	dreamed, dreamt
drink	drank	drunk
drive	drove	driven
eat	ate	eaten
fall	fell	fallen
feed	fed	fed
feel	felt	felt
fight	fought	fought
find	found	found
fit	fit, fitted	fit, fitted
flee	fled	fled
fling	flung	flung
fly	flew	flown
forbid	forbade, forbade	forbidden
forecast	forecast, forecasted	forecast, forecasted
foresee	foresaw	foreseen
foretell	foretold	foretold
forgive	forgave	forgiven
forget	forgot	forgotten
forgo	forwent	forgone
forsake	forsook	forsaken
freeze	froze	frozen
frolic	frolicked	frolicked
get	got	got, gotten
give	gave	given
go	went	gone
grind	ground	ground
grow	grew	grown
hang	hung (hanged for "*execute*")	hung, hanged
hear	heard	heard
hide	hid	hidden
hit	hit	hit
hold	held	held
hurt	hurt	hurt

basic or present form	***past-tense form***	***past participle***
input	inputted, input	inputted, input
keep	kept	kept
kneel	knelt, kneeled	knelt, kneeled
knit	knitted, knit	knitted, knit
know	knew	known
lay	laid	laid
lead	led	led
leap	leaped, leapt	leaped, leapt
leave	left	left
lend	lent	lent
let	let	let
lie ("recline")	lay	lain
light	lit, lighted	lit, lighted
lose	lost	lost
make	made	made
mean	meant	meant
meet	met	met
mimic	mimicked	mimicked
mislead	misled	misled
mistake	mistook	mistaken
misunderstand	misunderstood	misunderstood
mow	mowed	mowed, mown
offset	offset	offset
overcome	overcame	overcome
overdo	overdid	overdone
panic	panicked	panicked
partake	partook	partaken
pay	paid	paid
prove	proved	proven, proved
put	put	put
quit	quit	quit
read	read (*changes pronunciation*)	read (*changes pronunciation*)
rid	rid	rid
ride	rode	ridden
ring	rang	rung
rise	rose	risen
run	ran	run
say	said	said
see	saw	seen
seek	sought	sought
sell	sold	sold
send	sent	sent
set	set	set

basic or present form	past-tense form	past participle
sew	sewed	sewn, sewed
shake	shook	shaken
shed	shed	shed
shine	shone (shined for *"polished"*)	shone, shined
shoot	shot	shot
show	showed	shown, showed
shrink	shrank, shrunk	shrunk
shut	shut	shut
sing	sang	sung
sink	sank, sunk	sunk
sit	sat	sat
slay	slew	slain
sleep	slept	slept
slide	slid	slid
sling	slung	slung
slink	slunk	slunk
slit	slit	slit
sneak	snuck, sneaked	snuck, sneaked
sow	sowed	sown, sowed
speak	spoke	spoken
speed	sped, speeded	sped, speeded
spend	spent	spent
spin	spun	spun
spit	spat, spit	spat, spit
split	split	split
spread	spread	spread
spring	sprang, sprung	sprung
stand	stood	stood
steal	stole	stolen
stick	stuck	stuck
sting	stung	stung
stink	stank, stunk	stunk
stride	strode	stridden
strike	struck	struck
string	strung	strung
strive	strove, strived	striven, strived
swear	swore	sworn
sweep	swept	swept
swell	swelled	swollen, swelled
swim	swam	swum
swing	swung	swung
take	took	taken
teach	taught	taught

basic or present form	past-tense form	past participle
tear	tore	torn
tell	told	told
think	thought	thought
thrive	thrived	thrived
throw	threw	thrown
thrust	thrust	thrust
traffic	trafficked	trafficked
tread	trod	trodden, trod
uphold	upheld	upheld
upset	upset	upset
wake	woke, waked	woken, waked
wear	wore	worn
weave	wove	woven
weep	wept	wept
wet	wet, wetted	wet, wetted
win	won	won
wind	wound	wound
withdraw	withdrew	withdrawn
wring	wrung	wrung
write	wrote	written

▲ 17d Inflection for Person and Number

In order to agree with its subject (see #18), a verb is inflected for *person* and *number*. To illustrate, here are four verbs inflected for person and number in the *present tense*, using personal pronouns as subjects (see #14a):

Singular				
Ist person	I walk	I move	I push	I fly
2nd person	you walk	you move	you push	you fly
3rd person	he walks	he moves	he pushes	he flies
	she walks	she moves	she pushes	she flies
	it walks	it moves	it pushes	it flies
Plural				
1st person	we walk	we move	we push	we fly
2nd person	you walk	you move	you push	you fly
3rd person	they walk	they move	they push	they fly

Note that the inflection occurs *only in the third-person singular*, and that you add *s* or *es* to the basic form (first changing final *y* to *i* where necessary; see #62e).

17e Auxiliary Verbs

Auxiliary or helping verbs go with other verbs to form verb phrases indicating tense, voice, and mood. The auxiliary *do* helps in forming questions (see #12t), forming negative sentences, and expressing emphasis:

> Did you arrive on time?
>
> I did not arrive on time.
>
> She doesn't care for asparagus.
>
> I did wash my face!
>
> I do admire that man.

Do works only in the simple present and simple past tenses (see #17g). The principal auxiliary verbs—*be*, *have*, *will*, and *shall*—enable us to form tenses beyond the simple present and the simple past, as illustrated in #17g and #17h. *Be* and *have* go with main verbs and with each other to form the perfect tenses and the progressive tenses; *will* and *shall* (see #17h.3) help form the various future tenses. *Be* also combines with main verbs to form the passive voice (see #17-o and 17p).

Modal auxiliaries

There are also what are called **modal auxiliaries**. The principal ones are *can*, *could*, *may*, *might*, *must*, *should*, and *would*. They combine with main verbs and other auxiliaries to express such meanings as ability, possibility, obligation, and necessity.

The following chart illustrates the principal modal verbs currently in use in North American English:

The Modal	*Used to express . . .*
can	
could	ability
may	
might	permission
ought to	
should	
must	obligation
shall	
will	probability, prediction
should	
would	condition

Consider the following examples:

> I can understand that.
>
> There could be thunderstorms tomorrow.
>
> I would tell you the answer if I could.
>
> The instructor may decide to cancel the quiz.
>
> I might attend, but then again I might not.
>
> You should have received the letter by now.
>
> Must we wear our uniforms?

The equivalent phrases *able to* (*can*), *ought to* (*should*), and *have to* (*must*) also function as modal auxiliaries.

- **could**, **might**: *Could* and *might* also serve as the past-tense forms of *can* and *may*, for example if demanded by the sequence of tenses after a verb in the past tense (see #17i):

  > He was sure that I could handle the project.
  >
  > She said that I might watch the rehearsal if I was quiet.

  (For the distinction between *can* and *may*, see **can, may** in the Usage Checklist, #72. For *should* and *would* as past-tense forms, see #17i.2.)

- **might**, **may**: *Might* and *may* are sometimes interchangeable when expressing possibility:

  > She may (might) challenge the committee's decision.
  >
  > He may (might) have finished the job by now.

  But usually there is a difference, with *may* indicating a stronger possibility, *might* a somewhat less likely one.

  > Since more rain is forecast, the flood waters may rise overnight. (That is, flood waters *may very well* rise.)
  >
  > The weather report forecasts sunshine, but the river might still rise overnight. (That is, flood waters *could* rise but probably won't.)

17e

To express a condition contrary to fact (see #17m.2), *might* is the right word:

> If you had edited your essay, you might [not *may*] have received a higher grade.

That is, you *didn't* edit carefully, and you *didn't* get a higher grade. *Might* is necessary for clear expression of a hypothetical as opposed to a factual circumstance. Consider the difference in meaning between the following two sentences:

> Reducing his speed might have prevented the accident.
>
> Reducing his speed may have prevented the accident.

In the first sentence, *might* is used again to express a condition contrary to fact: the driver did not reduce his speed and the accident was not prevented, but the writer suggests the accident could have been prevented had the driver reduced his speed. The substitution of *may* for *might* in the second sentence changes the situation: in this case, the accident was prevented, and the writer is speculating that this fortunate occurrence may be attributable to the driver's having reduced his speed. See also **may**, **might** in #72.

Like forms of *do*, modal auxiliaries can join with the contraction *n't*: *can't, couldn't, shouldn't, wouldn't, mustn't.* In addition, *can* can join with the word *not*: *cannot.* Unlike other verbs (see #17d), modal auxiliaries are not inflected for third-person singular:

> I can go.
>
> You can go.
>
> He or she or it can go.

Nor do these verbs have any participial forms, or an infinitive form (one cannot say *to can*; instead, one must use another verb phrase, *to be able*). But modal auxiliaries can work as parts of perfect tenses as well as of simple present and simple past tenses (see #17g). (For more on modal auxiliaries, see #17n.)

▲ 17f Inflection of *do*, *be*, and *have*

Do, *be*, and *have* are different from the other auxiliaries in that they can also function as main verbs. As a main verb, *do* most often has the sense of *perform, accomplish*:

> I do my job. He did what I asked. She does her best.

Have as a main verb most often means *own, possess, contain*:

> I have enough money. July has thirty-one days.

And *be* as a main verb can mean *exist* or *live* (a sense seldom used: "I think; therefore I *am*"), but most often means *occur, remain, occupy a place*:

> The exam is today. I won't be more than an hour.
> The car is in the garage.

(See your dictionary for other meanings of these verbs.)

Even when functioning as auxiliaries, these verbs are fully inflected. Here are the inflections for *do* and *have*, which, as you can see, are irregular:

Singular		
1st person	I do	I have
2nd person	you do	you have
3rd person	he does	he has
	she does	she has
	it does	it has
Plural		
1st person	we do	we have
2nd person	you do	you have
3rd person	they do	they have
past-tense form	did	had
past participle	done	had
present participle	doing	having

The most common verb of all, *be*, is also the most irregular:

Singular	***present tense***	***past tense***
1st person	I am	I was
2nd person	you are	you were
3rd person	he / she / it is	he / she / it was
Plural		
1st person	we are	we were
2nd person	you are	you were
3rd person	they are	they were
past participle	been	
present participle	being	

For a fuller discussion of tense, see the next two sections.

▲ 17g Time and the Verb: Inflection for Tense

Even though verbs must agree with their subjects in person and number (see #17d, #18), they are still the strongest elements in sentences because they not only indicate action but also control time. The verb by its inflection indicates the *time* of an action, event, or condition. Through its **tense** a verb shows *when* an action occurs:

past tense: Yesterday, I practised.

present tense: Today, I practise.

future tense: Tomorrow, I will practise.

Here the adverbs *yesterday*, *today*, and *tomorrow* emphasize the *when* of the action, but the senses of past, present, and future are clear without them:

I practised. I practise. I will practise.

▲ 17h The Functions of the Different Tenses

Following are brief descriptions and illustrations of the main functions of each tense. Although these points are sometimes oversimplifications of very complex matters, and although there are other exceptions and variations than those listed, these guidelines should help you to use the tenses and to take advantage of the possibilities they offer for clear expression.

Tense	*Verb Form*	
1. Simple Present	I / you he / she / it we / you / they	**dance** **dances** **dance**
2. Simple Past	I / you / he / she / it / we / you / they	**danced**
3. Simple Future	I / you / he / she / it / we / you / they	**will dance**
4. Present Perfect	he / she / it I / you / we / you / they	**has danced** **have danced**
5. Past Perfect	I / you / he / she / it / we / you / they	**had danced**
6. Future Perfect	I / you / he / she / it / we / you / they	**will have danced**
7. Present Progressive	I you he / she / it we / you / they	**am dancing** **are dancing** **is dancing** **are dancing**
8. Past Progressive	I you he / she / it we / you / they	**was dancing** **were dancing** **was dancing** **were dancing**

9. Future Progressive	I / you / he / she / it / we / you / they	**will be dancing**
10. Present Perfect Progressive	I / you	**have been dancing**
	he / she / it	**has been dancing**
	we / you / they	**have been dancing**
11. Past Perfect Progressive	I / you / he / she / it / we / you / they	**had been dancing**
12. Future Perfect Progressive	I / you / he / she / it / we / you / they	**will have been dancing**

1. Simple present

Generally, use this tense to describe an action or condition that is happening now, at the time of the utterance:

> The pitcher throws. The batter swings. It is a high fly ball . . .
>
> The day is very warm. I am uncomfortable. Are you all right? I can manage.

But this tense has several other common uses. It can indicate a general truth or belief:

> Ottawa is one of the coldest capitals in the world.
>
> Cheetahs can outrun any other animal.
>
> The bigger they are the harder they fall.

or describe a customary or habitual or repeated action or condition:

> I paint pictures for a living.
>
> Anne spells her name with an *e*.
>
> I always eat breakfast before going to school.
>
> In Yellowknife, snow starts falling before Halloween.

or describe the characters or events in a literary or other work, or what an author does in such a work (see #17k):

> Oedipus searches for the truth almost like a modern detective.
>
> In a famous children's book, owls deliver the mail to the school.
>
> Dante with the help of Virgil ascends to paradise.

or even express future time, especially with the help of an adverbial modifier of time (see also number 7 on the present progressive below):

He arrives tomorrow. (adverbial modifier: *tomorrow*)

We leave for London next Sunday. (adverbial modifier: *next Sunday*)

17h

2. Simple past

Use this tense for a single or repeated action or condition that began and ended in the past (compare number 4 on the present perfect below):

She earned a lot of money last summer.

I was happy when I received my paycheque.

I painted a picture yesterday.

I painted pictures last year.

He went to Paris three times last year.

3. Simple future

Although there are other ways to indicate future time (see, for example, number 1 on the simple present above and number 7 on the present progressive below), the most common and straightforward is to use the simple future, putting *will* or *shall* before the basic form of the verb:

She will arrive tomorrow morning.

I will paint pictures next year.

We'll have a nice picnic if it doesn't rain.

Shall, once considered the correct form to use with a first-person subject (*I*, *we*), is now, in North American English, restricted largely to expressing emphasis or determination or to first-person questions asking for agreement or permission or advice, where *will* would sound unidiomatic:

Shall we go?

With negatives, the contracted forms of *will not* and *shall not* are *won't* and *shan't:*

Won't we arrive on time?

No, I shan't be able to attend.

Note, however, that *shan't* is uncommon in Canadian English.

4. Present perfect

Use this tense for an action or condition that began in the past and that continues to the present (compare number 2 on the simple past above); though commonly considered "completed" as of the moment, some actions or conditions referred to in this tense could continue after the present:

> I have earned a lot of money this summer.
>
> James Bond has just entered the casino.
>
> The weather has been lovely lately.
>
> The autobiography course has lasted for two months.

You can use this tense for something that occurred entirely in the past if you feel that it somehow impinges on the present—that is, if you intend to imply the sense of "before now" or "so far" or "already":

> I have painted a picture; take a look at it.
>
> She has told us how she wants our assignments done.
>
> I have visited Greece three times.
>
> We have beaten them at tennis seven out of ten times.

5. Past perfect

Use this tense for an action completed in the past before a specific past time or event. Notice that there are at least two actions taking place in the past:

> I had painted a picture just before they arrived.
>
> Though I had seen the film twice before, I went again last week.
>
> They got to the station only a minute late, but the train had already left.

6. Future perfect

Use this tense for an action or condition that will be completed before a specific future time or event:

> By this time next week I will have painted a self-portrait.
>
> I will already have eaten when you arrive.

Sometimes simple future works as well as future perfect:

> Some experts predict that by the year 2015 scientists will have found a cure for diabetes.

7. Present progressive

17h

Use this tense for an action or condition that began at some past time and is continuing now, in the present:

> I am writing my rough draft.
>
> Global warming is causing a significant rise in sea levels around the world.

Sometimes the simple and the progressive forms of a verb say much the same thing:

> We hope for snow. We are hoping for snow.
>
> I feel giddy. I am feeling giddy.

But usually the progressive form emphasizes an activity, or the singleness or continuing nature of an action, rather than a larger condition or general truth:

> A tax hike hurts many people.
> The tax hike is hurting many people.
>
> I walk to work.
> I am walking to work.

Like the simple present, the present progressive tense can also express future time, especially with adverbial help:

> They are arriving early tomorrow morning.

You can also express future time with a form of *be* and *going* before an infinitive (see #21a):

> They are going to walk around Stanley Park on New Year's day.

Stative verbs, verbs that express sense, cognitive, or emotional states, don't often appear in the progressive form. Because they express a state of being or mental activity, they are usually found describing static or relatively constant situations. Unless the stative verb is expressing an action, do not use it in the progressive tense.

incorrect: After being sprayed by the skunk, the dog is smelling bad now. (condition)

The odour of the dog is a condition, not an action. Therefore, you should write, "the dog smells bad." However, if you want to imply the dog's ability to smell is not functioning, you could write the following:

correct: After having its nose injured, the dog is smelling poorly. (activity)

Here is a short list of some common stative verbs:

appear	appreciate	be	believe	dislike
feel	hear	imagine	know	like
look	love	remember	resemble	seem
smell	understand	want	wish	

8. Past progressive

Use this tense for an action that was in progress during some past time, especially if you want to emphasize the continuing nature of the action:

I remember that I was painting a picture that day.

He was driving very fast.

They were protesting the city council's decision.

Sometimes the past progressive tense describes an interrupted action or an action during which something else happens:

When the telephone rang I was making tempura.

Just as he was stepping off, the bus started moving.

9. Future progressive

Use this tense for a continuing action in the future or for an action that will be occurring at some specific time in the future:

I will be painting pictures as long as I can hold a brush.

You will be learning things for the rest of your life.

They will be arriving on the midnight plane.

17h

10. Present perfect progressive

Use this tense to emphasize the continuing nature of a single or repeated action that began in the past and that has continued at least up to the present. This tense is suitable for showing trends in the sense of showing changes over time.

> I have been working on this sketch for an hour.
>
> The profits have been increasing in the last quarter.
>
> Our book club has been meeting once a week since January.

11. Past perfect progressive

Use this tense to emphasize the continuing nature of a single or repeated past action that was completed before or interrupted by some other past action:

> I had been painting landscapes for three years before I finally sold one.
>
> We had all been expecting something quite different.
>
> I had been pondering the problem for an hour when suddenly the solution popped into my head.

12. Future perfect progressive

This tense is seldom used in academic writing. Use it to emphasize the continuing nature of a future action before a specific time in the future or before a second future action:

> If she continues to dance, by the year 2013 she will have been dancing for over half her life.
>
> You will already have been driving for about nine hours before you even get to the border.

Exercise 17h (1) Using verb tenses

Choose a few fairly standard verbs, ones that you find yourself using often—say, three regular verbs and three from the list of irregular verbs (#17c)—and run them through their paces: that is, compose substantive sentences using them in all the tenses illustrated in #17g and #17h.

Exercise 17h (2) Using auxiliary verbs

Select ten or so of the sentences you wrote for the preceding exercise and try using *do* and some of the *modal auxiliaries* (see #17e) with them to produce different meanings.

Example:

I do paint pictures.	I should be painting the garage.
I did paint pictures.	I should have been painting pictures.
Didn't you paint pictures?	I shouldn't have tried painting the ceiling.
I may have painted pictures.	Could I have been painting in my sleep?
Can you paint?	They must have been painting all night.

17i Sequence of Tenses

When two or more verbs occur in the same sentence, they will sometimes be of the same tense, but often they will be of different tenses.

1. Compound sentences

In a compound sentence, made up of two or more independent clauses (see #12z), the verbs can be equally independent; use whatever tenses the sense requires:

> I am leaving [present progressive] now, but she will leave [future] in the morning.
>
> The polls have closed [present perfect]; the clerks will soon be counting [future progressive] the ballots.
>
> He had made [past perfect] his promise, and the committee decided [past] to hold him to it; therefore they will expect [future] his cooperation in drafting a new business plan in the weeks ahead.

2. Past tense in independent clauses

In complex or compound-complex sentences, if the verb in an independent clause is in any of the past tenses, the verbs in any clauses subordinate to it will usually also be in one of the past tenses. For example:

> I told her that I was sorry.

> They agreed that this time the newly elected treasurer would not be a gambler.

Refer to a time *earlier* than that of the main verb in the past tense by using the *past perfect* tense:

> By Monday, Maria had finally finished the speed-reading textbook that I lent her on Friday.

17i

But there are exceptions. When the verb in the subordinate clause states a general or timeless truth or belief, or something characteristic or habitual, it stays in the present tense:

> Einstein showed that space, time, and light are linked.

> They discovered the hard way that money doesn't guarantee happiness.

And the context of the sentence sometimes dictates that other kinds of verbs in subordinate clauses should not be changed to a past tense. If you feel that a tense other than the past would be clearer or more accurate, use it; for example:

> I learned yesterday that I will be able to get into the new program in the fall.

The rule calls for *would,* but *will* is logical and clear. Notice that the adverbial marker "in the fall" tells us the action will occur in the future.

> In an interview yesterday, Smith said that he is determined to complete the series of concerts.

To use *was* rather than *is* here would be ambiguous, implying that Smith's determination was a thing of the past; if it definitely *was* past, then *had been* would be clearer.

And here is one more example of a sentence in which the "sequence of tenses" rule is best ignored:

> The secretary told me this morning that Professor Barnes is ill and will not be teaching class this afternoon.

17j Verb Phrases in Compound Predicates

When a compound predicate consists of two verb phrases in different tenses, don't omit part of one of them:

> ***t:*** The leader has never and will never practise nepotism.

Rather, include each verb in full or rephrase the sentence:

> ***revised:*** The leader has never practised and will never practise nepotism.

> ***revised:*** The leader has never practised nepotism and will never do so.

17k Tenses in Writing about Literature

When discussing or describing the events in a literary work, it is customary to use the present tense (see also #17h.1):

> While he is away from Denmark, Hamlet arranges to have Rosencrantz and Guildenstern put to death. After he returns he holds Yorick's skull and watches Ophelia being buried. He duels with Laertes and dies. Without a doubt, death is one of the principal themes in the play.

For the tenses of infinitives and participles, see #21b and #21e.

Proofreading Tip

On Verb Tense and Conventions of Literary Analysis
It is also customary to speak even of a long-dead author in the present tense when one is discussing his/her techniques in a particular work; another example:

> In *Pride and Prejudice*, Jane Austen shows the consequences of making hasty judgments of others.

17-l Mood

English verbs are usually considered to have three moods. The mood of a verb has to do with the nature of the expression in which it's being used. The most common mood is the **indicative**, which is used for statements of fact or opinion and for questions:

> The weather forecast for tomorrow sounds promising.

> Shall we proceed with our plans?

The **imperative** mood is used for most commands and instructions (see #12u):

> Put the picnic hamper in the trunk.

> Don't forget the bubbly.

The **subjunctive** mood in English is less common, and it presents some difficulty. It is discussed below.

17m Using the Subjunctive

The subjunctive has almost disappeared from contemporary English. It survives in some standard expressions or idioms such as "*Be* that as it may"; "*Come* what may"; "Heaven *forbid*!" and "Long *live* the Queen!" Otherwise, you need consider only two kinds of instances where the subjunctive still functions.

1. Use the subjunctive in a *that*-clause after verbs expressing demands, obligations, requirements, recommendations, suggestions, wishes, and the like:

   The doctor recommended that she take a sea voyage.

   Ruth asked that the door be left open.

   I wish [that] I were in Paris.

2. Use the subjunctive to express conditions that are hypothetical or impossible—often in *if*-clauses or their equivalents:

   He looked as if he were going to explode. (But he didn't explode, we hope.)

   If Lise were here she would back me up. (But she isn't here.)

   An *as if* or *as though* clause almost always expresses a condition contrary to fact, but not all *if*-clauses do; don't be misled into using a subjunctive where it's not appropriate:

   wrong: He said that if there were another complaint he would resign.

   The verb should be *was*, for the condition could turn out to be true: there may be another complaint.

Since only a few subjunctive forms differ from those of the indicative, they are easy to learn and remember. The third-person-singular subjunctive form loses its *s*:

indicative: I like the way she paints.
subjunctive: I suggested that she paint my portrait.

The subjunctive forms of the verb *be* are *be* and *were:*

indicative: He is friendly. (I am, you / we / they are)
subjunctive: The judge asked that she be excused. (that I / you / we / they be)

indicative: I know that I am in Edmonton.
subjunctive: I wish that I were in Florence.

Note that both *be* and *were* function with either singular or plural subjects. Note also that the past tense form *were* functions in present tense expressions of wishes and contrary-to-fact conditions. Other verbs also use their past tense as a subjunctive after a present-tense wish:

I wish that I shopped less.

After a past-tense wish, use the standard past perfect form:

He wished that he had been more attentive.

She wished that she had played better.

17n Using Modal Auxiliaries and Infinitives Instead of Subjunctives

The *modal auxiliaries* (see #17e) offer common alternatives to many sentences using subjunctives; they express several of the same moods.

The doctor told her she should [ought to] live in a less polluted area.

I wish that I could be in Paris.

He looked as if he might explode.

If Lise could have been here, she would back me up.

Another alternative uses the *infinitive* (see #21a):

It is necessary for us to be there before noon.

The judge ordered Ralph to attend the hearing.

Ruth asked us to leave the door open.

Exercise 17n Using subjunctives

Suppose that you are giving a friend some advice about how to deal with noisy neighbours. Compose ten sentences using a variety of subjunctive forms. One sentence may start "If I were you, I would . . ." Then try to revise each so that it uses a modal auxiliary or an infinitive instead of a subjunctive. You should be able to change most if not all of them.

17-o

17-o Voice

There are two voices, *active* and *passive*. The active voice is direct: *I made this toy boat*. The passive voice is less direct, reversing the normal subject–verb–object pattern: *This toy boat was made by me* (see #12e). Passive voice is easy to recognize; the verb uses some form of *be* followed by a past participle: *was made*. What in active voice would be a direct object (*boat*) in passive voice becomes the subject of the verb. And passive constructions often leave unmentioned the agent of the action or state they describe: *The toy boat was made* (by whom isn't specified). You may sometimes see this referred to as a truncated passive.

17p The Passive Voice

pas Using the passive voice, some people can promise action without committing themselves to perform it, and they can admit error without accepting responsibility:

> ***passive:*** Be assured [by whom?] that action will be taken [by whom?].
> ***active:*** I assure you that I will act.

> ***passive:*** It is to be regretted [by whom?] that an error has been made [by whom?].
> ***active:*** I am sorry we made an error in your account. I will look into the matter and correct it immediately.

Although the passive voice has its uses, it is not often preferable to the active voice. When possible, use the direct and more vigorous active voice. Here are some examples from students' papers:

> ***pas:*** All of this <u>is communicated</u> by Tolkien by means of a poem rather than prose. The poetry <u>is shown</u> as a tool which Tolkien employs in order to foreshadow events and establish ideas which otherwise <u>could not be</u> easily <u>communicated</u> to us.

The wordiness of this passage results largely from the passive voice. A change to active voice shortens it, clarifies the sense, and produces a crisper style. Begin by making the agent the subject; the rest then follows naturally and logically:

> ***active:*** Tolkien communicates all this in poetry rather than prose because with poetry he can foreshadow events and establish ideas that would otherwise be difficult to convey.

> ***pas:*** Mixing the chemicals, hydrogen sulphide <u>was formed</u>.

In the second example, describing the experiment, the passive not only is ineffective but it also leads to a *dangling modifier* (see #36); there is no subject in the sentence to explain who is doing the mixing. The frequency of such errors is itself a good reason to be sparing with passive voice. The active voice eliminates the grammatical error:

> ***active:*** By mixing the chemicals, the chemist produced hydrogen sulphide.

When to use the passive voice (see also #29f)
Use the passive voice when the active voice is impossible or when the passive is for some other reason clearly preferable or demanded by the context. Generally, use passive voice

- when the agent, or doer of the act, is indefinite or not known;
- when the agent is less important than the act itself;
- when you want to emphasize either the agent or the act by putting it at the beginning or end of the sentence.

For example:

> It was reported that there were two survivors.

Here the writer doesn't know who did the reporting. To avoid the passive by saying "Someone reported that there were two survivors" would oddly stress the mysterious "someone." And the fact that *someone reported* it is less important than the content of the report.

> The accident was witnessed by more than thirty people.

Here the writer emphasizes the large number of witnesses by putting them at the end of the sentence, the most emphatic point in the utterance.

No doubt you'll want to use passive voice on other sorts of occasions as well, but don't use it unwittingly or uncritically. Remember: a verb in the passive consists of some form of *be* followed by a past participle (*is shown, was accompanied, to be announced, has been decided, are legalized, will be charged, is being removed*). Whenever you find yourself using such verbs, stop to consider whether an active structure would be more effective.

Note: Like mood, voice operates regardless of tense. Don't confuse passive constructions with the past tense just because the past participle is used. Passive constructions can appear in any of the tenses.

17p

Exercise 17p Revising passive voice

In the following, change passive voice to active voice wherever you think the revision improves the sentence. Retain the passive wherever you think it is preferable.

1. By planning a trip carefully, time-wasting mistakes can be avoided.
2. The car was driven by Denise, while Yves acted as map-reader.
3. Another factor that makes the Whistler ski resort so popular is the variety of après-ski entertainment that can be found there.
4. Some went swimming, some went on short hikes, some just lay around, and volleyball was played by others.
5. According to scientists, it is hoped that the oil spill will be cleaned up by the turbulence of the water.

18 Agreement Between Subject and Verb

agr A verb should agree with its subject in number and person. We say *I see*, not *I sees*; *he sees*, not *he see*; and *we see*, not *we sees*. Sometimes people have trouble making verbs agree with subjects in *number*. Here are the main circumstances to watch out for while editing a first or subsequent draft:

18a Words Intervening Between Subject and Verb

When something plural comes between a singular subject and its verb, the verb must still agree with the subject:

> Far below, a landscape of rolling brown hills and small trees lies among the small cottages.
>
> Each of the poems has certain striking qualities.
>
> Neither of the parties was willing to compromise.
>
> The whole experience—the decision to go, the planning, the journey, and especially all the places we went and things we saw—was consistently exciting.

Similarly, don't let an intervening singular noun affect the agreement between a plural subject and its verb.

18b Compound Subject: Singular Nouns Joined by *and*

A compound subject made up of two or more singular nouns joined by *and* is usually plural:

> Careful thought and attention to detail are essential.

> Coffee and tea were served on the loggia.

Occasional exceptions occur. If two nouns identify the same person or thing, or if two nouns taken together are thought of as a unit, the verb is singular:

> A common-law spouse and father has an obligation to share the domestic responsibilities.

> Macaroni and cheese is a student favourite.

But if you feel an urge to use a singular verb after a two-part subject joined by *and*, make sure you haven't used two nouns that mean the same thing and that are therefore *redundant* (see #71c):

> ***red:*** The strength and power of her argument is undeniable.

Remove one or the other, or replace the two nouns with some other single word, such as *force* in this particular example.

Proofreading Tip

Agreement When a Subject Is Followed by a Particular Phrase

Phrases such as *in addition to*, *as well as*, and *together with* are prepositions, not conjunctions like *and*. A singular subject followed by one of them still takes a singular verb:

> The cat as well as the dog comes when I whistle.

> Ms. Hondiak, along with her daughters, is attending law school this year.

Compound subjects preceded by *each* or *every* take a singular verb:

> Each dog and cat has its own supper dish.

18c Compound Subject: Parts Joined by *or* or a Correlative

When the parts of a subject are joined by the coordinating conjunction *or* (see #23a) or by the correlative conjunctions *either . . . or, neither . . . nor, not . . . but, not only . . . but also, whether . . . or* (see #23b), the part nearest the verb determines whether the verb is singular or plural:

18c

> One or the other of you has the winning ticket. (both parts singular: verb singular; note that the subject is *one or the other*, not *you*)
>
> Neither the artists nor the politicians feel the arts funding is adequate. (both parts plural: verb plural)
>
> Neither the mainland nor the islands are interested in building the bridge. (first part singular, second part plural: verb plural)
>
> Neither my parents nor I was to blame. (first part plural, second part singular: verb singular)

Try to avoid the construction in the previous example, since it usually sounds incorrect (see also #15b). It's easy to rephrase:

> Neither I nor my parents were to blame.
>
> My parents were not to blame, nor was I.

18d Agreement with Indefinite Pronouns (see also #14g, #15c)

Most indefinite pronouns are singular: *another, anybody, anyone, anything, each, either, everybody, everyone, everything, much, neither, nobody, no one, nothing, one, other, somebody, someone, something*. A few, (namely *all, any, more, most, none, some*) can be either singular or plural, depending on whether they refer to a single quantity or to a number of individual units within a group:

> Some of the pasta is eaten. (a single amount; *pasta* is singular, a mass noun)
> Some of the cookies are missing. (a number of cookies; *cookies* is plural)
>
> All of this novel is good. (a whole novel; *novel* is singular)
> All of his novels are well written. (a number of novels; *novels* is plural)
>
> Most of the champagne was drunk. (a single mass; *champagne* is singular)
> Most of the cases of champagne have been exported. (a number of cases; *cases* is plural)

None of the work is finished. (a single unit; *work* is singular)
None of the reports are ready. (a number of reports; *reports* is plural)

18e Subject Following Verb

When the normal subject–verb order is reversed, the verb still must agree with the real subject, not some word that happens to precede it:

There is only one answer to this question.
There are several possible solutions to the problem.

Here comes the judge.
Here come the clowns.

Thirty days has September.
Sitting in the coffee shop were my archenemy and his pet turtle.

When compounded singular nouns follow an opening *there* or *here*, most writers make the verb agree with the first noun:

There was a computer and a copier in the next room.

There was still an essay to be revised and a play to be studied before he could think about sleep.

There was still the play to be read and his lines to be memorized.

But others find this kind of syntax awkward sounding. By rephrasing the sentence you can easily avoid the issue and save a few words as well:

A computer and a copier were in the next room.

He still had an essay to revise and a play to study before he could think about sleep.

He still had to read the play and memorize his lines.

In expletive patterns, *it* takes a singular verb—usually a linking verb (see #17a)

It is questions like these that give the most trouble.

For more on the expletives *it* and *there,* see #12k and #71a.

Proofreading Tip

Agreement and Predicate Nouns:
Don't let a predicate noun determine a verb's number; the verb must agree with the subject of the sentence, not the complement (see #12h and #17a):

> The last word in style that year was platform shoes and bell bottom jeans.

18f

18f Agreement with Collective Nouns

Collective nouns (see #13) are collections or groups that are considered as units and therefore usually take singular verbs:

> The government has passed the legislation.

> The company is planning several events to celebrate its centennial.

But when such a noun denotes the individual members of a group, the verb must be plural:

> His family comes from Korea. (singular)

> His family come from Jamaica, India, and Southern Europe. (plural)

> The audience was composed and attentive. (singular)

> The audience were sneezing, coughing, blowing their noses, and chatting with one another. (plural)

Such words as *number*, *half*, and *majority* can also be considered collective nouns and either singular or plural. In the following examples, notice how the article—*a* or *the*—changes the verb agreement:

> A number of optimistic skiers are heading to the slopes. (*a number of*: plural)

> The number of skiers here is quite large. (*The number of*: singular)

(See also **amount, number** in #72.)

18g Nouns That Are Always Singular or Always Plural

Some nouns, because of their meanings, cannot be inflected for number and will always be either singular or plural. Do not be fooled by some singular nouns that look plural because they end in "s." Some examples of uninflectable nouns include:

The gold comes from the Yukon. (always singular)

Oxygen is essential to human life. (always singular)

Economics is difficult for some people. (always singular)

Good news is always welcome. (always singular)

The scissors are in the kitchen. (always plural)

His glasses are fogged up. (always plural)

Her clothes are very stylish. (always plural)

For more on *mass* and *countable* nouns, see #13a and #19c.6.

18h Plurals: *criteria, data, media,* etc.

Words of Greek and Latin origin ending in *a* look like singular words but are in fact plural. The following words are plural; they can't be used with singular verbs (see #62t.7):

criteria (singular is *criterion*)

phenomena (singular is *phenomenon*)

strata (singular is *stratum*)

While *criteria, phenomena,* and *strata* should always be treated as plural forms, some similar nouns may take either a singular or plural verb depending on the context. For instance, *data* should be treated as a plural noun in scientific contexts (the singular form is *datum*); in non-scientific practice, it may take a singular verb:

Vertical meteorological data are collected using a parachute-borne sensor. (plural)

Data from the poll has been tabulated and entered in the system. (singular)

It was once considered incorrect to use *media* as anything but a plural noun. But some dictionaries and usage guides have reduced their opposition to its use as a singular noun, arguing that it can be regarded in some contexts as a collective noun and thus followed by either a plural or singular verb, depending on whether it's being used to mean TV, print, and radio journalists or bloggers collectively or individually.

18h

> Some argue that the media is responsible for making health care the number-one concern among voters. (singular)
>
> A local newspaper broke the story, but other media were quick to report it. (plural)

18i Agreement with Relative Pronouns

Whether a relative pronoun is singular or plural depends on its antecedent (see #15). Therefore when a relative clause has *who*, *which*, or *that* as its subject, the verb must agree in number with the pronoun's antecedent:

> Her success is due to her intelligence and perseverance, which have overcome all obstacles. (The antecedent of *which* is *intelligence and perseverance*.)

Questions about agreement most often occur with the phrases *one of those . . . who* and *one of the . . . who*:

> He is one of those people who have difficulty reading aloud.
>
> He is one of the few people I know who have difficulty reading aloud.

Have is correct, since the antecedent of *who* is the plural *people*, not the singular *one*. The only time this construction takes a singular verb is when *one* is preceded by *the only*; *one* is then the antecedent of *who*:

> He is the only one of those attending who has difficulty reading aloud.

You can avoid the problem by simplifying:

> He has difficulty reading aloud.
>
> Of those attending, he alone has difficulty reading aloud.

18j Titles of Works: Words Referred to as Words

Titles of literary and other works and words referred to as words should be treated as *singular* even if they are plural in themselves:

> *The Two Gentlemen of Verona* is one of Shakespeare's lesser-known comedies.
>
> *The Four Seasons* is probably Vivaldi's best-known work.
>
> *Nervous Nellies* is an out-of-date slang term.

Exercise 18 (1) Choosing correct verbs

Underline the correct form in each pair of verbs:

1. Neither Jason nor Melinda (is, are) interested in moving in.
2. There (is, are) fresh coffee and muffins on the kitchen table.
3. The committee (intends, intend) to table its report today.
4. Unexplained natural phenomena (fascinates, fascinate) the scientific community.
5. Most critics agree that Timothy Findley's *The Wars* (is, are) an important Canadian novel.

Exercise 18 (2) Correcting faulty subject–verb agreement

Revise the following sentences to correct any lack of agreement between subject and verb.

1. Recent studies of the earth's atmosphere indicates that there are more than one hole in the ozone layer.
2. Juliet's love and courage is evident in this scene.
3. Post-modern architecture in North America and Europe have been changing urban skylines.
4. In Canada, the media is largely based in Ottawa and Toronto.
5. This economist writes of the virtue of selfishness, but it seems to me that she, along with those who share her view, are forgetting the importance of cooperation.
6. Everything in this speech, the metre, the repetition of vowels, and the vibrant imagery, lead us to believe that this is the high point of Othello's love and, as far as we know from this play, of his life.

Exercise 18 (2) Correcting faulty subject–verb agreement – *cont.*

7. The migration of whales attract many tourists to this coastal community.
8. Indeed, the exercise of careful thought and careful planning seem to be necessary for the successful completion of the project.
9. But scandal, unfair politics, and the "big business" of politics has led to the corruption of the system.
10. With innovation comes a few risks.

19 Adjectives

ad An **adjective** modifies—limits, qualifies, or particularizes—a noun or pronoun. Adjectives generally answer the questions *Which? What kind of? How many? How much?*

The black cat was hungry; he ate five sardines and drank some milk.

19a Kinds of Adjectives

Adjectives fall into two major classes: **non-descriptive** and **descriptive.**

1. Non-descriptive adjectives

The several kinds of **non-descriptive** adjectives include some that are basically *structure words* (see #12-l):

- **articles**: *a*, *an*, *the* (see #19c)
- **demonstrative adjectives** (see also #14f):

this hat   that problem   these women   those books

- **interrogative and relative adjectives** (see also #14c–d):

Which book is best?   What time is it?

Whose opinion do you trust?

She is the one whose opinion I trust.

- **possessive adjectives**—the possessive forms of personal and impersonal pronouns (see #14a–b) and of nouns (see #13b):

my book	her car	its colour	their heritage
one's beliefs	a man's coat	the river's mouth	
Hamlet's ego	Shirley's job	the car's engine	

(Note: People who think of *form* rather than *function* prefer to call these "possessive pronouns" and "possessive nouns.")

- **indefinite and numerical adjectives** (see #14g):

some money	any time	more fuel	several keys
three ducks	thirty ships	the fourth act	much sushi

2. Descriptive adjectives

Descriptive adjectives give information about such matters as the size, shape, colour, nature, and quality of whatever a noun or pronoun names:

a hybrid car	a delicate balance
an Impressionist painting	a brave woman
a tempting dessert	a well-done steak
a once-in-a-lifetime chance	Canadian literature
an experimental play	composted leaves
a fascinating place to visit	kitchen towels
a dictionary definition	looking refreshed, he . . .
the festival to exceed all others	the man of the hour

the rabbits who caused all the trouble
a large, impressive, three-storey, grey, Victorian house

As these examples illustrate, adjectival modifiers can be single (*hybrid*, *delicate*, *Impressionist*, etc.), in groups or series (*large*, *impressive*, *three-storey*, *grey*, *Victorian*), or in compounds (*three-storey*, *well-done*, *once-in-a-lifetime*); they can be proper adjectives, formed from proper nouns (*Victorian*, *Canadian*, *Impressionist*); they can be words that are adjectives only (*delicate*, *large*) or words that can also function as other parts of speech (*hybrid*, *brave*, *tempting*, etc.), including nouns functioning as adjectives (*kitchen*, *dictionary*); they can be present participles (*tempting*, *fascinating*), past participles (*composted*), or infinitives (*to visit*); they can be participial phrases (*looking refreshed*), infinitive phrases (*to exceed all others*), or prepositional phrases (*of the hour);* or they can be relative clauses (*who caused all the trouble*). For more examples see #26a. On the punctuation of nouns in series, see #49; on the overuse of nouns as modifiers, see #71g; on infinitives and participles, see #21a and #21d; on prepositions, see #22; on relative clauses, see #14d, #30c.2, and #48a.

19b Comparison of Descriptive Adjectives

19b

Most descriptive adjectives can be inflected or supplemented for *degree* in order to make *comparisons*. The basic or dictionary form of an adjective is called its **positive** form: *high, difficult, calm.* Use it to compare two things that are equal or similar, or with qualifiers such as *not* and *almost* that are dissimilar:

This assignment is <u>as difficult as</u> last week's.

It is <u>not nearly so difficult as</u> I expected.

To make the comparative form, add *er* or put *more* (or *less*) in front of it: *higher, calmer, more difficult, less difficult.* Use it to compare two unequal things:

My grades are <u>higher</u> now than they were last year.

Your part is <u>more difficult</u> than mine.

For the **superlative** form, add *est* or put *most* (or *least*) in front of it: *highest, calmest, most difficult, least difficult.* Generally, use it to compare three or more unequal things:

Whose talent is the <u>greatest</u>?

He is the <u>calmest</u> and <u>least pretentious</u> person I know.

It is difficult to set rules for when to add *er* and *est* and when to use *more* and *most.* Some dictionaries tell you when *er* and *est* may be added to an adjective; if you have such a dictionary, and it doesn't give those forms for a particular adjective, use *more* and *most.* Otherwise, you can usually follow these guidelines:

- For adjectives of one syllable, usually add *er* and *est*:

Positive	*Comparative*	*Superlative*
short	shorter	shortest
low	lower	lowest
rough	rougher	roughest
dry	drier	driest
grim	grimmer	grimmest
brave	braver	bravest

You can also use *more* and *most, less* and *least* with many of these positive forms. (And note the spelling changes in the last three examples; see #62d–f.)

- For adjectives of *three or more* syllables, usually use *more* and *most* (or *less* and *least*):

beautiful	more beautiful	most beautiful
tiresome	more tiresome	most tiresome
sarcastic	more sarcastic	most sarcastic
fabulous	more fabulous	most fabulous

- For most adjectives of two syllables ending in *al*, *ect*, *ed*, *ent*, *ful*, *ic*, *id*, *ing*, *ish*, *ive*, *less*, and *ous* (and any others where an added *er* or *est* would sound wrong), generally use *more* and *most* (or *less* and *least*):

formal	more formal	most formal
direct	more direct	most direct
polished	more polished	most polished
potent	more potent	most potent
tactful	more tactful	most tactful
manic	more manic	most manic
soothing	more soothing	most soothing
childish	more childish	most childish
restive	more restive	most restive
reckless	more reckless	most reckless

- For other adjectives of two syllables, you usually have a choice; for example:

gentle	gentler, more gentle	gentlest, most gentle
bitter	bitterer, more bitter	bitterest, most bitter
lively	livelier, more lively	liveliest, most lively
silly	sillier, more silly	silliest, most silly

When there is a choice, the forms with *more* and *most* will usually sound more formal and more emphatic than those with *er* and *est*. In fact, you can use *more* and *most* with almost any descriptive adjective, even one-syllable ones, if you want a little extra emphasis or a different rhythm:

> Of all my sister's friends, she is by far the most brave.

But the converse isn't true: adjectives of three or more syllables, and even shorter ones ending in *ous* and *ful* and so on, almost always require *more* and *most* unless you want to use very informal dialogue, or to create a humorous effect, as when Alice finds things in Wonderland to be growing "curiouser and curiouser."

Because of their meanings, some adjectives should not be compared: see **unique** in the Usage Checklist, #72. See also #42 and #38, on faulty comparison, and ***comp*** in Appendix 2.

19b

Proofreading Tip

Avoiding "Doubling-Up" Errors in Adjective Forms

Don't double up a comparative or superlative form as in *more better* or *most prettiest*. If you want emphasis, use the adverbial intensifiers *much* or *far* or *by far*.

much livelier	much more lively
far livelier	far more lively
livelier by far	by far the liveliest
much the liveliest	much the livelier of the two

Proofreading Tip

Irregular Comparative and Superlative Adjective Forms

A few commonly used adjectives form their comparative and superlative degrees irregularly:

good	better	best
bad	worse	worse
far	farther, further	farthest, furthest
little	littler, less, lesser	littlest, least
much, many	more	most

(And see **farther**, **further** in the Usage Checklist, #72.)

Good dictionaries list all irregular forms after the basic entry, including those in which a spelling change occurs.

Exercise 19b Comparing adjectives

Come up with five exceptions: adjectives that don't fit neatly into the guidelines. For example, would you use *er* and *est* with *pat*, *chic*, *prone*, and *lost*? Or with *sudden*, *thorough*, *malign*, and *sanguine*? Do *er* and *est* work with *slippery*? Do some longer adjectives take *est* comfortably, but not *er*? Think of some descriptive adjectives (other than *unique*, etc.) that for some reason don't lend themselves to comparisons at all. (Try some past-participial forms, for example, or words that function primarily as nouns or other parts of speech.)

▲ 19c Articles: *a*, *an*, and *the*

Articles—sometimes considered separately from parts of speech—can conveniently be thought of as kinds of adjectives. Like adjectives, they modify nouns. Like demonstrative and possessive adjectives, they are also sometimes called *markers* or *determiners* because an article indicates that a noun will soon follow.

The definite article *the* and the indefinite articles *a* or *an* are used idiomatically, and therefore, they often challenge people whose first language doesn't include articles. That is why an advanced learner's dictionary can be invaluable in helping you decide which article, if any, to use. If you are having difficulty proofreading for articles, keep your dictionary handy. For example, in these two entries from the *Oxford Advanced Learner's Dictionary of Current English* (*OALD*), we are informed that a noun can be countable (would most likely need an article in its singular form), uncountable (would probably not take the indefinite article but might take the definite), or that the noun has both countable and uncountable forms depending on context.

> **equi•nox** /ˈiːkwɪnɒks; ˈek; *NAmE* nɑːks/ noun one of the two times in the year (around 20 March and 22 September) when the sun is above the equator and day and night are of equal length: *the* ***spring/autumn equinox***
>
> **dem•oc•cracy** /dɪˈmɒkrəsi; *NAmE* ˈmɑːk/ noun (*pl.* **-ies**)
> **1** [*U*] a system of government in which all the prople of a country can vote to elect their representatives: *parliamentary democracy* ◇ *the principles of democracy.*
> **2** [*C*] a country which has this system of government: *Western democracies* ◇ *I thought we were supposed to be living in a democracy.*
> **3** [*U*] fair and equal treatment of everyone in an organization, etc., and their right to take part in making decisions; *the fight for justice and democracy.*
>
>

It is almost impossible to set down all the rules for article use, but here are some guiding principles.

1. Using the indefinite article

The form *a* of the indefinite article is used before words beginning with a consonant (*a dog, a building, a computer, a yellow orchid*), including words beginning with a pronounced *h* (*a horse, a historical event, a hotel, a hypothesis*) and a word beginning with a *u* or *o* whose initial sound is that of *y* or *w* (*a useful book, a one-sided contest*).

The form *an* is used before words beginning with a vowel sound (*an opinion, an underdog, an ugly duckling*). If the "h" is not pronounced, we use "an" as in *an honour*. Similarly, the pronunciation of *the* changes from "thuh" to "thee" before a word beginning with a vowel sound.

Generally a person or thing designated by the indefinite article is not specific:

> He wants to buy a racehorse.
>
> This town needs a new bridal shop.
>
> Each class has a projector.

The indefinite article *a* is like *one*: it is often used before singular countable nouns. Sometimes it even means *one*:

> I lasted only a week at my new job.
>
> This will take an hour or two.

2. Using the definite article

Generally, the definite article designates one or more particular persons or things whose identity is established by context (familiarity) or a modifier (clauses, phrases, superlative adjectives, ordinal numbers). Also, the definite article is used with some proper nouns.

The can occur with names for objects the reader is familiar with or that you share knowledge about, indicating that the object is something unique for a given situation.

> Go to the bookstore (the one we both know about) and get the required textbook (the one that is unique to the course).

In these examples, the definite article is used because **context** is understood or your reader is familiar with the noun being modified.

> The black racehorse is in the barn.
>
> The bridal shop is on the corner.
>
> The projector faces the front of the class.

If the noun is followed by a **modifying clause** or **phrase**, the definite article is often used.

> My parents gave me the scooter I wanted. (*scooter* is particularized by the modifying clause *I wanted*)

Compare to the use of the indefinite article:

> My parents gave me a scooter. (unspecified)

The definite article can also be used to indicate exclusiveness; *the* is then equivalent to *the only* or *the best*. In fact, we often use *the* in front of **superlative adjectives**.

> He is the happiest person I know.
>
> She is the most diligent student.

We also can indicate exclusiveness with the use of **ordinals**. Ordinals are numerical adjectives such as first, second, third, and so on.

The first act of the play takes place in Vienna.

The third sequel appealed to adolescent tastes.

3. Using articles with proper nouns

Definite articles go with some **proper nouns** but not with others. Strangely, *the* often goes with place names that are plural. Others have modifying phrases that begin with "of."

We say	*But also*
Canada	the Dominion of Canada
Great Britain	the United Kingdom
Gabriola Island	the Thousand Islands
Mount Baker	the Rockies
Western University	the University of Saskatchewan

4. Using articles with uncountable nouns or plural nouns

Uncountable nouns, whether mass nouns or abstract nouns, take no article if the mass or abstract sense governs. In addition, plural countable nouns rarely take indefinite articles.

art: The poem features a direct simple praise of nature.

Here *a* must be removed because praise in this context is uncountable. But notice the difference if the concrete noun "hymn" is inserted.

The poem features a direct, simple hymn of praise to nature.

Also avoid using *a* with plural countable nouns.

art: She wanted a writing notebooks.

revised: She wanted writing notebooks.

However, you can use *the* with plural nouns if they are particularized by a modifier.

revised: She wanted the writing notebooks that are made in Italy. (Here *notebooks* are particularized by *that are made in Italy*.) See above.

5. Using articles with abstract nouns

If a usually abstract noun is used in a countable but not particularized sense, the indefinite article precedes it; if in a particularized way, the definite article:

> This is an honour. (countable)
>
> He did me the honour of inviting me. (uncountable, specific)

6. Using the definite article in front of nouns that represent groups

The definite article usually precedes an adjective functioning as a noun that represents a group (see #19f):

> The young should heed the advice of the elderly.
>
> The poor will always have an advocate on city council.

This rule can also be applied to species of animals or inventions when emphasizing the class.

> The horse is a beautiful animal.
>
> The computer is a prominent feature of our lives.

7. Using articles with titles of artistic works

Titles of artistic works are not usually preceded by articles, but usage is inconsistent, and some idiomatically take the definite article. It would be incorrect to say:

> ***art:*** Donne's poetic power is evident in the Sonnet X.

Either omit *the* or change it to *his*. And one wouldn't say "the *Alice in Wonderland*" or "the *Paradise Lost*." But it would be natural to refer to "the *Wind in the Willows*" and "the *Adventures of Huckleberry Finn*." (Of course, if *A* or *The* is part of the title, it should be included: *A Midsummer Night's Dream*, *The Voyage Out*.) If a possessive (or pronominal) adjective or possessive form of the author's name precedes the title, no article is needed: "Milton in his *Areopagitica*," "in Milton's *Areopagitica*."

8. Using articles with names of academic fields and courses

With names of academic fields and courses, whether proper nouns or abstract common nouns, no article is used:

> She is enrolled in Psychology 301.
>
> He reads books on psychology.
>
> He is majoring in communications.

9. Using the definite article before names of ships and trains

Use the definite article (lower case) before the names of ships and trains:

the *Beagle*	the *Titanic*	the *Mary Ellen Carter*
the *St Roch*	the *Super Chief*	the *Orient Express*

Exercise 19c Using articles

In each blank, place *a*, *an*, or *the*; or put *O* if no article is needed. If two articles could be used, put a slash (/) between them. If an article could be used, but need not, put parentheses around it. Some of the answers will be debatable, and we hope you will debate them.

1. In _____ Canadian society, everyone is considered _____ equal.
2. After five years in _____ business, she decided to enrol in _____ International Relations.
3. My sister got _____ award for her work in _____ genetics.
4. There was _____ controversial documentary about _____ drug addiction on _____ television last night.
5. I think you should put _____ onion in _____ stew.
6. _____ art books were worth _____ small fortune, but there was no space for them in _____ Centre.
7. At _____ climactic moment of _____ violin solo, _____ man in _____ audience started to have _____ coughing fit.
8. Currently, _____ city council is divided on its decision whether to bid for _____ Olympics or to invest its energies in _____ clean water policy.
9. In his usual exuberant style, _____ scantily clad chef smashed _____ various condiments and spices on _____ counter in front of _____ hungry and curious studio audience.
10. _____ true happiness is found within us and not in _____ external objects, circumstances, or relationships.

19d Placement of Adjectives

Adjectival modifiers usually come just before or just after what they modify. Articles always, and other determiners almost always, precede the nouns they modify, usually with either no intervening words or only one or two other adjectives:

> Trying to save <u>some</u> money, <u>the</u> manager decided to close <u>his</u> store early.

The wise manager decided not to hire his scatterbrained nephew.

Predicate adjectives (see #12g) almost always follow the subject and linking verb:

The forest is cool and green and full of mushrooms.

Shortly after his operation he again became healthy.

19d

Adjectives serving as *objective complements* usually follow the subject–verb–direct object (see #12i):

I thought the suggestion preposterous.

Most other single-word adjectives, and many compound adjectives, precede the nouns they modify:

The tall, dark, and handsome hero lives on only in romantic fiction.

The weather map shows a cold front moving into the northern prairies.

Phrases like "the map weather" or "a front cold" or "the prairies northern" are unidiomatic in English. (Note that order can determine meaning; for example, a *cold head* is not the same thing as a *head cold*: here, adjective and noun exchange functions as they exchange positions.)

But deviations are possible. Poetry, for example, often uses inversions for purposes of emphasis and rhyme:

Red as a rose is she . . . .

And he called for his fiddlers three.

Such inversions also occur outside of poetry, but don't use them often, for when the unusual ceases to be unusual it loses much of its power. But if you want a certain emphasis or rhythm, you can put a predicate adjective before a noun (see also #17a):

Frustrated I may have been, but I hadn't lost my wits or my passport.

or a regular adjective after a noun:

She did the only thing possible.

There was food enough for everyone.

Compound adjectives and adjectives in phrases are often comfortable after a noun:

> His friend, always faithful and kind, came at once.
>
> Elfrida, radiant and delighted, left the room, secure in her victory.

Relative clauses and various kinds of phrases customarily follow the nouns they modify:

> He is one detective who believes in being thorough.
>
> The president of the company will retire next month.
>
> The time to vote is now!

The only adjectival modifier not generally restricted in its position is the participial phrase (see #21d):

> Having had abundant experience, Kenneth applied for the job.
>
> Kenneth, having had abundant experience, applied for the job.
>
> Kenneth applied for the job, having had abundant experience.

This movability makes the participial phrase a popular way to introduce variety and to control emphasis (see #29e). But be careful: writers sometimes lean too heavily on *ing*-phrases to begin sentences; and such phrases can be awkward or ambiguous, especially in the form of a *dangling modifier:*

> ***dm:*** Having had abundant experience, the job seemed just right for Kenneth. (This sentence implies it is the job, not Kenneth, that has the abundant experience.)

See #36; see also #35, on misplaced modifiers.

▲ 19e Order of Adjectives

Adjectives usually follow an idiomatic order: a determiner (an article, possessive, or demonstrative) comes first, then numbers, then adjectives that express a general description, followed by physical-state adjectives, proper adjectives, and then noun adjuncts before the main noun.

The following chart shows the common order of adjectives:

Determiner	*Number*	*General Description*	*Physical State including age, size, shape, colour, and temperature*	*Proper Adjectives*	*Noun Adjuncts including adjectives ending in "ic(al)" or "al"*	*Main Noun*
the	one	brilliant	young	Canadian	movie	star
their	third	expensive	white		impractical	chesterfield
a		sophisticated	small	Indian		restaurant
your	four	new	square		sushi	dishes
Sue's	two	funny daring		Swedish	theatrical	friends

Adjectives expressing an inherent quality (general description) can be reversed in order. For example, you could write: Sue's two daring, funny Swedish theatrical friends met her. Notice that "daring" and "funny" are separated by commas because they are interchangeable in order. See #38f.

19f Adjectives Functioning as Nouns

If preceded by *the* or a possessive, many words normally thought of as adjectives can function as *nouns*, usually referring to people, and usually in a plural sense (see #19c.6); for example:

the Swedish	the British	the Chinese	the Lebanese
(but Canadians, not *the* Canadians)			
the free	the brave	the poor	the sick and dying
the powerful	the wealthy	the uneducated	the unemployed
the starving	the enslaved	the deceased	the badly injured
the abstract	the metaphysical	the good	the true
the underprivileged		the high and the mighty	
the more fortunate		the big and the small	

20 Adverbs

ad Adverbs are often thought of as especially tricky. This part of speech is sometimes called the "catch-all" category, since any word that doesn't seem to fit elsewhere is usually assumed to be an adverb. Adverbs, therefore, are a little more complicated than adjectives.

20a Kinds and Functions of Adverbs

Whereas adjectives can modify only nouns and pronouns, adverbs can modify *verbs* (and *verbals*; see #21), *adjectives*, other *adverbs*, and *independent clauses* or whole *sentences*. Adverbial modifiers generally answer such questions as *How? When? Where? Why?* and *To what degree?* That is, they indicate such things as *manner* (How?); *time* (When? How often? How long?); *place* and *direction* (Where? In what direction?); *cause*, *result*, and *purpose* (Why? To what effect?); and *degree* (To what degree? To what extent?). They also express affirmation and negation, conditions, concessions, and comparisons. Here are some examples:

> Fully expecting to fail, he slumped disconsolately in his seat and began the examination.

To what degree? *Fully*: the adverb of degree modifies the participial (verbal) phrase *expecting to fail*. How? *Disconsolately*: the adverb of manner modifies the verb *slumped*. Where? *In his seat*: the prepositional phrase functions as an adverb of place modifying the verb *slumped*.

> For many years they lived very happily together in Australia.

How? *Happily* and *together*: the adverbs of manner modify the verb *lived*. To what degree? *Very*: the intensifying adverb modifies the adverb *happily*. Where? *In Australia*: the adverbial prepositional phrase modifies the verb *lived*. How long? *For many years*: the prepositional phrase functions as an adverb of time or duration modifying the verb—or it can be thought of as modifying the whole clause *they lived very happily together in Australia*.

> Fortunately, the cut was not deep.

To what effect? *Fortunately*: a sentence modifier. To what degree? *Not*: the negating adverb modifies the adjective *deep*.

> Because their budget was tight, they eventually decided not to buy a car.

Why? *Because their budget was tight*: the adverbial clause of cause modifies the verb *decided* or, in a way, all the rest of the sentence. When? *Eventually*: the adverb of time modifies the verb *decided*. The negating *not* modifies the infinitive (verbal) *to buy*.

> Last November it seldom snowed.

When? *Last November*: the noun phrase functions as an adverb of time modifying the verb *snowed*. How often? *Seldom*: the adverb of time or frequency modifies the verb *snowed*.

Driving fast is often dangerous.

How? *Fast*: the adverb of manner modifies the gerund (verbal) *driving*. When? *Often*: the adverb of time or frequency modifies the adjective *dangerous*.

If you're tired, I will walk the dog.

The conditional clause modifies the verb (*will walk*).

Although she dislikes the city *intensely*, she agreed to go *there* in order to keep peace *in the family*.

Intensely (degree) modifies the verb *dislikes*. *There* (place) modifies the infinitive *to go*. *Although she dislikes the city intensely* is an adverbial clause of concession. The prepositional phrase *in order to keep peace in the family* is an adverb of purpose modifying the verb *agreed*. The smaller adverbial prepositional phrase *in the family* modifies the infinitive phrase *to keep peace*, answering the question *Where?*

Meredith was better prepared than I was.

The adverb *better* modifies the adjective *prepared*; it and the clause *than I was* expresses comparison or contrast.

Adverbs as condensed clauses

Some single-word adverbs and adverbial phrases, especially sentence modifiers, can be thought of as reduced clauses:

Fortunately [It is fortunate that], the cut was not deep.

When possible [When it is possible], let your writing sit before proofreading it [before you proofread it].

Other kinds of adverbs: relative, interrogative, conjunctive

1. The **relative adverbs** *where* and *when* are used to introduce relative (adjective) clauses (see #14d):

    She returned to the town where she had grown up.

    Adam looked forward to the moment when it would be his turn.

2. The **interrogative adverbs** (*where*, *when*, *why*, and *how*) are used in questions:

    Where are you going? Why? How soon? How will you get there? When will you return?

3. **Conjunctive adverbs** usually join whole clauses or sentences to each other and indicate the nature of the connection:

> It was an important question; therefore they took their time over it.
>
> Only fifteen people showed up. Nevertheless, the promoter didn't let his disappointment show.
>
> The tornado almost flattened the town; however, only Dorothy and her dog were reported missing.

For more on conjunctive adverbs, see #44h.

20b Forms of Adverbs

1. Adverbs ending in *ly*

Many adverbs are formed by adding *ly* to descriptive adjectives, for example *roughly*, *happily*, *fundamentally*, *curiously*. Don't use an adjectival form where an adverbial form is needed:

> She is a careful driver. (adjective modifying *driver*)
>
> She drives carefully. (adverb modifying *drives*)

2. Adverbs not ending in *ly*

Some adverbs don't end in *ly*, for example *ahead*, *almost*, *alone*, *down*, *however*, *long*, *now*, *often*, *quite*, *since*, *soon*, *then*, *there*, *therefore*, *when*, *where*. Others without the *ly* are identical in form to adjectives, for example *far*, *fast*, *little*, *low*, *more*, *much*, *well*:

> He owns a fast car. (adjective)
> He likes to drive fast. (adverb)
>
> They have a low opinion of him. (adjective)
> They flew low over the coast. (adverb)

Well as an adjective means *healthy* (I am quite *well*, thank you) or sometimes *satisfactory*, *right*, or *advisable* (all is *well*; it is *well* you came when you did). When someone asks you about your health, don't say you are *good* (unless you want to imply you are the opposite of *bad* or *evil*). You should say "I am well." Otherwise *well* is an adverb and should be used instead of the frequently misused *good*, which is an adjective. Similarly, *bad* is an adjective, *badly* an adverb. Be careful with these often misused forms:

> She did a good coaching job. The team played well.

> They felt bad for the child, who had played badly in the game. (*Felt* is a linking verb here and requires a predicate adjective—*bad*—as its subjective complement.)

See also **good, bad, badly, well** in the Usage Checklist, #72.

20b

3. Adverbs with short and long forms

Some common adverbs have two forms, one with *ly* and one without. The form without *ly* is identical to the adjective, but the two do not mean the same thing. Check a dictionary if you aren't sure of the meanings of such pairs as these:

even, evenly	fair, fairly	hard, hardly	high, highly
just, justly	late, lately	near, nearly	right, rightly

With some of the others, the short form, although informal, is equivalent, sometimes even preferable, to the longer form; for example:

> Don't talk so loud.
>
> Look deep into my eyes.
>
> Come straight home.

As for the rest, words such as *cheap*, *clear*, *close*, *direct*, *loose*, *quick*, *quiet*, *sharp*, *smooth*, *strong*, *tight*, and *wrong* are often used as adverbs, but in formal contexts you should use the *ly* form.

But if you're writing instructions, avoid the opposite error, one found in many cookbooks. It's right to tell readers to "stir the sauce *slowly*," but wrong to tell them to "slice the onion *thinly*." You wouldn't tell someone to "sand the wood *smoothly*," but *smooth*—that is, until it is smooth; so slice the onion [so that it is] *thin*, and chop the nuts [until they are] *fine*, and so on. In such phrases, the modifier goes with the noun, not the verb.

4. *Real* and *really*, *sure* and *surely*

Don't use the adjectival form where the adverbial is needed:

> Her suggestion was really [not *real*] different.
>
> He surely [not *sure*] was right about the weather.

But the second example may sound odd. Most people would stick with *sure* in a colloquial context and use *certainly* in a formal one. And *really* is seldom needed at all: see **very** in the Usage Checklist, #72.

5. Adjectives ending in *ly*

Some common adjectives end in *ly*, among them *burly, curly, early, friendly, holy, homely, leisurely, likely, lively, lovely, lowly, orderly, silly, surly, ugly*. Adding another *ly* to these inevitably sounds awkward. And though some dictionaries label such adjectives as adverbs as well (he walked *leisurely* toward the door; she behaved *friendly* toward the strangers), that usage also often sounds awkward. You can avoid the problem by adding a few words or rephrasing:

> He walked toward the door in a leisurely manner.
>
> She behaved in a friendly way toward the strangers.
>
> She was friendly toward the strangers.

In a few instances, however, the *ly* adjectives do also serve idiomatically as adverbs; for example:

> He spoke kindly of you.
>
> She rises early.
>
> He exercises daily.
>
> The tour leaves hourly.
>
> Most magazines are published weekly or monthly.

20c Comparison of Adverbs

Like descriptive adjectives, most adverbs that are similarly descriptive can be inflected or supplemented for degree (see #19b). The following are some guidelines on how adverbs are inflected:

- Some short adverbs without *ly* form their comparative and superlative degrees with *er* and *est*; for example:

positive	*comparative*	*superlative*
fast	faster	fastest
hard	harder	hardest
high	higher	highest
late	later	latest
low	lower	lowest
soon	sooner	soonest

Less and *least* also sometimes go with these; for example:

> Students work least hard on the days following an exam.
>
> They still ran fast, but less fast than they had the day before.

(Note, however, that the second example would be more effective if *less fast* were replaced with *slower.*)

- Adverbs of three or more syllables ending in *ly* use *more* and *most*, *less* and *least*; for example:

happily	more happily	most happily
stridently	less stridently	least stridently
disconsolately	more disconsolately	most disconsolately

- Most two-syllable adverbs, whether or not they end in *ly*, also use *more* and *most*, *less* and *least*, though a few can also be inflected with *er* and *est*; for example:

slowly	more slowly	most slowly
grimly	less grimly	least grimly
fully	more fully	most fully
alone	more alone	most alone
kindly	kindlier, more kindly	kindliest, most kindly
often	more often	most often

- Some adverbs form their comparative and superlative degrees irregularly:

badly	worse	worst
well	better	best
much	more	most
little	less	least
far	farther, further	farthest, furthest

- A few adverbs of place use *farther* and *farthest* (or *further* and *furthest*; see **farther**, **further** in the Usage Checklist, #72); for example:

down	farther down	farthest down
north	farther north	farthest north

- As with adjectives, the adverbs *much*, *far*, and *by far* serve as intensifiers in comparisons:

> Bob and Louise live much more comfortably than they used to.

They flew far lower than they should have.

He practises harder by far than anyone else in the orchestra.

20d Placement of Adverbs

1. Adverbs modifying adjectives or other adverbs

An intensifying or qualifying adverb almost always goes just before the adjective or adverb it modifies:

almost always	strongly confident	very hot
only two	most surely	

2. Modifiers of verbs

Whether single words, phrases, or clauses, most modifiers of verbs are more flexible in their position than any other part of speech. Often they can go almost anywhere in a sentence and still function clearly:

Proudly, he pointed to his photo in the paper.

He proudly pointed to his photo in the paper.

He pointed proudly to his photo in the paper.

He pointed to his photo in the paper proudly.

But notice that the emphasis (and therefore the overall effect and meaning) changes slightly. Here is another example; note how much you can control the emphasis:

Because she likes movies, Sue often goes to the cineplex.

Sue, because she likes movies, often goes to the cineplex.

Sue often goes to the cineplex because she likes movies.

And in each version, the adverb *often* could come after *goes* or after *cineplex*.

3. Adverbs of place

The preceding example also illustrates the only major restriction on adverbial modifiers of the verb. A phrase like *to the cineplex*, like a direct object, almost has to follow the verb immediately or with no more than an *often* or other such word intervening. But sometimes an adverb of place or direction can come first if a sentence's usual word order is reversed to emphasize place or direction:

Off to market we shall go.

There she stood, staring out to sea.

Where are you going? (but: Are you going *there*?)

Downward he plummeted, waiting until the last moment to pull the ripcord.

4. Sentence modifiers

Sentence modifiers usually come at the beginning, but they, too, can be placed elsewhere for purposes of emphasis or rhythm:

Fortunately, the groom was able to stand.

The groom, fortunately, was able to stand.

The groom was, fortunately, able to stand.

The groom was able to stand, fortunately.

With longer or more involved sentences, however, a sentence modifier at the end loses much of its force and point, obviously; obviously it works better if placed earlier, as this sentence demonstrates.

See also #44h, on the placement and punctuation of conjunctive adverbs, and #35, on misplaced modifiers.

Exercise 19–20 (1) Recognizing adjectives and adverbs

Underline all the single-word adverbs and circle all the single-word adjectives (including articles) in the following sentences:

1. It was hard work, so he decided to work hard.
2. Although she felt happy in her job, she decided, reluctantly, to express very forcefully her growing concern about office politics.
3. The fireplace screen was too hot to touch.
4. When the hikers were fully rested, they cheerfully resumed the leisurely pace of their climb.
5. Surely the government can find some way to raise the necessary revenues fairly.

Exercise 19–20 (2) Correcting misused adjectives and adverbs

Correct any errors in the use of adjectives and adverbs in the following sentences:

1. She concentrated so hardly that she got a headache.
2. The promotion usually goes to the determinedest and skilfullest employee.
3. The temperature had risen considerable by noon.
4. We enjoyed a real good vacation in the Gatineau Hills.
5. He preferred to wear his denim blue old jacket.
6. Nira isn't writing as good as she usually does.
7. Condos are more costlier this year than they were last.
8. The slowlier you drive, the less fuel you use.
9. He treats his closest friends worstest of all.
10. Which member of the opposition party is the more ambitious politician?

Exercise 19–20 (3) Using adjectival and adverbial modifiers

Enrich and elaborate each of the following basic sentences by adding a variety of adjectival and adverbial modifiers. Use phrases and clauses as well as single words. Try several versions of each, and experiment with placement. (Change tenses of verbs if you wish, and add auxiliaries.) Label the elements you add as adjectives or adverbs.

1. Buskers sing.
2. Politicians lose elections.
3. The goalie was hit by the puck.
4. MP3 players are tools.
5. There are lessons in childhood.

Exercise 19–20 (4) Using adjectives and adverbs

Make a list of ten adjectives (other than those listed or discussed above) that can also serve as or be changed into adverbs. Use each adjective in a sentence; then make each an adverb and use it in a sentence. Then choose two of the words and compose sentences using them in their comparative and superlative forms as both adjectives and adverbs.

21 Verbals: Infinitives, Participles, and Gerunds

Infinitives, participles, and gerunds are called **verbals**, forms that are derived from verbs but that cannot function as main or finite verbs. Verbals are **non-finite** forms, not restricted by person and number as finite verbs are (see #17d, and the note at the end of #17b). They function as other parts of speech yet retain some characteristics of verbs: they can have objects, they can be modified by adverbs, and they can express tense and voice. Verbals often introduce *verbal phrases*, groups of words that themselves function as other parts of speech (see #12p). Verbals enable you to inject much of the strength and liveliness of verbs into your writing even though the words are functioning as adjectives, adverbs, and nouns.

21a Infinitives

We sometimes use a form called the **infinitive** to identify particular verbs. We may speak of "the verb *to be*" or "the verb *to live*." (In this book, however, we usually use just the basic or dictionary form: *be*, *live*; see note in #17b.) An infinitive usually consists of the word *to* (often called "the sign of the infinitive") followed by the basic form: *to be*, *to live*. Infinitives can function as *nouns*, *adjectives*, and *adverbs*.

1. Infinitives as nouns

> To save the wolves was Farley Mowat's primary intention.

The infinitive phrase *To save the wolves* is the subject of the verb *was*. The noun *wolves* is the direct object of the infinitive *To save*.

> She wanted to end the game quickly.

The infinitive phrase *to end the game quickly* is the direct object of the verb *wanted*. The infinitive *to end* is modified by the adverb *quickly* and has the noun *game* as its own direct object.

She wanted me to stop the game.

Here *me to stop the game* is the object of the verb *wanted.*

2. Infinitives as adjectives

His strong desire to be a doctor made him studious.

The infinitive phrase *to be a doctor* modifies the noun *desire.* Since *be* is a linking verb, the infinitive is here followed by the predicate noun *doctor.*

The cappuccino coupons are the ones to save.

The infinitive *to save* modifies the pronoun *ones.*

3. Infinitives as adverbs

She was lucky to have such a friend.

The infinitive phrase *to have such a friend* modifies the predicate adjective *lucky*. The noun phrase *such a friend* is the direct object of the infinitive *to have.*

He went to Niagara-on-the-Lake to experience the Shaw Festival.

The infinitive phrase *to experience the Shaw Festival* is an adverb of purpose modifying the verb *went*; *the Shaw Festival* is the direct object of the infinitive *to experience.*

21b Tense and Voice of Infinitives (see #17g–h, #17o–p)

Infinitives may be either *present* (to indicate a time the same as or later than that of the main verb):

She wants me to go to Egypt with her.

I was pleased to meet you.

or *present perfect* (to indicate a time before that of the main verb); the *to* then goes with the auxiliary *have,* followed by the verb's past participle:

I was lucky to have met the manager before the interview.

Each of these may also take the *progressive* form, using the auxiliaries *be* and *have*:

> I expect to be travelling in Europe this summer.
>
> He was said to have been planning the takeover for months.
>
> I look forward to meeting you.

Infinitives may also be in the *passive voice,* again putting *to* with the appropriate auxiliaries, then adding a past participle:

> The children wanted to be taken to see Cirque du Soleil.
>
> He was thought to have been motivated by sheer ambition.

Proofreading Tip

Verb Idioms That Omit *TO* Before the Infinitive Verb Form
After some verbs, an infinitive can occur without the customary *to*; for example:

> Let sleeping dogs lie.
> We saw the man *jump*.
> I helped her (to) decide.
> It made me cry.
> He felt the house shake.

Make and *let*, verbs used frequently in writing, are of particular note here.

21c Split Infinitives

split Since an infinitive is a unit, separating its parts can weaken it and often results in lack of clarity.

> ***split:*** He wanted to quickly conclude the business of the meeting.
>
> ***split:*** She claimed that it was too difficult to very accurately or confidently solve such a problem in the time allowed.

You can usually avoid or repair such splits by rephrasing or rearranging so the adverbs don't interrupt the infinitive:

> He wanted to conclude the business of the meeting quickly.
>
> She claimed that it was too difficult, in the time allowed, to solve such a problem with any degree of accuracy or confidence.

Occasionally, it is better to split an infinitive than to sound overly formal.

> The space crew vowed to boldly go where no one has gone before.

This split sounds more natural than the formal *boldly to go*, and *boldly* can't be moved to the end of the sentence.

If the infinitive includes a form of *be* or *have* as an auxiliary, an adverb before the last part is less likely to sound out of place:

> The demonstration was thought to have been carefully planned.

> We seem to have finally found the right road.

21d Participles

The **past participle** and **present participle** work with various auxiliaries to form a finite verb's *perfect* and *progressive* tenses (see #17g–h). But without the auxiliaries to indicate *person* and *number*, the participles are non-finite and cannot function as verbs. Instead they function as *adjectives*, modifying nouns and pronouns:

> Beaming happily, Josef received his well-deserved and hard-won diploma.

Present participles always end in *ing*, regular past participles in *ed* or *d*. Irregular past participles end variously: *made*, *mown*, *broken*, etc. (see #17b–c). A regular past participle is identical to the past-tense form of a verb, but you can easily check a given word's function in a sentence. In the example above, the past-tense form *received* clearly has *Josef* as its subject; the past participle *well-deserved*, with no subject, is an adjective modifying *diploma*. More examples:

> Painted houses require more care than brick ones.

The past participle *painted* modifies the noun *houses.*

> Impressed, she recounted the film's more thrilling episodes.

The past participle *impressed* modifies the subject, *she*; the present participle *thrilling* modifies the noun *episodes* and is itself modified by the adverb *more.*

> The subject discussed most often was the message behind the song.

The past participle *discussed* modifies the noun *subject* and is itself modified by the adverbial *most often*.

Suddenly finding himself alone, he became very flustered.

The present participle *finding* introduces the participial phrase *finding himself alone*, which modifies the subject, *he*; *finding*, as a verbal, has *himself* as a direct object and is modified by the adverb *suddenly*. The past participle *flustered* functions as a predicate adjective after the linking verb *became*; it modifies *he* and is itself modified by the adverb *very*.

21e Tense and Voice of Participles (see #17g–h, #17o–p)

The standard present or past participle indicates a time the same as that of the main verb:

Being the tallest, Luzia played centre.

Strictly speaking, a past participle by itself amounts to passive voice:

Worried by what he'd heard, Joe picked up the phone.

With *ing* attached to an auxiliary, participles can also be in the perfect or perfect progressive tense, indicating a time earlier than that of the main verb:

Having painted himself into a corner, George climbed out the window.

Having been painting for over two hours, Leah decided to take a break.

Participles in the present progressive and the perfect tenses can also be in the passive voice:

The subject being discussed was the environment.

Having been warned, she knew better than to accept the offer.

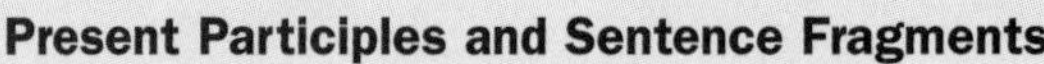

Proofreading Tip

Present Participles and Sentence Fragments
It is particularly important that you know a present participle when you write one. If you use a present participle and think it's functioning as a finite verb, you may well produce a **fragment** (see #12x).

Examples:

The parking lot being paved . . . (fragment)

The meal being prepared for the wedding reception . . . (fragment)

Exercise 21d–e Using participles

Compose sentences using—as single-word adjectives—the present and the past participles of each of the verbs below. Then add auxiliaries and use them as finite verbs.

Example: *stun – stunning – stunned*

She looked *stunning.* It was a *stunning* blow.
The *stunned* boxer hit the mat. He lay there, *stunned.*

He *was stunning* us with his revelations.
He *has stunned* others before us.
One *can be stunned* by a jolt of electricity.

1. interest
2. love
3. trouble
4. grow
5. change
6. ride
7. excite
8. dry
9. bake

21f Gerunds

When the *ing* form of a verb functions as a noun, it is called a **gerund**:

André gave himself a good talking to.

Moving offices can be hard work.

Sylvester has a profound fear of flying.

Careful preparation—brainstorming, organizing, and outlining—helps produce good essays.

The gerund *talking* is a direct object and is itself modified by the adjective *good*. The gerund *Moving* is the subject of the sentence, and has *offices* as a direct object. The gerund *flying* is the object of the preposition *of*. In the final example, the three gerunds constitute an appositive or definition of the subject noun, *preparation* (see #12q).

21g Tense and Voice of Gerunds (see #17g–h and #17-o–p)

As with infinitives and participles, the *perfect* form of a gerund indicates a time earlier than that of the main verb:

My having answered the phone myself may have secured the contract.

And a gerund can be in the passive voice:

> His being praised by the supervisor gave him a big lift.

Be aware, though, that using either the perfect or the passive gerund can produce awkward results:

> The misunderstanding resulted from our not having received the latest information.

> He was proud of her being awarded the gold star for excellence.

Rephrasing such examples to avoid the gerund will produce clearer sentences:

> The misunderstanding resulted because we didn't receive the latest information.

> He was proud of her for receiving the gold star of excellence.

21h Possessives with Gerunds

In formal usage, a noun or a personal pronoun preceding a gerund will usually be in the possessive case:

> His cooking left much to be desired.

> She approved of Bob's cleaning the house.

> Can you explain the engine's not starting?

If the gerund is the subject, as in the first example, the possessive is essential. Otherwise, if you are writing informally, and especially if you want to emphasize the noun or pronoun, you don't need to use the possessive:

> She approved of Bob cleaning the house.

> Can you explain the engine not starting?

Further, in order to avoid awkward-sounding constructions, you usually won't use a possessive form when the noun preceding a gerund is (a) abstract, (b) plural, (c) multiple, or (d) separated from the gerund by modifiers (other than adverbs like *not* or *always* when they sound almost like part of the verbal):

a. He couldn't bear the thought of love striking again.

b. The possibility of the thieves returning to their hide-out was slim.

c. There is a good chance of Alberto and Maria agreeing to your proposal.

d. One might well wonder at a man with such expertise claiming to be ignorant.

Proofreading Tip

The Gerund Followed Immediately by Another Noun

A gerund followed immediately by another noun will sometimes sound awkward or ambiguous unless you interpose *of* or *the* or some similar term to keep the gerund from sounding like a participle:

his building (of) boats	your organizing (of the) material
my practising (the) piano	his revealing (of, the, of the) sources.

21i Verbals in Absolute Phrases

Infinitives and participles (but not gerunds) can function in **absolute phrases** (see #12r):

To say the least, the day was memorable.

Strictly speaking, their actions were not legal.

All things considered, the meeting was a success.

21i

Exercise 21 (1) Recognizing verbals

Identify each verbal in the following sentences as an infinitive, a past or present participle, or a gerund:

1. Coming as he did from the prairies, he found the coastal scenery to be stunning.
2. She wanted to snowboard, and learning was easier than she had expected.
3. Trying to study hard on an empty stomach is usually not very rewarding.
4. The party was certain to last until midnight, permitting everyone to eat and drink too much.
5. Sent as she had been from one office to another, Cindy was tired of running back and forth and up and down; she was now resolved to go straight to the top.

Exercise 21 (2) Using verbals

Here are some exercises to help you become familiar with verbals and recognize some of the things you can do with them.

A. In short sentences, use three infinitives as nouns, adjectives, and, if possible, adverbs (they are less common). Then use each in three longer sentences, again as noun, adjective, and adverb, but expanded into infinitive phrases. You needn't simply build on the short sentences, but you may.

   Example: ***to meditate***

   noun: To meditate is restful. (subject)
   I like to meditate. (object)
   One relaxation technique is to meditate. (predicate noun)

   adjective: I need a place to meditate.

   adverb: She cleared a space in order to meditate.

   noun phrase: To meditate, feet up, before a quietly crackling fire on a cold winter night, staring into the embers, is one of the more relaxing pleasures available to human beings.

B. Compose ten sentences using present and past participles to modify different kinds of nouns—subjects, direct objects, indirect objects, objects of prepositions, predicate nouns, objective complements, appositives.

Exercise 21 (3) Reducing clauses to infinitive phrases

By reducing clauses to phrases, you can often get rid of unnecessary heaviness and wordiness. Practise by reducing each italicized clause in the following sentences to an infinitive phrase that conveys basically the same meaning. Change or rearrange words as necessary.

Example: We wondered *what we should do next.*
We wondered *what to do next.*

1. Remember *that you should be at the computer lab by 3:30.*
2. The quarterback's problem was *that he had to decide* what play *he should use next.*
3. My charismatic cousin gestured *that we should follow him into the restaurant.*
4. The time *that you should worry about* is the hour before the race.
5. After her motorbike came to a grinding halt, Abigail pondered *what her next move would be.*

Exercise 21 (4) Reducing clauses

This time reduce each italicized clause to the kind of phrase specified in parentheses after each sentence.

Example: *As she changed her mind,* she suddenly felt much better. (present participial)
Changing her mind, she suddenly felt much better.

1. Sometimes the best part of a vacation is *when you plan it.* (gerund)
2. Earning the respect of children is something *that you can be proud of.* (infinitive)
3. *Because they felt foolish*, they decided to leave early. (present participial)
4. *The fact that she had won the contest* came as something of a shock to her. (gerund)
5. The bank manager *who wore the colourful wig* started doing the samba. (present participial)

Exercise 21 (5) Using absolute phrases

Absolute phrases are useful for expressing cause–effect relationships or for providing vivid descriptive details. Since they considerably heighten style, don't use them often. But do use them sometimes. For practice, combine each of the following pairs of sentences by reducing one of them (usually the first) to an absolute phrase consisting of a noun and a participle (along with any modifiers). Remember that if the participle is *being*, it can sometimes be omitted (see #12r).

Example: Everyone present agreed. The motion passed unanimously.
Everyone present agreeing, the motion passed unanimously.

Dinner was over and the dishes were washed. They sat down to watch a movie on television.
Dinner (being) over and the dishes (being) washed, they sat down to watch a movie on television.

1. The toddler was very sleepy. Her father carried her upstairs to her bedroom.
2. His nose was running and his eyes were watering. He sat down, hoping he had chopped enough onions.
3. The lights flickered, and the computer groaned. The 100-page report disappeared from the screen.
4. The day was breezy yet warm. They decided to take their golden retriever for a walk in Hyde Park.
5. Extra money was hard to come by. He was forced to curtail his marathon shopping trips to New York City.

22 Prepositions

Prepositions are structure words or function words (see #12-l); they do not change their form. A preposition is part of a prepositional phrase, and it usually precedes the rest of the phrase, which includes a noun or pronoun as the object of the preposition:

This is a book about flirting.

She sent an e-mail to her spouse.

Make a question of the preposition and ask *what* or *whom* and the answer will always be the object: *About* what? Flirting. *To* whom? Her spouse.

22a Functions of Prepositions and Prepositional Phrases

A preposition *links* its object to some other word in the sentence; the prepositional phrase then functions as either an *adjectival* or an *adverbial* modifier:

> He laid the camera on the table.

Here, *on* links *table* to the verb *laid*; the phrase *on the table* therefore functions as an adverb describing *where* the camera was laid.

> It was a time for celebration.

Here, *for* links *celebration* to the noun *time*; the phrase therefore functions as an adjective indicating *what kind of* time.

22b Placement of Prepositions

Usually, like articles, prepositions signal that a noun or pronoun soon follows. But prepositions can also come at the ends of clauses or sentences, for example in a question, for emphasis, or to avoid stiffness:

> Which backpack do you want to look at?
>
> Which friend are you buying the backpack for?
>
> She is the one I want to give the backpack to.
>
> They had several issues to contend with.
>
> This is the restaurant I was telling you about.
>
> The problem he was dealing with seemed insurmountable.

Some would prefer "with which he was dealing," especially in a formal context. But it isn't wrong to end a sentence or clause with a preposition, in spite of what many people have been taught; just don't do it so often that it calls attention to itself. Remember that Sir Winston Churchill is supposed to have said that repeated use of the preposition in this way was the sort of usage "up with which I will not put."

22c

22c Common Prepositions

Most prepositions indicate a spatial or temporal relation, or such things as purpose, concession, comparison, manner, and agency. Here is a list of common prepositions; note that several consist of more than one word:

about	beneath	in front of	past
above	beside	in order to	regarding
according to	besides	in place of	regardless of
across	between	in relation to	round
across from	beyond	inside	since
after	but	in spite of	such as
against	by	into	through
ahead of	by way of	like	throughout
along	concerning	near	till
alongside	considering	next to	to
among	contrary to	notwithstanding	toward(s)
apart from	despite	of	under
around	down	off	underneath
as	during	on	unlike
as for	except	on account of	until
at	except for	onto	up
away from	excepting	on top of	upon
because of	for	opposite	with
before	from	out	within
behind	in	outside	without
below	in addition to	over	

A learner's dictionary will be extremely helpful in guiding you in the use of prepositions.

Exercise 22a–c (1) Recognizing prepositional phrases

Identify each prepositional phrase in the following sentences and note whether each is adjectival or adverbial:

1. Josh went into town to buy some back bacon for his breakfast.
2. There stood the famous pianist of about thirty, in the hot sunshine, wearing a heavy jacket with the collar turned up.
3. In the morning the president called her assistant on the telephone and told her to come to the office without delay.
4. The bulk of the presents was sent ahead in trunks.
5. The Siamese cat looked under the table for the ball of yarn that had fallen from the chair.

Exercise 22a–c (2) Using prepositional phrases

Prepositional phrases are essential components of writing, but they can be overdone. These exercises will give you practice both in using them and in avoiding their overuse.

A. REDUCING CLAUSES TO PREPOSITIONAL PHRASES
You'll use prepositional phrases without even thinking about them; but sometimes you should consciously try to tighten and lighten your style by reducing some clauses to prepositional phrases. Reduce the italicized clauses in the following sentences to prepositional phrases. Revise in other ways as well if you wish, but don't change the essential meaning.

Example: The cold front *that is over the coast* will move inland overnight.
The cold front *over the coast* will move inland overnight.

1. *If you have enough stamina*, you can take part in the triathlon.
2. *Because she was so confident*, she entered every race.
3. Students *who have part-time jobs* must budget their time carefully.
4. We need advice *that only a grandmother can give us*.
5. The time *when you should eat* is three hours before you go to sleep.

B. REDUCING CLAUSES TO PREPOSITIONAL PHRASES USING GERUNDS
Gerunds (see #21f–g) are often used as objects of prepositions. Convert the italicized clauses in the following sentences to prepositional phrases with gerunds.

Example: Before she submitted the essay, she proofread it carefully.
Before submitting the essay, she proofread it carefully.

1. *When I had run* only half a block, I felt exhausted.
2. *Although Petra trained rigorously*, she didn't get past the preliminaries.
3. You can't hope to understand *unless you attend all the classes*.
4. *They checked the luggage carefully* and found nothing but a pair of toe nail clippers.
5. He deserves some credit *because he tried so hard*.

22c

Exercise 22a–c (2) Using prepositional phrases – *continued*

C. GETTING RID OF EXCESSIVE PREPOSITIONAL PHRASES
When prepositional phrases come in bunches, they can contribute to wordiness. Practise revising to get rid of clutter: cut the number of prepositional phrases in each of the following sentences (shown in parentheses) at least in half.

Example: Some of the ministers in the Cabinet are in danger of losing their appointments because of the poor quality of their relations with the media and deficits in their department budgets. (8)
Because they have poor media relations and departmental budget deficits, some Cabinet ministers may lose their appointments. (reduced to zero)

1. Sarah got to the top of the mountain first by using several trails unknown to her competitors in the race, which was held during the celebration of the centennial of the province's entry into confederation. (9)
2. The feeling of most of the people at the meeting was that the committee chair spoke in strident tones for too long about things about which he knew little. (7)
3. The irritated ghost at the top of the stairs of the old house shouted at me to get away from his door in a hurry. (6)
4. One of the most respected of modern historians has some odd ideas about the beginning of the war between European nations that broke out, with such devastating consequences, in early August of 1914. (8)
5. Economists' predictions about the rise and fall of interest rates seem to be accurate for the most part, but only within the limits of a period of about three or four weeks, at most, and even at that you have to take them with a grain of salt. (10)

▲ 22d Two-part Verbs; Verb Idioms

English has many two-part and even three-part verbs consisting of a simple verb in combination with another word or words—for example *cool off, act up, blow up, find out, hold up, carry on, get on with, stick up for.* You may think of the added words as prepositions, adverbs, or some sort of "particle." Indeed, sometimes it is difficult to say whether a word like *down* in *sit down* is functioning as part of the verb or as an adverb describing how one can sit; but the *down* and *up* in "sit down to a good meal" and "sit up in your chair" seem more like parts of the verbs than, say, the preposition *at* in "He sat at his desk." Usually you can sense a difference in sound: in "He *took over* the operation" both parts are stressed when said aloud, whereas in "He *took* over three hours to get here" only the *took* is stressed; *over* functions separately. Often, too, the parts of a verb can be separated and still mean the same, whereas the verb and preposition or adverb cannot:

> The children were won over by the actor's exuberance.
> The actor's exuberance won the children over.
> **Compare:** He won over his nearest opponent by three points.

> The construction crew blew up the remains of the old factory.
> The construction crew blew the remains of the old factory up.
> **Compare:** The wind blew up the chimney.

Some two-part verbs cannot be separated, for example *see to*, *look after*, *run across*, *sit up*, *turn in* (as in *go to sleep*). Some simple verbs can take two or more different words to form new verbs; for example:

> try out – try on
> think out – think up
> fill up – fill in – fill out
> fall out – fall in – fall off

Some verbs can use several different words to form idiomatic expressions, as you will discover by looking them up in a learner's dictionary:

> let alone – let down – let go – let loose – let off – let on – let up
> turn up – turn down – turn in – turn loose – turn off – turn on – turn out – turn over – turn to – turn up
> bring about – bring around – bring down – bring forth – bring forward – bring in – bring off – bring on – bring out – bring over – bring to – bring up

See #62r on the spelling of two-part verbs.

22e Using Two-part Verbs: Informality and Formality

By consciously using or avoiding these verbs in a piece of writing, you can help control tone. Most of these verbs are standard and idiomatic, but some are informal or colloquial or even slangy, for example *let up*, *mess up*, *shake up*, *trip up* (and see #64). Even the standard ones are often relatively informal; that is, they have more formal equivalents; for example:

informal	*formal*
give away	bestow; reveal, betray
give back	return
give in	yield, concede
give off	discharge, emit
give out	emit; distribute; become exhausted
give over	relinquish, abandon; cease
give up	despair; stop, renounce; surrender, cede
give way	withdraw, retreat; make room for; collapse

If you choose *buy* as more appropriate to your context than *purchase*, you'll probably also want to use some two-part verbs rather than their more formal, often Latinate, equivalents; for example you'd probably say *buy up* rather than *acquire*. But if you're writing a strictly formal piece, you may want to avoid the informal terms, or limit yourself to just a couple for contrast or variety.

Exercise 22d–e Using two-part verbs

A. Draw up a list of two-part (and three-part) verbs and their more formal equivalents. Draw on those listed above, but add as many more as you can think of. Take common verbs like *come, go, put, take, get,* and *set,* and try adding on such common prepositions and adverbs as *about, at, away, back, down, in, off, out, over, through, to, up, upon,* and *with.* Consult your dictionary, where these are often treated separately under the entry for the basic verb. If you don't find many listed, look in a bigger dictionary, or a learner's dictionary, such as the *Oxford Advanced Learner's Dictionary.*

B. Compose several sentences—or, better yet, compose two or three separate paragraphs on different kinds of topics, using as many verbs from your list as you can squeeze in. Read them over, aloud, to see how they sound.

C. Rewrite your sentences (or paragraphs), wherever possible substituting more formal verbs for your originals. Now how do they sound?

23 Conjunctions

Conjunctions are another kind of structure word or function word (see #12-l). As their name indicates, conjunctions are words that "join together." There are three kinds of conjunctions: *coordinating, correlative,* and *subordinating.*

23a Coordinating Conjunctions

There are only seven **coordinating conjunctions**, so they are easy to remember:

and but for nor or so yet

When you use a coordinating conjunction, choose the appropriate one. *And* indicates addition, *nor* indicates negative addition (equivalent to *also not*), *but* and *yet* indicate contrast or opposition, *or* indicates choice, *for* indicates cause or reason, and *so* indicates effect or result. (See also #41, on **faulty coordination**.)

Bear in mind that some coordinating conjunctions can also be other parts of speech: *yet* can be an adverb (It's not *yet* ten o'clock); *so* can be an adverb (It was *so* dark that . . .), an adjective (Is that *so*?), a demonstrative pronoun (I liked him, and I told him *so*), and an interjection (*So!*); *for* is also a common preposition (*for* a while, *for* me); and *but* can be a preposition, meaning *except* (all *but* two).

Coordinating conjunctions have three main functions, which are discussed below.

1. Joining words, phrases, and subordinate clauses

And, *but*, *or*, and *yet* join coordinate elements within sentences. The elements joined are usually of equal importance and of similar grammatical structure and function. When joined, they are sometimes called compounds of various kinds (see #12z.1). Here are examples of how various kinds of sentence elements may be compounded:

> I saw Jean and Ralph. (two direct objects)
>
> Jean and Ralph saw me. (two subjects)
>
> They whooped and hollered. (two verbs)
>
> The gnome was short, fat, and melancholic. (three predicate adjectives)
>
> He ate fast and noisily. (two adverbs)
>
> The bird flew in the door and out the window. (two adverbial prepositional phrases)
>
> Tired but determined, the hiker plodded on. (two past participles)
>
> The lovely children cooked the dinner and washed the dishes. (two verbs with direct objects)
>
> People who invest wisely and who spend carefully often have boring lives. (two adjective clauses)
>
> I travel when I have the time and when I have money. (two adverbial clauses)
>
> The career coach told him what he should wear and how he should speak. (two noun clauses)

Obviously the elements being joined won't always have identical structures, but don't disappoint readers' natural expectations that compound elements will be parallel. For example it would be weaker to write the last example—*The career coach told him what he should wear and how he should speak*—with one direct object as a clause and the other as an infinitive phrase (see #40, on faulty parallelism):

23a

> The career coach told him what he should wear and how to speak.

When three or more elements are compounded, the conjunction usually appears only between the last two, though *and* and *or* can appear throughout for purposes of rhythm or emphasis:

> There was a tug-of-war and a sack race and an egg race and a three-legged race and . . . well, there was just about any kind of game anyone could want at a picnic.

And occasionally *and* can be omitted entirely also for emphasis (see also #49d):

> There were flowers galore—fuschias, snap dragons, jonquils, dahlias, azaleas, tulips, roses, lilacs, camellias—more kinds of flowers than I wanted to see on any one day.

2. Joining independent clauses

All seven coordinating conjunctions can join independent clauses to make compound (or compound-complex) sentences (see #12z). The clauses will be grammatically equivalent, since they are independent; but they needn't be grammatically parallel or even of similar length, though they often are both, for parallelism is a strong stylistic force. Here are some examples:

> The players fought, the umpires shouted, and the fans booed.

> The kestrel flew higher and higher, in ever-wider circles, and soon it was but a speck in the sky overhead.

> Jean saw me, but Ralph didn't.

> I won't do it, nor will she. (With *nor* there must be some sort of negative in the first clause. Note that after *nor* the normal subject–verb order is reversed.)

> There was no way to avoid it, so I decided to get as much out of the experience as I could.

Proofreading Tip

On Using the Conjunction *SO*
The conjunction *so* is informal; in formal writing, you can almost always indicate cause-effect relations with a *because* or *since* clause instead:

> Because there was no way to avoid it, I decided to get as much out of the experience as I could.

And so, however, is acceptable, but don't overuse it because it is a weak transition:

> We overslept, and so we missed the keynote address.

3. Joining sentences

In spite of what many of us have been taught, it isn't wrong to begin a sentence with *And* or *But*, or for that matter any of the other coordinating conjunctions. Be advised, however, that *For*, since it is so similar in meaning to *because*, often sounds strange at the start of a sentence, as if introducing a fragmentary subordinate clause (see #23c). Another coordinating conjunction, *And so*, often sounds too colloquial. But the rest, especially *And* and *But*, make good openers—as long as you don't overuse them. An opening *But* or *Yet* can nicely emphasize a contrast or other turn of thought (as in the preceding sentence). An opening *And* can also be emphatic:

> He told the employees of the company he was sorry.
> And he meant it.

Both *And* and *But* as sentence openers contribute to paragraph coherence (see #5d). And, especially in a narrative, a succession of opening *Ands* can impart a feeling of rapid pace, even breathless excitement. Used too often, they can become tedious, but used carefully and when they feel natural, they can be effective.

For punctuation with coordinating conjunctions, see chapter V, especially #44a–c and #55d.

Exercise 23a Using coordinating conjunctions

Put an appropriate coordinating conjunction in each blank. If more than one is possible, indicate that.

1. Uma was late for the meeting, _____ she had a good excuse.
2. There is only one solution to this problem, _____ I know what it is.
3. No one likes noise pollution, _____ some people insist that we have to live with it.
4. Her brother is not cynical, _____ is he insensitive.
5. We were puzzled by the professor's humorous comments, _____ we had expected her to speak seriously on the subject.
6. The tuba solo came as a surprise, _____ Tomas and Uli were expecting an organ concerto.

23b Correlative Conjunctions

Correlative conjunctions come in pairs. They *correlate* ("relate together") two parallel parts of a sentence. The following are the principal ones:

either . . . or	neither . . . nor
whether . . . or	both . . . and
not . . . but	not only . . . but also

Correlative conjunctions enable you to write sentences containing forcefully balanced elements, but don't overdo them. They are also more at home in formal than in informal writing. Some examples:

Either Rodney or Elliott is going to drive.

She accepted neither the first nor the second job offer.

Whether by accident or by design, the number turned out to be exactly right.

Both the administration and the student body are pleased with the new plan.

She not only plays well but also sings well.

Not only does she play well, but she also sings well.

Notice, in the last two examples, how *also* or its equivalent can be moved away from the *but*. And in the last example, note how *does* is needed as an auxiliary because the clause is in the present tense. Except for these variations, make what follows one term exactly parallel to what follows the other: *by accident* || *by design*; *the first* || *the second*; *plays well* || *sings well*. (See also #40, on faulty parallelism.)

Further, with the *not only . . . but also* pair, you should usually make the *also* (or some equivalent) explicit. Its omission results in a feeling of incompleteness:

incomplete: He was not only smart, but charming.
complete: He was not only smart, but also charming.
complete: He was not only smart, but charming as well.

To ensure that you use this correlative pairing effectively, keep in mind the following:

1. For clauses containing compound verbs (one or more auxiliary verbs attached to a main verb), place *not only* at the beginning of the clause and then place the first auxiliary verb before the subject. Then, place *but* before the subject of the second clause and *also* after the auxiliary verb.

   He has been a great star and he has served his fans well.

   Not only *has* he been a great star, **but** he has **also** served his fans well.

2. For sentences in the simple present or simple past tenses (other than those in which the main verb is *to be*), you must add the appropriate form of *do/does/did* before the subject of the *not only* clause when *not only* appears at the beginning of the clause.

   She looks rested and she looks happy.
   Not only *does* she look rested, **but** she **also** looks happy.

   She looked rested and she looked happy.
   Not only *did* she look rested, **but** she **also** looked happy.

   She is rested and she is happy.
   Not only *is* she rested, **but** she is **also** happy.

3. When *not only* appears inside the clause, you do not have to reverse the order of the auxiliary verb and subject, nor do you have to add *do/does/did*.

   She has worked hard at her job and at her hobbies.

   She has worked hard **not only** at her job **but also** at her hobbies.

See #18c for *agreement* of verbs with subjects joined by some of the correlatives.

23c Subordinating Conjunctions

A **subordinating conjunction** introduces a *subordinate* (or *dependent*) clause and links it to the *independent* (or *main* or *principal*) clause to which it is grammatically related:

> She writes because she has something to say.

The subordinating conjunction *because* introduces the adverbial clause *because she has something to say* and links it to the independent clause whose verb it modifies. The *because*-clause is *subordinate* because it cannot stand by itself: by itself it would be a *fragment* (see #12x). Note that a subordinate clause can also come first:

> Because she has something to say, she writes articles for magazines.

Even though *Because* does not occur between the two unequal clauses, it still links them grammatically.

> That Raj will win the prize is a foregone conclusion.

Here *That* introduces the noun clause *That Raj will win the prize*, which functions as the subject of the sentence. Note that whereas a coordinating conjunction is like a spot of glue between two structures and not a part of either, a subordinating conjunction is an integral part of its clause. In the following sentence, for example, the subordinating conjunction *whenever* is a part of the adverbial clause that modifies the imperative verb *Leave*:

> Leave whenever you feel tired.

Here is a list of the principal subordinating conjunctions:

after	if	that	where(ever)
although	if only	though	whereas
as	in case	till	whether
as though	lest	unless	which
because	once	until	while
before	rather than	what	who
even though	since	whatever	why
ever since	than	when(ever)	

There are also many terms consisting of two or more words ending in *as*, *if*, and *that* that serve as subordinating conjunctions, including *inasmuch as*, *insofar as*, *as long as*, *as soon as*, *as far as*, *as if*, *even if*, *only if*, *but that*, *except that*, *now that*, *in that*, *provided that*, *in order that*.

Some subordinating conjunctions can also function as adverbs, prepositions, and relative pronouns. But don't worry about parts of speech at this point. Think of all these terms as *subordinators*, including the relative pronouns and relative adverbs (*who*, *which*, *that*, *when*, *where*) that introduce adjective clauses. If you understand their *subordinating* function, you will understand the syntax of complex and compound-complex sentences (see #12z) and will be able to avoid *fragments* (see #12x).

Exercise 23c (1) Recognizing subordinate clauses

Identify the subordinate clauses in the following passage and indicate how each is functioning: as adjective, adverb, or noun. (Remember that sometimes relative pronouns are omitted; see #14d and #48a.) What words do the adjectival and adverbial clauses modify? How does each noun clause function? (You might begin by identifying the *independent* clauses.)

> Once upon a time, when he was only eight, Selwyn decided he wanted to be a marine biologist. He especially liked to play in the numerous tide pools found outside the Peggy's Cove cabin where his family stayed every summer. As he grew older, he discovered that in order to become a marine biologist, one had to study many different and difficult subjects that seemed far removed from ocean life. Whenever he worked on his math, statistics, or computer problems in stuffy rooms, he kept longing to walk on the beach. That he became a successful field scientist and expert on the microorganisms found in tide pools is, therefore, not surprising. What most people don't know is that when Selwyn became a full professor, he didn't need to worry about doing analysis anymore because he had graduate students who enjoyed working with numbers and who derived satisfaction from developing new approaches to data analysis. So while they crunched numbers, Selwyn puttered around happily ever after on shorelines all over the world looking deep into tide pools.

23c

Exercise 23c (2) Writing subordinate clauses

Combine each of the following pairs of simple sentences into a single complex sentence by subordinating one clause and attaching it to the other with one of the subordinators listed on pages 208 and 209. You may want to change, delete, or add some words, reverse the clauses, or otherwise rearrange words. Experiment with different subordinators.

Example: The technological revolution has affected many business and professional people. Its largest impact may prove to have been on the young.
(Though, Although) the technological revolution has affected many business and professional people, its . . .
The technological revolution has affected many business and professional people, (though, even though) its . . .

1. The art gallery won't open until next week. The leak in the roof hasn't been repaired yet.
2. Canada's gun laws are still stricter than those in the United States. We should defend this.
3. Some students may not have paid all their fees. They would not yet be considered officially registered.
4. First you should master the simple sentence. Then you can work on rhyming couplets.
5. The children ate most of their Halloween candy. They are bouncing off the walls.

24 Interjections

An **interjection** is a word or group of words *interjected* or dropped into a sentence in order to express emotion. Strictly speaking, interjections have no grammatical function; they are simply thrust into sentences and play no part in their syntax, though sometimes they act like sentence modifiers. They are often used in dialogue and are not that common in academic writing.

But—good heavens!—what did you expect?

Gosh, what fun!

It was, well, a bit of a disappointment.

A mild interjection is usually set off with commas. A strong interjection is sometimes set off with dashes and is often accompanied by an exclamation point (see #50b and #53c). An interjection may also be a minor sentence by itself (see #12w):

> Ouch! That hurt!
>
> Well. So much for the warm up. Now comes real aerobic exercise.
>
> Thanks John! Your advice on the project was most helpful.

Review Exercises Chapter III
Recognizing and using parts of speech

A. RECOGNIZING PARTS OF SPEECH

To test yourself, see if you can identify the part of speech of each word in the following sentences. Can you say how each is functioning grammatically? What kinds of sentences are they?

1. The skyline of modern Toronto provides a striking example of what modern architecture can do to distinguish a major city.
2. Waiter, there's a fly doing the back crawl in my soup!
3. Well, to tell the truth, I just did not have the necessary patience.
4. Why should anyone be unhappy about paying a fair tax?
5. Neither the captain nor the crew could be blamed for the terribly costly ferry accident.
6. The elevator business has been said to have its ups and downs.
7. Don, please put back the chocolate cake.
8. While abroad, I learned to make do with only three large suitcases and one full-time chauffeur.
9. In a few seconds, the computer told us much more than we needed to know.
10. Help!

B. USING DIFFERENT PARTS OF SPEECH

For fun, write some sentences using the following words as different parts of speech—as many different ones as you can. Each is good for at least two different parts of speech.

shed	plant	still	wrong	round	cross
best	before	train	last	set	near
left	study	cover	fine	rose	down

Writing Effective Sentences

IV

Chapter IV deals with the way the various elements work together in sentences. It is designed to enable you to understand how sentences work and how to avoid common problems. If you have difficulty with the terms and concepts discussed in this chapter, you may need to review previous chapters on sentences and parts of speech.

25–26 Basic Sentence Elements and Their Modifiers

25 Subject, Verb, Object, Complement

Consider again the bare bones of a sentence. The two essential elements are a *subject* and a *verb* (see #12a).

25a Subject

The subject is what is talked about. It is the word or phrase answering the question *who?* or *what?* before the verb. More precisely, it is the source of the action indicated by the verb, or the person or thing experiencing or possessing the state of being or the condition indicated by the verb and its complement:

> Osman watched the performance. (*Who* watched? Osman. Osman is the source of the action of watching.)
>
> We are happy about the outcome. (*Who* is happy? We are. We are experiencing the state of being happy.)
>
> Bernice is a physician. (*Who* is a physician? Bernice. Bernice is the person in the state or condition of being a physician.)
>
> Recycling is vital. (*What* is vital? Recycling. Recycling possesses the condition of being vital.)

The subject of a sentence will ordinarily be one of the following: a basic noun (see #13), a pronoun (see #14), a gerund or gerund phrase (see #21f), an infinitive or infinitive phrase (see #21a), or a noun clause (see #12-o):

> British Columbia joined Confederation on 20 July 1871. (noun)
>
> He is a Manitoba historian. (pronoun)
>
> Skydiving is a risky activity. (gerund)
>
> Visiting the website is part of our daily routine. (gerund phrase)

To travel is to enjoy life. (infinitive)

To order tofu is to make a healthy choice. (infinitive phrase)

That British Columbia joined Canada because of the railway is common knowledge. (noun clause)

Rarely, a prepositional phrase serves as subject; see #22a.

25b Finite Verb

The **finite verb** is the focal point of the clause or the sentence. It indicates both the nature and the time of the action (see #17a):

The prime minister will respond during Question Period. (action: responding; time: the future)

Lewis Carroll invented the adventures of Alice for a child named Alice Liddell. (action: inventing; time: past)

Cape Breton's fiddlers have a distinctive musical style. (action: having, possessing; time: present)

Syntax is word order. (state of being: being something; time: present)

25c Direct Object

If a verb is *transitive* (see #17a), it will have a **direct object** to complete the pattern (see #12d). Like the subject, the direct object may be a noun, a pronoun, a gerund or gerund phrase, an infinitive or infinitive phrase, or a noun clause:

The CD features Bruce Cockburn. (noun)

The increase in gasoline taxes worried us. (pronoun)

Our economy needs farming. (gerund)

He enjoys writing reports. (gerund phrase)

We wanted to participate. (infinitive)

You need to define your terms. (infinitive phrase)

The reporter revealed that his source feared retaliation. (noun clause)

Along with a direct object, there may also be an indirect object or an objective complement (see #12f, #12i, and #12j).

We gave you a blank cheque. [*you*: indirect object; *cheque*: direct object]

She judged the situation untenable. [*situation*: direct object; *untenable*: objective complement]

25d Subjective Complement

Similarly, a *linking verb* (see #17a) typically requires a **subjective complement** to complete the pattern. This complement will usually be either a *predicate noun* or a *predicate adjective* (see #12g and #12h). A predicate noun may be a noun or a pronoun, or (especially after *be*) a gerund or gerund phrase, an infinitive or infinitive phrase, or a noun clause:

We are friends. (noun)

Was he the one? (pronoun)

His passion is travelling. (gerund)

His passion is travelling the back country. (gerund phrase)

My first impulse was to run. (infinitive)

Our next challenge will be to take action. (infinitive phrase)

She remains what she has long been: a loyal friend. (noun clause)

A predicate adjective will ordinarily be a descriptive adjective, a participle, or an idiomatic prepositional phrase:

His music has become joyful. (descriptive adjective)

The novel's plot is intriguing. (present participle)

They seem dedicated. (past participle)

The government is out of ideas. (prepositional phrase)

The linking verb *be* (and sometimes others) can also be followed by an adverbial word or phrase (I am *here*; he is *in his office*).

These elements—**subject**, **finite verb**, and **object** or **complement**—are the core elements of major sentences. They are closely linked in the ways indicated above, with the verb as the focal and uniting element. (For a discussion of the *order* in which these elements occur, see #12s–u.)

26 Modifiers

Modifiers add to the core grammatical elements listed above. They limit or describe other elements so as to modify—that is, to change—a listener's or reader's idea of them. The two principal kinds of modifiers are *adjectives* (see #19) and *adverbs* (see #20). Also useful, but less frequent, are *appositives* (see #12q) and *absolute phrases* (see #12r and #21i). An adjectival or adverbial modifier may even be part of the core of a sentence if it completes the predicate after a linking verb (Recycling is *vital*; Peter is *home*). An adverb may also be essential if it modifies an intransitive verb that would otherwise seem incomplete (Peter lives *in a condominium*). But generally modifiers do their work by adding to—enriching—a central core of thought.

26a

26a Adjectival Modifiers (see #19–19b, #19e–f)

Adjectival modifiers modify nouns, pronouns, and phrases or clauses functioning as nouns. They commonly answer the questions *which? what kind of? how many?* and *how much?* An adjectival modifier may be a single-word adjective, a series of adjectives, a participle or participial phrase, an infinitive or infinitive phrase, a prepositional phrase, or a relative clause:

> Early settlers of western Canada encountered sudden floods, prolonged droughts, and early frosts. (single words modifying nouns immediately following)

> We are skeptical. (predicate adjective modifying the pronoun *We*)

> That the author opposes globalization is evident in his first paragraph. (predicate adjective modifying the noun clause *That the author criticizes globalization*)

> Four ambitious young reporters are competing to work on this front-page story. (series modifying *reporters*)

> The train station is filled with commuters and tourists. (noun functioning as adjective, modifying *station*)

> Grinning, he replied to her e-mail message. (present participle modifying *he*)

> Brimming with confidence, they began their performance. (present participial phrase modifying *they*)

> They continued the climb toward the summit, undaunted. (past participle modifying *they*)

Gisele applied for the position, having been encouraged to do so by her adviser. (participial phrase, perfect tense, passive voice, modifying *Gisele*)

They prepared a meal to remember. (infinitive modifying *meal*)

Our tendency to favour jazz is evident in our CD collection. (infinitive phrase modifying *tendency*)

The report on the evening news focused on forest fires in northern British Columbia. (prepositional phrase modifying *report*)

The soccer team, which was travelling to a tournament in Mexico, filed slowly through airport security. (relative clause modifying *team*)

26b Adverbial Modifiers (see #20–20d)

Adverbial modifiers modify verbs, adjectives, other adverbs, and whole clauses or sentences. They commonly answer the questions *how? when? where?* and *to what degree?* An adverbial modifier may be a single word, a series, an infinitive or infinitive phrase, a prepositional phrase, or an adverbial clause:

Mix the chemicals thoroughly. (single word modifying the verb *mix*)

As new parents, we are completely happy. (single word modifying the adjective *happy*)

They planned their future together quite enthusiastically. (single word modifying the adverb *enthusiastically*)

Apparently, the stem cell experiment is being delayed. (single word modifying the rest of the sentence)

He loves her truly, madly, deeply. (series modifying the verb *loves*)

To succeed, you must work well with others. (infinitive modifying the verb *must work*)

She was lucky to have been selected for the exchange program. (infinitive phrase modifying the predicate adjective *lucky*)

The passenger ship arrived at the port. (prepositional phrase modifying the verb *arrived*)

We disagreed because we were taking different theoretical approaches to the text. (clause modifying the verb *disagreed*)

The election results trickled in slowly because the ballots were being counted by hand. (clause modifying the adverb *slowly*, or the whole preceding clause, *The election results trickled in slowly*.)

Shut off your computer when you leave on vacation. (clause modifying the preceding independent clause)

26c Overlapping Modifiers

The preceding examples are meant to illustrate each kind of adjectival and adverbial modifier separately, in tidy isolation from the other kinds. And such sentences are not uncommon, for relative simplicity of sentence structure can be a stylistic strength. But many sentences are more complicated, largely because modifiers overlap in them. Modifiers occur as parts of other modifiers: single-word modifiers occur as parts of phrases and clauses, phrases occur as parts of other phrases and as parts of clauses, and subordinate clauses occur as parts of phrases and as parts of other clauses. Here are examples illustrating some of the possible structural variety. (You may want to check sections #12c–k in order to match these sentences and their clauses with the various patterns they include.)

They walked briskly toward the waiting car.
briskly – adverb modifying *walked*
toward the waiting car – adverbial prepositional phrase modifying *walked*
waiting – participial adjective modifying *car*

He purchased a few of the off-the-rack suits.
of the off-the-rack suits – adjectival prepositional phrase modifying a *few*
off-the-rack – hyphenated prepositional phrase, adjective modifying *suits*

Hoping to learn to perform brilliantly, the cast rehearsed until dawn.
Hoping to learn to perform brilliantly – participial phrase modifying *cast*
to learn to perform brilliantly – infinitive phrase, object of the participle *hoping*

to perform brilliantly – infinitive phrase, object of the infinitive *to learn*
brilliantly – adverb modifying infinitive *to perform*
until dawn – adverbial prepositional phrase modifying *rehearsed*

It was daunting to think of the consequences that might ensue.
to think of the consequences that might ensue – infinitive phrase, delayed subject of sentence
of the consequences – adverbial prepositional phrase modifying infinitive *to think*
that might ensue – relative clause modifying *consequences*
daunting – participle, predicate adjective modifying subject

The students developed the argument, an intriguing one for them, that postmodern architecture might someday become a distant memory.
an intriguing one for them – appositive phrase further defining *argument*
intriguing – participle modifying *one*
for them – adverbial prepositional phrase modifying *intriguing*
someday – adverb modifying *might become*
that postmodern architecture might someday become a distant memory – relative clause modifying *argument*

With several generous donations, we purchased what the homeless shelter had needed since October: warm blankets to distribute in cold weather.
With several generous donations – adverbial prepositional phrase modifying *purchased*
several generous – adjective series modifying *donations*
what the homeless shelter had needed since October – noun clause, direct object of *purchased*
since October – adverbial prepositional phrase modifying *had needed*
warm blankets to distribute in cold weather – appositive phrase modifying the noun clause *what the homeless shelter had needed since October*
to distribute – adjectival infinitive modifying *blankets*
in cold weather – adverbial prepositional phrase modifying *distribute*

Because she wanted to become better educated, she enrolled in night school.
Because she wanted to become better educated – adverbial clause modifying the independent clause *she enrolled in night school* (or just the verb *enrolled*)

to become better educated – infinitive phrase, direct object of *wanted*
better – adverb modifying *educated*, the predicate adjective after *become*
in night school – adverbial prepositional phrase modifying *enrolled*
night – noun functioning as adjective to modify *school*

He was a child who, being quite introverted in large groups of adults, chose a quiet corner where he could read a book.

who chose a quiet corner where he could read a book – relative clause modifying the predicate noun *child*
where he could read a book – adverbial clause modifying *chose*
being quite introverted in large groups of adults – participial phrase modifying the relative pronoun *who*
introverted – past participle, predicate adjective after *being*
quite – adverb modifying *introverted*
in large groups of adults – adverbial prepositional phrase modifying *introverted*
of adults – adjectival prepositional phrase modifying *groups*

The book being one of the kind that puts you to sleep, she laid it aside and dozed off.

The book being one of the kind that puts you to sleep – absolute phrase
of the kind that puts you to sleep – adjectival prepositional phrase modifying *one*
that puts you to sleep – relative clause modifying *kind*
to sleep – adverbial prepositional phrase modifying *puts*

I am the only member who knows what must be done when parliament reconvenes.

who knows what must be done when parliament reconvenes – relative clause modifying *member*
what must be done when parliament reconvenes – noun clause, direct object of *knows*
when parliament reconvenes – adverbial clause modifying verb *must be done*

These examples suggest the richness of structure that is possible, the kind you undoubtedly create at times without even thinking about it. But think about it. Try concocting sentences with these sorts of syntactical complexities. Working with sentences in this way can help you to develop greater variety in your writing.

26d Using Modifiers: A Sample Scenario

Suppose you were asked to write a short paper on your reading habits. In getting your ideas together and taking notes, you might draft a bare-bones sentence such as this:

> Recently, I've been reading fiction.

It's a start. But you soon realize that it isn't exactly true to your thoughts. It needs qualification. So you begin modifying its elements:

> Recently, I've been reading <u>historical</u> fiction.

The adjective specifies the kind of fiction you've been reading—you're focused on novels and short stories written about the past. Then you add an adjectival prepositional phrase to further limit the word *fiction*:

> Recently, I've been reading historical fiction <u>about the First World War</u>.

Then you realize that while the fiction you've been reading has been primarily historical and about World War I, you haven't read it all; therefore you insert another adjective to further qualify the noun *fiction*:

> Recently, I've been reading <u>Canadian</u> historical fiction about the First World War.

Then you realize that *Canadian historical fiction* implies that you are familiar with all such fiction. But you quickly see a way to revise the sentence to convey your thoughts accurately; you put the adjective *much* in front of the verb:

> Recently, I've been reading <u>much</u> Canadian historical fiction about the First World War.

So far so good. But you're not entirely satisfied with the sentence; you suspect that a reader might want a little more information about your reference to Canadian fiction about the First World War. You could go on to explain in another sentence or two, but you'd like to get a little more substance into this sentence. Then you have this thought: you can help clarify your point and at the same time inject some rhythm by adding a participial phrase modifying *fiction*:

> Recently, I've been reading much Canadian historical fiction <u>representing our longstanding ambivalence</u> about the First World War.

You rather like it. But working at this one sentence has got you thinking. Before you leave it you consider your reasons for reading such fiction.

You decide that you're doing this reading because this fiction focuses on a major event of the twentieth century, and because it tells stories of a time when Canada is said to have earned its national independence but when it also experienced deep political divisions over conscription. You feel the words beginning to come, and you consider your options: you can put the explanation in a separate sentence; you can join it to your present sentence with a semicolon or a colon or a coordinating conjunction like *for*, creating a compound sentence; or you can integrate it more closely by making it a subordinate clause, turning the whole into a complex sentence. You decide on the third method, and put the new material in a *because*-clause modifying the verb *have been reading*. And while you're thinking about it, you begin to feel that, given the way your sentence has developed, the word *reading* now sounds rather bland, weak because it doesn't quite reveal your seriousness. So you decide to change it to the more precise verb *studying*. Now your sentence is finished, at least for the time being:

> Recently, I've been studying much Canadian historical fiction about the First World War, because this fiction focuses on a major event of the twentieth century and because it tells stories of a time when Canada is said to have earned its national independence but also to have experienced deep political divisions over conscription.

By adding modifiers, a writer can enlarge the reader's knowledge of the material being presented and impart precision and clarity to a sentence, as well as improve its style. Minimal or bare-bones sentences can themselves be effective and emphatic; use them when they are appropriate. But many of your sentences will be longer. And it is in elaborating and enriching your sentences with modifiers that you as author and stylist can exercise much of your control: you take charge of what your readers will learn and how they will learn it.

Exercise 26 Using modifiers

Choose five of these bare-bones sentences and flesh them out with various kinds of modifiers. Compose several expanded sentences for each. Use some single-word modifiers, but try to work mainly with phrases and clauses, including some noun clauses. Identify each modifier. Keep the sentences simple or complex, not compound or compound-complex (see #12z). (If you don't like these core sentences, make up some of your own.)

Air travel can be an ordeal.
Recycling requires planning.
Think globally.
Hollywood movies follow trends.
The restaurant was reviewed.
Stop.
We are investigating.
Time is passing.
Canadians puzzle Americans.
Punctuation matters.

27–29 Length, Variety, and Emphasis

27 Sentence Length

How long should a sentence be to achieve its purpose? That depends. A sentence may, in rare cases, consist of one word, or it may go on for a hundred words or more. There are no strict guidelines to tell you how long to make your sentences. If you're curious, do some research to determine the average sentence length in several pieces of writing you have handy—for example this and other textbooks, a recent novel, a collection of essays, newspapers and magazines, e-mail messages, websites you visit regularly, a piece of your own recent academic writing. You'll probably find that the average is somewhere between 15 and 25 words per sentence, that longer sentences are more common in formal and specialized writing, and that shorter sentences are more at home in informal and popular writing, in e-mail, and in narrative and dialogue. There are, then, some general guidelines, and you'll probably fit your own writing to them. But if you're far off what seems to be the average for the kind of writing you are doing, you may need to make some changes to adapt to the writing situation.

27a Short Sentences

If you receive feedback that you're writing an excessive number of short sentences, try

- building them up by elaborating their elements with modifiers, including various kinds of phrases and clauses (see #26d);
- combining some of them to form compound subjects, predicates, and objects or complements;
- combining two or more of them—especially if they are simple sentences—into one or another kind of complex sentence. (Since compound sentences are made up of simple sentences joined by punctuation and coordinating conjunctions, they often read like a series of shorter, simple sentences.)

27b Long Sentences

If you find yourself writing too many long sentences, check them for two possible problems:

1. You may be rambling or trying to pack too much into a single sentence, possibly destroying its unity (see #41) and certainly making it difficult to read. Try breaking it up into more unified or more easily manageable parts.
2. You may be using too many words to make your point. Try cutting out any deadwood (see #71).

In either of these kinds of unwieldy sentence, check that you haven't slipped into what is called "excessive subordination"—too many loosely related details obscuring the main idea, or confusing strings of subordinate clauses modifying each other. Try removing some of the clutter, and try reducing clauses to phrases and phrases to single words (see Exercises 21.3, 21.4, and 22a–c (2).

28 Sentence Variety

Both to create emphasis (see #29) and to avoid monotony you should vary the lengths and kinds of your sentences. This is a process you should engage in when revising your draft to strengthen its style. Examine some pieces of prose that you particularly enjoy or that you find unusually clear and especially readable: you will likely discover that they contain both a pleasing mixture of short, medium, and long sentences and a similar variety of kinds and structures.

28a Variety of Lengths

A string of short sentences will sound choppy and fragmented; avoid the staccato effect by interweaving some longer ones. On the other hand, a succession of long sentences may make your ideas hard to follow; give your readers a break—and your prose some sparkle—by using a few short, emphatic sentences to change your pace occasionally. Even a string of medium-length sentences can bore readers into inattention. Impart some rhythm, some shape, to your paragraphs by varying sentence length. Especially consider using a short, emphatic sentence to open or close a paragraph, and occasionally an unusually long sentence to end a paragraph.

28b Variety of Kinds

A string of simple and compound sentences risks coming across to a reader as simplistic. In a narrative and in certain technical and business documents, successive simple and compound sentences may be appropriate for recounting a sequence of events, but when you're writing prose in other modes and especially in academic writing, let some of the complexity of your ideas be reflected in complex and compound-complex sentences. On the other hand, a string of complex and compound-complex sentences may become oppressive. Give your readers a breather now and then by changing pace.

28c Variety of Structures

Try to avoid an unduly long string of sentences that use the same syntactical structure. For example, though the standard order of elements in declarative sentences is subject–verb–object or –complement, consider varying that order occasionally for the purpose of emphasis (see #12s and #29). Perhaps use an occasional interrogative sentence (see #12t), whether a rhetorical question (a question that doesn't expect an answer) or a question that you proceed to answer as you develop a paragraph. An occasional expletive pattern or passive voice can be refreshing—if you can justify it on other grounds as well (see #12e, #12k, #17p, and #29f).

In particular, try not to begin a string of sentences with the same kind of word or phrase or clause—unless you are purposely setting up a controlled succession of parallel structures for emphasis or coherence (see #5a). Imagine the effect of several sentences beginning with such words as *Similarly . . . Especially . . . Consequently . . . Nevertheless. . . .* Whatever else the sentences contained, the sameness would be distracting. Or imagine a series of sentences all starting with a subject-noun, or with a present-participial phrase. To avoid such undesirable sameness, take advantage of the way modifiers of various kinds can be moved around in sentences (see #12q, #12r, #19d, #20d, #22b, and #29e).

29 Emphasis in Sentences

To communicate effectively, make sure your readers perceive the relative importance of your ideas the same way you do. Learn to control emphasis so that what you want emphasized is what gets emphasized.

You can emphasize whole sentences in several ways:

- Set a sentence off by itself, as a short paragraph. (Use this strategy judiciously.)
- Put an important sentence at the beginning of a paragraph or, even better, at the end.
- Put an important point in a short sentence among several long ones, or in a long sentence among several short ones.
- Shift the style or structure of a sentence to make it stand out from those around it (see #6).

In similar ways, you can emphasize important parts of individual sentences. The principal devices for achieving emphasis *within* sentences are position and word order, repetition, stylistic contrast, syntax, and punctuation.

29a Endings and Beginnings

The most emphatic position in a sentence is its ending; the second most emphatic position is its beginning. Consider these two sentences:

> Kerr's new play features seven young actors.
>
> Seven young actors appear in Kerr's new play.

Each sentence emphasizes both *Kerr's new play* and the *seven young actors*, but the first emphasizes the *seven young actors* a little more, whereas the second emphasizes *Kerr's new play* a little more. Further, the longer the sentence, the stronger the effect of emphasis by position. Consider the following:

a. The best teacher I've ever had was my high-school chemistry teacher, a brilliant woman in her early fifties.

b. A brilliant woman in her early fifties, my high-school chemistry teacher was the best teacher I've ever had.
c. My high-school chemistry teacher, a brilliant woman in her early fifties, was the best teacher I've ever had.
d. The best teacher I've ever had was a brilliant woman in her early fifties who taught me chemistry in high school.

Each sentence contains the same three ideas, but each distributes the emphasis differently. In each the last part is the most emphatic, the first part next, and the middle part least. Think of them as topic sentences (see #4a): sentence *a* could introduce a paragraph focusing on the quality of the teacher but emphasizing her intelligence, her age, and her gender; sentence *b* could introduce a paragraph focusing more on the quality of her teaching; sentence *c* could open a paragraph stressing the quality of the teaching and the nature and level of the subject; details of age, gender, and intelligence would be incidental; sentence *d* may seem the flattest, the least emphatic and least likely of the four, but it could effectively introduce a mainly narrative paragraph focusing on the writer's good experience in the class.

Note that in all four versions the part referring to "the best teacher I've ever had" comes either first or last, since the superlative *best* would sound unnatural in the unemphatic middle position—unless one acknowledged its inherent emphasis in some other way, for example by setting off the appositive with a pair of dashes (see #50b):

> My high-school chemistry teacher—the best teacher I've ever had—was a brilliant woman in her early fifties.

29b Loose Sentences and Periodic Sentences

Loose is not a pejorative term when it describes a sentence. It simply means that the sentence makes its main point in an early independent clause and then adds modifying subordinate elements:

> The concert began modestly, minus special effects and fanfare, with the performers sitting casually onstage and taking up their instruments to play their first song.

Such sentences—also called *cumulative* or *right-branching*—are common, for they are "loose" and comfortable, easygoing, natural. In contrast to the loose is the *periodic* (or "*left-branching*") sentence, which wholly or partly delays its main point, the independent clause, until the end:

> With the performers sitting casually onstage and taking up their instruments to play their first song, the concert began modestly, minus special effects and fanfare.

Full periodic sentences are usually the result of careful thought and planning. However, they can sometimes sound contrived, less natural, and therefore should not be used without forethought. They can also be dramatic and emphatic, creating suspense as the reader waits for the meaning to fall into place. When you try for such suspense, don't separate subject and predicate too widely, as a writer did in this sentence:

> ***ineffective:*** The abrupt change from one moment when the air is alive with laughing and shouting, to the next when the atmosphere resembles that of a morgue, is dramatic.

Many sentences delay completion of the main clause only until somewhere in the middle rather than all the way to the end. To the degree that they do delay it, they are partly periodic.

29c The Importance of the Final Position

Because the end of a sentence is naturally so emphatic, readers expect something important there; it is best not to disappoint them by letting something incidental or merely qualifying fall at the end, for then the sentence itself will fall: its energy and momentum will be lost, its essential meaning distorted. For example:

> ***emph:*** That was the best job interview I've had, I think.

The uncertain *I think* should go at the beginning or, even less emphatically, after *That* or *was.*

> ***emph:*** Cramming for exams can be counterproductive, sometimes.

The qualifying *sometimes* could go at the beginning, but it would be best after *can*, letting the emphasis fall where it belongs, on *cramming* and *counterproductive*.

29d Changing Word Order

Earlier sections point out certain standard patterns: for example, subject–verb–object or –complement (#12c–j); single-word adjectives preceding nouns —or, if predicate adjectives, following them (#19d); and so on. But variations are possible, and because these patterns are recognized as standard, any departures from them stand out (see #12s and #19d for examples). Be careful, for if the inverted order calls attention to itself at the expense of meaning, the attempt may backfire. In the following sentence, for example, the writer strained a little too hard for emphasis. Can you achieve it in some less risky way?

> It is from imagination that have come all the world's great literature, music, architecture, and works of art.

29e Movable Modifiers

Many modifiers other than single-word adjectives are movable, enabling you to shift them or other words to where you want them. Appositives, for instance, can sometimes be transposed (see #12q). And you can move participial phrases, if you do so carefully (see #19d). Absolute phrases (see #12r), since they function as sentence modifiers, can usually come at the beginning or the end—or, if syntax permits, in the middle.

But adverbial modifiers are the most movable of all (see #20d). As you compose, and especially as you revise your drafts, consider the various possible placements of any adverbial modifiers you've used. Take advantage of their flexibility to exercise maximum control over the rhythms of your sentences and, most important, to get the emphases that will best serve your purposes. Some examples:

> The creature made its way slowly and stealthily through the labyrinth.

Would the adverbs be more emphatic at the end? Try it:

> The creature made its way through the labyrinth slowly and stealthily.

A little better, perhaps. Now try them at the beginning, and instead of *and,* use punctuation to emphasize the slowness:

> Slowly, stealthily, the creature made its way through the labyrinth.

Another example, from a rough draft:

> ***draft:*** When I entered university I naturally expected it to be different from high school, but I wasn't prepared for the impact it would have on the way I lived my day-to-day life.

Clear enough. But the writer decided to try separating the independent clauses and using a conjunctive adverb to get a little more of the emphasis he felt he needed:

> ***revised:*** When I entered university I naturally expected it to be different from high school. However, I wasn't prepared for the impact it would have on the way I lived my day-to-day life.

But that sounded too stiff (as *However* oftentimes does at the beginning of a sentence). After some further tinkering with the adverbs, he came up with this:

> ***revised:*** When I entered university I expected it to be different from high school—naturally. I was not, however, prepared for the impact it would have on the way I lived my day-to-day life.

Setting *naturally* off with a dash at the end of the first sentence added a touch of self-mockery. And moving *however* a few words into the second sentence not only got rid of the stiffness but also, because of the pause produced by its commas, added a useful emphasis to *not,* now spelled out in full. (For more on *however,* see #44h.)

29f Using the Expletive and the Passive Voice for Emphasis

Two of the basic sentence patterns, the *expletive* (#12k) and the *passive voice* (#12e, #17p), can be weak and unemphatic in some contexts. Used strategically, however, they can enable you to achieve a desired emphasis. For example:

> Passive voice can be used to move a certain word or phrase to an emphatic place in a sentence.

Here, putting the verb in the passive voice (*can be used*) makes *Passive voice* the subject of the sentence and enables this important element to come at the beginning; otherwise, the sentence would have to begin less strongly (for example, with *You can use passive voice*). And consider this next example, which makes strategic use of the expletive pattern:

> There are advantages to using the expletive pattern for a deliberate change of pace in your writing.

In this case, opening the sentence with *There* is preferable to opening with these long and unwieldy alternatives:

> <u>Advantages to using the expletive pattern for a deliberate change of pace in your writing</u> are significant.

or

> <u>Using the expletive pattern for a deliberate change of pace in your writing</u> can be advantageous.

Use expletives and passive voice when you need to delete or delay mention of the agent or otherwise shift the subject of a sentence. But use these patterns only when you have good reason to do so.

29g Emphasis by Repetition

You may wish to repeat an important word or idea in order to emphasize it, to make it stay in your readers' minds. Unintentional repetition can be wordy and tedious (see #71b); but intentional, controlled repetition—used sparingly—can be very effective, especially in sentences with balanced or parallel structures:

> We particularly enjoy his lyrics—his witty, poignant, brilliant lyrics.
>
> If you have the courage to face adventure, the adventure can sometimes give you courage.
>
> If it's a challenge they seek, it's a challenge they'll find.
>
> Many Vancouver shops are filled with souvenirs: souvenir T-shirts, souvenir postcards, souvenir coffee mugs.

29h Emphasis by Stylistic Contrast

A stylistically enhanced sentence—for example, a periodic sentence (#29b), a sentence with parallel or balanced structure (#40, #29g), or a richly metaphorical or allusive sentence (#65)—stands out beside plainer sentences. For that reason, such a sentence may be most effective at the end of a paragraph (see #4c). In the same way, a word or phrase that differs in style or tone from those that surround it may stand out (and note that such terms often gravitate toward that position of natural emphasis, the end of the sentence):

> When the judge chastised the defence attorney for her sarcasm, her client went ballistic.
>
> The chef—conservative as her behaviour sometimes appears—dazzles the kitchen staff with her gutsy culinary experiments.
>
> My grandmother may be almost ninety years old, but she approaches each day with a child's *joie de vivre*.

Terms from other languages naturally stand out, but don't make the mistake of using them pretentiously, for some readers are unimpressed by them or even resent them; use one only after due thought, and preferably when there is no satisfactory English equivalent. And be careful not to overshoot: too strong a contrast may jar; the first example above works only because the emphasis deriving from the shift to colloquialism is deliberate.

29i Emphasis by Syntax

Put your most important claims in independent clauses; put lesser claims in subordinate clauses and in phrases. Sometimes you have more than one option, depending on what you want to emphasize:

> Reading the menu, she frowned at the high prices.
>
> Frowning at the high prices, she read the menu.

But more often the choice is determined by the content. Consider the way subordination affects emphasis in the following pairs of sentences:

original: I strolled into the laboratory, when my attention was attracted by the pitter-pattering of a little white rat in a cage at the back.
revised: When I strolled into the laboratory, my attention was attracted by the pitter-pattering of a little white rat in a cage at the back.

original: Choosing my courses carefully, I tried to plan my academic schedule around my co-op work placement.
revised: Because I was trying to plan my academic schedule around my co-op work placement, I chose my courses carefully.

original: I had almost finished the last chapter of my novel when the power failed and the computer screen went blank.
revised: When I had almost finished the last chapter of my novel, the power failed and the computer screen went blank.

Granted, the original version of the last example could be appropriate in a particular context; but unless you have a good reason, don't distort apparently logical emphasis by subordinating main ideas.

See also #41 and #23c.

29j Emphasis by Punctuation

An exclamation point (!) denotes emphasis. But using exclamation points is not the only way, and usually not the best way (especially in academic writing), to achieve emphasis with punctuation. Try to make your sentences appropriately emphatic without resorting to this sometimes artificial device. Arrange your words so that commas and other marks fall where you want a pause for emphasis (see #29e). Use dashes, colons, and even parentheses judiciously to set off important ideas (see #29a). Occasionally use a semicolon instead of a comma in order to get a more emphatic pause (but only in a series or between independent clauses).

Avoiding Artificial Emphasis
As much as possible, avoid emphasizing your own words and sentences with such mechanical devices as underlining, italics, quotation marks, and capitalization. See #58r and #60d.

Exercise 27–29 Sentence length, variety, and emphasis

29j

Below are four paragraphs from draft versions of student essays. For practice, revise each one to improve the effectiveness of sentence length, variety, and emphasis. Try not to change the basic sense in any important way, but make whatever changes will make the paragraphs effective.

(a) My father drove up to the campsite and chose an empty spot close to the lake, up against the thickly covered mountainside. We had just unpacked our equipment and set up our tent when an elderly man walked up our path. He introduced himself and told us that he was camped farther up the mountain, about a hundred yards away. He told us that only an hour before, as he walked toward his campsite, he saw a huge black bear running away from it. He said he then drew closer and saw that his tent was knocked down and his food scattered all over the ground. He suggested that we might want to move our camp to a safer place, not so close to this bear's haunts.

(b) The sky promised hot and sunny weather as we quickly finished closing side-pockets and adjusting straps on our packs in preparation for our hike up Black Tusk, which is in Garibaldi Park, a hike which was to be on a trail I had never seen before and which I therefore had been looking forward to with great enthusiasm. And that's what I felt as we set off in the early morning light on the first leg of the journey which would take us to the top in a few hours.

(c) The way time passes can be odd. The mind's sense of time can be changed. I remember an experience which will illustrate this. It happened when I was nine. I rode my bike in front of a car and got hit. I don't remember much about this experience. However, a few details do come to mind. These include the

Exercise 27–29 Sentence length, variety, and emphasis – *cont.*

way the car's brakes sounded suddenly from my right. I never even saw the car that hit me. And I remember flying through the air. It was a peculiar feeling. The ground seemed to come up slowly as I floated along. Time seemed almost to have stopped. But then I hit the ground. And then time speeded up. A neighbour ran up and asked if I was all right. My parents pulled our car up. They carefully put me in it. And all of a sudden I was at the hospital, it seemed. It all must have taken twenty or thirty minutes. To me it seemed that only a minute or two had passed since I had hit the ground.

(d) It's not so difficult to repot a houseplant, although many plant-owners procrastinate about doing this because they think it's too messy and time-consuming, when actually repotting takes very little time and effort if you follow a simple set of instructions such as I'm about to give you. And you'll find that when you've done the repotting both you and your plant will benefit from the process because the plant will then be able to receive fresh minerals and oxygen from the new soil which will make it grow into a healthier plant that will give you increased pleasure and enjoyment.

30 Analyzing Sentences

Practise analyzing your own and others' sentences. The better you understand how sentences work, the better able you will be to write effective and correct sentences.

You should be able to account for each word in a sentence: no essential element should be missing, nothing should be left over, and the grammatical relations among all the parts should be clear. If these conditions aren't met, the sentence in question is likely to be misleading or ambiguous. If words, phrases, and clauses fit the roles they are being asked to play, the sentence should work.

The first step in analyzing a sentence is to identify the main parts of its basic structure: the *subject*, the *finite verb*, and the *object* or *complement*, if any. (If the sentence is other than a simple sentence, there will be more than one set of these essential parts.) Then determine the modifiers of these elements, and then the modifiers of modifiers.

30a The Chart Method

Here is a convenient arrangement for analyzing the structure of relatively uncomplicated sentences:

The veteran coach warmly praised the young goalie.

Subject	*Finite Verb*	*Object or Complement*	*Adjectival Modifier*	*Adverbial Modifier*
Coach	praised	goalie (direct object of verb *praised*)	The (modifies *coach*) veteran (modifies *coach*) the (modifies *goalie*) young (modifies *goalie*)	warmly (modifies verb *praised*)

This most beautiful summer is now almost gone.

Subject	*Finite Verb*	*Object or Complement*	*Adjectival Modifier*	*Adverbial Modifier*
Summer	is (linking verb)	gone (predicate adj.)	This (demonstrative adj. modifying *summer*) beautiful (modifies *summer*)	most (modifies adj. *beautiful*) now (modifies verb *is*) almost (modifies *gone*)

The very befuddled Roger realized that learning Sanskrit was not easy.

Subject	*Finite Verb*	*Object or Complement*	*Adjectival Modifier*	*Adverbial Modifier*	*Other*
Roger	realized	that . . . easy (noun clause as direct object)	The, befuddled (modify *Roger*)	very (modifies *befuddled*)	
. . . . . .	. . . . . .	. . . . . .	. . . . . .	. . . . . .	. . . . . .
learning	was (linking verb)	easy (predicate adj.) Sanskrit (obj. of gerund *learning*)		not (modifies *easy*)	that (sub. conj.)

In the last example, the items below the dotted line belong to the subordinate clause of this complex sentence.

30b The Vertical Method

For more complicated sentences, you may find a different method more convenient, for example one in which the sentence is written out vertically:

When the canoe trip ended, Philip finally realized that the end of his happy summer was almost upon him.

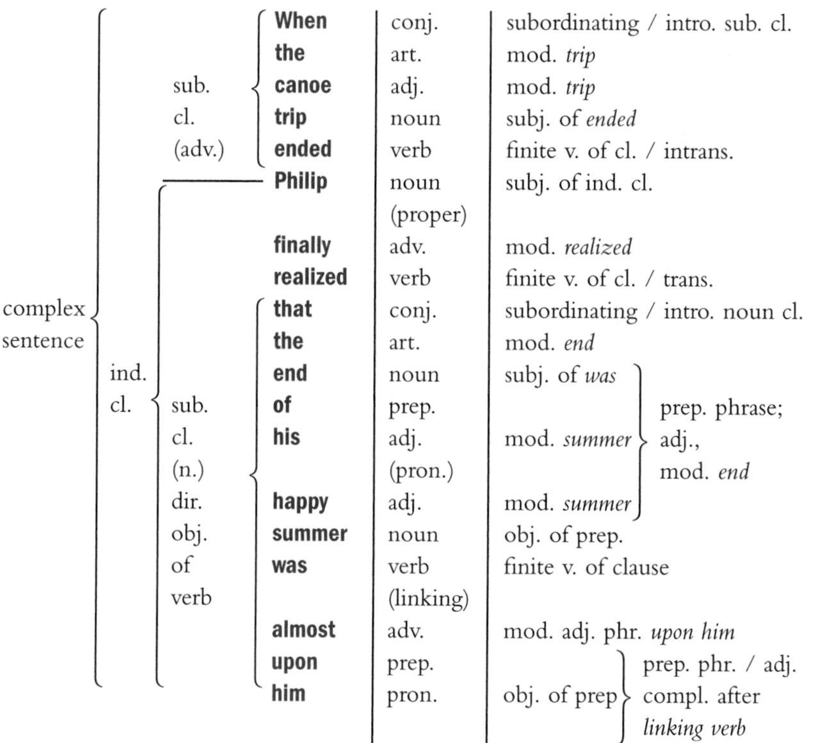

As you can see, this method challenges you to account for the grammatical function of every word in the sentence.

30c The Diagramming Method

Grammatical analysis, by whatever method, is not an end in itself (though some people enjoy it as a kind of game). Its purpose is to give you insight into the accepted structures of the basic unit of communication, the sentence, so that you can construct clear sentences and discover and eliminate weaknesses in your writing. As you become more familiar with such analyses and with the complexity and variety of sentence structure, you should find the process of composing, revising, and editing your sentences becoming clearer for you.

30c

Here are sample diagrams of the most common kinds of sentences:

1. Simple sentences

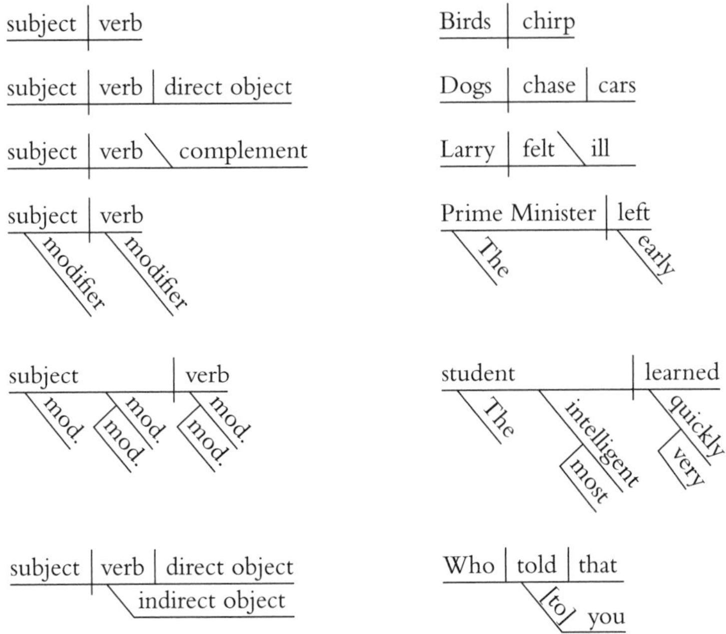

Compound Subject:

Compound Verb:

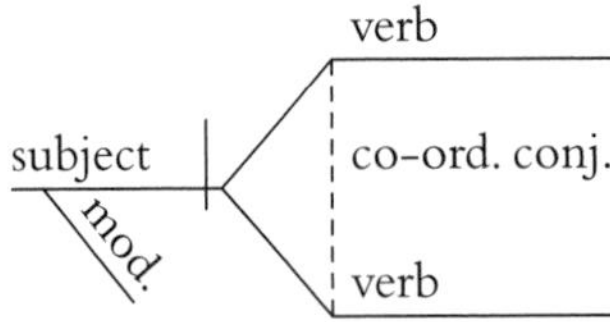

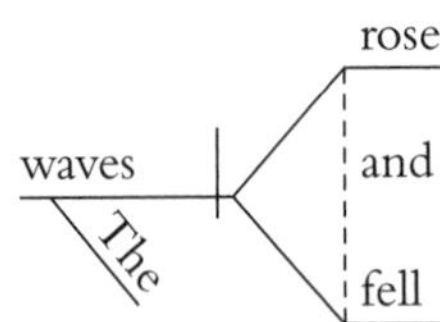

Compound Object:

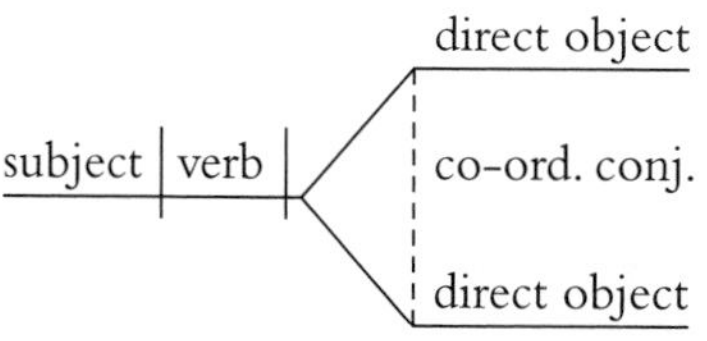

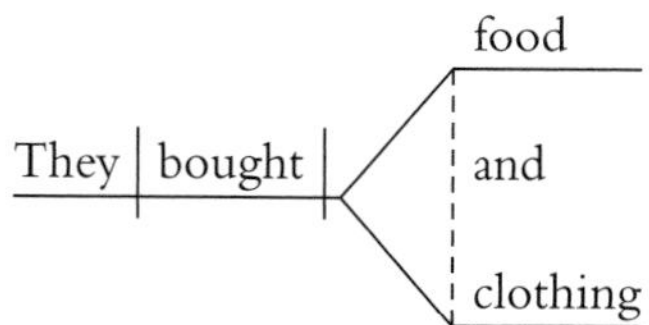

Prepositional Phrases:

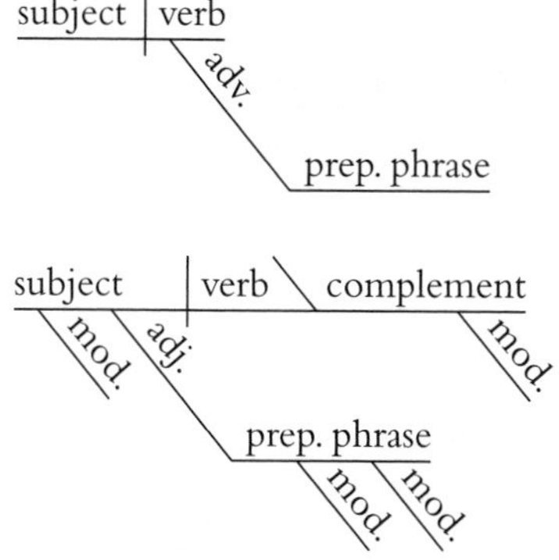

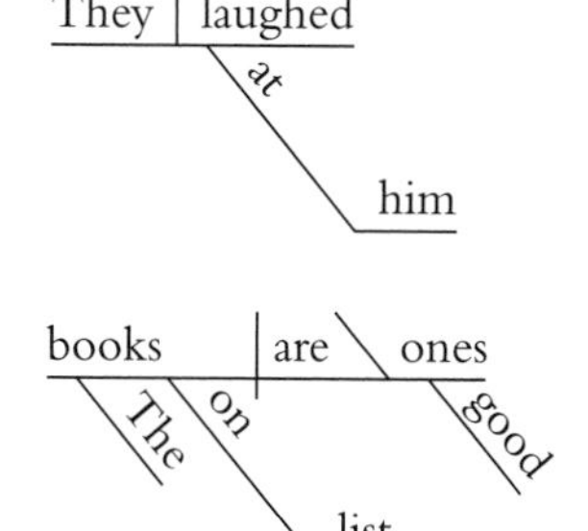

Participial Phrase:

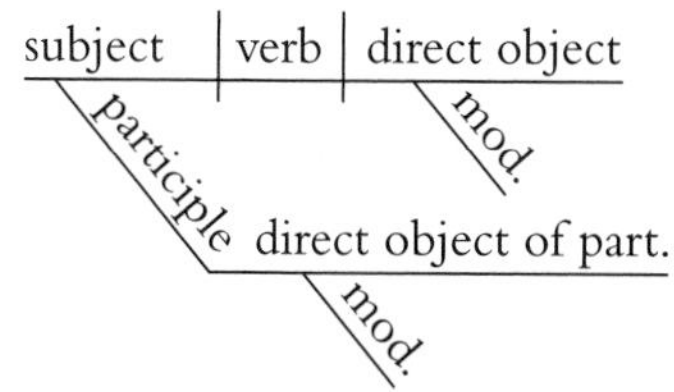

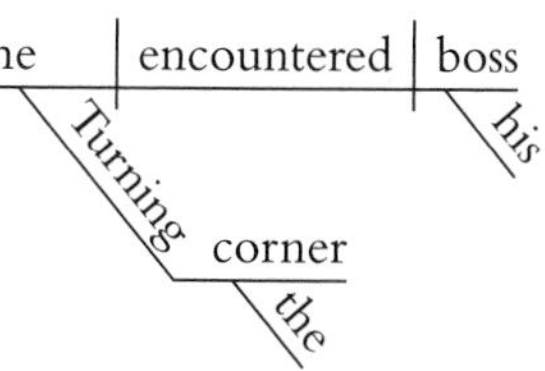

Gerund Phrase as Subject:

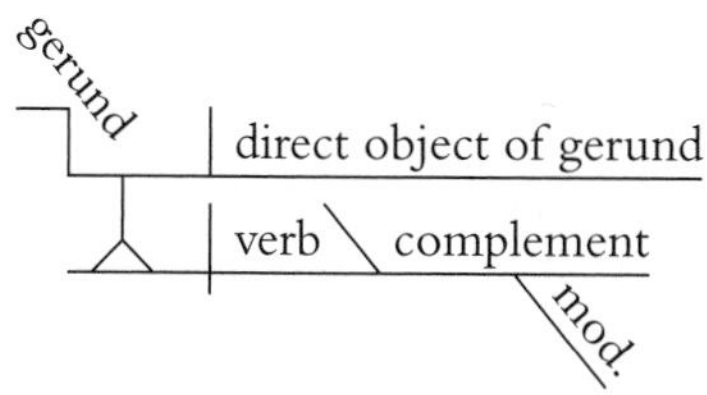

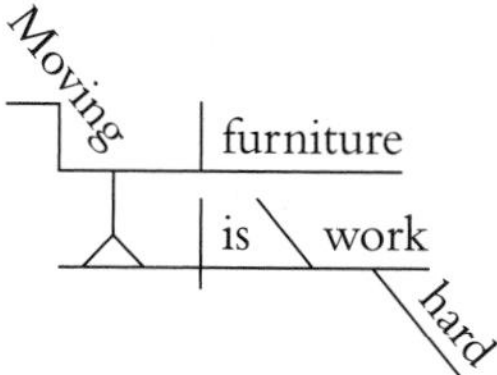

30c

Infinitive Phrase as Noun:

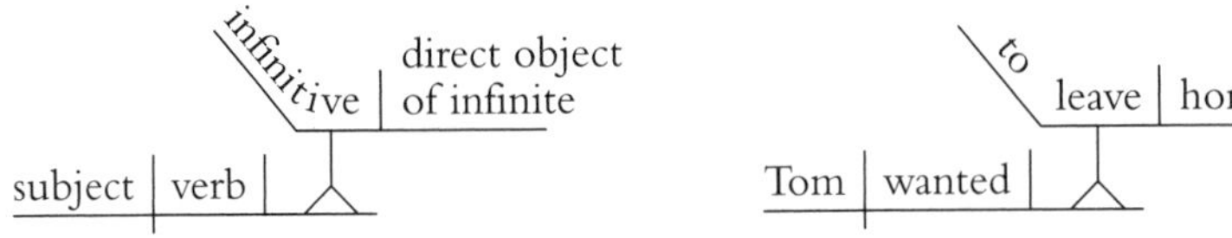

Infinitive Phrase as Adjective:

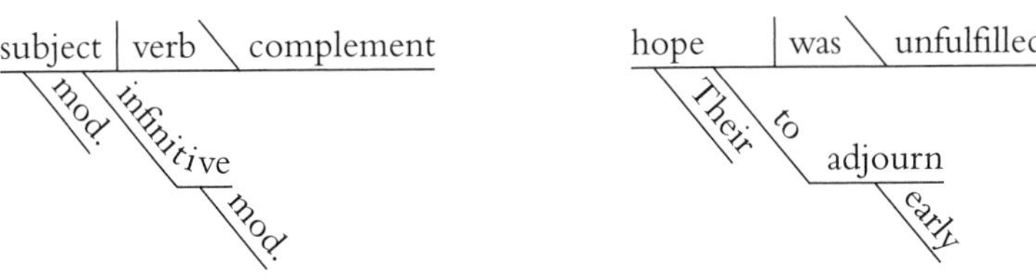

Infinitive Phrase as Adverb:

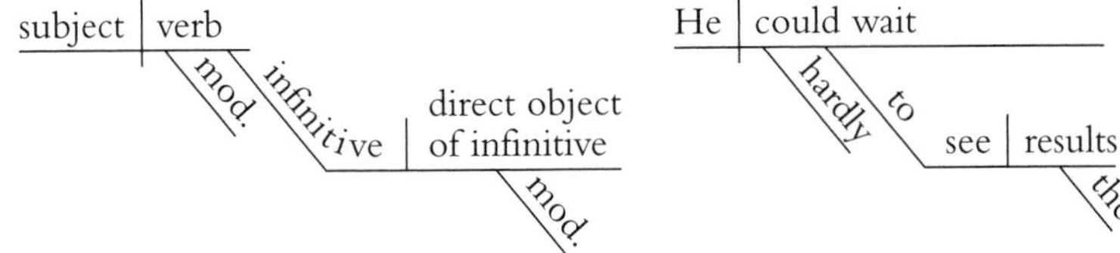

2. Complex sentences

Noun Clause as Direct Object:

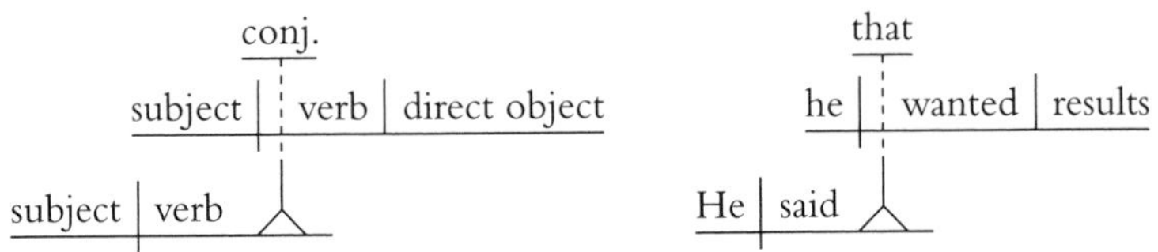

Noun Clause as Object of Preposition:

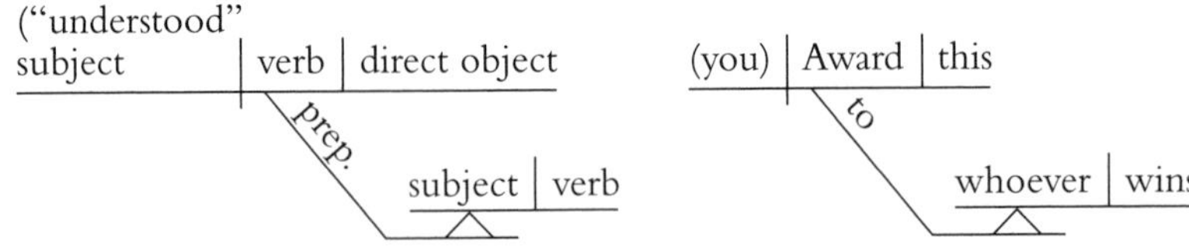

Relative Clause Modifying the Subject:

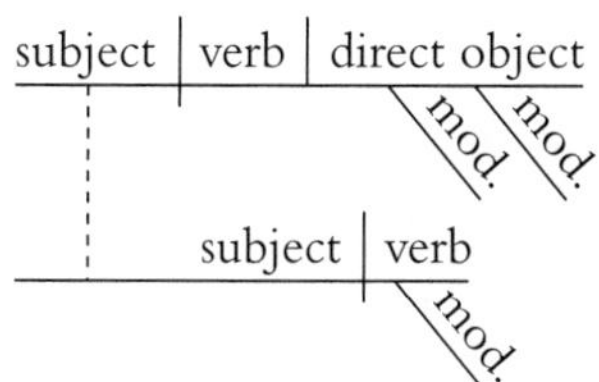

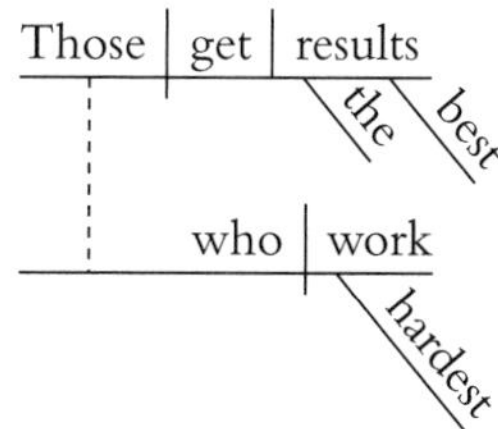

Relative Clause Modifying a Direct Object:

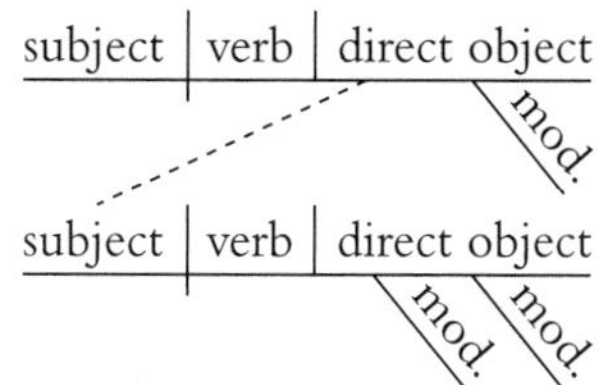

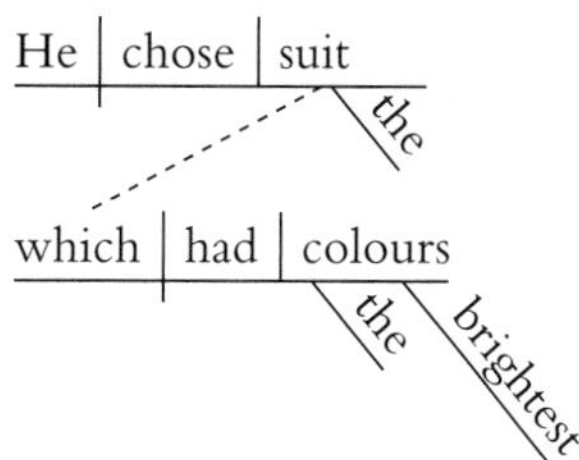

Relative Clause Modifying a Complement:

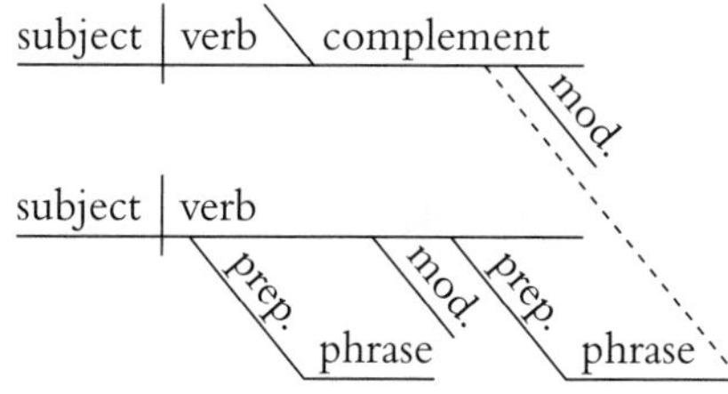

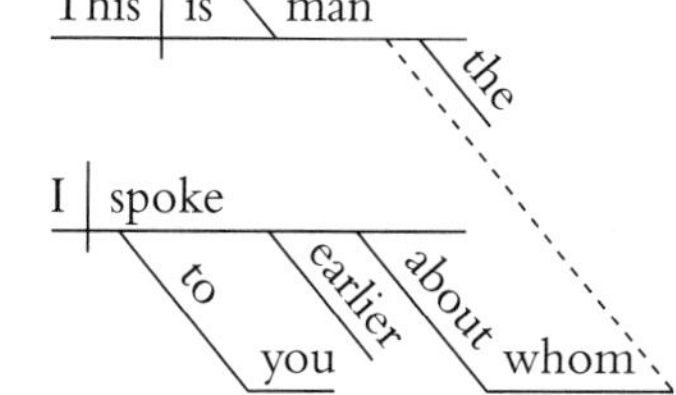

Adverbial Clause:

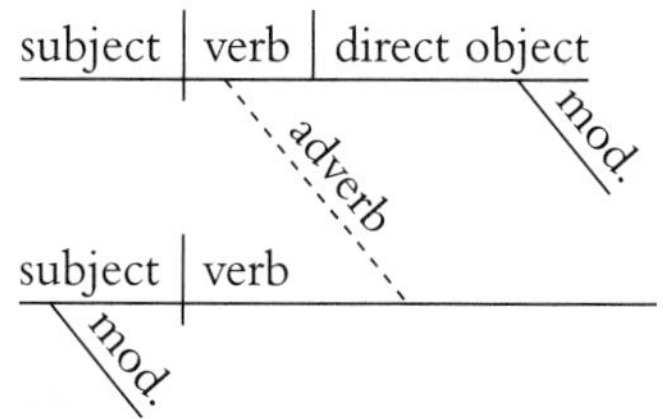

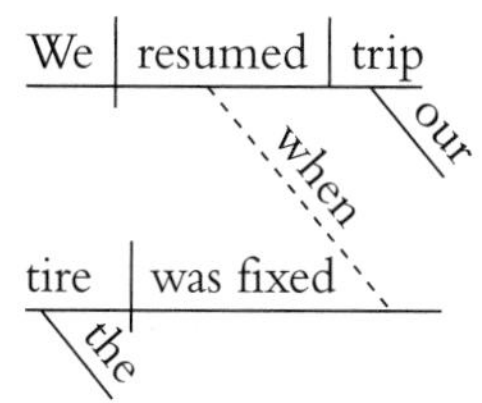

30c

3. Compound sentences

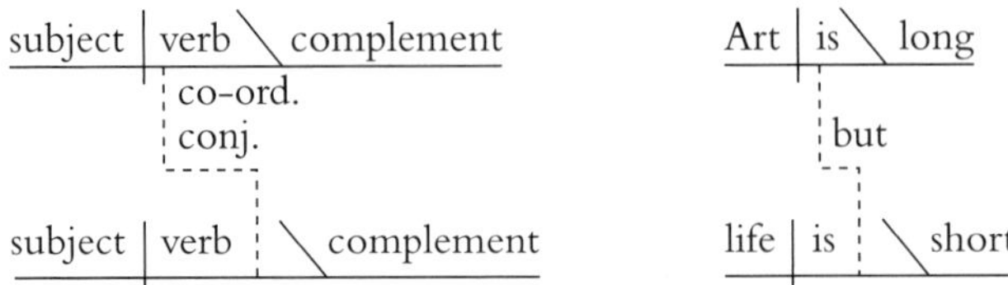

4. Compound-complex sentences are diagrammed following similar patterns.

30c

The traditional but still serviceable diagramming method has its drawbacks: there is no way to distinguish between adjective and adverb, for example, unless you label each one; and it also requires learning a rather complicated system. Nevertheless, it can prove useful by revealing the workings of a sentence. For visual learners—those who learn and understand best when presented with visual representations of abstract or complex verbal patterns—diagrams can make clearer the relationships of modifiers to the main elements (subjects, verbs, and objects) of a clause. They can also demonstrate visually the relationships between and among types of clauses in compound, complex, and compound-complex sentences. If you are taking courses in English language studies—for example, in traditional grammar or syntax—sentence diagrams will be a regular feature of lessons and exercises in sentence analysis.

Exercise 30 Analyzing sentences

A. Try analyzing the following sentences by each of the three suggested methods. Doing so should give you a sense of the advantages and disadvantages of each; you can then use or adapt the one you prefer, or use different methods for different kinds of sentences. You may even want to invent your own method.

1. Children danced to the music of the piper.
2. A chinook is a warm wind blowing eastward off the Rocky Mountains.
3. Many potentially good films are spoiled by sensationalism.
4. Both the beaver and the maple leaf are Canadian emblems.
5. Although she was discouraged, Suki persevered, and after a few more tries she succeeded in clearing the two-metre bar.

B. Here is a longer, more complicated sentence. For such sentences, the "vertical" method is probably the most convenient. Try it. (You may want to challenge a classmate: see which of you can write down the greatest number of grammatical facts about the sentence.)

Exercise 30 Analyzing sentences - *continued*

Constructed of stone and cedar, the large house that the Smiths built on the brow of Murphy's Bluff—an exposed promontory—was so sturdy that even the icy blasts of the continual north wind in December and January made no impression on it.

31–42 Common Sentence Problems

In the remaining sections of this chapter we define some common problems that can affect the clarity of sentences and suggest ways to avoid or correct them.

The three sentence errors that can most impede clear communication in your writing are the *fragment*, the *comma splice*, and the *run-on sentence*. Some readers consider these three errors to be serious signs of flawed writing. Edit closely for them.

31 Sentence Coherence

coh Although the word *coherence* usually refers to the connection between sentences and between paragraphs (see #3–5, #8b), the parts of a sentence must also cohere. Each sentence fault discussed in the next sections (#32–42) is capable of making a sentence incoherent. If a sentence lacks coherence, the fault probably lies in one or more of the following: faulty arrangement (*faulty word order, misplaced modifier*), unclear or missing or illogical connections and relations between parts (*faulty reference, lack of agreement, dangling modifier, faulty coordination, faulty logic, incongruous alignment*), syntactic shift from one part to another (*mixed construction, shift in point of view, faulty parallelism*); or the weakness may be due to something that can only be labelled *unclear* (see ***cl*** in Appendix 2). Consult these specific sections as necessary to ensure that your sentences are coherent within themselves.

32 Fragments

frag A **fragment** is a group of words that is not an acceptable sentence, either major or minor, but that is punctuated as if it were a sentence (that is, started with a capital letter and ended with a period). The fragment is discussed along with the minor sentence, which it sometimes resembles: see #12w and #12x. See also ***frag*** in Appendix 2.

33 Comma Splices

cs A **comma splice** occurs when two independent clauses are joined with only a comma, rather than with a semicolon. Although the error usually stems from a misunderstanding of sentence structure, it is discussed under *punctuation*, since it requires attention to punctuation marks: see #44e–h. See also ***cs*** in Appendix 2.

34 Run-on (Fused) Sentences

run-on fs A **run-on sentence**, sometimes called a **fused sentence**, is in fact not a single sentence but two sentences run together with neither a period to mark the end of the first nor a capital letter to mark the beginning of the second. An error most likely to occur when a writer is rushed, it can sometimes, like the comma splice, result from a problem in understanding how sentences work. And since a run-on sentence occurs with the same kind of sentence structure as does the comma splice, and like it requires attention to punctuation, we discuss it alongside the other error: see #44j. See also ***run-on*** in Appendix 2.

mm 35 Misplaced Modifiers

35a Movability and Poor Placement

As we point out in the introduction to chapter II, part of the meaning in English sentences is conveyed by the position of words in relation to each other. And though there are certain standard or conventional arrangements, a good deal of flexibility is possible (see #12s, #12t, #19d, #22b, and #26). Adverbial modifiers are especially movable (see #20d and #29e). Because of this flexibility, writers sometimes put a modifier where it conveys an unintended or ambiguous meaning, or where it is linked by juxtaposition to a word it can't logically modify. To say precisely what you mean, you have to be careful in placing your modifiers—especially adverbs. Note the changes in meaning that result from the different placement of the word *only* in the following sentences:

> Only her daughter works in Halifax. (No other member of her family works there.)

> Her only daughter works in Halifax. (She has no other daughters.)

> Her daughter only works in Halifax. (She doesn't live in Halifax, but commutes.)

> Her daughter works only in Halifax. (She works in no other place.)

The following sentence demonstrates how misplacement can produce absurdity:

> ***mm:*** While testifying before the Transport Committee, the minister denied allegations heatedly concerning inadequate passenger screening reported recently in a CBC documentary at Pearson airport.

The adverb *heatedly* belongs before *denied*, the verb it modifies. The adjective phrase *reported in a recent CBC documentary* belongs after *allegations*, the noun it modifies. And the adverbial phrase *at Pearson airport* belongs after the phrase *concerning inadequate passenger screening*.

Usually it is best to keep modifiers and the words they modify as close together as possible. Here is an example of an adjective out of place:

> ***mm:*** Love is a difficult emotion to express in words.

> ***clear:*** Love is an emotion (that is) difficult to express in words.

and an example of a misplaced relative clause:

> ***mm:*** Every year the Royal St John's Regatta is held on Quidi Vidi Lake, which has been called "the world's largest garden party."

Is it the lake that has been called "the world's largest garden party"? The writer likely meant something else:

> ***clear:*** Every year the Royal St John's Regatta, which has been called "the world's largest garden party," is held on Quidi Vidi Lake.

35b *Only*, *almost*, etc.

Pay particular attention (as illustrated in the preceding section) to such adverbs as *only*, *almost*, *just*, *merely*, and *even*. In speech, we often place these words casually, but in writing we should put them where they clearly mean what we want them to:

> ***mm:*** Hardy only wrote novels as a sideline; his main interest was poetry.
>
> ***clear:*** Hardy wrote novels only as a sideline; his main interest was poetry.

> ***mm:*** The students almost washed fifty cars last Saturday.
>
> ***clear:*** The students washed almost fifty cars last Saturday.

35c Squinting Modifiers

squint A **squinting modifier** is a word or phrase put between two elements either of which it could modify. That is, a modifier "squints" so that a reader can't tell which way it is looking; the result is ambiguity:

> ***squint:*** It was so warm for a week we did hardly any skiing at all.

Which clause does the adverbial phrase modify? It is ambiguous, even though the meaning would be about the same either way. A speaking voice could impart clarifying emphasis to such a sentence, but a writer must substitute words or structures for the missing vocal emphasis. Here, adding a simple *that* removes the ambiguity:

> ***clear:*** It was so warm that for a week we did hardly any skiing at all.

> ***clear:*** It was so warm for a week that we did hardly any skiing at all.

Another example:

> ***squint:*** My sister advised me now and then to travel in the Rockies.

This time, rearrangement is necessary:

> ***clear:*** My sister now and then advised me to travel in the Rockies.

> ***clear:*** My sister advised me to travel now and then in the Rockies.

Even a modifier at the end of a sentence can, in effect, squint. When rearrangement doesn't work, further revision may be necessary:

> ***ambig:*** He was overjoyed when she agreed for more reasons than one.

> ***clear:*** He was overjoyed for more reasons than one when she agreed.

> ***clear:*** He had more than one reason to be overjoyed when she agreed.

> ***clear:*** He was overjoyed because she had more than one reason for agreeing.

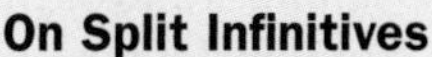

Proofreading Tip

On Split Infinitives
An awkwardly split infinitive—*to* + an adverb + a verb—is also caused by a kind of misplaced modifier; see #21c.

Exercise 35 Correcting misplaced modifiers

Revise the following sentences to eliminate awkwardness resulting from misplaced modifiers.

1. Our submissions were accepted if they were postmarked only by midnight.
2. I pledged to always listen to my children when I became a parent.
3. She decided that on this day she would skip dinner entirely in the morning.
4. I could see my grandmother coming through the window.
5. They discussed booking a trip around the world for two days but decided against it.
6. A piano stood in the centre of the stage with its outline only visible to the audience in the darkness.
7. The newspaper only published three letters to the editor yesterday.
8. It merely seemed a few days before he returned from his journey to Nepal.

36 Dangling Modifiers

dm Like a pronoun without an antecedent, a **dangling modifier** has no word in the rest of the sentence to attach to; instead it is left dangling, grammatically unattached, and so it often tries to attach itself, illogically, to some other word. Most dangling modifiers are *verbal phrases*; be watchful for them in editing drafts of your work.

36a Dangling Participial Phrases (see #21d)

dm: Strolling casually beside the lagoon, my eyes fell upon two children chasing a pair of geese.

Since the adjectival phrase wants to modify a noun, it tries to link with the subject of the adjacent clause, *eyes*. One's eyes may be said, figuratively, to "fall" on something, but they can scarcely be said to "stroll." To avoid the unintentionally humorous dangler, simply change the participial phrase to a subordinate clause:

> ***revised:*** As I strolled casually beside the lagoon, my eyes fell upon two children chasing a pair of geese.

Or, if you want to keep the effect of the opening participial phrase, rework the clause so that its subject is the logical word to be modified:

> ***revised:*** Strolling casually beside the lagoon, I let my gaze fall upon two children chasing a pair of geese.

Here is another example, one with no built-in absurdity:

> ***dm:*** Living in a small town, there was a strong sense of community among us.

To correct the dangling participle, you need to provide something for the phrase to modify, or revise the sentence in some other way:

> ***revised:*** Living in a small town, we had a strong sense of community among us.

> ***revised:*** Since we lived in a small town, there was a strong sense of community among us.

In the next example, passive voice causes the trouble (see #17p):

> ***dm:*** Looking up to the open sky, not a cloud could be seen.
> ***revised:*** Looking up to the open sky, I could not see a cloud.
> ***revised:*** There wasn't a cloud to be seen in the open sky.

36b Dangling Gerund Phrases (see #21f)

When a gerund phrase is the object of a preposition, it can dangle much like a participial phrase:

> ***dm:*** After being informed of the correct procedure, our attention was directed to the next steps.

It isn't "our attention" that was "informed." The use of the passive voice contributes to the confusion here.

> ***revised:*** After being informed of the correct procedure, we were directed to attend to the next steps.

But this revision is still passive and somewhat awkward. Such a sentence can be better revised another way:

> ***revised:*** After informing us of the correct procedure, the instructor directed our attention to the next steps.

36c Dangling Infinitive Phrases (see #21a)

> ***dm:*** To follow Freud's procedure, the speaker's thoughts must be fully explored.

Ineffective passive voice is again the issue, depriving the infinitive phrase of a logical word to modify.

> ***revised:*** To follow Freud's procedure, one must explore the speaker's thoughts fully.

The next example is more complicated:

> ***dm:*** To make the instructor's lab demonstration successful, it requires the students' cooperation.

Here the infinitive phrase seems to be the antecedent of *it*. Dropping the *it* lets the phrase act as a noun; or the sentence can be revised in some other way:

> ***revised:*** To make the instructor's lab demonstration successful will require the students' cooperation.

> ***revised:*** If the instructor's lab demonstration is to succeed, the students will have to cooperate.

36d Dangling Elliptical Clauses

An **elliptical clause** is an adverbial clause that has been abridged so that its subject and verb are only understood, or implied rather than stated; the subject of the independent clause then automatically serves also as the implied subject of the elliptical clause. If the implied subject is different from the subject of the independent clause, the subordinate element will dangle, sometimes illogically.

> ***dm:*** Once in disguise, the hero's conflict emerges.

It isn't "the hero's *conflict*" that is in disguise, but the *hero*. Either supply a logical subject and verb for the elliptical clause, or retain the elliptical clause and make the other subject logically agree with it:

> ***revised:*** Once the hero is in disguise, his conflict emerges.

> ***revised:*** Once in disguise, the hero begins to reveal his conflicts.

Another example:

> ***dm:*** When well marinated, put the pieces of chicken on the barbecue.

Here the understood subject is *the pieces*, but the subject of the independent clause of this imperative sentence is an understood *you*. Give the elliptical clause a subject and verb:

> ***revised:*** When the pieces of chicken are well marinated, put them on the barbecue.

36e Dangling Prepositional Phrases and Appositives (see #22 and #12q)

A prepositional phrase can also dangle. In this example, an indefinite *it* (see #16e) is the issue:

> ***dm:*** Like a child in a toy shop, it is all she can bear not to touch everything.

> ***revised:*** Like a child in a toy shop, she can hardly bear not to touch everything.

And so can an appositive prove to be problematic:

> ***dm:*** A superb racing car, a Ferrari's engine is a masterpiece of engineering.

The phrase seems to be in apposition with the noun *engine*, but it is illogical to equate an engine with an entire car (the possessive *Ferrari's* is adjectival). Revise it:

> ***revised:*** A superb racing car, a Ferrari has an engine that is a masterpiece of engineering.

Exercise 36 Correcting dangling modifiers

Revise the following to eliminate dangling modifiers.

1. Sitting quiet and fascinated, the hyperactive hummingbird was gazed at by the baby in her playpen.
2. By using first-person narration, readers are led by the author to wonder about the reliability of the story.
3. In order to cook, one must be creative, thereby being adept at substituting one ingredient for another.

Exercise 36 Correcting dangling modifiers – *continued*

4. Looked at in this light, one has to find Hamlet very much like other people.
5. Reamur introduced the idea of testing small sample rods and then studying their structure when fractured.
6. Being the youngest member of the community, it is harder for me to convince the elders of my experience.
7. When not going to school or working, my activities range from playing tennis to surfing the Internet.
8. By using this style it added more tension to the dialogue.
9. The colonel began to send groups of reinforcements to the weakened position only to be ambushed in the mountain passes.
10. Whispering in the darkened theatre, our popcorn spilled onto the floor.

▲ 37 Mixed Constructions

mix Avoiding mixed constructions is a particular challenge for anyone whose first language has a different sentence structure than English. To begin a sentence with one construction and then inadvertently shift to another can create confusion for one's readers:

> ***mix:*** Eagle Creek is a small BC community is located near Wells Gray Provincial Park.

The writer here sets up two clauses beginning with *is* but then omits a subject for the second occurrence of *is*. Either drop the first *is* and add commas around the resulting appositive phrase ("a small BC community"), or add *that* or *which* before the second *is*.

> ***mix:*** Since the hockey rink is in use all day, therefore we have to rent it for use at midnight.

Here the writer begins with a subordinating *Since* but then uses *therefore* to introduce the second clause, which would be correct only if the first clause were independent. Fix this by dropping either the *Since* or the *therefore* (if you drop *Since*, change the comma to a semicolon to avoid a comma splice: see #44e).

Exercise 37 Correcting mixed constructions

Revise the following to eliminate mixed constructions.

1. The reason for the decrease in tourism was due to the fear of terrorism.
2. Soccer happens to be a sport is very popular in Brazil.
3. I found that the children's literature website to be very useful.
4. The new styles were popular with both men or women alike.
5. Since, for most of us, our earliest recollections are mere fragments of things that made up our childhoods, we therefore must rely on the objects or ideas around us to trigger the past.
6. Just because people like to watch reality television programs is not a sign of a decadent society.

38 Faulty Alignment

Poor **alignment** results when two or more elements in a sentence are illogically or incongruously aligned with each other. Such errors often take the form of a verb saying something illogical about its subject—an error sometimes called *faulty predication*; that is, what is predicated about the subject is an impossibility. For example:

> ***al, pred:*** Many new inventions and techniques occurred during this period.

An invention could, with some strain, be said to *occur,* but *techniques* do not *occur.* Revision is necessary; one possibility is to use an expletive and the passive voice:

> ***revised:*** During this period there were many new inventions, and many new techniques were developed.

In the next example the verb repeats the meaning of the subject:

> ***al, pred:*** The setting of the play takes place in Verona.
>
> ***revised:*** The play takes place in Verona.
>
> ***better:*** The play is set in Verona.

Errors in predication often occur with a form of *be* and a complement:

> ***al, pred:*** The amount of gear to take along is the first step to consider when planning a long hike.

But an *amount* cannot be a *step*; revision is needed:

> ***revised:*** The first step in planning a hike is to decide how much gear to take along.

Note that this also removes the other illogicality: one does not *consider* a *step*; rather the considering, or deciding, is itself the step. Another example:

> ***al, pred:*** The value of good literature is priceless.

It is not the *value* that is priceless, but the *literature* itself. Here is a similar error, of a common kind:

> ***al, pred:*** The cost of my used car was relatively inexpensive.
>
> ***revised:*** The cost of my used car was relatively low.
>
> ***revised:*** My used car was relatively inexpensive.

Other errors in alignment aren't errors in predication, but are similar to them in using words illogically:

> ***al:*** In narrative, the author describes the occurrences, environment, and thoughts of the characters.

It is logical to speak of characters having thoughts and an environment, but not *occurrences*; substitute *experiences*.

> ***al:*** Its fine texture was as smooth and hard as a waterworn rock.

This, which illogically equates texture and rock, is also a form of incomplete comparison. Insert *that of* after *hard as*. (See **comp** in Appendix 2; see also #29.)

> ***al:*** Professions such as a doctor, a lawyer, or an engineer require extensive post-secondary education.

But *being* a doctor, a lawyer, or an engineer is not a *profession*. Change *profession* to *professional*:

> ***revised:*** Professionals such as doctors, lawyers, and engineers require extensive post-secondary education.

Or recast the sentence completely:

> ***revised:*** Professions such as medicine, law, or engineering require extensive post-secondary education.

Exercise 38 Improving alignment

Revise the following sentences to remove illogical or incongruous alignment.

1. I decided not to buy it, for the price was too expensive.
2. Even religious principles were being enlightened during this period.
3. It is clear that this general conception of his ability is greatly underestimated.
4. The only source of light in the house came through the windows.
5. Its shape is a rectangle about three times as long as it is wide.
6. The poem expresses the meaningless and useless achievements of war.
7. The character of the speaker in the poem seems euphoric and energetic.
8. The need for such great effort on the part of the reader represents serious weakness in the writing.
9. Life and death was a constant idea in the back of the pioneers' minds.
10. She started university at a very young age.

39 Shifts in Perspective: Inconsistent Point of View

shift, pv Be consistent in your point of view within a sentence and, except in special cases, from one sentence to the next. Avoid illogical shifts in the *tense*, *mood*, and *voice* of verbs, and in the *person* and *number* of pronouns.

39a Shifts in Tense (see #17g–h)

shift: The professor explained what she expected of us and then she sits in her chair and tells us to begin.

All of the events described in this sentence occurred at a particular time in the past. So, change *sits* and *tells* to the past tense to coincide with *explained*.

39b Shifts in Mood (see #17-l–m)

shift: If it were Sunday and I was through with my work, I would go skiing with you.

This sentence begins and ends in the subjunctive, but *was* is indicative. Correct this by changing indicative *was* to subjunctive *were*.

shift: First put tab A in slot B; next you will put tab C in slot D.

Omit *you will* to correct the shift from imperative to indicative.

39c Shifts in Voice (see #17-o–p)

shift: Readers should not ordinarily have to read instructions a second time before some sense can be made of the details.

shift: We drove thirty kilometres to the end of the road, after which five more kilometres were covered on foot.

Such shifts from active to passive could also be marked ***pas***. In this case, stay with active voice (and the same subject):

revised: Readers should not ordinarily have to read instructions a second time before they can make sense of the details.

revised: We drove thirty kilometres to the end of the road and then covered another five kilometres on foot.

39d Shifts in Person of Pronoun (see #14a–b)

Shifts in person from words such as *one*, *a person*, *somebody*, or *someone* to the second-person *you*, while common in informal conversation, are likely to be questioned in print, and particularly in the more formal contexts of academic writing. Edit to produce consistency in person.

shift: If one wants to be a cautious investor, you should not invest in the stock market.

revised: If you want to be a cautious investor, you should not invest in the stock market.

revised: If one wants to be a cautious investor, he or she should not invest in the stock market.

While *you* is an ineffective replacement for *someone*, it can be used effectively in the first revision suggested above. To avoid gender bias in references to *one* of unspecified gender, use *he or she* as in the second revision above.

39e Shifts in Number of Pronoun (see #14a)

> ***shift:*** If the committee wants its recommendations followed, they should have written their report more carefully.

The committee changed from a collective unit (*it*) to a collection of individuals (*they*, *their*); the committee should be either singular or plural throughout. See also #15e and #18f. (The errors in #39d and #39e could also be marked ***agr***: see #15.)

40 Faulty Parallelism

40

fp, // Parallelism, the balanced and deliberate repetition of identical grammatical structures (words, phrases, clauses) within a single sentence, can be a strong stylistic technique. Not only does it make for vigorous, balanced, and rhythmical sentences, but it can also help develop and tie together paragraphs (see #5a). Like any other device, parallelism can be overdone, but more commonly writers underuse it. Of course, if you're writing an especially serious piece, like a letter of condolence, you probably won't want to use lively devices like parallelism and metaphor. But in most writing, some parallel structure is appropriate. Build parallel elements into your sentences, and now and then try making two or three successive sentences parallel with each other. Here is a sentence from a paper on computer crime. Note how parallelism (along with alliteration) strengthens the first part, thereby helping to set up the second part:

> Although one can distinguish the malicious from the mischievous or the harmless hacker from the more dangerous computer criminal, security officials take a dim view of anyone who romps through company files.

Be careful as you experiment, for it is easy to set up a parallel structure and then lose track of it. Study the following examples of **faulty parallelism.** (See also #23a–b.)

40a With Coordinate Elements

Coordinate elements in a sentence should have the same grammatical form. If they don't, the sentence will lack parallelism and therefore be ineffective.

> ***fp:*** Reading should be engrossing, active, and a challenge.

The first two complements are predicate adjectives, the third a predicate noun. Change *a challenge* to the adjective *challenging* so that it will be parallel.

The coordinate parts of compound subjects, verbs, objects, and modifiers should be parallel in form.

> ***fp:*** Eating huge meals, too many sweets, and snacking between meals can lead to obesity.

This sentence can be corrected either by making all three parts of the subject into gerunds:

> ***revised:*** Eating huge meals, eating too many sweets, and snacking between meals can lead to obesity.

or by using only the first gerund and following it with three parallel objects:

> ***revised:*** Eating huge meals, too many sweets, and between-meal snacks can lead to obesity.

Another example:

> ***fp:*** He talks about his computer in terms suggesting a deep affection for it and that also demonstrate a thorough knowledge of it.

Simply change the participial phrase (*suggesting . . .*) to a relative clause (*that suggests . . .*) so that it will be parallel with the second part.

It is particularly easy for a writer to produce faulty parallelism by omitting a second *that*:

> ***fp:*** Marvin was convinced that the argument was unsound and he could profitably spend some time analyzing it.

A second *that*, before *he*, corrects the error and clarifies the meaning, for this slip is not only a breakdown of parallelism but also an implied shift in point of view (see #39); it could be marked ***shift*** or ***pv*** as well as ***fp***; it could also be marked ***ambig***. The omission of a second *that* invites a reader to take *he could profitably spend some time analyzing it* as an independent clause (expressing the writer's own opinion about what Marvin should do) rather than a second subordinate clause expressing a part of Marvin's opinion, which is what the writer intended. (See also ***pv*** in Appendix 2.)

40b With Correlative Conjunctions (see #23b)

Check for parallel structure when using correlative conjunctions:

> ***fp:*** Whether for teaching a young child the alphabet or in educating an adult about the latest political controversy, television is probably the best device we have.

The constructions following the *whether* and the *or* should be parallel: change *in* to *for.*

The correlative pair *not only . . . but also* can be particularly troublesome:

> ***fp:*** She not only corrected my grammar but also my spelling.

The error can be corrected either by repeating the verb *corrected* (or using some other appropriate verb, such as *criticized* or *repaired*) after *but also*:

> ***revised:*** She not only corrected my grammar but also corrected my spelling.

or by moving *corrected* so that it occurs before *not only* rather than after it:

> ***revised:*** She corrected not only my grammar but also my spelling.

Either method makes what follows *not only* parallel in form to what follows *but also.* The second version is more economical. See also #23b, on "not only . . . but also."

40c In a Series

In any series of three or more parallel elements, make sure that little beginning words like prepositions, pronouns, and the *to* of infinitives precede either the first element alone or each of the elements. And don't omit needed articles:

> ***fp:*** The new library is noted for a large auditorium, state-of-the-art computer lab, an impressive collection of journals, and brilliant, hard-working staff.

The article *a* is missing before the second and fourth items and should be added to make the items parallel. Another way to fix this would be to remove the articles and insert the possessive pronoun *its* before the first item.

> ***fp:*** She urged her teammates to obey the rules, to think positively, and ignore criticism.

Since *to* occurs in the first two phrases, it should lead off the third phrase as well—or else be omitted from the second one. If necessary, check your work by jotting down the items in such a series in a vertical list after the word that introduces them: any slips in parallelism should then be clearer to you.

> ***correction:*** She urged her teammates to obey the rules,
> to think positively,
> **and** to ignore criticism.

Exercise 40 Correcting faulty parallelism

Revise the following in order to repair faulty parallelism.

1. Disagreements over the war were not only apparent between elected officials and voters, but between various elements of the armed forces as well.
2. People adopt roles in life that they are most comfortable with, or will benefit them the most.
3. Not only was our trip like an adventure, but also very much like a marathon.
4. It is significant that the prosecutor ignored the jury and to try to address his comments to the judge.
5. Part of the report is not only concerned with the present situation but also prepares the way for the important reforms that are ahead.
6. We are told that we should eat more fibre, less fat, and exercise regularly.
7. The homeless are a neglected group in our society, and our own lives.
8. About 1750, it became clear to the French that the arrival of the few English traders was only the beginning and soon masses of settlers would follow and overwhelm the French empire in North America.
9. He says that when he graduates he wants to be a teacher, a home owner, and travel.
10. A pet not only gives an older person something to care for, but also a sense of companionship.
11. Today, even newspapers from across the world can be read on the same day of publication via the Internet rather than a magazine shop.
12. The mountaineers had to cope with obsolete or too few pieces of new equipment.
13. The speaker narrates the poem as if he has walked along the streets at night more than once before and that he is acquainted with what goes on around him during his walks.

Exercise 40 Correcting faulty parallelism – *continued*

14. There are many kinds of smiles. For example there are smiles of pleasure, compassion, humour, contempt, winning, competitive, shared secrets, idiotic grins, leers, gloating, sneers, recognition, friendliness, greeting, social, professional, gratification, spontaneous, contagious, deliberate, suppressed, courtesy, anger, humility, rebellion, embarrassment, and surprise.

15. Everything the fortuneteller told me was happy and exciting: I would marry an intelligent man, have two children, one who will become a famous author, and the other will be a doctor, travel all over the world, and live until I'm ninety-five, healthy as a young woman.

41 Faulty Coordination: Logic, Emphasis, and Unity

fc, log, emph, u If unrelated or unequal elements—usually clauses—are presented as coordinate, the result is **faulty coordination**.

> *fc:* Watches are usually water-resistant and some have the ability to glow in the dark.

There is no logical connection between the two clauses—other than that they both say something about watches. The ideas would be better expressed in separate sentences. Coordinating two such clauses produces a sentence that also lacks **unity.** Here is another example, from a description of a simple object; the lack of unity is even more glaring:

> *fc:* One might find this kind of a jar in a small junk shop and it can be used for anything from cotton balls to rings and things, or just to stand as a decoration.

The suggestion about the junk shop should either be in a separate sentence or be subordinated.

Similarly, if two elements are joined by an inappropriate coordinating conjunction, the result is again faulty coordination—sometimes referred to as "loose" coordination. Here is an example of this more common weakness:

> *fc:* Nationalism can affect the relations between nations by creating a distrustful atmosphere, and an ambassador's innocent remark can be turned into an insult by a suspicious listener.

The *and* misrepresents the relation between the two clauses; the second is not an additional fact but rather an example or result of the fact stated in the first. It would be better either to join the two clauses with a semicolon or colon, or to change *and* to *in which*, and to drop the comma, thereby subordinating the second clause. (The first clause could be made subordinate by adding an opening *Because*, but this would distort **emphasis**, since the first clause appears more important; see #29i). Here is another example, from a description of how a particular scene in *Hamlet* should be staged:

> ***fc:*** In this scene Rosencrantz is the main speaker of the two courtiers; therefore he should stand closer to Hamlet.

This sentence could be sharpened. The first clause would be better subordinated:

> ***revised:*** Because in this scene Rosencrantz is the main speaker of the two courtiers, he should stand closer to Hamlet.

The original *therefore* does express this relation, but the sentence was nonetheless a compound one, tacitly equating the two clauses. Emphasis and clarity are better served by letting the syntax acknowledge the logically subordinate nature of the first clause.

Sometimes faulty coordination produces a sentence that lacks not just clarity but also **logic** (***log***):

> ***fc, log:*** Alliteration is a very effective poetic device when used sparingly but appropriately.

The meaning expressed by *but* here is entirely illogical. *But* implies opposition, yet it is likely that a poet who uses alliteration sparingly would also use it appropriately. *And* would be a better coordinator here.

A particularly weak form of loose coordination overlaps with the overuse of *this* (see #16c, and Appendix 2 under ***ref***):

> ***fc:*** The poem's tone is light and cheery, and this is reinforced by the mainly one-syllable words and the regular rhythm and rhyme.

If you ever find such an *and this* in your draft, try to revise it, for not only is the coordination weak, but the demonstrative *this* is weak as well, since it has no antecedent:

> ***revised:*** The poem's light and cheery tone is reinforced by the mainly one-syllable words and the regular rhythm and rhyme.

Another kind of faulty coordination links several short independent clauses with coordinating conjunctions, mostly *and*'s; the result is a loose string of seemingly unrelated parts. Such sentences tend to ramble on and on, emphasizing very little.

> ***fc, rambling:*** The ferry rates were increased and the bigger commercial vehicles had to pay more to use the ferry service and so the cost of transporting goods rose and the consumers who bought those goods had to pay more for them but they had to pay higher fares on the ferries as well and naturally most people were unhappy about it.

41

The information needed to make the point is here, but ineffective syntax leaves the reader floundering, trying to decipher the connections and the thoughts behind the whole utterance. The *but* seems to be used less for logic than for variety, and the vague *it* at the end effectively dissipates any emphasis the sentence might have had. A little tinkering sorts out the facts, shortens the sentence by almost half, reduces the five coordinating conjunctions to a pair of correlative conjunctions, reduces the six independent clauses to two independent and one subordinate, and achieves some emphasis at the end:

> ***revised:*** Not only did the increased ferry rates cost travellers more, but, since the operators of commercial vehicles also had to pay more, the cost of transported goods rose as well, affecting all consumers.

See also #29i and #27b.

Exercise 41 (1) Using subordination

Convert each of the following pairs of sentences into a complex sentence by subordinating one or the other.

1. The book was well written. I did not find it rewarding.
2. The wind was very cold. She wore a heavy sweater.
3. It stopped snowing. We shovelled the driveway.
4. She read a good book. He played solitaire.
5. The meeting was contentious. A consensus was reached.

Exercise 41 (2) Correcting faulty coordination

Revise the following sentences to eliminate faulty or loose coordination; aim for good subordination, unity, emphasis, and logic. You may also find that you can reduce wordiness.

1. There are no windows in the room, and all lighting is from fluorescent fixtures.
2. At this point Ophelia becomes confused, and this becomes evident when she speaks her next line.
3. Patrick Lewis is a compelling character, and *In the Skin of a Lion* is a great novel about early twentieth-century Toronto.
4. The last appearance of the ghost is in the "closet" scene and the purpose of its appearance is to prevent Hamlet from diverging from his "blunted purpose."
5. Her experiments with chimpanzees were unusual but they were interesting.
6. Older people have already been through what others are experiencing, and this enables them to help.
7. Experts are not always right, and they are seldom wrong.
8. The city's streets are well paved and some of them badly need repair.
9. He is a genius; some people claim that he is an imposter.
10. The stores are usually the first to remind us that Christmas is coming and set the mood with decorations, music, and advertising.

42 Faulty Logic

log Clear and logical thinking is essential to clear and effective writing. For example, avoid sweeping statements: over-generalization is one of the most common weaknesses in writing. Precise claims and statements of fact will make your writing clearer. Make sure that the evidence you use is sound and that the authorities you cite are credible, current, and reliable. Such matters are particularly important in argumentative writing—as much writing, especially academic writing, is argumentative to some degree. Weak reasoning will hurt your attempt to convince the reader of the point you're trying to argue. You will want to avoid such logical missteps as begging the question, reasoning in a circle, jumping to conclusions, and leaning on false analogies, which can seriously decrease the effectiveness of an essay (see #10e–h).

There are many ways in which logic is important even in something so small as a sentence. The problems discussed in the preceding sections, from *Misplaced Modifiers* on, are in many instances problems in logic. Following are some examples of other ways in which sentences can be illogical. Unsound reasoning leads to sentences like this:

> ***log:*** You could tell that James's father was proud of him, for he had the boy's picture on his desk.

42

The conclusion may seem reasonable, but it should at least be qualified with a *probably*, or more evidence should be provided; for there are other possible reasons for the picture's being on the desk. James's mother could have put it there, and the father not bothered to remove it; perhaps he's afraid to. Or he could feel love for his son, but not pride. Or he could be feigning love and pride for appearances' sake, knowing inside that he doesn't feel either. Here's another example:

> ***log:*** Wordsworth is perhaps the first English Romantic poet, for his major themes—nature and human life—are characteristic of the Romantic style of poetry.

To begin with, the word *perhaps* is ineffective: either the writer is making a point of Wordsworth's primacy and there is no "perhaps" about it, or there is no point to be made and the whole clause is superfluous. Even more serious is the way evidence is given to substantiate the statement: if the mere presence in his poetry of themes common to Romanticism makes him first, then all Romantic poets are first. The writer probably meant something like "Wordsworth is the first English Romantic poet to develop the major themes of the Romantic movement." As for these "major themes," just how valid is the implication that "human life" is especially characteristic of Romantic writers? No amount of revision can repair this muddy thinking.

Even if writers know clearly what they want to say, they have to choose and use words thoughtfully:

> ***log:*** The town is surrounded on one side by the ocean.

If the town were indeed *surrounded* by the ocean, it would be an island. The correct word here is *bounded*. This error might equally well be designated an error in diction: see #69 and ***ww*** (wrong word) in Appendix 2.

Faulty logic can also affect the way writers put sentences together:

> ***log:*** Having a car with bad spark plugs or points or a dirty carburetor causes it to run poorly and to use too much gas.

This sentence could just as easily be marked ***ss*** (sentence structure, or sentence sense). The intention is clear, but the verb, *causes*, has as its subject the gerund *having*; consequently the sentence says that the mere possession of the afflicted car is what causes it to run poorly—as if one could borrow a similar car and it would run well. A logical revision:

> ***revised:*** Bad spark plugs or bad points or a dirty carburetor cause a car to run poorly and to use too much gas.

Faulty comparisons are another cause of illogicality:

> ***log, comp:*** French painting did not follow the wild and exciting forms of Baroque art as closely as most European countries.

Again the meaning is apparent, but the syntax faulty; readers would be annoyed at having to revise the sentence themselves in order to understand it. The sentence says either that "European countries followed the wild and exciting forms of Baroque art" to some degree or that "French painting followed most European countries more closely than it followed the wild and exciting forms of Baroque art," neither of which makes sense. Simply completing the comparison straightens out the syntax and permits the intended meaning to come through unambiguously:

> ***revised:*** French painting did not follow the wild and exciting forms of Baroque art as closely as did that of most European countries.

See also ***comp*** in Appendix 2.

Another kind of ambiguity appears in this sentence:

> ***log:*** Numerous scientific societies were founded in every developed country.

The intended meaning is probably that every developed country had at least one scientific society—but it could just as well mean that there were numerous such societies in each country. See also ***ambig*** and ***cl*** (clarity) in Appendix 2.

Here's another kind of illogical sentence:

> ***log:*** His lack of cynicism was visible in every paragraph of his essay.

The meaning is clear, but a reader might find it odd to think of a *lack* being *visible*. Put it more logically:

> ***revised:*** Every paragraph of his essay revealed his idealism.

Make sure that nouns are inflected to agree logically with the context:

> ***log:*** All the legislators appeared at the committee to express their view on health care reforms.

Clearly the legislators expressed their *views*, not just one *view.*

Sometimes an extra word creeps in and weakens an otherwise logical sentence:

> ***log:*** Alexander Graham Bell is known as the modern inventor of the telephone.

42

The writer was probably thinking subconsciously of the telephone as a *modern* invention, and the word just popped into the sentence. Thinking critically, one sees that the word *modern* implies that there have been one or more earlier, perhaps even ancient, inventors of the telephone.

Finally, make sure your sentences actually say something worth saying. Here's one that doesn't:

> ***log:*** The mood and theme play a very significant part in this poem.

This could be called an "empty" sentence (the weak intensifier *very* suggests that the writer subconsciously felt the need to prop it up). It would be illogical for the *theme* of a poem to play other than a significant part in it.

Exercise 42 Improving logic

Revise the following sentences to eliminate errors in logic.

1. As he approached the shore, he felt a challenge between himself and the sea.
2. Milton's influence on other subsequent poets was very great.
3. Some auto accidents are unavoidable, but can be prevented by proper maintenance.
4. Shakespeare fashioned *A Midsummer Night's Dream* around the theme of love and created the characters and situations to illustrate it in the best possible way. Thus he freely used a variety of comic devices in developing the theme.
5. By the use of imagery, diction, symbolism, and sound, we may also see the structure of the plot.
6. It employed the technique of using projected images on a screen and a corresponding taped conversation which visually enforced the lesson.

Exercise 42 Improving logic – *continued*

7. Throughout history philosophers have been discussing and proposing theories about our purpose on earth, and thus far they can be divided into three general camps.
8. Through the use of too much abstract language, jargon, and clichés, the clarity and effectiveness of this article have been destroyed.
9. As I think back to the days when we were in our early teens, we had a lot of fun together.
10. After his wife died, his paintings of excited forms changed to quiet ones.

Review Exercise, Chapters II, III, and IV Sentence errors and weaknesses

The following sentences contain various kinds of errors and weaknesses discussed in the preceding chapters. Decide what is wrong with each sentence, label it with the appropriate correction symbol, and then revise the sentence in order to eliminate the problem. Some of the sentences have more than one thing wrong with them.

1. Our coach is overbearing, tall, overpaid, and over forty.
2. One receives this impression when the colour of the picture is considered.
3. Many organic diseases present symptoms that are very similar to autism.
4. Great distances now separate he and his father.
5. The writer's skill was very good.
6. It's true that love and romance come when you least expect it.
7. No player in our school has ever scored as highly as Schmidt did this year.
8. The poem is separated into two parts. The first being his memories and an account of how he reacted to his father's death.
9. Its shape is rounded somewhat resembling a keyhole.
10. I pulled over to the side of the road in a green truck I had borrowed from my roommate, and because the weather was warm I was dressed only in a bathing suit and a bandana, which I had tied around my head.

Review Exercise, Chapters II, III, and IV
Sentence errors and weaknesses – *continued*

11. Borelli supposed that there was a tendency for celestial bodies to attract each other but a fluid pressure prevented this.
12. Shakespeare's *Othello* is a brilliant but tragic story of the betrayal of the Moor of Venice by his most trusted lieutenant, Iago.
13. The whole meaning of Housman's poem is that it is better to die young with honour and glory intact than to have someone take it away from you.
14. The forefinger along with the other digits of the hand have enabled us to evolve to the position of being a creative and destructive species.
15. He says he would like to have another chance at being premier; but if he couldn't run the government right the first time, how can anyone think he's about to do it right again?
16. Smitty is so eager about Michael's friendship, and this is easy to understand even the first time one reads the story.
17. Those who are actually involved in this holiday frenzy may find themselves feeling like getting in touch with old friends, making peace with people they haven't been getting along with, giving to their loved ones and even to strangers, decorating, and enjoying each other's company.
18. They preferred to go out with friends to movies and parties than to stay home and watch TV with their families.
19. By creating an atmosphere of concern for the main character we are more open to the message of the story.
20. What a university stands for more than anything else is an institution where one furthers his education.
21. He has an old worn coat which is far too big for him, but alterations are something he has neither money for nor feels the need to get done.
22. I feel faint; the reason is because I am hungry.
23. Her success is credited to her slyness and wit which always prevails over her daughter's weakness.
24. Physical activity of any kind is always beneficial for the individual.
25. At present the fees are already very expensive.

Punctuation

V

43 Internal Punctuation: Comma, Semicolon, Colon, Dash

How to Use Commas, Semicolons, Colons, and Dashes

44 Between Independent Clauses

45 To Set Off Adverbial Clauses

46 To Set Off Introductory and Concluding Words and Phrases

47 To Set Off Concluding Summaries and Appositives

48 To Set Off Nonrestrictive Elements

49 Between Items in a Series

Punctuation Marks That Come in Pairs: Commas, Dashes, and Parentheses

50 Punctuating Sentence Interrupters

51 Parentheses

52 Brackets

53 End Punctuation: Period, Question Mark, and Exclamation Point

54 Punctuation with Quotations: Using Quotation Marks

55 Avoiding Common Errors in Punctuation

p There are two common misconceptions about punctuation: first, punctuation is of no importance—it has little to do with the effectiveness of written English—and second, good punctuation is a mystery whose secrets are available only to those with a special instinct. Those who believe one or both of these misconceptions may punctuate poorly, whether through fear or lack of concern or both.

First, good punctuation is essential to clear and effective writing. It helps writers clarify meaning and tone and, therefore, helps readers understand what writers communicate: try removing the punctuation marks from a piece of prose, and then see how difficult it is to read it. Punctuation points to meaning that in spoken language would be indicated by pauses, pitch, tone, and stress. In effect, punctuation helps readers *hear* a sentence the way a writer intends. Commas, semicolons, colons, and dashes help to clarify the internal structure of sentences; often the very meaning or beauty of a sentence depends on how it is punctuated.

Second, the principles of good punctuation are not mysterious; mastering them shouldn't be difficult. Even the most inexperienced writers depend on punctuation to help them understand what they read; becoming more aware of the way punctuation operates in the writing of others will help writers generally control punctuation in their own writing.

And here yet another misconception needs to be examined: what are often called the "rules" aren't rules but conventions. For example, English-speakers agree that the word for a small domestic feline animal is *cat*. If you wrote about a *kat*, your readers would probably understand you, but they would wonder why you had strayed from the conventional spelling, and to that extent you would have lost touch with them. But if you chose to call the animal a *zyb*, you would have departed completely from the convention, and you would have lost your readers entirely. The "rule" that *cat is* spelled *c-a-t* is not a moral or legal restraint; no one is going to sue you for spelling it *z-y-b*. But in exercising your freedom of choice you would only be defeating your purpose: clear and effective communication.

Similarly, the conventions of punctuation have come to be agreed upon by writers and readers of English for the purpose of clear and effective communication. Although good writers do sometimes stray from these conventions, they usually do so because they have a sufficient command of them to break a "rule" in order to achieve a desired effect.

A good way to improve your punctuation sense is to become more aware of others' punctuation. Look not only for weaknesses but strengths as well. If you do this consciously as you read, you will soon acquire a better sense of what punctuation does and how it does it.

The following discussions cover the common circumstances and even some relatively uncommon ones. If you find it hard to grasp the principles, you may need to review the appropriate sections on grammar and sentence structure in the preceding chapters. Note that many of the principles not only allow but even invite you to exercise a good deal of choice.

Hyphens and *apostrophes* are dealt with in the discussion of spelling in chapter VI: see #62-o–s and #62v, respectively.

43 Internal Punctuation: Comma, Semicolon, Colon, Dash

43a Comma ,

The **comma** is a light or mild separator. It is the most neutral punctuation mark and the most used mark. A comma makes a reader pause slightly. Use it to separate words, phrases, and clauses from each other when no heavier or more expressive mark is required or desired.

Main functions of commas

43a

Basically commas are used in three ways; if you know these conventions, you should have little trouble with commas:

1. Generally, use a comma between independent clauses joined by a coordinating conjunction (*and*, *but*, *or*, *nor*, *for*, *yet*, *so*; see #23a; see also #44a and #44e–g):

   We went to the National Gallery, and then we walked to the Parliament Buildings.

   Most of us went back to college in the fall, but Dorothy was tempted by an opportunity to travel, so she took off for Italy.

2. Generally, use commas to separate items in a series of three or more (see #49a–b):

   It is said that early to bed and early to rise will make one healthy, wealthy, and wise.

   Robert Bateman, Emily Carr, and Mary Pratt are three Canadian painters.

See #55c on a common error with such constructions.

3. Generally, use commas to set off parenthetical elements, such as interruptive or introductory words, phrases, and clauses and nonrestrictive appositives or nonrestrictive relative clauses (see #45–48 and #50a):

   There are, however, some exceptions.

   Grasping the remote control firmly, she walked away.

E.M. Forster's last novel, *A Passage to India*, is both serious and humorous.

Caffè latte, which has always been a popular drink in Europe, is now popular in North America.

Other conventional uses of the comma

1. Use a comma between elements of an emphatic contrast:

   This is a practical lesson, not a theoretical one.

2. Use a comma to indicate a pause where a word has been acceptably omitted:

   Ron is a conservative; Sally, a radical.

   To err is human; to forgive, divine.

3. Use commas to set off a noun of address (see #13b):

   Simon, please write a thank-you note to your grandparents.

   Tell me, my darling, how you think I should handle this.

4. Generally, use commas with a verb of speaking before or after a quotation (see also #54d–e):

   Then Dora remarked, "That book gave me nightmares."

   "It doesn't matter to me," said Alain laughingly.

5. Use commas after the salutation of informal letters (Dear Gail,) and after the complimentary close of all letters (Yours truly,). In formal letters, a colon is conventional after the salutation (Dear Mr. Eng:).

6. Use commas with dates. Different forms are possible:

   She left on January 11, 2003, and was gone a month.
   (Note the comma *after* the year.)

   You may also place the date before the month—a style preferred by some writers in Canada and Britain—in which case no comma is required:

   She left on 11 January 2003 and was gone a month.

Whichever style you choose, make sure you use it consistently.

When referring only to month and year, you may use a comma or not, but again, be consistent:

> The book was published in March, 2007, in Canada.

> It was published here in March 2007.

7. Use commas to set off geographical names and addresses:

> She left Fredericton, New Brunswick, and moved to Hamilton, Ontario, in hopes of finding a better-paying job. (Note the commas *after* the names of the provinces.)

> Their summer address will be 11 Bishop's Place, Lewes, Sussex, England.

For some common errors with commas, see #55a–h.

43b Semicolon ;

The **semicolon** is a heavy separator, often almost equivalent to a period or "full stop." It forces a much longer pause than a comma does. And compared with the comma, it is used sparingly. Basically, semicolons have only two functions:

1. Generally, use a semicolon between closely related independent clauses that are not joined by one of the coordinating conjunctions (see #23a.1 and #44d):

> Tap water often tastes of chemicals; spring water imported from France usually does not.

> The lab had 20 new laptop computers; however, there were 25 students in the class.

See #55j on common misuses of the semicolon.

2. Use a semicolon instead of a comma if a comma would not be heavy enough; for example, if the clauses or the elements in a series have internal commas of their own (see #44b and #49c).

> Their class presentation examined three novels written by Canadian authors and set largely outside Canada: Edeet Ravel's *Wait for Me*, which is set in Israel and the Palestinian territory; Michael Ondaatje's *Anil's Ghost*, which takes place primarily in Sri Lanka; and David Bergen's *The Time in Between*, set principally in Vietnam.

43c Colon :

Colons are commonly used to introduce lists, examples, and long or formal quotations, but their possibilities in more everyday sentences are often overlooked. The reason a colon is useful is that it looks forward or anticipates: it gives readers a push toward the next part of the sentence. In the preceding sentence, for example, the colon sets up a sense of expectation about what is coming. It points out, even emphasizes, the relation between the two parts of the sentence (that is, a second part clarifies what the first part says). A semicolon in the same spot would bring readers to an abrupt halt, leaving it up to them to make the necessary connection between the two parts. Here are more examples; in some, the anticipatory function of the colon is perhaps less obvious, but it is there:

> Vita's garden contained only white flowers: roses, primulas, and primroses.

> Let me add just this: anyone who expects to lose weight must be prepared to exercise.

> It was an unexpectedly lovely time of year: trees were in blossom, garden flowers bloomed all around, the sky was clear and bright, and the temperature was just right.

> The rain came down during the race: we soon started slipping on the slick pavement.

Nevertheless, don't get carried away and overuse the colon: its effectiveness would wear off if it appeared more than once or twice a page. And see #55k on how to avoid a common misuse of the colon.

Spacing after a Colon
One space after a colon is the norm. And only one space follows colons setting off subtitles or in footnotes or bibliographical entries.

43d Dash —

The **dash** is a popular punctuation mark, especially in e-mail and other more informal communications. Hasty writers often use it as a substitute for a comma, or where a colon would be more emphatic. Use a dash only when you have a definite reason for doing so. Like the colon, the dash sets up expectations in a reader's mind. But whereas the colon sets up an expectation that what follows will somehow explain, summarize, define, or otherwise comment on what has gone before, a dash suggests that what follows will be somehow surprising, involving some sort of twist, or at least a contrary idea. Consider the following sentence:

> The teacher praised my wit, my intelligence, my organization, and my research—and penalized the paper for its poor spelling and punctuation.

Here the dash adds to the punch of what follows it. A comma there would deprive the sentence of much of its force; it would even sound odd, since the resulting matter-of-fact tone would not be in harmony with what the sentence was saying. Only a dash can convey the appropriate *tone* (see the introduction to chapter VII). Another example:

> What he wanted—and he wanted it very badly indeed—was the last piece of chocolate cake.

To set off the interrupting clause with commas instead of dashes wouldn't be "incorrect," but the result would be weaker, for the content of the clause is clearly meant to be emphatic. Only dashes have the power to signal that emphasis; commas would diminish the force of the clause (see #50c).

The dash is also handy in some long and involved sentences, for example after a long series before a summarizing clause:

> Our longing for the past, our hopes for the future and our neglect of the present moment—all these and more go to shape our everyday lives, often in ways unseen or little understood.

Even here, the emphatic quality of the dash serves the meaning, though its principal function in such a sentence is to mark the abrupt break.

As with colons, don't overuse dashes. They are even stronger marks, but they lose effectiveness if used often.

44–49 How to Use Commas, Semicolons, Colons, and Dashes

44 Between Independent Clauses

44a Comma and Coordinating Conjunction

Generally, use a comma between independent clauses joined by one of the coordinating conjunctions (*and*, *but*, *or*, *nor*, *for*, *yet*, and sometimes *so*; see #23a.3):

> The revision of the text proved difficult, and she found herself burning the midnight oil.

> It was a serious speech, but Gordon included many jokes along the way, and the audience loved it.

> Naieli could go into debt for the sports car, or she could go on driving her old jalopy.

> Don knew he shouldn't do it, yet he couldn't stop himself.

If the clauses are short, or if only one of a pair of clauses is short, the comma or commas may be omitted:

> The road was smooth and the car was running well and the weather was perfect.

> We studied all night so we were ready.

But sometimes even with a short clause, the natural pause of a comma may make the sentence read more smoothly and clearly:

> The building was respectably old, for the ivy had climbed nearly to the top of its three storeys.

When the clauses are parallel in structure the comma may often be omitted:

> Art is long and life is short.

> He smirked and she simpered.

When two clauses have the same subject, a comma is less likely to be needed between them:

> It was windy and it was wet. (A comma here would detract from the effect produced by the parallel structure and alliteration of these two short clauses.)

> The play was well produced and it impressed everyone who saw it.

When the subject is omitted from the second clause, a comma should not be used (see #55d):

> It was windy and wet.

Proofreading Tip

Using Commas between Independent Clauses of Contrast and Before *FOR* and *SO*

Independent clauses joined by *but* and *yet*, which explicitly mark a contrast, will almost always need a comma, even if they are short or parallel, or have the same subject:

> It was windy, yet it was warm.

And when you join two clauses with the coordinating conjunction *for*, always put a comma in front of it to prevent its being misread as a preposition:

> Amanda was eager to leave early, for the restaurant was sure to be crowded.

The conjunction *so* almost always needs a comma, but remember that *so* is considered informal (see #23a.2).

44b

44b Semicolon and Coordinating Conjunction

You will sometimes want to use a semicolon between independent clauses even though they are joined by a coordinating conjunction. A semicolon is appropriate when at least one of the clauses contains other punctuation:

> Distracted as he was, the English professor, Herbert, the best cryptic crossword player in the district, easily won the contest; and no one who knew him—or even had only heard of him—was in the least surprised.

44c Dash and Coordinating Conjunction

When you want a longer pause to create extra emphasis, a dash placed before a coordinating conjunction would produce a stronger effect than either a comma or a semicolon:

> Sameer protested that he was sorry for all his mistakes—but he went right on making them.

For a different rhetorical effect, change *but* to the more neutral *and*; a dash then takes over the contrasting function:

> Sameer protested that he was sorry for all his mistakes—and he went right on making them.

Similarly, consider the different effects of these two versions of the same basic sentence:

> It may not be the easiest way, but it's the only way we know.

> It may not be the easiest way—but it's the only way we know.

Even a period could be used between such clauses, since there is nothing inherently wrong with beginning a sentence with *And* or *But*. Even as sentence openers, they are still doing their job of coordinating. See #23a.3.

44d Semicolon Without Coordinating Conjunction

To avoid a *comma splice* (see the next section), generally use a semicolon between independent clauses that are not joined with one of the coordinating conjunctions (*and*, *but*, *or*, *nor*, *for*, *yet*, *so*):

> The actual prize is not important; it is the honour connected with it that matters.

> Leanna was exhausted and obviously not going to win; nevertheless, she persevered and finished the race.

44e Comma Splice

Using only a comma between independent clauses not joined with a coordinating conjunction results in a **comma splice** (*cs*):

> *cs:* The actual prize is not important, it is the honour connected with it that matters.

> *cs:* Being a mere child I didn't fully understand what I had witnessed, I just knew it was wrong.

> *cs:* He desperately wanted to eat, however he was too weak to get out of bed.

A semicolon signals that an independent clause comes next. But a comma tells readers that something subordinate comes next; an independent clause coming instead would derail their train of thought. A comma with a coordinating conjunction is enough to prevent the derailment of thought:

> The prime minister is elected, but the senate members are not.

With few exceptions (see below), a comma *without* a coordinating conjunction is not enough. In most such sentences, then, in order to avoid seriously distracting your readers, use semicolons:

> Being a mere child I didn't fully understand what I had witnessed; I just knew it was wrong.
>
> Adverbs can usually move around in a sentence; conjunctions are not as flexible.
>
> Vancouver, the largest city in British Columbia, is not the capital; Victoria has that distinction.

For a discussion of ways to correct comma splices, see ***cs*** in Appendix 2.

44f–g Exceptions: Commas Alone Between Independent Clauses

44f Commas with Short and Parallel Clauses

If the clauses are short enough that a reader can take them both in with a single glance, and especially if they are also parallel in structure, a comma rather than a semicolon may be enough:

> He cooked, she ate.
>
> Lightning flashed, thunder roared.

44g Commas with Series of Clauses

Relatively short independent clauses in a series of three or more, especially if they are grammatically parallel, may be separated by commas rather than semicolons:

> I saw, I shopped, I bought.
>
> He cooked, she ate, they fell in love.
>
> If you want to do well, you must read carefully, you must write thoughtfully, and you must revise thoroughly.

44h Semicolons with Conjunctive Adverbs and Transitions

Be sure to use a semicolon and not just a comma between independent clauses that you join with a conjunctive adverb, and yes, that includes *however* and *therefore*. Here is a list of most of the common ones:

accordingly	finally	likewise	similarly
afterward	further	meanwhile	still
also	furthermore	moreover	subsequently
anyway	hence	namely	then
besides	however	nevertheless	thereafter
certainly	indeed	next	therefore
consequently	instead	nonetheless	thus
conversely	later	otherwise	undoubtedly

The same caution applies to common transitional phrases such as these:

after this	if not	in the meantime
as a result	in addition	on the contrary
for example	in fact	on the other hand
for this reason	in short	that is

Conjunctive adverbs often have the *feel* of subordinating conjunctions, but they are not conjunctions, although some dictionaries label them as conjunctions for these meanings. Think of them as adverbs doing a joining or "conjunctive" job:

> The text was convoluted; therefore, she got a headache as she read it.

Here *therefore* works very much like *so*; nevertheless, *therefore* is a conjunctive adverb and requires the semicolon.

> He felt well enough to go; however, his doctor ordered him to stay in bed.

Here *however* works very much like *but*; nevertheless, *however* is a conjunctive adverb and requires the semicolon.

Proofreading Tip

On the Comma Following *HOWEVER*
Note that whereas other conjunctive adverbs will often, but not always, be followed by commas, *however* as a conjunctive adverb (unless it ends a sentence) is followed by a comma to prevent its being misread as a regular adverb meaning "in whatever way" or "to whatever degree," as in "However you go, just make sure you get there on time."

However sometimes sounds overly formal at the beginning of a sentence or clause. Unless you want special emphasis on it, put it at some other appropriate place in the clause. Often, delaying it just one or two words works best:

> His doctor, however, ordered him to stay in bed.

Since conjunctive adverbs can easily be shifted around within a clause, you may find it helpful to apply this test if you aren't sure whether a particular word is a conjunctive adverb or a conjunction. Just remember that adverbs can move around in the sentence; conjunctions cannot.

> His doctor ordered him, however, to stay in bed.

44i Dashes and Colons Without Coordinating Conjunctions

Dashes and colons may also be used between independent clauses not joined by coordinating conjunctions. Use a dash when you want stronger emphasis on the second clause; use a colon when the second clause explains or enlarges upon the first (see #43c and #43d). In many sentences, either a dash or a colon would work; the choice depends on the desired tone or emphasis:

> The film was dreadful from beginning to end: a plausible plot must have been the last thing on the director's mind.
>
> The proposal horrified Jon—it was ludicrous.
>
> Derek took the evolutionary way out: he turned and ran.
>
> It was a unique occasion—everyone at the meeting agreed on what should be done.

Note that a comma would not be correct in any of these examples. A semi-colon would work, but it would be weak and usually inappropriate (except perhaps in the first example). But note that a *period*, especially in the second and third examples, would achieve a crisp and emphatic effect by turning each into two separate sentences.

44j Run-on (Fused) Sentences

Failure to put any punctuation between independent clauses where there is also no coordinating conjunction results in a **run-on** or **fused** sentence:

> ***run-on:*** Philosophers' views did not always meet with the approval of the authorities therefore there was constant conflict between writers and the church or state.

A semicolon after *authorities* corrects this serious error. See #34; see also ***run-on*** in Appendix 2.

> Philosophers' views did not always meet with the approval of the authorities; therefore, there was constant conflict between writers and the church or state.

Exercise 44 (1) Punctuating between independent clauses

Insert whatever punctuation mark (other than a period) you think works best between the independent clauses in the following sentences. You may decide that some need no punctuation. Could some be punctuated in more than one way?

1. Everyone thought the technological revolution would reduce our use of paper we were wrong.
2. Jamil needed some help with his lab report so he thought he would make an appointment with a tutor.
3. Cartoons are enjoyed by both children and adults sometimes adults enjoy them more.
4. Some people eat to live others live to eat.
5. It was a fascinating hypothesis but it was greeted with silence.
6. His belly shook he had a red nose he was surrounded by reindeer.
7. The hurricane warning went up and most people sauntered to their shelters others continued to watch TV.
8. Easy come easy go.
9. You live you learn.
10. The strike was over the people were jubilant.

Exercise 44 (2) Correcting comma splices and run-ons

Correct any comma splices and run-on sentences in the following:

1. I had not been back in ages therefore I was surprised to see all the changes.
2. We started to edit the next edition of the newsletter, soon the office was littered with coffee cups and paper.
3. Atwood uses figurative language, however the literal sense is sufficiently clear.
4. But we sat silent the scene before us on the stage had left us stunned.
5. They make faces at each other each time they pass on the street.
6. This sales letter doesn't acknowledge women exist therefore they will never buy the product.
7. Life in those days was a gruelling chore, but at least life was short.
8. The dictator's statue stood for almost thirty years however it was toppled in less than an hour.
9. We pushed off from the shore the canoes were buffeted by the waves we found ourselves unexpectedly in the water.
10. Things went suspiciously well the first person to look at the house wanted to buy it.

45 To Set Off Adverbial Clauses

45a Commas with Introductory Clauses

Generally, use a comma between an introductory adverbial clause and an independent (main) clause:

> After I had selected all the items I wanted, I discovered that I had left my wallet at home.
>
> Since she was elected by a large majority, she felt that she had a strong mandate for her policies.
>
> When the party was over, I went straight home.

When the introductory clause is short and when there would be no pause if the sentence were spoken aloud, you may often omit the comma. But if omitting the comma could cause misreading, retain it:

> Whenever I wanted, someone would bring me something to eat.
>
> After the sun had set, high above the mountains came the fighter jets.

Whenever you're not sure the meaning will be clear without it, use a comma.

45b Commas with Concluding Clauses

A comma may or may not be needed between an independent clause and a following adverbial clause. If the subordinate clause is essential to the meaning of the sentence, it is in effect *restrictive* and should not be set off with a comma; if it is not essential but contains only additional information or comment, it is *nonrestrictive* and should be set off with a comma (see #48). Consider the following examples: 45b

> I went straight home when the party was over.
>
> She did an excellent job on her second essay, although the first one was a disaster.

In most cases final clauses such as these will be necessary and won't require a comma. When in doubt, try omitting the clause to see if the sentence still says essentially what you want it to. See also #48c.

Exercise 45 Punctuating adverbial clauses

Insert commas where you think necessary in the following sentences. Indicate any places where you think a comma would be optional.

1. Although it was almost midnight he knew he had to stay up and finish writing the report.
2. You may begin now if you want to.
3. You may begin whenever you wish.
4. The snowboarding is especially good this year because the snow is plentiful.
5. Because the snow is plentiful this year the snowboarding is especially good.
6. Before you move to Paris you should study French.

Exercise 45 Punctuating adverbial clauses – *continued*

7. Sleeping in on the weekend is a fundamental right though my family does not recognize the fact.
8. Some people can tell where commas are required when they read the sentences aloud and listen for the natural pauses.
9. After Anne finished the report which showed marked improvement in profits she seemed less happy than she had before she began the report.
10. However you look at it the solution needs to be simple and practical or the boss will not approve of it.

46 To Set Off Introductory and Concluding Words and Phrases

46a Adverbs and Adverbial Phrases

Generally, set off a long introductory adverbial phrase with a comma:

> After many years as leader of the union, Jean retired gracefully.
>
> To get the best results from your ice cream maker, you must follow the instruction manual carefully.
>
> Just like all the other long-time employees, Radha felt loyal to the company.

Generally, set off a word or short phrase if you want a distinct pause, for example, for emphasis or qualification or to prevent misreading:

> Unfortunately, the weather didn't cooperate.
>
> Generally, follow my advice about punctuation.
>
> Usually, immature people are difficult to work with.

Of the conjunctive adverbs, *however* is most often set off, though the others frequently are as well (see #44h and #55f).

When such words and phrases follow the independent clause, most will be restrictive and therefore not set off with commas:

> Jean retired gracefully after many years as leader of the union.

You must follow the instruction manual carefully to get the best results from your ice cream maker.

Aarti moved to Calgary in 2003.

If you intend the concluding element to complete the sense of the main clause, don't set it off; if it merely provides additional information or comment, set it off. The presence or absence of punctuation tells your readers how you want the sentence to be read.

46b Participles and Participial Phrases

Always set off an introductory participle or participial phrase with a comma (see #21d):

Finding golf unexpectedly difficult, Kevin sought extra help.

Feeling victorious, Shirin left the room.

Having been in the computer lab so long, Jason scarcely recognized the world when he emerged.

Puzzled, Karen turned back to the beginning of the chapter.

Closing participles and participial phrases almost always need to be set off as well. Read the sentence aloud; if you feel a distinct pause, use a comma:

Kevin sought extra help, finding golf unexpectedly difficult.

Higher prices result in increased wage demands, contributing to inflationary pressures.

Occasionally such a sentence will flow clearly and smoothly without a comma, especially if the modifier is essential to the meaning:

Shirin left the room feeling victorious.

She sat there looking puzzled.

If the closing participle modifies a predicate noun or a direct object, there usually should not be a comma:

He was a man lacking in courage.

I left him feeling bewildered. (He was bewildered.)

But if the participle in such a sentence modifies the subject, if it could also conceivably modify the object, then a comma is necessary:

> I left him, feeling bewildered. (I was bewildered.)

Only the presence or absence of the comma tells a reader how to understand such a sentence.

46b

Proofreading Tip

Commas and Gerunds; Commas and Participial Phrases
Don't mistake a gerund for a participle (see #21d and #21f). A gerund or gerund phrase functioning as the subject should not be followed by a comma (see #55a):

> ***participle:*** Dancing in the street, we celebrated the arrival of summer.
>
> ***gerund:*** Dancing in the street is a wonderful release of energy.

Proofreading Tip

Commas and Infinitive Phrases
Don't mistake a long infinitive phrase functioning as a subject noun for one functioning as an adverb (see #21a):

> ***noun:*** To put together a meal for six without help is a remarkable feat.
>
> ***adverb:*** To put together a meal for six without help, you need to be very organized or a professional chef.

46c Absolute Phrases

Always set off absolute phrases with commas (see #12r and #21i):

> The doors locked and bolted, they went to bed feeling secure.
>
> Timmy went on stage, head held high, a grin spreading across his face.

Exercise 46 Punctuating opening and closing words and phrases

Insert commas where you think necessary in the following sentences. Indicate any places where you think a comma would be optional.

1. In December my family always goes skiing.
2. We walked slowly soaking up the sights and sounds along the waterfront.
3. At the end of the lecture I had no clearer understanding of the subject than I had when I came in.
4. The dog walked and fed I decided to relax with a murder mystery.
5. The brain regulates and integrates our senses allowing us to experience our environment.
6. Raising prices results in increased wage demands adding to inflation.
7. Following the instructions I poured the second chemical into the beaker with the first and shook them shutting my eyes in the expectation of something unpleasant.
8. As usual before going to bed I turned on the eleven o'clock news.
9. To make a long story short I found my aunt looking healthier than I'd ever seen her before.
10. Looking pop-eyed and furious the coach stared back at the referee without saying a word.

47 To Set Off Concluding Summaries and Appositives

Both dashes and colons can set off concluding summaries and appositives. Some writers think dashes are best for short concluding elements and colons for longer ones; but what matters isn't their length but their relation to the rest of the sentence. Use colons for straightforward conclusions, dashes for emphatic or unexpected ones. For example, the following sentences express a conventional idea, with the colon straightforwardly, with the dash somewhat emphatically:

> He wanted only one thing from life: happiness.
>
> He wanted only one thing from life—happiness.

But with a less expected final word the tone changes:

> He wanted only one thing from life—money.

Here a colon would do, since a colon followed by a single word automatically conveys some emphasis, but the strength of the idea would not be as well served by the quietness of a colon as it is by the dash. The same principles apply to setting off longer concluding appositives and summaries, though colons are more common; use a dash only when you want to take advantage of its special emphasis.

48 To Set Off Nonrestrictive Elements

Words, phrases, and clauses are nonrestrictive when they are not essential to the principal meaning of a sentence; they should be set off from the rest of the sentence, usually with commas, though dashes and parentheses can also be used (see #50). A restrictive modifier is essential to the meaning and should not be set off:

> ***restrictive:*** Anyone wanting a refund should see the manager.
>
> ***nonrestrictive:*** Alex, wanting a refund, asked to see the manager.

The participial phrase explains why Alex asked to see the manager, but the sentence is clear without it: "Alex asked to see the manager"; the phrase *wanting a refund* is therefore not essential and is set off with commas. But without the phrase the first sentence wouldn't make sense: "Anyone should see the manager"; the phrase *wanting a refund* is essential and is not set off. The question most often arises with *relative clauses* (see #12-o and #14d); *appositives*, though usually nonrestrictive, can also be restrictive, and some other elements can also be either restrictive or nonrestrictive (see #45b and #46a–b).

48a Restrictive and Nonrestrictive Relative Clauses

Always set off a nonrestrictive relative clause; do not set off restrictive relative clauses:

> She is a woman who likes to travel.

The relative clause is essential and is not set off.

> Carol, who likes to travel, is going to Greece this summer.

Now the relative clause is merely additional—though explanatory—information: it is not essential to the identification of Carol, who has been explicitly named, nor is it essential to the meaning of the main clause. Being nonrestrictive, then, it should be set off. Consider the following pair of sentences:

> ***incorrect:*** Students, who are hard-working, should expect much from their education.
>
> ***correct:*** Students who are hard-working should expect much from their education.

Set off as nonrestrictive, the relative clause applies to all students, which makes the sentence untrue. Left unpunctuated, the relative clause is restrictive, making the sentence correctly apply only to students who are in fact hard-working.

> The book, which I so badly wanted to read, was not in the library.
>
> The book which I so badly wanted to read was not in the library.

With the clause set off as nonrestrictive, we must assume that the book has been clearly identified in an earlier sentence. Left unpunctuated, the clause identifies "The book" as the particular one the speaker wanted to read but which the library didn't have.

Proofreading Tip

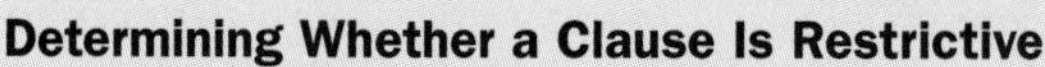

Determining Whether a Clause Is Restrictive

If you can use the relative pronoun *that*, you know the clause is restrictive; *that* cannot begin a nonrestrictive clause:

> The book that I wanted to read was not in the library.

Further, if the pronoun can be omitted (see #14d) altogether, the clause is restrictive, as with *that* in the preceding example and *whom* in the following:

> The person [whom] I most admire is the one who works hard and plays hard.

Don't omit *that* when it is necessary to prevent misreading:

> ***incorrect:*** Different varieties of tea shops sell are medicinal.

A *that* after *tea* prevents misreading the subject of the verb as "different varieties of tea shops."

> ***correct:*** Different varieties of tea that shops sell are medicinal.

Proofreading Tip

Using *THAT* and *WHICH* in Relative Clauses
That is much more common than *which* in restrictive clauses. Indeed, some writers prefer to use *which* only in nonrestrictive clauses. But the use of *which* in both nonrestrictive and restrictive clauses is becoming the norm.

48b Restrictive and Nonrestrictive Appositives

Always set off a nonrestrictive appositive:

48b

> Jan, our youngest daughter, keeps the lawn mowed all summer.
>
> Karl—my current accountant—is very imaginative.
>
> *King Lear* is a noble work of literature, one that will live in human minds for all time.
>
> Virginia is going to bring her sister, Vanessa.

In the last example, the comma indicates that Virginia has only the one sister. Left unpunctuated, the appositive would be restrictive, meaning that Virginia has more than one sister and that the particular one she is going to bring is the one named Vanessa.

Don't mistake a restrictive appositive for a nonrestrictive one:

> ***incorrect:*** The proceedings were opened by union leader, Peter Smith, with remarks attacking the government.

The commas are wrong, since it is only his name, Peter Smith, that clearly identifies him; the appositive is therefore restrictive. But alter the sentence slightly:

> The proceedings were opened by the union's leader, Peter Smith, with remarks attacking the government.

Now the phrase *the union's leader*, with its definite article, identifies the person; the name itself, *Peter Smith*, is only incidental information and is therefore nonrestrictive. This example works only if the union has been introduced in an earlier sentence.

> ***incorrect:*** According to spokesperson, Janina Fraser, the economy is improving daily.

revised: According to spokesperson Janina Fraser, the economy is improving daily.

revised: According to the spokesperson, Janina Fraser, the economy is improving daily.

The definite article makes all the difference. But even the presence or absence of the definite article is not always a sure test:

incorrect: One of the best-known mysteries of the sea is that of the ship, *Mary Celeste*, the disappearance of whose entire crew has never been satisfactorily explained.

correct: One of the best-known mysteries of the sea is that of the ship *Mary Celeste*, the disappearance of whose entire crew has never been satisfactorily explained.

The phrase *the ship* is insufficient identification; the proper name is needed and is therefore restrictive. This error most often occurs when a proper name follows a defining or characterizing word or phrase. In the reverse order, such a phrase is set off as a nonrestrictive appositive:

> Janina Fraser, the spokesperson, said the economy is improving daily.

See #55g for more on restrictive appositives.

48c *Because*-Clauses and Phrases

Adverbial clauses or phrases beginning with *because* (or otherwise conveying that sense) can be a problem when they follow an explicit negative. When *because* follows a negative, punctuate the sentence so that it means what you want it to:

> Mary didn't pass the exam, because she had stayed up all night studying for it: she was so groggy she couldn't even read the questions correctly. (She didn't pass.)

> Mary didn't pass the exam just because she had stayed up all night studying for it. Last-minute review may have helped, but her thorough grasp of the material would have enabled her to pass it without the cramming. (She would have passed anyway.)

Often you can best avoid the possible awkwardness or ambiguity by simply rephrasing a sentence in which *because* follows a negative.

48d Modifiers with *such as*

Nonrestrictive modifiers beginning with *such as* should be set off with commas:

> Johan played all kinds of sports, such as hockey, baseball, and lacrosse.

But be careful not to mistake a nonrestrictive *such as* modifier for a restrictive one. Consider the following example:

> Antibiotics, such as penicillin, are ineffective against the disease.

48d

Because the modifier *such as penicillin* is set off, the sentence implies that *all* antibiotics (of which penicillin is an example) are ineffective against the disease. If the commas were removed, the modifier would become restrictive, and the meaning would change: the sentence would imply that only those antibiotics that are like penicillin are ineffective, though other antibiotics might not be.

Exercise 48 Punctuating nonrestrictive elements

Decide whether the italicized elements in the following sentences are restrictive or nonrestrictive and insert punctuation as required.

1. The student *who takes studying seriously* is the one *who is most likely to succeed.*
2. The novels *I like best* are those page turners *you can buy at the drugstore.*
3. This movie *which was produced on a very low budget* was a popular success.
4. Whitehorse the *capital of Yukon* has a thriving arts community.
5. Pliny *the Elder* wrote about some interesting herbal remedies *involving bat dung and garlic.*
6. Sentence interrupters *such as parenthetical definitions* should be set off with commas.
7. Michel Tremblay *the playwright* is a Quebec writer with a national reputation.
8. Life of Pi *written by Yann Martel* is about a boy and a tiger on a lifeboat.
9. My twin brother *Greg* is very proud of his partner *Martin.*
10. In the view of the small-town newspaper editor *James Borred* the 12-foot worm was nothing to get excited about.

49 Between Items in a Series

49a Commas

Generally, use commas between words, phrases, or clauses in a series of three or more:

> He sells books, magazines, candy, and life insurance.
>
> He stirred the sauce frequently, carefully, and hungrily.
>
> She promised the voters to cut taxes, to limit government spending, and to improve transportation.
>
> Carmen explained that she had visited the art gallery, that she had walked in the park, and that eventually she had gone to a movie.

For information about special cases involving commas between adjectives, see #49f.

49b Comma Before Final Item in a Series

The common practice of omitting the final comma (known as the Oxford comma—found before the conjunction) can be misleading. That final pause will give your sentences a better rhythm, and you will avoid the kind of possible confusion apparent in sentences like these (try adding the final comma and then reading them again):

> The manufacturers sent us shirts, wash-and-wear slacks and shoes. (The shoes were wash-and-wear?)
>
> They prided themselves on having a large and bright kitchen, a productive vegetable garden, a large recreation room with a huge fireplace and two fifty-foot cedar trees. (The trees were in the recreation room?)
>
> The Speech from the Throne discussed international trade, improvements in transportation, slowing down inflation and the postal service. (Do we need to slow down the postal service?)

49c Semicolons

If the phrases or clauses in a series are unusually long or contain other internal punctuation, you might want to separate them with semicolons rather than commas:

> How wonderful it is to awaken in the morning when the birds are clamouring in the trees; to see the bright light of a summer morning streaming into the room; to realize, with

> a sudden flash of joy, that it is Sunday and that this perfect morning is completely yours; and then to loaf in a deckchair without a thought of tomorrow.

> Saint John, New Brunswick; Victoria, British Columbia; and Kingston, Ontario, are all about the same size.

49d Dashes

You can also emphasize items in a series by putting dashes between them—but don't do it often. The sharpness of the breaks greatly heightens the effect of a series:

> Rising taxes—rising insurance rates—rising gas costs—skyrocketing food prices: it is becoming more and more difficult to live decently and still keep within a budget.

Here the omission of *and* before the final item, together with the repetition and parallel structure, heightens the stylistic effect by adding to the stridency; even the colon adds its touch. But dashes can also be effective in a quieter context:

> Upon rounding the bend we were confronted with a breathtaking panorama of lush valleys with meandering streams—flower-covered slopes—great rocks and trees—and, overtopping all, the mighty peaks with their hoods of snow.

49e Colons

Colons, too, can be used in a series but even more rarely than dashes. Colons add emphasis because they are unusual, but mainly their anticipatory nature produces a cumulative effect suitable when successive items in a series build to a climax:

> He held on: he persevered: he fought back: and eventually he won out, regardless of the punishing obstacles.

> It blew: it rained: it hailed: it sleeted: it even snowed—it was a most unusual June even for Medicine Hat.

(Note how the dash in the last example prepares for the final clause.)

49f Series of Adjectives

Use commas between two or more adjectives preceding a noun if they are parallel, each modifying the noun itself; do not put commas between adjectives that are not parallel:

> He is an intelligent, efficient, ambitious officer.

> She is a tall young woman.

She wore a new black felt hat, a long red coat, and a woollen scarf with red, white, and black stripes.

In the first sentence, each adjective modifies *officer.* In the second, *tall* modifies *young woman*; it is a *young woman* who is *tall,* not a *woman* who is *tall* and *young.* In the third, *new* modifies *black felt hat, black* modifies *felt hat,* and *long* modifies *red coat*; *red, white,* and *black* all separately modify *stripes.*

But it isn't always easy to tell whether or not such adjectives are parallel. It often helps to think of each comma as substituting for *and*: try putting *and* between the adjectives. If it sounds logical there, the adjectives are probably parallel and should be separated by a comma; if *and* doesn't seem to work, a comma won't either. For example, you wouldn't say *a black and felt hat* or *a long and red coat,* whereas *red and white and black stripes* is natural. Another test is to change the order of the adjectives. If it sounds odd to say *a felt black hat* instead of *a black felt hat,* then the adjectives probably aren't parallel. A final aid to remember: usually no comma is needed after a number (*three blind mice*) or after common adjectives for size or age (*tall young woman; long red coat; new brick house*). But sometimes you'll have to rely on instinct or common sense. For example, the following sentences seem fine without commas:

49f

There was an ominous wry tone in her voice.

What caught our eye in the antique shop was a comfortable-looking tattered old upholstered leather chair.

See also #55c.

Exercise 49 Punctuating series

Punctuate the following sentences as necessary.

1. The things I expected from my education were maturity spiritual growth and a career.
2. Parsnips sardines and peanut butter were the ingredients for my new culinary creation.
3. The cheerful conscientious young man wore a tight purple shirt embossed with a white drawing of a skull and crossbones very long black dirty trousers and a dangling silver necklace consisting of various small sharp household objects.
4. The smiling cherubic baby with the chubby cheeks soon began to crawl fall and squall.
5. The recital was over the audience leapt to their feet they applauded wildly and the pianist pleased with his performance bowed.

Punctuation Marks That Come in Pairs: Commas, Dashes, and Parentheses

50 Punctuating Sentence Interrupters

Sentence interrupters are parenthetical elements—words, phrases, or clauses—that interrupt the syntax of a sentence. Although we discuss some of these under other headings, here we stress two points: (1) interrupters are set off at *both* ends; (2) you can choose from among three kinds of punctuation marks to set them off: a pair of commas, a pair of dashes, or a pair of parentheses.

50a

50a Interrupters Set Off with Commas

Set off light, ordinary interrupters with a pair of commas:

Robert Munsch, a children's book author, is a favourite with the preteen crowd. (nonrestrictive appositive phrase)

This document, the lawyer says, will complete the contract. (explanatory clause)

Thank you, David, for this much needed advice and the martini. (noun of address)

Mr. Hao, feeling elated, left the judge's office. (participial phrase)

At least one science course, such as botany or astronomy, is required of all students. (prepositional phrase of example)

You may, on the other hand, wish to concentrate on the final examination. (transitional prepositional phrase)

Could you be persuaded to consider this money as, well, a loan? (mild interjection)

Grandparents, who are wise and loving, should be allowed to spend a lot of time with their grandchildren. (nonrestrictive relative clause)

Jet lag, it now occurs to me, may after all be responsible for our falling asleep at dinner. (clause expressing afterthought)

It was, all things considered, a successful concert. (absolute phrase)

50b Interrupters Set Off with Dashes

Use a pair of dashes to set off abrupt interrupters or other interrupters that you wish to emphasize. An interrupter that sharply breaks the syntax of a sentence will often be emphatic for that very reason, and dashes will be appropriate to set it off:

> The increase in enrolment—over fifty per cent—demonstrates the success of our program.
>
> The stockholders who voted for him—quite a sizable group—were obviously dissatisfied with our recent conduct of the business.
>
> He told me—believe this or not!—that he would never drink beer again.
>
> Stephen Jay Gould—the well-known scientist—began his career by studying snails.

In the last example, commas would suffice, but dashes work well because of both the length and the content of the appositive. Wherever you want emphasis or a different tone, you can use dashes where commas would ordinarily serve:

> The employee of the year—Denise Dione—was delighted to receive the prize.
>
> The modern age—as we all know—is a noisy age.

Dashes are also useful to set off an interrupter consisting of a series with its own internal commas, such as our first sentence in this section; set off with commas, such a structure can be confusing:

> ***confusing:*** Sentence interrupters are parenthetical elements, words, phrases, or clauses, that interrupt the syntax of a sentence.
>
> ***clear:*** Sentence interrupters are parenthetical elements—words, phrases, or clauses—that interrupt the syntax of a sentence.

50c

50c Interrupters Set Off with Parentheses

Use parentheses to set off abrupt interrupters or other interrupters that you wish to de-emphasize; often interrupters that could be emphatic can be played down in order to emphasize the other parts of a sentence:

The stockholders who voted for him (quite a sizable group) were obviously dissatisfied with our recent conduct of the business.

It is not possible at this time (it is far too early in the growing season) to predict with any confidence just what the crop yield will be.

Speculation (I mean this in its pejorative sense) is not a safe foundation for a business enterprise.

Some extreme sports (hang-gliding for example) involve unusually high insurance claims.

50c

By de-emphasizing something striking, parentheses can also achieve an effect similar to that of dashes, though by an ironic tone rather than an insistent one.

Proofreading Tip

Punctuation Marks That Occur in Pairs
Remember, punctuation marks that set off sentence interrupters come in pairs. If you put down an opening parenthesis you shouldn't omit the closing one. But sometimes writers accidentally omit the second dash or—especially—the second comma. Reading aloud, perhaps with exaggerated pauses, can help you spot that a mark is missing.

Exercise 50 Punctuating sentence interrupters

Set off the italicized interrupters with commas, dashes, or parentheses. Be prepared to defend your choices.

1. It was seven o'clock in the evening *a mild autumn evening* and the crickets were beginning to chirp.
2. No one *at least no one who was present* wanted to disagree with the speaker's position.
3. Early one Sunday morning *a morning I will never forget* the phone rang unexpectedly.
4. Since it was only a mild interjection *no more than a barely audible snort from the back of the room* he went on with scarcely a pause but with a slightly raised eyebrow and finished his speech.
5. And then suddenly *out of the blue and into my head* came the only possible answer.

51 Parentheses ( )

Parentheses have three principal functions in non-technical writing: (1) to set off certain kinds of interrupters (see #50c above), (2) to enclose cross-reference information within a sentence, as we just did and as we do throughout this book, and (3) to enclose numerals or letters setting up a list or series, as we do in this sentence. Note that if a complete sentence is enclosed in parentheses within another sentence (here is an example of such an insertion), it needs neither an opening capital letter nor a closing period. Note also that if a comma or other mark is called for by the sentence (as in the preceding sentence, and in this one), it comes *after* the closing parenthesis, not before the opening one. Exclamation points and question marks go inside the parenthesis only if they are a part of what is enclosed. (When an entire sentence or more is enclosed, the terminal mark of course comes inside the parenthesis—as does this period.)

52 Brackets [ ]

Brackets (often referred to as "square brackets," since some people use the term *brackets* also to refer to parentheses) are used primarily to enclose something inserted in a direct quotation: see #54j. And if you have to put parentheses inside parentheses—as in a footnote or a bibliographical entry—change the inner ones to brackets.

53 End Punctuation: Period, Question Mark, and Exclamation Point

The end of every sentence must be marked with a period, a question mark, or an exclamation point (but see the note at the end of this paragraph). The period is the most common terminal punctuation; it ends the vast majority of sentences. The question mark is used to end direct questions or statements that are intended as questions. The exclamation point is used to end sentences that express strong emotion, emphatic surprise, or even emphatic query. Sometimes you will need to consider just what effect you want to achieve. Note for example the different effects of the following; in each instance, the end punctuation would dictate the necessary tone of voice and distribution of emphasis and pitch with which the sentence would be said aloud:

> We won. (matter-of-fact)
>
> We won! (surprised or emphatic)
>
> We won? (skeptical or surprised)

53a Period .

Use a **period** to mark the end of statements and neutral commands:

> Canadians use the telephone more than any other people in the world.
>
> Ezra Pound, the author of *The Cantos*, died in 1972.
>
> Don't let yourself be fooled by cheap imitations.

Use a period after most abbreviations:

abbr. Mr. Ms. Dr. Jr.
Ph.D. B.A. St. Mt. etc.

Generally use a period in abbreviated place names:

B.C. P.E.I. Nfld. N.Y. Mass.

But note that two-letter postal abbreviations do not require periods:

BC PE NL NY MA

Periods are not used after metric and other symbols (unless they occur at the end of a sentence):

km cm kg mc^2 ml
kJ C Hz Au Zr

Periods are often omitted with initials, especially of groups or organizations, and especially if the initials are acronyms—that is, words or names made up of initials (AIDS, NATO, CEGEP):

UN UNICEF WHO RCMP RAF
CBC TV APA MLA MP

When in doubt, consult a good dictionary. If there is more than one acceptable usage, be consistent: stick with the one you choose.

Proofreading Tip

On Abbreviations and Periods

(1) Although *Ms.* is not a true abbreviation, it is usually followed by a period.

(2) Some Canadian writers and publishers follow the British convention of omitting the period after abbreviations that include the first and last letter of the abbreviated word: Mr, Mrs, Dr, Jr, St, etc. (And note in the preceding sentence that a period after an abbreviation at the end of a sentence serves as the sentence's period.)

53b Question Mark ?

Use a **question mark** at the end of direct questions:

Who is the greatest poet of all time?

When will the lease expire?

Do not use a question mark at the end of an indirect question: see #55i.

Note that a question mark is necessary after questions that aren't phrased in the usual interrogative way (as might occur if you were writing dialogue):

You're leaving so early? (i.e. "Are you leaving so early?")

You want him to accompany you? (i.e. "Do you want him to accompany you?")

A question appearing as a sentence interrupter still needs a question mark at its end:

I went back to the beginning—what else could I do?—and tried to get it right the second time.

The man in the scuba outfit (what was his name again?) took a rear seat.

Since such interrupters are necessarily abrupt, dashes or parentheses are the appropriate marks to set them off.

See also #12t.

53c Exclamation Point !

Use an **exclamation point** after an emphatic statement or after an expression of emphatic surprise, emphatic query, or strong emotion:

> He came in first, yet it was only his second time in professional competition!
>
> What a loser!
>
> You don't say so!
>
> Isn't it beautiful today!
>
> Not again!
>
> Gosh!

Occasionally an exclamation point may be doubled or tripled for emphasis. It may even follow a question mark, to emphasize the writer's or speaker's disbelief:

> She said what?!
>
> You bought what?! A giraffe?! What were you thinking?!

This device should not be used in formal and academic writing.

Proofreading Tip

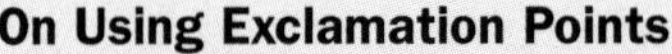
On Using Exclamation Points

Use exclamation points sparingly, if at all, in formal writing. Achieve your desired emphasis by other means: see #29j.

Proofreading Tip

Ending a Sentence with a Dash or Ellipsis

The dash and the three dots of an ellipsis (see #54i) are sometimes used at the end of a sentence, especially in dialogue or at the end of a paragraph or a chapter in order to indicate a pause, a fading away, or an interruption, or to create mild suspense.

54 Punctuation with Quotations: Using Quotation Marks " "

There are two kinds of quotation: dialogue or direct speech (such as you might find in a story, novel, or nonfiction narrative or other essay) and verbatim quotation from a published work or other source (as in a research paper). For the use of quotation marks around titles, see #59a and c.

54a Direct Speech

Enclose all direct speech in quotation marks:

> I remember hearing my mother say to my absentminded father, "Henry, why is the newspaper in the fridge?"

In written dialogue, it is conventional to begin a new paragraph each time the speaker changes:

> "Henry," she said, a note of exasperation in her voice, "why is the newspaper in the fridge?"
>
> "Oh, yes," he replied. "The fish is wrapped in it."
>
> She examined it. "Well, there may have been a fish in it once, but there is no fish in it now."

Even when passages of direct speech are incomplete, the part that is verbatim should be enclosed in quotation marks:

> After only two weeks, he said he was "fed up" and that he was "going to look for a more interesting job."

54b Direct Quotation from a Source

Enclose in quotation marks any direct quotation from another source that you run into your own text:

> According to Anthony Powell, "Books do furnish a room."

1. Prose

Prose quotations of no more than four lines are normally run into the text. Quotations of more than four lines should be treated as "block quotations": they should be indented ten spaces and double-spaced (like the text of your essay):

> When asked why she writes about food, M.F.K. Fisher answers directly:
>
> > It seems to me that our three basic needs, for food and security and love, are so mixed and mingled and entwined that we cannot straightly think of one without the others. So it happens that when I write of hunger, I am really writing about love and the hunger for it, and warmth and the love of it and the hunger for it . . . and then the warmth and richness and fine reality of hunger satisfied . . . and it is all one.

Do not place quotation marks around a block quotation, but do reproduce any quotation marks that appear in the original:

> Budgets can be important. As Dickens has Mr. Micawber say in *David Copperfield*,
>
> > "Annual income twenty pounds, annual expenditure nineteen nineteen six, result happiness. Annual income twenty pounds, annual expenditure twenty pounds ought and six, result misery."

If you're quoting only a single paragraph or part of a paragraph, do not include the paragraph indentation. If you are quoting a passage that is longer than one paragraph, include the indentations for the second and subsequent paragraphs; use three additional spaces for an indentation. If you are quoting a passage of multiple paragraphs that are in quotation marks in the original, include the quotation marks at the beginning of each paragraph, but at the end only of the last one.

2. Poetry

Set off quotations of four or more lines of poetry in the same way. A quotation of one, two, or three lines of poetry may be set off if you want to give it special emphasis; otherwise, run such a quotation into your text.

When you run in more than one line of poetry, indicate the line-breaks with a slash mark or virgule—with a space on each side:

> Dante's spiritual journey begins in the woods: "Midway this way of life, we're bound upon / I woke to find myself in a dark wood / Where the right road was wholly lost and gone."

54c Single Quotation Marks: Quotation Within Quotation ' '

Put single quotation marks around a quotation that occurs within another quotation; this is the only standard use for single quotation marks:

> In Joseph Conrad's *Heart of Darkness*, after a leisurely setting of the scene by the unnamed narrator, the drama begins when the character who is to be the principal narrator first speaks: "'And this also,' said Marlow suddenly, 'has been one of the dark places of the earth.'"

54d With Verbs of Speaking Before Quotations

When verbs of speaking precede a quotation, they are usually followed by commas:

> Helen said, "There is something nasty growing in my fridge."
>
> Adriana fumbled around in the dark and asked, "Now where are the matches?"

(Note that when a quotation ends a sentence, its own terminal punctuation serves also as that of the sentence.)

With short or emphatic quotations, commas often aren't necessary:

> He said "Hold your horses," so we waited a little longer.
>
> Someone shouted "Fire!" and we all headed for the exits.

Again, punctuate a sentence the way you want it to be heard; your sense of its rhythm should help you decide. On the other hand, if the quotation is long, especially if it consists of more than one sentence, or if the context is formal, a colon will probably be more appropriate than a comma to introduce it:

> When the movie was over, Joanna turned to her companion and said: "We have wasted ninety minutes of our lives. The movie lacked an intelligent plot, sympathetic characters, and an interesting setting. Even the soundtrack was pathetic."

If the introductory element is itself an independent clause, then a colon or period must be used:

> Joanna turned to her and spoke: "What a waste of time."

Spoke, unlike *said*, is here an intransitive verb.

If you work a quotation into your own syntax, don't use even a comma to introduce it; for example, when the word *that* follows a verb of speaking:

> It is often said that "[s]ticks and stones may break my bones, but words will never hurt me"—a singularly inaccurate notion.

54e With Verbs of Speaking After Quotations

If a verb of speaking or a subject–verb combination follows a quotation, it is usually set off by a comma placed inside the closing quotation mark:

> "You attract what you manifest in your personality," said the speaker.

> "I think there's a fly in my soup," she muttered.

But if the quotation ends with a question mark or an exclamation point, no other punctuation is added:

> "What time is it?" asked Francis, looking up.

> "I insist that I be heard!" he shouted.

If the clause containing the verb of speaking interrupts the quotation, it should be preceded by a comma and followed by whatever mark is called for by the syntax and the sense. For example,

> "Since it's such a long drive," he said, "we'd better get an early start."

> "It's a long drive," he argued; "therefore I think we should start early."

> "It's a very long way," he insisted. "We should start as early as possible."

54f With Quotations Set Off by Indention

Colons are conventionally used to introduce "block" quotations:

> Jane Austen begins her novel *Pride and Prejudice* with the observation:
>
> > It is a truth universally acknowledged, that a single man in possession of a good fortune must be in want of a wife. However little known the feelings or views of such a man may be on his first entering a neighbourhood, this truth is so well fixed in the minds of the surrounding families, that he is considered as the rightful property of some one or other of their daughters.

54g Words Used in a Special Sense

As we do with "block" in #54f above, put quotation marks around words used in a special sense or words for which you wish to indicate some qualification:

> What she calls a "ramble" I would call a twenty-mile hike.
>
> He had been up in the woods so long he was "bushed," as Canadians put it.

Proofreading Tip

On the Use of Quotation Marks to Call Attention to Words

Some writers put quotation marks around words referred to as words, but it is sometimes better practice to italicize them (see #60c):

> The word *toboggan* comes from a Mi'kmaq word for sled.

Don't put quotation marks around slang terms, clichés, and the like. If a word or phrase is so weak or inappropriate that you have to apologize for it, you shouldn't be using it in the first place. And the last thing such a term needs is to have attention called to it. Even if a slang term is appropriate, putting quotation marks around it implicitly insults readers by presuming that they won't recognize slang when they see it. And avoid using quotation marks for emphasis; they don't work that way.

54h Other Marks with Quotation Marks

Put periods and commas inside closing quotation marks; put semicolons and colons outside them:

> "Knowing how to write well," he said, "can be a source of great pleasure"; and then he added that it had "one other important quality": he identified it simply as "hard work."

We recommend this standard North American practice.

In British usage, periods and commas also are put outside quotation marks unless they are part of what is being quoted, and single rather than double quotation marks are conventional. Some Canadian writers and publishers follow British practice, putting periods and commas inside closing quotation marks only when they are actually in the material being quoted, as for example with a period at the end of a sentence. Question marks and exclamation points go either outside or inside, depending on whether they apply to the quotation or to the whole sentence:

54h

> 'Knowing how to write well', he said, 'can be a source of great pleasure.'

> 'What smells so good?' she asked.

> Who said, 'Change is inevitable except from a pop machine'?

> Did you find out who shouted 'See you in court, toad breath!'?

54i Ellipses for Omissions . . .

If when quoting from a written source you decide to omit one or more words from the middle of the passage you are quoting, indicate the omission with the three *spaced* periods of an **ellipsis**. For example, if you wanted to quote only part of the passage from Austen quoted at length earlier (#54f), you might do it like this:

> As Jane Austen wryly observes, "a single man in possession of a . . . fortune must be in want of a wife."

Note that you need not indicate an ellipsis at the beginning of a quotation unless the quotation could be mistaken for a complete sentence—for example, if it began with *I* or some other capital letter.

When the ellipsis is preceded by a complete sentence, include the period (or other terminal punctuation) of the original before the ellipsis points.

Similarly, if when you omit something from the end of a sentence, what remains is grammatically complete, a period (or question mark or exclamation point, if either of these is more appropriate) goes before the ellipsis. In either case, the terminal punctuation marking the end of the sentence is closed up:

> As Jane Austen wryly observes, "a single man in possession of a good fortune must be in want of a wife. . . . this truth is so well fixed in the minds of surrounding families, that he is considered the rightful property of some one or other. . . ."

Other punctuation may also be included before or after the ellipsis if it makes the quoted material clearer:

> However little known the feelings or views of such a man may be . . . , this truth is so well fixed in the minds of the surrounding families.

Three periods can also indicate the omission of one or more entire sentences, or even whole paragraphs. Again, if the sentence preceding the omitted material is grammatically complete, it should end with a period preceding the ellipsis.

An ellipsis should also be used to indicate that material from a quoted line of poetry has been omitted. When quoting four or more lines of poetry, use a row of spaced dots to indicate that one or more entire lines have been omitted:

> E.J. Pratt's epic "Towards the Last Spike" begins:
>
> > It was the same world then as now—the same,
> > Except for little differences of speed
> > And power, and means to treat myopia.
> > . . . .
> > The same, but for new particles of speech. . . .

Note that some instructors may ask that all ellipses added to quotations be enclosed in square brackets. Check with the reader of your work for his or her preference.

Proofreading Tip

On Ineffective Omission of Material from a Quotation
Don't omit material from a quotation in such a way that you distort what the author is saying or destroy the integrity of the syntax. Similarly, don't quote unfairly "out of context"; for example, if an author qualifies a statement in some way, don't quote the statement as if it were unqualified.

54j Brackets for Additions, Changes, and Comments [ ]

54j

Keep such changes to a minimum, but enclose in square brackets any editorial addition or change you find it necessary to make within a quotation, for example, a clarifying fact or a change in tense to make the quoted material fit the syntax of your sentence:

> The author states that "the following year [2000] marked a turning point in [his] life."

> One of my friends wrote me that her "feelings about the subject [were] similar to" mine.

Use the word *sic* (Latin for *thus*) in brackets to indicate that an error in the quotation occurs in the original:

> One of my friends wrote me: "My feelings about the subject are similiar [*sic*] to yours."

See also #78e. For further information on quotations, see the most recent edition of the *MLA Handbook for Writers of Research Papers.*

55 Avoiding Common Errors in Punctuation

55a Unwanted Comma Between Subject and Verb

Generally, do not put a comma between a subject and its verb unless some intervening element calls for punctuation:

> ***no p:*** His enthusiasm for the project and his desire to be of help, led him to add his name to the list of volunteers.

Don't be misled by the length of a compound subject. The comma after *help* in the last example is just as wrong as the comma in the following sentence:

> ***no p:*** Kiera, addressed the class.

But if some intervening element, for example an appositive or a participial phrase, requires setting off, use a *pair* of marks (see #50):

> His enthusiasm for the project and his desire to be of help, both strongly felt, led him to add his name to the list of volunteers.

> Kiera—the exchange student—addressed the class.

55b Unwanted Comma Between Verb and Object or Complement

Although in Jane Austen's time it was conventional to place a comma before a clause beginning with *that*, today this practice is considered an error. Do not put a comma between a verb and its object or complement unless some intervening element calls for punctuation. Especially, don't mistakenly assume that a clause opening with *that* always needs a comma before it:

> ***no p:*** Hafiz realized, that he could no longer keep his eyes open.

The noun clause beginning with *that* is the direct object of the verb *realized* and should not be separated from it. Only if an interrupter requires setting off should there be any punctuation:

> Hafiz realized, moreover, that he could no longer keep his eyes open.

> Hafiz realized, as he tried once again to read the paragraph, that he could no longer keep his eyes open.

Another example:

> ***no p:*** Ottawa's principal claim to fame is, that it has the world's longest skating rink.

Here the comma intrudes between the linking verb *is* and its complement, the predicate noun consisting of a *that*-clause.

55c Unwanted Comma after Last Adjective of a Series

Do not put a comma between the last adjective of a series and the noun it modifies:

> ***p:*** How could anyone fail to be impressed by such an intelligent, outspoken, resourceful, fellow as Jonathan is?

The comma after *resourceful* is wrong, though it may briefly feel right because a certain rhythm has been established and because there is no *and* before the last of the three adjectives.

55d Unwanted Comma Between Coordinated Words and Phrases

Generally, don't put a comma between words and phrases joined by a coordinating conjunction; use a comma only when the coordinate elements are clauses (see #44a):

> ***no p:*** The dog and cat circled each other warily, and then went off in opposite directions.
>
> ***no p:*** I was a long way from home, and didn't know how to get there.
>
> ***no p:*** She was not only intelligent, but also very kind.

The commas in these three sentences are all unnecessary. Sometimes a writer uses such a comma for a mild emphasis, but if you want an emphatic pause a dash will probably work better:

> The dog and cat circled each other warily—and then went off in opposite directions.

Or the sentence can be slightly revised in order to gain the emphasis:

> She was not only intelligent; she was also very kind.
>
> I was a long way from home, and I had no idea how to get there.

55e Commas with Emphatic Repetition

If the two elements joined by a conjunction constitute an emphatic repetition, a comma is sometimes optional:

> I wanted not only to win, but to win overwhelmingly.

This sentence would be equally correct and effective without the comma. But in the following sentence the comma is necessary:

> It was an object of beauty, and of beauty most spectacular.

Again, sounding a sentence over to yourself will sometimes help you decide.

55f Unwanted Comma with Short Introductory or Parenthetical Element

Generally, do not set off introductory elements or interrupters that are very short, that are not really parenthetical, or that are so slightly parenthetical that you feel no pause when reading them:

> ***no p:*** Perhaps, she was trying to tell us something.
>
> ***no p:*** But, it was not a case of mistaken identity.
>
> ***no p:*** Therefore, he put on his mukluks.
>
> ***no p:*** We asked if we could try it out, for a week, to see if we really liked it.

When the pause is strong, however, be sure to set it off:

> It was only then, after the very formal dinner, that we were all able to relax.

Often such commas are optional, depending on the pattern of intonation the writer wants:

> In Canada(,) the change of the seasons is sharply evident.
>
> In Canada(,) as elsewhere, money talks.
>
> Last year(,) we went to Quebec City.
>
> The committee(,) therefore(,) decided to table the motion.
>
> After dinner(,) we all went for a walk.
>
> As she walked(,) she thought of her childhood in Cabbagetown.

Sometimes such a comma is necessary to prevent misreading:

> ***incorrect:*** After eating the cat Irene gave me jumped out the window.
>
> ***revised:*** After eating, the cat Irene gave me jumped out the window.

See also #46a.

55g Unwanted Comma with Restrictive Appositive

Don't incorrectly set off proper nouns and titles of literary works as non-restrictive appositives (see #48b). For instance, it's "Dickens's novel *Great Expectations*," not "Dickens's novel, *Great Expectations*." Dickens, after all, wrote more than one novel.

> ***p:*** In her poem, "Daddy," Sylvia Plath explores her complicated relationship with her father.

> ***p:*** The home port of the Canadian Coast Guard icebreaker, *Terry Fox*, is Dartmouth, Nova Scotia.

The punctuation makes it sound as though Plath wrote only this one poem and that the *Terry Fox* is the only icebreaker in the Canadian Coast Guard's fleet. The titles are restrictive: if they were removed, the sentences would not be clear. If the context is clear, the explanatory words often aren't needed at all:

55g

> In "Daddy" Plath explores . . .

> The home port of the *Terry Fox* is . . .

If Sylvia Plath had in fact written only one poem, or if the Canadian Coast Guard had only one icebreaker, it would be correct to set off the title. Similarly, it would be correct to set off a title after referring to an author's "first novel" or the like, since an author, regardless of how many novels she or he has written, can have only one *first* novel. The urge to punctuate before titles of literary works sometimes leads to the error of putting a comma between a possessive and the title.

> ***no p:*** I remember enjoying Elise Partridge's, "To a Flicker Nesting in a Telephone Pole."

55h Unwanted Comma with Indirect Quotation

Do not set off indirect quotations as if they were direct quotations:

> ***no p:*** In his last chapter the author says, that civilization as we have come to know it is in jeopardy.

> ***no p:*** If you ask Tomiko she's sure to say, she doesn't want to go.

In an indirect quotation, what was said is being reported, not quoted. If Tomiko is quoted directly, a comma is correct:

> If you ask Tomiko she's sure to say, "I don't want to go."

See also #54a and #54d.

55i Unwanted Question Mark after Indirect Question

Don't put a question mark at the end of indirect questions—questions that are only being reported, not asked directly:

> I asked what we were doing here.
>
> She wanted to find out what had happened in the parking lot.
>
> What he asked himself then was how he was going to explain it to the shareholders.

55j Unwanted Semicolon with Subordinate Element

Do not put a semicolon in front of a mere phrase or subordinate clause. Use such a semicolon only where you could, if you chose to, put a period instead:

> ***p:*** They cancelled the meeting; being disappointed at the low turnout.
>
> ***p:*** Only about a dozen people showed up; partly because there had been too little publicity and no free muffins.

Those semicolons should be commas. Periods in those spots would turn what follows them into fragments (see #12x); in effect, so do semicolons. Since a semicolon signals that an *independent* clause is coming, readers are distracted when only a phrase or subordinate clause arrives. If you find yourself trying to avoid comma splices and overshooting in this way, devote some further study to the comma splice (#44e) and to learning how to recognize an independent clause (see #12m–n and p). Similarly, don't put a semicolon between a subordinate clause and an independent clause:

> ***p:*** After the show, when they got home, tired and with their eardrums ringing; Sheila said she was never going to another musical again.
>
> ***revised:*** After the show, when they got home, tired and with their eardrums ringing, Sheila said she was never going to another musical again.

Change the semicolon to a comma. The presence of earlier commas in the sentence doesn't mean that the later one needs promoting to semicolon; there is no danger here of confusing the reader as there sometimes is when a coordinating conjunction without a preceding comma is used to join two independent clauses (see #44b).

55k Unwanted Colon after Incomplete Construction

Do not use a colon after an incomplete construction; a colon is appropriate only after an independent clause:

> ***p:*** She preferred comfort foods such as: potatoes, bread, and pasta.

The prepositional *such as* needs an object to be complete. Had the phrase been extended to "She preferred such foods as these" or ". . . as the following," it would have been complete, an independent clause, and a colon would have been correct.

> ***revised:*** She preferred comfort foods such as the following: potatoes, bread, and pasta.

55k

Here is another example of this common error:

> ***p:*** His favourite pastimes are: swimming, hiking, and sipping fine cognac by the fire.

> ***revised:*** His favourite pastimes are swimming, hiking, and sipping fine cognac by the fire.

Since the linking verb *are* is incomplete without a complement, the colon is incorrect. Remember in academic writing not to use a colon after a preposition or after a form of the verb *be*. Scientific and business writing does allow for the use of a colon after the verb *be* or a preposition if the colon introduces a list that begins on a separate line.

55-l Unwanted Double Punctuation: Comma or Semicolon with a Dash

Avoid putting a comma or a semicolon together with a dash. Use whichever mark is appropriate.

Review Exercises, Chapter V Punctuation

A. CORRECTING PUNCTUATION

Correct any errors in punctuation in the following sentences—many of which come from students' papers. You may also want to make other improvements: practise your revising techniques.

1. Rainer Maria Rilke says love occurs when two solitudes protect and touch and greet each other.
2. I believe, that for a number of reasons, genetically modified food should be carefully regulated.
3. He was not a frightening poltergeist but an irritating one he hid the remote control and moved the coffee table.
4. Many of his plays are about royalty, as in the Lancastrian tetralogy *Richard II Henry IV (1) Henry IV (2)* and *Henry V.*
5. His childlike features were deceptive as we discovered when the alien from the planet Zotar began to give us detailed instructions on how to build a time machine.
6. When you spend time with close friends you get a different perspective life seems less narrow and serious.
7. With him too, she felt comfortable.
8. I would like to wake up in the morning especially a beautiful morning such as this and not feel the burden of work.
9. The encounter that deepened his feelings more, occurred at age nine.
10. Therefore one must always remember to be polite when encountering a ghostly stranger in a train station.
11. This then, was the plan. Return to our campsite for the night, and tackle Black Tusk the next morning.
12. I joined in; dancing haltingly at first and then more confidently.
13. As a person exercises the muscle of the heart becomes stronger therefore, it can pump more blood while beating less.
14. However I always wake up the next day with the worst sort of headache the emotional headache.
15. The meal started with grilled artichokes followed by mushroom ravioli and finished with a lemon tart.
16. It was after all, exactly what he had asked for.
17. Crisp memories of laughing eyes, loving smiles and peaceful easy feelings still linger.
18. A computer hard drive is easy to install just remember to ground yourself before you touch the hard drive.
19. Did Sheila Watson write *The Double Hook.*

Review Exercises, Chapter V Punctuation – *continued*

20. Eighteenth-century mathematicians unlike their counterparts in the seventeenth century, were able to develop both pure and applied mathematics. Leonhard Euler, a notable genius in both these fields contributed invaluably to every branch of mathematics.
21. Another classic film, that explores the effects of war on individual lives, is *Casablanca*.
22. It began to rain, nevertheless, since they were on the sixteenth fairway they went ahead and finished the round.
23. When the tyrant stood up and said you rascals you will get what you deserve a brick fell on his head.
24. To me this indicates, that although he remembers the details of the events he describes, there is an enormous space of time, between them and the present, that makes them intangible.
25. The sounds of the sonata are soft and never harsh which helps create the melancholy mood.

B. Using punctuation

Punctuate the following sentences as you think best, indicating possible alternatives and places where you think punctuation is optional. Be prepared to defend your choices. Some sentences may not need punctuating.

1. When the meeting ended he went to a pub for a drink.
2. Doggedly Peyvand finished his essay.
3. Soon those parts became unappealing and she decided to fire her current agent.
4. In 2000 he moved to Halifax Nova Scotia and bought a small reputable art gallery specializing in expensive striking white minimalist plastic sculpture.
5. She felt uneasy about the trip yet she knew she had to go and meet her sister flying in from Hong Kong.
6. I took the book that I didn't like back to the library but I still had to pay a fine.
7. Mary Winnie and Cora came to the party together but left separately.
8. He had a broad engaging smile even though he had three teeth missing.
9. Having heard all she wanted Bridget walked out of the meeting.
10. But once you've taken the first few steps the rest will naturally be easy.

Review Exercises, Chapter V Punctuation – *continued*

11. The poem was short the novel was long the poem was good the novel better.
12. Perhaps we can still think of some way out of this mess.
13. But Canadians don't think that way they prefer to sit back and wait.
14. Last summer we visited Hastings the site of the battle won by William the Conqueror in 1066.
15. A warm bath a good book and freshly laundered sheets were all she wanted.
16. There are only three vegetables I can't tolerate turnips turnips and turnips.
17. In the good old days the doctor a specialist in family practice made house calls all morning.
18. August 16 1977 is when Elvis Presley died.
19. He had to finish the novel quickly or he wouldn't get his advance.
20. We arrived we ate we partook in boring conversation we departed and that's all there was to the evening.
21. You must plan your budget carefully in times of inflation so remember to buy lottery tickets.
22. She is the only woman I know who wears pantyhose every day whatever the season.
23. His several hobbies were philately woodworking chess and fishing.
24. The two opponents settled the question amicably at the meeting and then went home to write nasty letters to each other and to the editor of the local newspaper.
25. He would rather make up a lie than stick to the boring truth that was his downfall.

Mechanics and Spelling

VI

56 Formatting an Essay

56a Format

Unless directed otherwise, follow these conventions when you are preparing a manuscript for submission:

1. Prepare your manuscript on recycled white paper of good quality, 8½ by 11 inches (or 21 by 28 cm). Use only one side of each page.

2. Choose a plain, readable typeface (12-point Times New Roman or 10-point Arial). Do not try to spruce up your essay with coloured paper or fancy fonts: these will only detract from the professional appearance of your work.

3. Double-space your essay throughout and leave margins of about 1 inch (2.5 cm) on all four sides of the page. Word-processed essays may be either fully justified or justified flush left with a ragged (i.e. unjustified) right-hand margin. Full justification may cause such typesetting problems as inconsistent spacing, gappy or loose lines, and ineffective word breaks. For these reasons, it is preferable to use only flush-left justification.

4. If you are submitting a handwritten document, as may be the case for an in-class essay or an examination, use medium- to wide-ruled white paper, and write on alternate lines. Do not use paper torn from a spiral notebook. Use black or blue-black ink, not pencil. Write as legibly as possible.

5. Label all pages after a covering title page at the right margin, about half an inch (1.25 cm) from the top. Include your surname before the page number, as a precaution against misplaced pages. Most word-processing software will enable you to generate these "headers" automatically. Page numbers should be set as Arabic numerals, without periods, dashes, slashes, circles, or other decorations.

6. For a long essay or research paper, begin about 1 inch (2.5 cm) from the top, at the left margin, and on separate double-spaced lines put your name, your instructor's name, the course number, and the date of submission; then double-space again and put the title, centred. (For an illustration, see chapter VIII, #80.) If you wish or are instructed to use a separate title page, centre the title about 1 inch (2.5 cm) from the top of the first page following the title page. (For the format of a title page, again see #80.)

7. Set the title in standard font size and in upper- and lowercase Roman letters, making sure to capitalize the title correctly (see #58m). Do not put the whole title in capital letters or in boldface type, and do not underline it or put a period after it. Do not put your title in quotation marks (unless it is in fact a quotation); if it includes the title of a poem, story, book, etc., or a ship's name, use italics or quotation marks appropriately (see #59). Do not use the title of a published work by itself as your own title. Some examples of effective titles:

    Of Pigoons and Wolvogs: Wildlife in *Oryx and Crake*

    The Structure of Dennis Lee's "Civil Elegies"

    Musical Allusions in *Fugitive Pieces*

    "How Are the Mighty Fallen": The Sinking of the *Titanic*

8. Indent each paragraph 1 inch (2.5 cm or 5 spaces) from the margin. Do not leave extra space between indented paragraphs. Indent long block quotations 2 inches (5 cm or 10 spaces) from the left margin. Do not leave any additional space before or after a double-spaced block quotation.

9. Leave only one space after any terminal punctuation, and remember to leave spaces before and after each of the three dots of an ellipsis (see #54i). If you are typing, use two unspaced hyphens to make a dash, with no space before or after them; most word-processing software will automatically convert two hyphens to a dash.

10. Never begin a line with a comma, semicolon, period, question mark, exclamation point, or hyphen. On rare occasions, a dash or the dots of an ellipsis may have to come at the beginning of a line, but if possible place them at the end of the preceding line.

11. As you write an essay on a computer, save your work frequently—every five minutes or so. Create a back-up disk, and save all drafts of your paper on that disk. Always keep a copy of the final draft of any paper you submit.

12. Print your document on an ink-jet or laser printer, making sure there is plenty of ink or toner in the cartridge.

13. Aim to produce documents with a professional appearance. If after proofreading you decide that you have to make changes to a word-processed document, call up the file, make the appropriate emendations, save the changes, and reprint the page or pages you have revised. To

change or delete a word or short phrase in a handwritten document, such as an examination paper, draw a single horizontal line through it and write the new word or phrase, if any, above it. If you wish to insert a word or short phrase, place a caret (‸) *below* the line at the point of insertion and write the addition *above* the line. If you wish to start a new paragraph where you haven't indented, put the symbol ¶ in the left margin and insert a caret where you want the paragraph to begin. If you wish to cancel a paragraph indention, write "No ¶" in the left margin.

14. Fasten the pages of an essay together with a paper clip. Do not use a staple. Long essays are sometimes submitted in folders.

56b Syllabication and Word Division

syl, div Generally, do not divide words at the end of a line. Inserting word breaks manually can be time-consuming, and relying on your computer to insert word breaks automatically can result in too many hyphens. Although you can control the guidelines to a certain extent, computer-generated hyphenation can produce undesirable word breaks that you will need to correct before printing the final copy of your essay. It is better to rely on the word-wrap feature of your word-processing software to shorten a line and to move a word that might otherwise be divided to the beginning of the next line.

One circumstance in which you may need to insert a word break is in a reference to an electronic source identified by its website or network address. When this address (also known as a *URL*, or *uniform resource locator*) is a long one, then it may need to be spread over two lines. The most recent edition of the *MLA Handbook* recommends that the break should appear only after one of the slashes in the URL. Introducing a hyphen or other punctuation, such as a period, into a URL is not recommended, for it will introduce an ambiguity into the data and make the website difficult for your reader to locate and access:

> To learn more about Sook-Yin Lee, one of CBC Radio's most lively and entertaining broadcasters, consult the entry for her program, *Definitely Not the Opera*, at <http://www.cbc.ca/dnto>.

> Jane Mayer has written an essay sure to provoke much discussion and debate. Entitled "Whatever It Takes," the piece takes a careful look at the use of torture in the television series *24*. The essay can be found online at <http://www.newyorker.com/
fact/content/articles/070219a_fact_mayer>.

On the *rare* occasions when you need to divide a word in a handwritten document, insert a hyphen at the end of a line, after the first part of the word, and begin the next line with the rest of the word. You should not begin a new line with a hyphen. Nor should you divide a word at the end of a page or at the end of a paragraph. Divide words only between syllables, and if you are uncertain, check your dictionary for a word's syllabication.

57 Abbreviations

abbr Abbreviations are expected in technical and scientific writing, legal writing, business writing, memos, reports, reference works, bibliographies and works cited lists, footnotes, tables and charts, and sometimes in journalism. The following relatively few kinds are in common use. (See also #79b.)

57a Titles before Proper Names

The following abbreviations can be used with or without initials or given names:

Mr.	(Mr. Eng, Mr. Marc Ramsay)
Mrs.	(Mrs. L.W. Smith, Mrs. Tazim Khan)
M.	(M. André Joubert; M. Stéphane Dion)
Mme.	(Mme. Girard; Mme. Nathalie Gagnon)
Mlle.	(Mlle. Stephanie Sevigny; Mlle. R. Pelletier)
Dr.	(Dr. Paula Grewal; Dr. P. Francis Fairchild)
St.	(St. John; St. Beatrice)

57b Titles before Proper Names with Initials or Given Names

In informal writing, abbreviations of professional or honorific titles can be used before proper names only with initials or given names:

Prof. Hana Jamalali (*but* Professor Jamalali)

Sen. H.C. Tsui (*but* Senator Tsui)

Gov. Gen. Michaëlle Jean (*but* Governor General Jean)

the Rev. Lois Wilson (*or, more formally*, the Reverend Lois Wilson)

the Hon. Ujjal Dosanjh (*more formally*, the Honourable Ujjal Dosanjh, the Honourable Mr. Dosanjh)

In formal writing, spell out these and similar titles.

57c Titles and Degrees after Proper Names

David Adams, M.D. (*but not* Dr. David Adams, M.D.)

Claire T. McFadden, D.D.S.

Martin Luther King, Jr.

Eva-Marie Kröller, Ph.D., F.R.S.C.

Academic degrees not following a name may also be abbreviated:

Shirley is working toward her B.A.

Amir is working on his M.A. thesis.

57d Standard Words Used with Dates and Numerals

720 B.C.

A.D. 231, the second century A.D.

7 a.m. (*or* 7 A.M.), 8:30 p.m. (*or* 8:30 P.M.)

no. 17 (*or* No. 17)

Note that *A.D.* precedes a date whereas *B.C.* follows one. Note also that some people now use *B.P.* ("before the present") or *B.C.E.* ("before the common era") and *C.E.* ("of the common era"), both following the date, instead of *B.C.* and *A.D.* respectively.

57e Agencies and Organizations Known by Their Initials (see also #53a)

Capitalize names of agencies and organizations commonly known by their initials:

UNICEF CAW CBC CNN RCMP NATO WHO

57f Scientific and Technical Terms Known by Their Initials

Some scientific, technical, or other terms (usually of considerable length) are commonly known by their initials (see also #53a):

BTU URL DDT DNA WMD FM

SARS ISBN HTML MP GST ISP

57g Latin Expressions Commonly Used in English

i.e. (that is)	etc. (and so forth)
e.g. (for example)	vs. (versus)
cf. (compare)	et al. (and others)

Note that in formal writing, it is better to spell out the English equivalent.

Proofreading Tip

57g

On Punctuating Latin Expressions and Abbreviations

(a) If you use e.g., use it only to introduce the example or list of examples; following the example or list, write out *for example*:

> Some provinces—e.g., Manitoba, Saskatchewan, and New Brunswick—supported a single national standard for homecare programs.
>
> Some provinces—Manitoba, Saskatchewan, and New Brunswick, for example—supported a single national standard for homecare programs.

Note also that if you introduce a list with *e.g.* or *for example* or even *such as*, it is illogical to follow it with *etc.* or *and so forth.*

(b) Generally use a comma after *i.e.*, just as you would if you wrote out *that is*. And usually use a comma after *e.g.* as well (test for the pause by reading it aloud as *for example*).

(c) The abbreviation *cf.* stands for Latin *confer*, meaning *compare*. Do not use it to mean simply "see"; for that, the Latin *vide* (*v.*) would be correct.

(d) Use *etc.* sparingly. Use it only when there are at least several more items to follow and when they are reasonably obvious:

> Evergreen trees—cedars, pines, etc.—are common in northern latitudes.
>
> Learning the Greek alphabet—alpha, beta, gamma, delta, etc.—isn't really difficult.

wrong: He considered several possible occupations: accounting, teaching, nursing, etc.

In the case of the last example, a reader can have no idea of what the other possible occupations might be.

Further, don't write *and etc.*: *and* is redundant, since *etc.* (*et cetera*) means "*and* so forth."

57h Terms in Official Titles

Capitalize terms used in official titles being copied exactly:

Johnson Bros., Ltd.	Ibbetson & Co.
Smith & Sons, Inc.	*Quill & Quire*

Proofreading Tip

Limiting the Use of the Ampersand (&)

Don't use the ampersand (&) as a substitute for *and*; use it only when presenting the title of a company or a publication exactly, as above.

58 Capitalization

cap, uc Generally, capitalize proper nouns, abbreviations of proper nouns, and words derived from proper nouns, as follows:

58a Names and Nicknames

Capitalize names and nicknames of real and fictional people and individual animals:

Nelson Mandela	Margaret MacMillan	Tiger Woods
Clive Owen	Clarissa Dalloway	Rumpelstiltskin
Cinderella	Barack Obama	Sidney Crosby
King Kong	Lassie	Washoe

58b Professional and Honorific Titles

Capitalize professional and honorific titles when they directly precede and thus are parts of names:

Professor Tamara Jones (*but* Tamara Jones, professor at Mount Allison)

Captain Janna Ting (*but* Janna Ting is a captain in the police force.)

Rabbi Samuel Singer (*but* Mr. Singer was rabbi of our synagogue.)

Proofreading Tip

On Capitalizing Titles After Names

Normally titles that follow names aren't capitalized unless they have become part of the name:

Shawn Graham, premier of New Brunswick
Stephen Harper, prime minister of Canada
Beverly McLachlin, justice of the Supreme Court
Romeo Dallaire, the senator

but

Catherine the Great
Peter the Hermit
Smokey the Bear

Some titles of particular distinction are customarily capitalized even if the person isn't named:

The Queen toured Canada to celebrate her fifty years on the Throne.

On Easter Sunday, the Pope will address the crowd gathered in St. Peter's Square.

The university was honoured with a visit by the Dalai Lama.

Opinion is divided on the question of whether "prime minister" and "president" are titles in the same category of distinction as "the Queen," "the Pope," and "the Dalai Lama." Some writers and news outlets make it a policy always to capitalize these titles. In your own writing, you should aim for consistency in whatever practices you adopt.

Prime Minister Howard met with President Bush at the White House. (In each case, the title is capitalized as part of the leader's name.)

The Prime Minister met with the President at the White House.

or

The prime minister met with the president at the White House. (Whichever practice you follow, be consistent in your choice.)

58c Words Designating Family Relationships

Capitalize words designating family relationships when they are used as parts of proper names and also when they are used in place of proper names, except following a possessive:

> Uncle Peter (*but* I have an uncle named Peter.)
>
> There's my uncle, Peter. (*but* There's my Uncle Peter.)
>
> I told Father about it. (*but* My father knows about it.)
>
> I have always respected Grandmother. (*but* Diana's grandmother is a splendid old woman.)

58d Place Names

Capitalize place names—including common nouns (*river*, *street*, *park*, etc.) when they are parts of proper nouns (see #13):

Active Pass	Alberta	the Amazon	the Andes
Asia	Banff	Buenos Aires	Mt. Etna
Hudson Bay	Japan	Lake Ladoga	Moose Jaw
Niagara Falls	Québec	Rivière-du-Loup	Yonge Street
the Gobi Desert	Vancouver Island	the Miramichi River	
the Suez Canal	Trafalgar Square	Kootenay National Park	

Usage Note

On Capitalizing North, South, East, West

As a rule, don't capitalize *north*, *south*, *east*, and *west* unless they are part of specific place names (North Battleford, West Vancouver, the South Shore) or designate specific geographical areas (the frozen North, the East Coast, the Deep South, the Northwest, the Wild West, the Far East).

Since writers in Canada usually capitalize East, West, North (and sometimes South) to refer to parts of the country (the peoples of the North, the settlement of the West), it makes sense to capitalize Eastern, Western, Northern, and Southern when they refer to ideas attached to parts of the country (Northern peoples, Western settlement). Otherwise, except for cases when they appear as parts of specific place names (the Eastern Townships), these adjectives should not be capitalized. This practice applies even to cases such as northern Canada, eastern Canada, western Canada, which are not specific place names but descriptions of geographic regions.

58e Months, Days, Holidays

Capitalize the names of the months (January, February, etc.) and the days of the week (Monday, Tuesday, etc.), but not the seasons (spring, summer, autumn, fall, winter). Also capitalize holidays, holy days, and festivals (Christmas, Canada Day, Remembrance Day, Hanukkah, Ramadan).

58f Religious Names

Capitalize names of deities and other religious names and terms:

God	the Holy Ghost	the Virgin Mary	the Bible
the Torah	the Talmud	the Dead Sea Scrolls	Islam
Allah	the Prophet	the Qur'an	Apollo
Jupiter	Vishnu	Taoism	

Note: Some people capitalize pronouns referring to a deity; others prefer not to. Either practice is acceptable as long as you are consistent.

58g Names of Nationalities and Organizations

Capitalize names of nationalities and other groups and organizations and of their members:

Canadian, Australian, Malaysian, Scandinavian,
South American, Iraqi, Somalian, Texan

New Democrats, the New Democratic Party

Liberals, the Liberal Party

Conservatives, the Conservative Party

Greens, the Green Party

Bloquistes, the Bloc Québécois, the Bloc

Roman Catholics, the Roman Catholic Church

Lions, Kiwanis

Teamsters

the Vancouver Canucks, the Toronto Blue Jays

the Taliban

58h Names of Institutions and Sections of Government, Historical Events, and Buildings

Capitalize names of institutions, sections of government, historical events and documents, and specific buildings:

McGill University, The Hospital for Sick Children

the Ministry of Health, Parliament, the Senate, the Cabinet, the Opposition

the French Revolution, the Great War, World War I, the Gulf War, the Cretaceous period, the Renaissance; the Magna Carta, the Treaty of Versailles, the Charter of Rights and Freedoms, the Ming Dynasty

the British Museum, the Museum of Civilization, Westminster Abbey

58i Academic Courses and Languages

Capitalize specific academic courses, but not the subjects themselves, except for languages:

Philosophy 101, Fine Arts 300, Mathematics 204, English 112, Food Writing, Humanities 101

an English course, a major in French (*but* a history course, an economics major, a degree in psychology)

58j Derivatives of Proper Nouns

Capitalize derivatives of proper nouns:

French Canadian, Haligonian, Celtic, Québécoise, Ethiopian, Kuwaiti

Confucianism, Christian

Shakespearean, Keynesian, Edwardian, Miltonic

Proofreading Tip

On Words Once But No Longer Capitalized

Some words derived from proper nouns—and some proper nouns themselves—are so much a part of everyday usage or refer to such common things that they were never or are no longer capitalized; some examples:

> bible (in secular contexts), biblical
> herculean, raglan, martial, quixotic, erotic, jeremiad, bloomers, gerrymander
> hamburger, frankfurter, french fries, champagne, burgundy, roman and italic, denim, china, japanned
> vulcanized, macadamized, galvanized, pasteurized, volt, ampere

58k Abbreviations of Proper Nouns

Capitalize abbreviations of proper nouns:

> PMO TVA CUPE CUSO P.E.I B.C. the BNA Act

Note that abbreviations of agencies and organizations commonly known by their initials do not need periods (see #57e), but that non-postal abbreviations of geographical entities such as provinces usually do. When in doubt, consult your dictionary. See also #53a.

58-l *I* and *O*

Capitalize the pronoun *I* and the vocative interjection *O*:

> O my people, what have I done unto thee? (Micah 6:3)

Do not capitalize the interjection *oh* unless it begins a sentence.

58m Titles of Written and Other Works

In the titles of written and other works, including student essays, use a capital letter to begin the first word, the last word, and all other important words; leave uncapitalized only articles (*a*, *an*, *the*) and any conjunctions and prepositions less than five letters long (unless one of these is the first or last word):

> *The Blind Assassin*
> *Pan's Labyrinth*
> "The Metamorphosis"
> *Through the Children's Gate*
> *Paris 1919*
> *Roughing It in the Bush*
> "The Dead"
> "O Canada"
> "Amazing Grace"
> *As for Me and My House*
> "Open Secrets"
> *In the Skin of a Lion*

But there can be exceptions; for example the conjunctions *Nor* and *So* are usually capitalized, the relative pronoun *that* is sometimes not capitalized (*All's Well that Ends Well*), and in Ralph Ellison's "Tell It Like It Is, Baby" the preposition-cum-conjunction *Like* demands capitalization. (See #59 for more on titles.)

If a title includes a hyphenated word, capitalize the part after the hyphen only if it is a noun or adjective or is otherwise an important word:

> *Self-Portrait*
> *The Scorched-Wood People*
> *Murder Among the Well-to-do*

Capitalize the first word of a subtitle, even if it is an article:

> *Beyond Remembering: The Collected Poems of Al Purdy*

See #59b for the use of italics in titles.

58n First Words of Sentences

Capitalize the first word of a major or minor sentence—of anything, that is, that concludes with terminal punctuation:

> Racial profiling. Now that's a controversial topic. Right?

58-o First Words of Quotations That Are Sentences

Capitalize the first word of a quotation that is intended as a sentence or that is capitalized in the source, but not fragments from other than the beginning of such a sentence:

> When he said "Let me take the wheel for a while," I shuddered at the memory of what had happened the last time I had let him "take the wheel."

If something interrupts a single quoted sentence, do not begin its second part with a capital:

> "It was all I could do," she said, "to keep from laughing out loud."

58p First Words of Sentences Within Parentheses

Capitalize the first word of an independent sentence in parentheses only if it stands by itself, apart from other sentences. If it is incorporated within another sentence, it is neither capitalized nor ended with a period (though it could end with a question mark or exclamation point: see #51 and #53).

> She did as she was told (there was really nothing else for her to do), and the tension was relieved. (But of course she would never admit to herself that she had been manipulated.)

58q First Words of Sentences Following Colons

An incorporated sentence following a colon may be capitalized if it seems to stand as a separate statement, for example if it is itself long or requires emphasis; the current trend is away from capitalization. Note that *The Globe and Mail*, Canada's newspaper of record, does capitalize the first letter following a colon.

> There was one thing, she said, which we must never forget: No one has the right to the kind of happiness that deprives someone else of deserved happiness.

> It was a splendid night: the sky was clear except for a few picturesque clouds, the moon was full, and even a few stars shone through. (The first *The* could be capitalized if the writer wanted particular emphasis on the details.)

58q

> It was no time for petty quarrels: everything depended on unanimity.

58r With Personification and for Emphasis

Although it is risky and should not be done often, writers who have good control of tone can occasionally capitalize a personified abstraction or a word or phrase to which they want to impart a special importance of some kind:

> In his quest to succeed, Greed and Power came to dominate his every waking thought.

> Only when it begins to fade does Youth appear so valuable.

Sometimes the slight emphasis of capitalization can be used for a humorous or ironic effect:

> He insisted on driving His Beautiful Car: everyone else preferred to walk the two blocks without benefit of jerks and jolts and carbon monoxide fumes.

And occasionally, but rarely, you can capitalize whole words and phrases or even sentences for a special sort of graphic emphasis:

> When we reached the excavation site, however, we were confronted by a sign warning us in no uncertain terms to KEEP OUT—TRESPASSERS WILL BE PROSECUTED.

> When she made the suggestion to the group, she was answered with a resounding YES.

Clearly in such instances there is no need for further indications, such as quotation marks or underlining, though the last one could end with an exclamation point.

59 Titles (see also #58m)

59a Quotation Marks for Short Works and Parts of Longer Works

title Put quotation marks around the titles of short works and of parts of longer works, such as short stories, articles, essays, short poems, chapters of books, songs, and individual episodes of television programs:

> Leonard Cohen's "Joan of Arc" and "Democracy" are songs featured in this documentary about the music of Canada.
>
> "A Wilderness Station" is an Alice Munro story that begins in Ontario in the 1850s.
>
> The final chapter of Carol Shields' last novel is called "Not Yet."
>
> "Her Gates Both East and West" is the final poem in Al Purdy's last collection of poems.
>
> Of the ten episodes in the CBC documentary *Hockey: A People's History*, I enjoyed the first one, "A Simple Game," the best.

There can be exceptions, however. For example, the title of each of the ten plays in volume 1 of *Modern Canadian Plays* deserves italicizing in its own right. And some works, for example Coleridge's *The Rime of the Ancient Mariner*, E.J. Pratt's *Towards the Last Spike*, and Conrad's *Heart of Darkness,* although originally parts of larger collections, are fairly long and have attained a reputation and importance as individual works; most writers feel justified in italicizing their titles.

59b Italics for Whole or Major Works

Use italics (see #60) for titles of written works published as units, such as books, magazines, journals, newspapers, and plays; for films and television programs; for paintings and sculptures; and for musical compositions (other than single songs), such as operas and ballets:

> *Paradise Lost* is Milton's greatest work.
>
> Have you read Michael Crummey's *The Wreckage*?
>
> *The New Yorker* is a weekly magazine.
>
> The scholarly journal *Canadian Literature* is published quarterly.

I prefer *The Globe and Mail* to the *National Post*.

I recommend that you see the Shaw Festival production of *The Circle*.

The Passionate Eye is a CBC program featuring the best in current documentaries.

One tires of hearing Ravel's *Bolero* played so often.

Michelangelo's *David* is worth a trip to Florence.

Picasso's *Guernica* is a disturbing representation of the Spanish Civil War.

We saw a fine production of Puccini's *La Bohème*.

Every spring, the CBC Radio website features information about *Canada Reads*, a program seeking to select the one book all Canadians should read.

Note that instrumental compositions may be known by name or by technical detail, or both. A title name is italicized (Beethoven's *Pastoral Symphony*); technical identification is usually not (Beethoven's Sixth Symphony, or Symphony no. 6, op. 68, in F).

In MLA documentation style, however, titles of works are underlined. (See #79a.)

59c Titles Within Titles

If an essay title includes a book title, the book title is italicized:

"Things Botanical in *The Lost Garden* and *A Student of Weather*"

If a book title includes something requiring quotation marks, retain the quotation marks and italicize the whole thing:

From Fiction to Film: James Joyce's "The Dead"

If a book title includes something that itself would be italicized, such as the name of a ship or the title of another book, either put the secondary item in quotation marks or leave it in roman type (i.e., not italicized):

The Cruise of the "Nona"

D.H. Lawrence and Sons and Lovers: *Sources and Criticism*

On Articles as Parts of Titles
Double check in the titles you cite for the role of the definite article, *the*: italicize and capitalize it only when it is actually a part of the title: Margaret Lawrence's *The Stone Angel*; Yann Martel's *Life of Pi*; Roman Polanski's *The Pianist*; the *Partisan Review; The Encyclopaedia Britannica*; the *Atlas of Ancient Archaeology*. Occasionally the indefinite article, *a* or *an*, bears watching as well.

Practice varies with the definite article as part of the name of a newspaper, and sometimes even with its city; try to refer to a newspaper the way it refers to itself—on its front page or masthead: the Victoria *Times Colonist*; the Regina *Leader-Post*; *The Vancouver Sun*; the *Calgary Herald*; *The Globe and Mail*.

60 Italics

ital *Italics* are a special kind of slanting type that contrasts with the surrounding type to draw attention to a word or phrase, such as a title (see #59b). The other main uses of italics are discussed below. In handwritten work, such as an exam, represent italic type by underlining.

60a Names of Ships and Planes

Italicize names of individual ships, planes, and the like:

the *Golden Hind*	*The Spirit of St. Louis*
the *St. Bonaventure*	*Mariner IX*
the *Lusitania*	the *Columbia*
the *Erebus* and the *Terror*	the *Orient Express*

60b Non-English Words and Phrases

Italicize non-English words and phrases that are not yet sufficiently common to be entirely at home in English. English contains many terms that have come from other languages but that are no longer thought of as non-English and are therefore not italicized; for example:

moccasin	prairie	genre	tableau
bamboo	arroyo	corral	sushi
chutzpah	spaghetti	goulash	eureka
litotes	hiatus	vacuum	sic

There are also words that are sufficiently Anglicized not to require italicizing but that usually retain their original accents and diacritical marks; for example:

cliché naïf fête façade Götterdämmerung

But English also makes use of many terms still felt by many writers to be sufficiently non-English to need italicizing, for example:

Bildungsroman	*au courant*	*coup d'état*	*chez*
joie de vivre	*jihad*	*raison d'être*	*savoir faire*
scheudenfreude	*verboten*	*Weltanschauung*	*carpe diem*

Many such expressions are on their way to full acceptance in English. If you are unsure, consult a good up-to-date dictionary.

60c Words Referred to as Words

Italicize words, letters, numerals, and the like when you refer to them as such:

The word *helicopter* is formed from Greek roots.

There are two *r*'s in *embarrass.* (Note that only the *r* is italicized; the *s* making it plural stays roman.)

The number *13* is considered unlucky by many otherwise rational people.

Don't use *&* as a substitute for *and.*

See also #54g. For the matter of apostrophes for plurals of such elements, see #62v.

60d For Emphasis

On rare occasions, italicize words or phrases—or even whole sentences—that you want to emphasize, for example, as they might be stressed if spoken aloud:

One thing he was now sure of: *that* was no way to go about the task.

Careful thought should lead one to the conclusion that *character*, not wealth or connections, will be most important in the long run.

If people try to tell you otherwise, *don't listen to them.*

Remember that *Fredericton*, not Saint John, is the capital of New Brunswick.

He gave up his ideas of fun and decided instead to finish his education. *And it was the most important decision of his life.*

Like other typographical devices for achieving emphasis (boldface, capitalization, underlining), this method is worth avoiding, or at least minimizing, in academic and other forms of writing. No merely mechanical means of emphasis is, ultimately, as effective as punctuation, word order, and syntax. Easy methods often produce only a transitory effect, and repeated use soon saps what effectiveness they have. Consider the following sentences and decide which of them you find most emphatic:

> Well, I felt just *terrible* when he told me that!
>
> I felt terrible, just terrible, when he told me that.
>
> I can think of only one way to describe how I felt when he told me that: I felt terrible.

61 Numerals

num Numerals are appropriate in technical and scientific writing, and newspapers sometimes use them to save space. But in ordinary writing certain conventions limit their use. Use numerals for the following purposes:

61a Time of Day

Use numerals for the time of day with *a.m.* or *p.m.* and *midnight* or *noon*, or when minutes are included:

> 3 p.m. (*but* three o'clock, three in the afternoon)
>
> 12 noon, 12 midnight (these are often better than the equivalents, *12 p.m.* and *12 a.m.*, which may not be understood)
>
> 4:15, 4:30 (*but* a quarter past four; half past four)

61b Dates

Use numerals for dates:

> September 11, 2001, *or* 11 September 2001

The year is almost always represented by numerals, and centuries written out:

> 2000 was the last year of the twentieth century, not the first year of the twenty-first century, wasn't it? (See #61h.)

Proofreading Tip 

Adding Suffixes to Numerals in Dates
The suffixes *st*, *nd*, *rd*, and *th* go with numerals in dates only if the year is not given; or the number may be written out:

May 12, 1955	May 12th
the twelfth of May	May twelfth

61c Addresses

61c

Use numerals for addresses:

2132 Fourth Avenue
4771 128th Street
P.O. Box 91
Apartment 8

61d Technical and Mathematical Numbers

Use numerals for technical and mathematical numbers, such as percentages and decimals:

31 per cent	31%
37 degrees Celsius	37°C
2.54 centimetres	2.54 cm

61e Pages and Chapters

Use numerals for page numbers and other divisions of a written work, especially in documentation (see #79 and #81):

page 27, p. 27, pp. 33–38	line 13, lines 3 and 5, ll. 7–9
Chapter 4, Ch. 4, chapter IV	section 3, section III
Part 2	Book IX, canto 120 (IX, 120)
2 Samuel 22: 3, II Samuel 19: 1	

(Note that books of the Bible are not italicized.)

61f Parts of a Play

Use numerals for acts, scenes, and line numbers of plays (some readers may prefer that you use roman numerals for acts and scenes):

In act 4, scene 2, . . .

See act IV, scene ii, line 77.

Remember Hamlet's "To be, or not to be" (3. 1. 56) or (III. i. 56).

61g Statistics and Numbers of More Than Two Words

Generally, spell out numbers that can be expressed in one or two words; use numerals for numbers that would take more than two words:

> four; thirty; eighty-three; two hundred; seven thousand;
> 115; 385; 2120
>
> one-third; one-half; five thirty-seconds
>
> three dollars, $3.48; five hundred dollars, $517

If you are writing about more than one number, say for purposes of comparison or giving statistics, numerals are usually preferable:

> Enrolment dropped from 250 two years ago, to 200 last year, to only 90 this year.

Don't mix numerals and words in such a context. On the other hand, if in your writing you refer alternately to two sets of figures, it may be better to use numerals for one and words for the other:

> We're building a 60-foot border; we can use either five 12-foot timbers or six 10-foot timbers.

61h Avoiding Numerals at the Beginning of a Sentence

Don't begin a sentence with a numeral. Either spell out the number or rewrite the sentence so that the number doesn't come first:

> ***num:*** 30–40% goes for taxes.
> ***revised:*** Thirty to forty per cent goes for taxes.
> ***revised:*** Taxes consume from 30 to 40 percent.
>
> ***num:*** 750 people showed up to watch the chess tournament.
> ***revised:*** As many as 750 people came to watch the chess tournament.
> ***revised:*** The chess tournament drew 750 interested spectators.

Dates are sometimes considered acceptable at the beginning of a sentence, but since some people object to the practice it is worth avoiding. In #61b above we could easily have rewritten the example:

> Wasn't 2000 the last year of the twentieth century, and not the first year of the twentieth-first century?

61i Commas with Numerals

Commas have long been conventional to separate groups of three figures in long numbers:

3,172,450   17,920

In the metric system, however, along with the rest of SI (Système Internationale, or International System of Units), groups of three digits on either side of a decimal point are separated by spaces; with four-digit numbers a space is optional:

7723 *or* 7 723
3 172 450
3.1416 *or* 3.141 6 (*but* 3.141 59)

There are two exceptions to this convention: amounts of money and addresses. Use commas to separate dollar figures preceding a decimal into units of three:

$3,500   £27,998.06   □ 30 000

Street addresses of four or more figures are usually not separated by commas or spaces:

18885 Bay Mills Avenue

For further information about SI consult the *Canadian Metric Practice Guide,* published by the Canadian Standards Association.

62 Spelling Rules and Common Causes of Error

sp Some writers have little trouble with spelling; others have a lot—or is that "alot"? Even confident writers must consult a dictionary or spell checker occasionally; poor spellers need to do this all the time. The good news is that good spelling comes with practice; taking the time to look up a word now will help you remember its proper spelling the next time you need to use it.

English spelling isn't as bizarre as some people think, but there are oddities. Sometimes the same sound can be spelled in several ways (fine, offer, phone, cough; or so, soap, sow, sew, beau, dough), or a single element can be pronounced in several ways (cough, tough, dough, through, bough, fought). When such inconsistencies occur in longer and less familiar words, sometimes only a dictionary can help us. And remember, a dictionary isn't *pre*scribing but *de*scribing: it isn't commanding us to be *correct* but simply recording the currently accepted *conventions*.

English has changed a great deal over the centuries, and it is still changing. Old words pass out of use, new words are added, conventions of grammar evolve, pronunciations and spelling change. Words in transition may have more than one acceptable meaning or pronunciation or spelling. The past tense of *dream* can be either *dreamed* or *dreamt*. The past tense of *slide* changed from *slided* to *slid* a century or so ago; will the past tense of *glide* someday be *glid*? Just a few years ago *dove* was considered unacceptable as the past tense of *dive*; now, it is at least as acceptable as *dived*. And so on. Dictionaries can tell you what is preferred or accepted right now—just make sure you're using an up-to-date dictionary and not an old one.

In Canada, we also have to contend with the influence of British and American spelling. Broadly speaking, Canadian conventions—whether of spelling, punctuation, usage, or pronunciation—are closer to American than to British, and where they are changing, they are changing in the direction of American conventions. Many of us, when we see the word *lieutenant*, still say "leftenant" instead of "lootenant," but we say and spell *aluminum* rather than *aluminium*. The alphabet still ends in *zed* rather than *zee* for most of us, though the distinction may be fading. Most Canadians write *centre* and *theatre* rather than *center* and *theater*; but we write *curb* rather than *kerb*, and "skedule" is replacing "shedule" as the pronunciation of *schedule*. Endings in *our* (colour, honour, labour, etc.) exist alongside those in *or*; either spelling is conventional in Canada. The same is true of endings in *ise* or *ize*, though the latter is clearly preferred. We have the useful alternatives *cheque* (bank), *racquet* (tennis), and *storey* (floor); Americans have only *check*, *racket*, and *story* for both meanings. But *draught* is losing ground to *draft*, and *program* and *judgment* are rapidly replacing *programme* and *judgement*.

62

Where alternatives exist, either is correct. But be consistent. If you choose *analyze*, write *paralyze* and *modernize*; if you choose *centre*, write *lustre* and *fibre*; if you spell *honour*, then write *humour*, *colour*, *labour*. But if you do choose the *our* endings, watch out for the trap: when you add the suffixes *ous*, *ious*, *ate* or *ation*, and *ize* (or *ise*), you must drop the *u* and write *humorous*, *coloration*, *vaporize*, *laborious*, and there is no *u* in *honorary*.

The point is, there is choice. In this book, for example, we use the *our* ending because we think it is still considered standard outside the popular media. And we use the *ize* ending (where the alternatives exist) because we believe it to be the dominant form. If a particular form is clearly dominant or an acknowledged standard, we think it should be used. (The Spelling List at the end of the chapter includes some words with alternative spellings that might occasionally be troublesome; the word listed first is preferred.)

But such dilemmas, if they are dilemmas, are infrequent. The real spelling difficulties, those shared by all writers of English, are of a different sort.

Many spelling errors can be prevented only with the help of a good dictionary. Many others, however, fall into clear categories. Familiarizing yourself with the main rules and the main sources of confusion will help you avoid these errors.

62a *ie* or *ei*

The old jingle should help: use *i* before *e* except after *c*, or when sounded like *a* as in *neighbour* and *weigh*.

ie:	achieve, believe, chief, field, fiend, shriek, siege, wield
ei* after *c:	ceiling, conceive, deceive, perceive, receive
ei* when sounded like *a:	eight, neighbour, sleigh, veil, weigh

When the sound is neither long *e* nor long *a*, the spelling *ei* is usually right:

counterfeit, foreign, forfeit, height, heir, their

62a

But there are several exceptions; memorize them by writing a sentence using all the words:

ei: either, neither; leisure; seize; weird
ie: financier; friend; mischief; sieve

When in doubt, consult your dictionary.

62b–i Prefixes and Suffixes

The more you know about how words are put together, the less trouble you will have spelling them. Many of the words that give writers difficulty are those with prefixes and suffixes. Understanding how these elements operate will help you avoid errors.

62b Prefixes

A **prefix** is one or more syllables added to the beginning of a root word to form a new word. Many common spelling mistakes could be avoided by recognizing that a word consists of a prefix joined to a root word. For example, *pre* is from a Latin word meaning *before*; *fix* is a root, meaning *fasten or place*: the new word, *prefix*, is then literally something fastened before. *Prefix* is not a difficult word for most writers to spell, but recognizing its prefix and root will ensure that it is spelled correctly.

One mistake writers often make is omitting the last letter of a prefix when it is the same as the first letter of the root. When a prefix ends with the same letter that the root begins with, the result is a double letter; don't omit one of them:

ad + dress = address	mis + spell = misspell
com + motion = commotion	un + necessary = unnecessary

(Similarly, don't omit one of the doubled letters in compounds such as *beachhead*, *bookkeeping*, and *roommate*.)

In some cases the first letter of a root has "pulled" the last letter of a prefix over. In other words, the first letter of the root is doubled to replace the last letter of a prefix in order to make the resulting word less difficult to pronounce. Writers unaware of the prefix sometimes forget to double the consonant. The Latin prefix *ad*, meaning *to, toward, near,* is commonly affected this way. For example, it became *af* in front of *facere* (a Latin verb meaning *to do*); hence our word *affect* has two *f*s. Here are some other examples:

ad	>	**ac**	in	*access, accept, accommodate*
		al	in	*alliance, allusion*
		an	in	*annul, annihilate*
		ap	in	*apprehend, apparatus, application*
com	>	**col**	in	*collide, colloquial, collusion*
		con	in	*connect, connote*
		cor	in	*correct, correspond*
ob	>	**op**	in	*oppose, oppress*
sub	>	**suc**	in	*success, succumb*
		sup	in	*suppress, supply, support*

Note the structure of the frequently misspelled *accommodate:* both *ac* and *com* are prefixes, so the word must have both a double *cc* and a double *mm*. It may help to think of the meaning of the word: *to make room for*. Be sure to *make room for* the double *cc* and the double *mm*.

Errors can also be prevented by correctly identifying a word's prefix. A writer who knows that the prefix of *arouse* is *a* and not *ar* will not be tempted to spell the word with a double *rr*. Knowing that the prefix of *apology* is *apo*, not *ap*, will curb the temptation to spell the word with a double *pp*. (Knowing that the root is from the Greek *logos* would also help.) Familiarize yourself with prefixes. The following are some of the more common prefixes, along with their meanings:

a not, without (*amoral*); onward, away, from (*arise, awake*); to, at, or into a particular state (*agree*); utterly (*abash*)
▶ VARIANT **an** before a vowel (*anaemia*)

ab off, away, from (*abduct, abnormal, abuse*)
▶ VARIANT **abs** before *c, t* (*abscess, abstain*)

ad denoting motion towards (*advance*), change into (*adapt*), or addition (*adjunct*)
▶ VARIANTS **ac** before *c, k, q* (*accept, accede; acknowledge; acquire*)
af before *f* (*affirm*)
ag before *g* (*aggravate*)
al before *l* (*allocate*)

an before *n* (*annotate*)
ap before *p* (*apprehend*)
ar before *r* (*arrive*)
as before *s* (*assemble*)
at before *t* (*attend*)

ante before (*antecedent*)

anti opposed to, against (*anti-hero, antibacterial*)

bi two, twice (*bicoloured, biennial*)
▶ VARIANT **bin** before a vowel (*binoculars*)

by subordinate, secondary (*by-election, by-product*)

com with, together (*combine, command*)
▶ VARIANTS **col** before *l* (*collocate, collude*)
con before *c, d, f, g, j, n, q, s, t, v*, and sometimes before vowels (*concord, condescend, confide*)
cor before *r* (*correct*)

de down, away, from (*descend, de-ice*); completely (*denude*)

di twice, two (*dichromatic, dilemma*)

dis not (*disadvantage*); denoting reversal (*disappear*), removal (*dismember*), or separation (*disjoin, dispel, dissect*)
▶ VARIANT **dif** before *f* (*diffuse*)

dys bad, difficult (*dysfunctional*)

e electronic (*e-mail, e-zine*)

en in, into (*ensnare, engulf; encrust; energy*); used in verbs ending in *en* (*enliven*)
▶ VARIANT **em** before *b, p* (*embed, embolden*)

epi upon, above (*epidemic, epicentre*); in addition (*epilogue*)

ex out (*exclude; exodus*); upward (*extol*); thoroughly (*excruciate*); into the state of (*exasperate*)
▶ VARIANTS **e** (*elect, emit*)

ef before *f* (*efface*)

for denoting prohibition (*forbid*), neglect (*forget*), or abstention (*forbear, forgo*)

fore in front, beforehand (*forebear; foreshadow; forecourt*)

hyper over, beyond, excessively (*hypersensitive*); relating to hypertext (*hyperlink*)

hypo under, below normal (*hypotension*)

in not, without (*infertile*); in, towards (*influx, inbounds*)
▶ VARIANTS **il** before *l* (*illegal, illegible*)
im before *b, m, p* (*immature, imbibe*)
ir before *r* (*irrelevant, irradiate*)

inter between, among (*interactive*)

intra on the inside (*intravenous, intramural*)

intro in, inwards (*introvert*)

mis wrongly, badly (*misapply, mismanage*); expressing negativity (*misadventure; mischief*)

multi more than one, many (*multicoloured, multiple*)

ob blocking, opposing, against (*obstacle, object*); to, towards (*oblige*)
▶ VARIANTS **oc** before *c* (*occasion*)
of before *f* (*offend*)
op before *p* (*oppose*)

para beyond or distinct from but analogous to (*paranormal, paramilitary*); protecting from (*parachute*)
▶ VARIANT **par** before a vowel (*parody*)

per through, all over, completely (*pervade, perforate, perfect*)

peri around, about (*perimeter*)

pre before (*precaution, precede*)

pro supporting (*pro-industry*); forwards or away (*proceed*); before (*proactive*)
▶ VARIANT **pur** (*pursue*)

re once more, afresh (*reactivate, restore, revert*); mutually (*resemble*); in opposition (*repel*); behind, back (*remain, recluse*)

se apart, without (*separate, secure*)

sub denoting subsequent or secondary action (*subdivision*); lower, less, below (*subalpine, subculture*)
▶ VARIANTS **suc** before *c* (*succeed*)
suf before *f* (*suffix*)
sug before *g* (*suggest*)
sup before *p* (*support*)

syn united, acting together (*synchronize*)
▶ VARIANT **sym** before *b, m, p* (*symbiosis, symmetry*)

uni one (*unicorn, unicycle*)

Proofreading Tip

Recognizing Prefixes

The following are some words with their prefixes in capital letters; after each is a common misspelling that knowing the prefix would have prevented:

Right	*Wrong*	*Right*	*Wrong*
AFOREmentioned	~~aformentioned~~	**MILLI**metre	~~milimetre~~
BY-product	~~biproduct~~	**MINI**ature	~~minature~~
CONTROversial	~~conterversial~~	**PEN**insula	~~penninsula~~
DEscribe	~~discribe~~	**PER**suade	~~pursuade~~
DIAlogue	~~diologue~~	**POR**traying	~~protraying~~
DISappointed	~~dissappointed~~	**PRO**fessor	~~proffessor~~

62c Suffixes

A suffix is one or more syllables added to the end of a root word to form a new word, often changing its part of speech. For example:

root	*suffix*	*new word*
appear (v.)	ance	appearance (n.)
content (adj.)	ment	contentment (n.)
occasion (n.)	al	occasional (adj.)
occasional (adj.)	ly	occasionally (adv.)

Suffixes, like prefixes, can give writers difficulty. For example, if you add *ness* to a word ending in *n*, the result is a double *nn*: *barrenness*, *openness*, *stubbornness*. And remember that the correct suffix is *ful*, not *full*: *spoonful*, *cupful*, *shovelful*, *bucketful*, *roomful*, *successful*. The following sections should help you avoid the common spelling mistakes that writers make when adding suffixes.

62d Final *e* Before a Suffix

When a suffix is added to a root word that ends in a silent *e*, certain rules generally apply. If the suffix begins with a *vowel* (*a*, *e*, *i*, *o*, *u*), the *e* is usually dropped:

desire + able = desirable	forgive + able = forgivable
sphere + ical = spherical	argue + ing = arguing
come + ing = coming	allure + ing = alluring
continue + ous = continuous	desire + ous = desirous
sense + ual = sensual	rogue + ish =roguish

(*Dyeing* retains the *e* to distinguish it from *dying*. If a word ends with two *e*'s, both are pronounced and therefore not dropped: *agreeing, fleeing.*)

If the suffix begins with *a* or *o*, most words ending in *ce* or *ge* retain the *e* in order to preserve the soft sound of the *c* (like *s* rather than *k*) or the *g* (like *j* rather than hard as in *gum*):

notice + able = noticeable	outrage + ous = outrageous

(Note that *vengeance* and *gorgeous* also have such a silent *e*.) Similarly, words like *picnic* and *frolic* require an added *k* to preserve the hard sound before suffixes beginning with *e* or *i*: *picknicked, picknicking, frolicked, frolicking, politicking*. (An exception to this rule is *arc*: *arced, arcing*.) When the suffix does not begin with *e* or *i*, these words do not add a *k*: *tactical, frolicsome.*

If the suffix begins with a *consonant*, the silent *e* of the root word is usually not dropped:

awe + some = awesome	effective + ness = effectiveness
definite + ly = definitely	hoarse + ly = hoarsely
immediate + ly = immediately	mere + ly = merely
immense + ly = immensely	separate + ly = separately
involve + ment = involvement	woe + ful =woeful

(But note a common exception: awe + ful = awful.)

And there is a subgroup of words whose final *e*'s are sometimes wrongly omitted. The *e*, though silent, is essential to keep the sound of the preceding vowel long:

completely	extremely	hopelessness	livelihood
loneliness	remoteness	severely	tasteless

But such an *e* is sometimes dropped when no consonant intervenes between it and the long vowel:

due + ly = duly	true + ly = truly	argue + ment = argument

62e Final *y* after a Consonant and Before a Suffix

When the suffix begins with *i*, keep the *y*:

baby + ish = babyish	carry + ing = carrying
try + ing = trying	worry + ing = worrying

(Note: Words ending in *ie* change to *y* before adding *ing*: die + ing = dying; lie + ing = lying.)

When the suffix begins with something other than *i*, change *y* to *i*:

happy + er = happier	duty + ful = dutiful
happy + ness = happiness	silly + est = silliest
harmony + ous = harmonious	angry + ly = angrily

Some exceptions: *shyly*, *shyness*; *slyer*, *slyly*; *flyer* (though *flier* is sometimes used); *dryer* (as a noun—for the comparative adjective use *drier*).

62f Doubling of a Final Consonant Before a Suffix

When adding a suffix, *double* the final consonant of the root if all three of the following apply:

(a) that consonant is preceded by a single vowel,
(b) the root is a one-syllable word or a word accented on its last syllable, and
(c) the suffix begins with a vowel.

One-syllable words:

bar + ed = barred	bar + ing = barring	
fit + ed = fitted	fit + ing = fitting	fit + er = fitter
hot + er = hotter	hot + est = hottest	
shop + ed = shopped	shop + ing = shopping	shop +er = shopper

Words accented on last syllable:

allot + ed = allotted	allot + ing = allotting	
commit + ed = committed	commit + ing = committing	
occur + ed = occurred	occur + ing = occurring	occur + ence = occurrence
propel + ed = propelled	propel + ing = propelling	propel + er = propeller

But when the addition of the suffix shifts the accent of the root word away from the last syllable, do not double the final consonant:

infer + ed = inferred	infer + ing = inferring	BUT inference
prefer + ed = preferred	prefer + ing = preferring	BUT preference
refer + ed = referred	refer + ing = referring	BUT reference

Do not double the final consonant if it is preceded by a single consonant (sharp + er = sharper) or if the final consonant is preceded by two vowels (fail + ed = failed, stoop + ing = stooping) or if the root word is more than one syllable and *not* accented on its last syllable (benefit + ed = benefited, parallel + ing = paralleling) or if the suffix begins with a consonant (commit + ment = commitment).

Proofreading Tip

On Doubling the Final Consonant *l* or *p*

Unlike *parallel*, other words often double a final *l*, even when they are of two or more syllables and not accented on the final syllable; for example, *labelled* or *labeled*, *traveller* or *traveler*. Either form is correct, though the Canadian preference is for the doubled *l*. (Some even double the *l* at the end of *parallel*, in spite of the present double *ll* preceding it.)

The word *kidnap* is a similar exception, for the obvious reason of pronunciation: either *kidnapped* or *kidnaped* is correct (and *kidnapping* or *kidnaping*). Another is *worship*: either *worshipped* or *worshiped*, *worshipping* or *worshiping*. In both instances, the double final consonant is preferred in Canada.

62g The Suffix *ly*

When *ly* is added to an adjective already ending in a single *l*, that final *l* is retained, resulting in an adverb ending in *lly*. If you pronounce such words carefully you will be less likely to misspell them:

accidental + ly = accidentally
incidental + ly = incidentally
natural + ly = naturally
cool + ly = coolly
mental + ly = mentally
political + ly = politically

If the root ends in a double *ll*, one *l* is dropped: full + ly = fully, chill + ly = chilly, droll + ly = drolly.

Proofreading Tip

On Adding the Suffix *-ally*

Many adjectives ending in *ic* have alternative forms ending in *ical*. But even if they don't, nearly all add *ally*, not just *ly*, to become adverbs—as do nouns like *music* and *stoic*. Again, careful pronunciation will help you avoid error:

alphabetic, alphabetical, alphabetically
basic, basically
cyclic, cyclical, cyclically
drastic, drastically
scientific, scientifically
symbolic, symbolical, symbolically

An exception: *publicly*.

62h Troublesome Word Endings

Several groups of suffixes, or word endings, consistently plague weak spellers and sometimes trip even good spellers. There are no rules governing them, and pronunciation is seldom any help; one either knows them or does not. Whenever you aren't certain of the correct spelling, check your dictionary. The following examples will at least alert you to the potential trouble spots:

62h

able, ably, ability; ible, ibly, ibility

It should be helpful to remember that many more words end in *able* than in *ible*; yet it is the *ible* endings that cause the most trouble:

-able		*-ible*	
advisable	inevitable	audible	inexpressible
comparable	laudable	contemptible	irresistible
debatable	noticeable	deductible	negligible
desirable	quotable	eligible	plausible
immeasurable	respectable	flexible	responsible
indispensable	syllable	forcible	tangible
indubitable	veritable	incredible	visible

ent, ently, ence, ency; ant, antly, ance, ancy

-en-		*-an-*	
apparent	independent	appearance	flamboyant
confidence	inherent	attendance	hindrance
coherent	permanent	blatant	irrelevant
consistent	persistence	brilliant	maintenance
excellent	resilient	concomitant	resistance
existence	tendency	extravagant	warrant

tial, tian; cial, cian, ciate

-tia-		*-cia-*	
confidential	influential	beneficial	mathematician
dietitian	martial	crucial	mortician
existential	spatial	emaciated	physician
expatiate	substantial	enunciate	politician

ce; se

-ce		*-se*	
choice	defence	course	expense
evidence	presence	dense	phrase
fence	voice	dispense	sparse

Proofreading Tip 

practice, practise; licence, license

Canadian writers tend to follow the British practice of using the *-ce* forms of *practice* and *licence* as nouns and the *-se* forms *practise* and *license* as verbs:

> We will practise our fielding at today's slo-pitch practice.
>
> Are you licensed to drive?
> Yes, I've had my driver's licence since I was sixteen.

American writers tend to favour the *-ce* spelling of *practice* and *-se* spelling of *license* regardless of whether each is being used as a noun or a verb.

Note also that Canadian as well as British writers generally prefer the *–ce* spelling for *offence* and *defence*, while American writers tend to use the *–se* spellings of these words.

ative; itive

-ative		***-itive***	
affirmative	informative	additive	positive
comparative	negative	competitive	repetitive
imaginative	restorative	genitive	sensitive

62i *cede*, *ceed*, or *sede*

Memorize if necessary: the *sede* ending occurs only in *supersede*. The *ceed* ending occurs only in *exceed*, *proceed*, and *succeed*. All other words ending in this sound use *cede*: *accede*, *concede*, *intercede*, *precede*, *recede*, *secede*.

62j Changes in Spelling of Roots

Be careful with words whose roots change spelling, often because of a change in stress, when they are inflected for a different part of speech, for example:

clear, clarity	maintain, maintenance
curious, curiosity	prevail, prevalent
despair, desperate	pronounce, pronunciation
exclaim, exclamatory	repair, reparable
generous, generosity	repeat, repetition

inherit, heritage, BUT heredity, hereditary

62k Faulty Pronunciation

Acquire the habit of correct pronunciation; sound words to yourself, exaggeratedly if necessary, even at the expense of temporarily slowing your reading speed. Here is a list of words some of whose common misspellings could be prevented by careful pronunciation:

academic
accelerate
accidentally
amphitheatre
analogy
approximately
architectural
athlete
authoritative
biathlon
camaraderie
candidate
celebration
conference
congratulate
controversial
definitely
deteriorating
detrimental
dilapidated
disgruntled
disgust
disillusioned
elaborate
emperor
environment
epitomize
escape
especially
etcetera
evident
excerpt
February
film
foliage
further
government
governor
gravitation
hereditary
hurriedly
immersing
insurgence
interpretation
intimacy
inviting
irrelevant
itinerary
larynx
lightning
limpidly
lustrous
mathematics
negative
nuclear
optimism
original
particular
peculiar
permanently
phenomenon
philosophical
predilection
prevalent
pronunciation
quantity
repetitive
reservoir
sacrilegious
separate
significant
similar
strength
subsidiary
suffocate
surprise
temporarily
triathlon
ultimatum
village
villain
visible
vulnerable
wondrous

Proofreading Tip

Spelling Unpronounced Sounds; Telescoping

Don't omit the *d* or *ed* from such words as *used* and *supposed*, *old-fashioned* and *prejudiced*, which are often pronounced without the *d* sound. And be careful not to omit whole syllables that are near duplications in sound. Write carefully, run a spell check when possible, and proofread, sounding the words to yourself. Here are some examples of "telescoped" words that occur frequently:

right	*wrong*	*right*	*wrong*
convenience	~~convience~~	institution	~~instution~~
criticize	~~critize~~	politician	~~politian~~
examining	~~examing~~	remembrance	~~rembrance~~
inappropriate	~~inappriate~~	repetition	~~repition~~

62-l Confusion with Other Words

Don't let false analogies and similarities of sound lead you astray.

A writer who thinks of a word like:	*may spell another word* ***wrong****, like this:*	*instead of* ***right****, like this:*
young	~~amoung~~	among
breeze	~~cheeze~~	cheese
conform	~~conformation~~	confirmation
diet	~~diety~~	deity
desolate	~~desolute~~	dissolute
exalt	~~exaltant~~	exultant
democracy	~~hypocracy~~	hypocrisy
ideal	~~idealic~~	idyllic
restaurant	~~restauranteur~~	restaurateur
comrade	~~comraderie~~	camaraderie
air	~~ordinairy~~	ordinary
knowledge	~~priviledge~~	privilege
size	~~rize~~	rise
religious	~~sacreligious~~	sacrilegious
familiar	~~similiar~~	similar
summer	~~grammer~~	grammar
prize	~~surprize~~	surprise
sink	~~zink~~	zinc
solid	~~solider~~	soldier

Proofreading Tip

On the Limitations of Spell Checking

Your word-processing program's spell check feature will help you catch spelling mistakes like "grammer" and "surprize", but it will *not* help you when you've used *principle* when you meant to use *principal, birth* instead of *berth, forth* instead of *fourth, to* or *two* instead of *too*, or *their* instead of *there* or *they're.* You will need to catch such slips in your own close checking of your documents.

62m Homophones and Other Words Sometimes Confused

1. Be careful to distinguish between **homophones** (or homonyms)—words pronounced alike but spelled differently. Here are some that can be troublesome; consult a dictionary for any whose meanings you aren't sure of; this is a matter of meaning as well as of spelling (and see #69):

aisle, isle	its, it's
alter, altar	led, lead
assent, ascent	manner, manor
bear, bare	meat, meet

birth, berth
board, bored
boarder, border
born, borne
break, brake
by, buy, bye
capital, capitol
complement, compliment
council, counsel
course, coarse
desert, dessert
die, dye, dying, dyeing
discreet, discrete
forth, fourth
hear, here
heard, herd
hole, whole
past, passed
patience, patients
piece, peace
plain, plane
pore, pour
pray, prey
presence, presents
principle, principal
rain, rein, reign
right, rite, write
road, rode, rowed
sight, site, cite
stationary, stationery
there, their, they're
to, too, two
whose, who's
your, you're

2. There are also words that are not pronounced exactly alike but that are similar enough to be confused. Again, look up any whose meanings you aren't sure of:

accept, except
access, excess
adopt, adapt, adept
adverse, averse
advice, advise
affect, effect
afflicted, inflicted
allude, elude
angle, angel
appraise, apprise
assume, presume
bizarre, bazaar
breath, breathe
choose, chose
cloth, clothe
conscious, conscience
custom, costume
decent, descent, dissent
decimate, disseminate
device, devise
diary, dairy
emigrate, immigrate
eminent, imminent, immanent
enquire, inquire, acquire
ensure, insure, assure
envelop, envelope
evoke, invoke
illusion, allusion
incident, incidence, instant, instance
incredulous, incredible
ingenious, ingenuous
insight, incite
later, latter
loose, lose
moral, morale
practice, practise
quite, quiet
tack, tact
than, then
whether, weather
while, wile

3. Be careful also to distinguish between such terms as the following, for although they sound the same, they function differently depending on whether they are spelled as one word or two:

already, all ready	awhile, a while
altogether, all together	everybody, every body
anybody, any body	everyday, every day
anymore, any more	everyone, every one
anyone, any one	maybe, may be
anytime, any time	someday, some day
anyway, any way	sometime, some time

62n One Word or Two?

Do not spell the following words as two or three separate or hyphenated words; each is one unhyphenated word:

alongside	lifetime	outshine	sunrise
background	nevertheless	setback	sunset
countryside	nonetheless	spotlight	throughout
easygoing	nowadays	straightforward	wrongdoing

The following, on the other hand, should always be spelled as two unhyphenated words:

a bit	at least	in order (to)
a few	close by	in spite (of)
after all	even though	no longer
all right (*alright* is informal)	every time	(on the) other hand
a lot	in between	(in) other words
as though	in fact	up to

Proofreading Tip

On *Cannot* and *Can Not*

The word *cannot* should usually be written as one word; write *can not* only when you want special emphasis on the *not*.

62-o

62-o Hyphenation

To hyphenate or not to hyphenate? That is often the question. There are some firm rules; there are some sound guidelines; and there is a large territory where only common sense and a good dictionary can help you find your way. Since the conventions are constantly changing, sometimes rapidly, make a habit of checking your dictionary for current usage. (For hyphens to divide a word at the end of a line, see #56b.) Here are the main points to remember:

1. Use hyphens in compound numbers from *twenty-one* to *ninety-nine.*

2. Use hyphens with fractions used as adjectives:

   A two-thirds majority is required to defeat the amendment.

   When a fraction is used as a noun, you may use a hyphen, though many writers do not:

   One quarter of the audience was asleep.

3. Use hyphens with compounds indicating time, when these are written out: *seven-thirty, nine-fifteen.*

4. Use a hyphen between a pair of numbers (including hours and dates) indicating a range: *pages 73–78, June 20–26.* The hyphen is equivalent to the word *to.* If you introduce the range with *from,* write out the word *to: from June 20 to June 26.* If you use *between,* write out the word *and: between June 20 and June 26.*

5. Use hyphens with prefixes before proper nouns:

all-Canadian	pan-Asian	pseudo-Modern
anti-Fascist	post-Victorian	semi-Gothic
ex-Prime Minister	pre-Babylonian	trans-Siberian
non-Communist	pro-Liberal	un-American

   But there are well-established exceptions, for example:

antichrist	postmodern	postcolonial
transatlantic	transpacific	

6. Use hyphens with compounds beginning with the prefix *self*: *self-assured, self-confidence, self-deluded, self-esteem, self-made, self-pity,* etc. (The words *selfhood, selfish, selfless,* and *selfsame* are not hyphenated, since *self* is the root, not a prefix.) Hyphens are conventionally used with certain other prefixes: *all-important, ex-premier, quasi-religious.* Hyphens are conventionally used with most, but not all, compounds beginning with *vice* and *by*: *vice-chancellor, vice-consul, vice-president, vice-regent,* etc., BUT *viceregal, viceroy*; *by-election, by-product,* etc., BUT *bygone, bylaw, byroad, bystander, byword.* Check your dictionary.

7. Use hyphens with the suffixes *elect* and *designate*: *mayor-elect, ambassador-designate.*

8. Use hyphens with *great* and *in-law* in compounds designating family relationships: *mother-in-law, son-in-law, great-grandfather, great-aunt.*

9. Use hyphens to prevent a word's being mistaken for an entirely different word:

   He recounted what had happened after the ballots had been re-counted.

   If you're going to re-strain the juice, I'll restrain myself from drinking it now, seeds and all.

   Once at the resort after the bumpy ride, we sat down to re-sort our jumbled fishing gear.

   Check out the great sale prices of the goods at the check-out counter.

10. Use hyphens to prevent awkward or confusing combinations of letters and sounds: *anti-intellectual, doll-like, e-book, e-learning, e-mail, photo-offset, re-echo, set-to.*

11. Hyphens are sometimes necessary to prevent ambiguity:

    ambig: The ad offered six week old kittens for sale.

    clear: The ad offered six week-old kittens for sale.

    clear: The ad offered six-week-old kittens for sale.

    Note the difference a hyphen makes to the meaning of the last two examples.

    In the following, hyphenating *levelling out* removes the possibility of misreading the sentence:

    To maintain social equality, we need a levelling-out of benefits.

62p

62p Compound Nouns

Some nouns composed of two or more words are conventionally hyphenated, for example:

free-for-all	half-and-half	jack-o-lantern	runner-up
merry-go-round	rabble-rouser	shut-in	trade-in
two-timer			

But many that one might think should be hyphenated are not, and others that may once have been hyphenated, or even two separate words, have become so familiar that they are now one unhyphenated word. Usage is constantly and rapidly changing, and even dictionaries don't always agree on what is standard at a given time. Some dictionaries still record such old-fashioned forms as *to-night* and *to-morrow* as alternatives; use *tonight* and *tomorrow.* Clearly it is best to consult a dictionary that is both comprehensive and up-to-date and use the form it lists first.

62q Compound Modifiers

When two or more words occur together in such a way that they act as a single adjective before a noun, they are usually hyphenated in order to prevent a momentary misreading of the first part:

a well-dressed man
middle-class values
a once-in-a-lifetime chance
greenish-grey eyes
computer-ready forms
a three-day-old strike

When they occur after a noun, misreading is unlikely and no hyphen is needed:

The man was well dressed.
Her eyes are greenish grey.

But many compound modifiers are already listed as hyphenated words; for example, the *Canadian Oxford Dictionary* lists these, among others:

first-class	fly-by-night	good-looking	habit-forming
open-minded	right-hand	short-lived	tongue-tied
warm-blooded	wide-eyed		

Such modifiers retain their hyphens even when they follow the nouns they modify:

The tone of the speech was quite matter-of-fact.

Proofreading Tip

On Hyphens and Adverbs Ending in *ly*

Since one cannot mistake the first part of a compound modifier when it is an adverb ending in *ly*, even in front of a noun, do not use a hyphen:

He is a happily married man.

The superbly wrought sculpture was the centre of attention.

Exercise 62p–q Checking hyphenation

What does your dictionary say about the following? Should they be two separate words, hyphenated, or one unhyphenated word? (As an experiment, look some of them up in more than one dictionary; you'll likely find differences.)

1. duty free
2. terror alert
3. half life
4. half moon
5. home stretch
6. long time
7. time out
8. world war
9. world wide
10. world weary

62r Hyphenated Verbs

Verbs, too, are sometimes hyphenated. A dictionary will list most of the ones you might want to use; for example:

double-click	pan-broil	pole-vault	re-educate
second-guess	sight-read	soft-pedal	two-time

But be aware that some two-part verbs can never be hyphenated. Resist the temptation to put a hyphen in two-part verbs that consist of a verb followed by a preposition (see #22c). Be particularly careful with those that are hyphenated when they serve as other parts of speech:

> I was asked to set up the display. (*but* Many customers admired the set-up.)

> Call up the next group of trainees. (*but* The rookie awaited a call-up to the big leagues.)

Proofreading Tip

Compounds that Change Their Spelling with the Part of Speech
Note that some expressions can be spelled either as two separate words or as compounds, depending on what part of speech they are functioning as; for example:

> He works full time. *but* He has a full-time job.
>
> If you get too dizzy you may black out. You will then suffer a blackout.

62s

62s Suspension Hyphens

If you use two prefixes with one root, use what is called a "suspension" hyphen after the first prefix, even if it would not normally be hyphenated:

> The audience was about equally divided between pro- and anti-Liberals.
>
> You may choose between the three- and the five-day excursions.
>
> You may either pre- or postdate the cheque.

Exercise 62o–s Using hyphens

Insert hyphens wherever they are needed in the following sentences. Consult your dictionary if necessary.

1. The ferry is thirty two and one quarter metres long.
2. The all Canadian team proved too much even for the ex champions.
3. The cold hearted vice president took up motor racing instead of profit sharing.
4. Is that an old fashioned and beautifully made antique salt cellar I see in your china cabinet?
5. The three tough looking youths were set to dish out some abuse.
6. I watched an interesting two hour documentary about an alien smuggling operation.
7. Avoid the scatter shot approach when writing a complaint email to part time employees.
8. The long lived queen has been a full time ruler from an early age.

62t Plurals (See also #62v. 1.)

1. Regular nouns

For most nouns, add *s* or *es* to the singular form to indicate plural number:

one building, two buildings	one box, two boxes
one cat, two cats	one church, two churches
one girl, two girls	one wish, two wishes

2. Nouns ending in *o*

Some nouns ending in *o* preceded by a consonant form their plurals with *s*, while some use *es*. For some either form is correct—but use the one listed first in your dictionary. Here are a few examples:

altos	echoes	cargoes *or* cargos
pianos	heroes	mottoes *or* mottos
solos	potatoes	zeros *or* zeroes

62t

If the final *o* is preceded by a vowel, usually only an *s* is added: *arpeggios*, *cameos*, *ratios*, *cuckoos*, *embryos*.

3. Nouns ending in *f* or *fe*

For some nouns ending in a single *f* or an *fe*, change the ending to *ve* before adding *s*, for example:

knife, knives	life, lives	shelf, shelves
leaf, leaves	loaf, loaves	thief, thieves

But for some simply add *s*:

beliefs	gulfs	safes
griefs	proofs	still lifes

Some words ending in *f* have alternative plurals:

dwarfs *or* dwarves	scarves *or* scarfs
hoofs *or* hooves	wharves *or* wharfs

The well-known hockey team called the *Maple Leafs* is a special case, a proper noun that doesn't follow the rules governing common nouns.

4. Nouns ending in *y*

For nouns ending in *y* preceded by a vowel, add *s*:

bays	buoys	guys
keys	toys	valleys

For nouns ending in *y* preceded by a consonant, change the *y* to *i* and add *es*:

city, cities
country, countries
cry, cries
family, families
kitty, kitties
trophy, trophies

Exception: Most proper nouns ending in *y* simply add *s*:

There are two Marys and three Henrys in my daughter's class.

From 1949 to 1990 there were two Germanys.

But note that we refer to the Rocky Mountains as the *Rockies* and to the Canary Islands as the *Canaries*.

62t

5. Compounds

Generally, form the plurals of compounds simply by adding *s*:

major generals
backbenchers
merry-go-rounds
shut-ins
lieutenant-governors
second cousins
prizewinners
webmasters
forget-me-nots
great-grandmothers

But if the first part is a noun and the rest is not, or if the first part is the more important of two nouns, that one is made plural:

governors general
mayors elect
poets laureate
daughters-in-law
jacks-of-all-trades
holes-in-one
passersby
townspeople

But there are exceptions, and usage is changing. Note for example *spoonfuls* (this is the form for all nouns ending in *ful*). And a few compounds conventionally pluralize both nouns, for example, *ups and downs.* And a few are the same in both singular and plural, for example, *crossroads*, *daddy-long-legs*, *underpants*.

6. Irregular plurals

Some nouns are irregular in the way they form their plurals, but these are common and generally well known, for example:

child, children
foot, feet
mouse, mice
woman, women

Some plural forms are the same as the singular, for example:

one deer, two deer
one moose, two moose
one series, two series
one sheep, two sheep

7. Borrowed words

The plurals of words borrowed from other languages (mostly Latin and Greek) can pose a problem. Words used formally or technically tend to retain their original plurals; words used more commonly tend to form their plurals according to English rules. Since many such words are in transition, you will probably encounter both plural forms. When in doubt, use the preferred form listed in your dictionary. Here are some examples of words that have tended to retain their original plurals:

alumna, alumnae
alumnus, alumni
analysis, analyses
basis, bases
crisis, crises
criterion, criteria
hypothesis, hypotheses
kibbutz, kibbutzim
larva, larvae
madame, mesdames
nucleus, nuclei
parenthesis, parentheses
phenomenon, phenomena
stimulus, stimuli
synthesis, syntheses
thesis, theses

Here are some with both forms, the choice often depending on the formality or technicality of the context:

antenna	antennae (insects) *or* antennas (radios, etc.)
apparatus	apparatus *or* apparatuses
appendix	appendices *or* appendixes
beau	beaux *or* beaus
cactus	cacti *or* cactuses
château	châteaux *or* châteaus
curriculum	curricula *or* curriculums
focus	foci *or* focuses (focusses)
formula	formulae *or* formulas
index	indices *or* indexes
lacuna	lacunae *or* lacunas
matrix	matrices *or* matrixes
memorandum	memoranda *or* memorandums
referendum	referenda *or* referendums
stratum	strata *or* stratums
syllabus	syllabi *or* syllabuses
symposium	symposia *or* symposiums
terminus	termini *or* terminuses
ultimatum	ultimatums *or* ultimata

And here are a few that now tend to follow regular English patterns:

bureau, bureaus
campus, campuses
sanctum, sanctums
stadium, stadiums
genius, geniuses (*genii* for mythological creatures)

Opinion, as well as usage, is divided on the spelling of the plurals of these and similar words. Most writers, for example, find *criterions* and *phenomenons* odd, preferring the original *criteria* and *phenomena*. On the other hand, some don't object to *data* and *media* as singular nouns. And *agenda*, originally the plural of *agendum*, is now simply a singular noun with its own plural, *agendas*. Your dictionary should indicate any irregular plurals; if you aren't sure of a word, look it up.

Proofreading Tip

Spelling Irregular Plural Nouns

When writing and speaking be mindful of the following usages:

62t

- *Data* is the plural of *datum*, but it has become acceptable in informal and non-scientific cases to treat it as if it were singular.
- *Strata* is plural; the singular is *stratum*.
- *Kudos* is singular; don't use it as if it were plural.
- *Bacteria* is plural; don't use it as if it were singular.
- *Media* is the plural of *medium*, but it has become acceptable to treat it as if it were singular in fields outside of science. (*Mediums* is the correct plural for *medium* when it refers to spiritualists who claim to communicate with the dead.)

Proofreading Tip

Spelling Accented Words from Other Languages

If you use or quote words from other languages that have such diacritical marks as the cedilla(¸), the circumflex(ˆ), the tilde(˜), the umlaut(¨), or acute(´) or grave(`) accents, write them accurately. For example:

façade	*fête*	*cañon*	*Götterdämmerung*
passé	*à la mode*	*cliché*	*résumé*

See also #60b.

Exercise 62t Forming plurals

Write out what you think is the correct plural form of each of the following nouns. Then check your dictionary to see if you are right.

1. aide-de-camp ________	15. museum ________
2. alley ________	16. octopus ________
3. bonus ________	17. ox ________
4. bus ________	18. plateau ________
5. cloverleaf ________	19. radius ________
6. embargo ________	20. serf ________
7. fifth ________	21. society ________
8. fish ________	22. solo ________
9. fly-by ________	23. speech ________
10. gloss ________	24. staff ________
11. goose ________	25. territory ________
12. handful ________	26. town ________
13. mongoose ________	27. wife ________
14. mosquito ________	28. yellow ________

62u Third-Person-Singular Verbs in the Present Tense

The third-person-singular, present-tense inflection of verbs is usually formed by following the same rules that govern the formation of plurals of nouns. For example:

I brief him. She briefs me.	I lurch. It lurches.
I buy. He buys.	I portray. He portrays.
I carry. She carries.	I run. He runs.
I wait. She waits.	I try. She tries.
I lift. The fog lifts.	I wish. He wishes.

But be careful, for there are exceptions; for example:

He loafs on weekends and wolfs his food.

She hoofs it to work every day.

Exercise 62u Inflecting verbs

Supply the present-tense, third-person-singular form of each of the following verbs:

1. atrophy ________
2. buy ________
3. chafe ________
4. choose ________
5. comb________
6. condone ________
7. convey ________
8. echo ________
9. go ________
10. grasp ________
11. leaf ________
12. mouth ________
13. rally ________
14. reach________
15. relieve________
16. revoke________
17. search ________
18. ski ________
19. swing ________
20. tunnel ________

62u

62v Apostrophes

1. For plurals

An apostrophe and an *s* may be used to form the plural, but only of numerals, symbols, letters, and of words referred to as words:

> She knew her *ABC*'s at the age of four.
>
> Study the three *R*'s.
>
> It happened in the 1870's.
>
> Indent all ¶'s five spaces.
>
> *Accommodate* is spelled with two *c*'s and two *m*'s.
>
> There are four *T*'s in my password.
>
> There are too many *and*'s in that sentence.
>
> Between them they have three Ph.D.'s.

Note that when a word, letter, or figure is italicized, the apostrophe and the *s* are not.

Many people prefer to form such plurals without the apostrophe: *R*s, *7*s, *1870*s, *and*s. But this practice can be confusing, especially with lowercase letters and words, which may be misread:

confusing: How many *s*s are there in Nipissing?

confusing: Too many *this*s can spoil a good paragraph.

In cases such as these, it is clearer and easier to use the apostrophe. Keep in mind that it is sometimes better to rephrase instances that are potentially awkward:

Accommodate is spelled with a double-*c* and a double-*m*.

And is used too many times in that sentence.

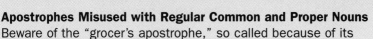

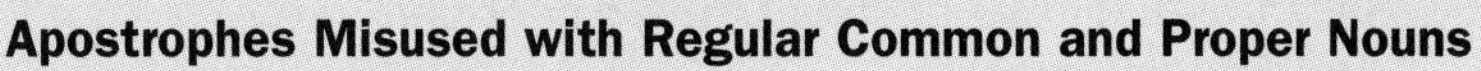

Proofreading Tip

Apostrophes Misused with Regular Common and Proper Nouns
Beware of the "grocer's apostrophe," so called because of its frequent appearance on signs in store windows:

incorrect: Escape the winter blah's with one of our romantic weekend getaway's.

correct: Escape the winter blahs with one of our romantic weekend getaways.

incorrect: Banana's and tomato's are sold here.

correct: Bananas and tomatoes are sold here.

Use 's only in cases such as those outlined above; don't use it to form any other kind of plural—that is, of regular common and proper nouns.

2. To indicate omissions

Use apostrophes to indicate omitted letters in contractions and omitted (though obvious) numerals:

aren't (are not)	they're (they are)
can't (cannot)	won't (will not)
doesn't (does not)	wouldn't (would not)
don't (do not)	goin' fishin' (going fishing)[informal]
isn't (is not)	back in '83
it's (it is)	the crash of '29
she's (she is)	the summer of '96

If an apostrophe is already present to indicate a plural, you may omit the apostrophe that indicates omission: the *20'*s, the *90'*s.

62w Possessives

1. To form the possessive case of a singular or a plural noun that does not end in *s*, add an apostrophe and *s*:

    Alberta's capital
    the car's colour
    the girl's teacher
    a day's work
    deer's hide
    Emil's briefcase
    yesterday's news
    children's books
    the women's jobs

2. To form the possessive of compound nouns, use *'s* after the last noun:

    The Solicitor General's report is due tomorrow.

    Sally and Mike's dinner party was a huge success.

    If the nouns don't actually form a compound, each will need the *'s*:

    Sally's and Mike's versions of the dinner party were markedly different.

3. You may correctly add an apostrophe and an *s* to form the possessive of singular nouns ending in *s* or an *s*-sound:

    the class's achievement
    the cross's meaning
    the congress's debates
    an index's usefulness
    Keats's poems
    a platypus's bill

    However, some writers prefer to add only an apostrophe if the pronunciation of an extra syllable would sound awkward:

    Achilles' heel
    for convenience' sake
    Moses' miracles
    Bill Gates' Foundation

    But the *'s* is usually acceptable: *Achilles's heel*; *for convenience's sake*; *Moses's miracles*; *Bill Gates's Foundation*. In any event, one can usually avoid possible awkwardness by showing possession with an *of*-phrase instead of *'s* (see number 5, below):

    for the sake of convenience
    the miracles of Moses
    the poems of Keats
    the bill of a platypus

4. To indicate the possessive case of plural nouns ending in *s*, add only an apostrophe:

    the cannons' roar
    the Joneses' garden
    the girls' sweaters
    the Chans' cottage

Proofreading Tip

On Forming/Spelling Possessive Pronouns

Do not use apostrophes in possessive pronouns:

hers (NOT her's)	its (NOT it's)
ours (NOT our's)	theirs (NOT their's)
yours (NOT your's)	whose (NOT who's)

(See also #14a.)

5. Possessive with *'s* or with *of*: Especially in formal writing, the *'s* form is more common with the names of living creatures, the *of* form with the names of inanimate things:

the cat's tail	the leg of the chair
the girl's coat	the contents of the report
Sheldon's home town	the surface of the desk

But both are acceptable with either category. The *'s* form, for example, is common with nouns that refer to things thought of as made up of people or animals or as extensions of them:

the team's strategy	the committee's decision
the company's representative	the government's policy
the city's bylaws	Canada's climate
the factory's output	the heart's affections
the law's delay	

or things that are "animate" in the sense that they are part of nature:

the dawn's early light	the wind's velocity
the comet's tail	the sea's surface
the plant's roots	the sky's colour

or periods of time:

today's paper	a day's work
a month's wages	winter's storms

Even beyond such uses the *'s* is not uncommon; sometimes there is a sense of personification, but not always:

beauty's ensign	at death's door
freedom's light	*Love's Labour's Lost*
time's fool	the razor's edge
the ship's helm	

If it seems natural and appropriate to you, go ahead and speak or write of a car's engine, a book's contents, a rocket's trajectory, a poem's imagery, and the like.

Conversely, for the sake of emphasis or rhythm you will occasionally want to use an *of*-phrase where *'s* would be normal; for example *the jury's verdict* lacks the punch of *the verdict of the jury*. You can also use an *of*-phrase to avoid awkward pronunciations (see above: those who don't like the sound of *Dickens's novels* can refer to *the novels of Dickens*) and unwieldy constructions (*the opinion of the minister of finance* is preferable to *the minister of finance's opinion*). Further, whether you use *'s* or just *s* to form the plural of letters, figures, and the like (see #62v.1), it is probably best, in order to avoid ambiguity, to form possessives of abbreviations with *of* rather than with apostrophes: *the opinion of the MLA, the opinion of the MLA's, the opinion of the MLAs.*

6. Double Possessives: There is nothing wrong with double possessive, showing possession with both an *of*-phrase and a possessive inflection. They are standard with possessive pronouns and can be used similarly with common and proper nouns:

a favourite of mine	a friend of the family *or* of the family's
a friend of hers	a contemporary of Shakespeare *or* of Shakespeare's

And a sentence like "*The story was based on an idea of Shakespeare*" is at least potentially ambiguous, whereas "*The story was based on an idea of Shakespeare's*" is clear. But if you feel that this sort of construction is unpleasant to the ear, you can usually manage to revise it to something like "*on one of Shakespeare's ideas.*" And avoid such double possessives with a *that* construction: *"His hat was just like that of Arthur's."*

Exercise 62v–w (1) Using apostrophes

Insert apostrophes where necessary in the following:

1. I dont know whether this book is hers, but theres no doubt its a handsome one and its value has increased since the 1930s.
2. Clearly he doesnt know whats going on: itll take him a weeks study to catch up.
3. Our end of term reports are ready but well have to revise them.
4. It isnt the resume that will get the job but whom you know that will count.

Exercise 62v–w (1) Using apostrophes – *continued*

5. Bonnies guess is closer than Jesss, but the jars full and accurate count of beans wont be verified till Monday.
6. The professors comments about Richs paper pointed out its errors.
7. I have two years experience in working with apostrophe problems.
8. It doesnt matter whether one wins or loses but how one plays the game.
9. When all the cars alarms started, the Joness neighbours had to shut their windows.
10. The Canadians approach to traffic is to stop for Canada geese and other passersby.

Exercise 62v–w (2) Using apostrophes

In the following sentences, supply any missing apostrophes and correct any instances of their misuse, and any associated errors.

1. Childrens toys are often made in countrys where the children do not play because theyre working.
2. He was taken aback by the spectacle of the St.Vituss Dance.
3. The two main characters are each others foils.
4. He acted without a moments hesitation.
5. We will meet again in three weeks time.
6. Have you read Herman Hesss *The Glass Bead Game*?
7. If its to perform it's duties properly, the committees agenda needs to undergo numerous changes.
8. You can buy boys and girls swim suits in many of the local malls shops.
9. The Harriss came to dinner.
10. When someone misuse's apostrophes's, it shows they dont understand the rules'.

62x Spelling List

In addition to the words listed and discussed in the preceding pages, other words often cause spelling problems. Following is a list of frequently misspelled words. If you are at all weak in spelling, you should test yourself on these words, as well as those discussed earlier. But you should also keep your own spelling list: whenever you misspell a word, add it to your list, and try to decide which rule the error violates or which category of error it falls into. Write only the correct spelling of the word: never write a misspelled word—even deliberately—when making your list, since this may reinforce the incorrect spelling in your mind when your goal should be to forget it. If a word continues to give you trouble, it can help to concentrate not on the rules that govern its spelling but on how the word looks, by taking a mental "photo" of it. Practise spelling the words on your list until you have mastered them.

absence
absorption
accessible
acclaim
accumulate
acknowledgement
acquaintance
acquire
additional
advertise
adviser (*or* advisor)
aesthetic (*or* esthetic)
affection
affidavit
aging
allege
alternately
always
amateur
amour
analogy
analyze (*or* analyse)
anonymous
anticipated
apartment
appall (*or* appal)
approach
architect
arctic
arithmetic
article
atmosphere
audience
automatically
auxiliary
axe (*or* ax)
background
beggar
beneficent
benefit
botany
bullet
buoyant
bureau
burglar
buried
cafeteria
calendar
Calvinist
camaraderie
candidate
cannibal
captain
careful
carnival
cartilage
catalogue
category
chagrin
challenge
champion
changeable
chocolate
cinnamon
clamour (*or* clamor)
clothed
coincide
colossal
committee
complexion
comprise
comrade
concomitant
conqueror
conscious
consensus
conservative
consider
consumer
continuing
control
controlled
convenient
court
courteous
create
criticism
criticize (*or* criticise)
curiosity
cylinder

decorative
decrepit
defence (*or* defense)
defensive
delusion
desperate
devastation
develop
diameter
dilemma
diminution
dining
diphtheria
dispatch
dissatisfied
dissipate
divide
doctor
drunkenness
eclectic
ecstasy
efficient
elegiac
eligible
emancipation
embarrassment
emphasize (*or* emphasise)
employee
emulate
encompass
encyclopedia
endeavour (*or* endeavor)
enforced
engraver
enterprise
epilogue
equip
equipment
equipped
erupt
euphonious
exaggerate
exalt
excel
exercise
exhausted
exhilarating
exorbitant
exuberant
facilities
fallacy
fascination
feasible
fervour (*or* fervor)
filter
flippant
flourish
flyer (*or* flier)
focuses (*or* focusses)
foreign
foresee
forty
fulfill
fundamentally
furor
gaiety
gauge
genealogy
gleam
goddess
grammar
grey (*or* gray)
grievous
guarantee
guard
harass
harmonious
height
heinous
heroin
heroine
hesitancy
hindrance
homogeneous
horseshoe
household
humorous
hygienist
hypocrisy
hypocrite
illegal
illegitimate
illiterate
imagery
imagination
imitate
immediate
impious
implementation
importance
imposter
improvise
inadequacy
incidentally
incompatible
indefinite
industrialization
inevitable
influence
initiative
injuries
innocent
inoculate
inquire (*or* enquire)
integrated
interrupt
intimate
intriguing
jealousy
jeweller (*or* jeweler)
jewellery (*or* jewelry)
judgment (*or* judgement)
knowledge
knowledgeable
laboratory
leeches
liaison
library
licence (*or* license) (n.)
license (*or* licence) (v.)
lieutenant
likelihood
lineage
liquefy
liqueur

liquor
luxury
magnificent
mammoth
manoeuvre (*or* maneuver)
manual
manufactured
marriage
marshal
mattress
meant
medieval
melancholy
menace
metaphor
mineralogy
minuscule
mischievous
misspelling
molester
monologue
monotonous
mould (*or* mold)
moustache (*or* mustache)
museum
naive, naïveté
necessary
ninety
nostrils
nosy (*or* nosey)
numerous
obstacle
occasion
occurred
occurrence
offence (*or* offense)
omniscient
oneself
operator
opulent
ostracize (*or* ostracise)
paralleled (*or* parallelled)
paralyze (*or* paralyse)
paraphernalia
parliament
partner
peculiar
peddler
perfectible
perseverance
personality
personify
personnel
persuade
pharaoh
phony (*or* phoney)
plagiarism
playwright
plough (*or* plow)
poem
pollution
porous
positioning
possession
practicality
practice (n.)
practise (v.)
predecessors
prejudice
prestige
pretense (*or* pretence)
primitive
procedure
proletariat
prominent
proscenium
psychiatry
psychology
pursue
putrefy
puzzled
quandary
quantity
quatrain
quizzically
rarefied
reality
recognize
recommend
reflection
registration
reminisce
repel
repetition
restaurant
rhythm
ridiculous
sacrifice
safety
scandal
sentence
separate
sheik
shepherd
sheriff
shining
shiny
signifies
simile
simultaneous
sincerity
siphon (*or* syphon)
skeptic (*or* sceptic)
skiing
skilful (*or* skillful)
smoulder (*or* smolder)
solely
soliloquy
species
spectators
speech
sponsor
storey (*or* story) (floor)
straddle
strategy
stretched
styrofoam
subconsciously
subsequent
subtly
superintendent
susceptible
suspense
symbolic
symbolize (*or* symbolise)

symmetry
synonymous
syrup
tariff
temperament
temperature
territory
theory
therein
threshold
tragedy
trailed
tranquility (*or* tranquillity)
transferred
troubadour
tyranny
unavailing
undoubtedly
unmistakable
until
usefulness
vehicle
veterinarian
weary
whisky (*or* whiskey)
wilful (*or* willful)
wintry
wistfulness
withdrawal
writing
written

Diction

VII

Introduction: Style and the Larger Elements of Composition

"Proper words in proper places make the true definition of a style": Jonathan Swift's definition of style may be the best, at least for simplicity and directness. In its broadest sense, style consists of everything that is not the content of what is being expressed. It is the manner more than the matter: everything that is a part of the way something is said constitutes its style.

But though many of us distinguish between style and content to facilitate discussion and analysis, the distinction is in some ways arbitrary, for the two are inseparable. Since the way in which something is expressed inevitably influences the effect, it is necessarily part of what is being expressed. "I have a hangover" may say essentially the same thing as "I'm feeling a bit fragile this morning," but the different styles of the statements create different effects, different meanings. The medium, then, if it is not the entire message, is a substantial part of it.

An important attribute of style is tone, often defined as a writer's attitude toward both subject matter and audience. Tone in writing is analogous to tone in speech. We hear or describe someone as speaking in a sarcastic tone of voice, or as sounding cheerful, or angry, or matter-of-fact. Writing, like speech, can "sound" ironic, conversational, intimate, morbid, tragic, frivolous, cold, impassioned, comic, coy, energetic, phlegmatic, detached, sneering, contemptuous, laudatory, condescending, and so forth. The tone of a piece of writing—whether an essay or only a sentence—largely determines the feeling or impression that writing creates.

The style of a piece of writing, including its tone, arises from such features as syntax, point of view, and even punctuation. But it is largely determined by diction: by choice of words, figurative language, and sounds. Diction, then, is near the heart of effective writing and style. This chapter isolates the principal challenges writers encounter in choosing and using words, and offers some suggestions for meeting them.

63 About Dictionaries

The first suggestion is the simplest one: when you think "diction," think "dictionary." Make sure you have a good dictionary, and use it to full advantage. Become familiar with it: find out how it works, and discover the variety of information it offers. A good dictionary doesn't merely give you the spelling, pronunciation, and meaning of words; it also offers advice on such matters as usage and idioms to help you decide on the best word for a particular context; it lists irregularities in the principal parts of verbs, in the inflection of adjectives and adverbs, and in the formation of plurals; it supplies etymologies (or word histories); it tells you if a word or phrase is considered formal, informal, slang, or archaic. And it usually has an interesting and useful introductory essay and relevant appendices. Take advantage of the many resources of your dictionary.

Whether you're browsing through the reference section of your library or its website, or considering the vast selection of dictionaries at your local bookstore, you may feel overwhelmed by the number of dictionaries available to you. The following sections offer some advice on how to find the dictionary that's most appropriate for your needs.

63a Kinds of Dictionaries

Dictionaries range in scope and function from multi-volume works offering detailed word histories to tiny word books designed to fit in your pocket for quick reference. Most of the information you will require as a student will be contained in one of three kinds of dictionary: an unabridged dictionary, an abridged dictionary, or a learner's dictionary for students of English as an additional language.

1. Unabridged dictionaries

Unabridged dictionaries, in one or more volumes, offer the most comprehensive view of English as it is now and has been used. The twenty-volume *Oxford English Dictionary* (2nd edn, 1989), the most famous of unabridged dictionaries, is based on historical principles, which means that it presents definitions for each word, accompanied by historical quotations, in the order of their first recorded use. The *OED* is most useful when you want to see how the meaning of a word has changed over time. For example, a look at the *OED*'s entry for *silly* will enable you to trace the word to its Old English roots, when it meant "fortunate; blessed by God," to Middle English, when it meant "deserving of compassion," to the sixteenth century, when it came to be used to mean "showing a lack of judgment or common sense." The *OED* is available on CD-ROM, and most libraries subscribe to the *OED Online*, which is updated quarterly and offers a convenient way to search for the information you might need.

Not all unabridged dictionaries are based on historical principles, nor do they all comprise multiple volumes. *Webster's Third New International Dictionary of the English Language* (2000) and the *Random House Webster's Unabridged Dictionary* (2003) are excellent single-volume unabridged dictionaries. Though the former is rather out of date, an updated version is available online for a monthly or annual fee. The latter is available on CD-ROM. (Be aware that there is no copyright on the name *Webster's*, so many American dictionary publishers use the name in their titles hoping that the good reputation of the famous American lexicographer Noah Webster will rub off on their own products.)

2. Abridged dictionaries

Although some questions will demand a check online or a trip to the library to consult an unabridged dictionary, an abridged dictionary is the most useful for the everyday needs of most students. An abridged dictionary may be as large as the two-volume *Shorter Oxford English Dictionary* or as small as a mini-dictionary, but the most practical is a "college" or "desk dictionary" that includes words and senses in current use, along with some historical senses, pronunciations, illustrative examples, etymologies, usage notes, and "encyclopedic" entries that provide information on people and places.

For years Canadians had to choose from among British and American dictionaries such as the *Concise Oxford Dictionary*, *Collins English Dictionary*, *Random House Webster's College Dictionary*, and *Merriam Webster's Collegiate Dictionary*. Today there are some very good desk dictionaries produced in Canada, including the *Canadian Oxford Dictionary* (2004) and the *Gage Canadian Dictionary* (2002), which offer a more accurate reflection of the language as it is spoken, written, and used by Canadians.

Some students find it useful to keep a dictionary on hand during lectures or, if permitted, during exams. Bear in mind, however, that although dictionary makers have certain methods of shrinking dictionaries without removing content—for example, by using more abbreviations or by reducing the type size—a smaller or abridged dictionary usually means some loss of useful material, and so some archaic or less common words may be removed, or etymologies may be truncated.

▲ 3. Learner's dictionaries

Although learner's dictionaries are designed especially for people whose first language is not English, the advice on usage and grammar and the defining style of several excellent learner's dictionaries make them enormously helpful even to native speakers of English. Some learner's dictionaries use a limited defining vocabulary of a few thousand words likely to be understood, or at least recognized, by readers of English as an additional language. This reduces the chances that a definition will contain words the user will have to look up.

A good learner's dictionary features numerous notes and examples to illustrate the idiomatic use of words. It may contain additional pages of information on such matters as understanding English grammar and spelling, and writing tests, essays, and letters. Some excellent learner's dictionaries include the *Oxford ESL Dictionary* (2004), the *Oxford Advanced Learner's Dictionary* (2005), the *Collins Cobuild Advanced Learner's English Dictionary* (2006), and the *Longman Dictionary of Contemporary English* (2003).

Writing Tip

Assessing the Size of a Dictionary
The standard way to gauge a dictionary's size is to count its **entries**. An entry is any word, form of a word, component of a word, or phrase that is presented explicitly as a distinct element of the English language. These elements are usually set in bold type. When a dictionary presents itself as having a certain number of entries, then, it is giving a total of all the words and phrases in bold type in the text.

Some dictionaries advertise themselves as including a certain number of definitions. Since there are usually several definitions for any defined word, a dictionary's definition count will be greater than its entry count: so don't compare one dictionary's entries with another's definitions.

63b Features of Dictionaries

Most people who consult a dictionary are looking for one of two things: the meaning of a word, or the spelling of a word. When assessing a dictionary, it is helpful to know how its editors made their decisions about meaning and spelling. Was their research based on analysis of a large corpus of English texts? An extensive reading program designed to capture new words and usages? If it is a Canadian dictionary, what kind of research was used to determine preferred Canadian spellings? All of this sort of information can usually be found on the inside dust jacket.

You will also want to make sure that the dictionary you're using is up to date and not just a recent reissue of an older work. When comparing dictionaries, have a list of newer words and see how many of them are included in each of the dictionaries you're considering. This should give you a good indication of whether or not a dictionary is sufficiently up to date.

Beyond meaning and spelling, a dictionary entry includes several features that may be useful. Deciding how important each of the following is to you will help you decide which dictionary is most appropriate for your needs.

1. Word breaks

Most North American dictionaries and some learner's dictionaries indicate syllable breaks or word breaks in headwords and other bold forms by means of points (·), pipes (|), or other symbols. Knowing an unfamiliar word's syllabication can make it easier to pronounce. It can also help if, when writing an essay, you need to hyphenate a long word at the end of a line. Remember, though, that not all syllable breaks are good places to insert a hyphen; in some multisyllabic words there is no desirable place to insert a hyphen, and these words should not be broken at all (see #56b, #62-o).

2. Pronunciations

All dictionaries contain pronunciations, though some may not provide pronunciations for all words. A dictionary may transcribe a word's pronunciation using the International Phonetic Alphabet, or IPA, so that various sounds are represented by specific symbols that are usually displayed across the bottom of the page. Or a dictionary may "respell" the word using a combination of letters and diacritical marks to indicate long and short vowels.

	IPA	*respelling*
curtains	'kɜrtənz	kûr′tnz
eavestroughing	'i:vz,trɒfiŋ	ēvz′trôfiŋ
shrivel	'ʃrɪvəl	shriv′əl
cookie	'kʊki	ko͝ok′ē

The IPA pronunciations, though they may appear at first confusing, produce the most accurate representations of a word's pronunciation. The respelling method is the easiest way to convey a reasonably accurate pronunciation without the user's having to learn a complicated set of symbols.

3. Examples and illustrations

Definitions for technical words can often be enhanced with illustrations. Consider the following definition, from *Webster's New World Dictionary*: "a lamp in which the light is produced by a filament of conducting material contained in a vacuum and heated to incandescence by an electric current." This definition, though accurate, likely will not produce for the reader a perfect idea of "incandescent lamp" the way the accompanying illustration of a standard light bulb does. Not all dictionaries contain illustrations, and of those that do, some provide illustrations to accompany definitions that don't really require them. If you are considering the suitability of a dictionary with illustrations, make sure the illustrations really benefit the definitions they accompany, bearing in mind that illustrations often take space away from definitions.

In a similar way, a definition may be greatly enhanced by an example that shows the way a word is used in a sentence. This is an important feature of learner's dictionaries, which strive to show their users not just what words mean but how they should be used in speech.

4. Usage information

An important thing to remember about dictionaries is that they are descriptive, not prescriptive. They record the language as it is actually used, not as some people think it should be used. As a result, a dictionary includes words or senses that may meet with the disapproval of some users. For example, most dictionaries include two nearly opposite definitions for the word *peruse*: "to read thoroughly or carefully" (the original sense), and "to read in a casual manner" (the more common sense). Many critics object to the second use, yet it would be inappropriate for a dictionary to exclude this sense, since it is the one most people have in mind when they use the word. A good dictionary will point out the usage issue in a brief note in the entry.

Most dictionaries also include register labels to indicate whether a word is formal, informal, slang, archaic, and so on.

5. Idioms and phrasal verbs

An idiom is an expression whose meaning is not easily deduced from the meanings of the words it comprises, for example *off the top of my head*, *out on a limb*, *be run off one's feet*. Idioms and phrasal, or two-part, verbs (see #22d) are often defined toward the end of a word's entry. Bear in mind that an idiom such as *off the top of my head* could be defined at the entry for *top* or the entry for *head*.

6. Derivatives

63b

A derivative is a word derived from another, such as *quickness* or *quickly* from *quick*. It is common for dictionaries to "nest" undefined derivatives at the main entry for a word if the derivatives' meanings can be easily deduced. For example, a word like *logically* does not require a separate definition as long as *logical* is well defined; the reader can safely assume that *logically* means "in a logical manner." But the word *practically* should not be nested in the entry for *practical*, since it has a sense beyond "in a practical manner." Be aware that some smaller dictionaries, in order to save space, nest derivatives that should be defined separately; this is something you should keep in mind when evaluating the usefulness of a dictionary.

7. Etymologies

Knowing a word's etymology, its original form and meaning, can sometimes help you remember or get a clearer idea of its meaning. For example, knowing that the word *recalcitrant* comes from a Latin word meaning "kicking back," from *calx*, "heel," may help you remember that it means "stubborn, uncooperative." And knowing that *peruse* comes from the prefix *per-*, meaning "thoroughly," plus *use* will help you understand why some critics object to its use to mean "read in a casual manner." A word's etymology can be fascinating as well as helpful: *climax* comes from a Greek word for ladder, *vegetable* comes from a Latin verb meaning "to be healthy," *pyjamas* comes from a Persian word meaning "leg clothing." If you find this kind of information interesting, make sure your dictionary goes into detail in its etymologies. Reading that *berserk* comes from an Old Norse compound meaning "bear coat" or that *amethyst* comes from a Greek word meaning "not drunk" without any accompanying explanation can be unsatisfying.

8. Canadian content

Because Canada has its own political, cultural, historical, and geographical realities, it has its own words to describe these realities. As a result of Canada's unique history and settlement patterns, Canadian English also includes words borrowed from languages that do not appear in other varieties of English. Since dictionaries inevitably describe and reflect the language and culture of the country in which they are edited, American dictionaries and British dictionaries overlook some words, senses, spellings, and pronunciations that are unique to Canadian English. Good Canadian dictionaries, such as the *Canadian Oxford Dictionary* and the *Gage Canadian Dictionary*, which are not merely Canadian adaptations produced in other countries, offer a more accurate view of Canadian English than either American or British dictionaries.

9. Encyclopedic entries

Some abridged dictionaries include entries for important people, places, and events. These may be quite short, consisting of little more than a person's years of birth and death or a city's population, or they can provide more information about a person's life and work or a city's importance. If you are considering dictionaries with encyclopedic entries, pick a couple of people or places and see how various dictionaries treat them.

63c Three Sample Dictionary Entries

The following three entries, from an abridged, a compact, and a learner's dictionary, illustrate some of the features just described. Dictionaries follow certain conventions, but each features a unique design. A final consideration when judging the suitability of a dictionary is how easy it is for you to navigate through it.

63c

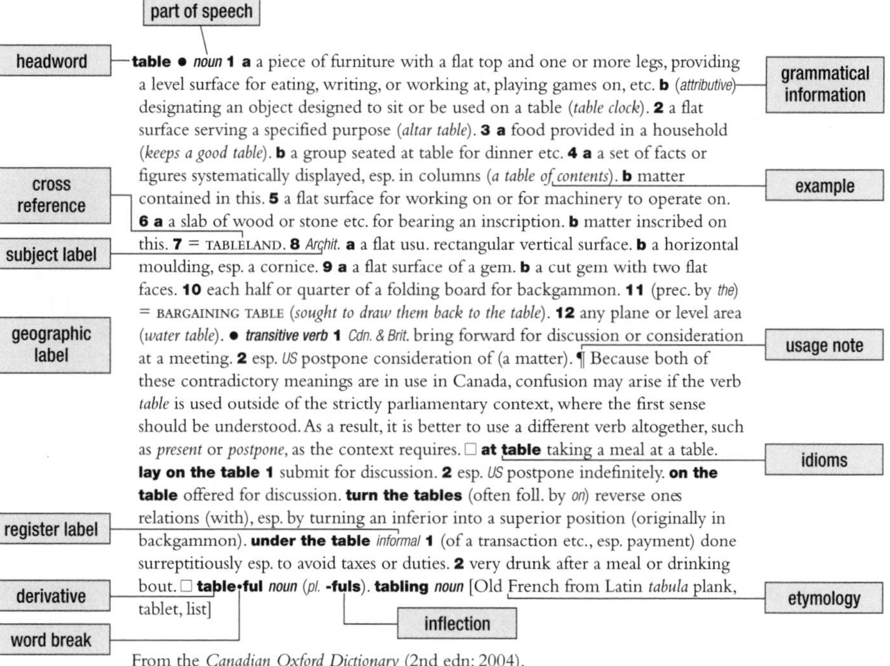

table • *noun* **1 a** a piece of furniture with a flat top and one or more legs, providing a level surface for eating, writing, or working at, playing games on, etc. **b** (*attributive*) designating an object designed to sit or be used on a table (*table clock*). **2** a flat surface serving a specified purpose (*altar table*). **3 a** food provided in a household (*keeps a good table*). **b** a group seated at table for dinner etc. **4 a** a set of facts or figures systematically displayed, esp. in columns (*a table of contents*). **b** matter contained in this. **5** a flat surface for working on or for machinery to operate on. **6 a** a slab of wood or stone etc. for bearing an inscription. **b** matter inscribed on this. **7** = TABLELAND. **8** *Archit.* **a** a flat usu. rectangular vertical surface. **b** a horizontal moulding, esp. a cornice. **9 a** a flat surface of a gem. **b** a cut gem with two flat faces. **10** each half or quarter of a folding board for backgammon. **11** (prec. by *the*) = BARGAINING TABLE (*sought to draw them back to the table*). **12** any plane or level area (*water table*). • *transitive verb* **1** *Cdn. & Brit.* bring forward for discussion or consideration at a meeting. **2** esp. *US* postpone consideration of (a matter). ¶ Because both of these contradictory meanings are in use in Canada, confusion may arise if the verb *table* is used outside of the strictly parliamentary context, where the first sense should be understood. As a result, it is better to use a different verb altogether, such as *present* or *postpone*, as the context requires. □ **at table** taking a meal at a table. **lay on the table 1** submit for discussion. **2** esp. *US* postpone indefinitely. **on the table** offered for discussion. **turn the tables** (often foll. by *on*) reverse ones relations (with), esp. by turning an inferior into a superior position (originally in backgammon). **under the table** *informal* **1** (of a transaction etc., esp. payment) done surreptitiously esp. to avoid taxes or duties. **2** very drunk after a meal or drinking bout. □ **table·ful** *noun* (*pl.* **-fuls**). **tabling** *noun* [Old French from Latin *tabula* plank, tablet, list]

From the *Canadian Oxford Dictionary* (2nd edn: 2004).

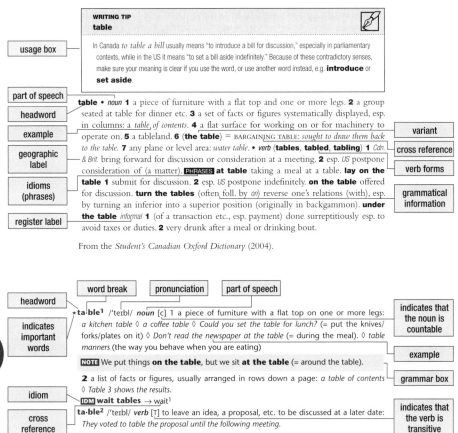

WRITING TIP
table

In Canada *to table a bill* usually means "to introduce a bill for discussion," especially in parliamentary contexts, while in the US it means "to set a bill aside indefinitely." Because of these contradictory senses, make sure your meaning is clear if you use the word, or use another word instead, e.g. **introduce** or **set aside**.

table • *noun* **1** a piece of furniture with a flat top and one or more legs. **2** a group seated at table for dinner etc. **3** a set of facts or figures systematically displayed, esp. in columns: *a table of contents*. **4** a flat surface for working on or for machinery to operate on. **5** a tableland. **6** (**the table**) = BARGAINING TABLE: *sought to draw them back to the table.* **7** any plane or level area: *water table.* • *verb* (**tables**, **tabled**, **tabling**) **1** *Cdn. & Brit.* bring forward for discussion or consideration at a meeting. **2** esp. *US* postpone consideration of (a matter). PHRASES **at table** taking a meal at a table. **lay on the table 1** submit for discussion. **2** esp. *US* postpone indefinitely. **on the table** offered for discussion. **turn the tables** (often foll. by *on*) reverse one's relations (with), esp. by turning an inferior into a superior position (originally in backgammon). **under the table** *informal* **1** (of a transaction etc., esp. payment) done surreptitiously esp. to avoid taxes or duties. **2** very drunk after a meal or drinking bout.

usage box
part of speech
headword
example
geographic label
idioms (phrases)
register label
variant
cross reference
verb forms
grammatical information

From the *Student's Canadian Oxford Dictionary* (2004).

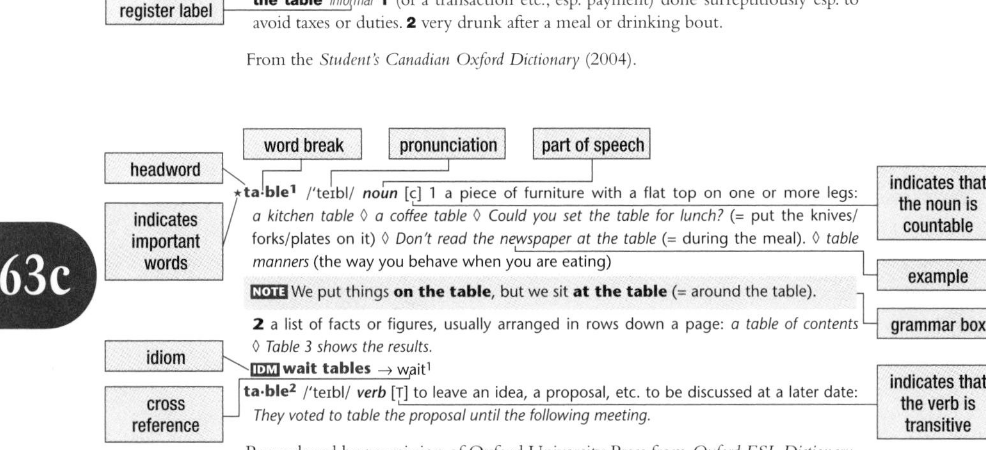

★**ta·ble¹** /ˈteɪbl/ *noun* [C] 1 a piece of furniture with a flat top on one or more legs: *a kitchen table* ◊ *a coffee table* ◊ *Could you set the table for lunch?* (= put the knives/forks/plates on it) ◊ *Don't read the newspaper at the table* (= during the meal). ◊ *table manners* (the way you behave when you are eating)

NOTE We put things **on the table**, but we sit **at the table** (= around the table).

2 a list of facts or figures, usually arranged in rows down a page: *a table of contents* ◊ *Table 3 shows the results.*

IDM **wait tables** → wait¹

ta·ble² /ˈteɪbl/ *verb* [T] to leave an idea, a proposal, etc. to be discussed at a later date: *They voted to table the proposal until the following meeting.*

63c

64 Level

lev In any piece of writing, use words that are appropriate to you, to your topic, and to the circumstances in which you are writing. That is, consider the *occasion*, the *purpose*, and the *audience*. Avoid words and phrases that call attention to themselves rather than to the meaning you want to convey. In writing a formal academic essay, adopt diction appropriate to the discipline *in which* and the audience *for which* you are writing. In other writing for your courses or for the workplace, avoid slang and colloquial or informal terms at one extreme, and pretentious language at the other. Of course there will be times when one or the other, or both, will be useful—for example to make a point in a particularly telling way, to achieve a humorous effect, or to make dialogue sound realistic. But it is usually preferable to adopt a straightforward, moderate style, a level of diction that both respects the intelligence of the reader and strives to communicate with the reader as effectively as possible. (See also #22e.)

64a Slang

Since **slang** is diction opposite to **formal diction**, it is seldom appropriate in a formal context. There is nothing inherently wrong with slang; it is undeniably a colourful part of the language and can help you express complicated ideas with clarity and force. But its very liveliness and vigour make it short-lived: some slang terms remain in vogue only for a few weeks, some linger on for a few years, and new ones are constantly popping up to replace those going out of fashion. Some slang terms eventually become part of the standard written language, but most slang is so ephemeral that dictionaries cannot keep up with it.

It is principally slang's transitoriness that makes it ineffective to use in the kind of writing you may be doing for your courses. A word or phrase that is *hot* (or *cool*) when you write it may sound stale and dated soon after. Much slang is also limited to particular social groups, classes, or professions, and it is often regional as well. Hence terms that may be vivid to you and your friends may be unintelligible to an outsider, such as someone older or from a different place. Or, given the nature of some slang words, a reader who finds them intelligible may also find them offensive.

If you are considering using slang in your writing, consult not only one or more good dictionaries but also members of your audience: trust your ear, your common sense, and your good taste.

Proofreading Tip

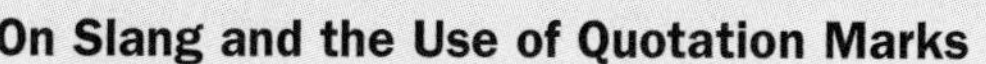

On Slang and the Use of Quotation Marks
If you do use a slang term, do not use quotation marks to call attention to it (see #54g).

Exercise 64a Thinking about slang

List as many slang terms as you can think of for each of the following. Which are current in your vocabulary? Which, if any, would you consider using in an academic essay? In a letter to a friend? In a letter to a parent or uncle or aunt?

1. criminal (n.)
2. mad (adj.)
3. intoxicated
4. cheat (vb.)
5. court (vb.)
6. bore (n.)
7. very good
8. talk (vb.)
9. stupid person
10. sweetheart
11. man
12. police officer
13. beautiful
14. food
15. inspiring

64b Informal, Colloquial

inf, colloq Even dictionaries can't agree on what constitutes slang versus **informal** or **colloquial** usage. Slang terms are in one sense simply extreme examples of the colloquial or informal. Nevertheless, there are many words and phrases that may be labelled *inf* or *colloq* in a dictionary, and although not slang, they do not ordinarily belong in formal writing. For example, unless you are aiming for a somewhat informal level, you should avoid such abbreviations as *esp.*, *etc.*, *no.*, *orig.*, and *OK*; and you may wish to avoid contractions (*can't, don't,* etc.), though they are common in our own discourse in this book and in everyday speech.

Here are more examples of informal or colloquial usages that would be out of place in strictly formal writing:

Informal or Colloquial	*Acceptable equivalents*
absolutely	very, thoroughly
a lot of, lots of, lots	much, many, a great deal of
anyplace, everyplace, noplace, someplace	anywhere, everywhere, nowhere, somewhere
around	approximately
awful	bad, ill, ugly, unpleasant, etc.
be sure and	be sure to
back of, in back of	behind
chance of + gerund (e.g., chance of getting)	chance + infinitive (chance to get)
expect (as in "I expect you want me here")	suppose, suspect, imagine
figure	think, believe, etc.
fix (verb)	prepare (food or drink); manipulate fraudulently (an election, a contract, a competition)
fix (noun)	predicament
funny	odd, peculiar, strange, unusual
guess (as in "I guess that…")	believe, suppose, think
mean	cruel, evil, deceitful, etc.
most (as in "most everyone")	almost, nearly
nice	agreeable, attractive, pleasant, etc.
nowhere near	not nearly, not at all, not anywhere near
out loud	aloud
over with	ended, finished, done
phone	telephone
photo	photograph
plan on + gerund (e.g., plan on going)	plan + infinitive (plan to go)
quite, quite a bit, quite a few, quite a lot	somewhat, rather, many, a large amount, much
real, really (as intensive adverb)	very, greatly, surely
right away, right now	immediately, at once
shape (good, bad, etc.)	condition
show up	appear, arrive; prove better than, best
size up	judge, assess

sure and (as in "be sure and call")	sure to
terrible, terribly (also as vague modifiers)	unpleasant, uncomfortable, very, extremely
try and	try to
wait on	await, wait for
where (as in "I see where we're in for fun")	that

In addition, many words have been so abused in advertising, used for gushy and exaggerated effect, that they can now seldom be used with precision in formal writing. For example:

awesome	fantastic	lifestyle	marvellous
stupendous	terrific	tremendous	

Exercise 64b Using formal diction

Provide formal substitutes for each of the slang or informal terms below. Use your dictionary or thesaurus as necessary. Then compose sentences for at least ten of the listed terms, using them in ways that you think would be acceptable in relatively formal writing.

1. bawl out
2. bellyache (vb. and n.)
3. cheapskate
4. chintzy
5. chump
6. con (vb.)
7. conniption
8. cook up
9. crackdown
10. crummy
11. jock
12. cute
13. ditch
14. down the tube
15. face the music
16. fall guy
17. high and mighty
18. hoot
19. hunch
20. jerk
21. miss out
22. monkey business
23. on the spot
24. scrounge
25. slapdash
26. slouch
27. southpaw
28. egghead
29. shocker
30. up the creek

64c

64c "Fine Writing"

Unnecessarily formal or pretentious diction is called "fine writing"—here, an ironic term of disapproval. Efforts to impress with such writing almost always backfire. For example, imagine yourself trying to take seriously someone who wrote "It was felicitous that the canine in question was demonstrably more exuberant in emitting threatening sounds than in attempting to implement said threats by engaging in actual physical assault," instead of simply saying "Luckily, the dog's bark was worse than its bite."

This is an exaggerated example; but it illustrates how important it is to be natural (within reason) and straightforward. Writers who overreach themselves often use supposedly elegant terms incorrectly. The individual who wrote "Riding majestically down the street on a magnificent float was the Festival Queen surrounded by all her courtesans" was striving for sophistication, but succeeded only in getting an undesired laugh from the reader who knew the correct meaning of *courtesans*.

Exercise 64c Thinking about "big" words

For each of the following words, provide one or more equivalents that are less formal and more natural. Use your dictionary or thesaurus as necessary. Which of these words do you recognize but not use yourself? Which do you consider to be in your working vocabulary? Mark any that you think should not necessarily be avoided as pretentious or overly formal in a non-academic context.

1. ablutions
2. assiduity
3. bellicose
4. cachinnation
5. circumambient
6. collation
7. colloquy
8. comminatory
9. compotation
10. concatenation
11. confabulate
12. conflagration
13. contumelious
14. crepuscular
15. defenestration
16. divagation
17. doff
18. egress
19. eleemosynary
20. equitation
21. erstwhile
22. frangible
23. gustatory
24. habiliments
25. hebdomadal
26. impudicity
27. ineluctable
28. jejune
29. lubricity
30. lucubrations
31. matutinal
32. mentation
33. objurgation
34. obloquy
35. oppugnant
36. orthography
37. otiose
38. pellucid
39. penurious
40. peregrinations
41. propinquity
42. raison d'être
43. rebarbative
44. repast
45. rubicund
46. salubrious
47. sartorial
48. serendipitous
49. sesquipedalian
50. superincumbent
51. tenebrous
52. transpontine
53. vilipend
54. visage
55. veridical
56. Weltanschauung

65 Figurative Language

fig Strictly speaking, **figurative language** includes mostly "figures of speech," such as personification, synecdoche, metonymy, hyperbole, litotes, and even paradox, irony, and symbolism. Generally, however, the term *figurative language* refers to *metaphoric* language, whose most common devices are the **metaphor** and the **simile**. A **simile** is an explicit comparison that is usually marked by *like* or *as*:

> The river is like a snake winding across the prairie.
>
> The Internet is like a highway without speed limits.

A **metaphor**, on the other hand, is an implicit comparison; the items being compared are assumed to be identical:

> The river is a snake winding its way across the prairie.
>
> The Internet is a highway without speed limits.

Often a metaphor is condensed into a *verb:*

> The river snakes its way across the prairie.

an *adjective:*

> The serpentine river meanders across the prairie.

or an *adverb:*

> The river winds snakily across the prairie.

Figurative language is often an important element of good style. Writing that lacks this kind of language will be relatively dry, flat, and dull. But remember that a good metaphor doesn't merely enhance style: it also sharpens meaning. Use metaphors not only for their own sake, but to convey meaning more effectively. For example, to say that "the hillside was covered with a profusion of colourful flowers" is clear enough; but if one writes instead that "the hillside was a tapestry of spring blossoms," the metaphor not only enriches the style but also provides readers with something *concrete* (see #65a), an *image* (that of the tapestry) that helps them visualize the scene.

65a Inappropriate Metaphors

If you force a metaphor into your writing just to embellish style, it will likely be inappropriate and call attention to itself rather than enhance the desired meaning. It will, to use a tired but still expressive simile, stick out like a sore thumb. For example, "the tide of emotion suddenly stopped" doesn't work, since tides don't start and stop; they ebb and flow. And a phrase like "bomb craters blossoming all over the landscape" works only if one intends the inherent discord between bombs and blossoms. And a simile such as "he ran like an ostrich in heat" may confuse the reader with inappropriate associations.

65b Overextended Metaphors

Extended metaphors can be effective, but don't let yourself become so enamoured with a metaphor that you extend it too far, to the point where it takes control of what is being said:

> When she came out of the surf her hair looked like limp spaghetti. A sauce of seaweed and sand, looking like spinach and grated cheese, had been carelessly applied, the red flower fastened in her tresses looked like a wayward piece of tomato, and globs of mud clung like meatballs to the pasty pasta of her face. The fork of my attention hovered hesitatingly over this odd dish. Clearly I would need more than one glass of the red wine of remembered beauty and affection to wash it all down.

65a

This may all be very clever, but after the first sentence—the spaghetti image itself being somewhat questionable—one quickly loses sight of the original descriptive intention and becomes mired in all the associated metaphors and similes; in short, a reader is likely to feel fed up, or in this case giddy, and turn to something less overdone.

65c Dead Metaphors

Guard against dead metaphors and clichés (see #71e). The language contains many dead metaphors like the "*leg* of a table," "*branching* out," and "*flew* to the rescue," which are acceptable since we no longer think of them as metaphors. But many other metaphors, whether altogether dead or only moribund but with little metaphoric force left, can be ineffective. Such overused phrases as *the ladder to success*, *making mountains out of molehills*, *nipped in the bud*, *flogging a dead horse*, and *between the devil and the deep blue sea* are usually muddying and soporific instead of enlivening and clarifying.

Occasionally, a dead or trite metaphor can be revivified if consciously used in a fresh way. For example, the hackneyed phrase *bit off more than he could chew* was given new life by the person who, discussing Henry James's writing, said that James "chewed more than he bit off." *Sound as a dollar* would these days be more appropriately rendered as "unpredictable as the loonie." Even a slangy phrase like *chew the fat* might be transformed and updated in a description of people sitting down to "chew the bad cholesterol." But take some care, for such attempts can misfire; like an overextended metaphor, they sometimes call attention to their own cleverness at the expense of the intended meaning.

65d Mixed Metaphors

Edit out of your writing incongruously mixed metaphors. The person who wrote, of the Great Depression, that "what began as a zephyr soon blossomed into a giant" had lost control of metaphor. The following paragraph about Shakespeare's *Othello* was written by one who obviously began with the good intention of using metaphors to describe the evil of Iago, but who became lost in a maze of contradictions and incongruities:

> Iago has spun his web and like a spider he waits. His beautiful web of silk is so fragile and yet it captures the souls of its victims by gently luring them into his womb. Unsuspecting are those unfortunate creatures who sense the poisonous venom oozing through their veins. It has a tranquil effect, for it numbs the mind with its magical potion. The victims are transformed into pawns as they satisfy the queen's appetite and so they serve their purpose.

Here, in contrast, is a paragraph that successfully uses a single extended metaphor to create its effect:

> I remember vividly my first days as a student teacher. They were the closest I have ever come to knowing what it must feel like to be part of a high-wire act. Walking into that high school classroom for the first time was like taking the first tentative steps onto the wire: the eyes of the audience were upon me, my knees were shaking, and I was struggling to keep my balance. But as that first morning went on and as my students and I moved forward into the lesson, I felt the exhilaration of the high-wire performer as she finds her equilibrium and moves with confidence to the middle and then the end of that tightrope. The only thing missing was the cheering.

Certainly, then, use figurative language. It can lend grace and charm and liveliness and clarity to your writing. But be alert to its potential pitfalls: inappropriate, overextended, and mixed metaphors.

66 Concrete and Abstract Diction; Weak Generalizations

66a Concreteness and Specificity

Concrete words denote tangible things, capable of being apprehended by our physical senses (*children, skyscraper, flowers, parks, broccoli, ice, fire, walking*). **Abstract** words denote intangibles, like ideas or qualities (*post modernism, agriculture, nature, health, creativity, progress*). Much of the writing you do is likely a blend of the abstract and the concrete. The more concrete your writing, the more readily your readers will grasp it, for the concreteness will provide images for their imaginations to respond to. If you write

> Transportation is becoming a major problem in our city.

and leave it at that, readers will understand you. But if you write, or add,

> In the downtown core of this city, far too many cars and far too few buses travel the streets.

you know that your readers will see exactly what you mean: in their minds they will see the traffic jams and the overloaded buses.

As your writing moves from generalizations to specifics, it will move from the abstract to the concrete. And the more specific your writing is, the clearer and more effective it will often be. *General* and *specific* are relative terms: a general word designates a *class* (e.g. *modes of transportation*); a less general or more specific word designates members of that class (*vehicles, ships, airplanes*); a still more specific word designates members of a still smaller class (*cars, trucks, bicycles, buses*); and so on, getting narrower and narrower, the classes and sub-classes getting smaller and smaller, until—if one wants or needs to go that far—one arrives at a single, unique item, a class of one, such as the particular car sitting in your own parking spot, driveway, or garage.

66a

Of course it is appropriate to write about "plant life," and then to narrow it, say, to "flowers"; and if you can write about "marigolds," "roses," "daffodils," and so on, you'll be more specific. Even the generalization "fire" is unquestionably vivid, but "forest fires" makes it sharper, and mentioning the specific example of "the huge bush fires in Queensland" will likely enable you to make your point even more sharply. Don't vaguely write "We experienced a warm day" when you could write more clearly, "We stayed outdoors all afternoon in the 25-degree weather," or "We basked in the warm spring sunshine all afternoon." Don't write "I found the city interesting" when you could write "I admired the city's architecture and enjoyed its night life," or, better still, "I was fascinated by the undamaged architecture in the city's French quarter, and I enjoyed the fine cafés, restaurants, and jazz clubs that I found there."

The following passage makes sense, but its abstractness and generality prevent it from being more memorable or effective:

> If one makes a purchase that a short time later proves to have been ill-advised due to the rapid deterioration of quality, then it is the opinion of this writer that one has every right to seek redress either by expressing one's displeasure to the individual who conducted the original transaction or, if it should prove necessary, by resorting to litigation.

Writers sometimes assume that this kind of language is good because it sounds formal and sophisticated. But notice how much more vivid a revised version is:

> If you buy a car on Thursday and the engine falls out of it on Saturday, I think you should complain to the dealer who sold it to you, and sue him if necessary to get back the good money you paid for what turned out to be a useless vehicle.

Of course, abstract and general terms are legitimate and often necessary, for one can scarcely present all ideas concretely, and the kind of concrete language illustrated in the above example is hardly appropriate to all situations. Try, though, to be as concrete and specific as your subject and the context will allow.

66b Weak Generalizations

gen A common weakness of student writing is an overdependence on unsupported generalizations. Consider: "Children today are reluctant readers." Few readers would or should accept such a general assertion, for the statement calls for considerably more illustration, evidence, and qualification. It evokes all kinds of questions: All children? Of all ages? In all countries? What are they reluctant to read? What is the connotation of "reluctant" here? Is such reluctance really something new? Merely stating a generalization or assumption is not enough; to be clear and effective it must be illustrated and supported by specifics.

Here are two essays on the same topic. Read the first one through:

> Travel can be a very broadening experience for people who go with the intention of having their eyes opened, which may often occur by unpleasant means. Culture shock can be a very unpleasant and hurtful experience to people who keep their eyes and minds closed to different attitudes or opinions. This problem of culture shock is an example of why people should prepare for the unexpected and try to learn from difficult experiences, rather than keeping a closed mind which will cause them to come away with a grudge or hurt feelings.

Besides causing negative attitudes, travel can also confirm the prejudices of people with narrow minds. For example, I once met a man from England who had travelled around the world visiting the last vestiges of the British empire. He had even travelled to apartheid South Africa, and still come away with his colonialist attitudes.

Even if one goes to a country with an open mind, one may still come away with a superficial perception of that country. It takes time to get to know a country and understand its people. The time one spends in a country will thus greatly affect one's perception of that country.

Time is also needed before travelling begins, for people to read and learn about the area they will be going to. This background will enable them to look for things they might otherwise never see, and they will appreciate more the things they do discover. For example, if one knows something about the architecture of a country before one visits it, one can plan one's trip to include visits to buildings of special interest.

Thus an open, well-prepared mind will benefit from the experiences of travel, but otherwise travel is likely to have a very negative, narrowing effect on people's minds.

Now, without looking back at the essay, ask yourself what it said. You will probably have a vague sense of its thesis, and chances are you will remember something about a well-travelled but still narrow-minded traveller from England, and perhaps something about the advisability of knowing something in advance about foreign architecture—for those are the only two concrete items in the essay. (Think how much more vivid and therefore meaningful and memorable the point about architecture would have been had it included a reference to a specific landmark, such as the Leaning Tower of Pisa or the Taj Mahal or the Parthenon or St. Paul's Cathedral.)

Now read the second essay, noting as you read how much clearer its points are than the relatively unsupported generalizations of the first essay:

> Travel can be broadening. The knowledge gained in the areas of historical background, cultural diversity, and the range of personalities encountered in foreign lands gives us a fuller outlook on ourselves, on Canada and Canadian issues, and on our position in the global context.
>
> The impact of history upon visitors to other lands is immense indeed. One cannot help but feel somewhat small when looking across valley upon valley of white crosses in France, coming face to face with the magnitude of death taking place in the world wars of the last century. Before long, one realizes that many of the events that took place years ago have an effect upon the way in which we live today. In some areas, scars of the recent past remain. The bits of rubble left from the once formidable Berlin Wall, for example, remind visitors that the way they live is not the same way others live, that, indeed, for decades millions lived grim and limited lives,

never dreaming that in their lifetimes revolutionary changes would bring freedom, if not immediate comfort and prosperity.

This is not to say that there are not pleasant aspects of history as well. Sixteenth-century cobblestone lanes, usually less than ten feet wide, still remain in many old English villages, surrounded by Tudor cottages, complete with thatched roofs, oil lamps, and sculpted wrought-iron fences. Standing in such an environment and thinking about the writings of masters like Shakespeare brings out a much deeper and richer taste than merely reading about them in a classroom at home. And places like this remind us of how our ancestors lived, making it easier to understand the customs and ideas of the past.

In going through different foreign lands, one cannot ignore the great cultural diversity. This is best illustrated by contrasting fiestas in Spain and *Oktoberfest* in Munich with Canadian celebrations. Many countries, besides having different languages (and dialects of those languages), also have their own dress, holidays, and religious beliefs. This variety is often startling to the tourist, who often takes it for granted that what is standard for him or her is also the norm throughout much of the rest of the world.

There is also a wide range of social habits within a country. This is especially true of Britain, which still shows signs of its once all-powerful class system. A visitor from Canada may find it hard to understand such a system, not realizing that it is a centuries-old tradition; a son does the same job as his father, whether knight or knave, and lives in the same place, and often dies there.

Above all, the differences among people from other countries are what leave a visitor with the most lasting impression. From the street person in the slums of Casablanca, to the well-dressed gentleman walking briskly in the streets of Hanover, to the British executive sipping beer in "the local" on Hyde Street, there are myriad personalities as one travels through other lands. When we look at the world from this perspective, realizing that we are *not* all the same, we are better equipped to understand many of the problems throughout the globe.

The first essay is not without a message, for unsupported generalizations do have content, do say something; but the message of the second is clearer, more forceful; readers will better understand and remember what it said because their minds have something concrete and specific to hang on to. (You may wish to compare these two non-academic essays in other ways, as well; for example, is the way the second concludes more effective than the way the first does?)

Exercise 66 (1) Using specific diction

For each of the following words, supply several increasingly specific terms; take at least a few all the way to a single specific item.

1. car
2. art
3. answered
4. said
5. food
6. drink (vb.)
7. drink (n.)
8. people
9. mythical thing
10. entertainment
11. creature
12. structure
13. see
14. moved
15. concept
16. freedom
17. music

Next, compose a paragraph in which you use one or two of these seventeen general terms in the first sentence and develop your idea by using increasingly specific terms.

Exercise 66 (2) Being concrete and specific

Rewrite this vague and abstract paragraph from a letter of application for an entry-level research position at a community newspaper. The ad for the position called for details of the applicant's educational and employment experience, so in your revision, try to make the paragraph sharp and vivid by supplying concrete and specific details wherever suitable.

> My education and job experience make me a good person to work in your organization. At university, I have been studying courses in arts and science, and I have done quite a bit of research and writing of various things along the way. I have worked as a volunteer in my community, and over the years, I have been employed in three jobs that have given me good experience working in a busy office setting.

67 Connotation and Denotation

Keep **connotation** in mind both to convey the meaning you intend and to enable yourself to convey particular shades of meaning you do intend. A word may **denote** (literally mean) what you want it to, yet **connote** (suggest) something you don't intend. For example, if you describe someone as "brash," your reader will understand the denotative meaning of "confident" but will also understand you to feel at least somewhat negative; if you in fact approve of the condition (and the person), you'll use a word like "self-assured," for its connotation is favourable rather than unfavourable.

Proofreading Tip 

On Using a Thesaurus
It is best not to use an online or book-form thesaurus without using a standard dictionary in conjunction with it. Words listed together in such books are not necessarily identical in meaning; they can be subtly different not only in denotation but, especially, in connotation as well. A thesaurus is a vocabulary-building tool, but it should be used with care, for it can trap unwary writers into saying things they don't mean. As an example, consider the fact that many of the words in each group in the following exercise were listed in a thesaurus simply as synonyms.

Exercise 67 Recognizing connotation

Label each of the following words as having an unfavourable (u), neutral (n), or favourable (f) connotation; it might help if you place the words in each group on a scale running from *u* to *f*. Explain cases where you think some could be labelled more than one way, depending on context. Use your dictionary if necessary.

1. artless crass dense dull dumb feeble-minded foolish green ignorant inept ingenuous innocent naive obtuse shallow simple slow stupid thick unsophisticated unthinking
2. bony gaunt lanky lean rawboned scrawny skinny slender slight slim spare spindly svelte thin trim twiggy underweight weedy
3. artful clever crafty cunning devious diplomatic foxy greasy guileful insinuating oily scheming slimy slippery sly smooth suave tricky unctuous wily
4. arrogance assurance audacity boldness brass brazenness cheek chutzpah effrontery gall highhandedness impertinence impudence insolence nerve pride presumption temerity
5. bookworm brain brainworker egghead genius highbrow intellectual mind pedant pundit sage savant scholar smarty thinker geek

68 Euphemism

euph **Euphemisms** are substitutes for words whose meanings are felt to be unpleasant and therefore, in certain circumstances, undesirable. In social settings we tend to ask for the location not of the toilet, which is what we want, but of the restroom, the bathroom, the washroom, or the powder room. Interestingly, the word *toilet* was itself once a euphemism.

But the euphemism is sometimes abused. Euphemisms used to gloss over some supposed unpleasantness may actually deceive. Innocent civilians killed in bombing raids are referred to as "collateral damage," and assassination squads are termed "special forces." What was once faced squarely as an economic depression is now, in an attempt to mitigate its negative implications, termed at worst a "recession," or an "economic downturn," or even a mere "growth cycle slowdown." Government officials who have patently lied admit only that they "misspoke" themselves.

Such euphemisms commonly imply a degree of dignity and virtue not justified by the facts. Calling genocide "ethnic cleansing" seriously distorts the meanings of both "ethnic" and "cleansing." Some euphemisms cloud or attempt to hide the facts in other ways. Workers are "laid off" or "declared redundant" or even "downsized" rather than "fired." A man who has died in a hospital is said to have "failed to fulfill his wellness potential" or undergone a "negative patient-care outcome." A spy is directed to "terminate with extreme prejudice" rather than "assassinate" or "murder." An escalation in warfare is described as a "troop surge"; a civil war is referred to as "factional unrest" or "an insurgency." George Orwell, in his 1946 essay "Politics and the English Language," referred to such usages as linguistic dishonesty.

Other euphemisms help people avoid the unpleasant reality of death, which is often called "passing away" or "loss"; the lifeless body, the cadaver or corpse, is deemed "the remains." Such usages may be acceptable, even desirable, in certain circumstances, since they may enable one to avoid aggravating the pain and grief of the bereaved. But in other circumstances, direct, more precise diction is preferable.

Euphemisms that deceive are obviously undesirable. Others may be acceptable if circumstances seem to justify them, but one must exercise taste and judgment.

Exercise 68 Avoiding euphemisms

Supply more straightforward equivalents for the following terms.

1. job action, work stoppage ____________________
2. revenue enhancement ____________________
3. repeat offender ____________________
4. correctional facility ____________________
5. underprivileged, deprived, disadvantaged ____________________
6. surveillance satellites ____________________
7. in custody ____________________
8. memorial chapel; memorial park ____________________

Exercise 68 Avoiding euphemisms – *continued*

9. untruth ______
10. friendly fire ______
11. indisposed ______
12. weather event ______

69 Wrong Word

ww Any error in diction is a "wrong word," but a particular kind of incorrect word choice is customarily marked **wrong word.** The use of *infer* where the correct word is *imply* is an example. Don't write *effect* when you mean *affect*. Don't write *ex-patriot* when you mean *expatriate.* (Such errors are also sometimes marked *spelling* or *usage:* see the lists of often-confused words, #62-l and #62m; and see the Usage Checklist, #72.) But other kinds of wrong word choices occur as well; here are a few examples:

ww: Late in the summer I met my best friend, which I hadn't seen since graduation.

ww: Most men would have remembered spending several days in an open ship with little water and under the tropic sun as a terrible hardship, but Marlow recalls only that he felt he could "last forever, outlast the sea, the earth, and all men."

ww: Many miles of beach on the west coast of Vancouver Island are absent of rocks.

Whom, not *which,* is the correct pronoun for a person (see #14d). The word *ship* won't do for a small open vessel like a rowboat; *boat* is the appropriate word here. The wrong phrase came to the third writer's mind; *devoid of* was the one wanted (and see #70, on idiom). See also ***nsw*** (no such word) in Appendix 2.

69

Exercise 69 Avoiding wrong words

Correct the wrong words in the following sentences.

1. The conference is intended to focus attention on the problems facing our effluent society.
2. The performance of our local orchestra was spirited and bombastic.

Exercise 69 Avoiding wrong words – *continued*

3. The company's representatives claimed to be authoritarians on the subject.
4. Politicians try to maintain an impressionable image in the eyes of the public.
5. We tried to convince her that her fear was entirely imaginative.
6. Some shoppers stopped buying coffee because they found the price so absorbent, if not gastronomical.
7. The premier of Alberta led his party to the best of his possibilities.
8. He was deciduously on the wrong track with that theory.
9. It was an incredulous display of manual dexterity.
10. The cat was very expansive, weighing over twenty pounds.

70

▲ 70 Idiom

id A particular kind of word choice has to do with **idiom**. An idiom is an expression peculiar to a given language, one that may not make logical or grammatical sense but that is understood because it is customary. The English expression "to sow one's wild oats," for example, if translated into another language, would not have its idiomatic meaning; but French has an equivalent expression, *jeter sa gourme,* which would make little sense if translated literally into English. Here are some other peculiarly English turns of phrase: *to have a go at, to be down in the dumps, to be at loose ends.* You will notice that these idioms have a colloquial flavour about them, and may even sound like clichés or euphemisms; but other similar idioms are a part of our everyday language and occur in formal writing as well; for example: to "do justice to" something, to "take after" someone, to "get along with" someone.

Most mistakes in idiom result from using a wrong preposition in combination with certain other words. For example, we get *in* or *into* a car, but *on* or *onto* a bus; one is usually angry *with* a person, but *at* a thing; one is *fond of* something or someone, but one has *a fondness for* something or someone. Here are some examples of errors in idiom:

incorrect: Her feelings toward her new job are mixed.
(*correct*: feelings about)

incorrect: She took the liberty to introduce herself to the group.
(*correct*: liberty of introducing)

incorrect: He plans to get married with my youngest sister. (*correct*: get married to)

incorrect: It is pleasant to live in the dorms and be in close proximity of everything on campus. (*correct*: proximity to)

Idiomatic expressions sometimes involve choosing between an infinitive and a prepositional gerund phrase. After some expressions either is acceptable; for example:

He is afraid to lose. He is afraid of losing.

They are hesitant to attend. They are hesitant about attending.

They plan to appeal. They plan on appealing. (informal)

But some terms call for one or the other:

They propose to go. They are prepared to go.

They insist on going. They are insistent on going.

And sometimes when a word changes to a different part of speech, the kind of phrase that follows must also change:

It was possible to complete the project in three days.
We agreed on the possibility of completing the project in three days.

Our tennis coach emphasized basic skills. Our tennis coach puts emphasis on basic skills.

It is pleasant to remember. She spoke of the pleasantness of remembering.

But it isn't always predictable:

He intended to go. He spoke of his intention to go.
He had every intention of going.

And sometimes a *that*-clause is the only idiomatic possibility:

I asked them to attend. I recommended that they attend.
I requested that they attend.

See also **different from, different than**; **let, make**; **recommend**; and **very** in #72.

Idiom is a matter of usage. But a good learner's dictionary such as the *Oxford Advanced Learner's Dictionary (OALD)* can often help. For example, if you look up *adhere* in the *OALD*, you will find that it is to be used with *to*, so you would know not to write "adhere on" or "adhere with." Or, should you be wondering about using the word *oblivious*, your dictionary will inform you that it can be followed by either *of* or *to*. (And see **agree** and **differ** in the Usage Checklist, #72; see also ***id*** in Appendix 2 for more examples.)

Other references that help with idiom (and with other matters) are *Fowler's Modern English Usage*, the *Canadian Oxford Dictionary* (and the *Student's Oxford Canadian Dictionary*), and the *Guide to Canadian English Usage*. Students for whom English is an additional language will benefit from using specialized learner's dictionaries, which offer a wealth of information about idiomatic uses of articles and prepositions and examples of idioms used in complete sentences (see #63a.3).

70

Exercise 70 Correcting idioms

Correct the unidiomatic usages in the following sentences.

1. She has an unusual philosophy towards modern technology.
2. He suggested me to use this new product.
3. Last summer I was bestowed with a scrawny, mangy mutt.
4. Desdemona had unquestioning faith of Iago's character.
5. Tanya made us to laugh with stories of her adventures in the Yukon.
6. The analysis is weak because it lacks in specific details.
7. I am amazed with the report's suggestions.
8. Lovers and poets create dream worlds in which only they can inhabit.
9. Ironically, although Huck fails, Tom succeeds to free Jim.
10. The generation gap between them is evident by their uneasiness of each other's boredom.
11. We discussed about global warming.
12. The class emphasized on mathematics skills.

71 Wordiness, Jargon, and Associated Problems

Avoid diction that decreases precision and clarity. Using too many words, or tired words, or fuzzy words weakens communication. We discuss and illustrate these weaknesses all in one section because they are related and sometimes overlapping. For example, phrases like "on the order of" and "on the part of" could be labelled ***w***, ***trite***, or ***jarg***. Jargonauts are fond of wordy and pretentious phrases like "make a determination" (instead of simply *determine*), or "at this point in time" (instead of *now*), or "due to the fact that" (instead of *because*), or "be of assistance to" (instead of *help*). They refuse to settle for the verb *support* when they can say instead that people "are supportive of" someone or something, and they increasingly use "characterize" rather than *call* or *name*, "necessitate" rather than "need."

Even without such overlapping, there is an inevitable family relationship among the several groupings of weaknesses—if only because one bad habit frequently leads to, or is accompanied by, others. Considering them all together rather than separately should give you a better sense of the kinds of difficulties they may cause. No lists such as those that follow can be exhaustive, because new words and phrases are making their way into these categories every day. But once you understand the principles, you will get a feeling for the kinds of impediments to good communication such terms represent. (If the reason for a given term's inclusion is not immediately apparent to you, the illustrations in the exercises may help to clarify the matter.)

71a

71a Wordiness

w Generally, the fewer words you use to make a point, the better. Useless words—often called *deadwood*—clutter up a sentence; they dissipate its force, cloud its meaning, blunt its effectiveness. The writer of the following sentence, for example, used many words where a few would have done a better job:

> ***w:*** What a person should try to do when communicating by writing is to make sure the meaning of what he is trying to say is clear.

Notice the gain in clarity and force when the sentence is revised:

> ***revised:*** A writer should strive to be clear.

Expletives

When used to excess, expletive constructions can be a source of weakness and wordiness (see #12k and #29f). There is nothing inherently wrong with them (there are many in this book—two already in this sentence), and they are invaluable in enabling us all to form certain kinds of sentences the way we want to. Nevertheless writers sometimes use them when a tighter and more direct form of expression would be preferable. If you can get rid of an expletive without creating awkwardness or losing desired emphasis, do it. Don't write

> *w:* There are several reasons why it is important to revise carefully.

when you can so easily get rid of the excess caused by the *there are* and *it is* structure:

> *revised:* Careful revision is important for several reasons.
> *revised:* For several reasons, careful revision is important.

> *w:* It is one of the rules in this dorm that you make your own bed.
> *revised:* One rule in this dorm requires you to make your own bed.
> *revised:* In this dorm you must make your own bed.

> *w:* In this small city, there are over a hundred people without housing.
> *revised:* Over a hundred people in this small city are homeless.

71a

The number of words you save may not always be great, but such changes can help strengthen your style. Note that you strengthen your style by using stronger verbs than the verb *to be.*

See also Exercise 22a–c(2c), on getting rid of the clutter of an excess of prepositional phrases, and #17p and #29f, on the passive voice.

71b Repetition

rep Repetition can be useful for coherence and emphasis (see #4b, #7b, #29g, #5). But unnecessary repetition usually produces wordiness, and often awkwardness as well. Consider this sentence:

> *rep:* Looking at the general appearance of the buildings, you can see that special consideration was given to the choice of colours for these buildings.

The sentence is wordy in general, but one could begin pruning by cutting out the needless repetition of *buildings.* Another example:

> *rep:* She is able to make the decision to leave her job and to abide by her decision.

It might be argued that the repetition of *decision* adds emphasis, but "make the decision" could be shortened to "decide," or the final "her decision" could be simply "it."

71c Redundancy

red Redundancy, another cause of wordiness, is repetition of an idea rather than a word. (The term "redundancy" can mean "excess" in general, but it is also used to designate the particular stylistic weakness known technically as "tautology.") Something is redundant if it has already been expressed earlier in a sentence. In the preceding sentence, for example, the word *earlier* is redundant, since the idea of *earlier* is present in the word *already*: repeating it is illogical and wordy. (Double negatives are a kind of redundancy, and also illogical: *can't never, don't hardly*.) To begin a sentence, "In my opinion, I think . . . " is redundant. The statement, "Tamiko is a personal friend of mine" is redundant, for a *friend* can scarcely be other than *personal*. To speak of a "new innovation" is to be redundant. The television writer describing a movie in which "Meryl Streep heads a stellar all-star cast" evidently didn't consider what "stellar" means. And the person who wrote, in a letter to a prospective employer, that "an interview would be mutually helpful to both of us" might not make a good first impression. Here are some other frequently encountered phrases that are redundant because the idea of one word is present in the other as well:

advance planning
added bonus
basic fundamentals
but nevertheless
character trait
climb up
close scrutiny
completely eliminate
consensus of opinion
continue on
enter into
erode away
general consensus
low ebb
mental attitude
more preferable
necessary prerequisite
new record
past history
reduce down
refer back
revert back

71c

One common kind of redundancy is called "doubling"—adding an unnecessary second word (usually an adjective) as if to make sure the meaning of the first is clear:

red: The report was brief and concise.

Either *brief* or *concise* alone would convey the meaning. Sometimes an insecure writer goes to even greater lengths:

red: The report was brief, concise, and to the point.

Exercise 71c Cutting redundancy

Revise the following sentences to eliminate redundancy.

1. If enough food cannot be supplied for all the people in the world, humankind will have to deal with hunger, starvation, and widespread famine.
2. He is adventurous in that he likes a challenge and is willing to try new experiences, but he is not adventurous to the point of insanity, though.
3. Looking ahead into the future, the economist sees even less rapid growth in Canada's national economy.
4. She approached the door with feelings of fear and dread.
5. Golding's *Lord of the Flies* concerns a group of young children, all boys, who revert back to savagery.
6. If one doesn't thoroughly examine every part of the subject fully, one is almost sure to miss something that could be vitally important.
7. Most people would rather flee away from danger than face it squarely.
8. Carol soon realized that she had to make a careful outline first, before she could expect an essay to be well organized.
9. She told him in exact and precise terms just what she thought of him.
10. The singer in the film does not fit the stereotyped image of a musician.

Exercise 71a–c (1) Removing wordiness

Revise the following sentences to eliminate wordiness.

1. Nature is a very strong, powerful image in this poem.
2. The courses being offered today require much more research and thought rather than the age-old memory work that used to plague the education system not too long a time ago.
3. These were the very things that caused him his puzzlement and his bafflement.

Exercise 71a–c (1) Removing wordiness – *continued*

4. Advances in developments of modern information technology greatly contribute to making the equipment necessary for computerization of machinery more and more feasible for potential users.
5. Since he has both positive and negative qualities of human nature, Othello is far from perfect and has many faults.
6. Her confidence in expressing her views caused her to develop her faith in herself, which added to her visible strength.
7. The president and the prime minister both shared that view of the foreseeable future.
8. Another device used by the playwright was one of repetition.
9. There were two hundred people outside the auditorium, pressing against the ropes.
10. In the past six months I have been subjected to moving from two locations to other surroundings.

Exercise 71a–c (2) Reducing wordiness by combining sentences

Often one can save many words by combining two or more drafted sentences. Try doing that with each of the following excerpts, from students' drafts; cut all the wordiness you can while you're at it.

1. Also, parents who wish to see a game live but do not want to be disturbed by their children have no choice except to leave them attended at home. In this case, the parents would have to hire a babysitter. As a result, the parents end up paying the babysitter as well as for the game.
2. At soccer practice, our coach would single out the players who had the least team spirit. An example of this would be the passing drills in practices. The players who lagged behind on the field would be asked to run laps after practice.
3. There are a surprising number of lawyers and stockbrokers playing the game. This may be because these people must thrive on strategic planning to be in those professions in the first place. [And see ***gr*** in Appendix 2.]

71d Ready-made Phrases

"Prefabricated" or formulaic phrases that leap to our minds whole are almost always wordy. They are a kind of cliché (see #71e), and many also sound like jargon (see #71h). You can often edit them out of a draft altogether, or at least use shorter equivalents:

a person who, one of those who
as of the moment
at the present time, at this time, at this point in time (use *now*)
at that time, at that point in time (use *then*)
at the same time (use *while*)
by and large
by means of (use *by*)
due to the fact that, because of the fact that, on account of the fact that, in view of the fact that, owing to the fact that (use *because*)
during the course of, in the course of (use *during*)
except for the fact that (use *except that*)
for the purpose of (use *for, to*)
for the reason that, for the simple reason that (use *because*)
in all likelihood, in all probability (use *probably*)
in a very real sense
in character, of a . . . character
in colour (as in "was blue in colour")
in fact, in point of fact
in height (use *high*)
in length (use *long*)
in nature
in number
in order to (use *to*)
in reality
in shape
in size
in spite of the fact that (use *although*)
in the case of
in the event that (use *if*)
in the form of
in the light of, in light of (use *considering*)
in the midst of (use *amid*)
in the near future, in the not too distant future (use *soon*)
in the neighbourhood of, in the vicinity of (use *about, near*)
in this day and age (use *now, today*)
manner, in a . . . manner
period of time (use *period, time*)
personal, personally

previous to, prior to (use *before*)
the fact that
up until, up till (use *until, till*)
use of, the use of, by the use of, through the use of
when all is said and done
with the exception of (use *except for*)
with the result that

And the prevalence of such ready-made phrases as *point of view* caused a student unthinkingly to tack *of view* onto *point* in the following sentence: "My dentist made the point of view that flossing is good for one's gums." Two-part verbs (see #22d) sometimes trip up writers in the same way: *fill in* is correct for "*Fill in* this form," but not for "The pharmacist *filled in* the prescription."

71e Triteness, Clichés

trite
cliché

Trite or hackneyed expressions, clichés, are another form of wordiness: they are tired, worn out, all too familiar, and therefore generally contribute little to a sentence. Since they are, by definition, prefabricated phrases, they are another kind of deadwood that can be edited out of a draft. Many trite phrases are metaphors, once clever and fresh, but now so old and weary that the metaphorical sense is weak at best (see #65c); for some, the metaphor is completely dead, which explains errors such as "tow the line" (for "toe the line") and "the dye is cast" (for "the die is cast"), "dead as a doorknob," and "tarnish everyone with the same brush." "To all intents and purposes" now sometimes comes out "to all intensive purposes"; "taken for granted" becomes "taken for granite"; "by a hair's breadth" turns up as "by a hare's breath"; and so on. A writer aiming for "time immemorial" instead wrote "time in memoriam." Another referred to the passage of a lifetime as "from dawn to dust." And another asserted that a particular poet's message was that "we should make hay while the tide's in." A reviewer of a novel imagined angry characters "tearing the author from limb to limb." Even the once-familiar proverb "The proof of the pudding is in the eating" is now often heard as the relatively meaningless "The proof is in the pudding."

71e

Some clichés are redundant as well: *first and foremost, few and far between, over and above, each and every, one and only, to all intents and purposes, ways and means, various and sundry, all and sundry, part and parcel, in this day and age, in our world today, in our modern world today*, and so on.

Of course clichés can be useful, especially in speech; they can help one fill in pauses and gaps in thinking and get on to the next point. Even in writing they can sometimes—simply because they are so familiar—be an effective way of saying something. And they can be used for a humorous effect. But in writing, in all such instances, they should only be used consciously. It isn't so much that clichés are bad in themselves as that the thoughtless use of clichés weakens style. Generally, then, avoid them, especially if you are aiming to communicate with an audience from another culture. No list can be complete, but here are a few more examples to suggest the kinds of expressions to edit from your work:

a bolt from the blue
a heart as big as all outdoors
a matter of course
all things being equal
as a last resort
as a matter of fact
as the crow flies
beat a hasty retreat
busy as a bee
by leaps and bounds
by no manner of means
by no means
clear as crystal (or mud)
conspicuous by its absence
cool as a cucumber
corridors of power
doomed to disappointment
easier said than done
from dawn till dusk
gentle as a lamb
good as gold
if and when
in a manner of speaking
in one ear and out the other
in the long run
it goes without saying
it stands to reason
last but not least
lock, stock, and barrel
love at first sight
many and diverse
moment of truth
needless to say
nipped in the bud
no way, shape, or form
off the beaten path, track
on the right track
one and the same
par for the course
pride and joy
raining cats and dogs
rears its ugly head
rude awakening
sadder but wiser
seeing is believing
sharp as a tack
slowly but surely
smart as a whip
strike while the iron is hot
strong as an ox
talk turkey
the wrong side of the tracks
when all is said and done

Edit for the almost automatic couplings that occur between some adjectives and nouns. One seldom hears of a circle that isn't a *vicious* circle, or a fog that isn't a *pea-soup* fog, or a tenement that isn't a *run-down* tenement. Mere insight is seldom enough: it must be labelled *penetrating* insight. A few more examples:

acid test
ardent admirers
budding genius
bulging biceps
blushing bride
consummate artistry
devastating effect
drastic action
festive occasion
hearty breakfast
heated opposition
knee-jerk reaction
proud possessor
sacred duty
severe stress
tangible proof
vital role

Several of this kind are redundant as well:

advance notice	foreseeable future
advance warning	just desserts
blazing inferno	perfectly clear
cozy (little) nook	serious concern
end result	serious crisis
final outcome	terrible tragedy
final result	total (complete) surprise

71f Overuse of Nouns

The over-reliance on nouns is another source of deadwood; it is also a form of jargon. The focus of a sentence or clause is its main verb; the verb activates it, moves it, makes it go. Too many nouns piled on one verb can slow a sentence down, especially if the verb is *be* or some other verb with little or no action in it. Consider the following:

> The opinion of the judge in this case is of great significance to the outcome of the investigation and its effects upon the behaviour of all the members of our society in the future.

The verb in this sentence must struggle to move the great load of nouns and prepositional phrases along to some kind of finish. One could easily improve the sentence by reducing the proportion of nouns to verbs and making the verbs more vigorous:

> The judge's decision will inevitably influence how people act.

The piling up of *-tion* nouns can also weaken style and bury meaning:

> The depredations of the conflagration resulted in the destruction of many habitations and also of the sanitation organization of the location; hence the necessity of the introduction of activation procedures in relation to the implementation of emergency preparations for the amelioration of the situation.

This example is not so exaggerated as you might think. In any event, here is a simpler version of it:

> Since the fire destroyed not only many houses but also the water-treatment plant for the town, emergency procedures had to be set up quickly.

The verbs in this revised sentence have a third as much noun-baggage to carry as the original verb *resulted* had. There is nothing inherently wrong with nouns ending in *tion*; the damage is done when they come in clusters.

Proofreading Tip

Checking on the Sound of Your Prose

Reading your work aloud can help you avoid other unpleasant patterns of sound and rhythm, such as excessive alliteration or too regular a metrical pattern:

> At the top of the tree sat a bird on a branch.

or jarring repetitions of sound:

> They put strict restrictions on lending, which constricted the flow of funds.

or accidental rhyme:

> At that time he was in his prime; the way he later let himself go was a crime.

71g Nouns Used as Adjectives

Another insidious trend is the unnecessary use of nouns as if they were adjectives. Many nouns have long functioned adjectivally, some even becoming so idiomatic as to form parts of compounds:

> school board, school book, schoolteacher
> bathing suit, bath towel, bathtub
> lunch hour, lunch box, lunchroom
> fire alarm, fire engine, firewood
> heart attack, heart monitor, heart-smart
> business school, business card, businessperson

Such nouns-cum-adjectives are quite acceptable, but the practice can be carried too far. "Lounge chair" is clearly preferable to "chair for lounging," but just as clearly "medicine training" does not conform to the usages of English as well as "medical training" or "training in medicine," nor "poetry skills" as well as "poetic skills" or "skill in poetry." In these last two examples, since there is a standard adjectival form available, the simple nouns need not and should not be so used.

But increasingly in recent years, speakers and writers—especially those in government, business, and the media—have settled for, or even actively chosen, noun combinations that contribute heavily to the jargon cluttering the language, cumbersome phrases such as *learning facilitation, resource person, demonstration organizer, cash flow position, opinion sampling, consumer confidence number.* Newspapers report that "a weapons of mass destruction update is expected next month," where "an update on weapons of mass destruction" would be better. The piling up of several nouns, as in such phrases as "the labour force participation rate," "the Resource Management Personnel Training and Development Program," and "a city park recreation facility area" can confuse or alienate readers.

Resist this tendency. Do not write, as a student did in a discussion of extracurricular activities, of their taking place "either in a school situation or a community-type situation"; refer not to "emergency situations" or "crisis situations," but to *emergencies* and *crises*. And try to avoid the unnecessary use of the word *situation* altogether.

Exercise 71g Evaluating nouns used as adjectives

Evaluate the following phrases in which nouns are used as adjectives. Are some unacceptable? If so, what alternatives can you suggest? Would some be acceptable only in certain contexts? Comment on them in other ways if you wish.

1. task fragmentation
2. worker injuries
3. child poverty
4. computer system
5. information technology
6. job description
7. resource planning
8. customer satisfaction
9. customer billing
10. customer complaints
11. staff organization
12. labour force
13. regime change
14. safety aspects
15. department manager
16. fear factor
17. work schedule
18. profit outlook
19. overkill situation
20. clean-up crew
21. soft interface
22. face time

Proofreading Tip

On Nouns Functioning as Verbs

Many nouns also function quite normally as verbs. But some usages have provoked criticism. For example, though it is now commonly accepted, some people once objected to the use of *chair* as a verb, as in "to chair a meeting" (see **man** in #72); and *contact*, meaning "get in touch with," was once criticized, although it is widely accepted today.

Certain other nouns have not received such widespread acceptance as verbs, and you may be best to avoid them. For instance, some critics accept *critique* as a verb, but some do not; some also continue to object to *parent* as a verb, and to its gerund *parenting*. Many wince when they hear *dialogue* used as a verb, or of something *transitioning*. And many still deplore referring to someone as having *gifted* another with a present, or *impacted* a process, or *authored* a piece of writing, or *suicided*. And unless you're writing specifically about using computers, it's probably best not to refer to *accessing*. And see **-ize** in the Usage Checklist, #72.

71h Jargon

jarg The word **jargon**, in a narrow sense, refers to terms peculiar to a specific discipline, such as psychology, chemistry, literary theory, or computer science, terms unlikely to be fully understood by an outsider. Here we use it in a different sense, to refer to all the incoherent, unintelligible phraseology that clutters contemporary expression. The private languages of particular disciplines or special groups are quite legitimately used in writing for members of those communities. Much less legitimate are the gobbledygook and bafflegab that so easily find their way into the speech and writing of most of us. Therefore, we should all be on guard against creeping bureaucratese and the like, baffling terms from other disciplines and from business and government that infiltrate everyday language. Bombarded by such words and phrases, we may uncritically use them in our own speech and writing, often assuming that automatic prestige attaches to such language. If you write to communicate rather than to impress, you will edit to avoid the pitfalls discussed and illustrated here and in the rest of section #71; you will then impress your readers in the best way.

The following list is a sampling of words and phrases that are virtually guaranteed to decrease the quality of expression, whether spoken or written. Some of the terms sound pretentious and technical, imported from specialized fields; others are fuzzy, imprecise, unnecessarily abstract; and still others are objectionable mainly because they are overused, whether as true clichés or merely popular jargon, or "buzz words" (which is itself a buzz word). If you are thinking of using these words or phrases in your writing, consider the context in which you are writing. Are you, for example, writing an academic essay in a particular discipline in which such language is appropriate? Are you addressing readers who will be familiar and comfortable with such language? Ask yourself whether another word or words would communicate your thoughts more effectively. If you don't come up with a more suitable alternative, then you are likely choosing well.

Several of these terms are discussed further in #72, the Usage Checklist that follows; and you will find more examples in the review exercises at the end of the chapter.

access (as a verb)
affirmative, negative
along the lines of, along that line, in the line of
angle
area (see Checklist, #72)
aspect
at that point in time (*then*)
at this point in time (*now*)
background (as a verb)
basis, on the basis of, on a . . . basis (see Checklist, #72)

bottom line
case
concept, conception
concerning, concerned
connection, in connection with, in this (that) connection
considering, consideration, in consideration of
definitely
dialogue (especially as a verb)
escalate
eventuate
evidenced by
expertise
facet
factor
feedback
hopefully (see Checklist, #72)
identify with
image
impact (especially as verb)
implemented, implementation
importantly
indicated to (for *told*)
infrastructure
input, output
in regard to, with regard to, regarding, as regards
in relation to
in respect to, with respect to, respecting
interface
in terms of (see Checklist, #72)
in the final analysis
-ize (-ise) verbs (see Checklist, #72)
lifestyle
marginal
meaningful, meaningful dialogue
mega-
motivation
ongoing
on stream
parameters
personage
phase
picture, in the picture
posture
profile, low profile

realm
relate to
relevant
replicate
scenario, worst-case scenario
sector
self-identity
situation
standpoint, vantage point, viewpoint
type, -type (see Checklist, #72)
viable
-wise (see Checklist, #72)
worthwhile (see Checklist, #72)

71h

Of course, many of these words can be used in normal and acceptable ways. But even such acceptable words can be used as jargon, and those in this list are among the most likely offenders. For example, *angle* is a good and useful word, but in such expressions as "looking at the problem from a different angle" it begins to become jargon. *Aspect* has precise meanings, but they are seldom honoured; the writer of the following sentence didn't know them, but just grabbed at an all too familiar word: "Due to money aspects, many high-school graduates would rather work than enter university." Here *aspects* has no real meaning at all (and see **due to** in the Checklist, #72). A phrase like "For financial reasons" or "Because of a need for money" would be far better. A student analyzing a poem fell into the jargon trap: "The third quatrain develops the aspect of time." In trying to revise, the writer fell right back into the trap: "The third quatrain brings in the factor of time," *factor* being nearly as ineffective here as *aspect*. Unless you use *case* to mean a box or container, a medical case, a legal case, or a grammatical case, or in phrases like "in case of fire," you are likely to create wordy jargon with it: "In most cases, students who worked hard got good grades." Why not "Most students who worked hard got good grades"? And why say "He replied in the affirmative" when "He said yes" would do? *Interface*, as a noun, has a precise technical meaning; but after some academic writers adopted it for their purposes, it began surfacing as jargon, used—even as a verb—by many who are evidently unaware of its meaning. *Realm* means a kingdom, and it can—or once could—be useful metaphorically in phrases like "the realm of poetry" or "the realm of ideas"; but it has long been so loosely and widely applied that most careful writers will avoid it except in its meaning of *kingdom*. Only as jargon does the verb *relate to* mean "understand" or "empathize" or "interact meaningfully with." And so on. If you read and listen carefully you will often find the listed terms, and others like them, being used in ways that impede clear, concise, and precise expression.

Proofreading Tip 

On Using Short Rather Than Long Word Forms

Writers addicted to wordiness and jargon will prefer long words to short ones, and pretentious-sounding words to relatively simple ones. Generally, choose the shorter and simpler form. For example, the shorter word in each of the following pairs is preferable:

analysis, analyzation
connote, connotate
consultative, consultitative
courage, courageousness
disoriented, disorientated
existential, existentialistic
(re)orient, (re)orientate
preventive, preventative
remedy (vb.), remediate
symbolic, symbolical
use (n. & vb.), utilize, utilization

▲ 72 Usage: A Checklist of Troublesome Words and Phrases

us This section features words and phrases that have a history of being especially confusing or otherwise troublesome. Study the whole list carefully, perhaps marking for frequent review any entries you recognize as personal problem spots. Like any such list, this one is selective rather than exhaustive; we have tried to keep it short enough to be manageable. (Even whole books on usage invariably leave out matters someone else would think important.) As with the list of frequently misspelled words, then, you should keep a list of your own for special study. You can often supplement the information and advice provided here by consulting a good dictionary—especially one that includes notes on usage. See also the index and the following lists and discussions: *Words Sometimes Confused* (#62-l–m), *Slang* (#64a), *Informal, Colloquial* (#64b), *Wordiness* (#71a), *Triteness, Clichés* (#71e), *Overuse of Nouns* (#71f), *Nouns Used as Adjectives* (#71g), and *Jargon* (#71h).

about (See **on**.)

above, below

Avoid stiff references to something preceding or following in an essay. Rather than "for the *above* reasons," write "for *these* (or *those*, or *the foregoing*, or *the preceding*) reasons"; instead of "for the reasons given *below*," write "for the *following* reasons." If you find yourself writing "as I said above" or "as I will explain below" and the like, the organization of your writing may need work; try revising your plan or outline.

absolute (See **unique etc.**)

actually (See **very**.)

advice, advise

Advice is a noun, usually used in uncountable form. *Advise* is the transitive verb form.

> My faculty advisor has given me good advice in planning my major. [noun]

> He advised his brother to consider studying abroad for a year. [transitive verb in past tense form; its direct object is *his brother.*]

affect, effect

Avoid the common confusion of these two words. *Affect* is a transitive verb meaning "to act upon" or "to influence"; *effect* is a noun meaning "result, consequence":

> He tried to affect the outcome, but his efforts had no effect.

Proofread carefully, since this error often appears in writing done under time pressures. (Note: *Effect* can also be a verb, meaning "to bring about, to cause"; see your dictionary for two other meanings of *affect,* one a verb and one a noun.)

afterward, afterwards (See **toward, towards**.)

aggravate

The verb *aggravate* is often colloquially or informally used to mean "annoy, irritate, anger, vex." But properly speaking, only a condition, not a person, can be *aggravated*, and only if it is already bad: *aggravate* means "make worse":

> Standing in the hot sun will aggravate your headache.

> The unexpectedly high tax bill aggravated the small company's already serious financial condition.

agree to, agree with, agree on

Use the correct preposition with *agree.* One agrees *to* a proposal or request, or agrees *to* do something; one agrees *with* someone about a question or opinion, and certain climates or foods agree *with* a person; one agrees *on* (or *about*) the terms or details of something settled after negotiation, or agrees *on* a course of action.

ain't

A nonstandard contraction, *ain't* is primarily equivalent to *aren't* and *isn't.* Avoid it in all writing unless for deliberate colloquial or humorous effect, as in "If it ain't broke, don't fix it."

all, all of (See **of**.)

along the lines of (See **in terms of**.)

alternate, alternative; alternately, alternatively
Alternate (adjective) means "by turns," or "every other one." *Alternative* (adjective or noun) refers to one of a number of possible choices (usually two). Don't use *alternate* or *alternately* when the sense has something to do with choice:

> In summer they could water their lawns only on alternate days.
>
> The squares on the board are alternately red and black.
>
> The judge had no alternative: he had to dismiss the charges.
>
> There is an alternative method, much simpler than the one you are using.
>
> She could meekly resign or, alternatively, she could take her case to the grievance committee.

Alternate is used legitimately to refer to a substitute or standby: "Each delegate to the convention had a designated *alternate*. She served as an *alternate* delegate."

although, though
These conjunctions introduce adverbial phrases or clauses of concession. They mean the same, but *although* with its two syllables usually sounds smoother, less abrupt, at the beginning of a sentence; *though* is more commonly used to begin a subordinate clause following an independent clause, though it can be slightly emphatic at the start of a sentence. But the two words are not always interchangeable: in *even though* and *as though* one cannot substitute *although*, and *although* cannot serve as an adverb at the end of a sentence or clause. (See also **despite that** and **while**.)

among (See **between, among**.)

amount, number
Use *number* only with countable things (i.e. with nouns that have both singular and plural forms), *amount* only with mass, uncountable nouns: a *number* of coins, an *amount* of change; a large *number* of cars, a large *amount* of traffic. *Number* usually takes a singular verb after the definite article, and a plural verb after the indefinite article (see #18f).

> The number of students taking the workshop is encouraging.
>
> A number of students are planning to take the workshop.

(See also **less, fewer**.)

and (See **while**.)

and/or
This is worth avoiding, unless you're writing legal phraseology. Write "We'll get there on foot or horseback, or both," rather than "We'll get there on foot and/or horseback." And with more than two items, *and/or* muddies meaning: "This bread can be made with wheat, barley, *and/or* rye."

angry (See **mad**.)

anxious
Anxious means much more than just "eager": use it only when there is at least some degree of real anxiety or angst.

any more, anymore
For the adverb meaning "now" or "nowadays," both spellings are common (though some dictionaries still don't recognize one or the other). Whichever spelling you use, use it only in negative statements (or positive statements with a negative implication) and in questions ("I don't get around much any more"; "I seldom attend sports events any more"; "Do you lie in the sun anymore?").

anyplace, someplace
These colloquial synonyms for *anywhere* and *somewhere* should be avoided in formal writing.

anyways, anywheres, everywheres, nowheres, somewheres
These are nonstandard forms. Use *anyway*, *anywhere*, etc.

approach (See **in terms of**.)

apt (See **likely, liable, apt**.)

area
The word *area* refers strictly to a physical division of space on a surface. Avoid using it as an unnecessarily vague term to refer to some abstract division, such as a field of study, a problem, or an activity (the *area* of the social sciences, the *area* of finance, the *area* of biblical interpretation). Weather forecasters and others are also fond of *area* as a substitute for *region*, *district*, *neighbourhood* (the eastern Alberta *area*, the Ottawa *area*). And journalists sometimes use it awkwardly as an adjective, e.g. in headlines ("Area man attacked by rabid dog"; "Area teenagers march in protest"). These usages, too, are worth avoiding.

as

To avoid ambiguity, don't use *as* in such a way that it can mean either "while" or "because":

> ***ambig:*** As I was walking after dark I tripped over a tree root.
>
> ***ambig:*** As I added the brandy, the cherries jubilee caught fire.
>
> ***ambig:*** The car gathered speed quickly as I pressed harder on the accelerator.

Because of such potential ambiguity, some writers have banished *as* in the sense of *because* from their vocabularies. Another awkward use of *as* occurs in sentences like

> ***awk:*** The book was considered as a threat to the state.

Here, *as* is unnecessary—or else needs something like "as a possible threat" to be clear. (See also **like, as, as if, as though,** and **so . . . as**.)

as . . . as (See **equally as** and **so . . . as**.)

as being

Don't follow with *being* when *as* alone is enough:

> He always thinks of himself as [not *as being*] the life of the party.
>
> She sees the deputy premier as [not *as being*] an incompetent legislator.

as far as . . . is (are) concerned, as far as . . . goes (go)

This construction has a wordy, jargon-like air about it, but if you feel that you need to use it anyway, don't leave it unfinished, as in this example:

> As far as financing my education, I'm going to have to get a summer job.

The error may stem from a confusion of *as far as* with *as for.*

as regards (See **in terms of**.)

as such

This phrase shouldn't be used as if it were equivalent to *thus* or *therefore*:

> ***us:*** My uncle wants to be well liked. As such, he always gives expensive gifts.

In this phrase, *as* is a preposition and *such* is a pronoun that requires a clear noun antecedent:

> My uncle is a generous man. As such, he always give me expensive gifts.

as though (See **like, as, as if, as though**.)

as to

This is a stiff jargon phrase worth avoiding; substitution or rephrasing will usually improve expression:

> ***ineffective:*** He made several recommendations as to the best method of proceeding.
> ***better:*** He made several recommendations with respect to the best method of proceeding.
> ***still better:*** He recommended several methods of proceeding.

> ***ineffective:*** I was in doubt as to which road to take.
> ***better:*** I was in doubt about which road to take.
> ***still better:*** I was not sure which road to take.
> *or*
> I did not know which road to take.

As to at the beginning of a sentence may seem more tolerable, but even there it usually sounds out of place; try changing it to *as for.*

(See also **in terms of**.)

awaiting for

Awaiting is not followed by the preposition *for*; *waiting* is:

> I was awaiting the train's arrival.

> I was waiting for the light to change.

awful, awfully

When used as intensifiers ("They were *awfully* kind to us") *awful* and *awfully* are colloquialisms that should be avoided in formal writing.

(See also **very** and #64b.)

a while, awhile
Most authorities object to the adverb *awhile* instead of the noun phrase *a while* in some positions, for example after a preposition such as *for*: sleep *awhile*; sleep for *a while*. Others contend that either form is acceptable.

backward, backwards (See **toward, towards**.)

bad, badly (See **good, bad, badly, well**.)

barely (See **can't hardly etc.)**

basis, on the basis of, on a . . . basis
Basis is a perfectly good noun, but some prepositional phrases using it are worth avoiding when possible, for outside of technical contexts they usually amount to wordy jargon.

> She made her decision on the basis of the committee's report.

This can easily be improved:

> She based her decision on the committee's report.

Again:

> He selected the furniture on the basis of its shape and colour.
> (by? for? according to? because of?)

The other phrase—*on a . . . basis*—is sometimes useful, but more often than not it can profitably be edited out: *on a daily basis* is usually jargon for *daily*; *on a yearly basis* or *on an annualized basis*, for *annually*; *on a temporary basis,* for *temporarily*; *on a regular basis*, for *regularly*; *on a voluntary basis,* for *voluntarily*; *on a political basis,* for *politically* or *for political reasons*; *We'll do this for a week on a trial basis* is jargon for *We'll try this for a week*; and so on. (See also **in terms of**.)

because (See **reason . . . is because**; see also #48c.)

because of (See **due to**.)

being that, being as, being as how
These are colloquial or dialectal substitutes for *because* or *since* to introduce a subordinate clause, as is *seeing as (how)*, though *seeing that* is acceptable.

believe (See **feel(s)**.)

below (See **above, below**.)

beside, besides

Beside, a preposition, means "next to, in comparison with"; *besides* as an adverb means "in addition, also, too, as well"; as a preposition, *besides* means "in addition to, except for, other than":

> She stood beside her car.
>
> Her objections were minuscule beside those of her brother.
>
> She knew she would have to pay the cost of repairs and the towing charges besides.
>
> Besides the cost of repairs, she knew she would have to pay towing charges.
>
> There was no one on the beach besides the three of us.
>
> Besides this, what am I expected to do?

between, among

Generally, use *between* when there are two persons or things, and *among*
72 when there are more than two:

> There is ill feeling between the two national leaders.
>
> There were predictable differences between the Liberal and Conservative leaders during the debate.
>
> They divided the cost equally among the three of them.

On occasion *between* is appropriate for groups of three or more, for example if the emphasis is on the individual persons or groups as overlapping pairs, or on the relation of one particular person to each of several others:

> It seems impossible to keep the peace between the nations of the world.
>
> One expects there to be good relations between a prime minister and the members of the caucus.

Between is also commonly used informally or colloquially to refer to more than two, as in the idiom "between you and me and the lamppost."

bi-

Bimonthly and *biweekly* usually mean "every two months" and "every two weeks." But since the prefix *bi* is sometimes also used to mean "twice," *bimonthly* and *biweekly* could mean the same as *semimonthly* and *semiweekly*, i.e. "twice a month" and "twice a week." In order to be clear, therefore, you may want to avoid *bi-* and spell out "every two months," "twice a month," etc. *Semiannually* clearly means "twice a year," and *biannual* ("twice a year") is distinguished from *biennial* ("every two years," "lasting two years")—but again you may want to use *semiannually* or the equivalent phrases, just to be sure.

but (See **can't hardly etc.**, and **while**.)

can, may (could, might)
Opinion and usage are divided, but in formal contexts it is still advisable to use *can* to denote ability, *may* to denote permission:

> May I have your attention, please?
>
> He can walk and chew gum at the same time.
>
> He knew that he might leave if he wished, but he could not make himself rise from his chair.

But both *may* and *can* are commonly used to denote possibility: "Things *may* (*can*) turn out worse than you expect. Anything *can* (*may*) happen." And *can* is often used in the sense of permission, especially in informal contexts and with questions and negatives ("*Can* I go?" "No, you *cannot*!") or where the distinction between ability (or possibility) and permission is blurred ("Anyone with an invitation *can* get in")—a blurring which, inherent in the concepts, is making the two increasingly interchangeable. (See also **may, might**.)

can't hardly etc.
Barely, *hardly*, *never*, *only*, and *scarcely* are regarded as negatives or as having a negative force. Therefore don't use words like *can't*, *don't*, *couldn't*, and *without* with them, for the result is an ungrammatical double negative. Use instead the positive forms: "I *can* hardly believe it. He *could* scarcely finish on time. He emerged from the ordeal *with* hardly a scratch." (Some writers also consider *but* a word not to be preceded by negatives, especially *can't* or *cannot*; others object only to *cannot but* or *can't help but* as redundant; but many consider both usages acceptable.)

centre around (or **about)**
This is an illogical phrase. The meaning of the word *centre* (or *focus*) calls for a different preposition:

> The discussion centred on the proposed amendment.

Or something can centre *upon*, *in*, or *at*. One can say *revolved around*, *circled around*, and be quite logical.

compare to, compare with

In formal contexts, use *compare to* to liken one thing to another, to express similarity:

> Shall I compare thee to a summer's day?

> He compared his work to flying a kite.

and *compare with* to measure or evaluate one thing against another:

> She compared the sports car with the SUV to see which would be best for her.

> He compared favourably with the assistant she had had the previous year.

> Compared with a desk job, farm work is more healthful by far.

complementary, complimentary

Complementary is the adjective describing something that adds to or completes something else. *Complimentary* is the adjective describing something free (*complimentary* tickets or passes) or comments intended to praise or flatter someone.

> Complementary exercises reinforcing the principles covered in this module are available on the course website. [the exercises will complete the module]

> We won complimentary passes to the Toronto Film Festival. [the passes are free]

> Their comments on our panel presentation were complimentary, and so we are eager to participate in next year's conference as well. [Those on the panel received praise for their presentation.]

complete (See **unique etc.**)

comprise, compose

Distinguish carefully between these words. Strictly, *comprise* means "consist of, contain, take in, include":

> The municipal region comprises several cities and towns.

> His duties comprise opening and shutting the shop, keeping the shelves stocked at all times, and making daily bank deposits.

Compose means "constitute, form, make up":

> The seven cities and towns compose the municipal region.

Don't use *comprise* in the passive voice—saying for example that some whole "is comprised of" several parts; use *is composed of*:

> The municipal region is composed of seven cities and towns.

continual, continuous

These words are sometimes considered interchangeable, but *continual* more often refers to something that happens frequently or even regularly but with interruptions, and *continuous* to something that occurs constantly, without interruptions:

> The speaker's voice went on in a continuous drone, in spite of the heckler's continual attempts to interrupt.

For something that continues in space rather than time, *continuous* is the correct adjective:

> The bookshelf was continuous for the entire length of the hallway.

convince, persuade

These words are often used interchangeably; both mean "to cause someone to believe or do something." But for many writers there is still a useful distinction between them: with *convince* the emphasis is more likely to be on the belief, with *persuade* on the action. You either *convince* or *persuade* someone *of* something or *that* something is so, but you *persuade* someone *to do* something. Further, *convince* implies appeal to reason, logic, hard facts; *persuade* implies appeal both to reason and to emotion. *Convince* also connotes an overcoming of objections, a change of mind. (The distinction is perhaps blurred by the fact that changing one's mind is itself a sort of action.)

could (See **can, may**.)

culminate

Many writers find this verb awkward when used with a direct object or in the passive voice:

> *us:* He culminated his remarks with strong support for the healthcare legislation.

> *us:* The building was culminated by a revolving restaurant and an observation deck.

It is better to use it only intransitively, usually with the preposition *in*:

> Our search culminates here.
>
> His speech culminated in strong support for the healthcare legislation.
>
> The building culminated in a revolving restaurant and an observation deck.

despite that
The phrase *despite that* is similar in meaning to *but, nevertheless, however*:

> The weather was cold. Despite that, we enjoyed our hike.

Don't use the phrase as if it were equivalent to *though* or *although*:

> ***us:*** Despite that the weather was cold, we enjoyed our hike.

To be used this way *Despite that* would have to be expanded to the wordy *Despite the fact that* (or *In spite of the fact that*); use the simpler alternatives *Although* or *Though* or *Even though*, or rephrase using *Despite* on its own:

> Despite the cold weather, we enjoyed the hike.

different from, different than
From is the idiomatic preposition after *different*:

> Your car is noticeably different from mine.

Than, however, is becoming increasingly common, especially when followed by a clause and when it results in fewer words:

> The finished sketch looks far different than I expected it to.

But to avoid the label "colloquial," use the construction with *from:*

> The finished sketch looks far different from what I intended.

differ from, differ with
To *differ from* something or someone is to be unlike in some way; to *differ with* someone is to disagree, to quarrel:

> She differed from her colleague in that she was less prone than he to differ with everyone on every issue.

disinterested

A much misused word, the adjective *disinterested* means "impartial, objective, free from personal bias." Although it is often used as a synonym for *uninterested, not interested* (no doubt partly because of increasing use of the noun *disinterest* to mean "lack of interest" as well as "impartiality"), in formal contexts retain the distinction between the two:

> It is necessary to find a judge who is disinterested in the case, for she will then try it fairly; we assume that she will not also be uninterested in it, for then she would be bored by it, and not pay careful attention.

due to

Use *due to* only as a predicate adjective + preposition after a form of the verb *be:*

> The accident was due to bad weather.

Many writers object to it as a preposition to introduce an adverbial phrase, especially at the beginning of a sentence; use *Because of* or *On account of* instead:

> Because of the bad weather, we had an accident.

As a substitute, *Owing to* is little if any better.

each other, one another

These are interchangeable, though *each other* more often refers to two, *one another* to more than two (see also **between, among**):

> The bride and groom kissed each other.

> The five boys traded hockey cards with one another.

effect, affect (See **affect, effect**.)

either, neither

As indefinite pronouns or adjectives, these usually refer to one or the other of two things, not more than two; for three or more, use *any* or *any (one)* or *none*:

> Either of these two advisers can answer your questions.

> Neither of the two answers is correct.

> Any (one) of the four proposals is acceptable.

> None of the four of us drove in today.

If *either* or *neither* is part of a correlative conjunction (see #23b), it can refer to more than two:

> Either Howard, Kiu, or Peter will act as referee.

empty (See **unique etc.**)

enormity
This noun does not mean "immensity, great size, enormousness," but rather "outrageousness, heinousness, atrocity," or at least "immoderateness, immorality."

> In pronouncing sentence, the judge emphasized the <u>enormity</u> of the arsonist's crime.

equal (See **unique etc.**)

equally as
Avoid this redundancy by dropping one word or the other or by substituting *just as*. In expressions like the following, *as* is unnecessary:

> Her first novel was highly praised, and her second is <u>equally</u> good.

> He may be a good high jumper, but she can jump <u>equally</u> high, if not higher.

In expressions like the following, *equally* is unnecessary:

> In a storm, one port is <u>as</u> good as another.

> His meat pies were <u>as</u> tasty as hers.

especially, specially
Especially means "particularly, unusually"; *specially* means "specifically, for a certain or special purpose":

> We <u>especially</u> want our parents to come; we planned the party <u>specially</u> for their wedding anniversary.

> It's <u>especially</u> cold today; I'm going to wear my <u>specially</u> made jacket.

-ess (See **man, woman, lady, etc.**)

essential (See **unique etc.**)

ever
Ever is not needed after *seldom* and *rarely.* Instead of *rarely ever*, you may say *hardly ever.*

farther, further
Although the distinction between these is often overlooked, use *farther* and *farthest* to refer to physical distance and *further* and *furthest* everywhere else, such as when referring to time and degree, and when used to mean something like "more" or "in addition":

> To go any farther down the road is the furthest thing from my mind.
>
> Rather than delay any further, he began his research, beginning with the book farthest from him.
>
> Without further delay, she began her speech.

Further, only *Further* can function as a sentence adverb, as in this sentence.

fatal (See **unique etc.**)

fatal, fatalistic (See **simple, simplistic**.)

feel(s)
Don't loosely use the word *feel* when what you really mean is *think* or *believe. Feel* is more appropriate to emotional or physical attitudes and responses, *think* and *believe* to those dependent on reasoning:

> The defendant felt cheated by the decision; she believed that her case had not been judged impartially.
>
> I feel the need of sustenance; I think I had better have something to eat.
>
> I feel good about starting my new job; given my previous experience, I think I will fit in well.

fewer (See **less, fewer**.)

figuratively (See **literally, virtually, figuratively**.)

firstly, secondly, etc.
Since some find the *ly* ending old-fashioned and unnecessary in enumerations, just say *first*, *second*, *third*, etc. Many object only to the word *firstly*, so even if you decide to use *secondly*, *thirdly*, etc., begin with *first*, not *firstly.*

focus (See **centre around**.)

following
If you avoid using *following* as a preposition meaning simply "after," you'll avoid both the criticism of those who object to it as pretentious and the possibility of its being momentarily misread as a participle or a gerund:

> ***ambig:*** Following the incident, she interviewed those involved to gain further details.

former, latter
Use these only when referring to the first or second of two things, not three or more (when *first* or *last* would be appropriate), and only when the reference is clear and unambiguous—i.e. when it is to something immediately preceding. Like *above* and *below*, they are worth avoiding if possible.

forward, forwards (See **toward, towards**.)

from the standpoint (viewpoint) of (See **in terms of**.)

frontward, frontwards (See **toward, towards**.)

72 **full** (See **unique etc.**)

fulsome
Although frequently used as if it meant "full, copious, abundant," especially in the phrase "fulsome praise," the word actually means "overfull, excessive" because insincere, and therefore "disgusting, offensive to good taste," and even "nauseating."

further (See **farther, further**.)

good, bad, badly, well
To avoid confusion and error with these words, remember that *good* and *bad* are adjectives, *badly* and *well* adverbs (except when *well* is an adjective meaning "healthy"). (See also #20b.2.)

> The model looks good in that business suit. (He is attractive.)
>
> That suit looks bad on you because it fits badly.
>
> Nathan acted bad. (He was naughty.)
>
> Nathan acted badly. (His performance as Hamlet was terrible.)
>
> I feel good. (I am happy, in good spirits.)

I feel bad. (I have a splitting headache.)

She feels bad about what happened. (She broke her mother's vase.)

Sophia looks well. (She looks healthy, not sick.)

This wine travels well. (It wasn't harmed by the long train journey.)

The infielders played especially well today; they are all good players.

The steak smells good. (My mouth is watering.)

Your dog doesn't smell well. (He's too old to hunt.)

half a(n), a half
Both are correct; use whichever sounds smoother or more logical. (Is *half a* loaf better than *a half* loaf? Is *a half* hour more formal than *half an* hour?) But don't use *a half a(n)*; one article is enough.

hanged, hung
In formal writing, use the past-tense form *hanged* only when referring to a death by hanging. For all other uses of the verb *hang*, the correct past form is *hung*.

happen, occur
These verbs sometimes pose a problem for students with English as an additional language. Both verbs are intransitive and cannot take the passive-voice form in any tense.

wrong: The revolution was happened in 1917.
right: The revolution happened in 1917.

wrong: My parents' wedding was occurred in September 1970.
right: My parents' wedding occurred in September 1970.

hardly (See **can't hardly etc.**)

have, of (See **of**.)

healthy, healthful
Although *healthy* is common in both senses, in formal writing it may be useful to preserve the distinction, using *healthy* to mean "in good health" and *healthful* to mean "contributing to good health":

> To stay healthy, one should participate in a healthful sport like swimming.

he or she, his or her, he/she, s/he (See #15d.)

herself, himself, myself, etc. (See #14h.)

hopefully
In formal writing, use this adverb, meaning "full of hope," only to modify a verb or a verbal adjective:

> "Will you lend me ten dollars?" I asked hopefully.

> Smiling hopefully, she began to untie the package.

To avoid potential ambiguity, don't use it as a sentence adverb (in spite of its similarity to such acceptable sentence adverbs as *Happily* and *Fortunately*):

> ***us:*** Hopefully, the sun will shine tomorrow.
> ***ambig:*** Hopefully, many people will come to the prize drawing.

72

Instead use *I hope* or *We hope* or *One hopes.*

hung (See **hanged, hung**.)

imply (See **infer, imply**.)

impossible (See **unique etc.**)

in, into
These are often interchangeable, but usually you will want to use *in* to indicate location inside of, or a state or condition, and *into* to indicate movement toward the inside of, or a change of state or condition; in other words, generally use *into* with verbs of motion and the like:

> He went into the kitchen, but she was in the den.

> We moved into our new home in the suburbs.

> After getting into trouble, he was understandably in a bad temper.

> I assured her I would look into the matter.

in connection with (See **in terms of**.)

individual

This is not simply a synonym for *person*. Reserve the word *individual* for times when the meaning "distinct from others" is present, or when certain people are being distinguished from a different kind of body or institution:

> The person [not *individual*] you are referring to is my aunt.

> Elsa is very much an individual in her behaviour.
> (i.e. she behaves like no one else.)

> The legal restrictions apply to the company itself, but not to the individuals within it.

It is often best to use *individual* as an adjective rather than as a noun. But see also **person, persons, people**.

infer, imply

Use *imply* to mean "suggest, hint at, indicate indirectly" and *infer* to mean "conclude by reasoning, deduce." A listener or reader can *infer* from a statement something that its speaker or writer *implies* in it:

> Her speech strongly implied that we could trust her.

> I inferred from her speech that she was trustworthy.

The word *inference*, then, means "something inferred, a conclusion"; it does not mean *implication* or *innuendo.*

infinite (See **unique etc.**)

in regard to (See **in terms of**.)

in relation to (See **in terms of**.)

in respect to (See **in terms of**.)

inside, inside of (See **of**.)

in terms of

This phrase is another example of contemporary clutter. Note that it is similar, sometimes even equivalent, to other wordy expressions (see **basis** and **-wise**). Although it is common in speech, and though occasionally it is the precisely appropriate phrase, it is more often vague; worse, it is capable of leading to such inane utterances as this (by a governor of a drought-stricken state): "We're very scarce in terms of water." If you can avoid it, especially in writing, do so; don't write sentences like these:

> He tried to justify the price increase in terms of [or *on the basis of*] the company's increased operating costs.
>
> In terms of experience [or *Experience-wise*], she was as qualified for the post as anyone else applying for it.
>
> In terms of fuel economy, this car is better than any other in its class.
>
> She first considered the problem in terms of the length of time it would take her to solve it.

Instead use sentences such as these:

> He tried to justify the increase in price by citing the company's increased operating costs.
>
> She was as experienced as anyone else applying for the post.
>
> 72 This car has the best fuel economy of any in its class.
>
> First she thought about how long it would take her to solve the problem.

And note the further family resemblance of this phrase to others like *along the lines of*, *in connection with*, *in relation to*, *in [with] regard to*, *as regards*, *regarding*, *in [with] respect to*, and *from the standpoint [viewpoint] of*. *Perspective* and *approach* are two more words often used in a similar way. (See also #71d and #71h.)

in (with) regards to
Drop the *s*: *in (with) regard to*. *As regards* is acceptable. But see #71h and **in terms of**.

into (See **in, into**.)

irregardless
This is nonstandard, as your dictionary should tell you. The prefix *ir* (= not) is redundant with *less*, forming a double negative (see **can't hardly**). The correct word is *regardless*.

is because (See **reason . . . is because**.)

is when, is where

Although often standard ("Early morning is when the cocks crow," "Home is where the heart is"), avoid these phrases in statements of definition, where adverbial clauses following linking verbs are considered ungrammatical:

> *us:* A double play is when two base runners are put out during one play.

> *rev:* In a double play, two base runners are put out during one play.

> *rev:* A double play occurs when two base runners are put out during one play.

Since *occurs* is not a linking verb, the adverbial clause beginning with *when* is acceptable. Compare **reason . . . is because**.

its, it's

Its—without the apostrophe—is the possessive form of *it*; *it's*—with the apostrophe—is the contracted form of *it is*, or occasionally of *it has* (as in "*It's* been a long day"). It's easy to slip when writing at speed, so proofread carefully for these usages.

-ize

The suffix *ize* (or *ise*) has long been used to turn nouns and adjectives into verbs (e.g. *democratize, galvanize, satirize, generalize, harmonize, idolize, modernize, theorize*). But like **-wise**, it is now sometimes overused, especially in business and other jargon (*finalize, concretize, prioritize*), leading even to such absurdities as this: "Let us not forget that the minister voluntarily resigned; had he not, he would surely have been *pressurized* to go." The *ize* ending remains acceptable in established words, but avoid using it to make new ones. (See **-wise**, and see also the Proofreading Tip in #71g.)

kind of, sort of

Used adverbially, as in "*kind of* tired" or "*sort of* strange," these terms are colloquial—as they are when followed by an article: "I had a bad *kind of an* afternoon"; "She was a rather peculiar *sort of a* guide." More formally, say "I had a bad afternoon" and "She was a rather peculiar guide." (See also **type**, and #15f.)

lack, lack of, lacking, lacking in

Lack in its various forms and parts of speech can sometimes pose problems for students with English as an additional language. Note the following standard usages:

> This paper lacks a clear argument. (*lack* as a transitive verb)

A major weakness of his argument was its lack of evidence.
(*lack* as a noun followed by the preposition *of*)

Lacking confidence, she gave up on her research.
(*lacking* as a present participle followed by a direct object)

Lacking in experience, they had difficulty in job interviews.
(*lacking* as a present participle in combination with the preposition *in*)

lady (See **man, woman, lady, etc.**)

latter (See **former, latter**.)

lay (See **lie, lay**.)

lend (See **loan**.)

less, fewer

72

Fewer refers to things that are countable (i.e. that appear as plural nouns); *less* is sometimes used the same way (e.g. on the signs at the express checkout lanes in supermarkets—"9 items or less"), but usually it is preferable to use it for things that are measured rather than counted or considered as units (i.e. with uncountable nouns):

fewer dollars, less money

fewer hours, less time

fewer shouts, less noise

fewer cars, less traffic

fewer bottles of wine, less wine

(See also **amount, number.**)

less, least; more, most (See #19b and #20c.)

let, make

The verbs *let* and *make* are parts of an idiom that causes problems, especially for those with English as an additional language. When *let* or *make* is followed by a direct object and an infinitive, the infinitive does not include the customary *to*:

id: They let me to borrow their new car.
revised: They let me borrow their new car.

id: Our professor made us to participate in the experiment.
revised: Our professor made us participate in the experiment.

(See also the Proofreading Tip in #21b.)

liable (See **likely, liable, apt**.)

lie, lay

Since *lay* is both the past tense of *lie* and the present tense of the verb *lay*, some writers habitually confuse these two verbs. If necessary, memorize their principal parts: *lie, lay, lain*; *lay, laid, laid*. The verb *lie* means "recline" or "be situated"; *lay* means "put" or "place." *Lie* is intransitive; *lay* is transitive:

> I lie down now; I lay down yesterday; I have lain down several times today.
>
> I lay the book on the desk now; I laid the book on the desk yesterday; I have laid the book on the desk every morning for a week.
>
> The book lies on the desk now; the book lay on the desk yesterday; the book has lain on the desk for an hour.

However common it may be colloquially, don't use *lay* for *lie,* or *laying* for *lying*. (See also **set, sit**.)

like, as, as if, as though

Like is a preposition:

> Roger is dressed exactly like Ray.

But if Ray is given a verb, then he becomes the subject of a clause, forcing *like* to serve incorrectly as a conjunction; use the conjunction *as* when a clause follows:

us: Roger is dressed exactly like Ray is.
revised: Roger is dressed exactly as Ray is.

In slightly different constructions, use *as if* or *as though* to introduce clauses:

> It looks like rain.
> It looks as if [or *as though*] it will rain.

72

He stood there like a statue.
He stood there as though [or *as if*] he were a statue.

She spent money as if [or *as though*] there were no tomorrow.

But don't hypercorrect: don't shun *like* for *as* when what follows it is not a clause:

us: Tiger Woods, just as last year's winner, sank a stunning birdie putt on the final hole.

correction: Tiger Woods, just like last year's winner, sank a stunning birdie putt on the final hole.

likely, liable, apt

Although often used interchangeably, especially in informal contexts, in formal writing use *likely* to mean "probable, probably, showing a tendency, suitable"; *liable* to mean "legally obligated, responsible, susceptible to (usually something undesirable)"; and *apt* to refer to probability based on habitual tendency or inclination:

A storm seems likely. He is likely to succeed. This is a likely spot.

She is liable for damages. Tom is liable to headaches.
He is liable to hurt himself.

Damon is apt to trip over his own feet.

Apt can also mean "exactly suitable" (It was an *apt* remark) and "quick to learn" (Maki is an *apt* pupil).

literally, virtually, figuratively

Literally means "actually, really." *Virtually* means "in effect, practically." *Figuratively* means "metaphorically, not literally." All too often the first two are used to mean their opposites, or as weak intensifiers:

us: She was literally swept off her feet. (i.e. *figuratively*)

us: They were caught in a virtual downpour. (It *was* a downpour; drop *virtual*)

loan, lend

Although some people restrict *loan* to being a noun, it is generally acceptable as a verb equivalent to *lend*—except in such figurative uses as "Metaphors *lend* colour to one's style" and "*lend* a hand."

mad
Although common in informal contexts to mean "angry," *mad* in formal contexts is usually restricted to the meaning "insane, crazy."

make (See **let, make**.)

man, woman, lady, -ess, Ms., etc.
Like the use of *he* as a generic pronoun (see #15d), the general or generic use of the word *man* causes difficulties. To avoid biased language, most writers now try to avoid the term *man* where it could include the meaning *woman* or *women*. If you're referring to a single individual, often simply substituting the word *person* will do, or in some contexts *human being*. If you're referring to the race, instead of *man* or *mankind*, use *human beings*, *humanity*, *people*, *humankind*, or *the human race*. Instead of *manmade*, use *synthetic* or *artificial* or *manufactured*. (Note that several words beginning with *man-*, such as *manufacture*, *manuscript*, *manoeuvre*, come not from the English word *man* but from the Latin *manus*, "hand.") Similarly, in compounds designating various occupations and positions, try to avoid the suffix *man* by using gender-neutral terms such as *firefighter*, *police officer*, *letter carrier*, *worker* or *labourer* (instead of *workman*), *supervisor* or *manager* (instead of *foreman*); and though some people object to it, the suffix *person* is becoming more and more common: *spokesperson*, *chairperson* (or just *chair*), *anchorperson* (or just *anchor*), *businessperson*, *salesperson* (but see #67). (See also **person, persons, people**.)

Another concern is the suffix *-ess*. Usefully gender-specific (and power-designating) terms like *princess*, *empress*, *duchess*, and *goddess* are firmly established, but there is seldom if ever any need to refer to an *authoress* or *poetess* when simply *author* or *poet* will serve; many now eschew *actress,* finding *actor* more suitable for both sexes. *Stewardess* has given way to *flight attendant*; and *waitress* and *waiter* have been replaced by *server*. The suffix *-ette*, as in *usherette*, is similarly demeaning; use *usher*. And don't use *lady* as a substitute for *woman*.

Further, don't thoughtlessly gender-stereotype occupations and other activities that are engaged in by both men and women; think about doctors, lawyers, business executives, secretaries, nurses, construction workers, cabdrivers, truckdrivers, family cooks, food-shoppers, fishing enthusiasts, and so on. And don't refer, for example, to a "woman doctor" unless gender is somehow relevant to the context, in which case you'll probably also refer to another doctor as a man, or "male." And don't, for example, highlight gender (as in *female athlete*, *female doctor*) unless it is somehow relevant to the context, in which case you would also refer to a *male athlete* or a *male doctor*. Similarly, if you're writing about English novelists and refer to Charles Dickens, refer also to Jane Austen, not "Miss Austen"; if you subsequently refer to him as simply *Dickens*, refer to her as *Austen*. Finally, use the title *Ms.* for a woman unless you know that a specific woman prefers *Miss* or *Mrs.*

Sources focused on issues of gender and English usage differ on the use of the word *woman* in phrases such as *woman doctor*, *woman judge*, *woman premier*. These sources suggest that it is only appropriate to use *woman* adjectivally if one would also use *man* in the same manner. And one would rarely, if ever, use *man* in this way. Instead, *male* would be the obvious choice. It follows, then, that *female* is preferable to *woman* in specific contexts calling attention to gender.

> The accident victim asked to be examined by a female doctor.
>
> The prime minister set a precedent by appointing the first female judge to the Supreme Court.
>
> She has been featured in a magazine story as the longest serving female premier in Canada.

material, materialistic

Don't use *materialistic* when all you need is the adjective *material*. *Material* means "physical, composed of matter," or "concerned with physical rather than spiritual or intellectual things"; it is often the sufficient word:

> Her life is founded almost entirely on material values.

Materialistic is the adjectival form of the noun *materialist*, which in turn denotes one who believes in materialism, a philosophical doctrine holding that everything can be explained in terms of matter and physical laws. A *materialist* can also be one who is notably or questionably concerned with material as opposed to spiritual or intellectual things and values:

> She is very materialistic in her outlook on life.

Unless you intend the philosophical overtones, use the simpler *material*. There is an analogous tendency to use *relativistic* rather than *relative* and *moralistic* rather than *moral*. Consult your dictionary. (See also **simple, simplistic**, and **real, realism, realist, realistic**.)

may (See **can, may**.)

may, might

Don't confuse your reader by using *may* where *might* is required:

(a) after another verb in the past tense:

> ***us:*** She thought she may get a raise. (use *might*)

In the present tense, either *may* or *might* would be possible:

> She thinks she may get a raise. (It's quite likely that she will.)
> She thinks she might get a raise. (It's less likely, but possible.)

(b) for something hypothetical rather than factual:

> *us:* This imaginative software program may have helped Beethoven, but it wouldn't have changed the way Mozart composed.

The word *may* makes it sound as if it is possible that the program *did* help Beethoven, which is of course absurd. Use *might*. (For other examples, see #17e.)

media (See #18h and #62t.7.)

might (See **may, might** and **can, may**.)

momentarily
Though often used to mean "in a moment, soon" ("We'll be eating *momentarily*"), many prefer to restrict it to meaning "for a moment" ("Her attention wandered *momentarily*"). Since the word is therefore sometimes capable of being misunderstood, some writers avoid it altogether. (See also **presently**.)

moral, moralistic (See **material, materialistic**.)

more, most; less, least (See #19b and #20c.)

more important, more importantly
Although *more importantly* is widely used as a kind of sentence adverb, many writers object to it on grammatical grounds, preferring *more important* (as if it were a shorter version of "what is more important").

Ms. (See **man, woman, lady, etc.**, and #53a.)

myself, herself, himself, etc. (See #14h.)

necessary (See **unique etc.**)

neither (See **either, neither**.)

never (See **can't hardly etc.**)

nowheres (See **anyways etc.**)

number (See **amount, number**.)

occur (See **happen, occur**.)

of

Keep in mind the following three points about the preposition *of*:

(a) legitimate use with *all* before some pronouns and some proper nouns:

> Bring all of them.
>
> We travelled across all of Canada.

(b) unnecessary use after the prepositions *off*, *inside*, and *outside*:

> She fell off the fence.
>
> He awoke to find himself inside a large crate.
>
> As requested, she remained in the hall outside the room.
>
> We had all the time in the world.

(c) incorrect use as a result of mispronunciation:

> We would of stayed for dinner if not for the weather. (have)
>
> The prime minister should of apologized for his remarks. (have)

Because of the way we sometimes speak, such verb phrases as "would have," "could have," "should have," and "might have" are mispronounced (*would've, could've, should've, might've*). Because of the way we hear these words, the *'ve* mistakenly becomes *of*.

(See also **on**.)

off, off of (See **of**.)

on

This preposition is sometimes unidiomatic when used as a substitute for *about* or *of*:

> ***id:*** She had no doubts on what to do next. (*about*)
>
> ***id:*** I am calling my essay "A Study on the Effects of Globalization." (*of*)

on account of (See **due to**.)

one another (See **each other, one another**.)

only (See **can't hardly etc.**)

oral, verbal (See **verbal, oral**.)

outside, outside of (See **of**.)

owing to (See **due to**.)

people (See **person, persons, people**.)

per
Although useful and at home in technical and business writing, the Latin *per* is usually out of its element in other writing, except when part of a Latin phrase (*per capita, per cent*); especially do not use it to mean simply "by, by means of, through" (as in business contexts: "per bearer") or "according to" ("per your instructions").

perfect (See **unique etc.**)

person, persons, people
Partly to avoid gender-biased language (*man, woman,* the generic *he*), some people overuse the word *person* in what often sounds a wordy, jargony way (for example, "The *persons* responsible for the accident have received a summons to traffic court"). Try to avoid it, or instead use *one*, or even *you* (see #15d). In the plural, use *persons* only when the number in question is small, say one or two or three ("Two *persons* refused to sign the petition") or when you want to emphasize the presence of *individuals* in a group ("Those *persons* wishing to attend the party should sign up now"), but even then the demonstrative pronoun *those* alone will often serve better ("*Those* wishing to attend . . ."). Otherwise, use *people,* which is normal even for referring to small numbers: "One or two *people* may object." (See also **man, woman, lady, etc.** and **individual**.)

perspective (See **in terms of**.)

persuade (See **convince, persuade**.)

plus (See ***d*** in Appendix 2.)

possible (See **unique etc.**)

presently
Since some people think that *presently* should mean only "in a short while, soon," and others think that it instead, or also, means "at present, currently, now," resulting in at least occasional ambiguity, many writers try to avoid the word altogether. Use the alternative terms and your meaning will be clear.

(See also **momentarily**.)

put forth (See **set forth**.)

quote
In contexts that are at all formal, use this only as a verb; don't use it as a noun, equivalent to "quotation" or "quotation mark."

raise, rise
The verb *raise* is transitive, requiring an object: "I *raised* my hand; he *raises* horses." *Rise* is intransitive: "The temperature *rose* sharply; I *rise* each morning at dawn." If necessary, memorize their principal parts: *raise*, *raised*, *raised*; *rise*, *rose*, *risen*.

real, realism, realist, realistic

If necessary, use your dictionary to help you keep these words straight. The person who wrote that "Huxley's novel is not about *realistic* people" was at best being ambiguous: does *realistic* here mean "lifelike," or "facing facts"? The one who wrote "He based his conclusions not on theory but on *realistic* observation" probably meant "observation of reality." (See also **material, materialistic**.)

real, really (See **very** and #20b.4.)

reason . . . is because
Although this construction has long been common, especially in speech, many people object to it as (a) redundant, since *because* often means simply "for the reason that," and as (b) ungrammatical, since adverbial *because* should not introduce noun clauses after a linking verb (critics for the same reason object to *it is because, this is because,* and the like). However common such phrases may be, we suggest that you avoid them, especially in formal writing, since they are likely to draw criticism—especially *the reason is because*.

reason why
The *why* in this phrase is often redundant, as in "The reason *why* I'm taking Spanish is that I want to travel in South America." Check to see if you need the *why*.

recommend

When this transitive verb appears in a clause with an indirect object, that object must be expressed as a prepositional phrase with *to* or *for*, and it must follow the direct object:

> ***id:*** She recommended me this restaurant.
>
> ***id:*** She recommended to me this restaurant.
>
> ***revised:*** She recommended this restaurant to me.

A number of other verbs fit the same idiomatic pattern as *recommend*. Among the most common are *admit*, *contribute*, *dedicate*, *demonstrate*, *describe*, *distribute*, *explain*, *introduce*, *mention*, *propose*, *reveal*, *speak*, *state*, and *suggest*. Note, however, that with several of these verbs, if the direct object is itself a noun clause, it usually follows the prepositional phrase:

> He admitted to me that he had been lying.
>
> She explained to me what she intended to do.

72

regarding (See **in terms of**.)

relative, relativistic (See **material, materialistic**.)

rise, raise (See **raise, rise**.)

round (See **unique etc.**)

scarcely (See **can't hardly etc.**)

seeing as (how), seeing that (See **being that, being as how**.)

sensual, sensuous

Although the meanings of these words overlap, and the two are often used interchangeably, *sensuous* is traditionally used to refer broadly to intellectual or physical pleasure derived from the senses, while *sensual*, on the other hand, usually refers to the gratification of physical—particularly sexual—appetites:

> Some Canadian poets, responding to the beauty of their natural environment, write sensuous poetry.
>
> We are studying the sensual features of contemporary love poetry.

set, sit

Set (principal parts *set, set, set*) means "put, place, cause to sit"; it is transitive, requiring an object: "He *set* the glass on the counter." *Sit* (principal parts *sit, sat, sat)* means "rest, occupy a seat, assume a sitting position"; it is intransitive: "The glass *sits* on the counter. May I *sit* in the easy chair?"—though it can be used transitively in expressions like "I sat myself down to listen," "She sat him down at the desk." (See also **lie, lay**.)

set forth

As a stiff, unwieldy substitute for *express(ed)* or *present(ed)* or *state(d),* this phrase is an attempt at sophistication that misfires. *Put forth* is similarly weak.

shall, will; should, would (See #17e, #17h.3, and #17i.2.)

she or he, her or his, she/he, s/he (See #15d.)

simple, simplistic

Don't use *simplistic* when all you want is *simple. Simplistic* means "oversimplified, unrealistically simple.":

> We admire the book for its simple explanations and straightforward advice.
>
> The author's assessment of the war's causes was narrow and simplistic.

Similarly, *fatalistic* does not mean the same as *fatal.* (See also **material, materialistic**.)

since

Since can refer both to time ("*Since* April we haven't had any rain") and to cause ("*Since* she wouldn't tell him, he had to figure it out for himself"). Therefore don't use *since* in a sentence where it could mean either:

> ***ambig:*** Since you went away, I've been sad and lonely.

sit, set (See **set, sit**.)

so, so that, therefore

As a conjunction, *so* is informal but acceptable (see #23a.3); just don't overwork it. To introduce clauses of purpose and to avoid possible ambiguity, you will often want to use *so that* or *therefore* instead:

> He sharpened the saw so that it would cut the boards properly.
>
> She cleverly changed her story several times, so that we couldn't be sure what actually happened.

She changed her story several times; therefore we couldn't be sure what actually happened.

so . . . as, as . . . as

In strictly formal contexts, use *so* or *so . . . as* with negative comparisons; use *as* or *as . . . as* only with positive comparisons:

Belinda was almost as tall as he was, but she was not *so* heavy.

He was not *so* light on his feet as he once was, but he was as strong as ever.

someplace (See **anyplace, someplace**.)

somewheres (See **anyways etc.**)

sort of (See **kind of, sort of**.)

specially (See **especially, specially**.)

square (See **unique etc.**)

72

state

State is a stronger verb than *say*; reserve *state* for places where you want the heavier, more forceful meaning of "assert, declare, make a formal statement."

straight (See **unique etc.**)

substitute

Don't use *substitute* when you mean *replace*—i.e. don't follow it with *by* or *with*; use it only with *for*:

us: The french fries were substituted by a tossed salad. (replaced)

us: I substituted the term paper with three shorter essays. (replaced)

revised: The server kindly substituted a tossed salad for the greasy french fries.

revised: I was permitted to substitute three short essays for the term paper.

Substitute can also be used intransitively:

> Because he is off his game this year, Stanley has only substituted.
>
> Mere cleverness cannot substitute for common sense.

sure, surely
Don't use *sure* as an adverb. (See #20b.4.)

suspect, suspicious
Though *suspicious* can mean *arousing suspicion*, it is sometimes best to reserve it for the person in whom the suspicions are aroused, using the adjective *suspect* for the object of those suspicions; otherwise ambiguity may result (unless the context makes the meaning clear):

> ***ambig:*** He was a very suspicious man.
>
> ***clear:*** I thought his actions suspect.
>
> ***clear:*** He was suspicious of everyone he met.
>
> ***clear:*** All of us were suspect in the eyes of the police.

72

tend, tends
This verb is often no more than a filler. Don't say "My French teacher *tends to* mark strictly" when what you mean is "My French teacher *marks* strictly."

therefore (See **so, so that, therefore**.)

these (those) kinds (sorts), this kind (sort) (See #15f.)

think (See **feel(s)**.)

though, although (See **although, though**.)

till, until, 'til
Till and *until* are both standard, and have the same meaning. *Until* is probably felt to be somewhat more formal, and (like the two-syllable *Although*) is usually preferable at the beginning of a sentence. The contraction *'til* is little used nowadays, except in markedly informal contexts, such as personal letters.

too

Used as an intensifier, *too* is sometimes illogical; if an intensifier is necessary in such sentences as these, use *very:*

> ***ww:*** I don't like my cocoa too hot.
> ***revised:*** I don't like my cocoa very hot.

> ***ww:*** She didn't care for the brown suit too much.
> ***revised:*** She didn't care for the brown suit very much.

But often you can omit the intensifier as unnecessary:

> She didn't care much for the brown suit.

(See **very**.)

toward, towards

These are interchangeable, but in North American (as opposed to British) English, the preposition *toward* is usually preferred to *towards,* just as the adverbs *afterward, forward* (meaning *frontward),* and *backward* are to their counterparts ending in *s.*

true facts

Any reference to *true facts* is an attempt to be emphatic that backfires into illogic. If there are such things as "true facts" or "real facts," what are "false facts" or "unreal facts"? Let the word *facts* mean what it is supposed to; trying to prop it up with *true* or *real* makes a reader or listener suspect it of being weak or insincere.

type, -type

Don't use *type* as an adjective or part of an adjective, as in "He is a very athletic *type* person." In any but a technical context, the word *type* has the ring of jargon, even when followed by the obligatory *of;* without the *of* it is colloquial at best. In general writing, if you can substitute *kind of* for *type of,* do so—but even then check to make sure you really need it, for often it is unnecessary, mere deadwood: "She is an intelligent [kind of] woman." As a hyphenated suffix, *-type* is similarly often unnecessary, as well as being one of the results of the impulse to turn nouns into adjectives: "This is a new-type vegetable slicer," or "He is a patriotic-type person." Avoid it. (See also **kind of, sort of**.)

unique, absolute, necessary, essential, complete, perfect, fatal, equal, (im)possible, infinite, empty, full, straight, round, square, etc.

In writing, especially formal writing, treat these and other such adjectives as absolutes that cannot logically be compared or modified by such adverbs as *very* and *rather.* Since by definition something *unique* is the *only one of its kind* or *without equal,* clearly one thing cannot be "more unique" than another, or even "very unique"; in other words, *unique* is not a synonym for *unusual* or *rare.* Similarly with the others: one thing cannot be "more necessary" than another. Since *perfect* means "without flaw," there cannot be degrees of perfection. Colloquially, expressions of degree or comparison with these terms are fairly common, especially those like *round, square, full, empty,* and *straight.* But strictly speaking, a thing is either *round* or not; one tennis ball cannot be "rounder" than another. And so on. And note that you can easily get around this semantic limitation by calling one thing, for example, "more nearly perfect," "more nearly round," or "closer to round" than another, or by referring to something as "almost unique" or "nearly unique" (but you could simply call it "very rare" or "highly unusual").

until (See **till, until, 'til.**)

usage, use, utilize, utilization

The noun *usage* is appropriate when you mean customary or habitual use, whether verbal or otherwise ("British usage," "the usages of the early Christians"), or a particular verbal expression being characterized in a particular way ("an ironic usage," "an elegant usage"). Otherwise the shorter
72 noun *use* is preferable. As a verb, *use* should nearly always suffice; *utilize,* often pretentiously employed instead, should carry the specific meaning "put to use, make use of, turn to practical or profitable account." Similarly, the noun *use* will usually be more appropriate than *utilization.* Phrases like *use of, the use of, by the use of,* and *through the use of* tend toward jargon and are almost always wordy.

verbal, oral

Although these words are commonly used interchangeably, you may want to preserve the still useful distinction between them. *Verbal* regularly means "pertaining to words," which could be either written or spoken. If you mean "spoken aloud," then *oral* is preferable. (In some special contexts *verbal* is often used to mean *oral* as opposed to written: "verbal contract, verbal agreement"—but even these usages can be ambiguous; *oral* and *written* would make the circumstances precisely clear.)

very

When revising, you may find that where you have used *very* you could just as well omit it. Often it is a vague or euphemistic substitute for a more precise adverb or adjective:

> It was very sunny today. (magnificently sunny?)
>
> I was very tired. (exhausted?)

He was very intoxicated. (falling-down drunk?)

Her embarrassment was very obvious. (It was either obvious or it wasn't; drop *very*, or change it to something like *painfully*.)

The same goes for *really* and *actually*. Such weak intensifiers sometimes even detract from the force of the words they modify.

Note that before some past participles, it is idiomatic to use another word (e.g. *much, well*) along with *very*:

You are very much mistaken if you think I'll agree without an argument.

Sharon is very well prepared for the role.

virtually (See **literally, virtually, figuratively**.)

way, ways

In formal usage, especially in writing, don't use *ways* to refer to distance; *way* is correct:

We were a long way from home.

They had only a little way to go.

well (See **good, bad, badly, well**.)

when, where (See **is when, is where**.)

whereas (See **while**.)

while

As a subordinating conjunction, *while* is best restricted to meanings having to do with time:

While Vijay mowed the lawn, Honoree raked up the grass clippings.

She played the piano while I prepared the dinner.

When it means *although (though)* or *whereas*, it can be imprecise, even ambiguous:

While I agree with some of his reasons, I still think my proposal is better. (*Although* would be clearer.)

While he does the lawn-mowing, she cooks the meals.
(Fuzzy or ambiguous; *whereas* would make the meaning clear.)

(See also **although, though**.)

will, shall (See #17h.3.)

-wise

Just as *-ize* (or *-ise*) has long been used to turn nouns and adjectives into verbs, *-wise* has been used to turn them into adverbs, e.g. of manner or position: *clockwise, crabwise, lengthwise, edgewise, sidewise, likewise, otherwise*. But this suffix, in its sense of "with reference to" (and equivalent phrases), is so overused in modern jargon (*moneywise, sales-wise, personnel-wise*, etc.) that it is now employed mainly as a source of humour ("And how are you otherwise-wise?"). Therefore do not tack it onto nouns, for it produces such inanities as what a politician once announced: "We've just had our best month ever, fundraisingwise." It is acceptable in established words but not, or seldom, in new coinages. You can easily find a way to say what you mean without resorting to it (see **in terms of**):

72

not: Grammarwise, Stephen is doing well.
but: Stephen is doing well with grammar.

not: Insurance-wise, I believe I am well enough protected.
but: I believe I have enough insurance.

not: This is the best car I've ever owned, powerwise.
but: This car has more power than any other I've owned.

with regard to (See **in terms of**.)

with respect to (See **in terms of**.)

woman (See **man, woman, lady, etc.**)

would, should (See #17e and #17i.2.)

Review Exercise, Chapter VII Diction

Revise the following sentences to strengthen the diction and normalize the usage; correct any other errors you find, as well.

1. They discussed the role of the psychiatrist in athlete motivation.
2. The team comprises a close-knit unit that functions on a collective basis.

Review Exercise, Chapter VII Diction – *continued*

3. Strategy-wise, we want to position union members in an advantageous situation.
4. Because this particular word occurs frequently throughout the course of the play, it achieves a certain importance.
5. In the winter even less tourist dollars are spent.
6. Her striving to be a perfectionist was evident in her business.
7. Hopefully, this weekend's events will turn out to be successful.
8. He was ignorant as to the proper use of the tools.
9. As is so often the case, one type of error leads to another.
10. This passage is a very essential one in the novel.
11. His metaphors really bring out a sinister feeling which one feels while reading it.
12. Eliot sees his poetry as occupying a kind of niche in a long conveyer belt of accumulated knowledge and poetry.
13. She has him literally at her beckon call.
14. He found himself in a powerless situation.
15. I resolved to do my best in terms of making friends and working hard.
16. The hulls of the tankers were ripped open in a majority of cases, dumping countless barrels of oil into the sea.
17. Hamlet spends the whole play trying to reach a situation where he can revenge his father's death.
18. This poem is concerned with the fact that one should grasp an opportunity quickly.
19. He is only in town on a once-in-a-while basis.
20. The prime minister is waiting for the premiers to show their bottom lines.
21. As she gave me so much money I thanked her profusely.
22. The deal may not have gone ahead if Anderson hadn't been so patient and persistent.
23. People in watching these shows or movies may develop a love for violence as a result of watching this type of program.
24. This man thought it was incumbent upon him to extract revenge.
25. In Olympic sports nationalism is increasingly becoming a more important factor.
26. She saw that this was the last remaining remnant of a very, very important species.
27. For more than a million Canadians, back pain is an incapacitating experience which slows ordinary movements and turns routine tasks into tortuous events.
28. We are all intensely involved in profiting on the expenses of other people.

Review Exercise, Chapter VII Diction – *continued*

29. The contribution of the coalition to the passage of the legislation was capitalized on by the opposition.
30. He is as equally at ease hobnobbing with celebrities as he is relaxing in his own home.
31. These instructions are contingent to your acceptance.
32. The prime minister's reply, he complained, was "warm and gratuitous but not very specific."
33. Iago is regarded by all as an honest, truthful man.
34. The character of Nicholas is recognizable to people who really exist in the world.
35. Thanks to your financial commitment, an alternate to on-air fundraising is possible.
36. This book about a politician will have a negative effect in terms of the interests of his opponents.
37. The premier has tried to pressurize the legislature to go along with his proposals.
38. After going only a hundred miles the ship was forced to return to its point of origination.
39. You'll also be amazed, too, at our low prices on basic apparel.
40. The new program will cost in the realm of five million dollars.
41. You can expect similar-type amounts of precipitation over the long weekend.
42. The minister said that he would not want to be categorized with respect to a reply to that statement.
43. There was a general consensus in the neighbourhood that ambulance service in the area was frequently inadequate regarding response time.
44. Today, environmentalists are trying to substitute the word "buy" with the word "recycle."
45. We have to reconsider the proposal in terms of the legal aspects of that situation.
46. I was playing my typical type of game.
47. It seems like he is rather mad at her for daring to try and deceive him.
48. Frodo continuously fretted about the Ring.
49. I denote a real sense of pride here.
50. One must judge the various proposals on an equal basis.

Omnibus Review Exercise, Chapters II–VII
Sentence errors and weaknesses

A. Each of the following sentences contains at least one error or weakness of a kind discussed in this book; many contain more than one. Practise your proofreading and revising. Label the sentences with the appropriate correction symbols.

1. The nature of his errors were not serious.
2. There was a clear increase in strength of Protestant power, especially in England and Prussia who had benefitted from the treaty of Utrecht.
3. In today's world it is becoming increasingly more difficult to find relatively inexpensive ways to use your leisure time.
4. As far as league standings, this string of successive losses has put the team in an insurmountable hole.
5. We at TSN want to feature a few more Canadian athletes at a young age.
6. There were artists which continued to study and produce classical works and there were artists which developed new ideas in their fields.
7. As for ancient man, being civilized was of no concern to one who was battling the many forces of nature such as hunting wild animals for food and shelter from the weather.
8. Argentina, more than any country in Latin America, was a place of massive immigration over relatively few decades.
9. The reason why their cars don't live as long is because most people have no idea of how to properly look after their cars.
10. There's no golfer who wouldn't give his life to don the coveted green jacket, symbolizing a Masters victory and an automatic lifelong membership into the Augusta National Golf Club.
11. This book provides what I think is indisputedly the best account of those troubled years.
12. Friends say the feisty newspaperwoman would have liked to have become an artist.
13. He was charged of embezzling over ten thousand dollars.
14. As a single parent with two high schoolers, it took two jobs to stay afloat.
15. During that period of time we talked to him on a nightly basis.
16. The poem's strange theme states that one is better off dying at a young age rather than growing old.

Omnibus Review Exercise, Chapters II–VII
Sentence errors and weaknesses – *continued*

17. An old Victorian mansion has a mysterious basement room which, by entering allows members of the household to travel through time.
18. I had truly scarred her while she had only embarrassed me.
19. At that point the immigration department closed the door tightly.
20. There's no question it was a tragedy, and there's also no question that it may have been prevented.
21. A hobby such as playing music in a band gives more than just enjoyment, it gives relaxation, self satisfaction, it is educational, and it is competitive.
22. During the long drought, many water areas, such as lakes and reservoirs, were drying up.
23. This evening's show features a family of nine who is competing in the National Karate Championships.
24. I felt a sudden needle like pain.
25. Based on her findings, she concluded that comedy was more healthful than tragedy.
26. The Board of Directors of *Design for Today* wishes to express their appreciation for assistance from many local individuals and businesses.
27. There are many arguments with respect to the importance of a university education in today's society.
28. In this modern day and age it is not unusual to find people who are ignorantly unaware of the technology of how things in our society work.
29. She had so many assignments over the holiday that she felt bogged under.
30. The police act against violators of this minor law only on a complaint basis.
31. They substituted butter with margarine in the belief that it was healthier.
32. As a soccer fan, recent events have been depressing.
33. The silver mentioned in the beginning and the end of the story not only symbolize freedom but they foreshadow a better future.
34. My grandfather was a very introspective-type individual.
35. He is one of those people, (and there are many of them) who does not understand economics.
36. When there never seems to be enough hours in a day, it's time to get yourself a cellular phone.

Omnibus Review Exercise, Chapters II–VII
Sentence errors and weaknesses – *continued*

37. Tonight's specialty is a dish that is a feast not only for the eyes but a treat for the palate as well.
38. Failure to produce efficiently together with failure to reduce imports have had serious economic consequences.
39. The show employs flashbacks to fill in the protagonists background as a former Vietnam veteran and ex-New Orleans cop.
40. Our opponent merely sights her party's ideology and says things are all right—but ask yourself, can you afford anymore?
41. The government permits the sale of surplus material abroad on an intermittent basis.
42. I hope you will forgive me pointing out certain weaknesses in your argument.
43. The poor woman had become addicted to the pain killing drug she was taking.
44. The laws were made by the parlament and enforced by a police force, which is a similar system to the present.
45. The room was furnished with the new chrome and plastic furniture but it wasn't very attractive.
46. We shouldn't act in terms of a knee-jerk reaction to the present situation.
47. She concluded from her investigation that under the new policy women employees may in fact receive a smaller increase than they may have otherwise received.
48. The English aristocracy, which was mainly comprised of wealthy landowners, did not however, in spite of their comfortable lifestyle, know the manners and etiquette that seemed to elevate the French aristocracy.
49. He promised he would take me to the movies, in spite of how much work that he hasn't finished yet, but has to do.
50. As a valued Acme Bank customer we are pleased to extend to you the opportunity to apply for a personal loan at exceptional fixed interest rates.

B. Here are ten more sentences, most slightly longer or more complicated than the others, that invite more drastic or thoroughgoing revision.

1. The fact that there are many people who I can relate to, adds to a sense of security for me because I feel that I am liked and I have a position with them in society, which enhances my self-identity.

72

Omnibus Review Exercise, Chapters II–VII
Sentence errors and weaknesses – *continued*

2. Further implications for disaster in postponing the driving experience to an older age could be encountered in those people wishing to use the car as their primary means of transportation to work or a post-secondary institution.
3. The poem mentions statues, pictures, and stairways, all of these seem to enable the reader to picture Prufrock better and the people he associates with.
4. An older person has already made a lot of mistakes in their life and sharing their mistakes with new generations will keep from every generation having to start from a beginning.
5. I am still not sure whether or not I did the right thing about coming here but everyone thought it was, so here I am.
6. Some people may view Hamlet as a feeble, gutless young man who can't make up his mind about anything and this is what I believed at first. But by reading the play carefully and by observing Hamlet's actions this can't be true.
7. A hobby is often a nice way to relax or to just sit down and read a favourite novel or listen to some music, anything, just as long as it is relaxing.
8. I'm lucky to live in a great country, have a family who I love and am loved in return, have caring relations acquaintances, and the opportunity to meet strangers who may someday be friends.
9. With no increase in salaries, increased teaching loads, and cutbacks in research facilities, faculty is starting to slip away that university has already lost at least seven faculty members since January, and there are strong indications of many more to come.
10. By portraying the Queen as being blind to the situation of hate between Hamlet and the King, and the fact that she does not seem to even consider the fact that the King killed her previous husband, the audience's attitude toward the King is made even stronger.

Research, Writing, and Documentation

VIII

A paper based on library research is still very much an essay, and so it should conform to the principles governing any good essay. It should represent you as a thinker, and it should contribute your distinctive perspectives on a question of interest to you. Research essays also call upon writers to seek out the findings and the views of others who have investigated a topic and to give full credit to those sources and at the same time to their own research efforts in careful documentation of materials both within and following the essay. This chapter discusses and illustrates the stages of writing a research essay and the details to keep in mind to do a good job. All the matters discussed are intended to produce a good essay without wasting time and energy. Some of the steps and details may seem mechanical, and some may look like unnecessary fiddling, but all of them are important, and all of them have proved useful to many writers.

Research and Writing Tip

On Methods of Research-based Writing

The techniques outlined here are, of course, not the only possible ones, but they are tested ones. An instructor may ask you to follow a different method, for example to take notes or to compile your bibliography in a different way or to cross-reference material in a special way. After some experience you may yourself devise or discover different or additional ways of safeguarding accuracy and increasing efficiency. No one method is sacrosanct: the important thing is to have a method. The alternative is likely to be confusion, error, and wasted effort.

73 The Library and the Internet

Doing effective research means learning your way around your library. It isn't enough to do your own research solely on the Internet. Consider following an online tutorial with a conducted tour of your library building(s). Or, on your own, explore the library's layout, its reference facilities, its other holdings, its catalogues, its whole system. And don't be afraid to ask librarians for help. Given good, specific questions from library users, reference librarians can be invaluable sources of help as you find your way through the myriad of non-electronic and electronic resources available to researchers and scholars in this information age. Once you feel reasonably at home in what may be a vast and complex building or group of buildings and databases, you can begin to use the library as it is intended to be used.

73a The Catalogues

You will find different kinds of cataloguing systems in different libraries, or even in a single library. Most college, university, and public libraries in Canada converted to computer catalogues during the 1990s. Searches for information in today's libraries typically follow the three major paths discussed in the remainder of this section.

An Internet search

Through links in your library's online catalogue you may access the search engines to which your library subscribes (such as *Google*, *Google Scholar Infomine*, or *Yahoo*). These will enable you to do keyword searches for information in the seemingly limitless number of websites that are part of the World Wide Web.

Research Tip

On the Critical Evaluation of Internet Sources

The Internet is a largely unregulated source of information. Thus, you need to evaluate carefully and critically the websites you locate in your research. Keep in mind the following suggestions in your use of the Internet:

1. Look for authoritative information on websites maintained by recognized researchers and scholars or by public and private institutions. Anonymous and personal websites are not considered as authoritative sources for scholarly research.
2. Look for the credentials of the identified authors of the website and consider them when weighing the research value of the site.
3. Peer-reviewed materials are the most credible sources of information for academic purposes. Consider using such search sources as Academic Search Premier and Google Scholar, databases that identify peer-reviewed articles online and in print form.
4. Check that the websites you plan to use are current—that is, recently updated—and that claims and evidence offered on the site are supported with detailed and accurate documentation.
5. Be cautious about using a website whose links to other sites are broken, as it may not be well maintained or particularly reliable in its content.

A simple search

You may search an online catalogue for a book, periodical (newspaper, magazine, journal), audio recording, video recording, or DVD actually housed in your library. In this **simple search**, as it is called, you can look for a book using one of four pieces of information: the last name of the author, the book's title, key words in the title, or the subject of the book. When you find a source in this way, the detailed catalogue entry will include a **call number**, which will allow you to locate the item in the library system.

An article search

You may look for relevant articles in a periodical source (a newspaper, a magazine, a print-based or electronic journal) by searching the indexes and databases listing the scholarly papers and popular essays published each year in Canada and around the world. The best way to conduct this kind of search is by using the key word or phrase identifying your topic or subtopic. In the late 1990s, many libraries began converting their indexes from book form to electronic databases, so while you may find yourself searching for some sources in the indexes housed in your library's reference section, you will likely access most information from the online databases. Once you have identified an article of interest, you may be able to access it online if your library has also begun converting its periodical collections to *e-form*; otherwise you may need to do a simple search to determine the call number and location of the print-based periodical on the library shelf.

73b Reference Sources

A library's reference section contains many sources of information. The website for this book offers a sampling to suggest the kinds of references usually available and some of the standard or more useful items in each category. (See www.oup.com/ca/he/companion/brownmontagnes5.) Find out for yourself what reference materials are in your library by making your own search through the reference section: you may be astonished at the quantity and variety of information available.

Find out as well about the computerized reference resources your library provides. In addition to online computer catalogues of their own holdings, libraries increasingly store their own reference materials electronically and subscribe to large electronic databases of reference materials (bibliographies, dictionaries, indexes, encyclopedias, and so on). Not only will learning how to access, evaluate, and use these materials put you in touch almost instantaneously with information and scholarship from around the world, it will make you a stronger, more well-read researcher.

Before you begin work on a project, browse through some of the relevant reference sources to get an idea of what kind of information is available. In addition, as you explore you will often find that an article in an encyclopedia or a book on a given subject will include its own bibliographical information; by following these leads or links you can save much of the time you might otherwise spend searching for sources.

74 The Research Plan: Collecting Data: Sources

As you get underway on a research project, you should begin by preparing a **research plan**, a strategy that will help you focus your research and especially to budget the right amount of time to spend on the assignment. Draft this plan early—that is, no more than a day or two after you first receive the assignment—and then be prepared, if necessary, to revise it as circumstances change.

Your plan should consist first of a **researchable question**. This question should be of sufficient interest and importance to sustain you through the research and writing process. As you move on and gain more insight into the topic, be confident enough to modify the original question.

As important as determining the researchable question is establishing a **realistic timeline** for the stages of your project. Consider, for example, how your assignment will fit in with other projects and commitments you have. Then ask yourself how much time you will give to each of the following:

- your search for sources
- your evaluation and reading of sources
- your notetaking, summarizing, and synthesizing of souces
- your organization and planning of the first draft
- your writing and revising of second and subsequent drafts
- your editing and polishing of the final draft

Try as much as possible to set a firm date for the end of your research and the beginning of your writing, and give yourself at least a week if possible for the writing and polishing of the drafts of your assignment.

74a The Preliminary Bibliography

Once you have decided on a researchable question, the first major step in gathering information is to compile a **preliminary bibliography**. By consulting various sources (for example, periodical indexes, essay indexes, general and particular bibliographies, encyclopedias and dictionaries, your library's own catalogues, and the Internet), make a list of books, articles, websites, and so on, that may be useful sources of information about your topic. Next, look in the appropriate part of the catalogue to find out which books and articles on your list are available in your library, and record the call number of each one; list the relevant websites with their URLs.

Research Tip

Recording the Date of Your Access to Electronic Sources

When you access a periodical article or website on the Internet, you must note the specific date of your access, as this information must be included in the MLA works-cited entry for the source. The reason for this requirement? Materials posted online are often updated, and so the date of your access will help to explain to a reader why the content of a source may have changed between the time the research is conducted and the time the paper is submitted.

74b Producing a Working Bibliography

When you begin looking at the actual books, articles, websites, and other sources on your preliminary list, you should do two things:

1. First, as you locate and evaluate a source, make out a **bibliography card** for it. (Use the small 8 × 12 cm or 3 × 5 inch index cards.) With cards you can keep track of material easily: you can keep them in handy alphabetical order, insert new cards as you find new sources, and put aside cards for sources you think are of no use to you. You will save time if you record the bibliographical information exactly as it will appear later in your bibliography (see #79a, #80, #81a, #81b, #81c). Record this information accurately and completely: double-check spellings, dates, page numbers, and so on.

   If you decide to record bibliographical information directly on a laptop rather than on index cards, consider enclosing bibliographical information for each separate source in its own text box. This practice will allow you to print copies of these notes in a form similar to that of the index card and will enable you to shuffle, sort, and arrange your information with ease as your list grows.

Research Tip

On Keeping Your Notes and Cards

Do not throw away any of these cards, even if you think they will be useless, for at a later stage you may decide to use some of them after all. In fact, don't throw anything away: keep all your notes, jottings, scribblings, lists, and drafts, for they may prove useful later when you want to check back on something or, in the light of new discoveries, restore something you earlier discarded. You may even find that something you are unable to use in one essay could turn out to be useful in another assignment.

Research Tip

Checking Actual Sources Against Initial Bibliographic Information

Some writers prefer not to make a preliminary bibliography (that is, a single alphabetical list of possible sources) but instead to enter each item on an index card as soon as they come across it in a bibliography, an online index, or other source. This does save one step, but if you choose to follow such a method, be careful: as soon as you come upon the actual book or article, or download material from the Internet, check your card against it for accuracy, because bibliographies and other lists sometimes contain errors, for example in spelling or punctuation or even dates. Since you will have to verify the accuracy of the information on any card prepared from a bibliography or index, you may find it takes as little (or even less) time to write up your bibliography card once you have the book, article, or web page right in front of you.

2. Second, study and evaluate the book or article to see how useful it looks, and jot down, on the card, a note to yourself about its likely worth as a source. This note is especially important if you are compiling an annotated bibliography. For example, note whether the source is scholarly and credible, whether it is promising or appears to be of little or no use, whether it looks good for a particular part of your project, or whether one part of it looks useful and the rest not. Be as specific as you can be, for a glance at such a note may later save you the trouble of a return trip to the library or the Internet. You may also want to write a label, called a **slug** (see #75c), on each card, indicating what part of your subject it pertains to. You may want to make each slug correspond to your preliminary outline (see #75); this information too could save you time. For the same reason, you might note on a card just how thorough your examination of the source was; that is, if you just glanced at it, you may want to return to it, but if you found it so interesting that you read it carefully and even took notes, then you will know that you need not return to it later. And, in case you do want to return to a source, save yourself time by recording the call number of each non-electronic item or the Internet path to each electronic item.

   Here are two sample bibliography records—one handwritten on an index card and the other typed on a laptop and saved in a text box. These records go with the sample MLA research paper appearing later in this chapter. Note the arrangement and completeness of the bibliographical information, the slugs in the upper right corners, the writer's notes to himself in the lower right, and the library call numbers in the lower left.

I. Genesis of the Novel

Findley, Timothy. Inside Memory: Pages from a Writer's Notebook.

Toronto: HarperCollins, 1990.

PR9271 - book source, autobiographical
I 638 - Findley's journals
Z 467 - 22 pages on the writing of
1990 Not Wanted on the Voyage!

II. Family warfare

York, Lorraine M. "Civilian Conflict: Systems of Warfare in Timothy Findley's Early Fiction." English Studies in Canada 15.3 (1989): 336–347.

–McMaster University professor, peer-reviewed article
–not directly focused on Not Wanted..., but useful on war as metaphor
–bibliographical information may be useful

PR 1
E 63 [downloaded in full text from Canadian Periodical Index (CPIQ online) 4 February 2000]

75 Taking Notes

Once you have compiled your working bibliography and begun consulting the items it lists, taking notes will become a priority for you. Initially, your notes will likely focus on brief descriptions of sources and of their relevance. As you become more engaged in reading and studying individual sources for their specific details, data, and arguments, your note-taking will accelerate as you prepare a working outline and write a first draft.

This taking of notes is by far preferable to cutting and pasting together materials you have duplicated or downloaded from the Internet, for it involves you actively from the beginning of the research process in filtering source material and in recording it as much as possible in your own terms. In fact, copying, cutting, and pasting at this stage delays your synthesis of sources and increases the risk of recording someone else's thoughts without any note of the original source. Whether inadvertent or not, the inclusion of such material in finished essays without proper acknowledgement constitutes plagiarism.

Your preliminary research should be relatively casual, for you will still be exploring your subject, investigating and weighing its possibilities, and attempting to limit it (see #9b) as much as necessary to meet the demands of time and length attached to the project. At some point during this early stage you should be able to construct a **preliminary outline or plan** (see #9f-j), which will, understandably, be subject to change as you go along. It may be only sketchy at first, but even a rough outline will help you decide what kinds of notes to take.

At first you may be uncertain about the usefulness or relevance of some of the material you come across. Be generous with yourself: take substantive notes. If you toss aside a source that doesn't look useful now, you may discover later that you need it after all; it is better to spend a few minutes taking some precise notes than to spend an hour or two on a return trip to the library only to find that the source has been borrowed by someone else. Use it while you have your hands on it.

For your notes you will need a separate stack of index cards. Try to use a different colour than you used for your bibliography cards, or else use the larger 10 × 15 cm (4 × 6 inch) cards, especially if your writing is large. On each **note card** you will need to include at least three things:

1. the note itself,
2. the exact source, and
3. a label or slug indicating just what part of your subject the note pertains to.

75a The Note Itself

1. **Include only one point on each card.** The reason for using cards is that it is easy to shuffle them around, to arrange them as you see fit at various stages. If you try to cram too much information onto one card, you won't be able to move it so easily; you may even have to recopy part of the material onto another card so that you can shift it to where you want it. Don't include two or three closely related points on one card unless you are certain that they will occur together in your essay.

2. **Be as brief as possible.** If for some reason your note must extend beyond one side of a card—if, for example, it is an unusually long summary or quotation—it can be continued on the back of the card. But write a large OVER in the bottom right-hand corner so that you won't forget that there is more to the note than appears on the front side. Or continue the note on another card. If you ever do use more than one card for a single note, repeat the listing of the source at the top of each card, and number the cards. For example, if a note extended to three cards, number them *1 of 3*, *2 of* 3, and *3 of 3*.

3. **Distinguish carefully between direct quotation and paraphrase or summary** (see #78)**.** Generally, quote only when you feel strongly that the author's own way of putting something will be especially effective in your essay. When you do quote directly, be careful: your quotation must accurately reproduce the original, including its punctuation, spelling, and even any peculiarities that you think might be incorrect (see item 10 below); do not "improve" what you are copying. In fact, it is a good idea to double check for absolute accuracy immediately after writing a note, and then to mark it as checked (a check mark, perhaps in red, at the right-hand edge will do). And when you do quote directly, put exaggeratedly large quotation marks around the quotation so that you cannot possibly later mistake it for summary or paraphrase. This safeguard is particularly important when a note is part quotation and part summary or paraphrase: the oversize quotation marks will help keep your work clear.

4. **Enclose your own ideas in square brackets.** If a note consists of a combination of (a) summary or paraphrase or quotation and (b) your own interjected thoughts or explanations or opinions, enclose your own ideas in square brackets—or, to be even safer, in double square brackets [[ ]] ; you might even want to initial them or to write MY OWN IDEA beside the note to reinforce your memory of the material as an insight of your own. This will prevent you from later assuming that the ideas and opinions came from your source rather than from you.

5. **Use your own words.** As much as possible, express the material in your own words when taking notes. The more you can assimilate and summarize information at the note-taking stage, the less interpreting you will need to do later—and it will never be fresher in your mind than at the time when you are taking the note. If you don't assimilate the information then, you may well have to return to the source to find out why you quoted it in the first place. It is all too easy to forget, over a period of days, weeks, or even months, just what the point was. This is especially true if you are working on two or three different papers at once, as many students often are.

6. **Quote from the original source.** When you quote, or even paraphrase or summarize, do so from the original source if possible. Second-hand quotations may be not only inaccurate but misleading as well. Seek out the most authoritative source—the original—whenever possible, rather than accept someone else's reading of it. Similarly, if more than one edition of a sourcebook exists, use the most authoritative or definitive one—usually the most recent.

7. **Distinguish between facts and opinions.** If you are quoting or paraphrasing a supposed authority on a subject, be careful not to let yourself be unduly swayed. Rather than note that "aspirin is good for heart and stroke patients," say that "Dr. Jones claims that aspirin is good for heart and stroke patients." Rather than write that "the province is running out of natural resources," say that "the premier believes, after reading the report given her by the investigating committee, that the province is running out of natural resources." The credibility of your own presentation may well depend on such matters of attribution.

8. **Be careful with the page numbers.** When you are quoting, or even just summarizing or paraphrasing from a paginated source, be careful with the page numbers. If a quotation runs over from one page to another in your source, be sure to indicate just where the page break occurs, for you may later decide to use only a part of the material, and you must know just which page that part came from in order to provide accurate documentation. A simple method is to indicate the end of a page with one or two slashes (/ or //).

9. **Enclose explanatory material in square brackets.** Whenever you insert explanatory material (for example, a noun or noun phrase to explain a pronoun in a quotation) use square brackets (see #54j).
10. **Use [*sic*].** When there is something in a quotation that is obviously wrong, whether a supposed fact or in the writing, such as a spelling error, insert [*sic*] after it (see #54j).
11. **Indicate ellipses.** Whenever you omit a word or words from a quotation, use three spaced periods to indicate the ellipsis (see #54i).

75b The Source

In the upper left-hand corner of each note card, identify the source. Usually the last name of the author and a page number will suffice. But if you are using more than one work by the same author, you must include at least a shortened title of the particular work from which the note comes. Indeed, it is always a good idea to include the title, for later in your note gathering you may come across a second work by an author you are already using. With a title on each card, no confusion can possibly arise. If the note comes from more than one page, indicate the inclusive page numbers; the note itself will show where the page changes (see #75a.8). (When the bibliography is complete, number the bibliography cards, if only to make it easier to put them back in order if you drop them or otherwise mix them up. But it is unwise to use this number alone to identify the source of a particular note. Be cautious: use the author's name and at least a short title.)

75c The Slug

In the upper right-hand corner of each note card, write a *slug*, the word or brief phrase identifying the topic of the note, and if possible indicating just what part of your essay the note belongs in. Be as specific as possible: this slug will be helpful when it comes to organizing the cards before writing the essay. If you've prepared a good outline, a key word or two from its main headings and subheadings with the corresponding numerals will be the logical choice to use as a slug on a card.

Research Tip

On the Legibility of Notes and Bibliographic Information

Do not use pencil to prepare your note and bibliography cards, since pencil writing can easily become smudged and illegible. Further, guard against the impulse to invent symbols and abbreviations; they may make the writing of notes easier at first, but over even a short time you can all too easily forget what your own code means. Except for standard abbreviations (but not even these in material you are quoting), write everything out in full. Similarly, if you don't use a laptop for your note-taking, be sure to write legibly.

75d Cross-Referencing: Numbering the Cards

If your project is long or unusually complex, you may want to devise some system for cross-referencing closely related note cards, or even ones you think might later prove to be closely related. One way to do this is to number the cards once you are through taking notes, and to make your cross-references to these numbers. Make sure that your cards are organized according to your outline, or that your outline has been changed to conform to the organization of your cards. Then, when the cards are all arranged, number them, say at top centre. Be sure to number your cards consecutively so that you can put them back into order should you drop or shuffle them.

75e Recording Your Own Ideas

In addition to taking notes from other sources, preserve your own ideas, insights, and flashes of inspiration as you go along. However fragmentary or tentative they may seem at first, they are likely to be valuable at a later stage. Even if you suddenly have so strong an idea about something that you feel sure you will remember it forever, *write it down*; otherwise there is a good chance you will forget it, for another strong idea may dislodge it a few minutes later. As with regular notes, restrict these to one idea per card. Even though there won't be an outside source listed in the upper left-hand corner, take the extra precaution of putting your initials there, or of putting double square brackets around the note, or both, so that you can't possibly later wonder where it came from. And, of course, put an appropriate slug in the upper right-hand corner.

76 Writing the Essay

When your research is complete and all the note cards you intend to use are in the desired order, you are ready to begin writing the essay. If your note-taking has been efficient—that is, if you have kept quotation to a minimum, assimilating and interpreting and evaluating as much as possible as you went along, and if you have included among the cards a sufficient number containing only your own ideas—then the essay may seem in some ways to write itself; you will need do little more than arrange material logically and compose necessary transitions as you move from card to card and follow your outline. (Of course the usual steps of revising and proofreading must follow the writing of the first draft, as described in chapter I; see #9m–o.)

76a Keeping Track of Notes in Your Drafts

As you write your first draft, proceeding from card to card, include in your text the information that will eventually become part of your documentation. That is, at the end of each quotation, paraphrase, summary, or direct reference, enclose in parentheses the last name of the author and the relevant page number or numbers—and also at least a short title if you are using more than one work by the same author. Similarly, if two or more authors have the same surname, you will also include the appropriate first name, or just an initial.

If you are using a system of parenthetical documentation, such as that of the MLA, which is the principal system illustrated in this text (see #79a), or that of the APA (see #81a), the final form of your notes will be the same as, or similar to, these parenthetical notes in your drafts.

If you are using the "number" method (see #81b), proceed in the same way until you prepare the final draft, at which point you will change each parenthetical reference to the appropriate number in the list of references. This number will appear in either parentheses or brackets, sometimes accompanied by a page number or date or author's name; and in some versions the number will be a superscript, like a footnote number.

If you are using the system of *The Chicago Manual of Style*, which calls for footnotes (or endnotes) and an alphabetized bibliographical list at the end (see #81c), do the same, converting to numbered footnotes or endnotes when you are preparing the final draft.

Research Tip

On Compiling Notes and Writing Drafts on a Computer

If you have access to a computer notepad, you may want to compile your bibliography and write your outline and notes by that method, though some writers with laptops still prefer to use index cards, both to have the actual physical objects in their hands and to steer away from the habit of cutting and pasting materials from various websites without ever engaging with the material in a critical way. You will find your computer especially helpful when drafting and revising your essay, since it will allow you to arrange and rearrange material easily. But do not rely on your computer to correct all of your spelling and grammatical errors. Further, writers do a better job of proofreading when they are looking at a hard copy of the essay rather than looking at the document on the screen. Remember to save files at frequent intervals, and when you rework material, always leave a back-up file on the hard drive. For example, when you revise a first draft, make sure to retain a copy of the original draft, just in case you aren't happy with the way the revision turns out; then you can retrieve the original and try again. And you will probably want to make back-up copies of everything on a separate disk as well, in case of virus, power failure, or printer problems.

77 Acknowledging Sources

The purpose of documentation is four-fold:

1. It demonstrates that you, the writer, are a genuine researcher who has done the considerable work of investigating authorities and experts in the field(s) assumed in your researchable question.
2. It acknowledges your indebtedness to particular sources.
3. It lends weight to your statements and arguments by citing experts and authorities to support them, and also demonstrates the extent of your investigation of a topic.
4. It enables an interested reader to pursue the subject further by consulting cited sources, or possibly to evaluate a particular source or to check the accuracy of a reference or quotation, should it appear questionable.

77a "Common Knowledge"

It is not necessary to provide documentation for facts or ideas or quotations that are well known, or "common knowledge"—such as the fact that Shakespeare wrote *Hamlet*, or that Hamlet said "To be or not to be," or that Sir Isaac Newton formulated the law of gravity, or that the story of Adam and Eve appears in the book of Genesis in the Bible, or that the moon is not made of green cheese. But if you are at all uncertain whether or not something is "common knowledge," play it safe: it is far better to over-document and appear a little naive than to under-document and engage in the unethical practice of plagiarism.

If a piece of information appears in three or more different sources, it qualifies as "common knowledge" and need not be documented. For example, such facts as the elevation of Mt. Logan, or the current population of the world, or the date of the execution of Louis Riel can be found in dozens of reference books. But it can be dangerous for a student, or any non-professional, to trust to such a guideline when dealing with other kinds of material. For example, there may be dozens of articles, websites, and books referring to or attempting to explain something like a neutrino, or the red shift, or black holes, or discoveries at the Olduvai Gorge, or Jungian readings of fairy tales, or the importance of the human genome project, or deep structure in linguistic theory, or the warnings about bio-terrorism, or neo-Platonic ideas in Renaissance poetry, or the nature and consequences of the great potato famine, or the origin of the name *Canada*; nevertheless, it is unlikely that a relatively non-expert writer will be sufficiently conversant with such material to recognize and accept it as "common knowledge." If something is new to you, and if you have not thoroughly explored the available literature on the subject, it is best to acknowledge a source. And when in doubt, check with your instructor.

When the question of "common knowledge" arises, ask yourself: *common to whom?* Your readers will probably welcome the explicit documentation of something that they themselves do not realize is, to a few experts, "common knowledge." Besides, if at any point in your presentation you give your readers cause to question your data, you will have lost their confidence. So be scrupulous: document anything about which you have the least doubt.

78 Quotation, Paraphrase, Summary, and Plagiarism

Quotation must be exact. A well-documented **paraphrase**, on the other hand, reproduces the content of the original, but in different words. Paraphrase is a second useful technique because it enables writers to make use of source material while still using their own words and thus to avoid too much direct quotation. But a paraphrase, to be legitimate, should give clear credit *at its beginning* to the source and should not use significant words and phrases from an original without enclosing them in quotation marks. In other words, begin your paraphrase by identifying your source (for example, "Biographer John English suggests . . ." or "John English, Pierre Trudeau's biographer, argues . . ."). End the paraphrase with an in-text parenthetical reference indicating the page number(s) for the material you have presented. A paraphrase will usually be a little shorter than the original, but it need not be. A **summary**, however, is by definition a condensation, a boiled-down version in one's own words that expresses the principal points of an original source. It is often the best evidence of a writer's effective synthesis of secondary source material.

78

Direct quotation must be documented: a reader of a passage in quotation marks will expect to be told who and what is being quoted. But some writers make the serious mistake of thinking that only direct quotations need to be documented; on the contrary, it is important to know and remember that *paraphrase and summary must also be fully documented*. Failure to document a paraphrase or summary is a breach of academic integrity known as **plagiarism**, a form of intellectual dishonesty for which there are serious academic penalties. To familiarize yourself with your institution's policies on academic integrity and on plagiarism, consult your institution's most recent academic calendar and other relevant sources and sites.

To illustrate the differences between a legitimate and illegitimate use of source material, here is a paragraph, a direct quotation, from Rupert Brooke's *Letters from America*, followed by

a. legitimate paraphrase
b. illegitimate paraphrase
c. combination paraphrase and quotation
d. summary, and
e. a comment on plagiarism

> Such is Toronto. A brisk city of getting on for half a million inhabitants, the largest British city in Canada (in spite of the cheery Italian faces that pop up at you out of excavations in

> the street), liberally endowed with millionaires, not lacking its due share of destitution, misery, and slums. It is no mushroom city of the West, it has its history; but at the same time it has grown immensely of recent years. It is situated on the shores of a lovely lake; but you never see that, because the railways have occupied the entire lake front. So if, at evening, you try to find your way to the edge of the water, you are checked by a region of smoke, sheds, trucks, wharves, storehouses, "depôts," railway-lines, signals, and locomotives and trains that wander on the tracks up and down and across streets, pushing their way through the pedestrians, and tolling, as they go, in the American fashion, an immense melancholy bell, intent, apparently, on some private and incommunicable grief. Higher up are the business quarters, a few sky-scrapers in the American style without the modern American beauty, but one of which advertises itself as the highest in the British Empire; streets that seem less narrow than Montreal [sic], but not unrespectably wide; "the buildings are generally substantial and often handsome" (the too kindly Herr Baedeker). Beyond that the residential part, with quiet streets, gardens open to the road, shady verandahs, and homes, generally of wood, that are a deal more pleasant to see than the houses in a modern English town. (Brooke 80–81)

The parenthetical reference for this block quotation begins one space after the final punctuation mark. It includes the author's surname and the page numbers on which the original appeared. The complete bibliographical entry for Brooke's work would appear in the list of "Works Cited" as follows (but double-spaced):

> Brooke, Rupert. Letters from America. London: Sidgwick and Jackson, 1916.

(For more information about handling quotations, see #54.)

78a Legitimate Paraphrase

> During his 1913 tour of the United States and Canada, Rupert Brooke sent back to England articles about his travels. In one of them, published in the 1916 book Letters from America, he describes Toronto as a large city, predominantly British, containing both wealth and poverty. He says that it is relatively old, compared to the upstart new cities further west, but that nevertheless it has expanded a great deal in the last little while. He implies that its beautiful setting is spoiled for its citizens by the railways, which have taken over all the land near the lake,

78a

> filling it with buildings and tracks and smell and noise. He also writes of the commercial part of the city, with its buildings which are tall (like American ones) but not very attractive (unlike American ones); one of them, he says, claims to be the tallest in the British Empire. (He pokes fun at Baedeker for being over-generous with his comments about the city's downtown architecture.) The streets he finds wider than those of Montreal, but not too wide. Finally, he compares Toronto's attractive residential areas favourably with those of English towns. (80–81)

This is legitimate paraphrase. Even though it uses several individual words from the original (*British*, *railways*, *tracks*, *American*, *British Empire*, *streets*, *residential*, *English town[s]*), they are a small part of the whole; more important, they are common words that would be difficult to replace with reasonable substitutes without distorting the sense. And, even more important, they are used in a way that is natural to the paraphraser's own style and context. For example, had the writer said "in the American style" or "the entire lake shore," the style (and words) would have been too much Brooke's. Paraphrase, however, does not consist in merely substituting one word for another, but rather in assimilating something and restating it in your own words and your own syntax.

The parenthetical reference contains only the page numbers, since the author is named in the text. Similarly, though it comes at the end of a long paragraph, it is clear because the paragraph begins by identifying its overall subject and because the writer has carefully kept Brooke's point of view apparent throughout by including him in each independent clause (a technique that also establishes good coherence): *Rupert Brooke*, *he describes*, *He says*, *He implies*, *He also writes*, *he says*, *He pokes fun*, *he finds*, *he compares*.

78b Illegitimate Paraphrase

An illegitimate paraphrase of Brooke's paragraph might begin like this:

> Brooke describes Toronto as a brisk kind of city with nearly half a million inhabitants, with some Italian faces popping up among the British, and with both millionaires and slums. He deplores the fact that the lake front on which it is situated has been entirely occupied by the railways, who have turned it into a region of smoke and storehouses and the like, and trains that wander back and forth, ringing their huge bells (80–81).

The parenthetical reference at paragraph's end does *not* protect such a treatment from the charge of plagiarism, for too many of the words and phrases and too much of the syntax are Brooke's own. The words and phrases we have underlined are all "illegitimate": a flavourful word like *brisk*; the intact phrases *half a million inhabitants* and *Italian faces popping up*, so little different from *pop up*; and so on. Changing *the railways have occupied the entire lakefront* to the passive *the lakefront . . . has been entirely occupied by the railways*, or *trains that wander up and down* to *trains that wander back and forth*, or *tolling . . . an immense . . . bell* to *ringing their huge bells*, does not make them the writer's: they still have the diction, syntax, and stylistic flavour of Brooke's original, and therefore constitute plagiarism.

Had the writer put quotation marks around "brisk," "Italian faces . . . pop[ping] up," "millionaires" and "slums," "lake front," "it is situated," "occupied," "a region of smoke," "trains that wander," and "bell[s]," the passage would, to be sure, no longer be plagiarism—but it would still be illegitimate, or at least very poor, paraphrase, for if so substantial a part is to be left in Brooke's own words and syntax, the whole might as well have been quoted directly: the writer would have done little more than lightly "edit" the original.

78c Paraphrase and Quotation Mixed

A writer who felt that a pure paraphrase was too flat and abstract, who felt that some of Brooke's more striking words and phrases should be retained, might choose to mix some direct quotation into a paraphrase:

> In Letters from America, Rupert Brooke characterizes Toronto as a "brisk," largely British city having the usual urban mixture of wealth and poverty. Unlike the "mushroom" cities farther west, he says, Toronto has a history, though he points out that much of its growth has been recent. He notes, somewhat cynically, that the people are cut off from the beauty of the lake by the railways and all their "smoke, sheds, trucks, wharves, storehouses, 'depôts,' railway lines, signals, and locomotives and trains" going ding-ding all over the place (80–81).

78d

This time the context is very much the writer's own, but some of the flavour of Brooke's original has been retained through the direct quotation of a couple of judiciously chosen words and the cumulative list quoted at the end. The writer is clearly in control of the material, as the writer of the preceding example was not. Here again, Brooke's name is excluded from the parenthetical reference because Brooke is named in the attribution in the first sentence of the paragraph. (See also #78f below.)

78d Summary

The purpose of a summary is to substantially reduce the original, conveying its essential meaning in a sentence or two. A summary of Brooke's passage might go something like this:

> Brooke describes Toronto as large and mainly wealthy, aesthetically marred by the railway yards along the lake, with wide enough streets and tall but (in spite of Baedeker's half-hearted approval) generally unprepossessing buildings, and a residential area more attractive than comparable English ones (80–81).

It is appropriate and usually preferable to refer to an author by name in your text—and the first time by full name, as in versions (a) and (c). If for some reason you do not want to bring the author's name into your text (for example if you were surveying a variety of opinions about Toronto and did not want to clutter your text with all their authors' names), then your text might read in part like this, with the author's surname tucked away in the parenthetical reference:

> Toronto was once described as "brisk," large, and encumbered with railways and tall but ugly buildings (Brooke 80–81).

78e Plagiarism

Had one of the foregoing versions of the passage not mentioned Brooke, nor included quotation marks, nor ended with documentation, it would have been plagiarism. A student doing research is part of a community of scholars (professors, investigators, instructors, other students, and researchers), all of whom are governed by the codes of academic honesty that identify plagiarism—whether intentional or accidental—as a serious offence against academic integrity. Your college or university calendar will no doubt include a detailed definition of plagiarism and a statement of policy on the academic discipline (failing marks, suspension, a note on one's academic transcript) arising from a finding of plagiarism. You should review this information and discuss any questions or concerns you have about your research practices with your instructors and academic advisers.

When you are working on a research project, keep in mind that you are ethically bound to give credit twice—*in the text* of the written document and *in the works cited list*—to all sources of information you have used (both print-based and electronic). All of the following kinds of material require acknowledgement whether they are drawn from print sources or from the Internet:

- direct quotations—whether short or long
- your summaries and paraphrases of sources
- ideas, theories, inspirations drawn from a source and expressed in your own words
- statistical data compiled by institutions (for example, think tanks and governmental or non-governmental organizations) and other researchers
- ideas and original findings drawn from course lectures and seminars
- graphic materials (diagrams, charts, photographs, illustrations, slides, film and television clips, audio recordings, video recordings, CD-ROMs, and DVDs)

Note that giving credit for this kind of material does not at all diminish your own work: it enhances the credibility of your claims and demonstrates just how much genuine research you have done on your project. It shows you adding your voice and your views to those of the community of scholars and researchers of which you are a part.

One final note. It is possible to commit self-plagiarism. This happens when a writer submits the same work—in whole or in part—for two different courses or assignments. If you are working in the same subject or topic area for two different courses or assignments, it is essential to discuss the ethical issues involved with both instructors to whom the work will be submitted.

See ***ack*** and ***doc*** in Appendix 2.

78f Altering Quotations to Fit Context

When you include quoted material within one of your own sentences, you may well have to alter it in one way or another to incorporate it smoothly. That is, you may have to change the grammar, syntax, or punctuation of a quotation to make it conform to the grammar and syntax of your own sentence. Note how the writers have altered the quoted material in the following examples. (See also #54j.)

The original quotation (from Mary Shelley's *Frankenstein; or, The Modern Prometheus*):

> I am by birth a Genevese; and my family is one of the most distinguished of that republic. My ancestors had been for many years counsellors and syndics; and my father had filled several public situations with honour and reputation. He was respected by all who knew him for his integrity and indefatigable attention to public business. He passed his younger days perpetually occupied by the affairs of his country; a variety of circumstances had prevented his marrying early, nor was it until the decline of life that he became a husband and the father of a family.

(a) altered for pronoun reference:

> Victor Frankenstein begins his story by stating that "[he is] by birth a Genevese; and [his] family is one of the most distinguished of that republic" (Shelley 31).

The first-person pronouns have been changed to third person in order to fit the third-person point of view in the sentence as a whole. The changed pronouns and the accompanying verb (*is* for *am*) appear in square brackets. (The opening *he is* could have been left outside the quotation, but the writer preferred to incorporate the parallelism within the quotation.)

(b) altered for consistent verb tense:

> As we first encounter him in the description at the beginning of his son's narrative, Victor's father is a man "respected by all who [know] him for his integrity and indefatigable attention to public business" (Shelley 31).

The verb in square brackets has been changed from past to present tense to conform with the tense established by the *is* of the student's sentence.

(c) altered for punctuation:

> The first words of Victor Frankenstein's narrative—"I am by birth a Genevese" (Shelley 31)—reveal a narrator preoccupied with himself, his birth, and his nationality.

The semicolon of the original has been dropped to avoid its clashing with the enclosing dashes of the student's own sentence.

(d) selective quotation:

> The first paragraph of Victor's narrative focuses more on Victor's father than on any other member of the Frankenstein family. Victor takes pains to describe him as a man of "honour and reputation . . . respected by all who [know] him for his integrity and indefatigable attention to public business" and "perpetually occupied by the affairs of his country" (Shelley 31). A first-time reader of the novel might well be forgiven for assuming that Victor's narrative will be more a tribute to his father than an account of his own creation of a monster.

Here, the student writer has selected key words and phrases from the opening paragraph of Victor Frankenstein's narrative in order to make a point about the novel's focus. The ellipsis indicates that material has been omitted in the interests of the student's own sentence structure.

78f

Exercise 78 Paraphrasing and summarizing

Here are two more paragraphs from Rupert Brooke's *Letters from America*. For each, write (a) a paraphrase, (b) a paraphrase with some quotation mixed in, and (c) a summary. Include an effective lead-in (attribution) for the material and a parenthetical reference in the MLA style for each piece you write.

(1) Ottawa came as a relief after Montreal. There is no such sense of strain and tightness in the atmosphere. The British, if not greatly in the majority, are in the ascendancy; also, the city seems conscious of other than financial standards, and quietly, with dignity, aware of her own purpose. The Canadians, like the Americans, chose to have for their capital a city which did not lead in population or wealth. This is particularly fortunate in Canada, an extremely individualistic country, whose inhabitants are only just beginning to be faintly conscious of their nationality. Here, at least, Canada is more than the Canadian. A man desiring to praise Ottawa would begin to do so without statistics of wealth and growth of population; and this can be said of no other city in Canada except Quebec. Not that there are not immense lumber-mills and the rest in Ottawa. But the Government farm, and the Parliament buildings, are more important.

Exercise 78 Paraphrasing and summarizing – *continued*

Also, although the "spoils" system obtains a good deal in this country, the nucleus of the Civil Service is much the same as in England; so there is an atmosphere of Civil Servants about Ottawa, an atmosphere of safeness and honour and massive buildings and well-shaded walks. After all, there is in the qualities of Civility and Service much beauty, of a kind which would adorn Canada. (54–55)

(2) Winnipeg is the West. It is important and obvious that in Canada there are two or three (some say five) distinct Canadas. Even if you lump the French and English together as one community in the East, there remains the gulf of the Great Lakes. The difference between East and West is possibly no greater than that between North and South England, or Bavaria and Prussia; but in this country, yet unconscious of itself, there is so much less to hold them together. The character of the land and the people differs; their interests, as it appears to them, are not the same. Winnipeg is a new city. In the archives at Ottawa is a picture of Winnipeg in 1870—Mainstreet, with a few shacks, and the prairie either end. Now her population is a hundred thousand, and she has the biggest this, that, and the other west of Toronto. A new city; a little more American than the other Canadian cities, but not unpleasantly so. The streets are wider, and full of a bustle which keeps clear of hustle. The people have something of the free swing of Americans, without the bumptiousness; a tempered democracy, a mitigated independence of bearing. The manners of Winnipeg, of the West, impress the stranger as better than those of the East, more friendly, more hearty, more certain to achieve graciousness, if not grace. There is, even, in the architecture of Winnipeg, a sort of *gauche* pride visible. It is hideous, of course, even more hideous than Toronto or Montreal; but cheerily and windily so. There is no scheme in the city, and no beauty, but it is at least preferable to Birmingham, less dingy, less directly depressing. It has no real slums, even though there is poverty and destitution. (102–03)

79

79 Documentation

In order to be effective, documentation must be complete, accurate, and clear. Completeness and accuracy depend on careful recording of necessary information as you do your research and take notes. Clarity depends on the way you present that information to your reader. You will be clear only if your audience can follow your method of documentation. Therefore, it is important that before you begin any research project, you investigate the method of documentation you need to use. There are four main methods:

1. The *name–page* method, currently recommended by the Modern Language Association (**MLA**), and in wide use in the humanities (see #79a, and also #80, the sample research paper);
2. the *name–date* method, recommended by the American Psychological Association (**APA**), and used in some of the social and other sciences as well as in education studies (see #81a, and its sample research paper);
3. the *number* method, used mainly in some of the sciences (see #81b); and
4. the *note* method, recommended by the MLA until 1984, and still preferred in some disciplines and by some individual writers and instructors (see #81c).

Which method you choose will depend on what discipline (field of study) you are writing in and on the wishes of the audience for whom you are writing. But you should familiarize yourself with all of them, or at least with those you will most often find in your textbooks and in your research for various courses.

In the examples and advice that follow, we place the greatest emphasis on the MLA's name–page method because it is the one you are most likely to encounter in your courses in the humanities. However, in #81a–c we provide descriptions and examples of the APA's name–date method, the number method, and the note method.

79a

79a The Name–Page Method (MLA Style)

The name–page method is detailed in the sixth edition of the *MLA Handbook for Writers of Research Papers* (2003). The virtues of this method of citation over the former note method are obvious: simplicity and efficiency. No footnotes or endnotes are needed. Using this method, you provide a short, usually **parenthetical** or **in-text reference** to each source as you use it in the body of your paper. Then, you provide complete bibliographical information about all the electronic and non-electronic sources you have used at the end of the essay, in a list titled "Works Cited," alphabetized by surnames of authors or editors (or title, when no author is named).

The pages that follow illustrate examples of the most common patterns of MLA documentation: each in-text parenthetical reference is accompanied by its works-cited entry. (See also the examples in #78a–d, and the sample research paper, #80.) Note that parenthetical references are usually placed at the end of the sentence in which the citation occurs; but if a sentence is necessarily long and complicated, a reference may be placed earlier, immediately after the citation itself.

Note also that in an actual paper, the examples that follow would be **double-spaced** rather than single-spaced.

Print Sources

A book by one author (or editor)

IN-TEXT REFERENCE

> The reaction in China to the end of World War I has been described by one historian as "popular rejoicing"—particularly among young people, who had "an uncritical admiration for Western democracy, Western liberal ideals, and Western learning" (MacMillan 322).

Note that when you don't mention the author by name in your actual sentence, the parenthetical reference includes the author's surname and a page reference, with *no intervening punctuation*, and that the page number is not preceded by the abbreviation "p." The closing period follows the parenthesis. If you can include the author's name and credentials in your text, however, the parenthetical reference will be shorter, the context of the quotation clearer, and the credibility of the point stronger:

> The reaction in China to the end of World War I has been described by historian Margaret MacMillan as "popular rejoicing"—particularly among young people, who had "an uncritical admiration for Western democracy, Western liberal ideals, and Western learning" (322).

WORKS-CITED REFERENCE

79a

> MacMillan, Margaret. Paris 1919: Six Months That Changed the World. New York: Random, 2001.

The works-cited reference for a book includes

- the author's name (surname, followed by a comma, and the full first name, followed by a period);
- the full title of the book (underlined) followed by a period that is *not* underlined; and
- the publication information—city of publication: short name of the publisher (words like "Company," "Inc.," "Ltd.," etc. are omitted, and a publisher's name can be reduced to a single name or word such as "McClelland"), and the year of publication—followed by a period. So punctuation here is city: publisher, year.

A book by two authors (or editors)

IN-TEXT REFERENCE

> The book's introduction argues that "schools have tended to represent and reproduce the interests of dominant classes" (Barman and Gleason 9).

WORKS-CITED REFERENCE

> Barman, Jean and Mona Gleason, eds. Children, Teachers and Schools in the History of British Columbia. 2nd ed. Calgary: Detselig, 2003.

When you have more than one author or editor in a works-cited entry, the names following the first name appear in first-name–last-name order. When a works-cited entry exceeds one line, the second and subsequent lines are indented by one tab (roughly five spaces) from the left margin.

A book by three authors (or editors)

IN-TEXT REFERENCE

> The essays in This Elusive Land are, according to the editors, "meant to identify how gender has contributed to experiences of the land" (Hessing, Raglon, and Sandilands xix).

WORKS-CITED REFERENCE

> Hessing, Melody, Rebecca Raglon, and Catriona Sandilands, eds. This Elusive Land: Women and the Canadian Environment. Vancouver: UBC Press, 2005.

A book by more than three authors (or editors)

79a

IN-TEXT REFERENCE

> The articles in Pacific Encounters: The Production of Self and Other are ordered neither chronologically nor geographically, a deliberate strategy on the part of the editors (Kröller et al. 11).

In the parenthetical reference, supply the name of the author or editor whose name appears first on the title page of the work, followed by the Latin abbreviation *et al.* (for Latin *et alii*, "and others").

WORKS-CITED REFERENCE

> Kröller, Eva-Marie, et al., eds. Pacific Encounters: The Production of Self and Others. Vancouver: Institute of Asian Research UBC, 1997.

The abbreviation "eds." indicates that the names listed are those of the book's editors. The abbreviation "ed." is used following the name of a single editor.

Two or more works by the same author

IN-TEXT REFERENCE

If you cite two different works by a single author in your writing, the in-text references must include title information to distinguish the two works.

Note that the pattern calls for the author's surname and then a comma, followed by the distinctive word or phrase from the title and then the page number. There is no comma between the title word and the page number. While it is preferable to include all of the required information, the "n. pag." notation can be used when the referenced page is not numbered.

> Both novels—Stanley Park and Story House—begin with searching looks into the past. Stanley Park's "Author's Note" recalls "January of 1953 [and] the skeletal remains of two children . . . found in Stanley Park" (Taylor, Stanley n.pag.). Story House begins with the cryptic chapter title, "17 Years Before the Beginning" (Taylor, Story 3).

WORKS-CITED REFERENCE

The two works by Taylor would be listed alphabetically according to the titles. In this case, the title beginning with "Sta" would precede the title beginning with "Sto."

> Taylor, Timothy. Stanley Park. Toronto: Knopf, 2001.
>
> ———. Story House. Toronto: Knopf, 2006.

Note that the second entry does not repeat the author's name but rather marks it with three consecutive hyphens followed by a period.

79a

A work by a government agency or a corporate author

A government agency is one of the many branches or departments of government at the international, federal, provincial, or municipal level. A corporate author is a group, association, or institute of authors who are not named individually on the title page of a work.

IN-TEXT REFERENCE

> A ninety-two-page report published in 2002 offers the views of individual Canadians on our national strategies for innovation in the decade ahead (Government of Canada).

Here, there is no page number because the reference is to the report as a whole.

WORKS-CITED REFERENCE

> Government of Canada. Canada's Innovation Strategy: Canadians Speak on Innovation and Learning. Ottawa: Government of Canada, 2002.

A work by an anonymous author

IN-TEXT REFERENCE

> When a magician dies, his or her friends and colleagues gather for a service known as "the broken-wand ceremony" ("Mere" 43).

This anonymous essay, entitled "Mere Stick," appeared in *The New Yorker* magazine in August 1993. A short version of the title moves into the position usually occupied by the author's surname in the parenthetical reference; there is no punctuation between it and the page number. In the list of works cited, such items are alphabetized by title.

WORKS-CITED REFERENCE

> "Mere Stick." The New Yorker 23–30 Aug. 1993: 43–44.

An anonymous article in a reference book

IN-TEXT REFERENCE

> One of the most distinctive sights to be seen off the shores of Pacific Rim National Park Reserve is that of the grey whales "migrat[ing] past the park on their travels between Baja California and the Bering Sea" ("Pacific" 525).

WORKS-CITED REFERENCE

> "Pacific Rim National Park Reserve." Encyclopedia of British Columbia. Ed. Daniel Francis. Madeira Park, BC: Harbour Publishing, 2000. 525.

Because Madeira Park, the place of publication, is not widely known, the works-cited entry includes "BC" (for British Columbia) to provide a fuller geographical marker. When including a province or state in the place of publication, two-letter postal abbreviations are used (e.g. AB for Alberta, SK for Saskatchewan, ME for Maine). The page number for the article follows the period that follows the year of publication.

A multivolume work

IN-TEXT REFERENCE

> In an entry dated 3 August 1908, she described her second book as "not nearly so good as Green Gables" (Montgomery 1: 338).

When you cite one volume from a work of two or more volumes, include the volume number in the parenthetical reference, followed by a colon and a space, and then the page number:

WORKS-CITED REFERENCE

> Montgomery, Lucy Maud. The Selected Journals of L.M. Montgomery. 5 vols. Eds. Mary Rubio and Elizabeth Waterston. Toronto: Oxford UP, 1985–2004.

The "UP" in the publication information is an abbreviation for "University Press." The year "1985–2004" indicates that the first volume of the journals was produced in 1985 and the last volume in 2004.

Quotation at second hand

IN-TEXT REFERENCE

Try as often as possible to quote from primary sources. If you quote from a secondary source, be careful to identify it and to give a full context (date, name of the speaker, identity of the audience, circumstances of the utterance) for the words you quote. Similarly, if the source of a quotation is not supplied or quite difficult to access, you may well have to rely on the secondary source:

> In 1753, Samuel Strickland, brother of Catharine Parr Traill, wrote these words of advice to new immigrants to Upper Canada: "I do not know any thing that gives a greater comfort to a farm, than a well-loaded orchard" (qtd. in Martin 49).

79a

WORKS-CITED REFERENCE

> Martin, Carol. A History of Canadian Gardening. Toronto: McArthur, 2000.

A work of literature

Many major works of pre-contemporary literature—fictional and non-fictional prose, plays, poems—have been published in several different editions. To enable readers to locate quotations in any edition they may have access to, parenthetical references to such works should include or consist of clear indications of text divisions other than the page numbers of the particular edition you happen to be using. If you begin with a page number, follow it with a semicolon and then add the other information, using clear abbreviations. Some examples:

(a) PROSE WORKS

IN-TEXT REFERENCE

> Jane Austen presents readers of Pride and Prejudice with the heroine's father, the likable Mr. Bennet, an "odd . . . mixture of quick parts, sarcastic humour, reserve, and caprice" (3; vol. 1, ch. 1); only much later do we learn that these in part contribute to his serious shortcomings as a father.

WORKS-CITED REFERENCE

> Austen, Jane. Pride and Prejudice. 1813. Oxford: Oxford UP, 1970.

(The year "1813" is listed here to indicate the year of the work's first publication.)

(b) A PLAY IN PROSE

IN-TEXT REFERENCE

> In Chekhov's The Cherry Orchard, Trofimov says to Anya, "The whole of Russia is our orchard" (59; act 2).

79a

WORKS-CITED REFERENCE

> Chekhov, Anton. Three Plays: The Cherry Orchard, Three Sisters, Ivanov. Trans. Elisaveta Fen. London: Penguin, 1951.

(c) A PLAY IN VERSE (see also #61f)

IN-TEXT REFERENCE

> The final act of As You Like It includes a memorable discussion about what it means to love. Silvius answers this question with these words:
>
> It is to be all made of fantasy,
> All made of passion, and all made of wishes,
> All adoration, duty, and observance,
> All humbleness, all patience and impatience,
> All purity, all trial, all obedience[.] (5.2.89–94)

With verse plays, you need not include page numbers at all, since act, scene, and line numbers clearly locate the citation.

WORKS-CITED REFERENCE

Shakespeare, William. As You Like It. Ed. Roma Gill. Oxford: Oxford UP, 2002.

(d) A POEM

IN-TEXT REFERENCE

> The most striking simile in Roo Borson's "Green World" occurs in these lines: "I'm like a toy that lies all day, / bad-tempered in the grass, and then the next morning / is found there, unrepentant, covered in dew" (lines 13–15).

The line number tells a reader precisely where in the work the quotation comes from; no page number is needed. Since the abbreviations *l.* and *ll.* could be confused with numerals, spell out *line* and *lines*. Subsequent references to the same poem need not include the words *line* or *lines*; the number will be enough.

WORKS-CITED REFERENCE

Borson, Roo. "Green World." Short Journey Upriver Toward Oishida. Toronto: McClelland, 2004. 64–66.

(e) A LONG POEM WITH DIVISIONS

79a

IN-TEXT REFERENCE

> Those who find Satan heroic are overlooking Milton's flat statements, for example that the Father of Lies is "in pain, / Vaunting aloud, but racked with deep despair," and that his "words . . . bore / Semblance of worth, not substance" (1.125–26, 528–29).

The second set of line numbers is separated from the first by a comma. Again, no page numbers are needed. When citing a range of numbers in references to lines or pages, list all digits for second numbers up to 99 (for example, *lines 5–88*; *pages 97–99*). When citing second numbers above 99, list only the last two digits unless more are necessary to prevent confusion (for example, *lines 108–22* for a range from 108 to 122, but *pages 385–485* for a range from 385 to 485.) Note the need for a space before and after the slash mark indicating a line break in the verse.

WORKS-CITED REFERENCE

Milton, John. Paradise Lost. Ed. Scott Elledge. New York: Norton, 1993.

(f) THE BIBLE

IN-TEXT REFERENCE

> In the biblical account of the Flood, Noah is presented as a dutiful servant of God, "a just man and perfect in his generations" (Gen. 6.9).

A standard abbreviation of the book is followed by a space, the chapter number, a period, and the number of the verse or verses being cited.

WORKS-CITED REFERENCE

> The Holy Bible. King James version. Nashville: Nelson, 1984.

Citing more than one source

IN-TEXT REFERENCE

If you wish to cite more than one source in a single parenthetical reference, simply write each in the usual way and separate items with a semicolon:

> The First World War left Canadians "a deeply divided people who had inherited a staggering debt," but it has also been said to have "mark[ed] the real birth of Canada" (Morton 226; Gwyn xxi).

WORKS-CITED REFERENCES

> Morton, Desmond. "First World War." The Oxford Companion to Canadian History. Ed. Gerald Hallowell. Toronto: Oxford UP, 2004. 226.

> Gwyn, Sandra. Tapestry of War: A Private View of Canadians in the Great War. Toronto: HarperCollins, 1993.

Using notes as well as parenthetical references

If circumstances demand, you may also use an occasional note along with the name–page method. For example, if you think that a reference requires some comment or explanation, make it an endnote rather than an obtrusive parenthetical reference. But keep such notes to a minimum; if you cannot comfortably include such discursive comments in your text, it may be that they aren't relevant after all. Try to limit such notes to (a) those commenting in some useful way on specific sources, such as a "See," "See for example," or "See also" note, and (b) those listing three or more sources, which might be unwieldy as a parenthetical reference.

In the text, insert a superscript numeral where you want to signal the note (usually at the end of a sentence). Begin the note by indenting five spaces, followed by a superscript numeral corresponding with the one in the text, then another space, and then the note. The most recent edition of *The MLA Handbook for Writers of Research Papers* recommends the use of endnotes over footnotes in such circumstances as we have just described. If you do use a footnote, put it at the bottom of the page, four lines below your text; the text of the note should be single-spaced, but double space between notes. If a note carries over to a second page, type a line across the page two spaces below the text and continue the note two spaces below the line. If you use endnotes, put them on a separate page with the heading *Notes*, following the text and before the list of works cited; they should be double-spaced.

Here are some examples of in-text references and corresponding works-cited listings for other kinds of print sources:

An essay in an edited collection of essays by various authors

IN-TEXT REFERENCE

> In "Resonant Lives: The Dramatic Self-Portraiture of Vincent and Emily," Anne Nothof examines plays that explore the life of the artist as "an imaginative expression of a series of possibilities" (149).

79a

WORKS-CITED REFERENCE

> Nothof, Anne. "Resonant Lives: The Dramatic Self-Portraiture of Vincent and Emily." Theatre and Autobiography: Writing and Performing Lives in Theory and Practice. Ed. Sherrill Grace and Jerry Wasserman. Vancouver: Talon, 2006. 137–51.

An article in a journal with continuous pagination throughout a volume

IN-TEXT REFERENCE

> That Canadians have increasingly sought out post-secondary education is supported by statistics such as these:
>
> > University enrollments increased gradually, doubling from 1920 to 1945, and then experienced explosive growth from 1960 to 1980 such that more than twenty times as many Canadians would receive a degree in 1990 as their grandparents had in 1920. (Harrigan 811)

WORKS-CITED REFERENCE

> Harrigan, Patrick. "The Schooling of Boys and Girls in Canada." Journal of Social History 23 (1990): 803–16.

Note that in the bibliographical entry the title of the journal is followed by a single space, then the volume number, another space, the year of publication in parentheses, a colon, another space, and the inclusive page numbers for the article. End the entry with a period. Do not include the issue number, the month, or the season of the issue.

An article in a journal with separate pagination for each issue

IN-TEXT REFERENCE

> Herb Wyile begins his article on The Colony of Unrequited Dreams with a brisk, engaging description of the debate between Rex Murphy and Wayne Johnston over the novel's fictional portrayal of the first premier of a Canadian Newfoundland, Joey Smallwood (69–70).

WORKS-CITED REFERENCE

> Wyile, Herb. "History versus Geography in Wayne Johnston's The Colony of Unrequited Dreams." Canadian Literature 189 (2006): 69–83.

This particular journal uses only issue numbers. Were there a volume number as well, the issue number would follow it in the entry. For example, 19.2 would mean that the article appeared in the second issue of volume 19.

An editorial

IN-TEXT REFERENCE

> "This attempt at an overt ideological makeover of the bench is unprecedented in the 25-year history of the Canadian Charter of Rights and Freedoms" ("As Charter" A18).

WORKS-CITED REFERENCE

> "As Charter turns 25, Harper tilts at judges." Editorial. The Globe and Mail 17 Feb. 2007: A18.

Newspaper editorials are not ordinarily attributed to a particular writer or editor. Without an author, the title moves into the author position and is used in short form in the parenthetical in-text reference and in full form in the works-cited entry.

A review

IN-TEXT REFERENCE

> The reviewer observes that "until recently theorists have been relatively silent about the ethical implications of telling the stories of our selves and/or others" (McNeill 159).

WORKS-CITED REFERENCE

> McNeill, Laurie. "Moral of the Life Story." Rev. of The Ethics of Life Writing, by Paul John Eakin. Canadian Literature 188 (2006): 159–161.

A newspaper article

IN-TEXT REFERENCE

> Devyani Saltzman evokes a vivid image in her opening comments on the holy rivers of India: "Frigid and tumultuous, the white water of the Ganges sped past a rocky bank where family friends had set up a bonfire and chairs overlooking the river" (T1).

WORKS-CITED REFERENCE

> Saltzman, Devyani. "At the water's edge." The Globe and Mail 17 Feb. 2007: T1+.

In this example, the page number T1+ indicates that the article begins on page 1 of section T of the newspaper and then continues not on page 2 but later in the section.

Interviews

This category includes interviews published in newspapers, magazines, books; interviews broadcast on radio or television; and interviews conducted by researchers themselves. In your text, include a parenthetical reference for a published interview; for a broadcast or for an interview you conduct for your own research include the necessary information, but without page numbers. In the works-cited entry, include the identification "Interview" for a published or broadcast interview, and "Personal interview," "Telephone interview," or "E-mail interview" for one you conducted yourself.

(a) A PUBLISHED INTERVIEW

IN-TEXT REFERENCE

In an interview with Susan Fisher, Frances Itani recalls the origins of her novel Deafening in a 1996 visit she made to the Ontario School for the Deaf, where her grandmother had once lived as a resident (40–41).

WORKS-CITED REFERENCE

Itani, Frances. "Hear, Overhear, Observe, Remember: A Dialogue with Frances Itani." Canadian Literature 183 (2004): 40–56.

(b) A BROADCAST INTERVIEW

IN-TEXT REFERENCE

In a recent CBC interview about her newly published book, journalist Chantal Hébert suggested that the federal Liberal and New Democratic parties will need to merge as the Conservative and Reform parties did several years ago.

WORKS-CITED REFERENCE

Hébert, Chantal. Interview. Mansbridge One on One. CBC Newsworld. Toronto. 3 March 2007.

(c) YOUR OWN RESEARCH INTERVIEW

IN-TEXT REFERENCE

Professor Joseph Atkinson reported that ideas of innovation in the teaching of science in British universities are a relatively new concern among his colleagues.

WORKS-CITED REFERENCE

Atkinson, Joseph. E-mail interview. 12 June 2003.

Here are some examples of works-cited entries for a few other kinds of print and non-print sources:

A book in translation

Tremblay, Michel. Birth of a Bookworm. Trans. Sheila Fischman. Vancouver: Talon, 2003.

A lecture

Greenstock, Jeremy. "Globalization or Polarization: Where Is the World Heading?" Vancouver Institute Lecture. University of British Columbia. 24 Feb. 2007.

A television program

"A Simple Game." Hockey: A People's History, Episode 1. CBC. 17 Sept. 2006.

A sound recording

Gaiman, Neil. Coraline. Read by Neil Gaiman. Harper Children's Audio, 2002.

Crossley-Holland, Kevin. Gatty's Tale. Read by Claudia Renton. Orion Audiobooks, 2006.

Young, Neil. "Falling Off the Face of the Earth." By Neil Young. Prairie Wind. Warner, 2005.

If a recording is a CD, that information need not be included; if it is an audiocassette, that information must be included.

A film

Begin with the underlined title (unless you are emphasizing a particular contributor, such as the writer or director, or a performer), followed by the director, the distributor, and the date:

Water. Dir. Deepa Mehta. Mongrel Media, 2006.

You may wish to include other information as well—whatever you think relevant to your use of the item; for example:

Mehta, Deepa, writ. and dir. Water. Perf. Seema Biswas. Mongrel Media, 2006.

A videocassette

Atwood and Family. Dir. Michael Rubbo. Videocassette. National Film Board of Canada, 1995.

Like the preceding entry, this one begins with the underlined title (unless you are emphasizing a particular contributor, such as the writer or director, or a performer), followed by the director, the format (videocassette), the distributor, and the date.

A painting

Hughes, E.J. Trees, Savary Island 1953. Museum of Fine Arts, Montreal.

If you are working from a published photograph rather than from a visit to Montreal's Museum of Fine Arts to see the painting, include the necessary data to indicate the print source in which you have studied the work.

Hughes, E.J. Trees, Savary Island 1953. E.J.Hughes. By Ian Thom. Vancouver: Douglas & McIntyre and the Vancouver Art Gallery, 2002. 117.

Electronic Sources

IN-TEXT REFERENCE

The in-text reference patterns for electronic sources follow those for print sources. Include the last name of the author and, if it is available, the number of the page in the electronic document. If the document is not paginated, include the paragraph number(s) from which you are quoting, and use "par."—the abbreviation listed in the current edition of the *MLA Handbook.* If neither page nor paragraph is available, use "n. pag."—the abbreviation for "no pagination." If the document you are referring to does not have an author, then the in-text reference would begin with a key word from the title of the document.

WORKS-CITED REFERENCE

An entire Internet site

Arts and Letters Daily. Ed. Dennis Dutton. 2007. 8 Jan. 2007 <http://www.aldaily.com>.

First, give the title of the site (underlined), followed by a period. Next, name the editor of the site followed by a period. Then comes the year of the site followed by a period. Next comes the specific date of your access to the site (this is important because the contents of a site are frequently updated, and so you need to indicate at what point you made your visit). Then, without intervening punctuation, cite the URL—the address—of the website enclosed within angled brackets < >. Follow the bracketed URL with a period.

A home page for a course

Baxter, Gisele M. English 468A/005: Children's Literature. Course home page. Sept.–Dec. 2006. Dept. of English, U of British Columbia. 20 Feb. 2007 <http://faculty.arts.ubc.ca/gmbaxter/4682006htm>.

Titles here are not underlined. "Sept.–Dec. 2006" indicates when the course was offered. That information is followed by information about where the course was offered. The citation ends with the date the site was accessed and the URL.

An online book

Grant, Jeannette. Through Evangeline's Country. Boston, 1894. Early Canadiana Online. 2007. CIHM. 2 February 2007 <http://www.canadiana.org>.

This book on the expulsion of the Acadians from Nova Scotia was originally published in Boston in 1894. CIHM is the acronym for the Canadian Institute for Historical Reproductions, which maintains this website for publications from early Canada.

An online government publication

Health Canada. Children's Sleepwear: Flammability Requirement Guidelines. 17 May 2004. 13 January 2007. <http://www.hc-sc.gc.ca/cps-spc/pubs>.

This report was published in May 2004 and accessed in January 2007.

An online newspaper or magazine

"Hamas orders ban on folk tale book." Jerusalem Post Online 5 March 2007. 6 March 2007 <http://www.jpost.com/servlet/Satellite?cid=1171894576974&pagename=JPost%2FJPArticle%2FShowFull>.

The article from the *Jeruselem Post* lists no author, and so the title of the article moves into the author position. Note that there is no period following the title of the newspaper or the magazine.

Faught, Brad. "A History of the Exam." Maclean's Online. 13 Nov. 2006. 8 Jan. 2007 <http://www.macleans.ca/education/universities/article.jsp?content=20061113_136509_136509>.

This magazine piece was first posted in November 2006 and accessed in January 2007.

An online review

Lanchester, John. “Other People’s Capital.” Rev. of Conrad and Lady Black: Dancing on the Edge, by Tom Bower. London Review of Books 14 Dec. 2006. 29 Dec. 2006 <http://www.lrb.co.uk/v28/n24/lanc01_html>.

An article from a journal available online

Golovakha-Hicks, Inna. “Demonology in Contemporary Ukraine: Folklore or ‘Postfolklore’?” Journal of Folklore Research 43.3 (2006): 219–240. Project Muse. 15 Jan. 2007 <http://muse.jhu.edu/journals/journal_of_folklore_research/v043/43.3golovakha-hicks.pdf>

The journal in this case is part of an online database called Project Muse, and so that information is included in the entry.

Griffin, Andrew. “The Banality of History in *Troilus and Cressida*.” Early Modern Literary Studies 12.2 (2006): 4.1–12. 4 Jan. 2007 <http://purl.oclc.org/emls/12-2/grifbana.htm>.

The article is available in a journal that publishes exclusively online and is available independently.

An online dissertation abstract

Rae, Ian Thomas. “Unframing the Novel: From Ondaatje to Carson (Michael Ondaatje, Anne Carson, George Bowering, Joy Kogawa, Daphne Marlatt).” Diss. U of British Columbia, 2003. Digital Dissertations June 2003. 27 July 2003 <http://www.lib.umi.com/dissertations/fullcit/NQ75069>.

A posting to an online forum

Etherington, Sarah. “Which panelist made the best case?” Online posting. 27 Feb. 2007. CBC Radio Canada Reads Message Board. 28 Feb. 2007 <http://www.cbc.ca/canadareads/yoursay/2007/02/which_panelist_made_the_best_c.html#comments>.

79b Some Abbreviations Commonly Used in Documentation and Notes (see also #57g)

abr.	abridgement
adapt.	adapted by, adaptation
anon.	anonymous
arch.	archaic
attrib.	attributed to
bk.; bks.	book; books
c., ca.	(Latin *circa*) about, approximately (with dates: c. 1737)
CD-ROM	compact disc read-only memory
cf.	compare
ch.; chs.	chapter; chapters (also chap.; chaps.)
col.; cols.	column; columns
comp.	compiler, compiled by
dir.	director, directed by
diss.	dissertation
distr.	distributor
DVD	digital videodisc
ed.; eds.	editor, edited by, edition; editors, editions
e.g.	(Latin *exempli gratia*) for example
e-mail	electronic mail
esp.	especially
et al.	(Latin *et alii*) and others
etc.	(Latin *et cetera*) and so forth
ex.	example
f.; ff.	and the following page(s) or line(s)—e.g., pp. 21ff.
fig.; figs.	figure; figures
fwd.	foreword, foreword by
i.e.	(Latin *id est*) that is
illus.	illustrator, illustrated by, illustrations
introd.	introduction, introduced by
HTML	Hypertext Markup Language
KB	kilobyte
l.; ll.	line; lines (but see example (d) on p. 501)
ms.; mss.	manuscript; manuscripts
n.; nn.	note; notes (usually with page numbers: 37n.; p.73, nn.2–4; or without periods: 37n, 73nn2–4)
natl.	national
N.B., n.b.	(Latin *note bene*) note well, take notice
n.d.	no date of publication given
no.; nos.	number; numbers
n.p.	no place of publication given, no publisher

n. pag.	no pagination
n.s.	new series
OED	*Oxford English Dictionary*
op.	opus, work
P	Press (see UP)
p.; pp.	page; pages
par., pars.	paragraph, paragraphs
perf.	performed by, performer
pl.	plate; plural
pref.	preface, preface by
prod.	producer, produced by
pub., publ.	publisher, published by
qtd.	quoted
q.v.	(Latin *quod vide*) which see
rev.	revision, revised, revised by, review, reviewed by
rpt.	reprint, reprinted by
sec., sect.	section
ser.	series
sic	(Latin) appears thus in the source (see #54j)
st.; sts.	stanza; stanzas
supp.; supps.	supplement; supplements
trans.	translated by, translator
ts., tss.	typescript, typescripts
U, Univ.	University
UP	University Press
URL	uniform resource locator (i.e. web address)
v	(Latin *vide*) see
VHS	video home system
vol.; vols.	volume; volumes
vs. (v.)	versus (v. used in legal contexts)
writ.	written by, writer
www	World Wide Web

80 A Sample MLA Research Paper with Comments

This sample research paper conveniently illustrates many of the details discussed in the preceding pages. The combined essay and commentary will repay your close attention. Try reading the paper and then constructing from it an outline of its structure. Then write a one-page summary of the paper.

Title Page

Although the *MLA Handbook for Writers of Research Papers* does not call for a separate title page, many instructors will prefer that you use one. Such was the case in the course for which the following paper, "Into the Battle: Timothy Findley's Not Wanted on the Voyage," was written.

Into the Battle

Timothy Findley's

Not Wanted on the Voyage

Eric Tung

Professor Brown

English 302

Section 002

3 April 2004

Other arrangements are possible, of course, but the one Eric Tung used for his paper is fairly standard: the title and subtitle are centred about a third or a fourth of the way down the page; the author's name, also centred, follows several lines lower; and the course, instructor, and date (each centred) come nearer the bottom of the page. Note the double spacing between the lines in each part.

If no title page is included, the information is grouped at the upper left of the first page, about 2.5 cm (1 inch) from the top (the surname plus page number, at upper right, should be 1.25 cm, or about half an inch, from the top):

Tung 1

Eric Tung

Professor Brown

English 302, Section 002

3 April 2004

Into the Battle: Timothy Findley's Not Wanted on the Voyage

[And the essay would begin here, double-spaced throughout.]

① Tung 1

② The last words written in Dr. Johnson's journal are these: "*Against despair.*" Nothing is harder . . . than staring down despair. But stare it down we must. (Findley, "My Final" 16)

③ **para. 1** When Timothy Findley first began work on the narrative that was to become Not Wanted on the Voyage, it was not a retelling of the biblical story of Noah's Ark at all (Findley, Inside 219). It was a tale about a man, a woman, their marriage, and a very old blind cat who was to become the unforgettable Mottyl of the book finally published in 1984. The man who later became Noah (*aka* Dr. Noyes) and the woman whom Findley later named Mrs. Noyes (and to whom he never did give a first name) and their long, complex, difficult marriage remain at the centre of the novel we read and study today. They invigorate a book that Findley wrote of in a "pep talk" to himself as based on a story everyone knows and so requiring the writer to
④ "tell . . . something new about its people and about the event" (Inside 222).

⑤ **para. 2** And so Findley tells the old story in a new way. He begins immediately with

80

"Against despair" (Not Wanted n.pag.). These—the last words Samuel Johnson is said to have written in his diary—become the first utterance of Findley's narrative. These two prophetic and disturbing words. Why does Findley include them? This is the question with which this paper begins. And my first answer is that the story of the old woman, the old man, and their centuries-long marriage is at the centre of this book of numerous battles against despair. Mrs. Noyes, while confronting her husband Noah, is the most prominent of the human and animal characters
⑥ battling against their own feelings of despair.

para. 3 Considered from a philosophical perspective, the battle between Dr. and Mrs. Noyes can be read in terms defined and described by Friedrich Hegel in his theory of the master and slave engaged in dialectical confrontation and caught up in a protracted—probably lifelong—struggle for what he calls recognition. What the novel investigates in the many scenes of combat between the patriarch Noah and
⑦ his spouse is what Lorraine York identified in her study of Findley's earlier fiction as "civilian conflict," for "polarity and conflict have always fascinated Findley as a writer" (336).

Comments on page 1 of "Into the Battle"

1. The first page following the title page is page 1 of the paper. In the upper right corner of this page the writer has set out an identifier or header. In MLA style, the header consists of the writer's family name, a space, and the number of the page. Headers run continuously from this first page up to and including the works cited page at the end.

2. The essay, which focuses in part on the significance of one of the epigraphs to Timothy Findley's novel *Not Wanted on the Voyage*, begins (appropriately) with an epigraph from a talk Findley gave in 1987. The address, entitled "My Final Hour," subsequently appeared in an issue of *Journal of Canadian Studies*. The opening epigraph to an essay should be formatted as a block quotation—doubly indented from the left margin and double-spaced. The final punctuation for a block quotation precedes the parenthetical reference. In this case, because the writer cites three different works by Findley in the paper, the parenthetical reference includes the author's last name followed by a comma, key words from the title (in quotation marks because the work is an article rather than a book), and the number of the page where the article can be found.

3. Sentence 1 of paragraph 1 summarizes in the student's own words a point Findley makes in excerpts from his journal, *Inside Memory: Pages from a Writer's Workbook*. The parenthetical reference cites the title in short form as *Inside*.

4. In the last sentence of paragraph 1, the second parenthetical reference to *Inside Memory*, this time a direct quotation, does not include Findley's name because he is identified as the writer in the brief introduction leading up to the direct quotation.

5. The student's core question—the question that launched him on his investigation of battles in Findley's novel—appears in paragraph 2 of the paper. The student focuses on the novel's first epigraph—"Against despair"; his question is why Findley included these words and why he began with these words. Interestingly, the answer to the question uses the first-person pronoun "my." Students often ask whether the use of the first person is appropriate in research-based or analytical writing of this sort. This essay shows an appropriate use, for the "my" fits the precise context, and the pronouns "I" and "my" are not used to excess or without purpose at any point in the paper.

6. The paper's thesis emerges at the end of paragraph 2 and the beginning of paragraph 3. In a longer paper, it is often the case that the argument is complex and that it should not be jammed into a single enormous thesis sentence. In this case, the paper is rooted in a question about the epigraph and then in the student's wish to bring to the discussion ideas from his studies in the discipline of philosophy. This accounts for the focus on the extent to which Hegel's philosophical speculations about conflict can be applied to Findley's story of battle in his re-telling of the biblical story of the world flood and Noah's ark.

7. The final quotation of paragraph 3 is a short passage drawn from an article in a scholarly journal. Because the author, Professor Lorraine York, is named in the part of the sentence introducing the quotation, her name need not be included in the parenthetical reference. Note that, in contrast to the placement of the final punctuation for a block quotation, the period here follows the parenthesis.

80

Tung 2

(1) **para. 4** Battles occur verbally in the novel when a character engages in discourse with or against another subject or subjects. One dramatic example occurs when Noah plans to ask his son Ham to kill a lamb as a sacrificial offering of thanks for the pending visit of Yaweh. Mrs. Noyes, who has been silent on other occasions, confronts him. "I know what you're going to do" (12), she says so quietly that she draws her husband's wandering attention to her almost immediately. The verbal battle begins: Noah responds by making her state exactly what she believes he is going to do, and she says: "You're going to ask Ham to perform the sacrifice" (12). When they start shouting at one another, the peacock nearby gives "a piercing scream" (13) and when Noah asserts that the peacock is affirming his decision, she retorts that the creature is "only calling to his mate, for God's sake!" (13). This scene foreshadows the pattern of many verbal battles to come, because when Mrs. Noyes uses God's name in vain, Noah becomes livid, intimidates her into apologizing, and makes her feel "contrite" (14). In this sense, Noah prevails because he invokes God as an authority figure and because Mrs. Noyes "mean[s] no harm to Yaweh" (14).

para. 5 Later, the combat between these two primary characters escalates when Mrs. Noyes, having for some time stayed away from home, boycotting the ark-building and the preparations for the apocalyptic flood, returns. Noah hurls down the verbal challenge, asking her whether she has "come to [her] senses at last" (187), and she replies in the affirmative. He then makes her answer again, and in doing so, he asserts his position as an authority figure over her. Hegel terms such a relationship one of "Lordship" and "Bondage"—or what we might term Master and Slave. In this important scene, Noah wins (again): he humiliates her, and experiences "an edge of amusement" (187) in the process. He reasserts God as
(2) an authority figure when he tells her that "Yaweh is pleased at [her] surrender to
(3) reality" (189); her only means of resistance is to remain silent. And so she does.

para. 6 It is only in part three of the novel, when the rains have begun, the ark is afloat, and the upper and lower deck divisions of the ark have been established by Noah, that the pattern of the so-called Master verbally bullying his so-called Slave is reversed. Banished below deck, Mrs. Noyes nevertheless gains the upper hand in matters culinary when Noah—amazingly and clumsily—asks her for her cheese dish recipe. She notices that her spouse "has the decency to be embarrassed" (221) at having to admit his hunger, his dissatisfaction with his
(4) daughter-in-law Hannah's cooking, and his dependency on his old and cast-off

Comments on page 2 of "Into the Battle"

1. Paragraph 4 shows the student summarizing his close reading of pages 12, 13, and 14 of *Not Wanted on the Voyage*, the primary text on which this paper is based. Note that each time the writer quotes words and phrases from the novel, he integrates them into his own sentence structure and provides page references in parentheses. References to the primary text that do not contain quotations are not given parenthetical citations.

2. The final quotation in paragraph 5 is one that has been altered to fit the context of the student's sentence. The pronoun "your" in the original quotation has been altered to "her" to ensure consistent point of view and pronoun reference, and the alteration has been signalled by the use of square brackets [ ] around the change.

3. Three paragraph breaks appear on this page. In revising an extended paper, the writer should consider the audience's need to pause in the course of reading to consider ideas raised and developed, and to prepare for ideas and evidence to come. This nine-page paper is nicely paced in its paragraphing. Its total of 21 paragraphs gives the reader a minimum of one or two breaks per page. The student here has moved past the formulaic approach some writers have that causes them to produce a paper of five paragraphs no matter how long or short the assignment.

4. One of the conventions of writing about a literary text calls for the use of the present tenses (simple present, present perfect) in the discussion of events taking place in the time of the narrative (or verse or drama). Note in each of paragraphs 4, 5, and 6, the writer's use of present-tense verbs in discussing scenes of verbal combat and confrontation between Dr. and Mrs. Noyes.

Tung 3

wife for nourishment and pleasure. Mrs. Noyes' reticence (she does not immediately share the recipe) shows her subtly savouring her modest victory–even if she does this for only a moment.

para. 7 Verbal battles also serve another Hegelian purpose: to enable characters to
① recognize themselves (i.e., they are speaking agents) and to become recognized as being autonomous (in their own eyes–self-consciously–or in the eyes of another character). What is a battle for autonomy? It is a paradox, for one thing. In The Phenomenology of Spirit, Hegel argues that the "[s]elf-consciousness achieves its satisfaction only in *another* self-consciousness" (110, emphasis added). Hegel believes that characters want recognition from others, but also yearn and strive for a kind of separateness when they assert their autonomy. This assertion can be difficult to achieve, as Findley's struggling characters so often demonstrate, or it can go unrecognized–particularly by members of Noah's Upper-Deck faction. For example, when Hannah, at the direction of Dr. Noyes, reads the rules of the New Order aboard the ark to the "factions at [the] treaty conference" (208), she refers to the animals aboard as "cargo" (210). By using this word, she implies that she does not see the animals as autonomous, since cargo, by definition, cannot be self-governing. Mrs. Noyes, not surprisingly, challenges Hannah's diction. And ironically, the narrative shows that the animals are
② cognizant–in fact self-conscious–beings. According to biographer Carol Roberts, Mottyl the cat, whom Findley modelled on Mottle, a stray cat that he found and cared for at his Stone Orchard home and whom he "admired for her courage and resourcefulness . . . as a fellow creature" (84), is the most memorable of these cognizant animals. She offers readers a cat's perspective on events and personalities aboard the ark; she recognizes that some of Noah's actions are "evil" (279). Mottyl never loses hold of her autonomy. Noah, in contrast, does lose his grip when, at the end of the novel, he calls out to God, wonders whether He, like everyone else, has died, and seems no longer the autonomous master he has always claimed to be.

para. 8 Hegel articulates the idea of individuals seeking to be autonomous in order to assert their self-consciousness and goes on to state that the "self-consciousness is Desire" (109). By having desire–by wanting others to recognize one's autonomy–a character in a work of fiction can become self-conscious or aware. And because of this demand for recognition, characters "are opposed to one another, one being only *recognized*, the other only *recognizing*" (Hegel 113). Thus characters, though opposed, are also co-dependent. They cannot bear living with one another, and yet they would cease to exist as cognizant beings if they chose to live isolated and apart from others. Mottyl, when acknowledging

Comments on page 3 of "Into the Battle"

1. Paragraph 7 offers a good example of a well-contextualized quotation. In sentence 4, the writer introduces a paradoxical passage from philosopher Friedrich Hegel's book *The Phenomenology of Spirit*. Mentioning the author and the title of the work in the main part of the sentence leading into the quotation helps to emphasize their importance and reduces the amount of information to be included in the parenthetical reference. Note that this strategy works best at the point when the work is first mentioned. In subsequent references, the writer adopts other strategies to ensure variety in his referencing. In this case, the parenthetical reference includes the words "emphasis added" following the page reference to indicate that the word *another* has been italicized by the writer and that italics did not appear in the original work.

2. Later in paragraph 7, the student introduces some background information about the character named Mottyl, the cat from whose point of view some of the events of Findley's flood story are observed. The details concerning Findley's own cat named Mottle are presented as summary in the student's own words and followed by words quoted from Carol Roberts, the secondary source. Note the strategy the student uses here to clearly mark the end of his own thought about the cognizance of animal characters in the text and the start of his summary and quotation of Carol Roberts' observations about Mottyl the fictional character and Mottle the Stone Orchard pet. The phrase "According to biographer Carol Roberts" is an attribution: it signals the beginning of her thought and identifies her credentials as a biographer. Her book on Findley, *Timothy Findley: Stories from a Life*, is from the Canadian Biography Series published by ECW Press.

Tung 4

Noah's evil character, indirectly enables Noah to exist, because she can see his self-consciousness as it really is. The idea of recognition requires the presence of self-consciousness:

> ① [It is] one which *knows* that it is the dual consciousness of itself, as self-liberating, unchangeable, and self-identical, and as self-bewildering and self-perverting, and it is the awareness of this self-contradictory nature of itself. (Hegel 126)

The self-consciousness is itself not autonomous to itself; that is, it requires the presence of others to assert and to recognize its autonomy. Gustavus Cunningham
② provides this exegesis of Hegel's complex paradox: "It is only when an object is fully known to be itself, that is, when it is seen to differ determinately from others . . . that it may legitimately be termed unique" (103).

③ **para. 9** Hegel did not likely have blind cats or any other non-human creatures in mind when he published The Phenomenology of Spirit in 1807. Still, Mottyl, whom Mrs. Noyes regards as a kindred spirit, shares with her human companion a past history of servitude to Dr. Noyes. She has surrendered her newborn kittens to him and his medical experiments, for "there was nothing she could do to stop him" (19). At the same time, she is one who achieves acute recognition of and insight into this man who, ironically, barely acknowledges her existence.

para. 10 In Hegel's system, once a self-consciousness recognizes its position or existence, it must then battle for recognition from other characters. In a battle of two, each one wants recognition from the other—each wants to obtain the other's desire. That is, a character will want his or her opponent to recognize his or her autonomy; conversely, the opponent will desire or wish to be recognized as well. Hegel asserts that "the self-consciousness must proceed to supersede the *other* independent being in order thereby to become certain of *itself* as the essential being" (111). During a battle, characters come to be differentiated hierarchically.
④ A master-and-slave confrontation ensues in the way pinpointed by philosopher Eric Steinhart:

> Tension builds. The symmetry of mutual recognition is unstable. The symmetry must be broken so that of the two opposed self-consciousnesses, one is going to be only recognized (master), the other only recognizing. The only way to settle the matter is in a fight to the death. (n. pag.)

Comments on page 4 of "Into the Battle"

1. The block quotation from page 126 of Hegel's *The Phenomenology of Spirit* appears at the mid-point of paragraph 8. Note that it is not segregated from the writer's own thoughts and words but rather integrated into his argument and his style with the introductory words "The idea of recognition requires the presence of self-consciousness." This strategy of integrating quoted material into one's own sentence structure is vital to the overall unity and coherence of the presentation. It is among the most important skills student researchers need to perfect in their research-based writing.

    Note as well that the block quotation itself has been altered. That is, the writer has added the words "It is" in square brackets to make Hegel's words fit grammatically into his own sentence structure.

2. At the end of paragraph 8, the student has used the word "exegesis" to describe the work of Gustavus Cunningham, a philosopher who has studied and written commentary on Hegel's works. This word is an apt descriptor for a source that offers explanation or interpretation of a complex or ambiguous text.

3. The opening sentence of paragraph 9 is noteworthy for two reasons. First, it serves as a transition, connecting the rather complex discussion of Hegel's philosophy back to Findley's work. And second, it shows the writer acknowledging the somewhat imperfect relationship he is aiming to draw (applying Hegel's theory to a cat) in a lighter tone that is refreshing in the midst of this complex material.

4. The source materials for this paper are primarily print-based, but the block quotation from Eric Steinhart, a professor of philosophy at William Patterson University, is drawn from a web-based document on Hegel's work. The *n.pag.* in the parenthetical reference is the abbreviation for "no page." Many online materials are unpaginated and so are represented in this way.

Also in this hierarchically organized world, characters subscribe to the idea of hegemony—they conform to expected roles. If they stray at all, Hegelians would say, the straying is short-lived.

① **para. 11** Findley's characters fit Hegel's model to a point. But in the world of Not Wanted on the Voyage, characters such as Mrs. Noyes, Mottyl, and the "rogue" (59) angel Lucy ultimately refuse to accept this idea of a hierarchical chain of being where Noah is the unchallenged master. The old woman, the blind cat, and the angel with feathers of bronze resist—ferociously and for longer than a moment—being classified as subordinates, inferiors, slaves.

② **para. 12** In the novel, the battle for recognition is a vital phase of the many struggles or confrontations between and among characters. In Book Two, the narrator tells us that once upon a time and long before the action of the novel, Mrs. Noyes had a "forbidden child," and that "[s]he killed it" (148). She had no choice—perhaps. The child was seen by her spouse and master as an aberration. And so she was a slave to Noah's wishes. However, in the present time of the narrative, when she brings Lotte to the ark, she has a chance—it seems—to enact revenge upon the master. By telling Emma about her slain baby Adam, she reveals Noyes' plan to ensure that future Lotte-like children will be blamed on Emma and forces him to acknowledge his intentions if not his past coercions. Mrs. Noyes gains the upper hand in this battle, because she is recognized, though this recognition does not initially seem to involve a battle for autonomy (and desire). But Hegel's idea of the battle for autonomy ultimately surfaces because Mrs.Noyes, by telling her story to Emma, asserts her autonomy or self-consciousness. She is her own master. To a point. But a scrupulous Hegelian might ask why, in the midst of this dialectic confrontation, Mrs.
③ Noyes "looks at him [Noah] almost tenderly" (161). Fascinatingly and revealingly, despite being locked in battle, Mrs. Noyes still, somewhere deep down, cares for her husband, at the same time as she hates him for coercing her into drowning Adam.

para. 13 Though Mrs. Noyes wins the confrontation with Noah when she tells Emma about the murder of Japeth's twin brother, she does not win the war. She is unable to prevent Lotte's death at the hands of Japeth and at the order of Dr. Noyes. When she holds the little girl's body in her arms, she sees "that Lotte has no eyes" (178). The irony here is that although Lotte has inspired Mrs. Noyes to tell the truth about Adam to force Noah to recognize his actions, her eyelessness alludes to Mrs. Noyes' lack of foresight in not realizing that Noah will ensure Lotte does not survive on the ark. Mrs. Noyes becomes the slave in this scene because she is unable to save Lotte. She now battles furiously against feelings of despair,

Comments on page 5 of "Into the Battle"

1. Paragraph 11, although short, represents a major turning point of the essay. The principal claim here is what is called a qualification. The writer emphasizes that although Findley's narrative fits Hegel's definition of conflict in many ways, it also resists or departs from the definition in others. The use of the phrase "to a point" signals that the writer is about to turn his attention (and ours) to the ways in which *Not Wanted on the Voyage* is not quite the neat fit with Hegel's world view that it might first appear to be.

   Interestingly, the phrase "to a point" is repeated—deliberately—in paragraph 12, where it appears as a fragment qualifying the idea that Mrs. Noyes is her own master.

2. In paragraph 12, the writer also departs from the practice of discussing the details of the literary text in the present tenses when he comments on the story of Dr. and Mrs. Noyes' "forbidden child." The reason for this departure is explained in the second sentence of the paragraph with the words "the narrator tells us that once upon a time long before the action of the novel Mrs. Noyes *had* a forbidden child." When alluding to events occurring before the time of the story being told, the shift into past tense is not only permissible; it is likely the most logical choice.

3. The last quotation appearing in paragraph 12 and drawn from page 161 of *Not Wanted on the Voyage* demonstrates the need to add information to a quotation to explain an ambiguous reference—particularly an ambiguous pronoun. The pronoun "him" is unclear, and so the writer has added [Noah] in square brackets to show the pronoun's antecedent.

while paradoxically, she sinks deeper into despair. She drinks her gin; she keens for the dead child; she bashes out hymns on the piano; she wonders who in heaven or on earth she can pray to. And then she says, "Well: I'm not drowned
① yet. Still here alive. Still me—and, in fact, a little more me than I was before all this began" (181).

② **para. 14** Does Mrs. Noyes achieve a feeling of superiority when she forces Noah to acknowledge their past murderous actions? No. Justice and truth are infinitely more important to her: she wants Emma to know the truth. Hegel argues that there is an inherent sense of superiority in recognition because one self-consciousness supersedes the other. However, he also insists on this complexity: that "[e]ach sees the *other* do the same as it does; each does itself what it demands of the other, and therefore also does what it does only insofar as the other does the same" (112). Each character sees a part of himself or herself in the eyes of the other. Though Mrs. Noyes did not want to kill Adam, she did the
③ deed. (This is evident in her monologue describing the atrocity: "'We killed him,' she said. 'I did . . .' She looked at Noah. 'We did'" (165).) She murdered him under protest. And when she tells Emma the truth about Adam, she and Noah see themselves in each other. The ultimate battle—for victory—is the next step in their war of attrition.

para. 15 Does Mrs. Noyes or Noah achieve ultimate victory? When she, Emma, Ham, and Lucy take over the upper deck of the ark, Mrs. Noyes brings out the sheep to sing. By singing, they are engaging in a vocal (if not a conventionally verbal) victory, because Noah and the others of his faction must *recognize* that the sheep are singing. Mrs. Noyes experiences a semblance of a victory because there is "self-certainty . . . from superseding [the] other" (Hegel 109). She is the master of language, and in her dialectical battle with Noah, she supersedes him and becomes the master, not the slave: she is in control when he asks her for her recipes; she exploits his shame when she reveals the truth about their secret child. And she receives recognition when the sheep sing for her.

para. 16 But does Mrs. Noyes win a true victory in the Hegelian sense? Hegel tells us that each self-consciousness "seeks the death of the other" (113), but the death of one or the other of these formidable antagonists does not occur in Not Wanted on the Voyage. The principal characters—Mrs. Noyes and Noah—do not die in the course of the plot, even as other characters do die (Lotte, the unicorn, the dolphins, Crowe, the demons, and the uncounted millions who die in the flood waters). And neither are they lifelong casualties in the way Japeth is when Lucy defeats him: instead of dying, he lives and suffers for his cruelty to others. The

Comments on page 6 of "Into the Battle"

1. The conclusion to paragraph 13 appearing at the top of this page offers examples of the paradox of despair the writer describes in his observations about Mrs. Noyes in the aftermath of the child Lotte's death. To demonstrate his point, he offers a list of Mrs. Noyes' actions. The list is precise; it is also compact. It demonstrates well the student's knowledge of the novel, and because he is writing in his own words about the primary text here, no parenthetical references are necessary. Note that the writer uses this same strategy of the compact list in paragraph 16, where he details in a parenthesis the characters who, unlike Dr. and Mrs. Noyes, die in the course of the plot.

2. Paragraphs 14 and 16 show the writer using a pattern of question and answer to introduce variety into sentence and paragraph patterns. Used strategically—that is, occasionally and in a way that allows the question to be followed directly by the answer—this pattern adds energy to the writing as it moves into its final paragraphs. Because longer essays sometimes end with a whimper of repetitiousness and sameness of diction and style, this is a strategy to keep in mind for your own longer assignments.

3. Paragraph 14 features the quotation of a passage of dialogue from page 165 of *Not Wanted on the Voyage*. Note the way in which the writer has handled the pattern of the quotation appearing within the quotation by using single quotation marks within double marks. Note as well the use of a parenthesis within a parenthesis.

Tung 7

threat of death in the Hegelian scheme is ominous to a subject, because "the self-consciousness learns that life is as essential to it as pure self-consciousness" (Hegel 115). If a self-consciousness dies, then it can neither recognize another nor be recognized. The horror of this realization is evident in one of those scenes in which non-human creatures are acknowledged in the narrative as equals. When the dolphins—or "PIRATES" (235)—approach the ark, Japeth slaughters them, while Mrs. Noyes watches in horror:

> ① The whole visage [of one of the dolphins] was a message [to Mrs. Noyes]
> ② of joy and of greeting. But in that moment of recognition, as Mrs. Noyes and the [dolphin] looked at one another and smiled—Japeth's sword descended—swiftly and fatally. (237)

Although Hegel argues that a self-consciousness seeks the death of another, in Not Wanted on the Voyage, the characters do not necessarily or always seek the deaths of their opponents; rather, they seek to become the master and seek recognition from the other (the opponent). They seek what Steinhart describes as "the symmetry of cooperation" (n.pag.).

③ **para. 17** Hegel's master-slave dialectic posits that a master wants recognition from a slave; that a slave must recognize the autonomy of the master; that each desires the other's desire. When Not Wanted on the Voyage opens, Noah appears to be the master and Mrs. Noyes the slave. The relationship—a marriage the 600-year old Noah speculates is 400 or 500 years old—is as longstanding as any reader might imagine. But why, given the myriad differences between the couple, has the union survived? Because according to Hegel, the slave has recognized the master's autonomy. At the start of Findley's story, when Noah argues with Mrs. Noyes about Ham performing the sacrifice, he wins by asserting his superiority and power over Mrs. Noyes (she recognizes that he will order Ham to kill the lamb). Each wants the other to recognize and assert his or her autonomy; both exist "only in being acknowledged" (Hegel 111). Each self-consciousness wants to interact with another consciousness, but only to abolish the otherness (or autonomy [truth of self-certainty]) of the other. The individual is certain of "its own self, but not of the other, and therefore its own self-certainty still has no truth" (Hegel 113). Hegel bases his philosophy on the interaction (or confrontation) between two self-consciousnesses—a dialectical struggle. The two "prove themselves and each other through a life-and-death struggle" (114). Each self-

Comments on page 7 of "Into the Battle"

1. The block quotation in paragraph 16 from page 237 of *Not Wanted on the Voyage*, even more than the quotation in paragraph 12 where [Noah] is added to explain an ambiguous pronoun, is carefully edited to provide vital detail about the dolphins and Mrs. Noyes. Note the addition of the phrase "[of one of the dolphins]," and then of "[to Mrs. Noyes]," and finally of "[dolphin]" to make clear just who is communicating what to whom in this scene.

2. The block quotation strategically placed at the mid-point of a body paragraph—here, mid-way through paragraph 16—is a consistent strategy of this writer. He has understood well the need to embed quoted material within a paragraph that introduces it, presents it, and then comments on its significance. He has avoided the problems caused when unexplained block quotations are positioned at paragraph's end and leave a reader with a sense of incompleteness and confusion.

3. In paragraph 17, the writer skilfully employs an alternating arrangement in which he moves confidently back and forth from thoughts of Hegel to thoughts of Findley. Note the effective use of coherence strategies (transitions, pronoun references, deliberate word repetitions, and synonyms) to achieve this pattern.

Tung 8

consciousness wants the other to *recognize* and acknowledge its superiority. Thus, whenever Noah and Mrs. Noyes confront one another, they engage in such a dialectical power struggle. Neither dies, but one—Mrs. Noyes—learns to live more fully than the other—Dr. Noyes (who seems pathetically reduced at the end).

para. 18 As the (initial) master, Noah needs Mrs. Noyes (as the slave) to recognize
① and to acknowledge him. But as Steinhart observes, "[t]he master wants to be
recognized by somebody that he respects as an equal, as a peer. Instead, the
master gets recognition from a slave, and the master knows that the slave doesn't
really respect him . . ., but resents and hates [him]" (n.pag.). Quite simply, Noah
is trapped at an impasse, because while battling with Mrs. Noyes, though she
recognizes him as a master in their initial confrontations, because she has a
presence as well, he (as the master) must also recognize her presence, even if, at
the same time, he recognizes that she is the slave. The truth (and complexity) of
self-certainty is that the confrontations actually force the master to recognize the
slave. Ironically, then, the unfolding narrative shows that Noah as the master is
not autonomous: he requires the presence of Mrs. Noyes to complement and to
acknowledge his existence. Hence, the distinction between the master and the
② slave becomes nebulous. In fact, in the latter half of the novel, Mrs. Noyes
80 captures the role of the master when she forces Noah to recognize his atrocious,
murderous actions.

para. 19 When the subjects finally exit from the ark, Noah no longer has autonomy, nor is he known to himself. The ambiguity of his final scene suggests that he may or may not be in charge of Mrs. Noyes and the other survivors. The circle is complete. Mrs. Noyes becomes the master, because in acknowledging and battling Noah, she gains the upper hand, for she is the one who must act in recognizing the other (Noah). Ironically, for Noah, Mrs. Noyes' resistance and her confrontations with him serve to elevate her. She is, at the end, the character who, with her cat companion, occupies the last scene, utters the last monologue, and undertakes the last action—her cryptic prayer for rain. She is, inarguably, the more important character in Not Wanted on the Voyage.

para. 20 In the last scene of the novel, when she is thinking about Noah reverting to his old ways, Mrs. Noyes says "No!" (352)—to herself, to Mottyl, to the skies, to us. With this single word, she asserts herself and is aware of her autonomy (and hence, her free will). Though Hegel might describe her battle (and most battles) as empty—victorless—(except for the fact of being recognized), Mrs. Noyes would not likely agree. She is the victor, but at a cost. She does not necessarily want Noah to recognize her autonomy (or wish that God would recognize her

Comments on page 8 of "Into the Battle"

1. The quotation from Eric Steinhart folded into the second sentence of paragraph 18 shows the use of square brackets around the single letter *t* in the word *the*; "[t]he master wants . . ." indicates that in the original, *the* was the first word in the sentence and was thus capitalized. The change to the lowercase *t* accommodates the student's sentence.

2. Paragraphs 18, 19, and 20 together comment on what may be the most important and yet the most-often ignored part of the literary text—the ending. This paper devotes three substantial paragraphs to an interpretation of the final scenes of *Not Wanted on the Voyage* and in doing so maintains the energy and momentum of the essay as a whole. The writer does not lapse into an ineffective re-hashing of ideas already well explored in earlier parts of the essay.

Tung 9

① self-consciousness), but rather, she wants her husband (and God) to acknowledge that there must be justice tempered with mercy in the world. If this involves recognition, then she is pragmatic: so be it. Judging by the tone of her last words, it is clear that if another Lotte-like child were to be born, she would not allow Noah to force her (or anyone else) to eliminate the child. She has made emotional and human progress. In the end, "[s]he pray[s] for rain" (352). These words signify that she will, if necessary, engage in battle with Noah again, without hesitation, because paradoxically, she is the victor in a victorless battle.

② **para. 21** In his thought-provoking discussion of critical commentary on Not Wanted on the Voyage, David Jefferess offers what he calls a "pacific" (138) re-reading of Findley's narrative. He argues that the novel has been read as "nothing more than the message contained within the epigraph, 'Against Despair' " (141). Fair enough. But the battle against despair, as it is enacted in the marital combat between Noah and his spouse of many centuries, resists the disparaging phrase "nothing more"—especially if it is read alongside Findley's words in his January 1987 address—"My Final Hour"— to the members of Trent University Philosophy Society:

> Nothing is harder, now in this present time, than staring down despair. But stare it down we must. Unless we do, there can be no reconciliation. Be grateful, in your final hour, for life. Not for your life alone, but for the fact of life: for everything that is. After all is said and done, I know I will have no answers. . . . What I will have . . . is questions. What I have done—what I have tried to do—is frame those questions—not with question marks—but in the paragraphs of books. (16)

That, as Mrs. Noyes might well say, is something.

Comments on page 9 of "Into the Battle"

1. Now that he has reached the end of his essay, the writer has earned the opportunity to be emphatic in his conclusions. A close study of the diction describing Mrs. Noyes in paragraphs 19 and 20 shows the student to be arguing energetically for Mrs. Noyes as a central, admirable, and paradoxically victorious character in her contests with her spouse.

2. The writer uses the last paragraph of his essay to introduce a comment about Mrs. Noyes and *Not Wanted on the Voyage* with which he wishes to take exception. He introduces the source—David Jefferess' article in the journal *Essays on Canadian Writing*—and quotes the somewhat dismissive comment about battling despair with which he disagrees. He then brings his paper full circle by using Timothy Findley's words from his address to a *philosophy* society (nicely coinciding with his paper's preoccupation with philosophical matters) and finishes with his own understated and witty speculation about what Mrs. Noyes herself might have to say about the value of battling against despair.

(1)

Tung 10

Works Cited

Cunningham, Gustavus W. Thought and Reality in Hegel's System. New York: Garland, 1984.

Findley, Timothy. Inside Memory: Pages from a Writer's Workbook. Toronto: HarperCollins, 1990.

(2)–(6) ---. "My Final Hour: An Address to the Philosophy Society, Trent University, Monday, 26 January 1987." Journal of Canadian Studies 22.1 (1987): 5–16.

---. Not Wanted on the Voyage. New York: Penguin, 1996.

Hegel, Georg Wilhelm Friedrich. The Phenomenology of Spirit. 1807. Trans. A.V. Miller. Toronto: Oxford UP, 1977.

Jefferess, David. "A Pacific (Re) Reading of Timothy Findley's Not Wanted on the Voyage." Essays on Canadian Writing 72 (2000): 138–157.

Roberts, Carol. Timothy Findley: Stories from a Life. Toronto: ECW, 1994.

(7) Steinhart, Eric, ed. "Master/Slave Dialectic." G.W.F. Hegel: *The Phenomenology of Spirit*. 1998. 14 Feb. 2000. <http://www.wpunj.edu/cohss/philosophy/courses/hegel/MASLAVE.HTM>.

York, Lorraine. "Civilian Conflict: Systems of Warfare in Timothy Findley's Early Fiction." English Studies in Canada 15 (1989): 336–347.

80

Comments on page 10 of "Into the Battle": the Works Cited page

1. The works-cited list—a list of all sources quoted, summarized, paraphrased, and alluded to in the paper—is part of the essay. Hence it is part of the pagination and here appears as page 10.

2. The works-cited list in MLA is alphabetically arranged and double-spaced. Entries are not numbered. Note carefully the indention of multi-lined entries and the punctuation within individual entries. All of these details are part of effective MLA documentation.

3. Of the nine items in the works-cited list, five are books (Cunningham, Findley's *Inside Memory* and *Not Wanted on the Voyage*, Hegel, and Roberts). Three works ("My Final Hour," Jefferess, and York) are journal articles in print form. One work (Steinhart's exegesis of Hegel) is an online source: a scholar's website.

4. This works-cited list features three works by one author—Findley. It includes a work in translation (Hegel), a title within a title (Jefferess and Steinhart), and journals with continuous (York) and separate (Findley, Jefferess) pagination.

5. The primary source for this particular assignment is *Not Wanted on the Voyage*. The remaining eight sources here are secondary.

6. Note that page references are included here for articles only.

7. The entry for Steinhart includes 1998 as the only date appearing on the site (ordinarily a site would include more specific information dating the posting or the most recent updating of the source. The date preceding the website address, 14 Feb. 2004, is the date of the student's access and should be noted and included in the entries for electronic sources. A full and usable/accessible web address must be included and should be enclosed in < >. If the web address (URL) is unusually long and extends beyond a single line, break it only after a slash. Do not add a hyphen at the line break, as to do so would alter the address and make it unusable. The most recent edition of the *MLA Handbook* also suggests that if an URL is unreasonably long (extending beyond two lines, for example), it is acceptable to use instead the URL of the website's search page.

81 Other Methods of Documentation

81a The Name–Date Method (APA Style)

The name–date system is common in the social sciences; the standard guide is the *Publication Manual of the American Psychological Association*, 5th ed. (2001). Like the name–page method, it uses parenthetical references in the text, but instead of listing the author and the page in the source where the cited material occurs, it lists the author and the date of publication of the source. The practice is the same whether the source is print-based or electronic. Since in the behavioural and social sciences reference is quite often made to the argument or evidence presented by an entire work, page numbers are not always necessary:

> There are many remarkable parallels between the way artists and scientists look at the world around us (Shlain, 1991).

But if you refer to a particular part of the source, or if you quote from it, supply the relevant page number or numbers:

> As Leonard Shlain (1991) reminds us, "Space, time, and light are of profound interest to both the physicist and the artist" (p. 28).

81a

Note that, as in the name–page method, if you name the author in the text, you don't include the name in the parenthetical reference.

Here are some further examples of name–date parenthetical references, followed by some examples of bibliographical entries. Were these examples to appear within an essay, they would be double-spaced:

A work with one author

> John Helliwell (2002) provides an incisive analysis of the effects of globalization.

A work with two or more authors

> Although it is true that "the religious and secular customs of the community sometimes helped women who had been assaulted or harassed, nothing could lessen the impact of war on the countryside and its inhabitants" (Anderson & Zinsser, 1988, 1: pp. 115–116).

The fact that the citation comes from volume 1 of a two-volume work could also be noted in the bibliographical list of references. Note that in

APA style an ampersand rather than *and* separates two authors in a reference, that author and date are separated by a comma, that the abbreviations "p." and "pp." are used for "page" and "pages," and that all three digits of the closing page number are included.

If a work has two authors, list both names in each reference you make to the source. If it has three, four, or five authors, list all of them the first time, but only the first and *et al.* (not italicized or underlined) thereafter. If it has six or more authors, list only the first and *et al.* each time, including the first.

Online sources

When citing electronic sources using APA style, you can follow most of the conventions you use to cite print sources. The one exception is that if your electronic source has no page numbers, identify the paragraph or section number instead. If page, paragraph, and section numbers are not used, identify the section by its heading and count the paragraphs following the heading to assign a number to the paragraph containing the material you are citing:

> Some of Pereira's views have recently been questioned (Freedman, 2004, para. 22).

> This recent development has many analysts perplexed (Hashemi, 2002, Further developments, para. 3).

Sample Works-Cited Entries

An entire book

> Helliwell, J. (2002). *Globalization and well-being.* Vancouver, UBC Press.

Note that initials are used instead of the author's full given name or names.

The MLA and APA styles differ in the treatment of titles. In MLA style, the titles of books and periodicals appearing in works-cited entries are underlined; in APA style, book and periodical titles are italicized. In MLA style, the first letters of all words in a title (with the exception of prepositions, articles, and conjunctions) are capitalized. In reference lists in APA style, only the first letters of a book or article title's first word, the first word after a colon or a dash, and proper nouns are capitalized. All other words begin with the lower case. The titles of periodicals are capitalized as they would be in MLA style. Finally, these capitalization practices apply to the APA reference (works-cited) list only. Titles appearing within the body of a paper capitalize all key words with the exception of prepositions, articles, and conjunctions.

An article in an edited book

Kaplan, A. (2003). Women, film, resistance: Changing paradigms. In J. Levitin, J. Plessis & V. Raoul (Eds.), *Women filmmakers: Refocusing* (pp. 15–28). Vancouver: UBC Press.

An article in a reference book

Fernandez, D. (2002). Rice cake of the Philippines. In A. Davidson (Ed.) *The Penguin companion to food* (pp. 792–797). London: Penguin.

A multivolume work

Smelser, N.J. & Baltes, P.B. (Eds.). (2001). *International encyclopedia of the social and behavioural sciences* (Vols. 1–26) Amsterdam: Elsevier.

An anonymous article

Riopel takes world junior silver. (2007, 24 February). *The Globe and Mail*, p. S5.

A republished book

McLuhan, M. (2002). *The mechanical bride: Folklore of industrial man*. Corte Madera, CA: Gingko Press. (original work published 1951).

A translated work

Benjamin, W. (2006). *Berlin childhood around 1900* (H. Eiland, Trans.). London: Belknap Press.

A review

Cohen, L. (2003). Metaphor and alienation. [Review of the book *The age of immunology: Conceiving the future in an alienating world*]. *Anthropological Quarterly, 76*, 343–350.

Woolley, P.J. (2002). Review of the book *Terrorism in the mind of God: The global rise of religious violence. The Journal of Conflict Studies, 22*, 152–153.

The first review by L. Cohen is entitled "Metaphor and alienation." The second review by P.J. Woolley is untitled, as are many reviews appearing in scholarly journals in the behavioural and social sciences.

A dissertation abstract

Ing, N.L. (2002). Dealing with shame and unresolved trauma: Residential school and its impact on 2nd and 3rd generation adults (Doctoral dissertation, University of British Columbia, 2001). *Dissertation Abstracts International 62/08*, 2664.

A letter

Wright, A. (2007, February 24). War cover-up? [Letter to the editor]. *The Globe and Mail*, p. A18.

An audio recording

Ma, Y. (2007). *Appassionato* [CD]. Toronto: Sony BMG Music Canada.

A musical recording (by musicians other than the original artist)

Foster, S. (1851). Sweetly she sleeps, my Alice fair [Recorded by C. LaRue, C. Norman, & K. Robertson]. On *Lullaby journey* [CD]. Troy, New York: Dorian. (1996)

A television program

Weissman, A. (Director). (2006, July 16). Blue Buddha: Lost secrets of Tibetan medicine [Television series episode]. In *The Nature of Things with David Suzuki.* Toronto: Canadian Broadcasting Corporation.

A videotape

Lapointe, P., Wong, G.Y.G., & Menard, J. (Producers) and Isacsson, M., & Lapointe, P. (Directors). (2002). *View from the summit: Quebec City—April 20–22, 2001* [Motion picture]. Canada. (Available from the National Film Board of Canada, P.O. Box 6100, Station Centre-Ville, Montreal, PQ H3C 3H5)

A film

Makhmalbaf, M. (Director). (2001). *Kandahar* [Motion picture]. Canada: Seville Pictures.

A journal article, one author

Fabian, E. (2002). On the differentiated use of humor and joke in psychotherapy. *Psychoanalytic Review, 89*, 399–412.

A journal article, two or more authors

Karras, J., Van Deventer, M.C., & Braumgart-Rieker, J.M. (2003). Predicting shared parent–child book reading in infancy. *Journal of Family Psychology, 17*, 134–146.

A government agency or corporate author

Canadian Radio-Television and Telecommunications Commission. (1995). *Competition and culture on Canada's Information Highway: Managing the realities of transition.* Ottawa: CRTC.

A magazine article

Orlean, S. (2007, February 19 & 26). The origami lab. *The New Yorker*, 112–120.

A newspaper article, no author

Cosmonaut's plans for nuptials up in the air. (2003, 19 July). *The Globe and Mail*, p. A14.

Electronic Sources

Works-cited entries for electronic sources should include, in addition to the details you would include for a print source, the date you retrieved the information and the URL.

An entire Internet site

Dutton, Dennis. (2003, March 23). *Arts and letters daily.* Retrieved June 29, 2003, from http://www.aldaily.com

In APA style, the name of the person or organization that has provided the content of the site comes first. The date in parentheses is the date the material was last updated. Note that the URL is not contained in angle brackets, and the entry does not conclude with a period.

An article from a journal available online

If the article you are citing comes from an online source that is identical to a print edition, you can use the same format you would for a print version of the article, adding "Electronic version" in square brackets after the title to indicate that you read the article online:

> Caldwell, M. (2001). Applying general living systems theory to learn consumers' sense making in attending performing arts [Electronic version]. *Psychology and Marketing, 18,* 497–511.

If the article is available in a journal that publishes exclusively online, then you must indicate the date you retrieved it and the URL:

> Gorton, L. (1998). John Donne's use of space. *Early Modern Literary Studies, 4*(2), 1–27. Retrieved April 10, 2001, from http://shu.ac.uk/emls/04.2/gortjohn.htm

An online government publication

> Health Canada. (2001, 12 November). Centres of excellence for children's well-being. Retrieved July 1, 2003, from http://www.hc-sc.gc.ca/english/media/releases/2000/2000_96ebk1.htm

This report was published in November 2001 and accessed in July 2003.

81a

A Sample Research Paper in Name–Date (APA) Style

The paper that follows is one written and formatted in the APA style. The writer, Kate Tracy, found her topic—the Slow Food Movement—while listening to a CBC radio documentary and proposed it for a dedicated writing course in which students were required to do a short research paper in the APA style.

Kate Tracy decided to focus her work on the meaning and implications of this movement, which arose in Europe in the 1980s as a reaction against fast food and the larger trend of homogenization of cultures attached to globalization. In her essay she attempts to define the Slow Food Movement, to recount its history, and to show how it differs from more militant recent movements against the effects of globalization. She sets out her thesis in these two sentences in the second paragraph:

> If Slow Food is a reaction to the fast food infiltration described by Schlosser (2002), it is a movement with a difference and a reaction without being reactionary. This investigation of recent commentary on the movement aims at explaining what it is and what it means for those who produce, prepare, and consume food.

Study the paper and construct a one-page outline of its structure. Then write a one-page abstract of the piece and/or a short comparison of this paper with the MLA-style paper appearing earlier in this chapter.

Slow Food 1

The Slow Food Movement

What It Is, What It Means

Kate Tracy

Professor R. Montagnes

Advanced Writing Workshop

Section 04C

30 July 2003

The Slow Food Movement

What It Is, What It Means

A recent documentary featured on CBC Radio One's *Ideas* series contrasted the low-profile Slow Food Movement with more high-profile movements against the forces of globalization by describing it as "a more positive challenge to global food and agriculture" and a "tantalizing mix of politics, environmentalism and the pursuit of pleasure" (Eisen, 2003). M. Holt has described Slow Food (a short form in common usage) as "a joke that turned into a movement" and goes on to quote founding president Carlo Petrini as saying, "We said, there's fast food, so why not slow food?" (2003, para. 8).

If Slow Food is a reaction to the fast food infiltration described by Schlosser (2002), it is a movement with a difference and a reaction without being reactionary. This investigation of recent commentary on the movement aims at explaining what it is and what it means for those who produce, prepare, and consume food—that staple that is "not only inseparable from the history of the human race, but basic to it" (Tannahill, 1988, p. xv).

Defining the Slow Food Movement first requires some historical and cultural context. Tannahill argues in *Food in History* that the story of food has been one marked by argument and struggle. It is a saga of "thousands of years of human choice set in the context of an almost Darwinian process of natural selection" (p. 363). The struggle implied by the reference to Darwin helps to explain why the idea of a Slow Food Movement first surfaced in Italy in 1986. It constituted a reaction to the powerful hold fast food has upon people in many regions of the world. In fact, Carlo Petrini's question and joke was delivered in specific response to the news that a McDonald's restaurant was about to open in Rome's Piazza di Spagna (Holt, 2003, para.8).

As Schlosser (2002) details in his book *Fast Food Nation: The Dark Side of the All-American Meal*, the fast-food empires, of which McDonald's is but one, developed in 1940s America as part of the car culture and the youth culture. In San Bernardino, California, brothers Richard and Maurice McDonald first developed a successful drive-in restaurant frequented primarily by teenaged boys and staffed primarily by teenaged girls. In 1948, Schlosser argues, the brothers became initiators of the fast-food revolution by closing their drive-in and opening a restaurant "designed to increase the speed, lower the prices, and raise the volume of sales" (p. 19). This first restaurant did away with cutlery and focused on hamburgers; it operated through a division of labour and an assembly-line model in which individual staff members worked on only one part of food preparation. Special orders were discouraged, and sameness of the product being served was a virtue. The organizational model was christened "The Speedee Service System" (p. 20), and the restaurant's first mascot was named Speedee.

From modest, small-business origins such as this, fast-food restaurants went on, according to Schlosser, to take hold across the United States and then to spread out across the world. Today, "fast food is . . . so commonplace that it has acquired an air of inevitability, as though it were somehow unavoidable, a fact of modern life" (p. 7), and individuals, as Schlosser discovered in his research, come from all over the world to seek their degrees in Hamburgerology at Hamburger University in Oak Park, Illinois. What causes Schlosser, Petrini, and others (Kummer, 2002; Holt, 2003) such concern in their critiques of fast-food culture is its particular hold on the younger generation. With the increased consumption of fast-food items—particularly beginning in the 1970s when franchised fast-food operations began to expand at dramatic rates—entire generations have grown up with no memory or experience of different sorts of diets and eating experiences. And as Schlosser observes, "fast food is heavily marketed to children and prepared by people . . . barely older than children. This is an industry that both feeds and feeds off the young" (p. 9).

It is common knowledge now to anyone who regularly listens to media reports or watches television news magazines that sedentary children raised on steady diets of fast food are obese at higher rates than ever before and that incidences of juvenile diabetes are escalating at alarming rates.

Given these circumstances, it is surprising perhaps, that something like the Slow Food Movement did not get its start until Carlo Petrini made his joke in 1986. By 9 November 1989, appropriately at the Opéra Comique in Paris, the Slow Food Movement was officially constituted and given the name, The International Movement for the Defence of and the Right to Pleasure. A 2003 article in *Ecologist* ("Slow Food") provides an ample and informative definition of this phenomenon.

Unlike the anti-World Trade Organization protests that have tended to take place spectacularly and sometimes violently in the streets of large venues like Seattle and Quebec City, the Slow Food Movement's early manifestations were more modest. At the founding meeting, for example, the group adopted as its symbol, the snail, described by Francesco L'Aquila in 1607 as a model for humans of "slow motion, to educate us that being fast makes man inconsiderate and foolish" (qtd. in "Slow Food," para. 2).

The Slow Food Movement's philosophy is embodied in its manifesto ("Slow Food," final section). It critiques "the fast life" as "an insidious virus" and argues for "a firm defence of quiet material pleasure" against those who "mistake frenzy for efficiency." Calling slow food "the only truly progressive answer," the declaration calls for an "international exchange of experiences, knowledge and projects" surrounding food—all under the symbol of "the little snail" ("Slow Food," final section, para. 1–10).

The core structure of this movement with members around the world is known as the convivium, a locally based chapter whose members gather to study, discuss, and practise the culture of the food indigenous to their region: "The convivium invites the wine maker or baker to explain to the members how the product is made and to share his or her personal history" (Kummer, 2002, p. 23). In 1996, the Movement announced the establishment of The Ark of Taste and the Presidium. The former is intended to identify in any community foods of local origin that are endangered—on the path to extinction. The methods of preparation for these foods, Kummer observes, "must be traditional and by hand, or as close to handmade as possible" (p. 23). The Presidia are said to be like "mini-SWAT teams that put at the disposal of the artisans the mighty publicity resources of Slow Food and look for inventive ways to help them" (Kummer, p. 23). Chief among the campaigns undertaken by Slow Food proponents are efforts to maintain the endangered raw milk cheeses subject to increasing regulation in Europe and North America (Bacon, 2002). Perhaps inevitably, the Movement announced in 2000 the creation of the annual Slow Food Award, which honours "people who preserve biodiversity as it relates to food—people who in the process save whole villages and ecosystems" (Kummer, p. 25).

81a

So much for what the Slow Food Movement is. What does it mean? In some Canadian communities, as Jill Eisen pointed out in her July 2003 radio documentary for CBC's *Ideas*, it has meant chefs and restaurateurs re-envisioning their menus to feature locally grown produce and to establish personal contacts with small local producers. In some schools, it has meant the creation of a communal garden to which all students contribute and which all students study as part of a curriculum focused on food as a vital element of culture and of course a vital part of one's health and livelihood.

Critics of the Movement have described its members as "semi-peculiar people" (Bacon, 2002, para. 5). In his Foreword to Corby Kummer's *The Pleasures of Slow Food: Celebrating Authentic Traditions, Flavors, and Recipes*, Eric Schlosser alludes to the critics of Slow Food, who call it "elitist and effete, too expensive for ordinary people, just the latest trend among foodies and gourmands" (p. 10). Given the economic and cultural

Slow Food 6

stakes in this current dialectic between the forces of speed and the forces of food history, such criticism is not surprising. Time and circumstances and the future adult health of children who are today growing up in "fast food nations" will tell whether Carlo Petrini's joke has the kind of staying power that serious humour has. The words of Eric Schlosser, investigator of fast food and admirer of the slow-food philosophy, are perhaps the most appropriate with which to end this consideration of the food we eat:

> The Slow Food movement stands in direct opposition to everything that a fast-food meal represents: blandness, uniformity, conformity, the blind worship of science and technology. . . . If fast food is the culinary equivalent of a sound bite, then Slow Food is an honest, thorough declaration of intent (Kummer, 2002, p.10).

Slow Food 7

References

Bacon, K. (2002, 14 November). The values of good food. *The Atlantic Online*. Retrieved July 18, 2003, from http://www.theatlantic.com

Eisen, J. (Producer). (2003, July 17 & 24). Slow food [Radio documentary, two parts]. In *Ideas*. Toronto: Canadian Broadcasting Company.

Holt, M. (2003). Slowing down our fast-food schools. *Education Digest, 68.6*, 4-13. Retrieved July 15, 2003, from EBSCO Research database.

Kummer, C. (2002). *The pleasures of slow food: Celebrating authentic traditions, flavors, and recipes.* San Francisco: Chronicle Books.

Schlosser, E. (2002). *Fast food nation: The dark side of the all-American meal.* New York: HarperCollins.

Slow food. (2003). *Ecologist, 33.3*, p. 42-. Retrieved July 23, 2003, from EBSCO Research Database.

Tannahill, R. (1988). *Food in history.* New York: Three Rivers Press.

81a

Note the following features in the above entries, and pay particular attention to the differences between the APA format illustrated here and the format used in the MLA's name–page system:

- The list is double-spaced throughout.
- Second and subsequent lines are indented only three spaces.
- Initials of authors and editors are used instead of first and middle names.
- The year of publication is placed immediately after the name of the author.
- In book and article titles, only the first word of the title and subtitles and any proper nouns are capitalized.
- The title of a periodical is capitalized except for prepositions, articles, and conjunctions within it; these items are left in lower case except when they begin a title or subtitle.
- There are no quotation marks around the title of an essay or article.
- Publishers' names are given in full, omitting only terms like "Company," "Co. ," or "Inc."
- The volume number of a journal is italicized.
- Sequences of page numbers are listed in full; digits are not dropped as they sometimes are in MLA style.

As with other systems, there will likely be variations among different disciplines. For more information and examples, consult the style manual recommended by the department that is offering the course you are writing for. If you're still uncertain, check with your instructor.

81b The Number Method (CSE Style)

Methods of documentation in the natural, physical, life, and applied sciences vary more than those in the social sciences and the humanities—though you may find that a course in one or another of these sciences asks you to use the name–page, the name–date, or even the note method, just as a course in one of the social sciences, or even one in the arts, may require you to use the number method.

Most of the sciences, and their scientific journals, use a form of the number method. Numbers in the text refer to specific items in a numbered list of "References" at the end. The numbers in the text may appear in parentheses or as superscript numbers, for example:

> Hawking (3) discusses black holes at some length.

> Hawking discusses black holes at some length.[3]

The reference may be to more than one source, listing the items in numerical order:

> Several recent articles have discussed this continuing investigation.[4,7,18,21]

Some versions call for the numbers to be underlined, which helps by distinguishing the item number from a page number if a specific passage is being referred to:

> Hawking says that the term "black holes" was coined in 1969, but that the idea goes back over two hundred years (<u>3</u>, 81).

And sometimes the numbers in the text will be in brackets rather than parentheses; sometimes the parenthetical reference will include not only a page number but a volume number, a date, or even an author's surname. The variations in method and format between one discipline and another, or even within one discipline, are so many that you should always find out what your instructor prefers. The following guidelines, which are used by the Council of Science Editors, are based on the sixth edition of *Scientific Style and Format: The CBE Manual for Authors, Editors, and Publishers* (1994). Superscript numbers in the text correspond to numbered references in a *References* section at the end of the document. These references are arranged according to the order in which they are first cited in the text. The information for each reference is presented in the following order:

1. the note number, followed by a period and two spaces
2. the author's last name, followed by initials without punctuation and then a period
3. the title of the work, followed by the title of the source, with no underlining or italics or quotation marks; only the first word of the title and proper nouns are capitalized
4. the place of publication, followed by a colon
5. the name of the publisher followed by a semicolon
6. the date of publication (or last update, if the source is online)
7. the date the information was retrieved (from an online source)
8. the range or total number of pages

The following are some examples of entries as they would appear in the *References* section of a document in CSE style.

A book by one author

1. MacMillan M. Paris 1919: six months that changed the world. New York: Random House; 2001. 288 p.

A book by two authors

2. Agnew K, Fox G. Children at war: from the First World War to the Gulf. London: Continuum; 2001. 227 p.

A book with an editor

3. Case-Smith J, editor. Pediatric occupational therapy and early intervention. 2nd ed. Boston: Butterworth-Heinemann; 1998. 324 p.

A selection in an edited book

4. Purdy A. Say the names. In: Bennett D, Brown R, editors. A new anthology of Canadian literature in English. Toronto: Oxford Univ Pr; 2002. p. 567.

An article in a journal

5. Harrigan P. The schooling of boys and girls in Canada. J Soc Hist 1990;23:803–16.

Note that the CSE uses abbreviations in names of journals.

A newspaper article

6. MacKinnon J. Paradise lost?: the Great Bear rain forest. Globe and Mail 2003 Jul 26; Sect T:1, 14.

In this example, the article begins on page T1 and continues on T14.

An entire Internet site

7. Centres of excellence for children's well-being [Internet]. Health Canada; 2001 Nov [cited 2003 Jul 1]. Available from: http://www.hc-sc.gc.ca/english/media/releases/2000/2000_96ebk1.htm

An article from a journal available online

8. Weagel, D. Musical counterpoint in Albert Camus' L'etranger. J Mod Lit [Internet]. 2002 [cited 2003 Jun 13]; 25:141–45. Available from: http://muse.jhu.edu/journals/journal_of_modern_literature/v025/25.2weagel.html

For further information consult the seventh edition of *Scientific Style and Format*, or visit the website of the Council of Science Editors at <http://www.councilscienceeditors.org>.

81c The Note Method (Chicago Style)

The note method, which uses either footnotes or endnotes and a bibliography, also appears in different versions. Although it is one traditionally used in some courses in the humanities, many disciplines that have used the note method in the past are moving away from footnotes and endnotes in favour of in-text references, which enable the reader to see the source being cited without having to stop reading to refer to the end of the paper or the foot of the page. Again, if your instructor wishes you to use this method, find out which version is required. The following guidelines are based on the fifteenth edition of *The Chicago Manual of Style*.

Notes—either footnotes or endnotes—should be single-spaced and formatted with either a first-line indent (as in the examples that follow) or a hanging indent. Although the note numbers in the text are superscript, the note numbers preceding each endnote or footnote are not. Notes should contain the name of the author, the name of the source, and the publisher and place of publication, as well as the page, chapter, or table number referred to if appropriate. If you are referring repeatedly to the same source, you can use the abbreviation "Ibid." and the page number for subsequent references, provided that there is no intervening reference to a different source. In cases where a different source intervenes, you can use a shortened citation, which should include enough information to lead the reader to the appropriate entry in the bibliography, and normally consists of the last name of the author and a shortened version of the title:

1. John Mercer and Kim England, "Canadian Cities in Continental Context: Global and Continental Perspectives on Canadian Urban Development," in *Canadian Cities in Transition: The Twenty-First Century*, ed. Trudi Buntin and Pierre Filion (Toronto: Oxford University Press, 2000), 59.
2. Ibid., 60.
3. Glen Williams, *Not For Export: The International Competitiveness of Canadian Manufacturing* (Toronto: McClelland & Stewart, 1994), 97.
4. Mercer and England, "Canadian Cities," 66.

All of the sources you have used in an essay, including those you may have consulted but not referred to directly, are listed in a bibliography at the end of the document. A bibliography may not be required if full bibliographic information has been included in the endnotes or footnotes; however, a bibliography allows the person reading your essay to see at a single glance all of the sources you have used.

The following examples illustrate the Chicago style for documenting sources in footnotes or endnotes and in the bibliography.

81c

A book by one author

FOOTNOTE OR ENDNOTE

5. Margaret MacMillan, *Paris 1919: Six Months That Changed the World* (New York: Random House, 2001), 322.

BIBLIOGRAPHY REFERENCE

MacMillan, Margaret. *Paris 1919: Six Months That Changed the World*. New York: Random House, 2001.

A book by two or more authors or editors

FOOTNOTE OR ENDNOTE

If the work you're referencing has two or three authors, list all of the authors' names:

6. Kathy Latrobe, Carolyn Brodie, and Maureen White, *The Children's Literature Dictionary: Definitions, Resources, and Learning Activities* (New York: Neil-Schuman, 2002), 16.

If the book has more than three authors, you can use the name of the first author only, followed by either "et al." or "and others":

7. Eva-Marie Kröller et al., eds., *Pacific Encounters: The Production of Self and Others* (Vancouver: Institute of Asian Research UBC, 1997), 126.

BIBLIOGRAPHY REFERENCES

If the book you are referencing has two or more authors, invert the name of the first author only:

Latrobe, Kathy, Carolyn Brodie, and Maureen White. *The Children's Literature Dictionary: Definitions, Resources, and Learning Activities*. New York: Neil-Schuman, 2002.

If the book has more than three authors, you may also follow the first author's name (inverted) with a comma and "et al." or "and others":

Kröller, Eva-Marie, et al., eds. *Pacific Encounters: The Production of Self and Others*. Vancouver: Institute of Asian Research UBC, 1997.

A work by a government agency or a corporate author

FOOTNOTE OR ENDNOTE

8. Government of Canada, *Canada's Innovation Strategy: Canadians Speak on Innovation and Learning* (Ottawa: Government of Canada, 2002), 22.

BIBLIOGRAPHY REFERENCE

Government of Canada. *Canada's Innovation Strategy: Canadians Speak on Innovation and Learning*. Ottawa: Government of Canada, 2002.

A book with an editor or translator

FOOTNOTE OR ENDNOTE

If the book you are citing has an editor and no author, give the editor's name first, followed by "ed.":

9. William Toye, ed., *The Concise Oxford Companion to Canadian Literature* (Toronto: Oxford University Press, 2001), 17.

If the book has a translator or editor as well as an author, the author's name should come before the title, with the translator's or editor's name following the title:

10. Denyse Baillargeon, *Making Do: Women, Family and Home in Montreal During the Great Depression*, trans. Yvonne Klein (Waterloo: Wilfrid Laurier University Press, 1999), 16.

BIBLIOGRAPHY REFERENCE

If the book has an editor and no author, give the editor's name first, followed by "ed.":

William Toye, ed. *The Concise Oxford Companion to Canadian Literature.* Toronto: Oxford University Press, 2001.

If the book has an editor or translator as well as an author, give the author's name first and give the translator's or editor's name after the title:

Baillargeon, Denyse. *Making Do: Women, Family and Home in Montreal During the Great Depression*. Translated by Yvonne Klein. Waterloo: Wilfrid Laurier University Press, 1999.

A work in an edited anthology

FOOTNOTE OR ENDNOTE

11. Al Purdy, "Say the Names," in *A New Anthology of Canadian Literature in English*, eds. Donna Bennett and Russell Brown, 567 (Toronto: Oxford University Press, 2002).

BIBLIOGRAPHY REFERENCE

Purdy, Al. "Say the Names." In *A New Anthology of Canadian Literature in English*. Edited by Donna Bennett and Russell Brown, 567. Toronto: Oxford University Press, 2002.

An article in a journal

FOOTNOTE OR ENDNOTE

12. Patrick Harrigan, "The Schooling of Boys and Girls in Canada," *Journal of Social History* 23 (1990): 803.

BIBLIOGRAPHY REFERENCE

Harrigan, Patrick. "The Schooling of Boys and Girls in Canada." *Journal of Social History* 23 (1990): 803–816.

A newspaper article

FOOTNOTE OR ENDNOTE

Since a newspaper may have several editions in a given day, and items may be moved or eliminated in various editions, page numbers should be omitted. If the section of the newspaper containing the article is identified, give its name, number, or letter.

13. J.B. MacKinnon, "Paradise Lost?: The Great Bear Rain Forest," Travel, *Globe and Mail*, 26 July 2003, sec T.

If the article is unsigned, begin with the title of the article.

BIBLIOGRAPHY REFERENCE

MacKinnon, J.B. "Paradise Lost?: The Great Bear Rain Forest." Travel, *Globe and Mail*, 26 July 2003, sec. T.

An Internet site

FOOTNOTE OR ENDNOTE

14. Dennis Dutton, ed., *Arts and Letters Daily* 29 (2006), http://www.aldaily.com (accessed June 29, 2006).

BIBLIOGRAPHY REFERENCE

Dutton, Dennis, ed. *Arts and Letters Daily* 29 (2006). http://www.aldaily.com (accessed June 29, 2006).

81c

An article from a journal available online

FOOTNOTE OR ENDNOTE

15. Deborah Weagel, "Musical Counterpoint in Albert Camus' *L'Etranger," Journal of Modern Literature* 25, no. 2 (2002): 141–145, http://muse.jhu.edu/journals/journal_of_modern_literature/v025/25.2weagel.html (accessed June 13, 2006).

BIBLIOGRAPHY REFERENCE

Weagel, Deborah. "Musical Counterpoint in Albert Camus' *L'Etranger*." *Journal of Modern Literature* 25, no. 2 (2002): 141–145. http://muse.jhu.edu/journals/journal_of_modern_literature/v025/25.2weagel.html (accessed June 13, 2006).

Appendix 1

Sample Student Essays with Comments and Grades

The student essays that follow were either written in response to specific assignments or developed under general instructions such as "Write an extended definition" or "Write an argument." The essays vary in length, kind, and quality, and some were written in class under a time constraint. The marginal and final comments focus on structure, content, and style following the criteria many instructors use in assessing a piece of writing. The final grades reflect the following system:

A	First Class	80–100%	Excellent
B	Second Class	68–79%	Good to Very Good
C–D	Pass	50–67%	Weak to Fair
F	Fail	0–49%	Unsatisfactory

Some comments on the individual essays that follow

The first two essays address the topic of drugs; one student chose to define a related term while another set up an argument. The third and fourth essays address the topic of animals. Both are arguments, but one is weak in its development whereas the other, though flawed, makes a far more persuasive argument. The fifth essay is a solid argument that is well-written with an engaging tone. The sixth essay is in need of significant revision. The seventh essay is from a student who has English as an additional language. Because this student is still in the beginning stages of writing at the university level, this essay has not been given a grade. The next two essays tackle the analysis of drama, and the last two essays deal with fiction. Essays 4, 9, and 11, unmarked and ungraded, are included for the purposes of practice in peer revising and discussion. Essays 1, 2, 8, 10, and 11 were written by second- and third-year university students; the rest (essays 3, 5, 6, and 7) were written by first-year university students.

Sample Essay No. 1

Addiction

A common definition of the word 'addiction' may read: the compulsive need for and use of a harmful, habit-forming substance characterized by recognizable, clearly-defined physiological reactions upon withdrawal of said substance. For most people, the formal definition of 'addiction' is a familiar one that conjures up images of drug addicts portrayed in popular movies such as Trainspotting. The problem with this narrow definition of 'addiction' is its focus entirely on the biological and physiological symptoms of withdrawal from chemical substances, to the exclusion of psychological addiction and a variety of other addictive 'substances'.

urce for this efinition?

good allusion

underline or italicize

clear thesis

this transition is overly formal and stiff

Considering almost everyone has had an experience with alcohol, I will use it to demonstrate both the physiological and the psychological symptoms of addiction. Alcohol is a chemical that is classified as a depressant because it slows down the functioning of the nervous system. When ingested, alcohol produces certain predictable physiological effects, including slurred speech, decreased reaction time, and loss of balance. In terms of addiction, alcoholism, and the associated physical withdrawal, symptoms include shivering and sweating, increased blood pressure, and a condition known as delirium tremens, a violent state of mental confusion accompanied by tremors.

italicize foreign words

Many people have experienced but may not consciously be aware of the psychological effects associated with the consumption of alcohol. Indeed, some individuals use alcohol as a kind of social anesthetic because it helps them relax, relieves their anxiety and erases their inhibitions. However, psychological addiction to alcohol (and many other 'substances') is not as widely recognized or understood, despite its importance and prevalence. Psychological withdrawal symptoms associated with alcohol include increased anxiety, agitation, anger, nervousness, uncontrollable urges, and a preoccupation with attaining alcohol to the exclusion of other things.

redundancy?

a good attempt at making a transition but you still need to make a logical connection between alcohol and other substances

By redefining addiction in terms of both psychological and physiological effects, we can now expand the list of 'substances' that could be classified as addictive. Have you ever gone shopping and purchased an article of clothing that you really liked, leaving you feeling happy and confident? Individuals who are addicted to activities such as shopping, gambling, or eating are in fact addicted to this euphoric high and the reduction of anxiety they get when they indulge in these behaviours. Those who suffer from an addiction to non-chemical 'substances' or behaviours also experience psychological withdrawal symptoms similar to those described in the example with alcohol: irritability, increased anxiety, agitation, nervousness, etc. *and so on*

good use of question

do they ever experience any negative feelings

can you think of a smoother, less mechanical way of ending the essay?

In conclusion, when you think of the word addiction, you should keep in mind that there are a large number of substances and behaviours that may be harmful and habit-forming, and, thus, are classifiable as addictive. In addition, remember that one of the critical features of addiction is the experience of withdrawal effects, either physiological or psychological, that occur when the substance is withdrawn or the behaviour is stopped.

B+ Melanie,

You have written a competent and well-organized definition of addiction. I like how you narrowed the focus to a specific addiction, the physical and psychological aspects of alcoholism. Do you think you could have narrowed the topic down even further? Also, make your transitions a little smoother, especially the transition to your conclusion, which is stiff and mechanical-sounding. The conclusion itself is a summary of the paper, but is it necessary to summarize when the essay is so short? (Readers will remember what you have written.) Perhaps you could end with a statement that focuses on the social implications of addiction or a prediction about what future studies on addiction might reveal?

Sample Essay No. 2

lower case

Handle With Care

Patent medicines and vitamins are bought in increasing quantities by people every day. They are placed on open shelves in stores to be bought without prescription by individuals who have little knowledge of what the chemical effects will be on their bodies. Many of the drugs are potentially harmful; they should be removed from the shelves, and their sales more strictly controlled. To be sure, many of the drugs that are so readily available to consumers are not harmful if administered properly. But people have come to believe that many drugs on the shelves are not harmful at all. Certain medicines have become so commonly used that they are taken as panaceas and administered for any discomfort. The drug universally known under one brand name, "aspirin," is an obvious example. People take one, or two, or several aspirin tablets for headaches, stomach pains, insomnia, nervous and emotional upsets—the whole range of disturbances—and many parents use aspirin to dose their

[Margin comments: ho? Can you be ore specific? / who? / ear position, ut is it placed the best art of your troduction? / who? / some? avoid generalizing / who? / Use examples in the body of your essay / This paragraph/intro needs editing / Perhaps some parents? Qualify your point here]

A1

children at the first sign of hyperactivity! These common cures are not safe when used in excess or when taken without being needed. *awk. how about unnecessarily?* Medicines are drugs and used incorrectly, drugs can be poison.

Is this a true premise? The government is expected to do this all the time. Of course, one might say that the government cannot be expected to pass regulations protecting people from themselves. Individuals are expected to exercise their own intelligence when using drugs. However, this reasoning assumes that the public is given information that will help it to act wisely. Unfortunately, that is not so. *good use of a simple emphatic statement* Most of the information received by society today is transmitted through popular media. What the public hears about patent medicines is conveyed via radio and television in the form of advertising. Drug companies have launched extensive campaigns designed to tell people *who?* how accessible drugs are and how little they cost. The advertisements are little more than popularity contests between brands. To the consumer, what is the value of a film *awk. sent. construction* clip showing a famous actor loading a shopping cart with fancy packages picked off a shelf in a drug store? It is all very well to be told that in a conveniently located store, *no punc.* the prices are always "right," but that says nothing about the drugs. The message is to buy.

A1

Of course, some may say that instructions about dosage are on the package of every medicine. *syntax: on every package of medicine* Moreover, individual drug companies often warn the public about misuse of their products. But in an advertisement, the warning against the detrimental effects of the drug is cleverly disguised. For example, there are several medicines on sale that are too strong for children's use. When one company says (boasts) *good word choice* that its product is "not even recommended for children," the message somehow gets mixed up. *interesting interpretation* Adults are made to feel that they are part of an exclusive class of people who can, and therefore should, rush out and buy the product. No one would rationally accept this line of reasoning, but this same principle, that kind of advertising appeals to the emotions, and people think what they are made to feel. *Is this necessary? A generalization?*

good concession ✓ Still, one must admit that many of these products are helpful in controlling ailments or in maintaining proper health, and that more stringent control of sales would cause prices to rise. This may be so, but after all, medicines are used by many people who do not need them. If these drugs—including vitamins—were less available or cost more, people would find alternative, more natural ways of maintaining good health. For instance, exercise can cure many ailments as quickly as aspirin; and regular exercise is a better preventive medicine than regular doses of patented bottled cure-alls. Moreover, many people would soon discover that the body functions very well on a proper diet with daily vitamin supplements. Indeed, the body is designed to assimilate what it needs from good food. In this age of technology, people are beginning to forget that the human race survived for generations before nourishment was compressed into little capsules, and the entire daily requirement swallowed with a drink of water in one gulp.

use comma *no punc.*

I will concede that there are individuals who do need to use these drugs or vitamins regularly, and other people who need to use them occasionally. Nevertheless, there is no good reason for the excessive use of medicine found in today's society. People have mistakenly concluded that if a drug can make them "better" when they are sick, then by the same principle, that drug will improve their condition when they are not sick. What could possibly be "better" than good health? Overdosing oneself with medicine is not the way to find out. In fact, excessive drug use will surely cause more harm than good. Drug companies have had ample time to warn the public about the need to take care when using their products. More stringent methods are obviously required. *word choice: controls*

be more specific *begging the question?*

A1

B- Alec,

This essay is a well-written and thought provoking argument. Although your introductory paragraph needs to be more focused, your thesis is strong. The body paragraphs are well developed, especially those in which you concede points. But your conclusion should have a stronger call-to-action. What exactly do you want the reader to do? What are the specific recommendations you want to make? Your argument would also be stronger if you used more specific words, avoided vague generalizations, and gave more examples. Keep these points in mind when doing your revision.

Sample Essay No. 3

Living with Animals — *your title indicates a process essay – is it?*

shift in person Human beings have always depended on animals to meet our needs. Animals have been used as food, labour, *for?* drug testing and even entertainment. All these uses for animals are useful, even vital for human needs, but management of animal uses must be responsible. *awk. repetition* *thesis: explain how*

Order? this doesn't follow the thesis Animals can be seen as the first slaves of man. Many pictures can be formed of oxen plowing fields *and* of horses pulling carts. I refered to animals as slaves, but no one opposed it as no one should. Animals were the only way to get things done faster and more economically. There weren't any harmful effects as the animals were well kept, for they were more important as labourers than broken down 'nags.' But as labour techniques were developed, animal labour became obsolete and is now very insignificant. *true? where?* *passive* *sp.* *Can animals = way? "using animals is one way"*

Order? this is your fourth point Animal entertainment is ever present in todays society as it was over a thousand years ago. Even as far back as Roman times, in events such as chariot racing and bear-baiting, animals have been a source of entertainment. Horse racing and the circus have substituted for entertainment of the past but the same enjoyment is there. Animal rights activists have spoken out against the poor treatment of animals in circuses. This is absurd. Why would the circus harm the things which make the circus thrive? It is, however, a reminder that we should not take advantage of the rights of animals as they are living beings as well. *apos* *now substitute* *punc* *vague ref* *You need to define "harm" to make this statement.* *You need to define "rights" and which groups believe in these rights*

order? After labour, animals are seen as food. Animals have provided mankind with food ever since we learned how to catch them. Some animals were hunted to extinction, which is sad as they will be lost forever but with better food management animals can be a food source *gender bias: "human kind"* *example?* *are being hunted?* *punc*

forever. It's sometimes sad to think that some animals live their whole life producing food or becoming food, but then again what did I eat today: eggs, milk, beef, so I can't really complain. *weak afterthought contradicts previous statement*

Killing animals may save human lives. Using test animals gives researchers better understanding of diseases and can also be used to test potentially life-saving drugs, all in search of a cure. It is true that hundreds of animals may die so that few humans live, but then the future will safer against disease and may result in a better world. The ends justify the means. *sweeping generalization*

does the subject fit the verb?

missing verb

Humans use animals to meet human needs. I do not oppose this, but we must understand that animals are a limited resource, and careful management of animal uses must be practiced so that the world will not feel the loss of another species. *You must be more specific. Which animals in particular are in danger? Are they being used for food, labour, or drug testing?*

F William,
You clearly have some ideas and opinions you wish to express about this topic, and this essay seems like a first draft of those ideas.
In revising the essay, you should consider the following:

1. Identify your purpose. What exactly do you want the paper to do? Do you want to persuade the audience to treat animals with more respect? Make sure your thesis and title reflect your purpose.
2. Develop a focused thesis, and use it to write your topic sentences and to determine the order of your paragraphs.
3. Proofread for sentence structure errors. Make sure your subjects and verbs "fit" together.

If you do the above, the essay will have a clear sense of direction and your writing will be more coherent.

A1

Sample Essay No. 4

Open Your Eyes

Frustrated and sad was the way I felt after reading about the death of Bjossa's calf in the Vancouver Sun several months ago. However, only part of the sadness came from the calf's actual death; the majority came from reading the response to such a tragedy. Bjossa, the killer whale at the Vancouver Aquarium, has given birth three times and all three have resulted in mortalities. This latest death has sparked animal rights extremists to go full fledged into the campaign to free whales from captivity. Keeping these animals in captivity helps to educate us about their lives which in turn, helps us understand the importance of preserving these creatures. Aquariums are not run by careless and cruel money-hungry opportunists, but rather, people who care about sea animals and only wish to educate the public about them.

As a regular volunteer at the Vancouver Aquarium, I have seen what this institution offers to the public. I must admit that before I started volunteering four years ago, I had the same views as many animal rights groups do today. What good could possibly come out of keeping these animals from their natural habitats? The answer to this question is obvious if you simply observe the public that visits the aquarium. To see the expression on the people's faces is amazing; they are in utter awe of these creatures, the majority of which they have never seen or knew existed before. That is precisely why I continue to volunteer at the Vancouver Aquarium; it provides a way for the public to become acquainted with these animals. It is one thing to talk about preserving the creatures in the oceans, lakes, and rivers, but it is another to actually see the creatures that you are referring to: the aquarium provides you with this opportunity.

Perhaps what frustrated and angered me the most about this article was the phrase: "abusive capture and captivity of orca whales" used by Lifeforce member Peter Hamilton to describe the treatment of these animals. As a member of the staff at the aquarium, I am very hurt by this comment. Nobody was anticipating the birth of this baby whale more than the staff who did everything possible to try to ensure that this was going to be a successful birth. This included such things as separating Bjossa from Finna, her mate, making a baby formula for the calf in case it had trouble nursing, and adding a new filtration system to the tank to improve the living environment. As an extra precaution a twenty-four hour monitoring system was set up by volunteers to make sure that nothing went wrong prior to the birth. However, nobody could have predicted a possible congenital defect in the baby. To imply that the aquarium staff doesn't care about these animals but "abuses" them is so untrue. Bjossa is a part of the Vancouver Aquarium family, so her loss was the loss of everyone at the aquarium too. Tears where shed by all, just as anybody would at the loss of a family member.

I know that Bjossa has lost three calves, but for people to suggest that we should release her back into the wild is irrational. Yes, it is true that these animals have become dependent on the aquarium for food, so to release them into the wild now is to send them to their death. In the name of education, these animals may have lost their hunting skills. We do not know this for sure, but I don't think that risking Bjossa and Finna's lives are worth it to find out. It's like leaving your child in the middle of the forest for a week to see if he/she could survive on their own. It's a cruel and dangerous experiment. These animals are treated with the utmost respect of everyone at the Vancouver Aquarium; they are not mistreated in any way. We have gathered valuable information about these animals such as mating behaviour, interactions with others, and general morphology, through close observation of them; however there is still so much more to know.

The death of Bjossa's third calf was very tragic, but unavoidable. We must realize that although killer whale births are rather rare, the infant mortality in the wild is very high (about 40 to 50 percent). The recent birth of a baby beluga whale at the Vancouver Aquarium demonstrates that babies do survive in captivity. All possible precautions were taken for this birth too. So yes, the aquarium cares very much for the animals it keeps. It also cares about bringing the public and animals together. The aquarium even has it own education department devoted to creating programs to help the public become acquainted with seal life and to help develop an understanding and respect for these animals. To truly understand my view of this whole topic, take some time to visit the Vancouver Aquarium and see for yourself. If you do, pay close attention to the other visitors there, talk to them and examine their expressions, it is then that you will understand the importance of having these animals available to the public.

Sample Essay No. 5

good title ✓ We're not alone, but we may as well be — upper case

The idea of extra-terrestrial life has become a minor obsession for our civilization. It is a wide-spread hope and belief that we will some day soon discover, and communicate with, aliens. People everywhere swear that aliens do exist, that there is evidence of other civilizations elsewhere in the universe. Much research has been done on the topic, involving serious amounts of time, expertise and money. Yet despite all this enthusiasm for extra-terrestrial civilizations, we have yet to discover proof of any such life-forms. This due to the sheer improbability of any life evolving at all, and to the massive distances between the stars. If there are any other life forms in our universe, it is highly improbable that we will ever communicate with them. ✓ clear thesis

fear? — missing word

Most people take life on earth for granted. We do not appreciate the incredible good luck involved in the creation of such a special planet as this one; the probability of another planet the could bear life forming within our galaxy is virtually zero. Frank D. Drake, the Dean of Natural Sciences at the University of Santa-Cruz, has formulated an equation to estimate the number of possible stars within our galaxy that have life-bearing planets around them (Snow 648). The equation is highly speculative, and answers obtained from it can range from zero to a very optimistic ten. That is, ten stars out of the ten billion in our galaxy could have life-supporting stars. Multiplied by the hundreds of thousands galaxies in the universe, that gives a large number of stars with life. Why don't they hurry up and call us? Unfortunately, it is not as simple as that, due to the enormous distances between the stars and galaxies in the universe.

ww: "that"? — good appeal to authority — qtd. in? — good use of a rhetorical question

A1

The average distance between the stars in our galaxy is twenty thousand light years—that is, one thousand, nine hundred trillion kilometers. That means any radio signals coming from extra terrestrials

emphasis: good use of dash — you can use numerals

would have to travel for twenty thousand years at the speed of light before arriving at our solar system. We have only been capable of receiving these radio signals for about fifty years—a very small window of time. If the theoretical other inhabitants of our galaxy had transmitted a signal to us nineteen thousand nine hundred and fifty years before we discovered radar, and if we did have the good luck to be looking in the right direction to receive these signals, we might have received a signal by now. Impossibilities of timing aside, if we did receive a signal from someone else, we would never be able to communicate with them. Their civilisation would probably have turned to dust aeons ago. It would be like a nightmare game of telephone tag, lasting thousands of years. At the most, we may discover some sign that there did exist, at one time, some other life in the universe. Any civilisations in our galaxy or universe that wished to ring us up would be so distant that the callers would be long dead by the time we got the message.

use numerals

good analogy

good refutation

Despite these facts, there are still people who are convinced that we have been contacted, even visited by extra terrestrials. People in magazine articles, in public and on television loudly proclaim that aliens have come to earth. The unlikelihood of aliens ever coming to visit us is underlined once again by the distances between the stars. Even if the aliens were traveling at the speed of light, it would take them a prohibitively long time to get here, ignoring the fact that it is impossible to move at light-speed. The fact is that nobody is going to visit us, and still obey the laws of physics. Numerous magazine articles and TV shows try to convince us to the contrary, that we have already been visited. The claims of these tabloids are undermined by a less than credible reputation. These "new" sources tend to inflate and embellish stories to improve readability, often at the expense of truth. One such story is the famous field-rings that appeared in English wheat fields on-and-off for twenty years. Areas of wheat, mysteriously flattened in elaborate circular patterns, caused wild speculation as to their source, and many people let

no punc

use colon

good but provide more examples

their imaginations run wild. It was believed by many that they were caused by aliens, until two men admitted to the hoax. With some long pieces of string and some plywood, they showed how they created the patterns and banished all thoughts of aliens. As of yet, there exists no real proof of alien life on earth, or elsewhere.

Still, much time and money has gone into the search for extra-terrestrial life. The first Voyager probe carried an encrypted message to any distant races that might stumble across it. High-powered signals are being transmitted to near-by star clusters, and to some even further away. At the same time, a highly sophisticated telescope in Harvard, sp. Massechusets has been entirely devoted to listening to nearby stars to try to detect artificial signals. Although it is not likely that we will ever see or communicate with an alien, we may still search for signs of their existence. If projects searching for extra-terrestrial life are to have any chance of success, they must operate for a time span that is many times greater than all of recorded human history; it highly unlikely that you or I *missing word* will be around to see any results. It is even more unlikely that we will ever make contact with an extra-terrestrial race. We must put aside all hopes of shaking hands with our celestial neighbours, and merely hope to pick out signs that they exist, signs to tell that we are not alone in the universe. We must search for an echoe of past life amongst the stars, *sp.* and leave our signature in the skies in the hopes someone else will record our passing.

Works Cited

"Listening for E.T." The Globe and Mail 4 November, 1995: D22.

Snow, Theodore. The Dynamic Universe. San Fransisco: West Publishing, 1988.

A1

A Cathy,

This essay was a pleasure to read. You made a valid argument, using authority to back your statements, and you acknowledged and refuted the opposition's views while keeping a friendly tone. In addition, the essay combines a variety of sentence types and styles that keeps the readers engaged with the topic.

For the next essay, however, you may want to proofread carefully for spelling mistakes.

Sample Essay No. 6

Contrasting Vancouver and Abbotsford

v.t. use present perfect

Unbelievably, I lived in almost 10 different places in Canada. When I first came to Canada, I lived in Lethbridge and then I moved to Calgary. After that my family moved to BC where I subsequently lived in Nanaimo, Langley, Aldergrove, Abbotsford, Walnut Grove, Surrey and Vancouver. Truthfully, I have attended about 15 different schools. Different places evoke a different atmosphere, due to the surrounding and the people. I moved from Abbotsford to Vancouver just a year ago; they are the two most recent places that I've lived in. Abbotsford and Vancouver have many similarities and differences.

correct verb tense *sp: "surroundings"* *can you list them? or explain why?*

Abbotsford is a rural place where agriculture is the main economy. Driving through the country, we can breathe in the fresh air and look at the farm animals grazing on the grass. I love the fresh open land of green grass everywhere and large spaces between the houses. Fortunately, houses here are much cheaper than the houses in Vancouver; hence, there is a lower demand for land in the country. The road is less crowded here because there are fewer occupants, less likely to get into car accidents.

unnecessary *art. (use "the" with a limiting phrase)* *one? or many? plural* *you need to add a conjunction & subject & verb*

Vancouver is an urban place where the land is more valuable. Everywhere on the sidewalk there would be people walking. I made many friends here because there are more opportunities for me to encounter them. Sometimes I feel that there is no fresh are here because of the busy traffic at every hour of the day, polluting the air. The houses here

idiom: "On the sidewalks everywhere" *use present tense – not conditional form* *people?* *sp* *transition*

A1

are very close together; in addition, there are no garages in the front of the house. *why is this significant?*

lower case In Conclusion, Vancouver and Abbotsford are unique in their own ways; therefore, I like both places. However, I wouldn't choose to live in Abbotsford for the rest of my life because there the shops and the mall are very far away. I would like to live in Vancouver and come back to Abbotsford every once in a while. Sometimes we need to travel to different places to learn the things that each place brings. *word choice: has? offers?*

can you use a more natural transition?

Is this feature of urban life important to you? Talk about it in the body of your essay.

use a more specific word

C- Amanda,
You certainly can speak from experience! You might however want to spend more time developing your thesis to take advantage of your experiences. Do you really want to focus on the urban vs. rural aspects of the two cities or is there some personal element you would like to add? Your thesis mentions similarities, but you don't really cover them in your paper. Continue proofreading for the occasional article and verb tense error in your next essay.

Sample Essay No. 7

Special Days

Chinese Lunar New Year, also known as Spring Festival, is the most important traditional holiday in China. It usually falls in January and February, lasting for fifteen days. These fifteen days are special days for people to celebrate the new start of a new year, visit friends and have fun. From government to individual family, various activities are held to observe the occasion. *Make your thesis into an opinion*

art. *plural*

Stronger topic sentence Several days before the new year, people are busy preparing for the holiday. They buy new clothes, food and other stuff. The houses are decorated with flashing lights, flowers and typical pictures with the character "fu" which means fortune. On New Year's Eve, family members get together to enjoy a feast. After dinner, married adults will give kids red envelopes with lucky money inside. At night, most Chinese watch the gala show broadcast by the Chinese Central Television and countdown the last minute to welcome the coming of a brand new year.

diction: can you be more specific?

diction

art. On the first day of the new year, parade take place in the street. *subj/verb agr.* *Have a stronger topic sentence* Lion dancing is a routine program. In parks, there are some exhibitions with topics like calligraphy and Chinese painting. Business takes *transition?* advantage of the festival. Tons of people can be seen in big shopping *art.* malls and department stores. Firework show is also an annual event. The *transition?* last day of the new year is the lantern festival. People will eat "Yuanxian" *transition?* which means reunion. It is also considered as the Chinese Valentine's Day because many young people came across their beloveds while *word choice: "future partners"* appreciating the beautiful lanterns in ancient China. After the last day of the Spring Festival, people are supposed to move back to their normal track of life. *idiom: "go back to their regular routines"*

art. Spring Festival has long history in China. It gives a break for Chinese *word choice: "provides" "allows the Chinese"* people to enjoy themselves and spend more time with their family. It makes life more meaningful and colorful. The holiday should be passed to the future generations.

Nicole,

Your essay is full of many interesting details regarding the Chinese Lunar New Year. The holiday sounds like a wonderful time. However, your thesis should be a little more focused. This would lead to stronger topic sentences for your paragraphs. Start your paragraphs with an "umbrella" statement that is your main idea. For example, if you want to emphasize that this holiday involves every member of the family, your topic sentence might be the following: Every member of the family contributes to the success of this holiday. Your paragraph would then support this statement with examples of the various activities.

With stronger topic sentences, your paragraphs will be more coherent, and you will have an easier time making transitions between your ideas. You can start by using more periodic sentences with transitional tags. (Too many of your sentences are loose, giving your essay a choppy feel.) Also proofread for the occasional article error.

A1

Sample Essay No. 8 (written for an examination)

Analysis of Hamlet's Remembrance Soliloquy (I. v. 92–112)

Hamlet. O all you host of heaven! O earth! What else?
And shall I couple hell? Oh fie! Hold, hold my heart,
And you, my sinews, grow not instant old,
But bear me stiffly up. Remember thee?
Ay thou poor ghost, while memory holds a seat
In this distracted globe. Remember thee?
Yea, from the table of my memory
I'll wipe away all trivial fond records,
All saws of books, all forms, all pressures past
That you and observation copied there,
And thy commandment all alone shall live
Within the book and volume of my brain,
Unmixed with baser matter. Yes, by heaven!
O most pernicious woman!
O villain, smiling damnèd villain!
My tables—meet it is I set it down
That one may smile, and smile, and be a villain.
At least I am sure it may be so in Denmark. [*Writes.*]
So, uncle, there you are. Now to my word:
It is "Adieu, adieu, remember me." I have sworn't.

It is a good strategy to begin with a question, but can you make it more focused?

What is Shakespeare's Hamlet? It is a tragedy, a calamity, and a gigantic puzzle, to begin with. The play's central character is a young man with great gifts of intellect, and yet all of his talents cannot save him or the people around him when he decides to follow a commandment of a ghost which haunts the night. In this, his second soliloquy, Hamlet, more alone than ever, expresses his horror at the truth, his rage at those who have betrayed his father, and his determination to remember his oath of vengeance against his father's killer.

necessary? cliché?

This thesis reflects character and his motivation; but you also need to address the themes of the passage.

This soliloquy in blank verse comes near the end of the first act, immediately following Hamlet's terrifying meeting with a figure whom he accepts as the tormented spirit of his dead father. The soliloquy marks the first turning point in the play, for from this point on, Hamlet is never quite the same. Now, Hamlet has some evidence—or at least testimony—to back up his previous suspicions about the evil nature of the new king, Claudius. Before this speech, Hamlet has been brooding about a marriage he regards as deeply sinful, but he has pledged to hold his tongue about it; now, he is committed to taking action against a murderer and an illegitimate king. From this point on, Hamlet's life of scholarship and romance and friendship is all but dead; he is about to become a man obsessed and an actor playing the role of a madman all too well. *good short summary of the soliloquy*

Hamlet's character is complex: he is brilliant, sad, funny, brutal, kind—an incredible mixture of elements. He is a man caught in a struggle between his reason and his passions. In this speech, the passion emerges first. In two exclamations and two questions, he begins his speech with strong emotions of shock and horror. He prays to heaven, shouts at earth and wonders about hell as he does elsewhere in the play when his passions overcome his reason. He speaks of his own physical weaknesses and described his mind metaphorically as "a distracted globe." In the first of many pledges, he promises to "wipe away all trivial fond records" and give up everything that has meant anything to him: his books, his sayings, his youthful interests. In a way, Hamlet becomes old and careworn before the audience's eyes as the ghost retreats with the rising of the sun. *good observation*

well said

wrong verb tense: use present

significance?

A1

The most emotional part of the soliloquy comes when Hamlet expresses his thoughts about his mother and his new stepfather. His mother is a "most pernicious woman," the word "pernicious" suggesting someone who is deeply evil. Claudius for his part is "a villain, a smiling villain," and Hamlet is having a hard time understanding how one so corrupt—so sinful—could appear to be so amiable, such a smiling, polished, perfect king.

This paragraph needs to be developed. Perhaps combine with the following one?

repetitious? unnecessary definition?

inaccurate quotation: a "villain, [a] smiling . . . villain"

Just when Hamlet's passion seems about to boil over into an act of public violence against his "aunt-mother" and "uncle-father," his mind asserts itself and reason prevails in him for the time being. The physical action of Hamlet in this passage matches this physical change. When Hamlet picks up his diary to write about his experience, he shows himself trying to organize the experience with his student's mind. He makes notes about what he has seen; he writes an essay about it. Such an action is but the first example of Hamlet's many attempts to make order out of a disordered, disjointed and rotten world.

Apart from revealing the complexities of Hamlet's character, this soliloquy presents the audience with several themes. It shows us Hamlet as a Dane deeply disgusted by his own country because it is a place where one may smile and prosper and be a villain. It shows us that the world for Hamlet has become, in just a few minutes on the battlements, a place in which the appearance of a man may not match at all the reality of his soul. In this passage, the word "memory" becomes a refrain, and the reader must wonder how Hamlet could ever forget what he has heard in the chill of the night. The last line, "I have sworn't," echoes other moments in the play in which characters swear oaths: the soldiers' pledge to keep the ghost secret; Ophelia's and Laertes's pledge to follow their father's advice; Gertrude's pledge to abandon Claudius's bed after Hamlet has "cleft [her] heart in twain" in the closet scene. Like the others, Hamlet has a dreadful time—a tragic time—living up to the pledge. In Denmark, it seems, pledges are made to be broken or at least forgotten.

good emphasis

good observation

This soliloquy is important to the play, then, as a contributor to the plot, the characterization and the theme. Without it, the audience would be deprived of a turning point in the plot; it would lose a glimpse at Hamlet's brilliant, embattled mind; it would lose an opportunity to understand the ironic gap between what is and what seems—even in the highest realms of government and power. [Without the remembrance soliloquy, in short, *Hamlet* just wouldn't be *Hamlet*.] *necessary?*

A- Robin,
Your essay is a thoughtful analysis of the soliloquy. Your observations about the language and placement of the soliloquy are both well put and interesting. However, your introduction needs to be more focused and your thesis more clearly stated. In fact, your conclusion should be your introduction! In your next home essay, you may want to write your introduction after drafting the body of essay.

Sample Essay No. 9

The Glory of It All

We live surrounded by music. What is more, modern technology has placed at our disposal every kind of music, from virtually every period in history and every corner of the globe. Of course, music from different eras serves as a link between people, a common ground. In Peter Shaffer's Amadeus, the audience is transported back in time to view the world of music as it was in the eighteenth century. Although Amadeus mirrors timeless real-to-life struggles, the play's major themes, revenge, fame versus talent, and jealousy are presented through ironies in character, plot, and language.

Throughout the play, Shaffer uses twists in character to present the theme of revenge. A prime example of character irony is presented when Salieri realizes that Mozart will be remembered as the most brilliant composer of his time. In order for Salieri to become "immortal" he must make it known that he murdered the brilliant Mozart, so that, "Whenever men say Mozart with love, they will say Salieri with loathing!" The irony is furthered at the end of the play, when Salieri overhears his claim is "believed in truth by no one but . . . himself," and realizes he will never be recognized for his efforts.

The theme of fame versus talent is emphasized through various examples of irony in plot. Right from the opening scenes, Salieri makes it clear that, "(he) want(s) fame," and although his talents do not compare to Mozart's, he pursues his goal with fierce determination, taking full advantage of his influential post as court composer. Knowing all along that Mozart is a musical genius, Salieri "get(s) the piece(s) cancelled" to delay Mozart's inevitable fame. Yet even as he does this, Salieri's fame continues to rise steadily "Almost as if (he) were being pushed deliberately from triumph to triumph!" above his talented victim Mozart. Though he dedicates his life to becoming famous, Salieri even admits, "Goodness could not make me a good composer."

The play's major theme, jealousy, is expressed primarily by means of ironies in language. At the beginning of the play, in retrospect, Salieri says ironically, "I wanted to blaze, like a comet, across the firmament of Europe," which is an apt description of his short-lived presence as a well-known eighteenth century composer. In addition, throughout the play, Salieri becomes increasingly envious of Mozart; he even describes a serene Adagio as ". . . pain! Pain as I had never known it." It is at this point in the play that the audience may be certain that Salieri has a mean and jealous passion for Mozart's work. After this point, Shaffer reinforces the theme of jealousy through further ironic speech when Salieri is seducing Mozart's wife: "Take a true look. I've no cunning," he tells her sympathetically. Salieri neatly sums up his feelings towards jealousy, "It's not a passion I understand," an extremely ironic understatement from a man whose world is consumed by it.

In Shaffer's Amadeus, the themes of revenge, fame versus talent, and jealousy are presented most effectively by means of twisted situations involving character, plot, and language.

Shaffer, Peter. Amadeus. Harmondsworth: Penguin, 1981.

Sample Essay No. 10

The Value of Emotional Intelligence in the Town of Avonlea ✓ *an excellent title*

How an author of children's literature defines and distinguishes a child's intelligence from that of an adult's reveals much about the author's (and his/her era's) beliefs about children's education. Moreover, how an author approaches the distinction between the minds of adults

Can one story affect a child both ways at different points?

and children may very subtly affect the child reader so that one story may empower a child while another story makes him/her feel impotent. Lucy Maud Montgomery's Anne of Green Gables offers the middle child reader an empowering experience, as they observe the triumph of a girl who faces a life of obstacles with good humour, good nature, good will and an innate insight into human nature. Lucy Maud Montgomery's portrayal of Anne shows her to be a funny, quirky, silly little girl who can't seem to stay out of trouble, but the author also manages to illuminate the young red-head's intelligence as distinct from and often more competent than that of the adults in the novel. Montgomery defines Anne's intelligence in a way that would be described today as "emotional intelligence," while the adults in the story have an intelligence based on varying degrees of (and often limitations of) long-acquired knowledge or wisdom. Montgomery begins the novel conveying the flaws of the story's key adult characters and uses these adults as contrasting characters to Anne, illustrating the differences between the intelligence of a child and that of an adult. The author also contrasts Anne and Gilbert with the other Avonlea children to demonstrate the value and potency of these two's dynamic young intelligence. *clear thesis*

pronoun agr.

good balanced sentence

Vary your sentence structure to avoid always starting with the author's name.

…original …ading of the …lue of …ucation/ …telligence in …e novel

awk. "their" or "this pair's"

A1

For the purposes of this paper, the psychological term, "emotional intelligence" should be defined and linked to Montgomery's approach to the intelligence of the child and adult characters in her novel. This paper will define "emotional intelligence" by using the definitions of two psychologists: Daniel Goleman and Howard Gardner. Daniel Goleman defines emotional intelligence as, "abilities such as being able to motivate oneself and persist in the face of frustrations; to control impulse and delay gratification; to regulate one's moods and keep distress from swamping the ability to think; to empathize and to hope" (Goleman 34). Howard Gardner defines emotional intelligence in terms of "personal intelligences":

no punc

no punc

> *Interpersonal intelligence* denotes a person's capacity to understand the intentions, motivations, and desires of other people and, consequently, to work effectively with others. . . . *Intrapersonal intelligence* involves the capacity to understand oneself, to have an effective working model of oneself—including one's own desires, fears, and capacities—and to use such information effectively in regulating one's own life. (Gardner 43)

good to define the terms but can you use paraphrases?

too informal: "Given that" Being that she wrote the novel in the early 1900's, Montgomery was not exposed to any such precise definitions of or likely even the term, "emotional intelligence"; however, in the late nineteenth and early twentieth centuries, the nature of children's intelligence was being examined and understood in new ways. Child psychology had emerged in the latter half of the nineteenth century, and "quasi-psychologists" such as Locke and Rousseau had been analyzing children since the seventeenth and eighteenth centuries (Tucker 158–159). So, while Montgomery may not have understood "emotional intelligence" in the same way as do today's child psychologists, she would have had (and apparently did have) her own informed opinions* about the uniqueness and value of children's intelligence, and an understanding about the distinctions between the way adults and children think.

**Were these opinions informed by reading of quasi-psychologists or by her own experience?*

A1

The first step Montgomery takes in her novel towards distinguishing the differences between adults' and children's intelligence is by characterizing the important adult characters in the novel as being flawed. She begins the novel by giving the reader some initial insight into the minds of the leading adult characters: Rachel, Marilla, and Mathew. *sp.* By exploring their intellect, views, and feelings, Montgomery conveys a message to the child reader: the wisdom and knowledge acquired by these adults has not seemed *v.t. "does not seem"* to have made them happier or better people. *What do you mean by "better"? Are the adult characters not good or virtuous anyway?*

Montgomery begins the novel with introductions to Rachel Lynde and Marilla Cuthbert in the first chapter. *well said* Both women seem to experience life through the guidance of scripture, being ever mindful of what is deemed respectable behaviour. Rachel Lynde occupies the first line of the novel and the narrator's description of her conveys a character with strict Victorian ideals who gives "due regard for decency and decorum . . . ," [MLA: misuse of ellipses] while occupying most of her spare time observing the comings and goings of the townsfolk (Montgomery 7). Rachel's character is representative of the town of Avonlea, where everyone knows everybody else's business. Marilla comes across as a no-nonsense utilitarian woman who spends her [good word choice] time putting herself to good use: keeping her house and her yard spotless, and rarely taking the time to sit down and relax (Montgomery 10). Neither woman seems very happy, and both seem to lack the ability to seek out pleasure in life by appreciating the little things; such as, the beauty of nature. Rachel believes "trees aren't much company . . ." [MLA] (Montgomery 9) and Marilla is "always slightly distrustful of sunshine, which seem[s] to her too dancing and irresponsible a thing for a world which [is] meant to be taken seriously . . . ." [MLA] (Montgomery 10). Neither of these women show great capacities of (in the words of Howard Gardner) [s-v agr: "shows" subject is "neither" not "women"] "Intrapersonal intelligence": [lower case] the ability to use one's self-knowledge to positively effect [sp] one's own life (Gardner 43).

[effective transition] Also in this first chapter, Montgomery gives the reader some insight into both women's levels of "interpersonal intelligence." Marilla's and Rachel's friendship seems somewhat cold and unaffectionate. ["Marilla and Rachel's"] On the day Mathew [sp] goes to fetch Anne, Rachel's main motivation for calling on Marilla is not to enjoy her friend's good company or to inquire if she's well, but to satisfy her own curiosity about where Mathew is going and why. In fact, Rachel must know or else won't have "a minute's peace of mind or conscience . . ." (Montgomery 9). Upon hearing their news, Rachel, instead of trying to be a good friend by listening to Marilla's and Mathew's reasons for taking in an orphan, immediately expresses her disapproval. Rachel's offer of a "Job's comforting" to Marilla is due either to the fact that Rachel does not care enough about her friend to extend [rewrite sentence removing "due to the fact that"]

A1

true comfort, or it is due to the fact that Rachel does not have a sense of how to help people during stressful times (Montgomery 13).* This failure to read Marilla's needs is indicative of Rachel's possession of a low level of interpersonal intelligence: the ability to read the needs of other people and to interact effectively with them (Gardner 43). This interaction between Rachel and Marilla also sheds some light on the way Marilla's mind works. As she complains about the lack of good labour in Avonlea, Marilla demonstrates a narrow, discriminatory outlook by making negative comments about "stupid, half-grown little French boys [. . . and] London street Arabs . . . ." (Montgomery 12). Overall, Marilla's and Rachel's discussion at Green Gables leaves both of them looking unhappy, close-minded, and intolerant.

*Which is th more likely explanation?

Throughout the novel, it is Mathew who comes across as the most forgiving adult character. In the beginning of the story, he seems to be the most emotionally intelligent adult, due to his natural shyness and apparent sensitivity. However, Montgomery is quick to point out his flaws. When the narrator first gets inside Mathew's head and discloses some of Mathew's feelings, the reader finds out about Mathew's phobia of women: "he [has] an uncomfortable feeling that the mysterious creatures [are] secretly laughing at him" (Montgomery 16). Mathew appears to be an unreliable adult character because of his timidness, and it makes his meeting with Anne humorous because they are such opposites. It is during Mathew's and Anne's meeting at the train station and their drive to Green Gables that Montgomery begins her contrasts of children's and adult's intelligences.

too strong a word?

good word choice

weak expleti

In her novel, Montgomery manages to distinguish between adult's and children's intelligence, showing the value and uniqueness of children's intelligence, without showing too much bias towards the child characters.* However, respect for the protagonist's intellect is important, and Montgomery begins her characterization of Anne by establishing her level of emotional intelligence immediately, contrasting her behavior with

*Would you say this is the case with other writers for children?

Mathew's. Anne shows "Intrapersonal intelligence" straight away by using her self-knowledge to comfort herself in a situation which is undoubtedly highly stressful for her. Having been dropped off at the train station, she waits for her new adoptive parents to pick her up, not knowing what to expect, and most likely expecting very little, considering her past experiences in orphanages and foster homes since her parents' deaths. Instead of worrying and brooding in the waiting-room, she chooses to wait outside because "'There [is] more scope for imagination'" (Montgomery 17). Here Anne takes what could be a distressing experience for herself, and turns it into an opportunity to delve into her world of fantasy and daydreams, which (Montgomery implies in the novel) has helped her through traumatic experiences throughout her eleven years. Goleman would say that Anne exhibits "self awareness." He says that "typical thoughts bespeaking emotional self-awareness include 'I shouldn't feel this way,' 'I'm thinking good things to cheer up,' and . . . 'Don't think about it' in reaction to something highly upsetting" (Goleman 47). Anne recognizes situations which cause her distress and takes a proactive approach towards keeping herself in good spirits. Anne also uses her Intrapersonal intelligence—the knowledge of her own "desires, fears, and capacities" on her drive home with Mathew (Gardner 43). Instead of mentally pushing against things that are strange to her, Anne begins renaming and romanticizing everything she sees in an effort to become enthusiastic about her new home.

good use of secondary source

Montgomery also uses the scene between Anne and Mathew to contrast Mathew's and Anne's "interpersonal intelligence," the ability to read other people's feelings and needs, and to effectively respond (Gardner 43). While Mathew appears helpless and at a loss about what to do about the problem (receiving a girl-orphan instead of a boy), Anne takes charge by rising and addressing Mathew first, instead of waiting for him to come to her. The narrator states that Anne "had been watching [Mathew]" throughout his upsetting conversation with the station-master

…a way Matthew's …rofound …ncertainty is … blessing that …llows Anne a …ot in the …oor of Green …ables.

A1

(Montgomery 18–19). It is entirely possible that Anne approaches Mathew first because she sees that he is uncomfortable and anxious. By reacting to the situation this way, Anne exhibits a high level of "interpersonal intelligence." She plays the role of comforter to Mathew, the adult, in a situation which would usually by much more stressful on her, the child. *oops. proofreading* Here Montgomery exhibits how extraordinary and valuable Anne's emotional intelligence is, and foreshadows how skilled and reliable Anne will be in future times of crisis. *an interesting observation*

Anne's emotional intelligence also comes through in her ability to learn from the adults in her life. While she teaches them, she is also grateful and heedful of what they have to teach her. Although the reader's initial view of Anne emphasizes her emotional intelligence, Montgomery is careful to portray her throughout the story as a realistic, imperfect character. She does have a temper which flares up on occasion. *ambiguous: real-life or practising realism?* *What is the transition here?* Conveying the findings of psychologist Dolf Zillmann, Goleman points out that a universal trigger for anger is the sense of being endangered. Endangerment can be signaled not just by an outright physical threat but also, as is more often the case, by a symbolic threat to self-esteem or dignity: being treated unjustly or rudely, being insulted or demeaned, being frustrated in pursuing an important goal (60).

A1

This transition implies a close connection to the previous paragraph. Perhaps you could restructure these paragraphs or change the topic sentence to avoid the vague "This"

This results in an energy surge that "lasts for minutes, during which it readies the body for a good fight or a quick flight, depending on how the emotional brain sizes up the opposition" (Goleman 60). It seems that in Anne's separate altercations with Rachel and Gilbert, she is ready for a good fight. In both situations, Anne faces from her antagonists a threat to her self-esteem because of their comparing the colour of her hair to carrots. It is clear to the reader that Anne over-reacts in both cases, and it isn't until she learns from Marilla and Mathew to work on managing her anger, and from Marilla not to be so sensitive about her appearance, that she becomes truly emotionally intelligent ~~(Montgomery 80–85)~~. While emotional intelligence may seem something innate, Goleman argues that

reference the primary text only when you are quoting from it

"there is ample evidence that emotional skills such as impulse control and accurately reading a social situation *can* be learned" (Goleman 83). If it weren't for Marilla's and Mathew's knowledge, life experience, role-modeling, and wisdom, Anne would not have grown into the extraordinary young woman she becomes.

not worldly wise but wise in the ways of Avonlea

Another of Anne's role-models, and the person who is closest to being Anne's equal in the novel, is Gilbert. In conveying the fact that Anne and Gilbert are connected in some way, Montgomery uses the other children of Avonlea to contrast their two characters. The novel portrays Gilbert as Anne's equal in terms of both emotional and academic intelligence. The other child characters: Diana, Ruby, Charlie, etc. are no match for Anne's and Gilbert's conventional intelligence (in terms of IQ), but neither are they any match for these two's emotional intelligence. Instead of emphasizing Anne's and Gilbert's IQ's, Montgomery emphasizes their emotional intelligence, one aspect of which is their abilities to hope. Goleman argues that the ability to hope is one of the most important indicators of a student's future success. He refers to C.R. Snyder's study of college students, where Snyder found that a student's hope about their academic performance or achievement "was a better predictor of their first-semester grades than were their scores on the SAT . . . . Emotional aptitudes make the critical difference [because . . .] 'students with high hope set themselves higher goals and know how to work hard to attain them'" (qtd. in Goleman 86). By characterizing Anne and Gilbert with higher emotional intelligence than the other children, and by showing them to have higher academic successes than the other children, Montgomery sends a message to the middle-child reader that hope, hard work, and determination are more the ingredients for success than is conventional intelligence.

no colon / *avoid: "and so on"* / *use double dashes around a list interrupting a sentence* / *reword* / *singular* / *noun-pronoun agr.* / *Where do the other children show themselves losing hope?* / *awk.*

Some of the most powerful evidence for Anne's emotional intelligence comes through in the fact that she feels absolutely no shame about her lack of religious education or spiritual connection to God. Daniel Goleman states that "there is growing evidence that fundamental ethical stances in life stem from underlying emotional capacities" (Goleman xii). Unlike the respectable citizens of Avonlea, Anne is not guided by religious and culture-based rules of life. She trusts her own instincts about the right ways to treat others and what is right for herself. She tells Marilla that "if [she] really wanted to pray . . . [she'd] go out into a great big field all alone or in the deep, deep woods, and . . . look up into the sky . . . and then . . . just feel a prayer" (Montgomery 58–59). Anne feels no shame about her lack of a relationship with God because she steadfastly believes in her own innocence. Her belief in her own innocence is remarkable because although Montgomery does not show the citizens of Avonlea blatantly persecuting Anne for her scandalous orphan status, her alienation by the townsfolk is implied by Rachel's assumptions about the evil nature of all orphans ~~(Montgomery 13)~~ and Mrs. Barry's belief that Anne intoxicated Diana with malicious intent ~~(Montgomery 144).~~ In those days it was generally thought that all orphans were criminals or just commonly bad or evil. Furthermore, since Anne faces humiliation on account of her lack of "puffed-sleeves," she must certainly face ostracism due to her lack of parents. So, although Montgomery doesn't show every act of cruelty, no matter how subtle, exacted on Anne by her schoolmates or the townspeople, the reader may infer that such occurrences are taking place.

good use of text

from other children or equally from children and adults?

a skilfully argued point

A1

Besides emphasizing the value of a child's intelligence as distinctive from that of an adult's intelligence, Montgomery succeeds in developing an important child-hero whom is of the most value to young girls. Anne's heroism is displayed through her ability to develop her own identity, sense of individualism, and intelligence. She works fiercely and steadily towards her ultimate goal of becoming a teacher, and she succeeds in life, no matter the obstacles. Obvious obstacles are her traumatic experiences from her past, which the reader only hears of briefly, and much of which the reader has to imagine: her parents' deaths, and the exploitation, and

who—subject of "is"

misplaced modifier

emotional and physical harm she experiences as an orphan and a foster child. But what the reader is most privy to are the less seedy, more *ordinary* obstacles that Anne shares with other girls of Avonlea, indeed with all girls and women in Western society.* She grows up in an age that still honours Victorian values. It is a world where men and women have separate domains: a man's place is in the public sphere, and a woman's place is in the private sphere. A man's intelligence is more highly valued than a woman's intelligence. Avonlea society's acknowledgment of a woman's value and place is reflected in the behaviour, expectations, and dreams of the other girls of Avonlea. Although Anne's desires for higher education are supported by Marilla—who, uncharacteristically for women of her time, believes a woman should always be able to support herself—it would likely have been perfectly acceptable for Anne to go the way of Diana: concentrating on becoming a competent housekeeper and maintaining her good looks in preparation for marriage. But Anne doesn't go that way, she chooses to put a value on her own intelligence equal to the value society puts on a man's intelligence. She chooses to take control of her own life and to strive towards becoming a better person, without becoming too distracted with conforming to the types of behaviour deemed by society as indicative of a "good woman." She is a good woman . . . as defined by Anne Shirley.✓ *excellent strong conclusion*

in what time period?

**Be cautious about sweeping statements*

to anyone but Anne!

comma splice

Works Cited

Gardner, Howard. Intelligence Reframed: Multiple Intelligences for the 21st Century. New York: Basic, 1999.

Goleman, Daniel. Emotional Intelligence. New York: Bantam, 1995.

Montgomery, L.M. Anne of Green Gables. Toronto: McClelland, 1992.

Tucker, Nicholas. "Good Friends, or Just Acquaintances? The Relationship between Child Psychology and Children's Literature." Literature for Children: Contemporary Criticism. Ed. Peter Hunt. London: Routledge, 1992. 156–173.

Tara,
I enjoyed reading your well-written and well-documented essay. Your strong opening and fresh approach to the text raise several thought-provoking issues and questions about the meaning of wisdom, including emotional wisdom, in literature for children. There are several potential future essays in this one essay! What you do need to work on for your next essay is proofreading. Be particularly careful with the spelling of characters' names, punctuation, and sentence structure.

Sample Essay No. 11

Green and Eden: Allusions that Raise Norma Joyce

In Elizabeth Hay's A Student of Weather, there is a division between the worlds of eastern and western North America. Hay uses an Eden motif to convey the contrast between the hardship of the west during the depression and the dustbowl of the 1930s and 40s with the apparently lush and abundance experienced at the same time in the east. But the motif is more significantly used to help the reader understand better the characters and their relationships in the story. Norma Joyce is on an almost life-long quest to end up in her own Eden, and Hay gives her an Eve-persona in order to draw parallels and connections between these two females. Hay also uses the colour green, allusions to the Tree of Knowledge, and to the Fall of Man in order to characterize Norma and to draw attention to her influences, inspirations, and motivations.

A1

Norma Joyce makes links between Eden and Ontario, which are formed from a few different sources during her childhood. One major source of this association is the shared view of most everyone living in Saskatchewan, at the time of the story, that while the west is sufferable, dry, and barren, the east is lush, green, and abundant. At age eight Norma pictures herself running away to the east because, as the narrator states, Saskatchewan "children grew up never tasting an apple and thinking Ontario was heaven" (Hay 3). Norma's exaggerated idea of Ontario has much to do with growing up in Saskatchewan, but it doesn't have everything to do with this. Her obsession with finding her own, personal Eden contrasts the preoccupations of her father and her sister who live the same bleak existence as she does. Hay implies that part of Norma's obsession comes from the encouragement and the spirit of her mother. The colour green is associated with Florida May, in a few things: a "blue-and-green afghan" (42) made by Norma's mother the year before she died; Florida's pale green notebook full of her creations and inspirations; and the scene where Norma and Florida are lying in the prairie grass, looking up in the starry sky. These three visions of green symbolize Florida's complicity in Norma Joyce's quest to get to Eden. Florida May's influence begins after little Norman's death, when she tries to protect Norma from Ernie's unspoken judgement of his youngest daughter, supposed murderer to his only son. When Florida "should have been outside helping Ernest and Lucinda . . . she stayed here instead, rocking her birthday girl and thinking about the caravans of Indians [. . .]" (44). This way, Florida shows Norma that it is good to dream, okay to imagine, fine not to give in to the blinding, mind-numbing work ethic of Ernie and Lucinda. Norma learns from her mother that it is acceptable to feel you deserve more, and it is all right to take more than someone else tells you that you deserve. This encouragement makes Norma feel okay about dreaming about Eden, planning a move east, and claiming her Adam. When she needs inspiration, Norma can take comfort under the blue-green afghan or flip through the pale green notebook.

A1

Hay solidifies the theme of Norma's quest for Eden by making connections between Norma and the biblical figure of Eve in order to draw parallels between the two. One effect of the connection is to relate what it feels like to carry the burden of blame and suspicion. Norma takes on a guilt—which illustrates the sinfulness historically fixed upon Eve—very early on in the novel. Very soon after an image of Norma Joyce's "[snaking]" arm—an allusion to the serpent tempting Eve in the Garden of Eden—comes the young girl's first documented act in the novel: sneaking "a heel of fruitcake" which she cannot let her sister "smell [on] her breath" (2); like Eve eating the forbidden apple. Norma's "Eve" image is also linked with her mother, who "choked to death on a piece of venison jerky snuck in the middle of the night" (23). After Florida's death, "Norma Joyce will be watched for sneakiness, and scolded for bolting food . . . she will feel like a sneak" (23). A "sneak" would be a very unique way of describing Eve. She did "sneak" the apple, but it is not the verb one usually turns to when describing the first woman's transgression. However, the sound of the word and its implications strongly convey the true psychological effect this particular label contains. It is an ugly label that likens the wearer to something less than human; say, a slinking fox, or, perhaps more fittingly, a slithering snake. But the reader also sees in this connection with the disobedience of Eve, that Norma, like Eve, has been chosen as scapegoat and wears that burden until the finger-pointers of her family die away.

Because Hay wants the reader to immediately see Norma as an Eve character, she begins the novel by painting Norma as having womanly characteristics, even when she is a child. Within the first few pages, the reader is told that Norma wants to run away to the east. Norma "pictures herself running away to the apple-strewn east like Claudette Colbert running lickety-split to Clark Gable" (2). And the first paragraph of the book has her "[wishing] for a man with straight white teeth and red lips" (1)—this, at eight years old. These images suggest that she wants her transportation to Eden to be the result of a chivalrous deed of a romantic, handsome man. Her dreams about men—not boys—at age eight seem out of place, and have the effect of taking away much of the innocence ascribed to the little girl she is supposed to be. In these first pages, her character is made so large; is fleshed out with substantial womanly desires and big dreams for herself that she takes on an Eve-like persona almost immediately.

The strength, depth, liveliness, and tenaciousness in Norma's character is conveyed throughout the novel through the use of the colour green. Many of the symbols, metaphors and images of the Eden motif are presented much more boldly than is the colour green, but that is what makes the mention of the colour in certain scenes so significant. Flickers and flashes of green taunt the reader, tempt and challenge the reader to think more deeply, find out more, care more about the Norma Joyce's path and development. Much of the green is found in the natural foliage of the novel's eastern settings, but green shows up in Saskatchewan as well. One of the first representations of green is in the grasses Maurice introduces to Norma from his botany manual. The grasses are suggested by Maurice as having a "tough, light, flexible existence" (33). The colour green, conveyed as being hardy (Hardy). This "Hardy-ness" Norma identifies with and sees reflected in her own character. These grasses, these depictions of green are described by Maurice as "puberulent . . . 'From the same root as puberty. Covered with fine hairs or down,'" (33)—like the prematurely pubescent and hairy Norma who claims to have "reached [her] sexual peak at the age of five" (35), deriving sexual pleasure from lying in long grass in the hot sun. This image of a sexual child seems premature; again, characterizing her as womanly, linking her with the image of Eve, and foreshadowing a strong sexual appetite in her future.

Besides characterizing Norma as tough, Hay draws attention to her thirst for knowledge through the theme of acquiring knowledge that is connected to the story of the Garden of Eden and the Tree of Knowledge. This theme is expressed through Maurice's and then Norma's quest for knowledge of all things, but particularly about plants and trees. One particular scene shows Norma's heightened quest for knowledge, now that she has arrived in her Eden, Ontario. During her initial meeting with Maurice's mother, Norma shows a desire to gain knowledge by compulsively enquiring about the names of Mrs. Dove's plants:

> 'What is the name of that vine?' . . .
>
> 'What about that bush?'
>
> 'Which? That one? I couldn't say.'

> No one could. No one knew anything. She had never wanted so badly to know the names of things . . . no one knew. Their ignorance was like an iron band around her heart. (124)

In the biblical story of the Garden of Eden, Adam is given the power, by God, to name all of God's new earthly creations. It is unclear whether or not at this point in the story Norma wishes for this same power—maybe believes she deserves this power—now that she has been brought to her own Eden, or whether she is simply missing the presence of her Adam, Maurice, who has been a great source of knowledge for her in the past. Whatever the case, it is clear that she wishes to engage with her surroundings, to take them in and understand them, to know them. She seeks knowledge about life, just like Eve, and she is showing herself to be growing into someone who will not tire until she gets it.

Another way Hay builds on the Eden motif is by using the colour green in the form of a type of grass to introduce the theme of the Fall of Man. Maurice's explanation of the "love grass" while they are still in Saskatchewan, is used by Hay as a type of foretelling; a symbol of the relentless way Norma will grow to live her life. This "love grass" is a grass, "'Often persistent after their fall'" (34). This definition alludes to the fall of man but really gets the reader thinking about what Norma's fall will be. The fall that occurs in Norma's Garden of Eden is not in the sexual acts that take place in the white tent or at the lake on the bed of wild strawberries. The fall that occurs in her Eden occurs in the Cranford Rose Garden in New York, when both Maurice and Norma gain an honest knowledge of one-another. Although Norma, almost without end throughout the novel, does not give up her romantic notions of love connected with Maurice, it is within this garden setting that she understands, honestly, how little she means to him compared with his own needs. When she tells him that she won't tell anyone that he's the father, "She [sees] the gratitude and shame on his face" (173). And it is in this garden that Maurice comprehends that Norma had the cleverness and the viciousness to trick him, fooling him by her claims of taking care of the contraception when she had only really "hoped" she was "safe." This is an unanticipated acquisition of knowledge about the evil that is existent in both of these characters. Norma is evil in the eyes of Maurice because she played so lightly with his future, possibly in an effort to trap him into marriage. Maurice is evil in the eyes of Norma because he cares more for his reputation and future than he does for her well-being. But, pregnant and alone, Norma goes on, persists after the fall, after the pain of knowledge is revealed to her.

Through all she learns in her quest, Norma Joyce realizes that there is no such place as Eden on earth. But there is happiness on earth; although, that is not something that is created for you in the way that God created the Garden of Eden. You have to make that for yourself, Adam or no. Norma always appreciated the value of knowledge and at the end of the novel she seems to have attained enough to warrant one more meaningful transformation. After her pilgrimage back home, Hay strips Norma of her fantastic Eve persona and transforms her into a strong, green grass, worthy of the stubble that survives droughts and protects from wind the dusty soil of the prairies.

Work Cited

Hay, Elizabeth. A Student of Weather. Toronto: McClelland, 2000.

Appendix 2

Marking Symbols Explained

Marking Symbols Explained

This chapter provides an alphabetical list of the marking abbreviations or correction symbols commonly used in marking students' essays, followed by a short list of other symbols and notations a marker might use. Most symbols we have listed are followed by brief explanations of their meaning and of the steps required to correct or revise particular errors or stylistic weaknesses, including one or more examples of each. We have included all the most common symbols and provided cross-references for those that have more than one form; some instructors, for example, will use ***fs*** (fused sentence) to indicate that error, but since we believe many will refer to it as a run-on sentence, we have made that the main entry.

When you approach a marked draft of your work for the purpose of correction and revision, you will probably find it helpful to consult this chapter first. If the brief explanation you find here doesn't enable you to make a correction or revision, follow the cross-reference to the fuller discussion elsewhere in the book; only a few of the categories listed below are not discussed specifically elsewhere.

Reminder: These symbols are also listed inside the back cover.

abbr Undesirable or Incorrect Abbreviation

Generally, avoid abbreviations in formal writing. Instead of *e.g.*, *i.e.*, *viz.*, *etc.*, use the more formal expressions *for example*, *that is*, *namely*, *and so forth*. Some abbreviations are so common that they are frequently used as substitutes for the full terms to which they correspond. For example, we often speak or write of British Columbia as *B.C.* and of Prince Edward Island as *P.E.I.*, but never of Alberta as *Alta.* or of Ontario as *Ont.* Abbreviations like *B.C.* and *P.E.I.* are acceptable in writing (but the name should be spelled in full the first time it appears), whereas *Alta.* and *Ont.* are not. Whenever you aren't sure, avoid the abbreviation; the full word or words will not be inappropriate.

A2

See #57 for more information about abbreviations.

ack Acknowledgement of Sources

Whenever you include in an essay information, statistics, ideas, diagrams and other graphic materials, or wording that you obtained from investigating any electronic or non-electronic source, you must acknowledge your indebtedness in accordance with the conventions of documentation; this is true even if you aren't writing a full-fledged research paper. Even specific information from lectures, interviews, online discussions, and conversations should be scrupulously acknowledged.

Failure to indicate fully the use of outside sources—whether you quote directly or paraphrase—is **plagiarism**. Instructors and institutions usually apply severe academic penalties for such unethical conduct.

See #77-81c, passim. See also ***doc*** (*Documentation*).

ad **Adjectives and Adverbs Confused or Misused**

The most common kind of mistake in this category is the use of either an adjective or an adverb where the other should appear. For example:

> ***ad:*** After eating three pepperoni pizzas, he didn't sleep very good.

Here the adjective *good* should be replaced by the adverb *well.* (See #20b.2 and **good, bad, badly, well** in #72).

See #19 and #20.

agr **Agreement**

1. *Agreement between subject and verb*: A finite verb agrees with its subject in person and number.

   > ***agr:*** This group of tourists are headed to Cape Breton.

   The singular *group*, not the plural *tourists*, is the subject; to agree in number, therefore, the verb should be *is*, not *are*.

   See #18.

2. *Agreement of pronouns with their antecedents*: A pronoun must agree in person and number with its antecedent, the word—usually preceding it—to which it refers.

   > ***agr:*** When the lab assistant asked for volunteers, nobody in the lecture hall raised their hand.

   The indefinite pronoun *nobody* is singular; to agree with it in number, the pronoun referring to it should also be singular. But to avoid gender-biased language, you would not use the formerly common *his*, but rather *his or her* (or *his/her*)—or avoid the problem by rephrasing the sentence: "When the lab assistant asked for volunteers, not a single hand went up" (see #15d).

   See #15. For shifts in the person and number of pronouns, see ***shift, pv*** (*Point of View*) and #39d–e.

al Illogical or Incongruous Alignment of Elements

If you find this mark on an essay it means that there is an illogicality that you must remove. The illogicality may be a matter of faulty predication:

> ***al, pred:*** The professions many undergraduates dream of pursuing are doctor and lawyer.

But *doctors* and *lawyers* are not professions; they are *professionals*. The sentence needs revising:

> ***revised:*** The professions many undergraduates dream of pursuing are medicine and law.

> ***revised:*** Many undergraduates dream of becoming doctors or lawyers.

Other alignment errors result from trying to make words behave in ways that their meanings don't permit:

> ***al:*** The general believed that acts such as courage and initiative should be recognized.

But *courage* and *initiative* are not acts.

> ***revised:*** The general believed that acts of courage and initiative should be recognized.

See #38; see also ***log*** (*Logic*) and ***comp*** (*Incomplete Comparison*).

ambig Ambiguous

A2

Ambiguity is a lack of clarity that permits a reader to understand a passage, sentence, or word in two different ways. Although ambiguity is sometimes intentional—for example in poetry, where it can enrich the meaning—it is generally unwelcome in expository prose, where it can obscure the meaning and confuse the reader.

> ***ambig:*** The prime minister was in favour of elimination of violent crime and gun control.

Here coordination appears to link eliminating violent crime and eliminating gun control—a highly unlikely political stance. The ambiguity can be removed by rearranging elements of the sentence or by changing the syntax:

clear: The prime minister was in favour of gun control and elimination of violent crime.

clear: The prime minister was in favour of maintaining gun control and eliminating violent crime.

In this second version, the parallel gerunds *maintaining* and *eliminating* help convey the intended meaning.

See also ***cl*** (*Clarity*), ***dm*** (*Dangling Modifier*) and #36, ***mm*** (*Misplaced Modifier*) and #35, ***fp*** (*Faulty Parallelism*) and #40, ***p*** (*Punctuation*) and chapter V, and ***ref*** (*Faulty Reference*) and #16b.

apos Apostrophe Missing or Misused

1. An apostrophe indicates the possessive inflection of nouns. Here the necessary apostrophe is omitted:

   apos: We noted the professors behaviour during the orientation for new students.

   Without an apostrophe, one can't tell whether the possessive *professors* is singular (*professor's*) or plural (*professors'*).

2. An apostrophe is not used for the possessive case of personal pronouns:

   incorrect: her's, your's, their's

3. An apostrophe indicates the omission of letters in contractions; omitting the apostrophe in a contraction results in a misspelling. Some examples of correctly contracted forms:

   he'll (he will)
   hasn't (has not)
   it's (it is)
   they're (they are)
   shouldn't (should not)
   we're (we are)
   you're (you are)
   who's (who is)

4. Don't confuse a contraction with a possessive form:

   wrong: Who's book is this? (*Whose*)

   wrong: Is this where your going to sleep? (*you're*)

   wrong: She put the dog in it's kennel. (*its*)

   See #62v–w for complete information on the apostrophe.

A2

Proofreading Tip

The Place of Contractions in Formal and Informal Writing
Contractions are usually out of place in formal writing. If you want a relatively informal tone, however, they are not only permissible but desirable. See #64b.

art Article Missing or Misused

> ***art:*** We are looking for computer lab where our class is scheduled to meet.

Supply the missing *the* before *computer lab*, which is made specific by the subordinate clause following it.

> ***art:*** My sister wants to write on an historical topic related to the city of Vancouver.

Change *an* to *a*.

> ***art:*** It was at this point in the life that he decided to reform.

Remove *the* or change it to *his.*

See #19c; see also ***id*** (*Idiom*) and #70.

awk Awkwardness

Awk is the symbol some use when they know something is wrong with a sentence but can't put a finger on a particular error, or when the combination of several faults is unusually complicated. *Awk* could be translated as something like "Revise this sentence in a significant way to make it clearer." Awkwardness can result from several causes, among them the following:

- haste under time pressure when you don't have time to edit or revise;
- overly elaborate or imprecise diction and wordiness (see ***w***—*Wordiness*—and #71);
- overly elaborate sentence structure;
- ineffective use of the passive voice (see ***pas*** and #17p);
- mistakes in punctuation (see chapter V);
- confused thinking and insufficient explanations.

Here are some examples of awkward sentences, each followed by an attempt to straighten the problem out:

awk: Caught up in this new way of life, I felt a closer existence to every thought of today.
revised: Caught up in this new way of life, I developed more interest in contemporary thought.

awk: Now, as I began to get some feeling of confidence restored in me, I thought how silly my previous experience had been.
revised: Now, as I regained confidence, I realized how foolish my response to the earlier experience had been.

awk: I looked for a familiar face among that great sea of faces, but this was done in vain.
revised: I looked in vain for a friend in that great sea of faces.

awk: The essay is written in a way that he relates his beliefs to the reader, but does not force the reader to digest his beliefs.
revised: The writer explains his beliefs although he does not expect the reader to share them.

awk: The poem also gives a sense of lightness in the way it rhymes and in its metre.
revised: The poem's rhymes and metre contribute to its light tone.

awk: During the eighteenth century, chemistry became a real science instead of the previous alchemy.
revised: In the eighteenth century, chemistry became a true science, evolving out of and replacing the pseudoscience of alchemy.

awk: In the poem, "To an Athlete Dying Young," by A.E. Housman, the author poses an argument of why the athlete benefited from dying young.
revised: In A.E. Housman's poem "To an Athlete Dying Young," the speaker argues that it was fortunate for the athlete to die so young.

ca **The Case of the Pronoun Is Wrong**

The case of a pronoun depends on its function in its own clause or phrase. A pronoun that is a subject or a complement must be in the subjective case:

> ***ca:*** Hans and me dug the ditch ourselves. (*I*)
>
> ***ca:*** He's the one whom I predicted would win the race. (*who*)
>
> ***ca:*** That is her. (*she*)

A pronoun that is an object of a verb or a preposition must be in the objective case:

> ***ca:*** They told Alberta and I to leave. (*me*)
>
> ***ca:*** It was up to Gillian and I to finish the job. (*me*)
>
> ***ca:*** It doesn't matter who you take with you. (*whom*)

See #14e. For information about the possessive case of nouns and pronouns, see #13a.2, #13b, #14a–d, #19a, #21h, and #62w.

cap **Capitalization Needed or Faulty**

> ***cap:*** Near Hudson bay in the Northwest Territories is the region known as the barrens.
>
> ***corrected:*** Near Hudson Bay in the Northwest Territories is the region known as the Barrens.

See #58; see also ***lc*** (*Lower Case*).

A2

cl **Lack of Clarity**

Like awkwardness, a lack of clarity can result from a number of causes. The parts of a sentence may fail to go together in a meaningful way, or the words chosen to express an idea may not do so adequately, or the writer may have expressed only a vague idea needing further thought and development. Sometimes, writers lacking confidence will add unnecessary qualifications that muddy or, at the very least, water down the ideas they are trying to convey:

> ***cl:*** There is also a general sense of irony in the plot or story behind the play.

What is a *general sense* as opposed to a *sense*? What is a *sense of irony* as opposed to *irony*? Why the choice of *plot or story*? And how is it that the plot (or story) is *behind* the play? It is impossible to be sure what the writer meant, but here is a clear sentence that uses the major features of the original: "There are ironic elements in the plot of the play."

> ***cl:*** This blessing is intended to restore faith in God when things happen such as death which you don't understand and want to blame God for letting them happen.

This sentence could also have been marked ***awk***, but the muddiness of the thought and its expression seem to be its principal problems. Sorting the sentence out and adding some logic as well as some careful syntax produce a clearer and more succinct version:

> ***revised:*** This blessing is intended to restore faith in God, which may be lost when incomprehensible events like death make one question God's justice.

But here is an example of an unclear sentence that remains impenetrable:

> ***cl:*** Absurdist plays work on the situation in much greater detail than the dramatic level.

Here is another sentence that goes astray; one can only wonder what the intended meaning was:

> ***cl:*** He compares the athlete's achievements and victories to that of death.

A2

Sometimes punctuation or the lack of it is part of the trouble:

> ***cl, p:*** Before I really had time to think they wanted me to report for work in the morning.

A comma after *think* makes it likely that a reader will understand the sentence on the first reading rather than on the second or third.

See also ***ambig*** (*Ambiguous*), ***awk*** (*Awkward*), #16, #31, and #35–42.

cliché **Cliché**

See ***trite*** (*Trite, Worn-out, Hackneyed Expression*). See #71e.

coh **Not Coherent; Continuity Weak**

Coherence is weak or faulty when there is insufficient transition between two sentences or two paragraphs. The first sentence of a paragraph, whether it is the topic sentence or not, should provide a connection to the preceding paragraph. Similarly, sentences within paragraphs should flow smoothly from one to another. Here, for example, are two sentences that are not smoothly connected:

> ***coh:*** Rachel is invited both to dine at Willard's and to go out with Calla. Despite her desire to accept one of the invitations she declines both of them because it is her mother's card night.

Although the idea of the invitations is present in both, and although a reader can more or less work out the connection, a *But* to begin the second sentence or a *however* (between commas) after the word *invitations* would make the two sentences more coherent and the reader's task much easier.

See #3–5d and #8b; see also ***tr*** (*Transition Weak or Lacking*) and #31.

colloq **Colloquialism**

See ***inf*** (*Informal, Colloquial*). See #64b.

comb **Combine Sentences**

An instructor may write ***coord*** (Coordinate) or ***sub*** (Subordinate), or even ***coord or sub*** together, to indicate that some kind of improvement (e.g. economy, coherence, logic, or just a decrease in choppiness) could be gained by putting two (or more) sentences together. Sometimes, however, rather than specify ***coord*** or ***sub***, an instructor may write ***comb***, meaning simply "Combine these sentences into one in the way you think best." In the following, for example, which could as well have been marked ***w*** (*Wordiness*), the improvement in the revision is apparent:

> ***w, comb:*** The whiteness of the snow piled on their outstretched branches gave their green colour an extra richness. This added attractiveness seemed to enhance their beauty.
>
> ***revised:*** The whiteness of the snow piled on their outstretched branches gave their green colour an extra richness, enhancing their beauty.

See ***coord*** (*Coordination Needed*), ***sub*** (*Subordination Needed*), #41, and Exercises 12q, 21(4,5), 23c (2) and 71a–c (2).

A2

comp Incomplete Comparison

Revise to correct incomplete or illogical comparisons.

comp: She is a better chef than any chef in the city.
revised: She is a better chef than any other chef in the city.
revised: She is the best chef in the city.

comp: Life in a small town is better than a big city.
revised: Life in a small town is better than (life) in a big city.

comp: I think cranberry juice is as good, if not better, than orange juice.
revised: I think cranberry juice is as good as, if not better than, orange juice.
revised: I think cranberry juice is as good as orange juice, if not better.

comp: Fresh vegetables have more vitamins.
revised: Fresh vegetables have more vitamins than canned or frozen ones.

comp: I like snowboarding more than Julie.
revised: I like snowboarding more than Julie does.
revised: I like snowboarding more than I like Julie.

Note that ***ambig*** (*Ambiguous*), ***cl*** (*Lack of Clarity*), or ***log*** (*Logic*) would be appropriate marks for some of these sentences.

See #38 and #42.

A2

conc Insufficient Concreteness

Revise by increasing the concreteness of your diction. Replace abstract words and phrases with concrete ones, or expand upon general and abstract statements with specific and concrete details.

conc: Seymour was a very deep young man.

The word *deep* here is suggestive, but too abstract to be very meaningful. *Deep* could mean any one of several different things here (consult your dictionary); more information, especially in the form of concrete examples, would enable a reader to understand precisely what the writer meant to convey. Here are two sentences whose vague abstractness and illogical circularity (see #10h, under *begging the question*) render them almost meaningless:

conc, log: The author makes the setting so good that it is very convincing.

conc, log: The characters are presented as fully described people.

Don't write empty sentences like those. Inject some specific, concrete content.

See #66.

coord Coordination Needed; Combine Sentences

When two sentences are closely related—for example, when they express a contrast—it is often preferable to combine them, using either punctuation or a coordinating conjunction (see #23a–b) or both.

coord: Life in a farming community can be very challenging. Life in a large city offers more variety.

revised: Life in a farming community can be very challenging, but life in a large city offers more variety.

Depending on context and desired emphasis, such sentences could also be joined with a semicolon, or one or the other could be subordinated with *though* or *whereas.*

See also ***sub*** (*Subordination*), ***comb*** (*Combine Sentences*), ***cs*** (*Comma Splice*), ***coh*** (*Coherence*), and ***fc*** (*Faulty Coordination*), and #41.

A2

cs Comma Splice

A comma splice results from putting a comma between two independent clauses that are not joined with a coordinating conjunction; "splicing" the clauses together with only a comma is not enough.

cs: The flight from Vancouver to Toronto takes only about four hours, it seems to last forever.

The comma is not enough. A semicolon (or period) would be correct, but a poor solution because the two clauses obviously are closely related. Here the desired contrast would best be emphasized either by using an appropriate coordinating conjunction along with the comma:

> ***revised:*** The flight from Vancouver to Toronto takes about four hours, but it seems to last forever.

or by using a subordinating conjunction to change one of the clauses to a subordinate clause:

> ***revised:*** Although the flight from Vancouver to Toronto takes only about four hours, it seems to last forever.

Another example:

> ***cs:*** Contemporary poetry is, if nothing else, plentiful, it pours daily from a number of small presses.

Here, since the second clause illustrates the idea expressed in the first, a coordinating conjunction would not be the most appropriate connector. Using *for* would work, but it would be better to emphasize the syntactic integrity of the second clause by simply changing the comma to a semicolon. Even a colon would work well (see #43c and #44i). The following is an instance where a colon would be the preferred mark to replace the comma:

> ***cs:*** Slavery took hold in the American South in part for economic reasons, large numbers of workers were forced to maintain white-owned plantations.

Comma splices, then, can be corrected by replacing the comma with an appropriate mark—usually a semicolon, sometimes a colon, or even a period if you decide to turn the clauses into two separate sentences—or by showing the relation between the two clauses with a precise coordinating or subordinating conjunction. One last solution is to reduce one of the clauses to a modifying phrase:

> ***cs:*** The poem gives us several clues to the speaker's attitude toward love, one of these is the imagery.

> ***revised:*** The poem gives us several clues to the speaker's attitude toward love, one of these being the imagery.

See #44e and h; for exceptions, see #44f–g. See also ***comb*** (*Combine Sentences*), ***coord*** (*Coordination*), ***fc*** (*Faulty Coordination*), ***sub*** (*Subordination*), and Exercises 21(3), 21(4), and 22a–c (2).

d **Faulty Diction**

Mistakes in diction are often marked with one or another specific symbol, such as ***ww*** (wrong word), ***nsw*** (no such word), ***inf*** (informal or colloquial), or ***id*** (idiom). But sometimes a reader will simply use ***d***, implying either that the error does not fall into one of the particular categories or that the writer is expected to find out just what the specific error is. In either event, the first thing the writer should do is consult a dictionary; ***d*** could be said to stand for *dictionary*.

> ***d:*** If we regard the poem in this way, the recurring images of the "unwatered," aimless, barren mind of modern man would be one of the musical themes, and the imagery of water plus its symbolism of replenishment would be another.

In this otherwise well-crafted sentence, the word *plus* creates a stylistic disturbance. *Plus* is normally a mathematical term; it is not a conjunction, nor appropriate to this context. In an expository context the meaning of *plus* is usually conveyed by the conjunction *and*; the preposition *with* would also serve the meaning here.

Diction can also be poor by being weak or imprecise. In the following sentence, for example, the word *done* is inadequate for the job it is being asked to do:

> ***d:*** The program should be done in such a way that learning can take place in the field as well as in the classroom.

A word like *designed*, *planned*, or *organized* would be better.

See chapter VII. See also ***inf*** (*Informal, Colloquial*), ***conc*** (*Concreteness*), ***id*** (*Idiom*), ***jarg*** (*Jargon*), ***nsw*** (*No Such Word*), and ***ww*** (*Wrong Word*).

A2

dev **Development Needed**

This mark indicates that an idea, point, or subject needs to be developed further, expanded upon. The weakness occurs most often in the form of an inadequately developed paragraph. Revise by supplying details, examples, or illustrations, by defining or explaining, or by some other method appropriate to the particular instance.

See #1b, #4b, #7b, and #66.

dm **Dangling Modifier**

> ***dm:*** Floating down the aisle to the strains of "Here Comes the Bride," the groom smiled nervously at his best man.

Correct a dangling modifier by changing it so that it no longer dangles:

> ***corrected:*** As the bridal party floated down the aisle to the strains of "Here Comes the Bride," the groom smiled nervously at his best man.

> ***corrected:*** Floating down the aisle to the strains of "Here Comes the Bride," the bridal party approached the groom, who was smiling nervously at his best man.

See #36.

doc Documentation

Use the correct forms for your notes (whether parenthetical, at the foot of the page, or collected at the end) and your works-cited list or bibliography. In chapter VIII you will find model notes and bibliographical entries.

See #79 and #81. See also #80. See also ***ack*** (*Acknowledgement of Sources*).

emph Emphasis Weak or Unclear

Make a marked sentence or paragraph emphatic by rearranging or by otherwise clarifying the relationships among its parts.

> ***emph:*** The older generation of our society, like the younger, is also continually confronted with both beneficial and harmful advertisements, which are effective on our society in some way or other.

This is a flabby sentence—and what strength it has is mostly dissipated by the final prepositional phrase; simply removing it would sharpen the end of the sentence, which should be its most emphatic part. But further improvement can be gained by sorting out and rearranging its content and by cutting the repetition and deadwood:

> ***revised:*** All of society—not just the young but the older generation as well—is bombarded by advertising, which can be beneficial as well as harmful.

This may not be the best possible version, but at least its emphasis is clear.

See #6, #8c and #29; see also ***fc*** (*Faulty Coordination*) and #41.

euph Euphemism

Avoid unnecessary *euphemism* ("good sounding," though not necessarily good in fact). Often directness and precision are preferable to even well-intentioned delicacy and vagueness. Is someone lacking money to buy enough food really made to feel better by being described as "disadvantaged" rather than "poor"?

When you are tempted to use a euphemism to avoid an unpleasant reality (for example, describing a person as "inebriated" or "in a state of intoxication" rather than "drunk"), consider the possible benefits of being direct and succinct instead.

See #68.

fc Faulty Coordination

Faulty coordination occurs when unrelated clauses are presented as coordinate, or when related clauses are linked by punctuation or coordinating conjunctions that fail to indicate the relation correctly.

> ***fc:*** Lawren Harris was born in 1885, and he was an influential member of the Group of Seven.

The coordinating conjunction *and* is misleading: Harris's birth date and his role as an influential Canadian painter are not significantly related or equal in value. The significant comment is contained in the second clause; the opening clause contains a minor fact that should be subordinated to the main statement:

> ***revised:*** Lawren Harris, who was born in 1885, was an influential member of the Group of Seven.

> ***revised:*** Lawren Harris (1885–1970) was an influential member of the Group of Seven.

Here is another example in which the second of two clauses is more important; the first clause should be subordinated or even changed to a participial phrase:

> ***fc:*** We are working together to write an evaluation of websites focusing on contemporary poetry, and we are spending hours searching the Internet.

> ***revised:*** Since we are working together to write an evaluation of websites focusing on contemporary poetry, we are spending hours searching the Internet.

revised: In working together to write an evaluation of websites focusing on contemporary poetry, we are spending hours searching the Internet.

See #41; see also ***comb*** (*Combine Sentences*), ***coord*** (*Coordination*), and ***sub*** (*Subordination*).

fig Inappropriate or Confusing Figurative Language

This mark is used to signify that some wording needs to be revised to change or remove figurative language (similes, metaphors) that is inappropriate or mixed.

> ***fig:*** The decline of the provincial economy is skyrocketing; tax reform is the path we need to follow to break through this wall of stagnation.

The image of a rocket hurtling through the sky clashes with the image of a decline or fall; the image of the path is inconsistent with both skyrocketing and decline, and it clashes with the image of the wall, which itself clashes with the idea of stagnation. The sentence can be recast using the single metaphor *remedy*:

> ***revised:*** The provincial economy is declining rapidly; the remedy for this problem is tax reform.

Or, two or more metaphors (*propping, sagging*) can be used as long as they are complementary:

> ***revised:*** Tax reform should help to prop up the sagging provincial economy.

A2

Here is another example:

> ***fig:*** Like a bolt from the blue the idea grabbed him, and it soon grew into one of his most prized pieces of mental furniture.

One of the troubles with clichés that are dead metaphors is that we can fail to visualize them; when used unthinkingly they can make writing absurd. The *bolt from the blue,* even if allowed, could scarcely *grab* anyone, nor could it grow (like a plant?) into a piece of furniture. The urge to be metaphorical here backfired on the writer.

See #65 and #71e.

fp
//

Faulty Parallelism

Revise by making coordinated elements grammatically parallel.

> ***fp:*** For me England brings back memories of pleasant walks in Cornwall on some windblown lea, looking out to sea dressed in warm woollen jerseys, and feeling a warmth brought about by being with my family in that place.

The three objects of the preposition *of* here are all nouns, but *looking* and *feeling,* unlike *walks*, are gerunds. Repeating *of* before each gerund would help, but it is better to make the three grammatically parallel (and the phrase "dressed in warm woollen jerseys" seems more appropriate to the windblown lea than to looking out to sea):

> ***revised:*** For me England brings back pleasant memories of walking on some windblown lea in Cornwall dressed in warm woollen jerseys, looking out to sea, and feeling a warmth brought about by being with my family in that place.

There is also the kind of awkwardness that occurs when a parallel structure breaks down—or isn't sufficiently built up:

> ***fp:*** During my trip I had the chance to learn some of the language and to help with the shopping and cooking—all of which helped make the experience enjoyable.

The sentence structure implies that we're going to be given more than two things—and the phrase "all of which" makes it sound as though we have been. Perhaps the writer subconsciously thought of "shopping" and "cooking" as separate items; but the parallelism is in the verbs *learn* and *help*. That is, the implied parallel series after *to* is not fulfilled.

> ***revised:*** During my visit I had the chance to learn some of the language and to help with the shopping and the cooking; these activities helped make the experience enjoyable.

Alternatively, a third element could be supplied, or *cooking* could be governed by a third verb, such as "participate in."

See #40.

frag **Unacceptable Fragment**

Word groups that are punctuated as sentences but don't fulfill the requirements of sentences are usually unacceptable. Apart from passages of dialogue, any word group that cannot stand by itself and communicate effectively is problematic.

> ***frag:*** Vancouver was chosen to be the site of the 2010 winter Olympics. The city being the second one in Canada to be awarded the winter games.

The second part here has no verb (*being* is a participle), nor is it an acceptable minor sentence. It should be set off with a comma as part of the preceding sentence.

> ***frag:*** The convention was held at the Chelsea Hotel. Because it has a large banquet room which would accommodate us all.

The second part is a subordinate clause dependent on the predicate of the preceding sentence, and should be set off with a comma.

See #12w, #12x, and #32.

Proofreading Tip

On Marking Stylistically Effective Fragments
Fragmentary patterns can sometimes be used effectively as a stylistic device by skilled writers. If you deliberately use a fragmentary pattern in the draft of an essay, perhaps indicate the fact in a marginal note so that your reader can comment on its effectiveness.

fs **Fused Sentence**

See ***run-on.***

gen **Inadequately Supported Generalization**

See #66b and ***conc*** (*Insufficient Concreteness*).

id **Faulty Idiom, Unidiomatic Usage**

Idiom refers to the structures and forms of expression particular to a given language. Idioms are not necessarily logical or explicable in grammatical terms. In English, errors in idiom most often occur with prepositions, as in the following examples:

id: The extent of television's influence towards our view of global issues is incalculable. (*on*)

id: Our university has a reputation of innovative undergraduate programs. (*for*)

See #70; see also ***art*** (*Articles*) and #19c.

inc **Incomplete Comparison**

See ***comp.***

inf **Inappropriate Informal or Colloquial Diction**

Replace the inappropriate word or words with something more formal.

inf: This is the goofiest plot I've read in some time. (*most improbable, most unlikely*)

See #64b.

ital **Italics Needed or Incorrect**

Correct by italicizing or by removing unwanted italics. (In handwritten material, italics are represented by underlining.)

ital: A Night to Remember is a film about the sinking of the Titanic.

corrected: *A Night to Remember* is a film about the sinking of the *Titanic.*

See #60; see also *Titles*, #59.

A2

jarg **Jargon**

Revise to avoid unnecessary jargon.

jarg: The research team utilized every methodological approach it could conceptualize to produce bottom-line outcomes.

revised: The research team used every method it could to produce results.

See #71h.

lc

Lower Case

Change incorrect capital letter(s) to lower case.

> ***lc:*** You can now find Champagne made elsewhere than in France. (*champagne*)

> ***lc:*** My grandmother was one of the first women in her community to get a University education. (*university*)

See #58.

leg

Legibility, Illegible

You are most likely to find this mark on an in-class paper or examination when your handwriting or revisions are difficult or impossible to decipher. If you are doing a revision, redo the illegible passages in consideration of your readers. Keep in mind that word-processed documents can be illegible if prepared too hastily. Don't, for instance, use whiteout and pen or pencil to correct typographical errors. Instead, make the correction in the document and print a clean copy of the page you have revised.

lev

Inappropriate Level of Diction

See #64.

log

Logic: Illogical as Phrased; Logicality of Reasoning Questioned

Illogic underlies many different problems in writing and thinking. Nevertheless, ***log*** is frequently the mark used to indicate an error of logic arising out of the way something has been phrased. For example:

A2

> ***log:*** Insecurity is a characteristic basic to Davies's nature, and it becomes a consistent weakness of his throughout the play.

If insecurity is a basic characteristic, it can't *become* consistent in the course of the play; and it can't *become* consistent *throughout* the play, since *throughout* logically contradicts the meaning of *become*. Here is another example:

> ***log:*** In giving a precise definition of what this mental science is, Asimov is very vague.

The illogicality is evident. At least three meanings are possible:

> ***clear:*** Asimov fails to provide a precise definition of this mental science.

> ***clear:*** Asimov's definition of this mental science is very vague.

> ***clear:*** Asimov deals only vaguely with this mental science and makes no attempt to define it.

See also #41, #42, ***al*** (*Alignment*) and #38, and #10e–h.

mix

Mixed Construction

This mark indicates a shift from one syntactical pattern to another within a single sentence:

> ***mix:*** The war was justified as a strike against terrorism was viewed skeptically by most Canadians.

In order to revise an error such as this, you must decide on one pattern or the other:

> ***revised:*** The war, which was justified as a strike against terrorism, was viewed skeptically by most Canadians.

> ***revised:*** The war, which was viewed skeptically by most Canadians, was justified as a strike against terrorism.

See #37.

A2

mm

Misplaced Modifier

Revise a misplaced modifier by moving the modifying word or phrase to the logical place in the sentence.

> ***mm:*** Sauron wished to be the Dark Lord of Middle-earth, and almost had enough power to succeed twice.

> ***revised:*** Sauron wished to be Dark Lord of Middle-earth, and twice had almost enough power to succeed.

See #35; see also ***wo*** (*Word Order*).

ms **Improper Manuscript Form or Conventions**

Conscientious writers are careful to follow certain conventions pertaining to the form and presentation of a manuscript. These include such things as indenting paragraphs clearly, double spacing and leaving adequate margins, paginating correctly, not underlining one's own title, and being consistent with punctuation marks.

See chapter VI.

nsw **No Such Word**

Don't make up words (unless perhaps for humorous purposes or other special effects). If you can't think of a particular word you want, try consulting a thesaurus. And if you use a word that looks or sounds unusual, that doesn't quite ring true, consult a good dictionary to see if it's there. A little extra care will enable you to avoid using such concoctions as these, all of which occurred in essays we have read:

ableness (use *ability*)
afraidness (use *fear*)
artistism (use *artistry*)
condensated (use *condensed*)
cowardism, cowardness (use *cowardice*)
deteriorized (use *deteriorated*)
disgustion (use *disgust*)
enrichen (use *enrich*)
freedomship (use *freedom*)
fruitition (use *fruition*)
infidelous (use *unfaithful*)
irregardless (use *regardless, irrespective*)
nonchalantness (use *nonchalance*)
prejudism (use *prejudice*)
prophesize (use *prophesy*)
skepticalism (use *skepticism*)
superfluosity (use *superfluity, superflousness*)

num **Incorrect Use of Numerals**

See #61 for the conventions governing the use of numerals.

A2

org **Organization Weak or Faulty**

Repetition, choppiness, lack of proportion or emphasis, haphazard order—all these and more can be signs of ineffective organization. It may be necessary to rethink your outline.

See #4, #9e–j, and #10d.

p **Error in Punctuation**

Punctuation marks are symbols that should be just as meaningful to readers as are the symbols of speech (words) with which they are associated in writing. In speech, "punctuation" takes the form of inflections of voice, pauses, and changes in pitch or intensity. In order to communicate clearly and effectively on paper, one must be as careful with punctuation as one is with words and syntax. When you find the letter ***p*** in the margin, refer to chapter V to find out not only *what* is wrong or weak, but also *why* it is so.

para ¶ **Paragraphing**

See #1–7.

pas **Weak Passive Voice**

This mark means that the sentence in question would be more effective with a verb in the active voice than with one in the passive voice—some form of *be* followed by a past participle, making the subject of a clause the receiver of the action: *Jo brought the ice* is active; *The ice was brought by Jo* is passive.

pas: This issue is being spotlighted by the leader of the opposition.
active: The leader of the opposition is spotlighting this issue.

pas: In this article, the styles of tennis stars Venus and Serena Williams are compared by the sports editor.
active: In this article, the sports editor compares the styles of tennis stars Venus and Serena Williams.

See #17p. See also #29f.

passim **Error Throughout**

This mark, which is Latin for *throughout*, is used to indicate that an error, such as the misspelling of a name, needs to be corrected throughout an essay.

pred **Faulty Predication**

See ***al*** (*Alignment*) and #38.

pron **Error in Use of Pronoun**

This abbreviation usually marks such errors and weaknesses as the use of an intensive pronoun as a casual substitute for a personal pronoun, or the overuse of vague demonstrative pronouns, or perhaps *which* to refer to a person.

See also ***agr*** (*Agreement*), ***ca*** (*The Case of the Pronoun Is Wrong*), ***ref*** (*Weak or Faulty Pronoun Reference*), ***shift*** (*Shift in Perspective*), and #14–16.

pv **Point of View Inconsistent**

See ***shift*** (*Shift in Perspective*).

Q Error in Handling Quoted Material or Quotation Marks

Sometimes this correction symbol will refer to nothing more than the omission of quotation marks (usually at the end of a quotation). But it could also refer to incorrect punctuation with quoted material, ineffectively introduced quoted material, and so on. If the error marked is not an obvious one, you may have to consult the section on quotation, #54, to find out what is wrong. See also #78, on handling quotations in research writing.

red Redundancy

Redundancy can mean simply wordiness, but it is often used to refer specifically to unnecessary repetition of the meaning of one word in another word. In the sentence "But he was not unfriendly though," *But* and *though* do the same job; one of them should go (omit *though*, since it is informal and also weakens the end of the sentence: see **although, though** in #72, and #29c). Here are two more examples:

> ***red:*** Throughout the entire story the tone is one of unrelieved gloom.

Since *throughout* means *all through, from beginning to end,* the word *entire* merely repeats what has already been said.

> ***revised:*** Throughout the story the tone is one of unrelieved gloom.

But this is still redundant, for if the tone is *unrelieved*, it must be constant throughout the story. Hence further tightening is possible:

> ***re-revised:*** The story's tone is one of unrelieved gloom.

A2

Again:

> ***red:*** Puck's playful pranks include tricks on housewives and village maids.

Here the writer's choice of the word *pranks* is accurate and effective, but since *pranks* are *frolicsome tricks*, the addition of the adjective *playful* is redundant and decreases the effectiveness. One might even want to get rid of the word *tricks*:

> ***revised:*** Puck plays pranks on housewives and village maids.

See #71c; see also ***w*** (*Wordiness*).

ref Weak or Faulty Pronoun Reference

Pronouns need to refer to their antecedents in a clear way. The following sentence, for example, is muddled because it isn't clear whom the pronouns refer to:

> ***ref:*** Because of all the attention which Seymour and Buddy gave to Franny and Zooey when they were young children, they never allowed them to develop their own ideas of life.

One can, by careful reading, extract the sense of this sentence, but it is the writer's job to make the meaning clear, not the reader's to puzzle it out.

> ***revised:*** When Franny and Zooey were young, Seymour and Buddy gave them so much attention that the children were never able to develop their own ideas of life.

The revised sentence contains just one clear pronoun instead of four confusing ones (and the redundant *young children* has been broken up as well). Here is another example:

> ***ref:*** Merlin's power, quite naturally, is partially a result of his "Sight" and what are thought to be his magical powers. An example of this is given during the battle between King Ambrosius and the Saxons.

Clearly one must also be careful with demonstrative pronouns: here the reference of *this* is obscure. Probably in the writer's mind *this* somehow referred to the entire idea expressed in the first sentence. In other words, *this* has no precise antecedent, and the reference is therefore loose at best. A clearer and more precise version (clearing up the problem with parallelism and the passive voice as well) is possible:

> ***revised:*** Merlin's power derives from a combination of his Sight and his reputed magic. The battle between King Ambrosius and the Saxons provides an illustration of this fact.

Changing the demonstrative pronoun to a demonstrative adjective usually makes things clearer. But the passage is still wordy. Try again, combining the sentences:

> ***revised:*** As the battle between King Ambrosius and the Saxons illustrates, Merlin's power derives from a combination of his Sight and his reputed magic.

See #16; see also #15.

rep Weak, Awkward, or Unnecessary Repetition

This mark indicates another kind of wordiness that requires pruning. Although repetition is often useful for achieving emphasis and coherence, unnecessary repetition only slows the writer's momentum and bogs the reader down.

> ***rep:*** The snow was falling heavily, but I didn't mind the snow, for I have always enjoyed the things one can do in the snow.

The repetition of *snow* at the end is all right, but the middle one must go; replace *the snow* with *it,* or—better yet—with nothing at all.

See #71b.

run-on Run-on or Fused Sentence

Failure to put any punctuation between two independent clauses not joined by a coordinating conjunction results in a run-on sentence. Since a run-on is often merely a slip caused by writing too fast and not proofreading, it should be relatively easy to prevent with strategies for close editing.

> ***run-on:*** Vancouver is the most beautifully situated city in Canada it also has some serious drug problems in a number of its neighbourhoods.

Like the comma splice, a run-on can be corrected by inserting a semicolon, by inserting a comma and a coordinating conjunction, by subordinating one of the clauses and inserting a comma, or even by inserting a period.

See #34 and #44j; see also ***cs*** (*Comma Splice*).

shift *pv* Shift in Perspective; Point of View Inconsistent or Unclear

Revise a passage marked ***shift*** or ***pv*** to remove the awkward or illogical shift in tense, mood, or voice of verbs, or person or number of pronouns.

shift: On winter hikes in the back country, one should never forget your snowshoes. (*one's*)

shift: It was four in the afternoon, beginning to get dark, and we are still only half-way down the mountain. (*were*)

See #39.

Perspective can also seem to shift because of a lack of parallelism:

shift, fp: Ralph said that it was raining and he preferred to stay home.

If "he preferred to stay home" is part of what Ralph said, then a second *that* is required after *and*; otherwise, "he preferred" could be taken as parallel to "Ralph said." That is, without the second *that*, "he preferred" would be from the writer's point of view rather than Ralph's.

See #40a.

sp Spelling

If you misspell a word, don't simply try to guess how it should be corrected, for you may get it wrong again. The spell-check function of your word-processing software can help, but don't rely on it alone. Check the word in your dictionary, and take the opportunity to find out all the dictionary can tell you about the word—not only for the sake of learning something, but also because studying the word will help fix it and its correct spelling in your mind. Then check chapter VI to see if your error fits any of the categories discussed there; if it does, study the principles involved. And keep a list of the words you misspell so that you can review them as often as necessary to become thoroughly familiar with their correct spellings.

A2

split Unnecessary Split Infinitive

See #21c.

squint Squinting Modifier

A squinting modifier is one that is ambiguous because it seems to look both ways, so that a reader can't be sure which of two elements it is supposed to modify. This kind of problem can usually be solved fairly simply by moving the modifier closer to the element you want it to apply to.

See #35c.

ss **Sentence Structure or Sentence Sense**

Sometimes an instructor will put ***ss*** (or just ***s***) in the margin opposite a sentence to indicate that something is wrong with its sense or its structure, leaving it to the writer to discover what the problem is. It may, for example, be a grammatical error, or a faulty arrangement, or a lack of clarity. Or the sentence may be faulty in some way not covered by any of the more specific categories. If this mark appears often, you may need to review the chapters II, III, and IV.

stet **Let it Stand**

This mark indicates that you were right the first time, that when you changed something, such as a punctuation mark or the spelling of a word, you should have left it the way it was. To correct, therefore, merely restore it to its original form. (Note that an instructor will be able to advise you this way only if you cancel a handwritten word or phrase with a single neat line through it; if you blot it out entirely, you may never find out that your first choice was correct.)

sub **Subordination Needed; Combine Sentences**

sub: Suzuki has also done a superb job in his use of examples. His examples are clear and precise.

revised: Suzuki has also done a superb job in his use of examples, which are clear and precise.

As two sentences (or even as one sentence consisting of two independent clauses) this example is wordy. Even the revised version could be tightened:

revised: Suzuki has also done a superb job of providing clear and precise examples.

Or even:

revised: Suzuki's use of clear and precise examples is superb.

See also ***coord*** (*Coordination*), ***comb*** (*Combine Sentences*), ***fc*** (*Faulty Coordination*) and #41, ***coh*** (*Coherence*), #12n–p, #23c, and #29i.

t **Error in Tense**

t: I often think back to the day, five years ago, when I bought my first horse. To many people this wouldn't be very exciting, but I have wanted a horse for as long as I can remember.

A2

Change the present perfect *have wanted* to the past perfect *had wanted*, and the present *can* to the past *could*.

See #17g–k.

title **Manuscript Conventions for Titles**
See #59.

tr **Transition Weak or Lacking**
This mark will appear where the transition between two sentences or two paragraphs is weak or non-existent. Revise by providing some kind of transitional word or phrase, by improving upon an existing one, or by otherwise improving the transition at the place indicated.

See ***coh*** (*Coherence*), #4, #4a.1, #5c–d, and #8b.

trite **Trite, Worn-out, Hackneyed Expression**
cliché As the following example illustrates, some clichés will simply be wordy and therefore wholly or partly expendable; others will have to be replaced with something fresher; and often the sentence will require other rewording as well:

> ***trite:*** It goes without saying that over the years many and diverse opinions have been held regarding the origin of the universe.
>
> ***revised:*** Ever since people began thinking about it, astronomers and others have held many different opinions about the origin of the universe.

Here the passive voice *have been held* also contributed to the sluggishness of the original sentence.

See #71e.

A2

u **Unity of Sentence, Paragraph, or Essay Is Weak**
See #2, #8a, and #41.

uc **Upper Case**
Change to upper-case (capital) letter(s). See ***cap*** and #58.

us **Usage**
A subcategory of diction, this refers specifically to the kinds of problems discussed in *A Checklist of Troublesome Words and Phrases*, #72.

var **Variety**

Try to improve the variety of lengths, kinds, and patterns of your sentences (see #28) or your paragraphs (see #7c).

vb **Verb Form**

This abbreviation will mark an error in the form of a verb, for example an incorrect inflection or an incorrect principal part of an irregular verb.

See #17b–g.

w **Wordiness**

If you find this mark in the margins of your essays, you may have to take drastic measures. Try thinking of words as costing money, say a loonie apiece; perhaps that will make it easier to avoid a spendthrift style. Mere economy, of course, is not a virtue; don't sacrifice something necessary or useful just to reduce the number of words. But don't use several words where one will not only do the same job but do it better, and don't use words that do no real work at all. Here are some examples of squandered words:

> ***w:*** In today's society, Canada has earned itself a name of respect with many in the world.
> ***revised:*** Canada has earned widespread respect. ($11 saved)

> ***w:*** His words have a romantic quality to them.

The phrase *to them* does no work. In fact, its effect is negative because it undermines the emphatic crispness of the meaningful part of the sentence. Cut it and save $2.

> ***w:*** Hardy regarded poetry as his serious work, and wrote novels only in order to make enough money to live on.
> ***revised:*** Hardy regarded poetry as his serious work, and wrote novels only to make a living. ($5 saved)

> ***w:*** Othello's trust in Iago becomes evident during the first encounter that the reader observes between the two characters.
> ***revised:*** Othello's trust in Iago becomes evident during their first encounter. ($8 saved)

w: The flash of lightning is representative of God's power.
revised: The flash of lightning represents God's power.

See #71, especially #71a; see also ***red*** (*Redundant*) and #71c, and ***rep*** (*Repetition*) and #71b.

wo

Word Order

A misplaced modifier is one kind of faulty word order, but there are other kinds not so easily classified.

wo: She was naturally hurt by his indifference.
revised: Naturally she was hurt by his indifference.

The potential ambiguity could also have been removed by putting commas around *naturally*, but that would slow the sentence down (though it would also emphasize the word).

wo: I will never forget the day July 17, 2002, when I began my first job.
revised: I will never forget July 17, 2002, the day I began my first job.

wo: The image created in the advertisement is what really makes us buy the product and not the product itself.
revised: The image created in the advertisement, not the product itself, is what makes us buy it.

This is not the only possible revision, of course, but it is the simplest, and the sentence is now clearer and less awkward.

A2

wo: Only at the end was clearly revealed the broad scope of the poem and the intensity of the emotions involved.

There seems no reason for the distortion of normal sentence order.

revised: Only at the end were the poem's broad scope and intensity of emotion revealed.

See ***mm*** (*Misplaced Modifier*) and #35, #12s–t, #19d–e, #20d, and #22b.

Proofreading Tip

Word Order in Comparisons Using *Similar To, Superior To, Inferior To*
In a stated comparison using *similar to, superior to,* or *inferior to,* a noun modified by the adjective should precede, not follow the comparative word (*similar, superior, inferior*):

> ***wo:*** The film has a similar plot to that of Shakespeare's *The Tempest.*
>
> ***revised:*** The film has a plot similar to that of Shakespeare's *The Tempest.*

ww **Wrong Word**

This category of diction error covers those mistakes that result from confusion about meaning or usage. For example:

> ***ww:*** Britain is a nation who has brought the past and the present together.

The pronoun *who* refers to persons, not things; usage demands *that* or *which* in this context (see #14d, and #48a, Proofreading Tip).

> ***ww:*** He came to the meeting at the special bequest of the chairperson.

A glance at the dictionary confirms that *bequest* cannot be the right word here; the writer probably confused it with *request* and *behest.*

See #69; see also #62-l–m.

The following are other symbols often used in marking essays:

- [delete mark] Delete, omit.
- ¶; no ¶ Paragraph; no paragraph; see ***para.***
- // Parallelism; see ***fp.***
- × Obvious error (e.g., typographical).
- ∧ Something omitted? Insert.
- =/ Insert hyphen.
- [transpose mark] Transpose.
- [close-up mark] Close up.
- # Space; more space.
- ? Something questionable or unclear: Is this what you mean?
- ✓ Something especially good.
- !! Something brilliant!

Appendix 3

Checklists for Use in Revising, Editing, and Proofreading

Omnibus Checklist for Planning and Revising

As you begin to prepare a piece of your writing for final submission to your reader(s), it is good strategy to ask yourself a series of questions designed to ensure that you have polished your work to the point where you can consider it a finished and appealing discourse. What we have listed here are the kinds of questions we ask ourselves in reading and evaluating students' writing. If you can ask and answer all of the questions we have listed here in the affirmative, your essay should be not just adequate, but very good.

1. During and after planning the essay, ask yourself these questions:

Subject

- ❑ Have I chosen a subject that sustains my interest? (**#9a**)
- ❑ If I am doing research, have I formulated a researchable question? (**#74**)
- ❑ Have I sufficiently *limited* my subject? (**#9b**)

Audience and Purpose

- ❑ Have I thought about audience and purpose?
- ❑ Have I written down a statement of purpose and a profile of my audience? (**#9c**)

Evidence

- ❑ Have I collected or generated more than enough material/evidence to develop and support my topic well? (**#9d**)

Organization and Plan

- ❑ Does my *thesis* offer a focused, substantive, analytical claim about the subject?
- ❑ Is my *plan* or *outline* for the essay logical in its content and arrangement? (**#9e–j**)
- ❑ Considering my plan or outline, do I have the right number of *main ideas*—neither too few nor too many—for the purpose of my essay?
- ❑ Are my main ideas reasonably *parallel* in content and development?
- ❑ Have I chosen the best *arrangement* for the main parts? Does it coincide with the arrangement of ideas in the thesis?

2. During and after your revision of the essay, ask yourself these questions:

Title

- ❑ Does the *title* of my essay clearly indicate the subject and topic?
- ❑ Is the *title* original?
- ❑ Does the *title* contain something to catch a reader's interest?

Structure

- ❑ Does my beginning engage a reader's curiosity or interest?
- ❑ Have I kept the *beginning* reasonably short and to the point? (**#9-1**)
- ❑ Have I clearly stated my *subject* (and my *thesis* as well) somewhere near the beginning? (**#9-1.3**)
- ❑ Does my *ending* bring the essay to a satisfying conclusion? (**#8c**, **#11.9**)
- ❑ Have I used the ending to do something other than rehash ideas already well presented in the rest of the essay?
- ❑ Have I kept my *ending* short enough, without unnecessary repetition and summary?

Unity
Development
Emphasis

- ❑ Is my essay *unified*? Do all its parts contribute to the whole, and have I avoided digression? (**#8a**)
- ❑ Have I been sufficiently *particular* and *specific*, and not left any generalizations unsupported? (**#66**)
- ❑ Have I devoted an appropriate amount of space to each part? (**#8c**)

Paragraphs

- ❑ Does the first sentence of each paragraph (except perhaps the first and last) somehow mention *the particular subject* of the essay? (**#4a.1**, **#8a**)
- ❑ Do the early sentences of each body paragraph clearly state the topic, or part of the topic? Or, is the topic sentence, when it isn't among the first sentences, effective where it is placed? (**#4a**)
- ❑ Is each body paragraph *long enough to develop its topic* adequately? (**#7b**)
- ❑ Does each paragraph *end* adequately, but not too self-consciously? (**#4c**)

Coherence

- ❑ Do the sentences in each paragraph have sufficient *coherence* with each other? (**#3–5**)
- ❑ Does the beginning of each new paragraph provide a clear *transition* from the preceding paragraph? (**#4a.1**, **#8b**)

- [ ] Is the coherence between sentences and between paragraphs smooth? Do I need to revise any unnecessary or illogical transitional devices? (**#5c–d**)

Sentences

- [ ] Is each sentence (especially if it is compound, complex, or long) internally *coherent*? (**#31**)
- [ ] Is each sentence clear and sufficiently *emphatic* in making its point? (**#29**)
- [ ] Have I used a variety of *kinds, lengths, and structures* of sentences? (**#28**)
- [ ] Have I avoided *the passive voice* except where it is clearly necessary or desirable? (**#17p**, **#29f**)

Diction **(ch. VII)**

- [ ] Have I used *words* whose meanings I am sure of, or checked the *dictionary* for any whose meanings I am not sure of?
- [ ] Is my diction sufficiently *concrete* and *specific?* (**#66a**)
- [ ] Have I avoided *unidiomatic* usages? (**#70**)
- [ ] Have I weeded out unnecessary repetitions and other *wordiness?* (**#71a–c**)
- [ ] Have I avoided *jargon* and unnecessary *clichés* and *euphemisms*? (**#71d–h**, **#68**)
- [ ] Have I avoided unintentional *slang* and *informal* diction, as well as *overformal* diction? (**#64**)
- [ ] Have I avoided inappropriate or confusing *figurative language?* (**#65**)
- [ ] Have I avoided *gender-biased, sexist language?* (**#15d**, **#72**)

Grammar

- [ ] Are my sentences *grammatically* sound—that is, free of dangling modifiers, agreement errors, incorrect tenses, faulty verb forms, incorrect articles and prepositions, and the like? (**chs. III and IV**)
- [ ] Have I avoided *run-on sentences* and *unacceptable fragments* and *comma splices?* (**#44j**, **#12x**, **#44e**)

Punctuation **(ch. V)**

- [ ] Is the *punctuation* of each sentence correct and effective?
- [ ] Have I proofread sentences slowly with special attention to the punctuation?

Spelling **(ch. VI)**

- [ ] Have I checked all my words—reading backwards if necessary—for possible *spelling* errors?
- [ ] Have I then used the spell-checker in my software package to check the essay?

Mechanics	❑	Have I carefully *proofread* my essay *in hard copy* and not just on the computer screen, and corrected all typographical errors? (**#9-o**)
	❑	Is my manuscript neat and legible? Does it conform to all *manuscript conventions* (esp. spacing, margins, font size, pagination, and headers)? (**ch. VI**)
	❑	Have I introduced and handled all *quotations* and *references* properly? (**#54**, **#78**)
	❑	Have I checked all *quotations* for accuracy? (**#78**)
Acknowledgement	❑	Have I *acknowledged* everything that requires acknowledgement according to the guidelines and rules of my university or college? (**#77**, **#78**)
	❑	Have I double-checked my *documentation* for accuracy, consistency, and correct form? (**#79a**, **#81**, **ch. VIII**)
The Last Step	❑	Have I read my essay aloud—preferably to a colleague—as a final check on how it sounds and made adjustments for clarity and emphasis?

Specialized Checklist for Writers with English as an Additional Language

What follows is an additional checklist we hope will be of particular help to those of you who are bilingual or multilingual and working to achieve fluency in English as your second, third, or fourth language. The questions we have listed are meant to help you target your editing on those issues that are often problematic for a writer whose own first language differs significantly from English in its grammatical patterns. For example, English is a language with a complex set of tenses that inflect or change verbs to express actions and states of being. In contrast, other languages may express changes in time through adverbial expressions and not change or inflect verb forms at all.

A3

When you take this targeted approach to checking a draft you have written, you need to re-read several times, checking each time for patterns with which you have had difficulty in previous writing. In each reading (ideally a slow check of a hard copy you read aloud), you should focus on one or two patterns in a sentence-by-sentence and paragraph-by-paragraph review. Your short-term objective is to polish the paper itself; your long-term objective is to become a self-sufficient proofreader who will not have to rely on others to edit your work.

Next to each of the questions that follow, you will find references to the sections of this book in which we have treated these various patterns. You will also see, in a number of cases, the acronym ***OALD***, our abbreviation for the *Oxford Advanced Learner's Dictionary*. This dictionary is an invaluable resource, and one we have used throughout our teaching careers in working with many students aiming to perfect their writing in their new language. The *OALD* can be of significant help to you in checking for verb forms, prepositional idioms, and accurate use of the indefinite articles *a* and *an*. You should take some time to read the introduction to the dictionary to learn how to use its specialized features.

Use the questions on this checklist and on the omnibus checklist preceding it *selectively*; that is, focus on the questions targeting problem areas you and your readers have identified in your recent writing. We hope that our cross-references here to particular sections of this book and to the *OALD* will help you to achieve mastery in your expression and confidence in your style.

Sentence Structure

- ❑ Have you checked your longer sentences for *mixed constructions*? (**#37**)
- ❑ Have you checked sentences for *faulty predications*? (**#38**)
- ❑ Have you checked for *ineffective fragments*—especially at points where you are introducing examples and illustrations into your work? (**#12x**, **#21e**, **#32**)
- ❑ Have you checked your compound sentences for *faulty coordination*? (**#41**)
- ❑ Have you checked your complex sentences for *faulty subordination*? (**#27b**, **#55j**)
- ❑ Have you checked your longer and balanced sentences for *faulty parallelism*? (**#40**)
- ❑ Have you checked your longer sentences for *comma splices* and *misused semicolons*? (**#33**, **#44e**, **#55j**)

Grammatical Patterns within Sentences

- ❑ Have you checked nouns for *countability* and *uncountability* and have you then checked as well for correct number form (singular or plural) for these nouns? (**#13a** and ***OALD***)
- ❑ Have you checked that *singular countable nouns* in an indefinite context are preceded by an *indefinite article*? (**#19c** and ***OALD***)
- ❑ Have you checked that *uncountable nouns* are in singular form and unaccompanied by *indefinite articles*? (**#19c** and ***OALD***)
- ❑ Have you checked that nouns made specific by their context are modified by the *definite article*? (**#19c**)
- ❑ Have you checked that *verbs* appear in their correct *regular* or *irregular forms*? (**#17b–f** and ***OALD***)
- ❑ Have you checked that you have used *gerund* and *infinitive* verbals correctly? (**#21**)

- ❑ Have you checked that *subjects* and *verbs* in your sentences *agree*? (**#18**)
- ❑ Have you checked that *noun antecedents* and *pronouns* referring to them *agree*? (**#15**)
- ❑ Have you checked that *verbs* used in *the passive voice* are *transitive*? (**#17-o–p** and ***OALD***)
- ❑ Have you checked that the *tenses* of your verbs are correct? (**#17g–h**, **#17k**)
- ❑ Have you checked for correct *sequence* of tenses in sentences where you have used more than one tense? (**#17i**)
- ❑ Have you checked that the *prepositions* you have used in combination with particular nouns or verbs are *idiomatic*? (***OALD***)

Diction

- ❑ Have you checked that the *level of your diction* fits your audience and purpose, and have you steered away from the kind of artificial diction created by overuse of a thesaurus? (**#64**)
- ❑ Have you checked that you are using words new to your vocabulary in their correct *parts of speech*? (**ch. III** and ***OALD***)

Composing

- ❑ Have you checked that you have used *transitions* correctly and in moderation? (**#5d**)
- ❑ Have you checked that your paragraphs position their *core or topic sentences* effectively and strategically? (**#4a**)

Index

List of Exercises